94

Manual of British Standards in
BUILDING CONSTRUCTION AND SPECIFICATION

Manual of
British Standards in
BUILDING
CONSTRUCTION AND
SPECIFICATION

second edition

Edited by Maxwell Smith

Deputy Director, Polytechnic of the South Bank

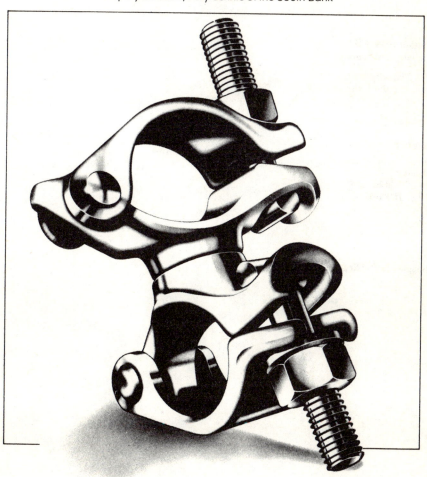

British Standards Institution
in association with Hutchinson

London Melbourne Sydney Auckland Johannesburg

Hutchinson Education

An imprint of Century Hutchinson Limited

62–65 Chandos Place, London WC2N 4NW

Longwood Publishing Group,
27 South Main Street, Wolfeboro, New Hampshire 03894-2069

Century Hutchinson Australia Pty Ltd
16–22 Church Street, Hawthorn, Victoria 3122, Australia

Century Hutchinson New Zealand Ltd
PO Box 40–086, Glenfield, Auckland 10, New Zealand

Century Hutchinson South Africa (Pty) Ltd
PO Box 337, Bergvlei 2012, South Africa

First published 1985
Second Edition 1987

Typeset in 9 on 10½pt VIP Times by
D P Media Limited, Hitchin, Hertfordshire

Printed and bound in Great Britain by
R. J. Acford, Chichester, Sussex

British Library Cataloguing in Publication Data

Manual of British Standards in building and
  construction and specification.—2nd ed.
  1. Building—Standards—Great Britain
  I. Smith, Maxwell, 1929– II. British
  Standards Institution
  692'.3'0941   TH420
ISBN 0-09-170760-9

Library of Congress Cataloging in Publication Data 87-3906

Contents

Foreword to second edition

British Standards save time, money, materials and energy in the production and exchange of goods and services.

Everybody concerned with building uses standards: manufacturers for the definition of the features which ensure products or services will be fit for their purpose; purchasers for the specification of products and materials; architects and engineers for accepted principles of design; and the end user for criteria of compliance with specification and for the procedures necessary to ensure the correct use of the product.

This manual answers the need to provide accessible, concise information about standards and standardization in one volume. It has been prepared by a team of lecturers to help the reader find essential information and, equally important, a method of guiding him or her into the topics where a knowledge of standards is essential.

I am delighted that a second edition of this manual is now available.

Dr. I. Dunstan
Director General, BSI

Readers can obtain up-to-date information on revisions, replacements and deletions by telephoning the BSI Enquiry Section: (0908) 320066.

Preface to first edition

This book is for students of disciplines within the built environment in the widest sense: students who will be users of products and materials, and concerned with the design and execution of building. It emphasizes dimensions rather than tolerances, performances rather than manufacture, the final product rather than constituent processes, site rather than factory tests.

Broadly, the range of this manual corresponds to the contents of *BS Handbook 3: Summaries of British Standards for Building*, but the format is different. The order adopted is the CI/SfB system as used in *BS Sectional List 16*. The CI/SfB classification is set out in the *CI/SfB Construction Indexing Manual* (RIBA Publications 1976). There are four departures. First this manual uses the titles in the CI/SfB Manual rather than the edited versions in the Sectional List. To give continuity, all main headings have been included, with an appropriate note where no standard is inserted under that heading. Second, the Sectional List duplicates references to particular standards as often as the classification justifies, while this manual normally covers a given standard once and refers back or forward if appropriate. Third, the order of treatment *within* a particular heading is decided by the author and often departs from the Sectional List. Finally, the authors and general editor have exercised discretion in including or excluding material in the Handbook or the Sectional List. It will be seen that significantly greater weight is given to services than is afforded in the Handbook. As in the Handbook, codes of practice are not treated in any depth.

The manual includes material drawn from the original standards rather than from the Handbook. The approach, throughout, is that a standard appears in an author's précis, only occasionally quoting or extracting titles, etc. from the standard. It follows that the standard must be referred to as the authoritative document and that this manual makes no claim to match either the standards or the Handbook in authority. The user of standards in the professional environment must also ensure that he or she refers to the most up-to-date edition of the British Standard.

Original material – introductory and linking sections, references and personal judgements – is included. Some mention of relevant legislation, Agrément certificates, international standards and codes produced by such bodies as the Institution of Civil Engineers is made where appropriate.

The summary of a given standard always quotes the number, title and date of publication in full, but other references are briefer.

Metric dimensions are given wherever possible, even where the standards are imperial – provided that some basis for metric equivalent is afforded. Some irrational elements persist, for example BS 1210 *Wood screws*, which gives screw size increments very obviously in inches, very awkward to follow in their metric version; and many pipes in Table 1(59) are cited in standards, and here, with mixed units.

The decimal marker is used in the form found in the source standard, and, in consequence, a number in Table 2(6 –) differ from the remainder.

Most illustrations are taken from standards. Some are adapted, but this is indicated, and others are original.

Tables and figures are numbered in sequence, with a note of the original standard reference as a subscript.

Thanks are due especially to Mr Stewart Sanson of BSI, who liaised with the Institution, the publishers and ourselves, and contributed the chapter which follows; and Miss Colette Collins, who prepared most of the typescript from a very varied group of manuscript drafts, and must have wished that handwriting conformed to a British Standard. The team of authors record their sense of loss at the death of Stephen Lane, and their gratitude that he had so far advanced his contribution despite illness.

Mrs Gillian Anderson played an important role in restoring order whenever disorder threatened the general editor. Mr K. Turner, Faculty Librarian at South Bank, gave help and advice that was greatly valued and contributed the index.

The authors are all members or former members of staff of the Polytechnic of the South Bank. They are as follows:

M. Smith,* TD, BSc.(Est. Man.), FRICS, MBIM, Deputy Director; general editor and author of the Prefaces, Table 2 and sections of Tables 1 and 4.

C. V. Y. Chong,* BSc. Chem., Ph.D, FRSC, Head of Division of Construction Science and Materials; author of Tables 3 and a section of Table 1.

H. B. Gerrity,* MSc., FIPHE, MCIOB, Senior Lecturer, Department of Building Administration; author of sections of Tables 1 and 4.

S. J. Lane, FRICS, FBIM, Dip. FE, Lately Head, Department of Building Economics; author of sections of Tables 1 and 4.

J. Scott, FRIBA, MBIM, Lately Senior Lecturer, Department of Architecture; author of a section of Table 4.

J. R. Slaney,* BSc. (Eng.), MPhil., CEng., MICE, FIStruct. E, Lately Head of Department of Civil and Structural Engineering; author of sections of Tables 0 and 1.

L. Wilder, MTech., FCIOB, Lately Head of Department of Building Administration; author of sections of Tables 1 and 4.

M. Young,* Dip. Arch., MSc., RIBA, FRAIA, Principal Lecturer, Department of Building Economics; author of sections of Tables 0, 1 and 4.

* involved in the second edition.

Preface to second edition

It is gratifying that a second edition is required within six months of publication of the first. There are some three hundred new entries, and an average of four or five revisions to each page. A large part of Table 4 has been rewritten or re-ordered.

The Building Regulations, 1985

Standards referred to in Approved Documents to the *Building Regulations, 1985* are distinguished by a symbol ■ and 'AD' followed by a note of the part or parts to which they relate. Where such standards have been superseded, summaries of the old standards or parts have been included as well as the new. As an extreme example, the 1958 version of Part 3 of BS 476 – which did *not* appear in the first edition of this book – is now summarized, together with the 1975 version – which is current.

British Standards and British Board of Agrément Certificates sometimes cover aspects of performance which go beyond the requirements of The Building Regulations: they may cover serviceability or recommendations for good practice. The guidance in Standards and Certificates is relevant to compliance with the Regulations where it concerns health and safety (Parts A-K), conservation of energy (Part L) or access for disabled people (Schedule 2). (References in brackets are to the Regulations.)

The work of the British Standards Institution

British Standards

British Standards are technical documents which, if used properly, save time, money, materials and energy in the production and exchange of goods and services.

Standards promote economy through variety reduction by rationalizing a range of product sizes, designations and test methods.

An acceptable *quality* – at an acceptable cost – is implicit in the use of standards because they define the features which ensure that a product or service will be *fit for its purpose*.

Standards promote *safety* which implies the definition of what is acceptable as a reasonable level of risk.

Benefits

Architects, engineers, manufacturers, surveyors, quantity surveyors, contractors, builders, specifiers and purchasers, users and regulatory authorities benefit from standards. They need to know the dimensions and other characteristics of products and materials, specify goods more simply by quoting a standard number, use standardized tests, refer to design criteria, check procedures for handling, storage and protection on site and for workmanship, and ascertain, from codes of practice, accepted principles of design.

Types of standard

Symbols and glossaries

Symbols and glossaries aid communications and understanding. Symbols and conventions, in particular, are useful in drawings and plans. For example, there are symbols for components of heating and ventilating installations, and fire-fighting appliances.

Methods

Methods state the way in which the activity is to be performed and how conclusions are to be drawn from it by calculation or otherwise. There are standardized methods of sampling, measurement, testing, analysis and specifying.

For example, a method of test to assess behaviour on impact is included in BS 6206 *Impact performance requirements for flat safety glass and safety plastics for use in buildings*. The test piece is held in a frame, an impactor is released from one of three prescribed heights and swung in a pendulum arc to strike the test piece. Then, if all of the requisite number of specimens do not break or break safely, as defined in the specification, the material is given a classification based on the drop height of the impactor.

Specifications

Specifications lay down the characteristics of a product in terms of its size, shape, materials, etc. or in terms of the functions it has to perform such as carrying loads or resisting the passage of sound. The procedures for checking compliance with these requirements are also stated.

The first type is prescriptive in nature – laying down materials and dimensions of wall ties, for example. An example of the second type is the standard which specifies the strength of concrete pipes.

The function of a British Standard specification is to provide an agreement between purchaser and supplier on verifying compliance, which reduces time in contract specification writing.

Many specifications provide ranges of characteristics and multichoice characteristics. The purchaser must then specify a grade or class when ordering.

Codes of practice

Codes of practice recommend accepted good practice as followed by competent practitioners. They bring together the results of practical experience and scientific investigation in a form that enables architects and engineers to make use of new developments and existing practices.

Codes of practice are written as guidance only, and are not generally intended to provide objective criteria by which compliance may be judged. They do not seek to provide necessarily exclusive solutions to particular requirements but to indicate recommended solutions which may be used as bases of comparison against which to judge the use of alternative procedures and materials.

Broadly speaking, two types of code may be distinguished. The first type details professional knowledge or practices, for example BS 5930 *Code of practice for site investigations*. Normally they would not be called up directly in a job specification, although they could be mentioned in a preamble requiring the contractor to have a general knowledge of them.

The second type is more specific, for example CP 118, which could be called up directly in a job specification using such words as 'The aluminium structure shall comply with . . .'.

Many codes make a contribution to safety, for example in relation to lift installations or fire precautions.

Categories of standards

British Standards (BS)

Each Standard has a number with the prefix BS, followed by the year in which the standard was issued.

Published Documents (PD)

These are often issued for guidance and to provide supplementary information to standards.

Drafts for Development (DD)

These are issued instead of a British Standard when firm requirements cannot be laid down because sufficient information is not available or because the subject is new. They can be converted into formal standards.

Preparation of standards

Standards are prepared by technical committees. The membership of these committees is firmly based on the principle of bringing together all those with an interest in a particular project, wherever possible through organizations representing the views of an industry, sector, trade, profession, government department, or other interest. This achieves, economically, a wide measure of consultation and support in standards work. The basic principles are that BSI should carry out its task in the national interest, take account of all significant viewpoints, and secure their representation at all levels, thus having an authoritative body of opinion behind every British Standard.

Proposals for new standards or revisions of existing standards may be put forward by any responsible body. Wherever possible, an initial draft is prepared outside the committee, preferably by a small panel or a single person.

Draft standards are issued for public comment and announced in *BSI News*. The technical committee then reviews all comments received, and when consensus has been achieved, the chairman finally records his or her approval. All standards are reviewed at intervals of not more than five years to determine whether a revision is needed.

Finance

BSI's income is derived from three sources: sales of standards; voluntary subscriptions from some 18,000 firms, trade associations, local authorities, individuals, professional institutions and other bodies; and a government grant which matches subscription income. Quality Assurance and Testing Services are entirely self-financing.

British Standards and the law

The publication of a standard by BSI does not, in itself, ensure its use. Its application depends on the voluntary action of interested parties. It becomes binding only if a claim of compliance is made, if it is invoked in a contract or if it is called up in legislation. References to standards in regulations may have one of two effects.

1 *Standards made mandatory*. The standard or part of it referred to must be followed, or a specific result in a standard test must be achieved in order to obey the statutory requirement.
2 *Standards approved* or *deemed to satisfy*. Here compliance with the standard is indicated as one way of fulfilling a regulatory requirement.

See also the notes on the *Building Regulations, 1985* and Approved Documents.

The Quality Assurance and Testing Services of BSI

The quality of a product or of a complete building or other construction is the totality of attributes which enable it to perform satisfactorily for an acceptable period of time. For building and civil engineering, as in many other industries, satisfactory products although necessary are not sufficient. They must be incorporated into the design and construction in a proper way. In buildings more defects and failures arise from inadequacies in the treatment of products in design and construction than arise from shortcomings in the products themselves. The achievement of quality therefore requires that everybody concerned with the manufacture and use of products understands clearly how they are intended to perform and what to do (or not do) to ensure that the intention is fulfilled.

The other aspect of standardization critical for quality is the means of ensuring that the resulting products do comply with requirements, that is, quality assurance.

BSI's Certification and Assessment Services are responsible for the certification of products and schemes for assessment of the capability of firms in manufacturing and service industries.

The *Buyers' Guide* lists the numerous building materials and products covered by these schemes, the most familiar of which is the Kitemark system for product certification. Increasing emphasis is now being put on registering firms of assessed capability in accordance with BS 5750 *Quality systems*.

The BSI Test Centre provides a wide range of testing facilities to industry and other clients. Tests are carried out to many national and international standards, regulations and directives, as well as to British Standards.

The Inspectorate is concerned with factory inspections and assessment, these services being also generally available.

CI/SfB Table 0: Physical environment

0 Planning areas (no entry)
1 Utilities, civil engineering facilities

12 Road transport facilities

The standards in this section are concerned with road lighting and road signs, and the structures required to support these facilities. Bituminous materials are covered in Table 1 Building elements (90) External elements; brickpavers in Table 2 Constructions: forms F Blockwork and brickwork.

BS 5489 *Code of practice for road lighting*
Parts 1–9: 1967–1980

This standard covers lighting for traffic routes up to 15 m in width (single carriageway) and up to 2 × 11 m (dual carriageway) together with subsidiary roads. Recommendations are given on choice of systems, planning, illumination levels, through to operation and maintenance. Precincts, footpaths and pedestrian areas are not covered due to the wide variety of specific requirements which will occur in practice. The standard goes on to deal with single and multi-level road junctions, bridges and elevated roads, underpasses and bridged roads. Additional requirements for street lighting for roads in the vicinity of airports, railways, docks and navigable waterways and for areas of special importance such as civic centres are given.

Examples of the type of diagrammatic information provided can be seen in Figure 1, which is concerned with the lighting of single level road junctions.

A further indication of the type of detail and recommendation covered by this standard can be seen from the following extract and Figure 2.

> **4.5.3.** *The individual bright patch.* An individual lantern suspended over the carriageway and viewed by a driver provides a patch of light on the carriageway of characteristic shape, generally in the form of a 'T' (figure 1 [of BS 5489 Part 1]) having a discernible 'head' and 'tail' and orientated always towards the observer. The shape and luminance of this patch is especially important. The head of the patch does not normally extend beyond the point on the road below the lantern. The shape and luminance depend upon the amount and distribution of the light, and markedly on the properties of the road surface; rough surfaces produce a more pronounced head and smooth surfaces a longer brighter tail. . . .

BS 5649 *Lighting columns* Parts 1 and 2: 1978

This standard covers the posts and, if necessary, the brackets for supporting one or more lanterns. It does not cover columns for suspended catenary type lighting. Part 1 carefully covers the definitions and terms used (including French and German). Part 2 covers the dimensions and tolerances for a chosen series of lighting columns adopted by the European Committee for Standardization. Post top lanterns as well as bracket support lanterns are catered for. Main dimensions cover columns from 3 to 20 m

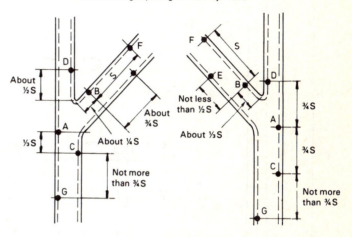

S is the design spacing for the major road

(Figure 5: BS 5489: Part 4: 1967)

Figure 1 *Examples of oblique T-junctions (turn in major road)*

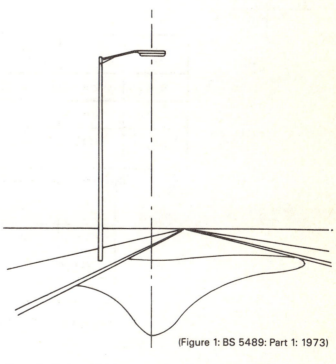

(Figure 1: BS 5489: Part 1: 1973)

Figure 2 *T-shaped bright area produced by semi-cut-off light distribution*

(Dimensions in millimetres)

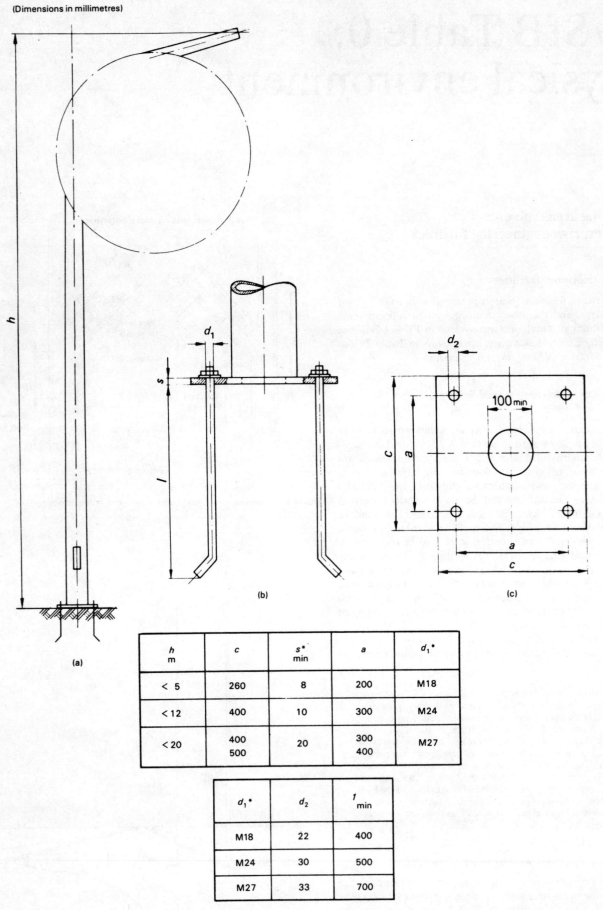

h m	c	s^* min	a	d_1^*
< 5	260	8	200	M18
< 12	400	10	300	M24
< 20	400 500	20	300 400	M27

d_1^*	d_2	l min
M18	22	400
M24	30	500
M27	33	700

* These dimensions shall be checked by calculation

(Figures 6 – 8: BS 5649: Part 2: 1978)

Figure 3 *Flange plate: lighting column*

high and requirements are specified for openings, cable entry slots, base plates, flange plates, lantern connections and tolerances.

Typical diagrammatic information is shown in Figure 3.

Parts 3–9: 1982–1985

These recently published parts give additional details for the same range of lighting columns dealt with dimensionally in Parts 1 and 2. The new parts of BS 5649 also affect some of the clauses to BS 1308 and BS 1840.

Part 3 deals with the materials to be used for steel, aluminium alloy and concrete columns together with the foundation bolts. Welding requirements for steel and aluminium are specified and suitable aluminium alloys suggested.

Part 4 covers corrosion protection of lighting columns after fabrication while Part 5 deals with the base compartments, cableways, protection and earthing.

Parts 6, 7 and 8 cover the requirements for evaluating design loads and the method for verification of structural design by calculation and testing.

Finally, Part 9 gives the special requirements for reinforced and prestressed concrete lighting columns in terms of materials, construction and quality control.

BS 1308: 1970, BS 1840: 1960 and BS 3989: 1966 deal specifically with street lighting columns in concrete, steel and aluminium respectively.

BS 873 *The construction of road traffic signs and internally illuminated bollards* Parts 1–8: 1973–1985

Parts 1 and 2 of this specification cover signs, signals and other devices for the purposes of regulating, guiding or informing road users. A miscellaneous collection of signs are covered: self-supporting, rigid and flexible portable signs, manually operated stop/go signs, school crossing patrol signs, traffic cones, road barriers, reflective markers, pedestrian crossing beacons and refuge beacons.

Part 3 is devoted to internally illuminated bollards to warn drivers of obstructions. These may also contain a prescribed traffic sign.

Part 4 is a section on road studs and covers the famous reflecting 'cats' eyes' as well as other non-reflecting studs.

Part 5 is a specification for internally illuminated signs and externally lighted luminaires, covering materials, construction, light sources and electrical requirements.

Part 6 contributes a further specification for retroreflective illuminated bollards, for example road traffic signs and internally illuminated bollards.

Part 7 provides a specification for parts and fittings.

Part 8 is a specification for traffic cones and cylinders.

Table 1 *Classes and design loads*

Class	Minimum design loads					
	Rails	End and 90° corner posts		Other posts		Infilling
		Parallel	Normal	Parallel	Normal	
	N/m	N	N	N	N	N
A	700	700	700	700	1400	500
B	700	700	700	700	1400	1000
C	1400	1400	1400	1400	2800	1000

Note: The following is a guide to the intended use of the various classes.
Class A: Normal duties.
Class B: Similar to class A but where greater resistance to vandalism is required.
Class C: Where heavy loads are expected, for example, in crowded streets outside certain classes of premises and on ceremonial routes.

(Table 1: BS 3049: 1976)

BS 3049: 1976 *Pedestrian guard rails (metal)*

In this standard the requirements relating to metal guard rails for restraining pedestrians using the footway from entering the carriageway may be found. Height of rails, centres of posts, rails, infilling, intermediate rails, foundations, gates, etc. are all covered. The standard requires that guard rails be classified according to the design loads they are required to carry. This requirement is embodied in Table 1.

BS 6044: 1981 *Specification for pavement marking paints*

This covers the requirements for paints, in containers, for use as markings on bituminous and concrete surfaces. These paints are capable of retaining a surface layer of reflectorizing glass beads to improve night visibility.

BS 6088: 1981 (1985) *Specification for solid glass beads for use with road marking compounds and other uses*

This is a specification for the bulk supplies of glass beads for road marking, impacting, plaster reinforcement and general industrial applications.

16 Power supply facilities

This section consists of two specialist standards which are simply listed without commentary in here to complete the record.

BS 4975: 1973 *Prestressed concrete pressure vessels for nuclear reactors*

BS 4485 *Water cooling towers* Parts 1–4: 1969–1975

13 Maritime structures

BS 6349: *Maritime structures* Part 1: 1984 *General criteria*

18 Civil engineering facilities

The main item in this section is a massive standard covering steel, concrete and composite bridges. There are two standards, one on composite construction in structural steel and concrete and the other on steel girder bridges. Finally there are two relatively new standards, one on safety in tunnelling work and the other is a code of practice for fixed offshore structures.

BS 153 *Steel girder bridges* Parts 1–3: 1972

This specification is intended to cover the superstructure of simply supported steel girder bridges up to spans of 100 m and should be used with great care for larger spans.

Parts 1 and 2 deal exclusively with materials, workmanship, erection and inspection together with measurement and marking for shipping.

Part 3 deals with the various loading conditions which must be accounted for in bridge design including the standard highway and railway loading tables.

BS 5400 *Steel, concrete and composite bridges*
Parts 1–10C: 1978–1984

This is a later and wider ranging standard than BS 153 and describes the application of the limit state principles. This standard also includes sections on analysis and foundation design, both of which are common to all bridge construction.

The standard is divided into ten parts. Parts 1 and 2 cover a general statement and specification for loading including wind loading.

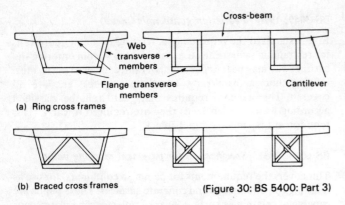

(a) Ring cross frames

(b) Braced cross frames

(Figure 30: BS 5400: Part 3)

Figure 4   *Internal intermediate cross frames in box girders*

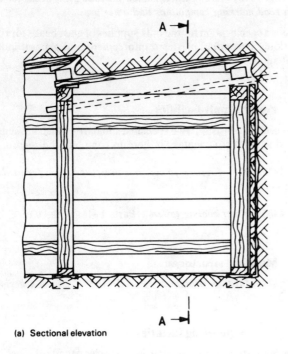

(a) Sectional elevation

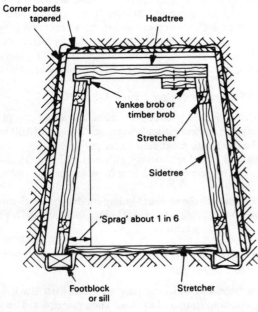

(b) Section A–A

(Figure 3: BS 6164: 1982)

Figure 5   *Piled heading: headboards and sideboards driven to full length*

Part 3 constitutes a 'code of practice for the design of steel bridges'. Recommendations are given for the design of structural steelwork in bridges and this is complementary to BS 153 in giving recommendations for a larger range of steel bridges (BS 153 refers to steel girder bridges only) and uses the limit state approach. Procedures are given for the design of steelwork components, assembly and connections. It includes recommendations for box girders of the type recently in the news due to certain modes of failure. Figure 4 illustrates the type of bracing recommended for box girders.

Part 4 is in fact a 'code of practice for the design of concrete bridges' and contains a great deal of information which may be found also in the major concrete code. Requirements are given for reinforced, prestressed and composite concrete construction and the associated structural elements.

Part 5 is a further 'code of practice for the design of composite bridges' and it is this section which supersedes Part 2 of CP 117. Composite construction here means the combination of structural steel and reinforced or prestressed concrete in such a way that they act together. Consideration is given to simply supported composite beams, composite columns and composite box beams. Prestressing and the use of formwork designed to act compositely with *in situ* concrete is also dealt with.

Parts 6, 7 and 8 cover specifications of the constituent materials including workmanship, handling and erection. Many of the clauses are suitable for incorporation into construction contract documents.

Part 9 sections 9.1 and 9.2 cover the design and specification of bridge bearings for steel, concrete and composite bridges. All types of bearings are covered: roller, rocker sliding, knuckle leaf and elastomeric laminated bearings. This section does not cover concrete hinges and special bearings for swing and lift bridges.

Part 10 constitutes a code of practice for fatigue giving methods for the fatigue assessment of parts of bridges subject to repeated fluctuations of stress.

Part 10C provides charts for classification of details for fatigue.

BS 6164: 1982   *Code of practice for safety in tunnelling in the construction industry*

This document gives recommendations for safe practice in tunnelling. It does not include cut and cover type tunnelling, immersed tube tunnels nor tunnels for the purposes of winning materials from the earth. There is a strong emphasis throughout on the safety of those engaged in tunnelling.

There are sections on planning and organization, including preliminary studies and assessment of hazards, emergencies, for example flooding, methane and explosions; working environment – ventilation, dangerous gases, dust, etc.; access and transport – shafts, cranes, hoists and carriage of persons; plant and equipment.

Appendix A of BS 6164 contains a wealth of first-class illustrations of which Figure 5 is typical.

BS 6235: 1982   *Code of practice for fixed offshore structures*

This is a large new code covering all the important aspects of the relatively new environment of sea operations for oil and gas. The document gives recommendations on the design, construction, sea operations and maintenance of fixed offshore structures. Civil, mechanical and electrical engineering aspects of offshore structures are dealt with but the specialized equipment associated with petroleum related operations is not covered.

Although concerned with fixed structures associated with the oil and gas industry the code does have certain applications to other offshore structures such as articulated structures and tethered buoyant platforms. While much of the information is common to other codes there is a wealth of information on environmental data wind speeds, water depths and tides. There are sections on loading and dynamic response, and on sea operations.

2 Industrial facilities
3 Administrative, commercial, protective service facilities
4 Health, welfare facilities

There are very few standards covering buildings for specific uses and these relate to fringe areas, for example BS 3632: 1981 *Mobile homes*. However, there are several which relate to specialist areas within the buildings, for example BS 3202: 1959 *Recommendations on laboratory furniture and fittings*. Regulation B1 of the Building Regulations 1985 applies to dwelling houses, flats, offices and shops.

Students should also refer to other parts of the manual, namely Table 1 'Building elements', for specific recommendations on parts of buildings, and to Table 4 'Activities, Requirements' especially (G), (H), (K), (M), (N), (P) and (U).

26 Agricultural facilities

The standards in this area are of marginal interest, for example BS 3445: 1981 *Fixed agricultural water troughs and water fittings*; BS 5061: 1974 *Cylindrical forage tower silos and recommendations for their use*; BS 5539: 1978 *Safety requirements in rotary milking parlours*; BS 5545 *Milking machine installations* Parts 1–3 *Construction and performance*; and BS 4903: 1979 *External colours for farm buildings*, which specifies preferred colours for roof and wall sheeting and is summarized in Table 4 'Activities, requirements' under section (G5) 'Colour'.

There is also BS 5502 *Code of practice for design of buildings and structures for agriculture* Part 1 *General considerations* (seven sections, most published in 1986), Part 2 *Special considerations* (in five sections) and Part 3 (twelve sections, most published in 1986), which gives recommendations for the design and construction of and provision of services to agricultural and horticultural buildings.

27 Manufacturing facilities

The *Factories Acts* generally apply, and the *Building Act, 1984* (S 65) in particular requires the provision of sanitary conveniences. There is only one standard on this subject, BS 5295 Parts 1–3: 1976 *Environmental cleanliness in enclosed spaces*. Part 1 relates to requirements applicable in clean rooms, clean work stations and clean air devices used in the industrial, medical and pharmaceutical fields to provide controlled environments suitable for the particular condition required in manufacture, processing and assembly and in surgery and nursing. Four classes of environmental cleanliness are identified according to the degree of control of airborne particulate matter present in the enclosed environment. Airflow, filters, temperature, humidity, lighting, noise, design, construction, testing and fire precautions are covered. Part 2 expands on construction and installation while Part 3 gives guidance to be followed in the operation and maintenance of clean rooms.

In addition to this standard there is BS 5908: 1980 *Code of practice for fire precautions in chemical plant* which is summarized in Table 4 Activities, requirements (K) Fire, explosion.

32 Office facilities: offices

The *Offices, Shops and Railway Premises Act 1963* covers this and 34 below. In particular, the scale of provision of sanitary conveniences and washing facilities is laid down. There are no British Standards for this subject, however BS 5588 *Fire precautions in the design and construction of buildings* Part 3: 1985 Office buildings applies and BS 6266 *Code of practice for fire protection for electronic data processing installations* (formerly CP 95) makes recommendations to users and installers of electronic data processing equipment on its protection from fire.

34 Trading facilities: shops

There are no British Standards for this subject but BS 5588 *Fire precautions in the design and construction of buildings* Part 2: 1985 Shops provides a similar valuable coverage for shops to that which Part 3 does for offices.

The *Food Hygiene (General) Regulations 1970* (S1N01172) apply to premises used for the purposes of a food business.

5 Recreational facilities

Under this heading standards fall into two categories. The first deals with the motion picture industry, namely BS 5363: 1976 *Method of measurement of reverberation time in auditoria*, and BS 5550: *Cinematography* where subsection 7.4.1: 1978 covers the specification and measurements for electro-acoustic response of motion picture control rooms and indoor theatres and section 8.1: 1980 provides a glossary of terms used in the motion picture industry.

In addition CP 1007: 1955 *Maintained lighting for cinemas* relates to the safety lighting and management of lighting in parts of cinema premises to which the public have access.

The second category is concerned with sporting and play equipment. BS 1892 *Gymnasium equipment* Part 1: 1972 covers general requirements while Part 2 sections 2.1–2.6: 1972 and section 2.7: 1974 covers the particular requirements, especially dimensions and construction, of various types of equipment such as wall bars, bucks and horses, spring boards and gymnastic competition equipment. In addition BS 5696 *Play equipment intended for permanent installation outdoors* Part 2: 1979 *Recommendations for minimizing hazards in equipment* is primarily intended for equipment set into or fixed on to concrete foundations and recommendations are given on materials, components and design for fixed and agility equipment with further information being given in Part 3: 1979 *Code of practice for installation and manufacture*.

6 Religious facilities (no entry)

7 Educational, scientific, information facilities

Virtually all standards in this area deal with equipment, the only exception being BS 4163: 1984 *Recommendations for health and safety in workshops of schools and colleges* which gives general guidance, together with more detailed information where necessary, on the procedures to be followed in order to ensure the safety of users in workshops of schools and departments of teacher training. Planning and environmental factors such as size and layout of workshop, illumination, storage and service installations are covered, together with safety in use of tools and equipment; the rather specialized BS 5454: 1977 *Recommendations for the storage and exhibition of archival documents* which applies to the long-term storage of archival documents in restricted areas; and BS 8205: 1985 *Code of practice for determining the design of learning spaces where audio-visual equipment will be used*.

Those standards dealing with equipment fall into three groups:

1 Those dealing with *catering equipment*, see Table 1 Building elements (73) Culinary fittings.
2 The one dealing with *playground equipment*, BS 3191 *Fixed playground equipment for schools* where Part 1: 1959 *General requirements* deals with steel tubular playground and rope appendages for use by school children up to the age of twelve years and fixed into the ground of enclosed premises. Materials, workmanship, assembly and maintenance are also dealt with. Part 2: 1959 covers rope equipment while Part 3 relates to special requirements for the following equipment: assault poles (3A: 1961); climbing apparatus (3B: 1964); climbing ropes, rope ladders, hand rings and trapeze bars (3C: 1964); horizontal bars (3D: 1964); horizontal ladders (3E: 1965); parallel bars (3F: 1965) and steel window ladders (3G: 1965).
3 Those dealing with *laboratory equipment*, namely the very useful BS 3202: 1959 *Laboratory furniture and fittings* which makes recommendations on laboratory design, benches, fume extraction and services while BS 4194: 1967 (1984) *Design requirements and testing of controlled-atmosphere laboratories* makes recommendations on the control of temperature and relative humidity in laboratories in which operators work with atmospheric sensitive materials or equipment. In addition there is a development draft, namely DD 80 *Laboratory fume cupboards* Part 1: 1982 *Safety requirements and performance testing*, Part 2: 1982 *Recommendations for information to be exchanged between purchaser, vendor and installer and recommendations for installation* and Part 3: 1982 *Recommendations for selection, use and maintenance* which gives assessment of risk from toxic material, the selection of construction material, face velocity and design features.

8 Residential facilities

81 Housing

The only standard for this subject is BS 5250: 1975 *Code of basic data for the design of buildings: the control of condensation in dwellings*. See also Table 4 'Activities, requirements' sections (G5), (H6), (K), (M2), (N), (P) and (U3).

87 Temporary, mobile residential facilities

There are a number of standards covering these, namely BS 3632: 1981 *Mobile homes* which specifies the requirements for a mobile home which is to be used as a permanent dwelling and BS 4989: 1984 *Permanent holiday caravans*, both of which deal with design, construction, equipment and fire precautions. For ventilation and heating of caravans, see Table 1 (57).

A glossary is given in BS 5264: 1975 *Glossary of caravan terms* while PD 6491: 1980 *Preferred exterior colours for static caravans* sets out the preferred range of body and trim colours for static residential and holiday caravans.

9 Common facilities, other facilities (no entry)

CI/SfB Table 1: Building elements

(1–) Ground, substructure

This section begins with earthworks and the soil tests associated with assessing the strength of soils. There are two standards on the methods of damp-proofing of floors and codes of practice covering retaining walls and foundations.

Part C (especially regulations C1, 2 and 3) is the relevant part of the *Building Regulations 1985*.

(11)   Ground

Site investigation is considered in BS 5930: 1981 (see Table 4 Activities, requirements A3s Site investigation, etc.).

BS 6031: 1981   *Code of practice for earthworks*

This is a recent revision of a previous well-known code of practice (CP 2003: 1959) and it deals with earthworks forming parts of general civil engineering construction such as highways, railways and airfields. Large excavations for major structures and excavations associated with pits, shafts and trenches for work such as foundations, pipelines and drainage are dealt with. It should be noted that the standard does not deal with a number of areas such as tunnels, dams, reservoirs, etc.

Of the three sections, section one is general and includes information on safety procedures. Section two covers cuttings, embankments, grading and levelling and gives methods of design and construction in relation to highways, railways and airfields, and bulk excavation in open ground is also covered. Section three deals with the methods of supporting the sides of trenches, pits and shafts. Figure 6 is typical of the illustrative detail given in the code.

One appendix describes plant for earthworks, namely excavation plant and compaction plant and a second appendix gives a useful list of references for further reading.

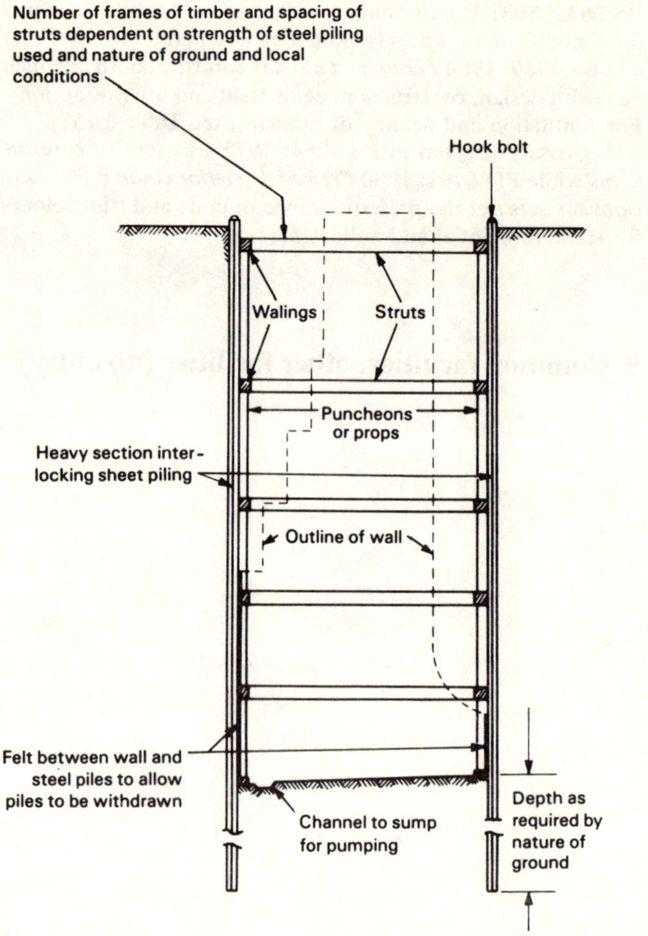

BS 1377: 1975   *Methods of test for soils for civil engineeering purposes*

This is the handbook for those involved in assessing the strength characteristics and load-bearing capacities of natural soils. The tests upon which the science of soil mechanics is based are set out in detail. The detail includes the sampling, preparation of samples, test procedure, apparatus, calculations and presentation of results. Types of test include soil classification, chemical, compaction and strength tests.

BS 1924: 1975   *Methods of test for stabilized soils*

Stabilization of a soil really means any process which either increases or maintains the natural strength of a soil. In particular, stabilization in the sense of this standard means either compaction of a well graded soil or the use of additives, such as cement, to increase stability. This standard is the handbook for

(Figure 28: BS 6031: 1981)

Figure 6   *Wide and deep trench using steel sheet piling*

carrying out the standard tests associated with this type of soil in order to ascertain the strength and durability of stabilized soil. Many of the tests are the same as those applied to natural soil but the tests do include the determination of the stabilizer content, determination of degree of pulverization and detection of organic matter able to interfere with the hydration of portland cement.

(13)   Floor beds

Part C of the *Building Regulations 1985* applies.

BS 2832: 1957   *Hot applied damp resisting coatings for solums*

The word 'solum' means the area of ground within the perimeter walls of a building. The specification is therefore concerned with the materials used for damp-proofing the ground floor area of a building which is in direct contact with the ground.

Part 1 of this standard deals with the delivery condition, certification and marking of coal tar pitch – Part 3 does the same for asphaltic bitumen.

Part 2 is concerned with soft pitch-sand suitable for spreading to provide a damp-proofing.

DD 86   *Damp-proof courses*

Part 1: 1983   *Methods of test for flexural bond strength and short-term shear strength*

Clearly the flexural and shear strength at a joint containing a damp course will be different and, indeed, less than that appertaining to a normal horizontal brick joint. This development draft suggests methods of test for flexural bond strength and short-term shear strengths.

Part 2:   1984 *Method of test for creep deformation*

Determines the creep deformation of damp-proof course materials.

(16)   Retaining walls, foundations

CP 101: 1972   *Foundations and substructures for non-industrial buildings of not more than four storeys*

This code is limited, as its title implies, and further deals only with simple foundations involving even dispersal of loads on to ground where the condition can be shown to be adequate.

Buildings of a specialist nature or buildings involving a large element of structural engineering are not intended to be covered.

This code gives recommendations on site exploration, weather effects, ground movement, bearing capacities and the selection and design of the appropriate foundation. There is a useful and simple table of bearing capacities for different types of rock and soil.

CP 102: 1973   *Protection of buildings against water from the ground*

■   AD (Reg. C4)

This code makes recommendations for keeping ground water and surface water out of buildings.

Recommendations cover the drainage of surrounding areas, special waterproof construction below ground level and the damp-proofing of walls and floors at or near ground level.

There is a section on methods of preventing the entry of ground water into buildings where ground or surface water may not be able to escape immediately. This protection may be provided by a continuous impervious membrane or by a very high quality concrete.

Figure 7 illustrates a few of the construction details recommended when using a membrane.

This code does not cover embedded heating in basements or the special requirements of cold stores.

CP 2004: 1972   *Foundations*

▨   AD (Reg. A1/2)

This is a very large and comprehensive code covering foundations for all types of buildings and engineering structures but does not cover special structures. This code takes over where CP 101 finishes and is a complete guide for most foundation problems.

Its comprehensive nature may be quickly appreciated by a glance at the list of sections into which it is divided:

Design of foundations and shallow foundations.
Deep and subaqueous foundations.

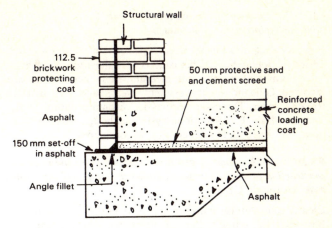

(a)   Externally applied asphalt tanking to brickwork

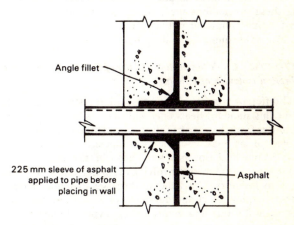

(b)   Asphalt tanking. Treatment of pipes

(Figures 3 and 4: CP 102: 1973)

Figure 7   *Asphalt tanking*

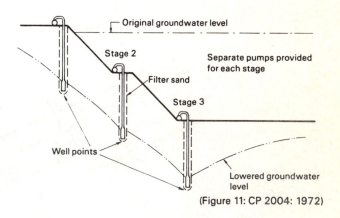

(Figure 11: CP 2004: 1972)

Figure 8   *Multi-stage well point system for deep excavation*

Cofferdams and caissons.
Geotechnical processes for dewatering and treatment of substrata.
Pile foundations.
Tide work, underwater concreting and diving.
Excavation, demolition, shoring and underpinning.
Durability of timber, metal and concrete structures.

There are a number of useful charts, tables and illustrations contained within the code of which Figure 8 is typical.

CP 2012　*Foundations for machinery*　Part 1: 1974　*Foundations for reciprocating machines.*

Reciprocating machinery needs special consideration when designing foundations. This code covers the rigid block type foundation where low and medium frequency ranges are involved. Guidance on data assembly, design and control of site work is given. The code restricts its recommendation to the undamped single-mass spring system although there will be occasions when damping needs to be considered.

BS 5573: 1978　*Code of practice for safety precautions in the construction of large diameter boreholes for piling and other purposes* (formerly CP 2011)

Clearly safety precautions are necessary in the construction of boreholes exceeding 0.75 m diameter into which a man may descend for working or inspection purposes. In addition to stating these precautions the code deals with safety requirements for the equipment normally used and the gas hazards which can be encountered in deep boreholes.

BS 6177: 1982　*Guide to selection and use of elastomeric bearings for vibration isolation of buildings*

Several different types of vibration isolation systems are available but this standard deals only with the resilient properties which derive from the use of an elastomeric (that is, rubber-like) substance or an elastomer-based composite. The standard reviews the practical aspects of providing vibration isolation but does not develop the theory involving the effectiveness of these bearings as isolators. The standard discusses dynamic characteristics, damping effect and durability of elastomers together with structural safety and serviceability. Types of elastomeric bearings, bonding and adhesions are covered. There is a final section on testing and identification of bearings.

DD 81: 1982　*Recommendations for ground anchorages*

Although not yet a standard this document is large and comprehensive. There has been a dramatic increase in the use of ground anchorages in the UK during the past ten years ranging

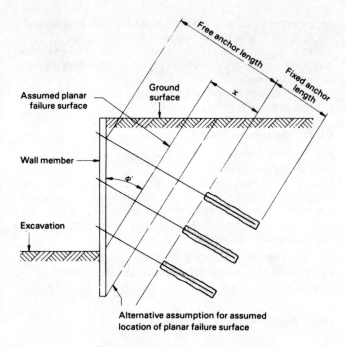

Alternative assumption for assumed location of planar failure surface

(Figure 4: DD 81: 1982)

Figure 9　*Typical anchorage geometry using wedge method of analysis*

from dam stressing and reinforcement of underground excavations in rock to tying back earth retaining structures and holding down tower and bridge foundations. This document seems to bring together current good practice and the appropriate elements of certain foreign standards in the absence of a current British Standard. There is a wealth of tabular evidence and some excellent diagrams in this development draft and Figures 9 and 10 are typical of the diagrammatic information.

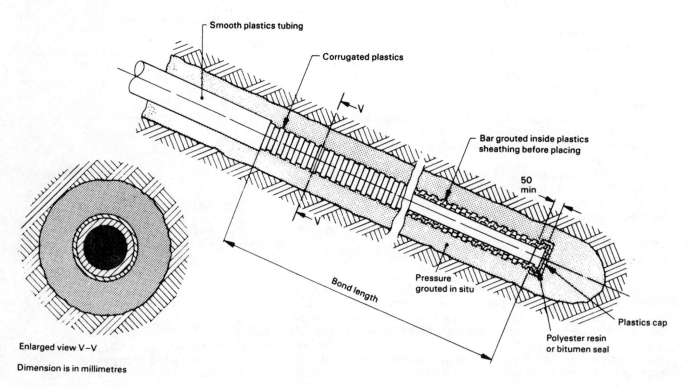

Enlarged view V–V

Dimension is in millimetres

Figure 10　*Typical acceptable fixed anchor detail for bar tendon*

(Figure 32: DD 81: 1982)

(2–) Structure, primary elements, carcass

This section covers some very important major standards involving the use of structural steel, reinforced concrete, precast concrete, prestressed concrete, aluminium, timber and masonry in building elements. Additionally there are standards covering partitions, floors, gallions stairs, ladders, roofs and chimneys.

BS 8110 *Structural use of concrete*

■ AD (Reg. A1/2 (all three parts) and Reg. A3 (Parts 1 and 2 only))

This standard is in three parts.
Part 1: 1985 *Code of practice for design and construction*
Part 2: 1985 *Code of practice for special circumstances*
Part 3: 1985 *Design charts for singly reinforced beams, doubly reinforced beams and rectangular columns*

This is the major standard used by designers of reinforced, precast and prestressed concrete structures. Its recommendations are deemed to satisfy the *Building Regulations*, and are superseding CP 110 as an Authorized Document upon publication. It has superseded CP 114, also an Authorized Document.

The design recommendations are written in limit-state terms and much of the information is presented in chart form for various components of structural framing and combinations of allowable concrete and steel stresses. Like most codes, Part 1 also gives guidance on specification and workmanship for concrete elements, the inspection and testing of structures and fire resistance of various forms of construction.

Parts 1 and 2 are under revision.

CP 110: *The structural use of concrete*

■ AD (Regs. A1/2 and A3. H1 (Part 1 only))

This code (including reference to CP 114, CP 115 and CP 116) consists of Part 1: 1972 *Design, materials and workmanship*, Part 2: 1972 *Design charts for singly reinforced beams, doubled reinforced beams and rectangular columns* and Part 3: 1972 *Design charts for circular columns and prestressed beams*.

A major code of practice used by designers of reinforced, precast and prestressed concrete structures. Although BS 8110 is intended to supersede it, still in general use. It refers to the use of concrete in buildings and other structures and is becoming the best known of all the concrete codes. CP 114 *Structural use of reinforced concrete in buildings*, CP 115 *Structural use of prestressed concrete in buildings* and CP 116 *Structural use of precast concrete* are all intended to be replaced in due course.

The main advance of CP 110 over the other codes (namely CP 114, CP 115 and CP 116) is that its design recommendations are written in limit state terms whereas the older codes are presented in elastic or load factor terms.

Much of the information in Parts 2 and 3 of CP 110 is presented in chart form for various components of structural framing. These charts are based on assumptions and methods laid down in Part 1 of the code. The charts cannot be used to obtain the complete detailed design of any member but can be an aid when analysing the cross-section of a member at ultimate limit state. Part 1 also gives guidance on the specification and workmanship of concrete elements, the inspection and testing of structures and the fire resistance of various forms of construction.

CP 114: 1969 *Structural use of reinforced concrete in buildings*

BS 4447: 1973 *The performance of prestressing anchorages for post-tensioned construction*

The reliability of anchorages used in post-tensioned prestressed concrete is clearly very important. Any failure could result in a serious situation. This standard describes the test procedures to be used in establishing the satisfactory performance of prestressing anchorages of various types. The results of these tests, if presented in a certified form, may be used in design.

The standard defines various types of anchorages, goes on to set out the minimum required performance, and concludes with the manner in which test reports must be presented.

BS 6089: 1982 *Guide to the assessment of concrete strength in existing structures*

This standard gives information on the tests which are available to assess the strength of existing concrete in a structure. The various tests are compared and their relative merits assessed together with the methods of carrying out these tests.

Reference is made to the fact that this specification amplifies the sections on testing in CP 110 Part 1.

Guidelines are given for engineers in interpreting results from these tests and the action to be taken in the event of non-compliance with the testing plan.

Information is also given on how to plan and carry out an investigation incorporating the tests. The standard concludes with a useful bibliography of references.

BS 5950 *Structural use of steelwork in buildings*

This standard is intended to be in nine parts. Three parts currently exist.

Part 1: 1986 *Code of practice for design in simple and continuous construction: hot rolled sections*

■ AD (Regs. A1/2 & A3)

Part 2: 1985 *Materials, fabrication and erection: hot rolled sections*

■ AD (Regs. A1/2 & A3)

Part 4: 1982 *Code of practice for design of floors with profiled steel sheeting*

■ AD (Reg. A1/2)

This is the major steel designers' code and, like BS 8110 for concrete, is deemed to satisfy the *Building Regulations 1985*.

Parts 1 and 2 of this standard cover materials, loading, design and details of construction, fabrication and erection and tests for the efficiency of welders.

Like the concrete code the design recommendations are written in limit-state terms and much of the information is in the form of tables which have been compiled using a combination of relevant theory and practical results. For example, Table 2 (part of Table 27(a) of the standard) is typical of this approach and gives the allowable stress in axially loaded columns for a range of slenderness ratios (λ) and design strength (P_y).

Part 4 is concerned with the use of profiled steel sheets in floor slabs as illustrated in Figure 11. The design recommendations cover two eventualities:

1 Where the steel sheet and concrete act compositely in supporting loads
2 Where the steel sheet is only a permanent shutter to support newly-placed concrete. The hardened concrete is designed to support the total loading.

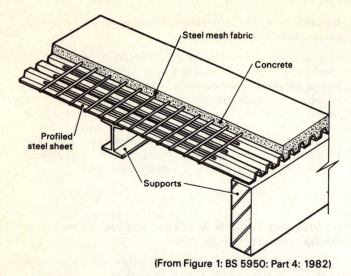

Steel mesh fabric

Concrete

Profiled steel sheet

Supports

(From Figure 1: BS 5950: Part 4: 1982)

Figure 11   *Typical floor, using profiled steel sheet*

Table 2 *Extract: Compressive strength,* p_c, *(in N/mm²) for struts*

λ \ p_y	225	245	255	265	275	305	320	325	335*
15	225	245	255	265	275	305	320	325	335
20	225	244	254	264	273	303	317	322	332
25	222	241	251	261	270	299	314	318	328
30	220	239	248	258	267	296	310	315	324
35	217	236	245	254	264	292	306	310	320
40	214	233	242	251	260	287	301	305	315
42	213	231	240	249	258	285	299	303	312
44	212	230	239	248	257	283	297	301	310
46	210	228	237	246	255	281	294	299	307
48	209	227	236	244	253	279	292	296	305
50	208	225	234	242	251	277	289	293	302
52	206	223	232	241	249	274	286	291	299
54	205	222	230	238	247	271	283	287	295
56	203	220	228	236	244	268	280	284	292
58	201	218	226	234	242	265	277	281	288
60	200	216	224	232	239	262	273	277	284
62	198	214	221	229	236	259	269	273	280
64	196	211	219	226	234	255	265	268	275
66	194	209	216	223	230	251	261	264	270
68	192	206	213	220	227	247	256	259	265
70	189	204	210	217	224	242	251	254	259
72	187	201	207	214	220	237	246	248	253
74	184	198	204	210	216	233	240	243	247
76	182	194	200	206	212	227	235	237	241
78	179	191	197	202	208	222	229	231	235
80	176	188	193	198	203	217	223	225	229
82	173	184	189	194	199	211	217	219	222
84	170	181	185	190	194	206	211	213	216
86	167	177	181	186	190	200	205	207	209
88	164	173	177	181	185	195	199	200	203
90	161	169	173	177	180	189	193	195	197
92	158	166	169	173	176	184	188	189	191
94	154	162	165	168	171	179	182	183	185
96	151	158	161	164	166	173	176	177	179
98**	147	154	157	159	162	168	171	172	173

* and 340, 355, 395, 410, 415, 430 and 450.
** and 100 (×2), 130 (×5), 200 (×10), 350.

Part of Table 27(a), BS 5950: Part 1: 1985 section four.

BS 449 *The use of structural steel in buildings* Part 2: 1969 *Metric units*

■ AD (Reg. A1/2)

This standard is well known to every structural steelwork designer and is on a par with CP 110 in being a major design guide extensively used in practice, deemed to satisfy the *Building Regulations 1985*, although superseded.

The standard covers materials, loading, design and details of construction, fabrication, erection and tests for the efficiency of welders.

Much of the design information is in the form of tables which have been compiled using a combination of relevant theory and practical results. For example Table 2 is typical of this approach and gives the allowable stress in axially loaded columns for a range of slenderness ratios.

The original standard dealt only with hot rolled steel sections, plates and normalized tubular shapes in various grades of steel. An addendum was issued to cover the use of cold formed steel sections formed from steel plate, sheet and strip not more than 6 mm thick.

BS 4395 *High strength friction grip bolts and associated nuts and washers for structural engineering* Parts 1–3: 1969–1973

BS 4604 *The use of high strength friction grip bolts in structural engineering* Parts 1–3: 1970–1973

It has been well-known for many years that when a bolt is tightened it has more strength than that which is attributable to shear and bearing. These standards enable the frictional properties between the bolts, washers and jointing plates to be utilized when designing joints in practice.

BS 4395 deals with the mechanical properties, dimensions, markings and testing of the bolts, nuts and washers and comes in three parts covering three grades of manufacture. See Table 2 'Constructions, forms' section Xt6 'Fasteners'.

BS 4604 which is also divided into three parts, covering the same three grades as BS 4395, deals specifically with the use of these bolts in structural steelwork. The rules are concerned with developing the correct relationship between bolt shank tension and the amount of tightening by torque wrench or other means.

The following extract illustrates one of the rules for tightening by part turn.

Table 3 *Final tightening*

Nominal size and thread diameter of bolt	Grip of bolt for rotation of the nut (relative to the bolt shank)	
	$\frac{1}{2}$ to $\frac{3}{4}$ turn	$\frac{3}{4}$ to 1 turn
	mm	mm
M 16	Up to 115	—
M 20	Up to 115	Over 115 to 225
M 22	Up to 115	Over 115 to 275
M 24	Up to 160	Over 160 to 350
M 27	Up to 160	Over 160 to 350
M 30	Up to 160	Over 160 to 350
M 33	Up to 160	Over 160 to 350

Note: With the amount of nut rotation specified in the above table, a bolt tension at least equal to the proof load will be attained.

(Table 3: BS 4604: Part 3: 1973)

4.2.1 *Tightening by part turn.* In tightening by the part-turn method the procedure shall be as follows:

On assembly of a joint, each bolt shall be given a preliminary tightening to bring the faying surfaces into close contact. This preliminary tightening is not intended, and shall not be used, as a corrective for poor workmanship in the preparation of the parts of the joint or in its assembly. Tightening by hand spanners will often suffice for bolts of diameters up to 24 mm, but for larger ones it will usually be necessary to use power-operated wrenches.

After all the bolts in the joint have been thus tightened, a permanent mark shall be made on each nut and another on the protruding thread of its bolt so as to record their relative positions.

Each bolt shall then be further and finally tightened, preferably with a power-operated wrench, so that a relative rotation, of the amount specified in Table 3, occurs between the bolt shank and the nut.

Table 4 *Grade stresses for softwoods: graded to BS 4978 rules: for the dry exposure condition*

Standard name	Grade	Bending parallel to grain*	Tension parallel to grain*	Compression		Shear parallel to grain	Modulus of elasticity	
				Parallel to grain	Perpendicular to grain†		Mean	Minimum
		N/mm²	N/mm²	N/mm²	N/mm²	N/mm²	N/mm²	N/mm²
Redwood/ whitewood (imported) and Scots pine (British grown)	SS/MSS	7.5	4.5	7.9	2.1	0.82	10500	7000
	GS/MGS	5.3	3.2	6.8	1.8	0.82	9000	6000
	M75	10.0	6.0	8.7	2.4	1.32	11000	7000
	MN50	6.6	4.0	7.3	2.1	0.82	9000	6000
Corsican pine (British grown)	SS/MSS	7.5	4.5	7.9	2.1	0.82	9500	6500
	GS/MGS	5.3	3.2	6.8	1.8	0.82	8000	5000
	M75	10.0	6.0	8.7	2.4	1.33	10500	7000
	M50	6.6	4.0	7.3	2.0	0.83	9000	5500
Sitka spruce and European spruce (British grown)	SS/MSS	5.7	3.4	6.1	1.6	0.64	8000	5000
	GS/MGS	4.1	2.5	5.2	1.4	0.64	6500	4500
	M75	6.6	4.0	6.4	1.8	1.02	9000	6000
	M50	4.5	2.7	5.5	1.6	0.64	7500	5000
Douglas fir (British grown)	SS/MSS	6.2	3.7	6.6	2.4	0.88	11000	7000
	GS/MGS	4.4	2.6	5.6	2.1	0.88	9500	6000
	M75	10.0	6.0	8.7	2.9	1.41	11000	7500
	M50	6.6	4.0	7.3	2.4	0.88	9500	6000
Larch (British grown)	SS	7.5	4.5	7.9	2.1	0.82	10500	7000
	GS	5.3	3.2	6.8	1.8	0.82	9000	6000
Parana pine (imported)	SS	9.0	5.4	9.5	2.4	1.03	11000	7500
	GS	6.4	3.8	8.1	2.2	1.03	9500	6000
Pitch pine (Caribbean)	SS	10.5	6.3	11.0	3.2	1.16	13500	9000
	GS	7.4	4.4	9.4	2.8	1.16	11000	7500
Western red cedar (imported)	SS	5.7	3.4	6.1	1.7	0.63	8500	5500
	GS	4.1	2.5	5.2	1.6	0.63	7000	4500
Douglas fir-larch (Canada)	SS	7.5	4.5	7.9	2.4	0.85	11000	7500
	GS	5.3	3.2	6.8	2.2	0.85	10000	6500
Douglas fir-larch (USA)	SS	7.5	4.5	7.9	2.4	0.85	11000	7500
	GS	5.3	3.2	6.8	2.2	0.85	9500	6000
Hem-fir (Canada)	SS/MSS	7.5	4.5	7.9	1.9	0.68	11000	7500
	GS/MGS	5.3	3.2	6.8	1.7	0.68	9000	6000
	M75	10.0	6.0	9.3	2.4	1.13	12000	8000
	M50	6.6	4.0	7.7	2.1	0.71	10500	7000
Hem-fir (USA)	SS	7.5	4.5	7.9	1.9	0.68	11000	7500
	GS	5.3	3.2	6.8	1.7	0.68	9000	6000
Spruce-pine-fir (Canada)	SS/MSS	7.5	4.5	7.9	1.8	0.68	10000	6500
	GS/MGS	5.3	3.2	6.8	1.6	0.68	8500	5500
	M75	9.7	5.8	8.5	2.1	1.10	10500	7000
	M50	6.2	3.7	7.1	1.8	0.68	9000	5500
Western whitewoods (USA)	SS	6.6	4.0	7.0	1.7	0.66	9000	6000
	GS	4.7	2.8	6.0	1.5	0.66	7500	5000
Southern pine (USA)	SS	9.6	5.8	10.2	2.5	0.98	12500	8500
	GS	6.8	4.1	8.7	2.2	0.98	10500	7000

* Stresses applicable to timber 300 mm deep (or wide); for other section sizes see **14.6** and **16.2**.
† When the specifications specifically prohibit wane at bearing areas, the SS grade compression perpendicular to the grain stress may be multiplied by 1.33 and used for all grades.

(Table 9: BS 5265: Part 2: 1984)

CP 118: 1969 *The structural use of aluminium*

■ AD (Reg. A1/2)

This is the design code for aluminium used in all forms of structures with the exception of special structures such as pressure vessels, lighting columns, etc. for which special individual codes exist.

The code deals with the principal alloys H30, N8 and H9, and a number of supplementary alloys but care must be taken since aluminium can appear in a large range of alloys.

The code gives recommendations for materials, loading, design, testing, fabrication and erection. It also deals with the protection of the material against corrosion.

Like many codes provision is made for acceptance of a structure by testing should stress analysis not be feasible. The design methods do not include limit state principles.

BS 5268 *Structural use of timber*

■ AD (Reg. A1/2)

It is intended that this standard will be in seven parts. Currently only Part 2: 1984 *Code of practice for permissible stress, design materials and workmanship*, Part 3: 1985 *Trussed rafter roofs* (see (27)), Part 4 section 4.1 *Fire resistance of timber structures* (see Table 4: Activities, requirements, (K) Fire, explosion), Part 5 *Preservation treatments for constructional timber* (see Table 3 Materials U3 Protective, etc. materials), and Part 7 *Recommendations for the calculation basis for span tables for joist* Section 7.3 *Ceiling joists*, have been issued.

Timber, being a natural material, has a number of variables and possible deficiencies which would not occur in a controlled material such as steel. Therefore considerable emphasis is placed upon modifications to allow for different species, the position of knots, graining and other defects which might occur. Thus the basic design stresses are subject to a number of modification factors which are not seen in standards relating to other materials. Some idea of the variables can be seen from Table 4 which relates to species of timber. The code includes recommendations for the minimum quality of materials, permissible stresses and modification factors when timber is used in simple solid members or as part of built-up components and structures incorporating other materials.

BS 6661: 1986 *Air supported structures*

This deals with the design, construction, operation and maintenance of single skin air supported structures and also the grading of those structures into distinct classes for safety. This type of structure may be seen as the covering for swimming pools and similar semi outdoor activities and provides a cheap efficient means of weather proofing fairly extensive areas.

CP 117 *Composite construction in structural steel and concrete* Part 1: 1965 *Simply-supported beams in buildings (Imperial units)*

■ AD (Reg. A1/2)

This code refers to beams composed of either rolled or built-up structural steel sections, with or without concrete encasement, acting in conjunction with *in situ* reinforced concrete slabs. It is in fact an amalgamation of the two main structural elements of structural steel and reinforced concrete.

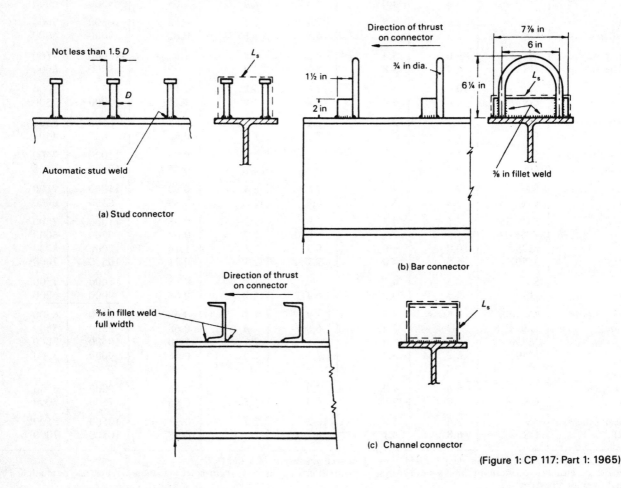

(a) Stud connector

(b) Bar connector

(c) Channel connector

(Figure 1: CP 117: Part 1: 1965)

Figure 12 *Steelwork: typical shear connectors*

Table 5 *Design values of shear connectors for different concrete strengths*

Types of connector		Connector material	Welds	Design values of connectors for concrete strengths U_w (lbf/in²)*		
				3000	4000	6000
Headed studs (Figure 11(a))		Minimum yield stress 25 tonf/in² Minimum TS 32 tonf/in²	See Figure 11(a)	Load per stud (P_c) tons		
Diameter	Height					
in	in					
1	4			11.9	13.1	15.5
$\frac{7}{8}$	4			9.8	10.8	12.8
$\frac{3}{4}$	4			7.8	8.6	10.2
$\frac{3}{4}$	3			6.7	7.4	8.8
$\frac{5}{8}$	3			5.7	6.3	7.5
$\frac{1}{2}$	$2\frac{1}{2}$			3.6	4.0	4.8
Bars with hoops (Figure 11(b))			See Figure 11(b)	Load per bar (P_c) tons‡		
$2 \times 1\frac{1}{2} \times 7\frac{7}{8}$ in bar		BS 15†		40	53	80

* Design values for concrete of intermediate strength can be obtained by linear interpolation.
† BS 15 *Mild steel for general structural purposes*.
‡ For bars and channels of length less than those quoted above, the values are propotional to the length.

Note 1: U_w is the specified cube strength of concrete.
Note 2: The heights of the studs quoted are the overall heights.
Note 3: The figures are 80 per cent of the ultimate capacities.
Note 4: Values in the table are not applicable where there is a concrete haunch between the top flange of the steel beam and the concrete slab with a slope steeper than 1 vertical and 3 horizontal.

Editor's note: In this table metric conversion is not appropriate.

(Table 1: CP 117: Part 1: 1965)

As the title implies it deals with simply supported beams in buildings but nevertheless it contains a wealth of information on the means of connecting the two basic elements to act as one, that is, the design of shear connectors.

Some typical shear connectors are illustrated in Figure 12 and Table 5 gives design values of shear connectors.

Part 2: 1967 *Beams for Bridges*
To be superseded by BS 5400 Part 5. See relevant entry under BS 5400 in Table 0 18 above.

(21) Walls, external walls

BS 5628 *Code of practice for the structural use of masonry*
Part 1: 1978 *Unreinforced masonry*

■ AD (Reg. A1/2)

This has been written in limit-state terms and takes its place, alongside BS 8110 and BS 5950 in the structural designer's 'tool kit'. The code deals with unreinforced walls which are a significant part of a structure and not just infilling. Brickwork, blockwork, masonry and concrete are covered giving recommendations for materials, permissible stresses as well as methods of design and construction.

Clearly, a large variety of bricks and blocks is available and they are defined in terms of crushing strength. Furthermore they may be jointed by various mortar mixes and factors are included to allow for this as well as construction control.

Recommendations other than structural but nevertheless essential may be found in Part 3.

Part 2: 1985 *Structural use of reinforced and prestressed masonry*
Like plain concrete, masonry is weak in tension but this can be overcome by either reinforcing or prestressing in a similar way to that of concrete. This code provides the necessary information for such an operation.

Part 3: 1985. *Materials and components, design and workmanship*

■ AD (Regs. A1/2 and C4)

This is a code of practice dealing with the design and construction of brickwork and blockwork in general walling construction. Its recommendations are general and apply to both load-bearing and non-load-bearing construction. It is concerned with matters such as stability, cracking, weathering, damp-proof courses, parapets, chimneys, durability, fire resistance, thermal properties, facing work, mortars and construction details.

The special provisions applicable additionally to load-bearing walls are to be found in Part 1 of the standard.

CP 111: 1970 *Structural recommendations for load-bearing walls*

■ AD (Reg. A1/2)

This code deals with walls which are a significant part of a structure, rather than just infilling. Brickwork, blockwork, masonry and concrete are covered, giving recommendations for materials, permissible stresses as well as the methods of design and construction. CP 111 is part of the structural designer's 'tool kit' in company with CP 110 and BS 449.

It is intended that BS 5628 Part 1 should eventually supersede CP 111 as it is written in modern limit state terms. Both are currently in use but one or the other (not both) must be used for each individual design. Still an Authorized Document under the Building Regulations 1985.

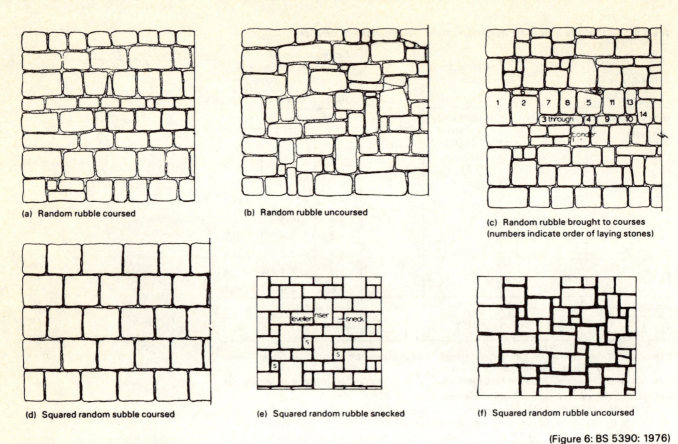

(a) Random rubble coursed

(b) Random rubble uncoursed

(c) Random rubble brought to courses (numbers indicate order of laying stones)

(d) Squared random subble coursed

(e) Squared random rubble snecked

(f) Squared random rubble uncoursed

(Figure 6: BS 5390: 1976)

Figure 13   *Types of rubble walling*

BS 5390:   *Code of practice for stone masonry*

■ AD (Regs. A1/2 and C4)

This is a guide to good design and construction of and the selection of materials for faced walls with stone or cast stone, rubble and rubble faced walls using stone or cast stone. The code recognizes that methods of construction, style and appearance will vary according to location and local traditions but the general principles suggested should nevertheless be adhered to.

Figure 13 shows examples of good practice in rubble walling.

BS 6073   *Precast concrete masonry units*   Parts 1 and 2: 1981

■ AD (Reg. A1/2)

The units covered by this standard are solid (including autoclave aerated concrete) cellular and hollow blocks not exceeding 650 mm in any work size dimension. Units where the height exceeds the length or six times the thickness are outside the scope of this standard.

The standard specifies materials, tolerances and minimum performance levels for precast masonry units within the size range stated above.

Various types of blocks and bricks are defined, there is a section on binders, aggregates and admixtures. Dimensional variation, strength, drying shrinkage and means of identification of units are covered.

The appendices deal with the determination of compressive strength, transverse strength and drying shrinkage.

BS 6178   *Joist hangers*   Part 1: 1982   *Joist hangers for building into masonry walls of domestic dwellings*

The practice of supporting timber joists on steel hanger supports which are in turn built into masonry walls is now accepted as normal within the building industry.

This standard specifies the requirements for joist hangers which are supported by or built into internal masonry walls or the inner skins of cavity walls of domestic dwellings in order to supply vertical support only to the timber joints. The standard does not cover in any way horizontal or horizontal components of inclined loads.

Matters specified are materials, construction, protective coatings, markings and testing. Figure 14 shows typical hangers made from sheet with a protective coating.

BS 8200: 1985   *Code of practice for design of non-load-bearing external vertical enclosures of buildings*

■ AD (Reg. C4)

Provides a systematic framework within which enclosures (including roof elements more than 75° to the horizontal) can be

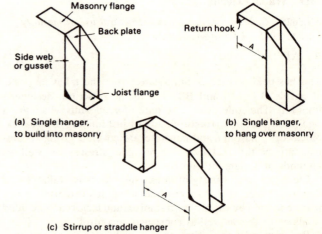

(a) Single hanger, to build into masonry

(b) Single hanger, to hang over masonry

(c) Stirrup or straddle hanger

(Figure 1: BS 6178: Part 1: 1982)

Figure 14   *Types of hanger*
Note: The diagrams are intended only to illustrate definitions, not to restrict or direct design forms nor to suggest a need for all the features illustrated

designed and constructed. Includes guidance on establishing initial performance requirements, maintaining them during the intended life of the enclosure and realizing the design on site. Insulation – see Table 4 Activities, requirements, (M2) Insulation.

(22) Internal walls, partitions

BS 5234: 1975 *Code of practice for internal non-load-bearing partitioning*

Even though partitions are usually non-load-bearing they will be required to have certain essential properties such as strength and stability against deflection and buckling, fire resistance, thermal and sound insulation, durability and provision for services.

This standard is a code of practice relative to these vital properties and it also includes recommendations for good practice to be followed during design, manufacture, erection and maintenance.

Movable partitions are not included in this code.

An abundance of materials is available for the manufacture of non-load-bearing partitions ranging from aerated concrete slabs to wood wool sections.

A sample of the type of information provided is illustrated by Table 6 and the following extract relating to the 'mass law' of various materials.

A.2.4. *Mass of materials.* The following list, which is not intended to be exhaustive, provides conservative estimates of the mass of various common building materials designed for use in assessing sound insulation by the 'mass law'. For this reason some of the values given will be found to be less than the equivalent quoted in BS 648 which is designed as information for calculating dead loads and therefore tends to provide some safety margin. All masses are in kilogrammes per square metre.

Figure 15 relates mass to insulation value.

Table 6 *Mass of materials*

Material	Nominal thickness	Mass
	mm	kg/m²
Asbestos 'insulating' board	12	8.5
Asbestos wallboard	12	14.1
Blockboard	25	12.2
Resin-bonded wood chipboard	19	13.5
Fibre insulating board	12.7	3.4
Flaxboard	25	10.4
Hardboard, standard	3.2	3.1
Hardboard, tempered	6.4	6.5
HM medium board (panelboard)	9	6.5
LM medium board	6.4	3.5
Plasterboard	12.7	10.0
Plasterboard plastered with 5 mm single coat plaster	–	17.0
Plywood	per 1.0	0.49
Straw (compressed)	50	18.5
Wood wool	50	23.0
Glass	6	14.6
Plaster, gypsum or lime	12	19.0
Metal lath (three coat plaster)	–	29.0
Aluminium	0.7	1.9
Asbestos cement	6.0	9.7
Copper	0.56	4.9
Steel	1.5	12.2
Zinc	0.9	6.3
Timber (average)		
seasonal softwoods	25	12.0
common hardwoods	25	18.0
Lightweight aerated concrete	per 10	8.0

(Adapted from *Sound insulation in buildings* (HMSO). Supplementary data have been added.)

(Clause A.2.4: BS 5234: 1975)

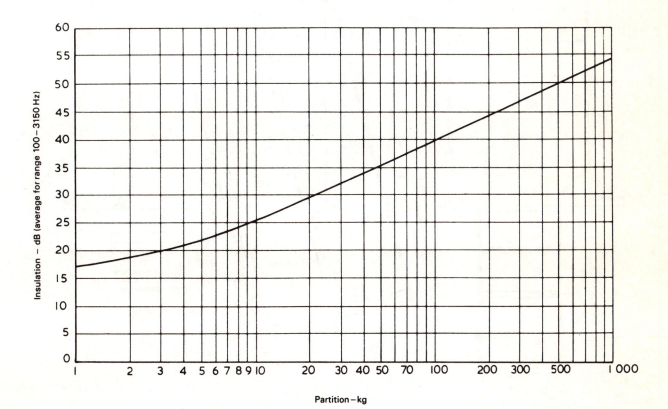

Figure 15 *Sound insulation values of partitions due to mass.*

(Figure 13: BS 5234: 1975)

(23)   Floors, galleries

BS 4592: 1970   *Industrial open type metal flooring and stair treads*

This standard covers industrial open type metal flooring panels and stair treads fabricated with metal load-bearing bars of uniform section. Materials, dimensions, design and testing are covered together with recommendations relating to fixing methods.

It is important to realize that this standard does not apply to flooring and stair treads used for escape stairways and ramps, neither does it apply to 'pressed metal' type flooring.

(24)   Stairs, ladders

BS 5578   *Building construction – stairs*

Part 1: 1978   *Vocabulary*
A most useful document for those starting out in construction technology since it defines all the special words, namely, the jargon, associated with stairs. What is a 'going', a 'riser', a 'string'? – all these and more are defined in this standard.

Part 2: 1978   *Modular co-ordination. Specification for co-ordinating dimensions for stairs and stair openings*
This is a very short standard giving general principles for co-ordinating dimensions of stairs and stair openings in buildings of all types. It does not specify or recommend actual modules as such.

BS 585:   *Wood stairs*

Part 1: 1984   *Straight-flight stairs and stairs with quarter or half*

landings for domestic use
This standard covers timber stairs and includes plywood risers; edge-to-edge jointed timber and glue-laminated wood components. An appendix gives recommendations for fixing stairs on site. Open risers flights with winder treads, stairs wider than 1220 mm and flights having a going in excess of 3800 mm are excluded.

Part 2: 1985   *Performance requirements for domestic stairs constructed of wood board materials*
This covers corkboard, chipboard, glue-laminated components, hardboard, laminboard, medium-density fibre board, plywood timber. Covers straight-flight stairs and stairs with quarter and half landings, intended for use inside one-family dwellings.

BS 4211: 1967   *Steel ladders for permanent access*

Steel ladders with single bar rings, permanently fixed to structures to provide a means of access are covered by this standard. The ladder may be of relatively short lengths between working platforms or of the type fixed to high structures in a continuous vertical length interspersed with landings.

Recommendations relating to materials, finishes, stringers, rings, safety hoops, etc. are provided. Figure 16 is typical of the working details provided.

BS 5395   *Stairs, ladders and walkways*

Part 1: 1977   *Code of practice for stairs*
■   AD (Reg. K1)

This is a general code covering the design of stairs and steps in a number of materials for all types of buildings.

The code does not cover ramps or ladders. Guidance is pro-

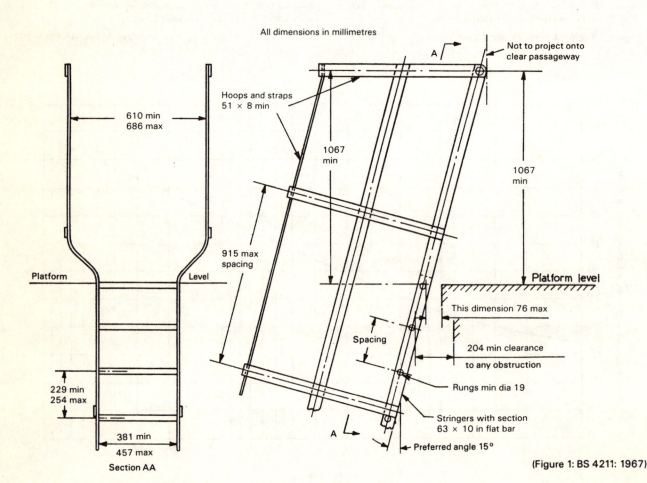

All dimensions in millimetres

Section AA

Figure 16   *Typical ladder to platform detail*

(Figure 1: BS 4211: 1967)

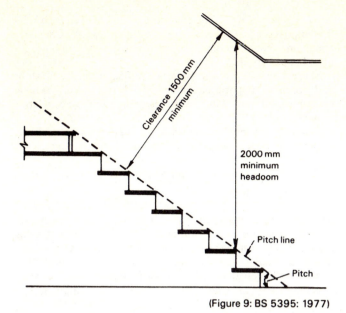

(Figure 9: BS 5395: 1977)

Figure 17 *Headroom: staircase*

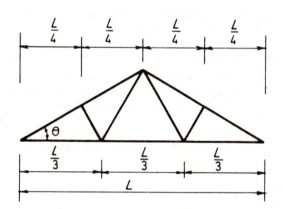

(From Figure 6: BS 5268: Part 3: 1985)

Figure 18 *Fink or 'W' trussed rafter*

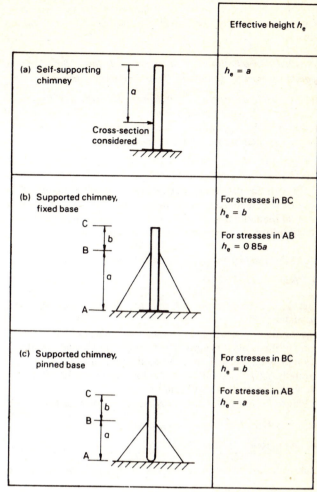

(Figure 1: BS 4076: 1978)

Figure 19 *Effective height of chimney shell*

vided on materials and components in concrete, metal and wood stairs, constructional design, protection and painting, maintenance and cleaning.

Much useful information is given in both tabular and sketch form, and Figure 17 is typical.

Part 2: 1982 *Code of practice for the design of helical and spiral stairs*

■ AD (Reg. K1)

This, too, gives constructional guidance.

(27) Roofs

BS 5268 *The structural use of timber* Part 3: 1985 *Code of practice for trussed rafters for roofs*

■ AD (Reg. A1/2)

Trussed rafters are in common use and Figure 18 shows a typical fink or 'W' truss with which this code mainly deals.

The design, fabrication and erection of trussed rafters for roofs of dwelling and similar buildings is provided for in this part of the code. It recommends maximum spans for a range of

member sizes under specified conditions with no requirement for calculation beyond an ability to assess the loading. The information in the code could be extended to apply to configurations other than the fink by engineers experienced in the use of structural timber.

BS 6229: 1982 *Code of practice for flat roofs with continuously supported coverings*

■ AD (Reg. F2)

Gives recommendations for the design and application of flat roofs with continuously supported roof coverings. Considers weather tightness, drainage, thermal and sound insulation, condensation control, structural support, fire precautions, maintenance and repair.

(28) Building frames, other primary elements

(28.8) Chimneys

BS 4076: 1978 *Steel chimneys*

The structural design and construction of steel chimneys is dealt with in this standard. It deals only with chimneys of circular cross-section either free-standing or guyed (see Figure 19). It covers the application of linings or cladding to such chimneys where required. Recommendations on inspection and maintenance are given. Proper warning is given that chimneys in pairs, rows or groups and those near structures of comparable height may be subjected to wind buffeting and consequently oscillation, not covered by this standard, would need to be seriously considered.

BS 6461: *Installation of chimneys and flues for domestic appliances burning solid fuels (including wood and peat)*

Part 1   *Code of practice for masonry chimneys and flue pipes*
Deals with design, construction and testing. Maximum heat output 45 kW. Appendices cover remedial action for defective chimneys, cleaning and maintenance.

Part 2: 1984   *Code of practice for factory-made insulated chimneys for internal application*
Deals with the installation of new factory-made insulated chimneys designed to serve appliances with chimneys of nominal internal diameter 100, 125, 150 and 200 mm with an appendix giving information on cleaning and maintenance.

BS 4543   *Factory-made insulated chimneys*

■ AD (Regs. J1/2/3)

Part 1: 1976   *Methods of test for factory-made insulated chimneys*
These chimneys are made in the factory and require no fabrication on site – only assembly. The tests covered include joint test, draught test, thermal shock test, thermal insulation test and strength test. Each is fully described and specified. The chimneys are valid for up to 45 kW rated output.

Figure 20 illustrates the installation for strength test.

Part 2: 1976   *Chimneys for solid fuel fired appliances*

■ AD (Regs. J1/2/3)

This standard refers to chimneys made up from the factory

components of Part 1. The chimneys are to be used with solid fuel appliances with a rated output of up to 45 kW. Chimneys complying with this standard might also be suitable for oil or gas fired appliances also.

Matters specified cover materials, erection, finish, firestops and spacers, support assemblies, wind resistance, terminal assembly and rain cap, joints, cleaning traps and relative dimensions.

Test requirements are specified for supports, joint leakage, draught, thermal shock, thermal insulation and strength.

Part 3: 1976   *Chimneys for oil fired appliances*

■ AD (Regs. J1/2/3)

This standard is largely the same as Part 2. The chimneys are again designed for a rated output of up to 45 kW but with a flue gas temperature at the appliance exit not to exceed 450 °C after any permanent draught break or before any stabilizer. The clauses are largely the same as for Part 2 but no cross-reference is made to CP 131, which covers only solid fuel appliances.

(29)   Parts, accessories, etc. special to primary elements, carcass

There are three standards under this classification, all of which deal with damp-proof courses, namely:

BS 743: 1970   *Materials for damp-proof courses*

This covers damp-proof course materials for normal situations. However, tanking of basements to withstand the penetration of water under pressure is not strictly within the scope of this standard.

Materials covered are lead, copper and bitumen-impregnated materials, as listed in Table 7, and mastic asphalt, polythene, slates and brick.

Table 7   *Composition of bitumen damp-proof courses and sheeting*

Type of damp-proof course			Minimum mass per unit area of complete material excluding packaging
			kg/m²
Hessian base			3.8
Fibre base			3.3
Asbestos base			3.8
Hessian base and lead	....	}	4.4
Fibre base and lead		}	4.4
Asbestos base and lead		}	4.9
Bitumen sheeting			5.4

(Table 1: BS 743: 1970)

Useful notes on the selection, laying and durability of damp-proof courses are given in Appendix C of the standard.

Reference should be made to CP 102: 1973 *Protection of buildings against water from the ground*.

BS 6515: 1984   *Polyethylene damp-proof courses for masonry*

This gives the requirements for the composition, thickness, finish and impregnating of polyethylene damp-proof courses

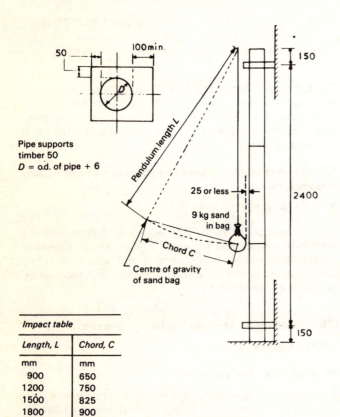

Pipe supports
timber 50
D = o.d. of pipe + 6

Impact table	
Length, L	Chord, C
mm	mm
900	650
1200	750
1500	825
1800	900

All dimensions in millimetres

(Figure 6: BS 4543: Part 1: 1976)

Figure 20   *Installation for strength test*

intended for use in masonry constructions. Appendices are included which give methods of determining the mass of material other than polyethylene, of measuring thickness and of assessing unfirmeability.

BS 6576: 1985 *Installation of chemical damp-proof courses*

Makes recommendations for the chemical treatment of rising damp in existing buildings with solid (single-leaf) walls, cavity walls, whether unfilled or filled, and random rubble-filled walls. It describes the procedures to be used for diagnosing rising damp and indicates essential precautions and procedures for installing chemical damp-proof courses. It does not cover treatment of walls below ground level or under hydrostatic pressure. Reference should be made to CP 102.

(3–) Secondary elements, completion of structure

(31) Secondary elements to walls, external walls

BS 493: 1970 *Airbricks and gratings for wall ventilation*

The standard classifies wall ventilating units as:

Class 1: airbricks, for use in external walls.
Class 2: wall ventilators or gratings for internal use.

Materials, design, workmanship and dimensions are specified. Coordinating sizes of airbricks and ventilators range from 225 × 75 mm to 300 × 300 mm. Examples of designs are shown in Figure 21.

BS 1243: 1978 *Metal ties for cavity wall construction*

■ AD (Reg. A1/2)

This standard covers wall ties manufactured from wire or strip and suitable for cavity walls. Where walls are constructed to dimensionally coordinated sizes the larger ties are adequate for the largest cavity.

Specifications for the following wall tie materials are provided: low carbon steel strip, low carbon steel wire, copper, copper alloys, stainless steel wire and stainless steel strip.

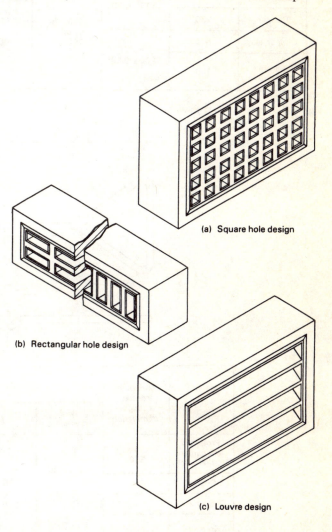

(a) Square hole design

(b) Rectangular hole design

(c) Louvre design

(Figure 31.1: BS 493: 1970)

Figure 21 *Typical examples of airbricks*

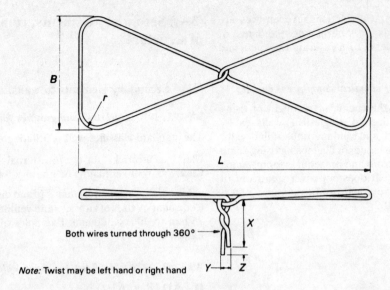

Both wires turned through 360°

Note: Twist may be left hand or right hand

Material	Minimum tensile strength of material	Dimensions and permissible deviations						
		Wire diameter	L	B	r (min)	X (min)	Y (max)	Z (max)
Protected low carbon steel wire	N/mm² 370	mm 3.15 ± 0.08	mm	mm	mm	mm	mm	mm
Copper	230		150 ± 5 or 200 ± 5	75 ± 5 or 100 ± 5	13	8 × wire diameter	3 × wire diameter	5
Copper alloy	530							
Stainless steel wire	460	2.60 ± 0.08						

Figure 22   *Butterfly type of wall tie*

(From BS 1243: 1978)

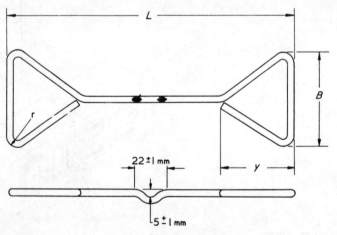

22 ± 1 mm

5 ± 1 mm

Material	Minimum tensile strength of material	Dimensions and permissible deviations				
		Wire diameter	L	B	r (min)	Y
Protected low carbon steel wire	N/mm² 370	mm 4.5 ± 0.08	mm	mm	mm	mm
Copper	250		150 ± 5 or 200 ± 5	65 ± 5	8	50 ± 5
Copper alloy	530					
Stainless steel wire	460	4.0 ± 0.08				

Figure 23   *Double-triangle type of wall tie*

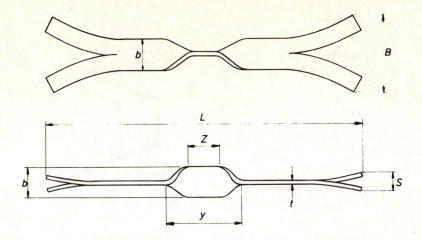

Material	Minimum tensile strength of material	Dimensions and permissible deviations						
		t	*b*	*L*	*B*	*Y* (max)	*Z* (min)	*S*
Protected low carbon steel strip	N/mm² 430	mm	mm	mm	mm	mm	mm	
Copper	280	Not less than 3.20 and not more than 4.83	20 ± 1	150 ± 5 200 ± 5 255 ± 5 305 ± 5	Not less than 30 and not more than 50	50		Split ends shall not be out of plane by more than 5
Copper alloy	460							
Austenitic stainless steel strip	510							

Figure 24 *Vertical-twist type of wall tie*

Ties are classified as butterfly wire wall ties (Figure 22), triangle wire wall ties (Figure 23) and vertical-twist strip wall ties (Figure 24).

Protective coatings are specified and the importance of the coating in relation to the life of the tie is stressed.

Valuable recommendations for fixing and jointing are given in Appendix F.

BS 5642 *Sills and copings*

Part 1: 1978 *Window sills of precast concrete, cast stone, clayware, slate and natural stone*
This standard deals with sills constructed in these materials

suitable for the use of windows complying with the requirements of BS 644 *Wood windows*, BS 990 *Steel windows generally for domestic and similar buildings* Part 2: 1972 *Metric units* and BS 4873: 1972 *Aluminium alloy windows*.

Dimensions, performance and construction details (cross-sections, jointing, damp-proof courses, groove for water bar and positions for fixings) are covered together with materials specifications for the various types of sill. Figure 25 illustrates two typical sills together with the standard's recommendations for the installation of damp-proof courses at sills.

Part 2: 1983 *Copings of precast concrete, cast stone, clayware, slate and natural stone*
This standard deals with the quality of the various materials

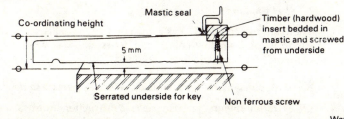

(a) Slate sill for metal windows

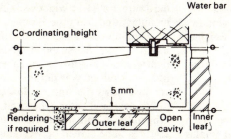

(b) Cast stone concrete or natural stone sill for timber windows

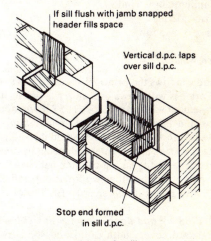

(c) Damp-proof course for sills

(Adapted from Figures 4, 5 and 8: BS 5642: Part 1: 1978)

Figure 25 *Types of sill*

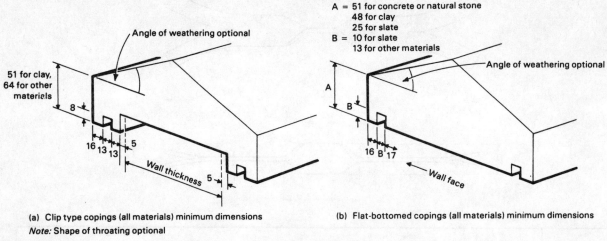

A = 51 for concrete or natural stone
48 for clay
25 for slate
B = 10 for slate
13 for other materials

Angle of weathering optional

51 for clay,
64 for other
materials

Angle of weathering optional

8

16 13 13   5

Wall thickness   5

A

B

16 B 17

Wall face

(a) Clip type copings (all materials) minimum dimensions
Note: Shape of throating optional

(b) Flat-bottomed copings (all materials) minimum dimensions

All dimensions in millimetres

Figure 26 *Types of copings*

together with the workmanship, functional requirements and the dimensions essential to meet them. No specific shape for copings is laid down although flat-bottomed and clip-type are identified (Figure 26).

BS 5977 *Lintels*

Part 1: 1981 *Methods for assessment of load*
This standard describes a method of assessing the load carried by lintels in masonry where lintels span up to 4.5 m in single storey buildings and up to 3.6 m in two- or three-storey buildings in normal domestic use and where no openings are wholly or partly within the load triangle defined as a 45° triangle having 1.1 times the clear span of the lintel at its base.

Part 2: 1983 *Prefabricated lintels*
This standard gives requirements for concrete, steel and timber prefabricated elements used in composite lintels for spans as above. Recommendations on materials protection against corrosion, design, workmanship and site installation are given.

(31.4) Windows (BS 6100 *Glossary of building and civil engineering terms* ss 1.3.5 *Doors, windows and openings* applies)

The standards for windows can be divided into five groups:

1 Wood windows.
2 Steel windows.
3 Aluminium alloy windows.
4 Security glazing.
5 Testing of windows.

1 *Wood windows*

For wood windows the principal standard is BS 644 *Wood windows*. Part 1 is withdrawn and under revision; it will deal with wood casement windows. Part 2: 1958 *Wood double-hung sash windows* and Part 3: 1951 *Wood double-hung sash and case windows (Scottish type)* cover wood double-hung sash windows with cased frames and counter-balancing by means of weights, or solid frames using spring counter-balancing devices.

Both parts require timber, workmanship and plywood to conform to BS 1186 and adhesives to BS 745 or BS 1204.

Part 2: 1958 *Wood double-hung sash windows*
This standard covers both cased and solid frame types with or without glazing bars. Overall dimensions for cased frames vary from 1146 mm high × 457 mm wide to 1756 mm high × 1143 mm wide for one light sash, 1822 mm wide for two light

sashes and 1828 mm wide for Venetian frame (three lights, outer sashes fixed and centre sashes hung). For solid frames overall dimensions are slightly smaller, however, provision is made for solid frames to be supplied with wider linings so that the overall sizes of such windows shall agree with the overall sizes of the cased frame types.

Recommendations are given for assembly, jointing and glazing bars for both types and also for axle pulleys for cased frames. Daylight areas of windows are given. Revision is in hand.

Part 3: 1951 *Wood double-hung sash and case windows (Scottish type)*
This standard differs from Part 2 in minor ways. First, terminology is suited to Scottish practice and, second, provision is made in the case of window with spiral sash devices for a Type H which enables the lower sash to open inwards to allow for cleaning.

Windows are available with or without astragals (glazing bars) and with astragals to the top sash only.

Working dimensions of one light windows range from 876 mm high × 368 mm wide to 1943 mm high × 1264 mm wide.

The specification for the construction of the actual frames and sashes is broadly similar to that contained in Part 2.

Linked to BS 644 Parts 2 and 3 is BS 6125: 1981 *Natural fibre cords, lines and twines*, which makes recommendations for the manufacture and subsequent finishing treatments of plaited cords, lines and twines. Table 1 of BS 6125 gives minimum breaking loads and strengths for plaited cordless sash cords.

2 *Steel windows*

There are two standards on steel windows. One deals with steel windows, sills, window boards and doors; and one with wood surrounds for steel windows and doors.

BS 6510: 1984 *Steel windows, sills, window boards and doors*

Gives requirements for materials, construction finishes and hardware for steel windows, sills, window boards and doors manufactured from the F range, or the heavier W20 range, of steel window sections. Weathertightness performance requirements for weatherstripped opening-light windows and fixed-light windows are also specified. Provision is included for glazing of frames but glass is not included. The standard also includes steel windows sills and window boards.

Window and door types and size limitations are given in Appendix A and summarized in Table 8. Details of optional features to be agreed between manufacturer and purchaser are given in Appendix B.

Recommendations for the site assembly of composites are

given in Appendix C and for marking in Appendix D.

Figure 27 shows a typical F range window and Figure 28 shows a typical W20 range window.

Table 8 *Window and door types and size limitations*

Window type	Maximum dimensions (mm)		
	Length	Height	Perimeter
F Range			
Fixed height	1800	1800	7200
Side-hung casement (open out)	600	1300	3800
Top-hung casement (open out)	1800	1300	4800
Bottom-hung casement (open in)	1200	1200	4800
Horizontally pivoted casement (reversible)	1500	1500	5200
Folder (fixed meeting rail) opening out	1200	1300	5000
Double door (open in or out)*	1200	2100	6600
Single door (as above)*	900	2100	6000
W20 Range			
Fixed light	3000	3000	9200
Side-hung casement (open in or out)	900	2400	6400
Top-hung casement (open out)	1800	1800	8400
Bottom-hung casement (open in)	1800	1500	6400
Horizontally pivoted casement (reversible)	1800	1800	6400
Vertically pivoted casement (open in or out one-thirds to two-thirds pivoted)	1150	2400	6500
ditto but centre pivoted	1500	2400	6500
Projected top-hung casement (open out)	1500	1200	4800
Folder (fixed meeting rail) (open in or out)	1800	2400	8000
Double door (open in or out)*	1800	2500	8400
Single door (open in or out)*	900	2500	6600

* Minimum height at kicking panel 300 mm

BS 1285: 1980 *Wood surrounds for steel windows and doors*

This covers subframes with both softwood and hardwood surrounds. Coordinating dimensions are designed to comply with windows and doors to which the surrounds are being fitted.

Recommendations are given on quality of timber, workmanship and jointing.

Typical details are shown in Figure 29.

3 Aluminium alloy windows

There is only one standard for these windows, namely BS 4873: 1972 *Aluminium alloy windows*, which covers single- and double-glazed units with various opening arrangements.

Recommendations are given for alloys, construction, finishes, weatherstripping and joint sealing materials, and hardware. Considerable stress is placed on ensuring that materials which are used in conjunction with the aluminium do not react with it. Specific reference is made to sliding devices, glazing, gaskets and hardware. Recommendations for the quality and preservation of timber where it forms an essential part of the windows are made.

Preferred coordinating sizes of windows range from 300 mm high × 600 mm wide to 2100 mm high × 1500 mm wide for fixed lights and from 500 mm high × 900 mm wide to 1500 mm high × 2400 mm wide for horizontally sliding windows. Preferred dimensions are also given for hinged, projecting, pivoted and vertically sliding windows.

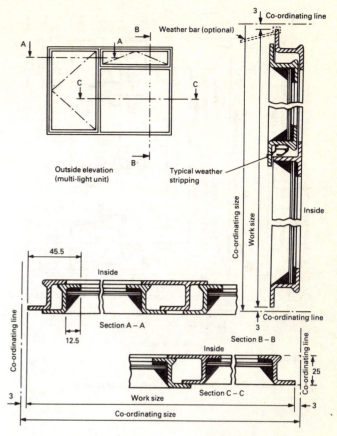

Figure 27 *Typical F range window*   (Figure 5: BS 6510: 1984)

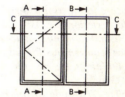

Outside elevation (multi-light unit)
NOTE: Putty or beads for glazing may be on an internal or external face.

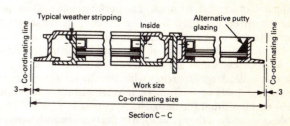

Figure 28 *Typical W20 range window*   (Figure 4: BS 6510: 1984)

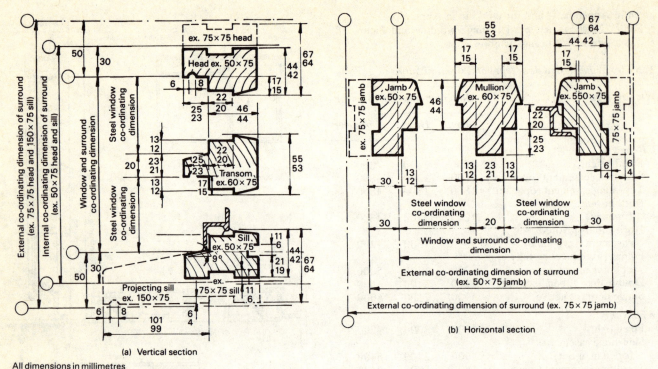

(a) Vertical section

All dimensions in millimetres

(Figure 31.4.4: BS 1285: 1980)

(b) Horizontal section

Figure 29 *Wood surround for steel windows and doors*

4 Security glazing

Three standards and one code of practice deal with security glazing. The standards BS 5051 *Security glazing* Part 1: 1973 *Bullet-resistant glazing for interior use* and Part 2: 1979 *Bullet-resistant glazing for exterior use*, BS 5544: 1978 *Anti-bandit glazing (glazing resistant to manual attack)* and BS 6206: 1981 *Impact performance requirements for flat safety glass and safety plastics for use in buildings* are covered in Table 3 'Materials' under section on 'Glass'.

Finally, BS 5357: 1976 *Code of practice for installation of security glazing* makes recommendations for installing anti-bandit glazing (framed) and bullet-resistant glazing (framed and unframed) for internal use.

5 Testing of windows

There are two standards and one draft for development dealing with testing of windows. They are dealt with in Table 4 'Activities, Requirements' under section (H1) 'Weather protection'.

In addition to the standards, BS 6262: 1982 *Code of practice for glazing for buildings* should be referred to. This contains much valuable information. Recommendations for the design, installation and maintenance of vertically glazed glass and plastic glazing sheet materials for the external walls and interiors of buildings are given. Design and performance are covered, including design and legislative requirements, effects of design on cost, glazing system, natural lighting, thermal sound and safety considerations – the latter including wind loading, fire, criminal attack and risk areas. The performance of glass, plastic glazing sheet materials, frame and sealing materials is considered in depth for each material including dimensional recommendations for glazing as well as glazing and fixing techniques.

Recommendations are also made on handling, storage and care on site, large openings with structural glass assemblies, frameless doors and entrances, mirrors and essential information required from the designer. Appendix A of BS 6262 provides guidance on the application of the recommendations of the code in some commonly occurring risk situations, namely the selection of glass and plastics for doors and side panels that can be mistaken for doors, and glass or plastics wholly or partially within 800 mm of the floor.

Reference should also be made to CP 153 *Windows and rooflights*, which is in three parts. Part 1: 1969 *Cleaning and safety* covers cleaning of glass and related problems of safety with regard to windows and rooflights. Recommendations are made covering not only the safety requirements for those who clean windows, whether professional or amateur, but also the precautions that need to be taken to safeguard people against the ordinary risks associated with glazing and glazed openings. Although the text refers only to glass, many of the recommendations, and particularly those relating to access to roof glazing, apply equally to other glazing material such as plastics.

The design information which is given on dangers associated with cleaning typical windows including maximum 'reaching' distances is very useful.

Part 2: 1970 *Durability and maintenance* deals with maintenance of wood and metal windows and roof glazing bars. Information is given on selection, protection on site, protective treatment required by timber and behaviour of metal window frames and roof glazing bars in different environments together with suggested requirements for washing and maintenance.

Part 3: 1972 *Sound insulation* covers sound transmission through windows, rooflights and glazed curtain walling. The code is to be regarded as an extension, in these particular directions, of the more basic information on sound transmission and insulation in buildings given in CP 3 Chapter III *Sound insulation and noise reduction*.

Guidance is given on the external noise levels likely to be experienced in various circumstances and on the degrees of sound insulation obtainable with various forms of glazing, so that noise penetrating indoors can be controled as may be desired.

Reference should also be made to BS 952 *Glass for glazing* Part 1: 1978 *Classification* and Part 2: 1980 *Terminology for work on glass* which is covered in Table 3 'Materials' under section o 'Glass'.

(31.5) Doors, doorsets, frames

In addition to BS 459 *Doors* Part 4 there are two standards on door frames, one standard on internal and external wood doorsets, door leaves and frames; one standard on aluminium framed sliding glass doors; one on locks and latches; two on measurement of defects in doors; and one on methods of testing doors for behaviour under humidity variations. Reference should also be made to PD 6512 Part 1: 1985, & BS 476 summarized in Table 4 Activities, requirements (K) Fire, explosion.

BS 459 *Doors*

Part 4: 1965 *Matchboarded doors*

This standard deals with ledged and braced doors, and framed, ledged and braced doors, the facing of both types consisting of tongued-and-grooved matchboarding. These doors are intended primarily for use as external doors. Recommendations are made for timber and adhesives.

Door sizes range from 1829 mm high × 610 mm wide to 1981 mm high × 762 mm wide for ledged and braced doors and from 1981 mm high × 686 mm wide to 2134 mm high × 1073 mm wide for framed, ledged and braced doors. Figure 30 shows the construction of each door type.

A revision is in hand (1986).

BS 1245: 1975 *Metal door frames (steel)*

Of the two standards on door frames one deals with metal and one wood. BS 1245: 1975 *Metal door frames (steel)* covers door frames fabricated from mild steel and protective coatings suitable for internal or external use. There are nine jamb profiles which are used to form the frames designed to accommodate walls or partitions of varying thickness. Frames with a coordinating height of 2100 mm are door height frames and those with greater coordinating heights are ceiling height frames and these include a transome and provision for glazing by means of putty or beads. Internal steel door frames are supplied with a base tie and external frames with a sill. Recommendations are made on manufacture, protective coatings and fixing lugs. Mild steel hinges are welded or screwed to frames as follows:

Mass of door leaf	No. of hinges	Method of application
Up to 30 kg	2	Welded
30 kg to 45 kg	3	Welded
Up to 45 kg	2	Screwed
45 kg to 60 kg	3	Screwed

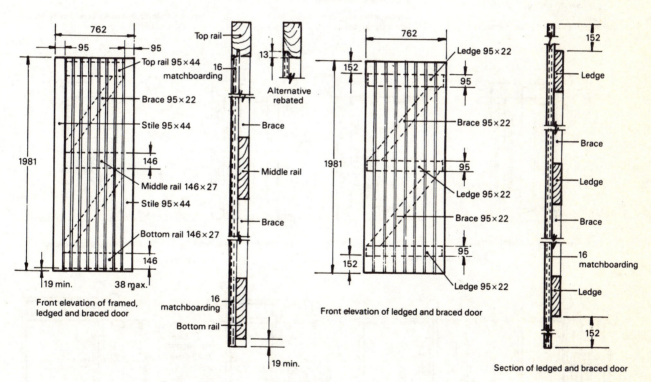

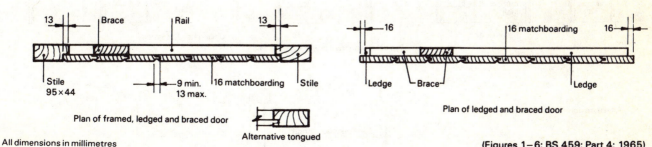

All dimensions in millimetres

(Figures 1–6: BS 459: Part 4: 1965)

Figure 30 *Matchboarded doors*

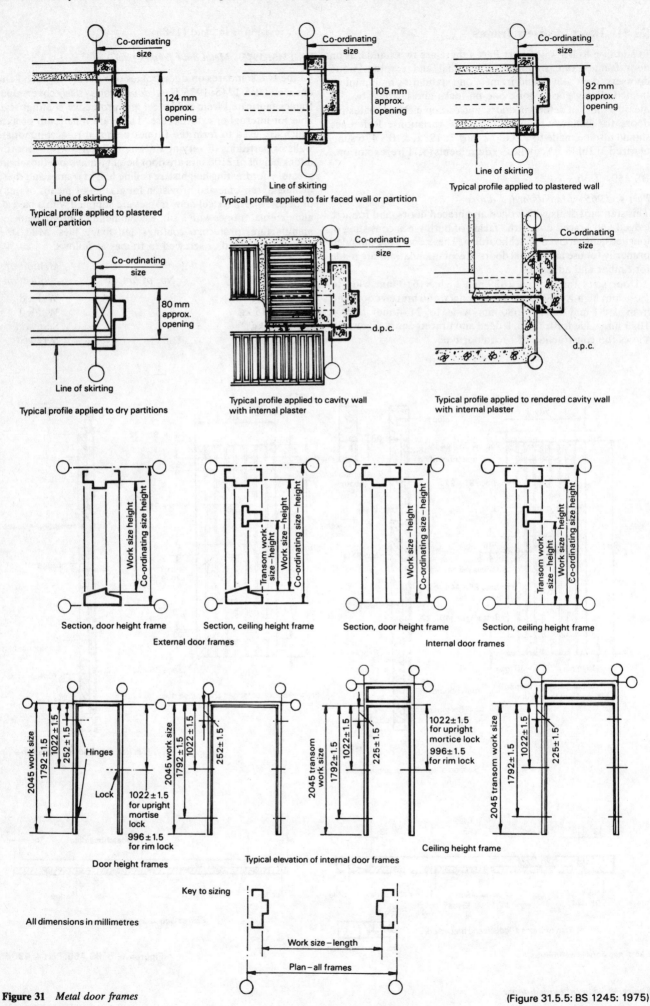

Figure 31   *Metal door frames*

(Figure 31.5.5: BS 1245: 1975)

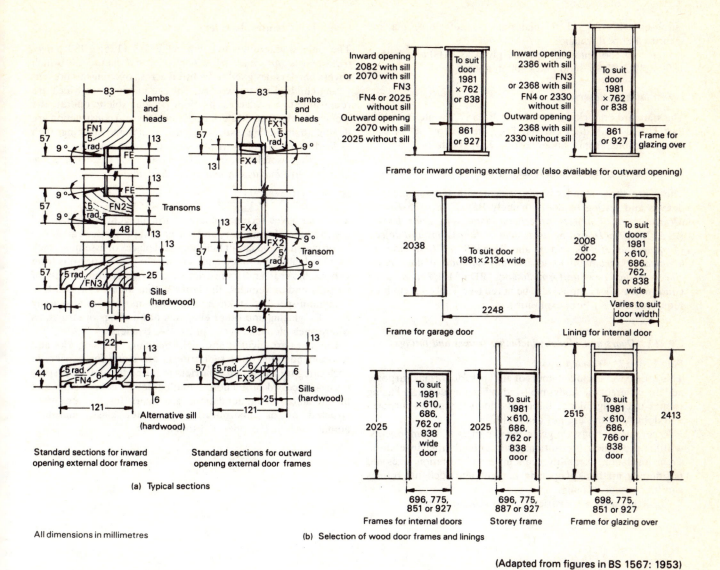

(a) Typical sections

All dimensions in millimetres

(b) Selection of wood door frames and linings

(Adapted from figures in BS 1567: 1953)

Figure 32 *Wood door frames and linings*

Frames are equipped with lock strike plates, mortar guards and rubber buffers.

Coordinating sizes for frames range from 2100 mm high × 900 mm wide (600 mm for internal frames) to 3000 mm high × 2100 mm wide.

Figure 31 shows typical door frames.

BS 1567: 1953   *Wood door frames and linings*

This covers standard wood frames and linings for external and internal doors. Recommendations are given for timber, adhesives, sills and winglights as well as for jointing and the provision of glazing beads for fanlights. Internal frames and linings are normally supplied unassembled except for storey height frames.

Figure 32 shows typical wood frames and linings.

BS 4787   *Internal and external wood doorsets, door leaves and frames*   Part 1: 1980   *Dimensional requirements*

This standard covers metric sizes for dimensionally coordinated internal and external wood doorsets, door leaves and frames suitable for internal door leaves for single doors 2040 mm high × 526, 626, 726, 826 and 926 mm wide × 40 or 44 mm thick and external door leaves for single doors 1994 mm high × 806 and 906 mm wide × 40 or 44 mm thick. The base co-

ordinating dimensions are given as:

Height of door leaf sets	2100 mm
Height of ceiling height sets	2300 mm
	2350 mm
	2400 mm
	2700 mm
	3000 mm
Width of all doorsets	600 S (internal only)
(S – single leaf set)	700 S (internal only)
(D – double leaf set)	800 S and D (internal only)
	900 S (D also internal only)
	1000 S (D also internal only)
	1200 D
	1500 D
	1800 D
	2100 D

All dimensions are given including doorstep width, rebate depth, clearances, permissible deviations, position of lock/latch (centre line to be centrally in height of leaf) and hinges. In addition minimum margins around glazing are given.

BS 5286: 1978   *Aluminium framed sliding glass doors*

This standard makes recommendations for single- and double-glazed aluminium framed sliding glass doors for general purposes with regard to materials, manufacture, glazing, security and performance.

Preferred coordinating sizes are given as 2100 mm high × 1800, 2400, 2700, 3600 and 4800 mm wide.

Locks, latches, closers, etc.

The standard on locks and latches is BS 5872, while BS 6459: Part 1 deals with door closers. They are covered in Table 2 'Constructions, forms' under section Xt7 'Hardware'.

Measurement of defects and testing of doors

There are three standards which deal with measurement of defects and testing of doors, namely BS 5277: 1976 *Doors. Measurement of defects of general flatness of door leaves*; BS 5278: 1976 *Doors. Measurement of dimensions and defects of squareness of door leaves*; and BS 5369: 1976 *Methods of testing doors; behaviour under humidity variations of door leaves placed in successive uniform climates*. PD 6512: Part 1: 1985 *Guide to fire doors* should also be noted (see Table 4 Activities, requirements (K) Fire, explosion).

CP 151   *Doors and windows including frames and linings*

Part 1: 1957   *Wooden doors*
This code covers wooden doors of all types for normal purposes and the different methods employed in hanging doors and fixing frames and linings, doors to fitments, doors for special purposes and door furniture are not dealt with.

Recommendations are given for materials and components, weather protection, precautions against fire, thermal insulation, sound insulation, durability, economy, pest infestation, sizes and positioning, methods of opening, fanlights and sidelights, frames and linings and hanging.

This code does not restrict itself to standard doors.

(35)   Suspended ceilings

There are no British Standards on suspended ceilings, however there is much useful information in CP 290: 1973 *Suspended ceilings and linings of dry construction using metal fixing systems* which deals with the design of suspended ceilings and lining systems for concealment of services, etc. including thermal insulation, acoustic absorption, sound insulation, illumination, heating and ventilating ceilings. It also recommends principles of design and construction to establish satisfactory design criteria for the purpose of fire protection and includes recommendations for tendering and measurement procedures, coordination of work on and off site and for care and maintenance.

Fixing systems for fibrous plaster panels are included.

(37.4)   Rooflights

There are no British Standards on rooflights, however there are three very useful codes of practice. Two of these, BS 6262: 1982 *Code of practice for glazing for buildings* and CP 153 *Windows and rooflights*, have been summarized under section (31.4) 'Windows'. The third code, BS 5516: 1977 *Code of practice for patent glazing*, deals with patent glazing, sloping and vertical, single and double. Recommendations are given for glazing bars, ancillary components and types of glass most commonly used. Information is also provided on such matters as fire resistance, thermal insulation and the use of special glasses. Systems supported on all four edges as well as the conventional two edge manner are covered.

(38)   Balustrades, barriers

The only standard on this subject is BS 4125: 1982 *Safety requirements for child safety barriers for domestic use* which covers barriers designed to be fitted across openings to prevent young children up to two years of age passing, but which are removable to allow access by older persons able to operate the locking mechanism. Materials, dimensions and construction are dealt with, including restrictions on coatings and finishings such as lead which are of particular importance in this case.

A further useful reference is BS 6180: 1982 *Code of practice for protective barriers in and about buildings*

■   AD (Regs. K2/3)

This code gives recommendations for the general design and construction of temporary and permanent protective barriers to be provided in and about buildings and places of assembly, such barriers being positioned and designed to protect persons from various hazards and to restrict or control the movements of persons and/or vehicles, the latter within areas restricted to a maximum speed of 16 km/h. The recommendations also apply to walls, glazing and other elements of buildings or structures where such elements act as protective barriers.

Buildings are divided into eight building-use categories and recommendations on design criteria are made for barriers in each category and also for barriers required for audience, spectator and crowd protection. Detailed design construction and maintenance recommendations are made for barriers, constructed of or incorporating concrete, glass, masonry, aluminium, steel, copper and timber.

(4–) Finishes to structure

(41) Wall finishes, external

Two British Standards deal with external wall finishes, one is a glossary of terms and the other relates to cladding colours. There are, however, standards dealing with specific materials, such as BS 690 *Asbestos-cement slates and sheets* Parts 2–6 which are summarized in Table 2 'Constructions, forms' under section N 'Rigid sheets for overlapping'. In addition there are several codes of practice which contain valuable information.

The standard relating to cladding colours is BS 4904: 1978 *External cladding colours for building purposes* which gives preferred colours for external cladding in aluminium, asbestos-cement, opaque glass (used with a back-up wall or similar arrangement), opaque plastics or steel.

The standard covers thirty-eight colours including black and white for vitreous enamel for building purposes selected from BS 4900: 1976 *Vitreous enamel colours for building purposes* and colours for opaque plastics for building purposes selected from BS 4901: 1976 *Plastics colours for building purposes*. Reference should be made to these standards. It is also necessary to consult BS 5252: 1976 *Framework for colour coordination for building purposes*. See Table 4 'Activities, requirements', section (G5) 'Colour'.

The other standard is BS 4049: 1966 *Glossary of terms applicable to internal plastering, external rendering and floor screeding*.

Of the codes of practice two deal with applied finishes (external rendering and ceramic tiles), two with heavy non-load-bearing claddings (pre-cast concrete and natural stone), one with glass and the other with light claddings which can be used for walls or roofs.

Applied finishes

BS 5262: 1976 *Code of practice for external rendered finishes*

■ AD (Reg. C4)

Covers external renderings on all common types of backgrounds.

The standard includes renderings on both new and old backgrounds and the maintenance and repair of existing work while BS 5385 *Code of practice for wall tiling* Part 2: 1978 *External ceramic wall tiling and mosaics* covers external ceramic wall tiling and mosaic (including glazed and unglazed ceramics, glass and marble) in normal conditions. The code deals with the types and classes of backgrounds and their suitability to receive a bedded finish using the following fixing methods, which also are described in the relevant sections:

1 Bedding in cement: sand mortar on rendering or as a direct bedding method.
2 Bedding in cement-based adhesives on an intermediate substrate or as a direct bedding method.
3 Bedding in organic-based adhesives on an intermediate substrate or as a direct bedding method.
4 Bedding in other adhesives on an intermediate substrate or as a direct bedding method.

Heavy claddings

CP 297: 1972 *Precast concrete cladding (non-load-bearing)*

■ AD (Reg. C4)

This deals with the design and use of precast concrete cladding in the form of:

1 An applied facing held to a solid background by mechanical means such as metal fixings.
2 Units supported by the structural frame of the building.
3 Permanent formwork held mechanically to a background of *in situ* concrete.

Load-bearing cladding or cladding held only by adhesion is not included, nor is any type of cladding supported or held in position around the perimeter of cladding units by metal framing.

The provisions contained in this code relate only to the best known conventional practices at the time of publication and are based on current cladding techniques, while CP 298: 1972 *Natural stone cladding (non-load-bearing)*

■ AD (Reg. C4)

This deals with the design and use of stone cladding in the form of:

1 An applied facing held to a solid background by mechanical means such as metal fixings.
2 Units supported by the structural frame of the building.
3 Permanent formwork held mechanically to a background of *in situ* concrete.

The code includes valuable information on materials, design considerations and workmanship in production and erection, moving, storage and protection.

Glass

The code dealing with glass is BS 6262: 1982 *Code of practice for glazing for buildings* which is summarized under section (31.4) 'Windows'.

Light claddings

For light claddings reference should be made to CP 143 *Sheet roof and wall coverings*

■ AD (Reg. C4)

Part 1: 1958 *Aluminium, corrugated and troughed*; Part 5: 1964 *Zinc*; Part 10: 1973 *Galvanized corrugated sheet. Metric units*; Part 11: 1970 *Lead. Metric units*; Part 12: 1970 *Copper. Metric units*; and Part 15: 1973 *Aluminium. Metric units* which are summarized under (47) 'Roof finishes'.

BS 5247 *Code of practice for sheet roof and wall coverings* Part 14: 1975 *Corrugated asbestos-cement*

■ AD (Reg. C4)

This deals with the design and construction of asbestos-cement, sheet coverings of various profiles to walls and roofs. Information is included on weather resistance, durability, thermal insulation, fire hazard and other characteristics, also recommendations for maintenance. This code is not applicable to small domestic buildings such as garages and garden sheds not exceeding 20 m² in floor area.

BS 5534 *Code of practice for slating and tiling* Part 1: 1978 *Design* covers the design and application of slating and tiling, underlay, loading, counter battens, flashings and their fixings. Weathertightness and thermal resistance are considered. This code does not deal with stone slab roofing or techniques peculiar to certain parts of the country.

For further reference BS 5427: 1976 *Code of practice for performance and loading criteria for profiled sheeting in building* is summarized under section (49) 'Parts, accessories, etc.'.

(42) Wall finishes, internal

There is only one British Standard relating to internal wall finishes and that is BS 4049: 1966 *Glossary of terms applicable to internal plastering, external rendering and floor screeding*. However, there are standards dealing with specific materials such as BS 1281: 1974 *Glazed ceramic tiles and tile fittings for internal walls* which is summarized in Table 2 'Constructions, forms' under section S 'Rigid tiles'.

Reference can also be made to BS 6452 *Beads for internal plastering and dry lining* Part 1: 1984 *Galvanized steel beads*, and to BS 6262: 1982 *Code of practice for glazing for buildings* which is summarized under (31.4) 'Windows', and CP 290: 1973 *Suspended ceilings and linings of dry construction using metal fixing systems* which is summarized under (35) 'Suspended ceilings'.

Wall tiling

For wall tiling, reference should be made to BS 5385 *Code of practice for wall tiling* Part 1: 1976 *Internal ceramic wall tiling and mosaics in normal conditions*. The code deals with the types and classes of backgrounds and their suitability to receive a bedded finish using the following fixing methods:

1 Bedding in cement-based adhesives on an intermediate substrate or as a direct bedding method.
2 Bedding in organic-based adhesives on an intermediate substrate or as a direct bedding method.
3 Bedding in other adhesives on an intermediate substrate or as a direct bedding method.

An appendix specifies test requirements for adhesives. This is included pending the issue of a British Standard.

Plastering

BS 5492: 1977 *Code of practice for internal plastering* makes recommendataions for internal plastering on all types of background for use under normal conditions.

The standard contains guidance on materials, types of background, preparation of the surface to be plastered, choice of a suitable plastering system, methods of application (including mechanical project plastering techniques) and maintenance.

A further reference is the draft for development DD 71 *Guide to sprayed mineral insulation* Part 1: 1981 *Sprayed mineral fibre* which is summarized in Table 4 'Activities, requirements' under section (M2) 'Thermal insulation'.

(43)   Floor finishes

Apart from a number of standards on the method of determination of thickness of various floor coverings there are some sixteen valuable standards which deal with particular types of covering. In addition there is one standard which deals with colours, namely BS 4902: 1976 *Sheet and tile flooring colours*

for building purposes, which gives preferred colours for the following types of flooring: sheet linoleum (calendered types), cork carpet and linoleum tiles, solid rubber flooring, felt backed linoleum, thermoplastic flooring tiles, PVC (vinyl) asbestos floor tiles, unbacked flexible PVC flooring, homogeneous flooring, backed flexible PVC flooring, needle-loom felt backed flooring, terrazzo tiles, precast terrazzo units, *in situ* terrazzo flooring, clay tiles for flooring and ceramic mosaic flooring. *See also* Table 4 'Activities, requirements' section (G5) 'Colour'.

The floor coverings which are described can be divided into six groups:

1 *In situ* floor finishes.
2 Tile flooring and slab flooring.
3 Sheet and tile flooring (cork, linoleum, plastics and rubber).
4 Flooring of wood and wood products.
5 Textile floor coverings.
6 Coir matting.

1   In situ floor finishes

There is one standard relating to *in situ* finishes. BS 776 *Materials for magnesium oxychloride (magnesite) flooring* Part 2: 1972 *Metric units* provides detailed specifications of the various materials – calcined magnesite, magnesium chloride, wood flour, sawdust, other aggregates and fillers and pigments for use in the manufacture of magnesium oxychloride flooring composition and is intended to be used in conjunction with the relevant part of CP 204. In addition requirements are specified for testing.

In addition reference should be made to CP 204 *In situ floor finishes* Part 2: 1970 *Metric units* which gives much valuable information including recommendations for the laying of the floor finish and for the bases on which it may be laid. In addition to magnesium oxychloride and pitch mastic the code deals with concrete (including granolithic), terrazzo, mastic asphalt and cement rubber-latex flooring.

2   Tile flooring and slab flooring

Reference should be made to BS 6431 *Ceramic floor and wall tiles*, in Table 2 Materials, S Rigid tile work.

Each of these types of flooring has its own specification. BS 1197 *Concrete flooring tiles and fittings* Part 2: 1973 (1980) *Metric units* covers hydraulically pressed flooring tiles made with cement and aggregate. The tiles may be plain or coloured, matt or polished. Specifications for cement, pigment, aggregate, additives and admixtures are given. Shape, finish, uniformity of colour and tolerances are specified.

Table 9 shows sizes of square tiles, Table 10 shows dimensionally coordinated tiles while Table 11 gives sizes of skirtings and fittings which are illustrated in Figure 33 .

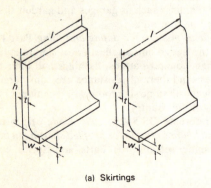

(a) Skirtings

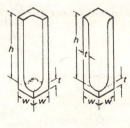

(b) Internal angles

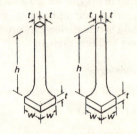

(c) External angles

(From BS 1197: Part 2: 1973)

Figure 33   *Concrete tiles: skirtings and fittings*

Table 9 *Sizes of square tiles*

Length of each side	Thickness
Work size	Work size
mm	mm
150	15
200	20
225	20
300	30
400	35
500	40
Permissible deviation ± 1 mm	Permissible deviation ± 3 mm

When laid, diagonal and rectangular half-tiles shall conform to the above sizes.

(Table 1: BS 1197: Part 2 1973 (1980))

Table 10 *Dimensionally co-ordinated sizes for tiles*

These sizes may be supplied by agreement between the purchaser and the supplier

Length of tile-side co-ordinating size	mm 300	mm 400	mm 500
Joint clearance	3	3	3
Work size	297	397	497
Permissible deviation on work size	± 1	± 1	± 1
Maximum limit of manufacturing size	298	398	498
Minimum limit of manufacturing size	296	396	496
Thickness, work size (not dimensionally co-ordinated)	30 ± 3	35 ± 3	40 ± 3

(Table 3: BS 1197: Part 2: 1973)

Table 11 *Sizes of skirtings and fittings*

Dimension (*see* Figure 36)		Work size	Permissible deviation
		mm	mm
Length of skirting	(*l*)	150	± 1
		200	± 1
		225	± 1
		300	± 1
		400	± 1
		450	± 1
		500	± 1
		600	± 1
		675	± 1
		750	± 1
		800	± 1
		900	± 1
Base width	(*w*)	40	± 1
Height	(*h*)	100	± 1
		150	± 1
Thickness	(*t*)	12	± 3
Radius of cove		25	± 3
Radius of bull-nose (if made)		8	± 4

(Table 2: BS 1197: Part 2: 1973)

BS 4131: 1973 *Terrazzo tiles* deals with hydraulically-pressed terrazzo floor and wall tiles. Requirements are specified for cement, aggregate, pigments and additives or admixtures together with recommendations on manufacture and surface treatment. Shape, tolerances, finishes, age at delivery (seven days minimum after pressing), uniformity of colour and freedom from defects or flaws are specified together with requirements for water absorption, transverse strength, protection in transit, stacking tiles on site, special use of tiles and maintenance of terrazzo tiling.

Tables 12 and 13 show normal and dimensionally coordinated sizes of tiles.

Table 12 *Sizes of tiles: terrazzo tiles*

Length of each side	Thickness
Work size	Work size
mm	mm
150 ± 1	15 ± 3
200 ± 1	20 ± 3
225 ± 1	20 ± 3
300 ± 1	30 ± 3
400 ± 1	35 ± 3
500 ± 1	40 ± 3

(Table 2: BS 4131: 1973)

Table 13 *Dimensionally co-ordinated sizes for tiles*

	Length of tile-side		
	mm	mm	mm
Co-ordinating size	300	400	500
Joint clearance	3	3	3
Work size	297	397	497
Permissible deviation from work size	± 1	± 1	± 1
Maximum limit of manufacturing size	298	398	498
Minimum limit of manufacturing size	296	396	496
Thickness (work size)	30 ± 3	35 ± 3	40 ± 3

Tiles made to these sizes should be laid in accordance with the recommendations given in CP 202 *Tile flooring and slab flooring* for jointing and laying floor tiles.

(Table 3: BS 4131: 1973)

BS 1286: 1974 *Clay tiles for flooring* deals with ceramic floor tiles and clay floor quarries, sills and associated fittings. Ceramic floor tiles differ from quarries in that while the former have a fine finish produced by compaction of blended ceramic powders the latter are of substantial uniform thickness, produced by extrusion or other plastic forming from any suitable clay or combination of clays and other minerals. Quality, colour, water absorption and deviations from facial size, work size thickness, squareness, warpage and curvature are specified for both types. Requirements for ceramic floor tiles being of a higher standard in each case than those for quarries.

Tiles are shown as modular and non-modular. Preferred coordinating sizes for modular tiles are as follows:

Ceramic tiles	Quarries
100 × 100 × 9.5 mm	200 × 100 × 19 mm
200 × 100 × 9.5 mm	100 × 100 × 19 mm and diagonal halves

Preferred sizes for non-modular tiles are also given, the predominant range of which is as follows:

Ceramic tiles	Quarries
152 × 152 × 12.5 mm	229 × 229 × 32 mm and diagonal halves
152 × 152 × 9.5 mm	229 × 114 × 32 mm
152 × 76 × 12.5 mm	152 × 152 × 16 mm and diagonal halves
152 × 76 × 9.5 mm	152 × 152 × 19 mm and diagonal halves
(Thicknesses of 16 and 19 mm are also acceptable.)	152 × 152 × 22 mm and diagonal halves
	152 × 76 × 16 mm
	152 × 76 × 19 mm
	152 × 76 × 22 mm
	150 × 150 × 15 mm
	(Thicknesses of 12.5, 25 and 29 mm are also acceptable.)

Note: Thicknesses quoted are exclusive of bedding.

A range of floor tile fittings is also quoted as follows:

Ceramic tiles		Quarries	
Modular	Non-modular	Modular	Non-modular
Round edge	Round edge	Round edge	Round edge
	Square top cove base		Round top cove base skirting
	Round top cove skirting		Square top cove base skirting
	Angle beads		
	Coves		
	Channels		
	Step treads		

Figure 34 shows modular and non-modular ceramic tile fittings while Figure 35 shows quarry fittings.

Reference should also be made to CP 202: 1972 *Tile flooring and slab flooring* which deals with all work involved in the laying of clay floor tiles, terrazzo tiles and slabs, brick floors, stone floors and asphalt tiles bedded on a solid base. Useful information on design considerations, maintenance, resistance of jointing materials to various liquids and solutions is given together with a guide to sealing compounds and recommendations on floor finish and bedding techniques for different traffic and base conditions.

3   Sheet and tile flooring

Cork

There are no specific standards dealing with cork flooring. However, BS 810: 1966 *Sheet linoleum (calendered types), cork carpet and linoleum tiles* refers to cork carpet manufactured as calendered sheet on a jute canvas backing designated in thicknesses of 8.0, 6.7, 4.5 and 3.2 mm, in widths of 1.83 m and in lengths not less than 9.3 m with a uniform surface free from streaks and marks. Requirements are specified for residual indentation, seasoning, flexibility, adhesion and marking.

Linoleum

There are two standards dealing with linoleum, namely BS 810: 1966 *Sheet linoleum (calendered types), cork carpet and linoleum tiles* and BS 1863: 1952 *Felt backed linoleum*. The former deals with plain, moiré, jaspé and marble linoleum and linoleum tiles manufactured as calendered sheet on a jute canvas backing. Thicknesses vary from 2.0 to 6.7 mm for plain and marble linoleum and from 1.6 to 6.7 mm for moiré and jaspé, in widths of 1.83 m and in lengths of not less than 9.3 m (4.6 m for 6.0 and 6.7 mm thickness). Linoleum tiles are 228 or 305 mm square. Requirements are specified for residual indentation, seasoning, flexibility, adhesion, water absorption and colour fastness.

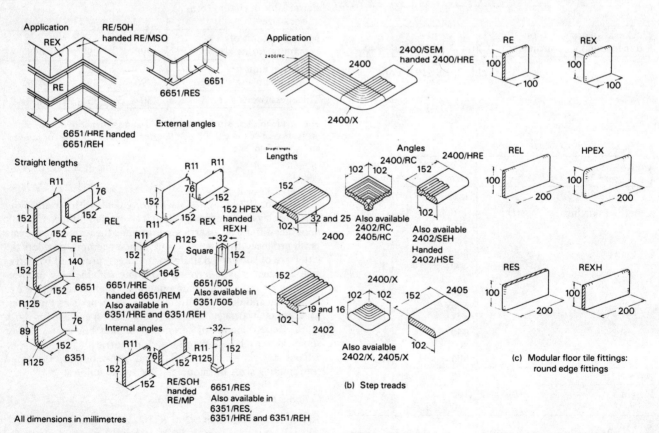

(Figures 1 and 2: BS 1286: 1974)

Figure 34   *Ceramic tile fittings*

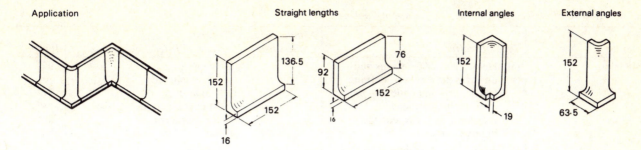

Application   Straight lengths   Internal angles   External angles

These fittings are also available with a height of 92 mm in order to match the straight lengths of that height

All dimensions in millimetres

(a) Non-modular floor quarry fittings: square top cove base skirtings

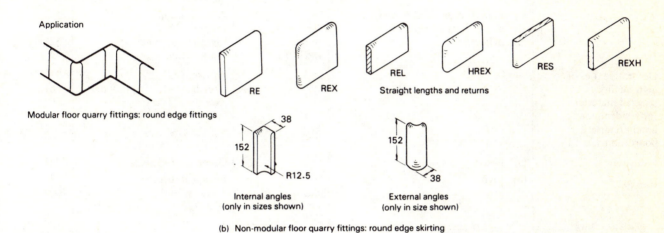

Application

Modular floor quarry fittings: round edge fittings

RE   REX   REL   HREX   RES   REXH

Straight lengths and returns

Internal angles
(only in sizes shown)

External angles
(only in size shown)

(b) Non-modular floor quarry fittings: round edge skirting

Figure 35 *Quarry fittings* (Adapted from BS 1286: 1974)

BS 1863: 1952 *Felt backed linoleum* covers flexible floor coverings comprising a wearing layer of linoleum composition united to a bituminized felt base. Requirements are specified for quality of materials, finishes and methods of testing.

Plastics

There are four standards dealing with plastic flooring; two cover tiles and two cover flexible flooring. BS 2592: 1973 *Thermoplastic flooring tiles* requires tiles to consist of a thoroughly blended composition of thermoplastic binder (mineral asphalt and/or thermoplastic resins such as those obtained from the distillation of coal or oil with or without polymers or copolymers of vinyl chloride), asbestos fibre, fillers and pigments. Tiles may be plain or mottled, 2.5 or 3 mm thick × 300 or 250 mm square. Requirements are specified for deflection and resistance to impact, indentation and curling. The other standard on tiles is BS 3260: 1969 *PVC (vinyl) asbestos floor tiles* which specifies requirements for homogeneous PVC (vinyl) asbestos floor tiles covering materials, colour and finish, dimensions and performance requirements.

Of the two standards dealing with flexible PVC flooring BS 3261 *Unbacked flexible PVC flooring* Part 1: 1973 *Homogeneous flooring* classifies the materials into two types. Type A materials meet specified requirements for elasticity and flexibility while Type B materials have no elasticity and flexibility requirements. The constituency of the flooring is of a thoroughly blended composition of thermoplastic binder (consisting substantially of vinyl chloride polymer and/or vinyl chloride copolymer), fillers and pigments (the polymeric material is compounded with suitable plasticizers and stabilizers). Flooring may be plain or patterned, with or without an embossed surface and of thickness 1.5, 2.0, 2.5 or 3.0 mm, in widths 1.2, 1.5, 1.8, 2.0 and 2.1 m. Provisions for tiles are also covered. Requirements are specified for colour fastness to daylight,

residual indentation, flexibility, ply adhesion, dimensional stability, curling, moisture movement, heat ageing, extrudation, resistance to various substances and elasticity.

The second standard, BS 5085 *Backed flexibility PVC flooring* Part 1: 1974 *Needle-loom felt backed flooring* and Part 2: 1976 *Cellular PVC backing*, deals with flexible PVC flooring with a wear layer, an underlayer and a backing layer. The materials and surface characteristics in the wear layer and underlayer are substantially as specified in BS 3261 Part 1: 1973. The backing layer for needle-loom felt backed flooring consists of natural fibres needled into a hessian support while that for cellular backed PVC flooring consists of a layer of plasticized vinyl chloride polymer and/or vinyl chloride copolymer, suitably stabilized and converted into a cellular state by chemical blowing or the physical entrapment of air. The backing may contain fillers and/or pigments. A reinforcing layer of woven or nonwoven fabric may be incorporated between the wear layer and the cellular backing. Thicknesses of cellular PVC backed flooring are given as 2.0, 2.5, 3.0 and 4.5 mm with a minimum wear layer thickness of 1.0 mm and minimum backing of 1.0 mm. Requirements are specified for both types for colour fastness to daylight, ply adhesion, residual indentation, low temperature flexibility, dimensional stability and resistance to heat ageing. Requirements for needle-loom felt backing also include mass per unit area of felt and PVC, resistance to staining and sheer strength of felt while those for cellular PVC backing include compressibility, moisture movement and elasticity.

Rubber

There are two standards which deal with rubber flooring, namely BS 1711: 1975 *Solid rubber flooring* and BS 3187: 1978 *Electrically conducting rubber flooring*. The former standard deals with solid rubber flooring composed of vulcanized rubber compounds with smooth or raised pattern, plain or marbled in either

Table 14   *Hardwoods and softwoods suitable for use in flooring*

Class of traffic	Type of traffic	Number of timbers listed	Random selection of timbers listed	Weight*
1 Pedestrian	(a) Heavy (i.e. 2000 persons and upwards per day: e.g. definite traffic lanes in public institutions, barracks, industrial canteens, corridors in large schools)	33	Banga wanga European oak Nakarati Malayan keruing Panga panga Purpleheart	993 705 977 785 801 865
	(b) Normal (i.e. less than 2000 persons per day, e.g. village halls, school classrooms, hotels, offices, shops)	65 (including all in 1(a))	Afzelia Gurjun Iroko Makoré Ramin Sapele/utile	753 705–37 657 609 657 641–64
	(c) Light (i.e. residential and domestic buildings, small offices)	88 (including all in 1(a) and 1(b))	African walnut Idigbo Light red meranti Parana pine	545 545 528 528
2 Decorative (i.e. of high quality, selected material for residential and hotel premises, boardrooms, etc.)	—	20	Afrormosia Grevillea/African silky oak Yew	737 561 609
3 Industrial	(a) Heavy	17	Greenheart	1041
	(b) Light	14 plus the hardwoods in 2	European beech Tallowwood	721 1009
4 Special	(a) High impermeability to acids, etc.	19	European oak Jarrah	705 865
	(b) Small movement. (i) Industrial processes involving wide temperature and humidity changes	6	Muhuhu	865
	(ii) Residences and other buildings with floor panel heating	14 plus hardwoods in 4(b)(i)	Agba Guarea Teak	497 609 689
	(iii) Gymnasia	18	Douglas fir, rift sawn only Pillarwood	457 737
	(iv) Ballrooms	13	Danta Yellow birch	737 689
	(v) Skating rinks	7	Rock maple	737

*In kg/m^3 at 12 % moisture content.

(Adapted from BS 1187: 1959)

Table 15   *Nominal dimensions of fingers, component squares and mosaic parquet panels*

Fingers			Component squares			Panels			Dimensions in millimetres
Thickness	Width	Length	Thickness	Width × length	Number of fingers	Thickness	Width × length	Number of component squares	
6	20	100	6	100 × 100	5	6	400 × 400	16	
8	22.4	112	8	112 × 112	5	8	448 × 448	16	
10	22.4	112	10	112 × 112	5	10	448 × 448	16	
10	25	125	10	125 × 125	5	10	500 × 500	16	

Note: On agreement between the interested parties, fingers, component squares and panels having other dimensions may be produced.

(Table 1: BS 4050: Part 1: 1977)

sheet or tile form. Thicknesses are 3, 4, 5 or 6 mm with widths of 0.9, 1.2, 1.5, 1.8, 2.0 and 2.1 m while tiles are 225, 250, or 300 mm square. Requirements are specified for composition of materials, colour fastness to cleaning materials and daylight, hardness and compression set.

BS 3187 also specifically covers the electrical resistance of the flooring both before and after laying.

For all floor coverings in this classification reference should also be made to CP 203: 1969 *Sheet and tile flooring (cork, linoleum, plastics and rubber)* Part 2: 1972 *Metric units* which makes recommendations for the selection, laying and maintenance of cork tiles and cork carpet, linoleum sheet and tiles, rubber sheet and tiles, thermoplastic and PVC (vinyl) asbestos tiles as well as flexible sheet and tiles.

In addition there is also a very useful code of practice, namely BS 6263 *Code of practice for care and maintenance of floor surfaces* Part 2: 1982 *Sheet and tile flooring*, which gives recommendations for the initial treatment and subsequent maintenance of cork, linoleum, plastics and rubber flooring in sheet and tile form. Guidance is given on the care and maintenance of flooring in particular environments such as computer rooms, clean rooms, sports and leisure centre playing surfaces, health care buildings and areas with under floor heating, with heavy traffic, with abnormal air temperature conditions, with high relative humidity, where accidental spillage of oil, grease or hazardous material may occur and where slip resistance is important.

4 Flooring of wood and wood products

There are three standards for wood flooring. One deals with wood blocks, one with mosaic parquet panels and one with the grading and sizing of softwood flooring.

BS 1187: 1959 *Wood blocks for floors* covers hardwood and softwood blocks for laying on level concrete or other types of rigid level bases. Blocks use an interlocking method of jointing such as the tongue and groove and have a chamfer or groove along the bottom of both longitudinal edges to take up surplus adhesive. Blocks have a finished thickness not less than 21 mm with a clear wearing thickness of not less than 10 mm above the interlocking system; the maximum width of the face should not exceed 89 mm and lengths should be not less than 152 mm nor more than 381 mm (common range 229 to 305 mm). The moisture content of the blocks should be adjusted to suit the conditions under which the building is ultimately to be used.

Type of heating	Ranges of moisture content at time of delivery
Intermittent heating	12–15%
Continuous heating	9–12%
Under floor heating (not suitable for softwood flooring)	6–10%

Hardwood blocks should be free from all signs of decay and insect attack, except for pinholes to the extent specified below, and should have the face free from all defects. Occasional tight sound knots and bright sapwood are not considered defects.

Softwood blocks should be free from all signs of decay and insect attack, except for pinholes to the extent specified below, and should have the face free from all defects. Occasional tight sound knots, with the overall dimension of the knot measured across the width of the face of the block (that is, the width between lines touching the knot and parallel to the edges of the block) not greater than 19 mm and bright sapwood are not considered defects.

On the back of any wood blocks defects other than decay and insect attack are permitted, provided they do not impair the fitting of the interlocking system or the laying of the floor.

Pinholes in both hardwoods and softwoods not greater than 1.6 mm in diameter are permitted, provided that they are not closely clustered and also that only 20 per cent of the piece or 25 per cent of the parcel is affected. (The pinworm is a borer which cannot live in timber after the tree is felled and dried.)

Colour variation in both hardwood and softwood blocks is permitted.

Table 14 shows hardwood and softwoods suitable for use as flooring not only in wood block but also in wood strip or board form.

Mosaic parquet panels are covered in BS 4050 *Mosaic parquet panels* Part 1: 1977 *General characteristics* and Part 2: 1966 *Classification and quality requirements*.

Part 1 describes mosaic parquet panels as being made up from wood fingers of the same species or of different species, laid on a single layer and pre-assembled by juxtaposition, either by means of a material temporarily fixed (for example paper glued on the face) or of a sufficiently flexible material permanently fixed. The panels are made up from component squares laid in a chequered pattern.

Nominal dimensions of fingers are 6, 8 and 10 mm thick (6 mm not suitable for softwood or softer grades of hardwood) by 18 to 25 mm wide (preferred widths 20, 22, 24 and 25 mm) with lengths of 100 to 165 mm (preferred lengths 100, 112, 120 and 125 mm).

Examples of nominal dimensions of fingers, component squares and mosaic parquet panels are shown in Table 15. See also Figure 36.

A national appendix showing botanical species, symbols and standard names for deciduous and coniferous trees is included.

Part 2 requires that the wood used is sound and free from any decay or damage caused by insects which may adversely affect the wearing properties of the wood.

Knot holes are not admissible.

The face sides of mosaic fingers should be free of ring shakes, which are admissible only on the backs provided that they are sound and do not penetrate within 5 mm of the face.

Any preservative treatment of sapwood against damage by insects should be the subject of special agreement between the

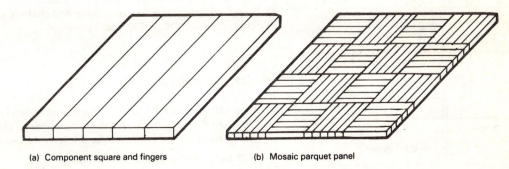

(a) Component square and fingers   (b) Mosaic parquet panel

Figure 36 *Mosaic parquet panels*

(From BS 4050: Part 1: 1977)

purchaser and the supplier and any treatment applied should not affect either the appearance or the bonding characteristics of the wood.

1 First quality (I) – wearing surface. The wearing surface should be free from sapwood, decay, seasoning checks, veins, pockets, abnormal coloration and knots, other than pin knots or black knots with a diameter not exceeding 2 mm. Not more than 5 per cent of the mosaic fingers may contain pin or black knots.

2 Second quality (II) – wearing surface. The wearing surface should be free from decay and from seasoning checks, veins, pockets, black knots and sound knots in excess of the limits shown in Table 16. Not more than one of these defects may be present in any mosaic finger.

Table 16   *Limits of defects*

Seasoning checks	Veins and pockets	Black knots	Sound knots
Length in mm	Width	Largest dimension	Largest dimension
30	$\frac{1}{25}$ width of mosaic finger	$\frac{1}{5}$ width of mosaic finger	$\frac{1}{2}$ width of mosaic finger

(Table 1: BS 4050: Part 2: 1966)

The third standard is BS 1297: 1970 (1980) *Grading and sizing of softwood flooring*

■ AD (Reg. A1/2)

This covers softwood which is suitable for use as tongued and grooved softwood boarding and strip floorings which are laid upon joists, fillets or subflooring and basically covers Canadian spruce, Douglas fir, Redwood, Whitewood and Western hemlock, all of which must be free of all signs of decay and insect attack. Requirements for moisture content (normal 16–22 per cent; special-kiln dried 12–15 per cent) are given together with acceptability in terms of sapwood, fissures, cup, knots, wane and manufacture. Finished dimensions should be as follows:

	mm	mm	mm	mm
Finished thicknesses	16	19	21	28
Finished widths of face	65	90	113	137

Table 17   *Tongue and groove dimensions*

		mm	mm	mm	mm
Finished thickness	A	16	19	21	28
Finished tongue thickness	B	4.5	6	6	6
Finished tongue top width	C	7	7	7	7
Face of board to top of tongue	D	7	7	8	12

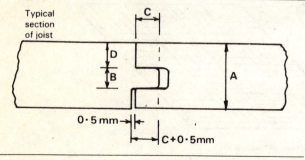

(Table 1: BS 1297: 1970)

Lengths unless otherwise specified should be 1.8 m and longer with a minimum average in any delivery of 3.0 m.

Dimensions for tongue and groove should be as shown in Table 17. The finished tongue bottom width should be 0.5 mm greater than that of the top width. The groove should be of suitable section to accommodate the tongue with a push fit, but should be not less than 1 mm deeper than the width of the upper face of the tongue.

Reference should also be made to CP 201 *Flooring of wood and wood products* Part 2: 1972 *Wood flooring (board, strip, block and mosaic)* which deals in metric units with the work involved in laying flooring and recommends the bases on which it should be laid. Appendix A lists hardwoods and softwoods suitable for use as flooring, mainly in wood strip, wood block or board form, and CP 209 *Care and maintenance of floor surfaces* Part 1: 1963 *Wooden flooring* which contains much useful information.

5   Textile floor coverings

There are only two standards referring to textile floor coverings. BS 5557: 1978 *Textile floor coverings: classification and terminology* relates to coverings with pile (pile carpet) and to those without pile while BS 5808: 1979 *Underlays for textile floor coverings* deals with underlays made of felt, cellular material, rubber crumb, or composites of these materials. No recommendations are made as to which type of underlay should be used in any particular application. Requirements are specified for breaking strength, extension under force, loss in thickness under static and dynamic loading and compression and resistance to breaking or cracking.

Reference should also be made to BS 5325: 1983 *Code of practice for installation of textile floor coverings* which deals with the installation of textile floor coverings, including the laying of fully adhered carpet tile and gives advice on the selection of materials and their properties.

6   Coir matting

The only standard on this subject is BS 3959: 1965 *Coir matting* which covers requirements for six standard widths of coir matting suitable for domestic and general-purposes and services requirements.

(45)   Ceiling finishes

There are no specific standards dealing with ceiling finishes although reference should be made to CP 290: 1973 *Suspended ceilings and linings of dry construction using metal fixing systems*, summarized under (35) 'Suspended ceilings', and BS 5492: 1977 *Code of practice for internal plastering*, summarized under (42) 'Wall finishes, internal'. A glossary of terms is to be found in BS 4049: 1966 *Glossary of terms applicable to internal plastering, external rendering and floor screeding*.

A further reference is the draft for development DD 71 *Guide to sprayed mineral insulation* Part 1: 1981 *Sprayed mineral fibre*, which is covered in Table 4 'Activities, requirements' under section (M2) 'Thermal insulation'.

(47)   Roof finishes

See entries under Table 2: *Constructions, forms*, sections L, N, R, S and T; and Table 4: *Activities, requirements* (M2) *Insulation* (BS 5803 *Thermal insulation for use in roof space in dwellings*)

CP 143   *Sheet roof and wall coverings*

■ AD (Reg. F2) (Parts 1, 5, 10, 11, 12, 15 and 16)

Part 1: 1958 *Aluminium, corrugated and troughed* deals with sheeting conforming to BS 4868: 1972 *Profiled aluminium sheets for building* (see Table 2 'Constructions, forms' section N 'Rigid overlap sheets, tiles'). The code contains information on weathering, contact with other materials, fire hazard and other characteristics, and makes recommendations relating to materials, design and construction. Part 5: 1964 *Zinc* gives recommendations for laying roofs on the roll cap system together with flashings and gutters in so far as they are integral parts of the roof covering. Part 10: 1973 *Galvanized corrugated steel. Metric units* covers the use of galvanized corrugated steel sheets for roofing and cladding in building.

Recommendations are given on materials and design, construction and maintenance, together with information on weathertightness, durability, thermal insulation, fire hazard, rainwater drainage from roofs and other characteristics.

Part 11: 1970 *Lead. Metric units* deals with lead coverings for roofs and walls following normal established practice. Recommendations are given in regard to the whole of the coverings above the wooden rafters for pitched roofs, and above the joists or the upper surface of the constructional base for flat roofs and walls.

Flashings and gutters are dealt with in so far as these are integral parts of the covering while Part 12: 1970 *Copper. Metric units* covers methods of covering a roof or wall with copper sheet or strip in accordance with established practice. There are alternative methods of laying which are not included in the techniques described as they are generally variations of traditional roof practice.

Recommendations are given in regard to the whole of the coverings above the wooden rafters for pitched roofs, and above the joists or the upper surface of the construction base for flat roofs and walls.

Flashings and gutters are dealt with in so far as they are integral parts of the covering.

Part 15: 1973 *Aluminium. Metric units* deals with the installation of aluminium fully-supported roof coverings in accordance with established practices.

The code includes information on appropriate alloys and forms of aluminium, durability, contact with other materials, sizes and weights of sheet and strip, protection and storage.

Gutters and flashings are dealt with in so far as they form an integral part of the main roof covering.

The code deals with coverings, substructures and accessories placed above the rafters or the upper surfaces of constructional bases, but does not apply to aluminium roof deckings or deck units.

Part 16: 1974 *Semi-rigid asbestos bitumen sheet. Metric units* makes recommendations based on accepted good practice for laying fully supported semi-rigid asbestos bitumen sheet roofs using the roll cap and rib systems.

Recommendations are given for the whole of the roof covering above the upper surface of the constructional base for both flat and pitched roofs.

Flashings and gutters are dealt with in so far as they are integral parts of the roof covering.

CP 144   *Roof coverings*

■ AD (Regs. B2/3/4)

Part 3: 1970 *Built-up bitumen felt* sets down requirements for materials, design and construction of roofs and the preparation of surfaces on which built-up bitumen felt roofing is to be laid and gives general recommendations to ensure a satisfactory roof covering while Part 4: 1970 *Mastic asphalt* deals with the use of mastic asphalt as a roof covering including situations designed to carry traffic, such as a roof car park.

The code covers recommendations for the preparation of the base to which the mastic asphalt is applied and sets out the site

practice. Subsidiary functions are given including the use of mastic asphalt as a waterproof lining to a roof reservoir for the storage of water.

BS 6229: 1982   *Code of practice for flat roofs with continuously supported coverings*

■ AD (Reg. F2)

This deals with the design and application of flat roofs with continuously supported roof coverings. Watertightness, drainage, thermal and sound insulation, fire precautions, maintenance and repair are considered.

The other two codes, namely BS 5247 *Code of practice for sheet roof and wall coverings* Part 14: 1975 *Corrugated asbestos-cement* and BS 5534 *Code of practice for slating and tiling* Part 1: 1978 *Design* are summarized under section (41) 'Wall finishes, external'.

(48)   Other finishes to structure

There is only one British Standard which falls under this classification, namely BS 4232: 1967 *Surface finish of blast-cleaned steel for painting* which specifies qualities of surface finish for all steels that are prepared by dry methods of blast-cleaning for the application of paints and non-metallic coatings. It applies both to uncoated steel, whether new or weathered, and to steel from which an old protective coating has to be removed.

First, second and third qualities of surface finish are defined. Recommendations are made regarding the selection of an appropriate quality of surface finish for a particular paint system or purpose, methods of inspection and control of the surface finish achieved, and blast-cleaning procedures.

There are, in addition, two very useful codes of practice, BS 5493: 1977 *Code of practice for protective coating of iron and steel structures against corrosion*

■ AD (Regs. J1/2/3)

This recommends methods of protection against corrosion of iron and steel structures exposed to environments commonly encountered. The code describes the various methods in detail and gives guidance on how to specify a chosen protective system, how to ensure its correct application, and how it should be maintained.

BS 6150: 1982 *Code of practice for painting of buildings* provides recommendations for good practice in the initial and maintenance painting of buildings, for example dwellings, offices, light industrial buildings, schools, hospitals, hotels and public buildings generally, in which decoration is a significant and often the major factor. In addition the need to protect many building materials against the weather or other forms of attack normally encountered in these types of building is taken into account.

Design, specification and organization are covered in section two and it is recommended that all users should refer to this section as a preliminary to the selection of coating systems.

The various materials and coatings employed in painting, together with application and practice, are covered as are the various paint systems recommended for wood, iron and steel, non-ferrous metals and metallic coatings, plaster, external rendering, concrete, brick and stone, cement-based sheets, boards and components, fibre building board, wood chipboard and plasterboard, paper and wallcoverings, plastics, glass and inorganic glazed surfaces, bituminous surfaces and materials.

Maintenance and health and safety requirements are also covered.

Finally, reference may be made to DD 24: 1973 *Recommendations for methods of protection against corrosion on light section steel used in building.*

(49)   Parts, accessories, etc. special to finishes to structure elements

Many of the standards and codes which fall into this classification are summarized in sections (41), (42), (43), (45) and (48), and reference should be made to these sections.

There is one valuable code, not summarized elsewhere, which falls into this section, namely BS 5427: 1976 *Code of practice for performance and loading criteria for profiled sheeting in buildings* which deals with design, performance and loading criteria for profiled weathering sheeting, in a range of materials used in building. Composite materials are not included but many of the principles apply. Special attention is given to identifying the various regulations that govern the use of profiled sheeting. There are particularly valuable tables dealing with the durability of sheet materials and the incompatibility of materials.

(5–) Services, mainly piped, ducted

The relevant parts of the Building Regulations 1985 are Part F – Ventilation; Part G – Hygiene; and Part L – Conservation of fuel and power. This group of sections includes a significant amount of material whose placement is relatively arbitrary. A typical case is BS 3456 *Safety of household and similar electrical appliances*, reference to which recurs in *Sectional List 16* within sections (5 –), (6 –) and (7 –). Repetitive cross-references would not be helpful. *Sectional List 16* is followed in the main, and users of this manual should refer to *all* appropriate subsections. Note that section (59) 'Parts, accessories and components', in particular, covers materials used in all other sections.

This general introduction will include a note on BS 5997 which is a guide to all the relevant British Standard codes on building services. The sequence then comprises: (52) 'Waste disposal, drainage', which is subdivided into (52.1) on refuse disposal; (52.5), (52.6) and (52.7) on drainage; (53) 'Liquids supply' which is subdivided into (53.1) and (53.2) on water supply; (54) 'Gases supply', which is subdivided into (54.1), (54.2) and (54.4) on gas supply and vapour supply; (55) 'Space cooling'; (56) 'Space heating', which has four subsections on heating; (57) 'Air conditioning and ventilation'; and (59) 'Parts, accessories and components'.

Specialist standards of which students should be aware include the following.

BS 4118: 1981   *Glossary of sanitation terms*

BS 6068   *Water quality*

Part 1 covers terms in two sections.

BS 5760   *Reliability of systems, equipment and components*
Part 2: 1981   *Guide to the assessment of reliability*

BS 1042   *Methods of measurement of fluid flow in closed conduits* (in three parts)

BS 3680   *Measurement of liquid flow in open channels* (in twenty-four parts)

BS 6199   *Methods of measurement of liquid flow in closed conduits using weighing and volumetric methods* (in one part)

BS 5997: 1980   *Guide to British Standard codes of practice for building services*

This document is a guide on the subject matter of other British Standard codes of practice which relate to building services.

Codes of practice are listed in numerical order. Against each reference a brief summary is given of the scope of the code and an indication in heading form of the areas covered ranging from water supply through to security protection.

(52)   Waste disposal, drainage

(52.1)   Refuse disposal

Refuse disposal is covered in some detail. A number of standards cover large and small dustbins in various materials, refuse chutes and large and small incinerators. Coverage includes trade and hospital waste.

BS 5906: 1980   *Code of practice for storage and on-site treatment of solid waste from buildings*

■   AD (Reg. H4)

This standard is concerned with the problem of the storage and

Table 18 *Commercial waste*

	Typical bulk density	Composition of waste (percentage by mass)				
		Multiple stores	Departmental stores	Supermarkets	Hotels	Offices
	kg/m³					
Folded newspaper; cardboard packed or baled	500 ⎫					
Loosely crumpled paper; office stationery	50 ⎬	81	65	50	8	80
Wastepaper (loose in sacks)	20 ⎭					
Mixed general refuse, similar to domestic (no solid fuel residues)	150	13	31	40	55	16
Separated food waste uncompacted vegetable waste well-compacted, moist pig swill	200 ⎫ 650 ⎭	4	2	—	33	4
Salvaged bones and fat	600	2	2	10	—	—
Empty bottles	300	—	—	—	4	—

(Table 1: BS 5906: 1980)

Table 19 *Output of waste per week*

Multiple stores	Department stores	Supermarket*		Hotels	Offices
		(1)	(2)		
kg	kg	kg	kg	kg	kg
1.0	0.54	1.8	5.8	3.0 Per head (staff and residents) 7-day week	1.68 Per employee 5-day week
Per m² of sales area, 6-day week					

* Supermarkets can be placed in one of two categories, depending on their output of refuse: (1) smaller stores with a small output; (2) stores in prime shopping areas.

(Table 2: BS 5906: 1980)

treatment of waste from large residential buildings, large and small commercial establishments and hospitals. It does not cover medical waste.

The standard records recommended good practices for collection and good hygiene. Information is provided on the composition and output of waste to be expected from residential buildings, multiple stores, departmental stores, etc. Tables 18 and 19 illustrate how this information is presented.

The methods of storage and collection are then covered, ranging from dustbins to chute systems and storage chambers. The need to have adequate roads and approaches to buildings is stressed. Transportation of containers, hygiene and on-site treatment such as compaction and shredding are covered together with incineration and pipeline collection.

BS 792: 1973 *Mild steel dustbins*

This standard covers the construction of four sizes of small dustbins: 0.028, 0.056, 0.071 and 0.092 m³.

These bins are the familiar type, circular in cross-section with tapered non-corrugated sides and having a removable lid.

Construction details include quality and thickness of steel plate, dimension and weight, seams, handles, lid and galvanizing.

BS 1136: 1972 *Mild steel refuse storage containers*

This gives the constructional details and requirements for large mild steel refuse storage containers and mechanical removal of refuse. Two shapes and capacities are provided: circular with nominal capacity of 0.95 m³ and flat sided with nominal capacity of 0.75 m³.

BS 3495: 1972 *Aluminium refuse storage containers*

Constructional details and requirements covering cylindrical storage containers of 1 m³ capacity in aluminium for use with mechanical removal systems.

BS 3654: 1963 *Galvanized steel dustbins for dustless emptying*

The purpose of these containers is for the transfer of the contents into the enclosed body of the refuse collection vehicle with the lid remaining closed at all times except when the loading aperture of the vehicle is closed by the mouth of the bin.

The standard therefore covers the constructional details of dustbins with hinged lids for this specific use. The standard covers two sizes 0.07 and 0.09 m³.

BS 3735: 1976 *Rubber components for refuse containers*

Many refuse containers are fitted with a rubber lid and rubber foot rim in order to reduce noise and impact damage. This standard covers the construction requirements of these parts to fit containers of 0.06, 0.07 and 0.09 m³ nominal capacities in steel and 0.12 m³ nominal capacity in plastic dustbins.

BS 4324: 1968 *Litter bins*

This standard gives dimensional, material and constructional requirements for litter bins of various capacities from 14 litres up to 170 litres.

Bins incorporating iron, steel, aluminium, concrete, timber and plastic are covered.

Recommendations for siting, selection, installation, servicing and maintenance are also provided.

BS 4998: 1985 *Moulded plastics dustbins (excluding lids)*

These bins are suitable for use with normal household refuse but not hot ashes. This standard covers the requirements for those bins for capacities not exceeding 0.12 m³. Important issues are impact resistance, strength of handles and deformation resistance.

BS 5832: 1981 *Compacted waste containers for lift-off vehicles*

This covers the large containers of approximately 10 m³ capacity containing compacted material which can be handled by vehicles equipped with lift-off equipment.

The containers must also be suitable for use with a range of compactors capable of applying a compaction pressure of 200 kPa over the input area. The containers are made of steel plate reinforced to withstand compaction and handling stresses and are of welded construction.

The standard lays down the requirements for materials, dimensions and construction details.

BS 1703: 1977 *Refuse chutes and hoppers*

These chutes and hoppers are a familiar feature in large blocks of flats. The chute is constructed to take refuse from successive floors and the hopper is the storage container.

Materials, dimensions, design, finishes, ventilation and shutters are all specified in respect of both chutes and hoppers.

BS 3107: 1973 *Small incinerators*

A range of incinerators using fuel gases or electricity for the combustion of sanitary towels, bandages, dressings and paper not exceeding a volume of 0.04 m³ combustion chamber are covered by this standard.

Matters specified include installation, operation and maintenance instructions, surface temperatures, combustion chambers, agitation and ashpan.

BS 3316: 1973 *Large incinerators for the destruction of hospital waste*

Hospital waste and infected materials include dressings, sputum containers, surgical waste, animal carcases, material from operating theatres and labour rooms, foodstuffs, etc. which, due to bulk or wetness or other characteristics, need to be disposed of by incineration.

The specified capacity rating of this type of incinerator is 120 kg/h/m² of grate area combustion with material having a density of 160 kg/m³.

The specification covers materials used in construction, and emphasis is rightly placed upon the construction of the flue and chimney together with regulations relating to the emission of smuts or other solids.

The appendices give useful information relating to the amount of waste and the size and type of hospital (see Figure 37) together with the correct siting of installations and transportation of waste.

(52.5)   Rainwater, surface water drainage

Rainwater and drainage goods such as gutters, pipes, fittings and accessories in various appropriate materials together with land drains are included.

BS 6367: 1983   *Code of practice for drainage of roofs and paved areas*

■   AD (Reg. H3)

Recommends design methods for roof and paved area drainage based on modern hydraulics and meteorological knowledge. Also deals with the choice of materials and with site-work, including inspection, testing and maintenance.

BS 460: 1964   *Cast iron rainwater goods*

■   AD (Reg. H3)

This standard gives detailed information on the dimensions of rainwater pipes and fittings and of half-round gutters, fittings and accessories. Ogee gutters, fittings and accessories are covered in Appendix A.

Figure 38 is typical of the amount of detail provided for a large number of elements.

The standard lays down requirements for material quality together with manufacturing processes, finishes, dimensions, weights and tolerances and markings.

BS 569: 1973   *Asbestos-cement rainwater goods*

This is a similar document to BS 460 but covers asbestos-cement products instead of cast iron ones. Again a large amount of information on sizes of pipes, gutters and fittings is provided as well as specification clauses.

BS 1091: 1963   *Pressed steel gutters, rainwater pipes, fittings and accessories*

■   AD (Reg. H3)

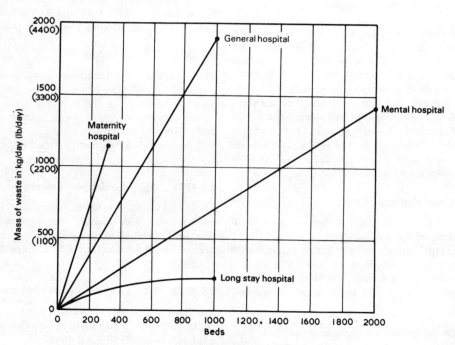

Curves showing relationship between total hospital waste
and the number of beds

(Figure 1: BS 3316: 1973)

Figure 37   *Relationship between total waste curves for types of hospital survey 1966–7*

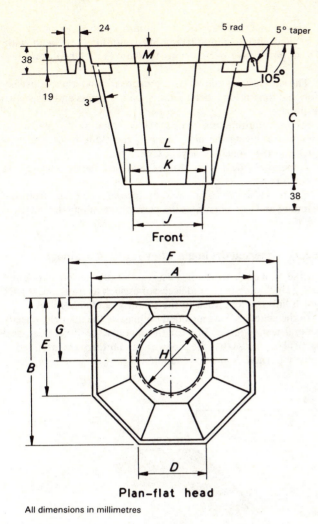

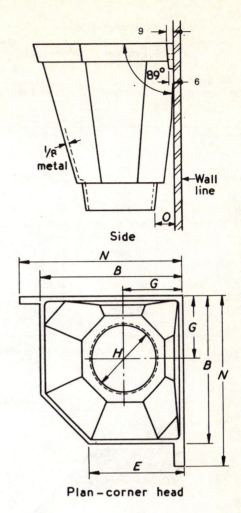

(Figure 8: BS 460: 1964)

Figure 38 *Rainwater heads. Hopper type (flat and corner patterns)*

This standard is in two sections. Section one deals with light pressed steel rainwater goods up to 10 mm diameter in pipes and 150 mm in half-round gutters.

Section two relates to heavy pressed steel boundary wall, valley, box and half-round gutters of 380 mm and over in girth. The materials, workmanship, effective length, finishes and joints are specified and a wealth of dimensional information of the various components is given in tabular form with reference diagrams.

BS 1431: 1960 *Wrought copper and wrought zinc rainwater goods*

■ AD (Reg. H3)

BS 2997: 1958 *Aluminium rainwater goods*

■ AD (Reg. H3)

BS 4576 *Unplasticized PVC rainwater goods*
Part 1: 1970 *Half-round gutters and circular pipes*

■ AD (Reg. H3)

The above three standards follow the patterns of specification and information already described in the previous few standards but relate in each case to a specific material. All are suitable for external use in appropriate situations.

BS 1194: 1969 *Concrete porous pipes for under-drainage*

These are pipes intended to admit water through the pipe wall throughout their entire length and full circumference but the

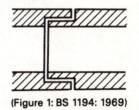

(Figure 1: BS 1194: 1969)   (Figure 2: BS 1194: 1969)

Figure 39 *Non-porous inverts*   **Figure 40** *Ogee or rebated joint*

standard also covers pipes with non-porous inverts, that is the lower half (see Figure 39). The moulds, methods of manufacture, lengths, dimension tolerances and permissible variation from straightness are all specified. The ends of these pipes are all ogee or rebated (see Figure 40).

The standard also gives a useful table relating crushing strength to porosity for various diameters of pipes (see Table 20).

BS 1196: 1971 *Clayware field drain pipes*

This standard covers the manufacture of unglazed clayware field drains of circular cross-section having plain butt joints.

Quality, workmanship and finish are specified. Requirements for dimensions, tolerances and straightness are given and a crushing strength test procedure.

BS 4962: 1982 *Plastic pipes for use as light duty subsoil drains*

This type of piping is used for normal field drainage and also in drainage situations where heavy wheel loadings do not occur.

Table 20 *Porosity and crushing strength (metric)*

Nominal diameter	Infiltration rate (minimum)	Crushing proof test load (min.)	
		Standard	Extra strength
		Type 1	Type 2
mm	1/min m	N/m	N/m
75	45	20 200	—
100	52	20 200	—
150	105	20 200	—
225	158	20 200	—
300	263	20 200	—
375	263	20 200	—
450	263	20 200	22 500
525	263	20 200	24 750
600	263	20 200	27 000
675	263	20 200	27 000
750	263	20 200	30 000
825	263	20 200	30 000
900	263	20 200	30 000

(Table 2: BS 1194: 1969)

Plastic pipes up to 200 mm nominal outside diameter for subsoil drainage under light duty conditions are dealt with. These pipes have perforations to allow the land to drain into them.

The standard lays down requirements for materials, construction and dimensions, perforations, pipe stiffness and resistance to impact.

Extra requirements are specified relating to particular methods of laying the pipes, namely the chute feeding techniques and the trenchless laying technique.

Appendices deal with storage and installation and testing procedure.

Figure 41 shows some bedding recommendations from the standard and also illustrates the perforations along the length of the pipe.

(52.6) Internal drainage, above ground drainage

This section deals with soil, waste and ventilating pipework and fittings including parts and accessories such as traps and wastes which link the pipework to the sanitary appliances.

In the specifications included on plastics the majority specify general test requirements for the manufactured product, and particularly stress that the pipework and fittings are intended to convey normal domestic effluent.

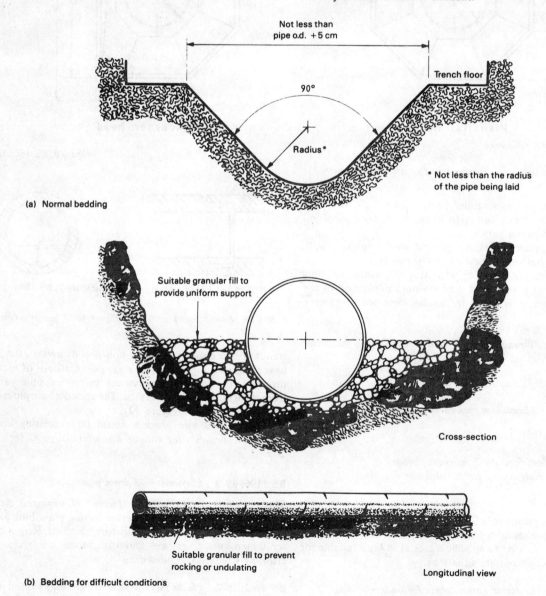

(a) Normal bedding

(b) Bedding for difficult conditions

Figure 41 *Bedding conditions for open-trench laying*

(Figure 8: BS 4962: 1982)

One code of practice, BS 5572, deals with general design principles applicable to the three standards on plastic pipes and fittings, the standard on cast iron pipes and fittings and the standard on galvanized mild steel drainage units. The three other standards in this section cover plastic traps, and waste fittings and traps in other materials.

BS 5572: 1978   *Code of practice for sanitary pipework*

■   AD (Reg. H1)

This is a comprehensive guide to the design, installation, testing and maintenance of above ground non-pressure sanitary pipework for domestic, commercial and public buildings. However the code does not purport to cover any special requirements of buildings such as may be found in hospitals, research and similar laboratories, or trade waste discharges. Neither does it cover the pumping/ejection of effluent from appliances incapable of being drained by gravity nor constraints imposed due to the consideration of fire hazards. The code includes useful data on flow rates from appliances and trap performance. The hydraulics and pneumatics of discharge systems are considered and illustrated with explanatory diagrams. Guidance is given in four diagrams, on various pipework layouts designed to meet different sanitary appliance arrangements, with a series of illustrations giving greater detail of branch discharge pipes.

The code contains eleven diagrams showing common arrangements of discharge stacks and branches for a number of types of buildings.

An important part of this code is the data, tables and procedures used for pipe sizing.

BS 416: 1973   *Cast iron spigot and socket soil, waste and ventilating pipes (sand cast and spun) and fittings*

■   AD (Regs. H1 and H3)

The standard specifies requirements for cast iron pipes, manufactured by the sand cast or spun process, with either Type A or Type B sockets (see Figure 42) together with requirements for sand cast fittings.

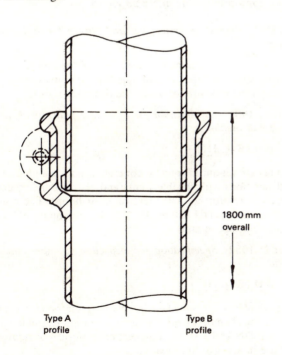

(Adapted from figures in BS 416: 1973)

Figure 42   *Straight pipes, sockets (Types A and B) and spigots. Optional features: alternative socket profile, spigot bead and ears*

The pipes and fittings are designed for use above ground for soil, waste and ventilating purposes in all types of building. All the pipes and fittings covered by this standard are illustrated in diagrams and dimensioned in tables. The range of diameters for the pipes and fittings is shown in Table 21.

Table 21   *Types of pipes and fittings*

	Nominal bore in mm						
	50	65	75	90	100	125	150
Pipes with Type A sockets	×	×	×	×	×	×	×
Pipes with Type B sockets	×	×	×	×	×	×	×
Fittings with Type A sockets	×	×	×	×	×	×	×
Fittings with Type B sockets	—	—	×	×	×	—	—

(Adapted from BS 416: 1973)

Details of bossed pipes and fittings for use in installations incorporating design techniques such as single stack plumbing are included. Some details of roof outlets for flat roofs are also given.

BS 4514: 1983   *Unplasticised PVC soil and ventilating pipes, fittings and accessories*

■   AD (Regs. B2/3/4, H1 and H3)

The specification deals with material appearance, dimensions and physical requirements for pipes, fittings and accessories including coated metal fittings, and jointing materials for use in above ground drainage systems. Although details of methods of jointing will differ from one system to another guidance may be obtained from BS 5572.

Dimension details and illustrations of the pipework and a number of fittings and accessories are given in a series of tables and diagrams, the range of nominal outside diameters being 82, 110 and 160 mm. Bossed pipes and fittings in this range are also included.

BS 5254: 1976   *Polypropylene waste pipe and fittings (external diameter 34.6 mm, 41.0 mm and 54.1 mm)*

■   AD (Reg. H1)

Detailed material requirements are not specified in this standard but there is a requirement for the pipework and fittings to withstand the long-term effects of the intermittent discharge of hot water.

The outside diameters specified are based upon superseded copper pipe sizes in accordance with BS 659, and as such may be unacceptable to some local authorities in the United Kingdom. The various jointing methods in use preclude at present the standardization of the lengths and configuration of fittings. However, 'O' ring, multi-vane and mechanical compression joint systems are covered.

BS 5255: 1976   *Plastics waste pipe and fittings*

This standard specifies requirements for waste pipe and fittings in nominal diameters of 32, 40 and 50 mm, manufactured from four different plastics materials:

1   Acrylonitrile-butadiene-styrene (ABS).
2   Modified unplasticized polyvinyl chloride (MUPVC).
3   Polypropylene (PP).
4   Polyethylene (PE).

Each material is dealt with separately, mainly covering tests required on specimens after manufacture. However, since requirements are given for pipes and fittings manufactured from materials which have different coefficients of expansion and design features, it is essential that manufacturers' fixing instructions are followed.

Two basic jointing methods are covered. The first, solvent cementing, is suitable for ABS and MUPVC only; the second, rubber ring jointing, is suitable for all four materials. Additional design features dealt with are multi-vane and mechanical compression joints.

BS 3943: 1979   *Plastics waste traps*

■ AD (Reg. H1)

Details of specific design and test requirements are given for plastics traps connecting to types of wastes complying with BS 3380 Part 1. Depth of seal, inlet and outlet connections, access, and angle of outlet are dealt with. Included along with the usual tests for plastics materials are further tests for leakage, water seal and flow of water.

BS 3868: 1973   *Prefabricated drainage stack units: galvanized steel*

■ AD (Reg. H1)

Requirements are specified for prefabricated drainage units for use above ground in plumbing systems for soil, waste and rainwater. They are manufactured from steel and galvanized after fabrication. Tables with associated diagrams give full details and dimensions of the components.

BS 1184: 1976   *Copper and copper alloy traps*

■ AD (Reg. H1)

Eighteen figures and 16 tables give comprehensive drawn details and dimensions information for copper and copper alloy traps as used with baths, basins, sinks, washtubs, tubs and sink sets. Included are details of associated components.

BS 3380: 1982   *Wastes (excluding skeleton sink wastes) and bath overflows*

This standard deals with the requirements for the materials, design, construction and dimensions of wastes for baths, basins, sinks and bidets. Included are details of plugs, chains and overflows for baths.

(52.7)   Below ground drainage

The Building Act 1984, s 21 gives local authorities power to require satisfactory drainage.

BS 6297: 1983   *Code of practice for design and installation of small sewage treatment works and cesspools*

■ AD (Reg. H2)

This document incorporates the subject matter previously covered by the codes of practice for small sewage treatment works CP 302 and cesspools CP 302: 200, and the scope has been extended to include treatment units capable of dealing with sewage from populations of up to 1000 persons. New processes developed since the publication of the previous code, such as the rotary biological contactor, are now also included. The aim of this code is to give guidance for those experienced in the design of small sewage treatment works but does not set out in detail the full operation and maintenance of such works. General guidance only is given on good design and installation practice for sewage treatment works suitable for the domestic discharge from domestic and industrial communities ranging from single households up to about 1000 population. It does not deal with the treatment of trade effluents or the effluent from chemical closets. The major part of this code deals with design of the work supported by three tables and fifteen figures.

BS 8301: 1985   *Code of practice for building drainage*

■ AD (Regs. C3, H1 and H3)

Sets out recommendations for the design, layout, construction, testing and maintenance of foul, surface water and ground water drainage systems constructed in the ground under and around any buildings and their connection to sewers, treatment works, cesspools, soakaways or watercourses.

CP 2005: 1968   *Sewerage*

The term sewerage covers the whole system – sewers, manholes, stormwater overflows, siphons, pumping stations, pumping mains, tidal outfalls and all works required to convey sewage, stormwater and surface water to the sewage treatment works or other places of final disposal.

This is a code covering good practice in the design and construction, under average conditions, of sewerage installations. Materials, design and construction, types of effluent, ancillary structures, pumping stations, tidal outfalls, are all covered.

BS 5178: 1975   *Prestressed concrete pipes for drainage and sewerage*

This standard covers the manufacture of prestressed concrete pipes and associated fittings for the construction of sewers, conduits and ducts to be used at atmospheric pressure.

A range of bores from 450 to 3000 mm in increments of 75 up to 1200 mm and increments of 150 up to 3000 mm are given.

The standard covers materials, dimensions and tolerances, pipe design and manufacture, and fittings. A final section on appropriate test procedures is also given. Specification requirements for bedding and backfill and the relationship between earth cover, superimposed loadings and pipe strength are not given.

Users are warned to satisfy themselves that a particular pipe will withstand the loading conditions likely to apply by reference to an appropriate table in NBSS report No. 7.

BS 5911   *Precast concrete pipes and fittings for drainage and sewage*

This is a standard aimed at covering the complete range of precast concrete pipes and fittings for the conveyance, under atmospheric pressure, of sewage and surface water.

Part 1: 1981   *Specification for pipes and fittings with flexible joints and manholes*

■ AD (Reg. H1)

Details are set out for precast concrete cylindrical pipes, bends and junctions with flexible joints and also manholes, unreinforced or reinforced, with steel cages or hoops. The range of nominal sizes is DN 150 to DN 3000 by increments of 75 (DN dimensions are in mm).

Part 2: 1982   *Specification for inspection chamber and street gullies*

■ AD (Reg. H1)

Requirements are specified in this part for precast concrete inspection chambers over a drain or sewer not exceeding nominal size DN 250 and street gullies, unreinforced or reinforced, for use in areas of light loading.

Part 3: 1982   *Specification for pipes and fittings with ogee joints*
This part deals with two categories of precast concrete cylindrical unit, each with ogee joints, unreinforced or reinforced, with steel cages or hoops, namely 'land drainage' units and 'sewage' units.

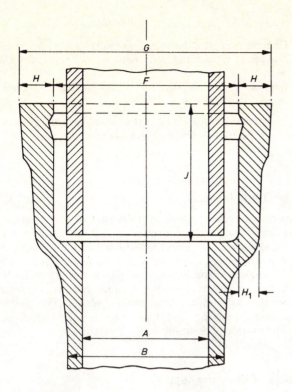

(Figure 1(b): BS 437: 1978)

Figure 43 *Centrifugally cast only: alternative dimensions*

The range of nominal sizes for both units is DN 150 to DN 1800 by increments of 75.

BS 3656: 1981 *Asbestos-cement pipes, joints and fittings for sewerage and drainage*

■ AD (Reg. H1)

The composition, geometrical characteristics, physical characteristics and classification of pipes by means of crushing strength related to diameter are specified in this standard.

Joint materials involving rubber rings and asbestos cement are specified. Fittings such as bends, junctions, saddles are specified and listed. Requirements are stated for crushing strength and chemical resistance.

Again the pipe line designer is made responsible for choosing the class of pipe or even whether asbestos-cement pipes would be suitable at all in the knowledge of the possible loading and bedding conditions.

BS 65: 1981 *Vitrified clay pipes, fittings and joints*

■ AD (Regs. H1 and J1/2/3)

This standard supersedes BS 640, BS 539 Part 1 and BS 1143.

Requirements for vitrified clay pipes and fittings, with or without sockets for the construction of drains and sewers operating at atmospheric pressure as gravity pipe lines for the following types of drains, are covered in both pipes and fittings.

Normal – suitable for all drains and sewers.
Surface water – suitable for surface water only.
Perforated – suitable for French drains and land drains.
Extra chemically resistant – suitable for drains and sewers in acid ground where extra resistance is required.

The standard covers materials, manufacturers, dimensions and tolerances, performance requirements including flexible mechanical joints.

An appendix gives test procedures for checking straightness and strength properties.

BS 437: 1978 *Cast iron spigot and socket drain pipes and fittings*

■ AD (Reg. H1)

Spigot and socket joints are best described by referring to Figure 43. This type of joint is suitable for caulking.

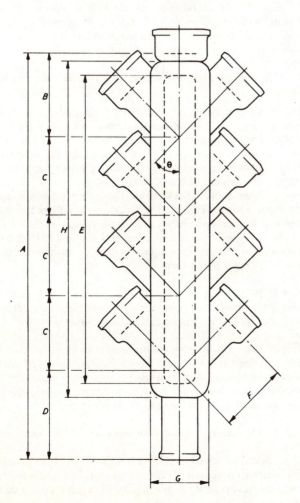

Figure 44 *Inspection chambers. The minimum throat radius at branch entry will be 50 mm*

	mm	mm	mm
Main bore	100	150	225
Branch bore	100	100	100
θ	45°	45°	45°
A	1270	1290	1450
B	240	260	330
C	250	250	250
D	280	280	370
E	1030	1030	1030
F	220	250	310
G	220	260	355
H	1120	1120	1195

For 414, 014, 410

(From Figure 65: BS 437: 1978)

The pipes and fittings may be manufactured by the sand cast or centrifugal cast (spun) processes. The pipes and fittings are suitable for drainage purposes where the hydrostatic pressure does not exceed 345 kPa in pipes and 170 kPa in fittings.

Requirements are specified for materials, permissible deviation on dimensions and masses, depth of seals, crushing requirement, protective coating and inspection.

Most of this standard is devoted to listing of the dimensions and shapes of a large variety of fittings to comply with the stated conditions and pressures. Figure 44 gives some idea of the detail provided.

BS 4660: 1973   *Unplasticized PVC underground drain pipe and fittings*

■ AD (Reg. H1)

PVC has proved to be a satisfactory material for pipes conveying normal domestic effluents and surface water. If it is proposed to use these pipes and fittings with untreated trade waste or with prolonged discharges at elevated temperatures reference should be made to CP 312 Part 1 and/or the pipe manufacturer. Matters covered are material, colour, defects, dimensions of pipes and fittings, lengths of pipes, markings and sealing components, together with an appendix on storage, handling and installation.

This standard applies to drain pipes to be laid under gardens, fields, driveways, yards and roads other than main roads. The pipe sizes are 110 and 160 mm diameter.

BS 5481: 1977   *Unplasticized PVC pipes and fittings for gravity sewers*

■ AD (Reg. H1)

Again PVC is suitable for publicly owned sewers if in conformity with this standard. Nominal diameters in the range 200 to 630 mm are covered together with the necessary joints and accessories. Care must be taken if the pipes are to convey untreated trade waste or prolonged discharges at elevated temperatures (refer to CP 312 Part 2).

Materials, dimensions, construction, fittings, marking, testing and sealing components are specified.

BS 2494: 1986   *Elastomeric joint rings for pipework and pipelines*

This standard applies to elastomeric components of composite or non-composite joint rings, sealing rings, jointing gaskets and similar components used to seal fluids in pipes and fittings. The performance requirements, manufacturing compounds and methods of test are specified for rings used in the following applications:

1 Potable water (W).
2 Drainage (D).
3 Gas and hydrocarbon fluids (G).
4 Hot water and low pressure steam for potable purposes (H).
5 Hot water and low pressure steam for non-potable purposes (S).

BS 497   *Manhole covers, road gully gratings and frames for drainage purposes*

Part 1: 1976   *Cast iron and cast steel*
This standard deals with cast iron manhole covers, inspection covers and the associated frames. It also includes cast iron and cast steel road gully covers and frames.

Matters specified include materials, manufacture, workmanship, protective coatings, design requirements and quality control. The various grades of manhole covers and gully gratings are defined in terms of their use and the loads to be carried.

BS 1247: 1975   *Manhole step irons*

This standard covers the testing and general requirements for manhole step irons for use in the following situations:

1 General purposes, that is, in brickwork and *in situ* concrete.
2 For use in precast concrete manhole and inspection chambers.
3 For use across the corners of rectangular manholes and inspection chambers.

The step irons are defined in terms of shapes and dimensions for each specific use. Finishes, treads and testing procedures are also specified.

(53)   Liquids supply

One code of practice deals with design, and one standard and one draft for development relate to cold water supply. Of the four codes of practice concerned with hot water supply one deals with centralized supplies, one with solar heating and one each with gas and electric hot water supplies. Seven standards are summarized. Five of them apply to water heaters, one refers to safety devices, and one to expansion vessels. Two drafts for development are included. One refers to solar collectors, the other to safety of domestic water heaters.

(53.1)   Cold water supply

CP 310: 1965   *Water supply*

The code is intended to give guidance to engineers, architects, surveyors and contractors, and should be of interest to the water user, particularly where large premises are concerned. The greater part of the code deals with the storage, distribution and use of water when supplied by a statutory water undertaking to premises. However the code also deals in a general way with private water supplies and treatment. A number of tables, figures, and appendices provide useful information on storage amounts, pipe sizing, fixings and insulation.

BS 5728   *Measurements of flow of cold potable water in closed conduits*

This British Standard applies to water meters of various metrological classes having nominal flow rates which lie in the range 0.6 to 4000 m³/h, with a nominal pressure of 10 bar and a working temperature up to 30 °C. Except for the connecting flange dimensions, the standard also applies to water meters subject to nominal pressures of 10 to 16 bar.

The water meters specified are those that employ a direct mechanical process involving either the use of volumetric chambers with mobile walls or the action of the velocity of the water to rotate a vaned rotor. They are self-contained integrating measuring instruments continuously determining the volume of water flowing through them.

Part 1: 1979   *Meters*
This part deals with terminology, technical characteristics, metrological characteristics and pressure loss.

Part 2: 1980   *Installation conditions for meters*
This part deals with selection of water meters, associated fittings, installation, special requirements for some meters and the first operation of new or repaired meters to ensure accurate constant measurement and reliable reading of the meter.

Part 2 Supplement 1: 1984   *Parallel and multiple meter operation*
This addendum specifies criteria additional to those given for single meter installations in ISO 4064/2 and applicable to single water meters operating either in parallel or grouped together in one location.

Part 3: 1984 *Methods for determining principal characteristics of meters*
This part specifies the best method and means to be employed in determining the principal characteristics of meters.

Part 4: 1986 *Combination meters*
This part defines the characteristics peculiar to combination meters consisting of:
One large meter (the meter with the larger nominal flow rate)
One small meter
One changeover device functioning automatically without using any source of energy other than that of the fluid being measured.

DD 82: 1982 *Specification of requirements of suitability of materials for use in contact with water for human consumption with regard to their effect on the quality of the water*

This draft is based on test methods adopted by the National Water Council and covers requirements for materials, lubricants, components or fittings for use in contact with water for human consumption. It deals separately with the support of microbial growth by non-metallic materials, toxic metals extracted from non-metallic materials, taste, odour, colour and turbidity from non-metallic materials, and toxic metals extracted from metal pipes and fittings.

(53.3) Hot water supply

CP 342 *Centralized hot water supply*

Part 1: 1970 *Individual dwellings*
Part 2: 1974 *Buildings other than individual dwellings*
Both parts offer guidance on the designing, planning, installation, inspection, testing and commissioning of systems of hot water supply. Part 1 confines its scope to individual dwellings where water may be treated by boilers burning solid, liquid or gaseous fuels or by electricity. Part 2 considers commercial, industrial or multiple dwelling buildings supplied from a central source, including district or group schemes. Installation work for the supply of steam or high pressure hot water to calorifiers is not included.

Each part of the code presents a general section giving definitions, and some useful details of exchange of information which should take place between the designers of the building and the designers of the hot water supply. This section is more extensive in Part 2, which makes recommendations for programming and prefabrication. Further common sections deal with materials, appliances and components, design, work on-site, inspection, testing and commissioning and maintenance.

Both parts give recommendations on water temperatures, character of water, delivery and storage of fuel, boiler siting, chimneys and flue pipes, pipework, pipe sizing and insulation. Part 2 offers further advice on standby plant, disposal of ash, ventilation of boiler houses, hot water storage vessels and their siting, safety and fire precautions, circuits, air eliminators and pumps.

BS 2883: 1964 *Domestic instantaneous and storage water heaters for use with liquefied petroleum gases*

The standard specifies performance requirements for appliances for use with commercial butane at a working pressure of 27.4 mbar and with commercial propane at a working pressure of 35 mbar. Appliances may be designed for use with either gas or both. Instantaneous and storage heaters are defined and section one covers constructional requirements which are mainly applicable to the manufacturer. Section two outlines the performance requirements for all heaters plus particular details of water pressure loss for instantaneous heaters and water temperatures related to storage heaters.

BS 5258 *Safety of domestic gas appliances*

Part 7: 1977 *Storage water heaters*

■ AD (Regs. J1/2/3)

Safety requirements and associated methods of test for storage water heaters with rated heat input up to and including 20 kW are dealt with.

The standard does not cover the special requirements necessary for appliances with fan-powered combustion circuits or fan-assisted flues or take into account the special hazards which exist in nurseries and other places where there are young children or aged or infirm persons without supervision; in such cases additional requirements may be necessary.

BS 5386 *Gas burning appliances* (see also Table 1.73)

Part 1: 1976 *Gas burning appliances for instantaneous production of hot water for domestic use*

■ AD (Regs. J1/2/3)

This part of the standard defines the main constructional and performance characteristics of gas burning appliances where the useful output meets the requirements of Table 22.

Table 22 *Output requirements*

Water heater	Nominal useful output range kW
Small	8 to 9
Large (bath water heater)	17 to 18 21 to 23 26 to 28

(From text, BS 5386: Part 1: 1976)

The appliances are accorded three further classifications:

1 Categories I, II and III, depending on the nature and family of the gas or gases the appliance is designed to use. Table 23 defines the families of gases.
2 Types A, B, C₁ and C₂, depending on the method of evacuating the products of combustion and admitting the combustion air.
3 Water pressure in the appliance:
  (a) Inlet control appliance designed to deliver a free flow of water.
  (b) Low pressure appliance designed for connection to a water supply at a pressure not exceeding 2.5 bar.
  (c) Normal pressure appliance designed for connection to a water supply at a pressure not exceeding 10 bar.
  (d) High pressure appliance designed for connection to a water supply at a pressure not exceeding 13 bar.

Table 23 *Gas families*

Gas family	Wobbe number range mJ/m³
1st manufactured gas of groups (a) and (b)	23.8 to 31.4

2nd natural gas
  group H
  group L
	
	48.1 to 57.9
	41.3 to 47.3

3rd LPG (liquefied petroleum gas)	77.4 to 92.4

(From text, BS 5386: Part 1: 1976)

Part 2: 1981 *Mini water heaters (2nd and 3rd family gases)*
Water heaters of less than 8 kW nominal useful output are covered, in the same way as their larger counterparts.

BS 5546: 1979   *Code of practice for installation of gas hot water supplies for domestic purposes (2nd family gases)*

■ AD (Regs. J1/2/3)

Recommendations are given for the selection and installation of appliances burning 2nd family gases supplied by a gas undertaking. The appliances considered supply hot water for domestic purposes in individual dwellings and other premises where a similar service is required. The standard does not apply to large scale hot water supply systems. It is also important to note that many of the recommendations made are obligatory under the current Gas Supply Regulations. Information is provided on system selection, installation planning along with details of water, gas and electricity supplies. Tables to assist in water pipe sizing are included and there are nine diagrams illustrating typical instantaneous and storage installations and systems using circulators.

BS 5978: 1983   *Gas-fired hot-water boilers (60 kW to 2 MW input)*

This standard has three parts:

Part 1 *General requirements*
Part 2 *Additional requirements for boilers with atmospheric burners*
Part 3 *Additonal requirements for boilers with forced- or induced-draught burners*

Part 1 sets out the general requirements for gas-fired hot-water boilers operating at internal pressures up to 4.5 bar and a heat input range of 60 kW to 2 MW inclusive calculated on the gross calorific value. It also applies to boilers designed for use with open flues, boilers used on normal low-pressure district supplies of 2nd and 3rd family gases and cast-iron and steel boilers constructed in compliance with BS 779, BS 855 or BS 2790. The performance and safety requirements of this part apply also to boilers constructed of other materials and for which there are no constructional standards.

Electrical requirements are given and requirements specified for testing, design, construction, flue systems and dampers, combustion air input dampers, gas soundness, temperature, heat input, valves, controls and electricity supply. Details are also included on the instructions the manufacturer should provide with the boiler regarding installation, commissioning, servicing and using.

Part 2 states that boilers with atmospheric burners shall comply with the requirements of Part 1 together with the additional requirements of this part which includes design, construction, combustion, ignition, flame stability, flue systems, and dampers, controls, flame supervision and ignition sequence.

Part 3 specifies additional requirements which together with those in Part 1 apply to boilers with forced- or induced-draught burners. Requirements are given for burners, combustion, ignition, flame stability, flue systems, flue dampers and controls.

DD 84: 1982   *Method of test for the resistance to freezing of gas-fired instantaneous water heaters*

The draft describes a method of test for the safety of domestic gas-fired instantaneous water heaters as covered in BS 5386 when the appliance is subjected to freezing conditions.

CP 324 202: 1951   *Domestic electric water-heating installations*

The code affords guidance on the provision in domestic premises of electric water heating installations, having a nominal storage capacity not exceeding 455 litres. It deals with systems relying solely on electric heaters, and also with those which use electric heaters in conjunction with fuel-fired boilers. In addition to dealing with purely electrical matters, the code enunciates certain general principles regarding installation layout, minimizing

of metallic corrosion, etc which should be observed to ensure satisfactory operation of an installation as a whole.

There are diagrams of four types of storage water heaters with associated tables of capacity, power requirements and dimensions. Typical solid fuel/electric hot water systems are illustrated, using a direct tank and indirect cylinder. The appendices contain information on heat losses from pipework and heaters, insulation, water volumes and pipe sizing data.

BS 843: 1976   *Thermal-storage electric water heaters (constructional and water requirements)*

The standard covers stationary non-instantaneous (thermal storage and non-thermal storage) electric water heaters. Included are cistern fed water heaters with cylindrical containers, and cistern-type and open outlet water heaters with cylindrical and non-cylindrical containers. There is also a useful list of definitions related to these type of water heaters.

BS 3999   *Methods of measuring the performance of household electrical appliances*

Part 2: 1985   *Thermal storage electric water heaters*
The principal performance characteristics of these domestic heaters of interest to the user are defined and the standard methods of measuring these characteristics are described.

BS 6144: 1981   *Expansion vessels using an internal diaphragm for unvented hot water supply systems*

The subject of this specification is the manufacture and testing of welded and non-welded expansion vessels made from steel, that have an internal flexible diaphragm and which are suitable for use in systems where the heated fluid is potable water. Two grades of vessel suitable for systems having a maximum stored volume of 150 litres are specified. Grade 1 relates to vessels which can operate up to pressures of 6 bar. Grade 2 vessels are intended for maximum working pressures up to 3 bar.

BS 5918: 1980   *Code of practice for solar heating systems for domestic hot water*

This code is the first standard to deal with the use of solar energy. It covers solar heating systems having flat plate collectors with liquid heat transfer media for heating water for domestic purposes in single family dwellings. It sets out a framework of recommended practice in the design, manufacture, handling, installation, operation, commissioning and maintenance of components and systems for domestic hot water preheating. It also provides a basis of estimating the performance to be expected of these systems. Emphasis is placed on general principles rather than matters of detail concerning particular systems so that development and innovation in this new field should not be unduly inhibited. However to allow layout, operation and design limitations to be discussed three systems are cited as shown in Figure 45.

There are four appendices which consider maintenance of weather tightness, structural safety, consideration and ventilation in roof spaces, and solar collector classification.

DD 77: 1982   *Methods of test for the thermal performance of solar collectors*

This draft describes a method of test for solar collectors for use where the solar irradiance varies during the test, that is, when the collector is subject to transient conditions. This 'transient' method of test has been prepared to complement the 'steady-state' method already developed in the USA.

A steady-state method of test for use in solar simulators is also described and requirements are given for the specification of the stimulator and for the correction necessary to take account of the extra thermal irradiance present indoors.

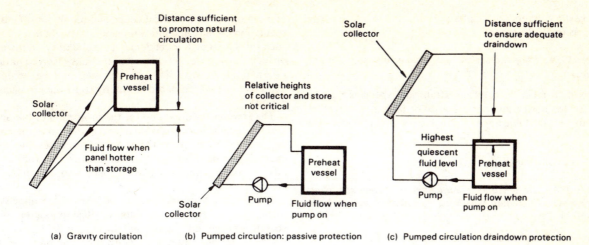

(a) Gravity circulation   (b) Pumped circulation: passive protection   (c) Pumped circulation draindown protection

Figure 45 *Examples of arrangements for solar preheating*

(Figure 2: BS 5918: 1980)

The requirements for test facilities, instrumentation and reporting formats used are as far as possible in accordance with the recommendations for European Solar Collector Test Methods.

The methods of test are for the thermal performance of a non-concentrating solar collector using a liquid heat transfer fluid which enters the collector at a single inlet and leaves the collector at a single output. The draft may also be applied to a collector with more than one inlet or outlet, or to a combination of collectors, provided that the external piping is connected so as to provide effectively a single inlet and a single outlet.

(54) Gases supply

The Building Regulations 1985 refer to one Approved Document: the Gas Safety (Installation and Use) Regulations 1984 SI 1984 No. 1358.

CP 331 *Installation of pipes and meters for town gas*

According to BS 1179, town gas is combustible gas normally supplied to the public by a utility undertaking in accordance with statutory requirements. The provisions of this code therefore apply to installations supplied with manufactured and natural gas of the 1st and 2nd families, including mixtures of liquified petroleum gas (LPG) and air distributed by a gas undertaking. They do not apply to installations using gases of the 3rd family (neat LPG).

Part 1: 1973 *Service pipes*
Recommendations are made for service pipes conveying town gas from the gas main to the meter control at pressures not exceeding 7 bar. Included are the provision of a service valve and service governor where necessary. The code deals with the interrelationship with other services, controls, sleeves, ducts and casings, protection against corrosion, excavation, identification and inspection and testing.

Part 2: 1974 *Low pressure metering*
This part deals with the siting and fixing of meters, cocks, valves, meter governors, filters and connections and arrangements for meter bypasses for town gas at low pressure. Low pressure in this contest refers to inlet pressures to the meter control not exceeding 0.075 bar.

Materials for meters and components, design considerations, installation and testing and purging are all covered.

Part 3: 1974 *Low pressure installation pipes*
Materials and methods of installing low pressure (not exceeding

0.075 bar) installation pipes in all types of buildings are covered. Materials and components, design considerations, installation and commissioning are the general areas considered.

BS 6400: 1985 *Installation of domestic gas meters (2nd family gases)*

This standard applies only to the installation of gas meters complying with BS 4161 Parts 1, 3 and 5, and supplied with 2nd family gases, including mixtures of liquified petroleum gas (LPG) and air distributed by a gas undertaking. Meters of unit construction up to 6 m³/h rating and tin plate meters up to P4 size are considered with specific reference to siting, fixing, meter controls and governors, filters and connections and the subsequent termination of supply for gas at inlet pressures to the meter control not exceeding 75 mbar.

BS 5482 *Code of practice for domestic butane- and propane-gas burning installations*

Part 1: 1979 *Installations in permanent dwellings*
This code deals with the installation in permanent dwellings of domestic systems using liquefied petroleum gases whether from cylinders or bulk supply at a pressure of 28 mbar for commercial butane and at 37 mbar for commercial propane. It gives guidance on the selection of materials, components and appliances, design considerations, installation requirements, inspection and testing, and consumer instruction.

An appendix contains basic user guidance on safe practice for inclusion in the instructions.

This standard does not cover the installation on-site of bulk supplies of LPG, for which guidance is given in a Home Office Code of Practice, *Storage of liquid petroleum gas at fixed installations* (1971).

Appliances incorporating their own gas supply are not considered to be part of the installation and are thus outside the scope of this code.

BS 4947: 1984 *Test gases for gas appliances*

Requirements are detailed for the composition and characteristics of test gases suitable for the testing of appliances designed to operate on one or more of the three gas families.

BS 669 *Flexible hoses, end fittings and sockets for gas-burning appliances*

Part 1: 1984 *Strip-wound flexible hoses, covers, end fittings and sockets for domestic appliances burning 1st and 2nd family gases*

The minimum requirements are specified for hoses and fittings for domestic cookers and appliances with gases at a nominal inlet pressure of 20 mbar.

BS 570: 1959 *Plug-and-socket gas connectors for portable appliances*

This standard makes recommendations and specifies requirements for the design and performance of plug-and-socket gas connectors for portable appliances using low pressure town gas.

(54.2)   Vapour supply

BS 1113: 1985 *Design and manufacture of water-tube steam generating plant (including superheaters, reheaters and steel tube economizers)*

This document applies to the following types of plant:

(a) Water tube boilers classified for the purposes of this standard into
(1) Natural-circulation boilers
(2) Forced-, assisted- or controlled-circulation boilers
(3) Once-through boilers
(b) Steam reheaters
(c) Independently fired steam superheaters
(d) Integral superheaters
(e) Steel tube economizers

Requirements are given for the design and manufacture of the above, including materials and design stresses, workmanship, testing, documentation amd marking, valves, gauges and fittings.

(54.4)   Medical, industrial gas supply

BS 349: 1974 *Identification of the contents of industrial gas containers*

This is the only standard included in this section and specifies requirements for the identification of gas containers. Traditional colours associated with particular gases in the 1932 edition of this standard have been retained but their use is additional to the prime requirement of marking the containers with the name of the gas and chemical formula and symbol.

(55)   Space cooling

BS 4434 *Requirements for refrigeration safety*

Part 1: 1980   *General*
This standard specifies requirements for the safety of refrigerating systems and ancillary equipment and is applicable to new refrigerating systems, extensions and modifications of existing systems and for used systems on being re-installed and operated on another site. Deviations are permissible only if equivalent protection is ensured. It also applies in the case of the conversion of a system for use with another refrigerant, for example R40 to R12 or ammonia to R22 (see BS 4580).

The standard applies, as pertinent, to all kinds of refrigerating systems in which the refrigerant is evaporated and condensed in a closed circuit, including heat pumps and absorption systems, but excluding systems using water or air as the working fluid. If special regulations exist, as for example for mines or transport (rail or road vehicles, ships and aircraft) they would take precedence over this British Standard in so far as they are more stringent.

This standard is intended solely to minimize possible hazards peculiar to refrigerating systems and ancillary equipment; it does not constitute a technical design manual.

Reference is directed to relevant standards, pressure-vessel

and piping codes, electrical codes and regulations, factory fire regulations, health and safety regulations, etc. In many countries such rules exist and, indeed, may be mandatory. In the absence of such rules a relevant document that has received national or international recognition is to be used and be accepted by agreement of all the parties properly concerned in each transaction.

The standard is drawn up for the protection of life and limb and the health of the individual, and also for the prevention of damage to property in the sense of premises but not, for example, goods in storage. In order to attain these objects, good design, construction, installation, operation and management are necessary.

Requirements are specified for occupancies, cooling systems, refrigerants, materials, working and test pressures, pressure vessels, refrigerant piping and fittings, miscellaneous parts, instrumentation, protection against excessive pressure, electrical installations, machinery rooms, miscellaneous special precautions, use of systems and refrigerants in relation to occupancies, distraction operating and maintenance and protective equipment.

(56)   Space heating

BS 5643: 1984 *Glossary of refrigeration, heating, ventilating and air-conditioning terms*

Defines the technical terms used in industry.

CP 3 Chapter VIII: 1949 *Heating and thermal insulation*

Conditions affecting the temperature of dwellings are dealt with and recommendations are given on standards of warmth for rooms and for indoor places of public assembly. The code also prescribes methods for calculating the degree of insulation appropriate to a building in terms of costs of structure, heating and expenditure on fuel. Information is also provided on the maximum permissible thermal transmittance for external parts of the structure.

The next two standards will help to ensure that the appliances covered by it are safe and will give good service, but it is necessary to point out that compliance with the standards does not in itself guarantee that satisfactory service will be obtained. Conditions of use vary greatly and it is necessary to relate the standards of performance to the actual use to which appliances will be subjected. There are also local preferences and customs which should be taken into account. For these reasons the cooperation of the local gas undertaking and of heating engineers concerned with the installation, maintenance and servicing of appliances should be sought when these are being selected.

BS 3561: 1962 *Non-domestic space heaters burning town gas*

This standard covers the construction and performance of non-domestic space heaters burning town gas, but not their installation.

Where performance standards are laid down for controls, they relate only to controls fitted as part of, or supplied with, particular appliances, they do not necessarily provide a complete specification for controls when they are intended for general use and are tested separately.

No specific reference is made to central heating boilers for non-domestic purposes, but it is intended that those rated over 43.5 kW shall satisfy the relevant requirements of BS 1250 Parts 1 and 3.

The general requirements specified include electrical requirements, gas soundness, connection, safety devices and controls, temperatures, thermal efficiency, flue system, built-in appliances, fitting, maintenance and operation, additional design features and working life and packaging.

Fan assisted air heaters, which are dealt with in Part 2, have requirements related to controls, flue buffers, air volume, temperature, inlet and outlet, motors and fans and installation. Part 3 considers overhead heaters, radiant-type, and provides information on temperature, controls, radiant elements, heat distribution and efficiency, flue system, installation and servicing.

Part 4 deals with flued convector heaters, natural convectors and requirements covered are air temperature, wall staining, installation, thermal efficiency and flame failure device.

Part 5 is divided into two sections providing details of room sealed heaters of the balanced flue and Se-duct types respectively. Requirements are specified for installation and servicing, ignition, thermal efficiency and sealing off heat exchangers. Additional requirements for balanced flue type heaters relate to the terminal and its guard, flame stability and fitting into walls of combustible material.

BS 4096: 1967 *Non-domestic space heaters burning liquefied petroleum gases*

This standard specifies the construction, operation, performance and safety requirements of non-domestic space heaters designed for use with either commercial butane or commercial propane, or both, but not their installation. It does not cover catalytic heaters and appliances for installation where special fire hazards are present, for example in garages or paint spray booths.

Where performance standards are laid down for controls they relate only to controls fitted as part of, or supplied with, particular appliances; they do not necessarily provide a complete specification for controls when they are intended for general use and are tested separately.

For low pressure operation the standard pressure for commercial butane should be 0.027 bar and for commercial propane should be 0.035 bar. For high pressure working above 0.035 bar the maximum working pressure should be 2 bar. Requirements are specified also for instructions to be supplied with appliances and the marking of appliances. The general requirements in section two cover workmanship, fitting and materials, design for maintenance, gas valves, controls, safety devices and soundness, electrical components, temperatures, flue system, safety requirements and stability of portable heaters. Fan assisted air heaters are dealt with in section three. The requirements specified in this section are controls, air temperatures, inlets and outlets, motor and fans, installation, thermal efficiency and guards. Radiant heaters are covered in section four and information is provided on ignition, temperatures, controls, radiant elements, heat distribution, and efficiency and installation and servicing.

Section five deals with natural convection heaters and requirements specified are for convected air temperatures, wall staining, installation, thermal efficiency and tests in vitiated atmosphere. Section six specifies requirements (additional to those given in sections three and five) for room-sealed heaters of the balanced flue or Se-duct types.

BS 6230: 1982 *Installation of gas-fired forced convection air heaters for commercial and industrial space heating of rated input exceeding 60 kW (2nd family gases)*

Requirements are specified for installations in commercial and industrial premises of direct and indirect gas-fired forced convection air heaters of rated input greater than 60 kW, and combination thereof for space heating. The standard applies to the following.

1 Installations supplied with 2nd family gases (for example natural gas) including mixtures of liquefied petroleum gas (LPG) and air, distributed by a gas undertaking.
2 Air heaters designed to supply make-up air to door curtain heaters, spray booth heaters, transportable air heaters and to direct-fired air heaters capable of providing full space heating.
3 Air heaters designed for use with and without ducting, and to those designed for permanent outdoor installation.

BS 5990: 1981 *Direct gas-fired forced-convection air heaters for space heating (60 kW up to 2 MW output): safety and performance requirements (excluding electrical requirements) (2nd family gases)*

BS 5991: 1983 *Indirect gas-fired forced-convection air heaters for space heating (60 kW up to 2 MW input): safety and performance requirements (excluding electrical requirements) (2nd family gases)*

These standards give details of design and construction, safety and performance requirements and methods of test for direct and indirect gas-fired convection air heaters intended for industrial and commercial applications. The standards cover heaters for use both with and without ducting and intended primarily for space heating, and those designed for permanent outdoor installation. BS 5990 specifies requirements for transportable gas heaters, but both standards apply to appliances designed to operate on normal low-pressure district supplies of 2nd family gas.

The appliances covered by BS 5990 are classified by category 1N (see BS 4947) and by Flue Type A, flueless appliances.

The appliances covered by BS 5991 are classified by category 1N (see BS 4947) and by Flue Type B, open-flued appliances.

BS 5258 *Safety of domestic gas appliances*

This standard is in a number of parts, each of which will apply to one particular type of appliance. It specifies the safety requirements and associated methods of test for domestic gas appliances burning 1st, 2nd and 3rd family gases. In the main the information given is for the use of the manufacturer but some details are included on installation and servicing and user instruction. The parts relevant to this section are:

■   AD (Regs. J1/2/3), with Part 2

Part 1: 1975 *Central heating boilers and circulators*
Part 4: 1977 *Fanned-circulation ducted-air heaters*
Part 5: 1975 *Gas fires*
Part 7: 1977 *Storage water heaters*
Part 8: 1980 *Combined appliances: gas fire/back boiler*
Part 10: 1980 *Flueless space heaters (excluding catalytic combustion heaters) (3rd family gases)*
Part 11: 1980 *Flueless catalytic combustion heaters (3rd family gases)*
Part 12: 1980 *Decorative gas log and other fuel effect appliances (2nd and 3rd family gases)*

BS 5986: 1980 *Electrical safety and performance of gas-fired space heating appliances with input 60 kW to 20 MW*

The standard details the electrical safety and performance and methods of test for the gas-fired space heating appliances that fall within the scope of BS 5918, BS 5990 and BS 5991. The principal concerns of the specification are the connection provisions, arrangements to external circuits, earthing and plug and socket outlets.

(56.4)   Central heating: hot water, steam distribution

(56.5)   Central heating: warm air distribution

(56.6)   Central heating: electrical distribution

These sections are conveniently linked together covering three aspects of central heating. There are four codes of practice. Two deal with hot water, one with gas-fired air heaters and one with electric floor warming. Of the four standards included under these headings, one covers expansion vessels in sealed systems, one deals with steam and hot water heaters, one relates to oil-fired heaters and one deals with gas-fired boilers.

(56.4)   Central heating: hot water, steam distribution

BS 6332   *Thermal performance of domestic gas appliances*

Part 1: 1983   *Thermal performances of central heating boilers and circulators*
Thermal efficiency requirements and associated methods of tests for boilers and for circulators of rated heat input up to and including 60 kW and 8 kW respectively burning 1st, 2nd and 3rd family gases. Partially suspersedes BS 1250: Part 3: 1963 which is to be withdrawn.

Part 2: 1983   *Thermal performance of gas fires*
Specifies thermal performance requirements and associated methods of test for open-flued gas fires burning 1st, 2nd and 3rd family gases. Partially supersedes BS 1250: Part 4.

Part 3: 1984   *Thermal performance of combined appliances: gas fire/back boiler*
Specifies thermal efficiency requirements and associated methods of test for combined appliances comprising a boiler or circulator and a gas fire and burning 1st, 2nd and 3rd family gases.

Part 4: 1983   *Thermal performance of independent convector heaters*
Specifies thermal efficiency requirements and associated methods of test for independent convector heaters operating under natural draught and burning 1st, 2nd and 3rd family gases. Partially supersedes BS 1250: Part 4.

Part 5: 1986   *Thermal performance of fanned circulation ducted air heaters*
Thermal efficiency requirements and associated methods of test are specified for heaters of rated heat input up to and including 60 kW and burning 1st, 2nd and 3rd family gases.

CP 341.300–307: 1956   *Central heating by low pressure hot water*

This code deals with the planning, designing and installation of systems of central heating by means of low pressure hot water, utilizing appliances such as column radiators, convectors, surface panels, unit heaters and pipe coils. The data included in this code applies to systems with a maximum 'flow' or upper working temperature of 82 °C. Variations from this condition may require adjustments to the data. A series of subcodes 301–307 give recommendations on boilers and calorifiers, storage vessels, pipework, fittings, valves, taps and cocks, column radiators, surface panels, convectors, unit heaters, power driven circulating pumps for these types of heating systems and thermal insulation. The code and subcodes are each divided into sections giving general information, and dealing specifically with materials, appliances, and components, design considerations, work on- and off-site, inspection and testing, and maintenance. Twenty-two tables are included in the data, thirteen of which were based on the IHVE guide and may be subject to revision from time to time.

BS 3528: 1977   *Convection-type space heaters operating with steam or hot water*

The equipment and procedures to be used for determining the thermal output of convection-type space heating appliances including radiators are detailed.

Two main tests for measuring the thermal output of the appliances are dealt with. The first test using measurements made on water or steam-fed primary circuits. The second using an air-cooled closed booth.

The materials for cast iron and steel radiators are specified and test pressures for all convection-type space heaters are given.

BS 5449   *Code of practice for central heating for domestic purposes*

Part 1: 1977   *Forced circulation hot water systems*
This part deals with the work involved in the general planning, designing and installation of forced circulation hot water central heating systems with heat requirements up to 45 kW, which may or may not include an indirect cylinder for domestic hot water. The following systems are considered:

1   Open vented smallbore and microbore.
2   Sealed smallbore and microbore.

Detailed information on materials, appliances and components, installation work on-site and commissioning is given. A full section on design considerations is also provided which includes diagrammatic arrangements for open vents and cold feeds. An appendix illustrates four tables of reference data to be used with this code.

BS 4814: 1976   *Expansion vessels using an internal diaphragm for sealed hot water heating systems*

BS 6144: 1981   *Expansion vessels using an internal diaphragm, for unvented hot water supply systems*

These standards specify requirements for both the manufacture and testing of expansion vessels manufactured from carbon steel only, that have an internal flexible diaphragm and are suitable for use in systems where the heating fluid is water. BS 4814 covers vessels that have a total volume of up to 1000 litres, have a diameter not exceeding 1000 mm and are suitable for operating at pressures up to 7 bar (grade 1) or 3 bar (grade 2). BS 6144 covers vessels up to 150 litres and 6 bar.

(56.5)   Central heating: warm air distribution

BS 4256   *Oil-burning air heaters*

This standard specifies the construction, operation, performance and safety requirements for air heaters burning oil.

Where special fire hazards exist, limitations on the location of the heater and the provision of special additional protective equipment can be required by the appropriate authority.

Where performance standards are specified for controls they relate only to controls fitted as part of, or supplied with, particular appliances; they do not necessarily provide a complete specification for controls when they are intended for general use and are tested separately.

Notwithstanding the requirements specified in this standard, any new designs, materials and methods of assembly, giving at least equivalent results to those specified in this standard, are acceptable.

Part 2: 1972   *Fixed, flued, fan-assisted heaters*
This part deals with fixed, flued, fan-assisted air heaters designed for use with liquid petroleum fuels such as kerosine, gas oil and heavy fuel oil. Such heaters are fitted with heat exchangers to give a supply of warm air to the immediate vicinity, or to ducting for distribution to different areas.

BS 5864: 1980   *Code of practice for the installation of gas-fired ducted-air heaters of rated input not exceeding 60 kW (2nd family gases)*

This code deals with the installation of gas-fired ducted-air heaters of rated input not exceeding 60 kW for heating one room, two or more rooms, or internal spaces simultaneously, in domestic premises and also in small commercial premises. It is concerned mainly with the type of heater that incorporates a fan to circulate the warm air by convection currents. The code also covers combined air heater/water heaters. Recommendations are given for the selection of a suitable appliance and its safe and satisfactory installation, ensuring that flueing and air supply arrangements are satisfactory, that the appliance is accessible for servicing and safe in operation. These recommendations are covered in six sections: general, selection of appliances, installation, air supply, commissioning, and servicing.

Attention is drawn to the fact that many of the practices recommended are obligatory under the Gas Safety Regulations.

(56.6) Central heating: electrical distribution

CP 1018: 1971 *Electric floor-warming systems for use with off-peak and similar supplies of electricity*

This code covers the following systems:

1 Heating cables, electrically insulated and operated at mains voltage, embedded in the floor.
2 Heating cables, electrically insulated and operated at mains voltage, drawn into ducts laid or formed in the floor.
3 Bare, uninsulated conductors embedded in the floor and energized at extra low voltage from a transformer.

The code gives recommendations on basic principles, heat requirements, electrical requirements, building requirements, temperature control, commissioning and maintenance.

(56.8) Local heating

This section contains codes of practice relating to solid fuel appliances and gas fires. Standards deal with open fires, room heaters, gas heaters, and electric room heaters. See also BS 6332: Parts 2, 3 and 4 (in 56.4).

CP 403: 1974 *Installation of domestic heating and cooking appliances burning solid fuel*

This code is a revision of CP 403: 1952 but does not supersede CP 403.101: 1952. In its preparation the opportunity has been taken to extend the types of appliances now covered by this code and this is reflected in the change of title. It deals with the selection and installation of various types of domestic heating appliances burning solid fuel in both new and existing buildings.

The appliances are considered in five main categories:

1 Open fires.
2 Room heaters.
3 Independent boilers.
4 Fanned warm air heater units.
5 Cookers.

Most of the appliances in these categories may incorporate provision for domestic hot water supply or space heating, or both. This code does not deal with the design or installation of hot water heating systems or hot water supply systems. It does, however, cover certain aspects relating to the safety of warm air heating systems.

BS 1251: 1970 *Open fireplace components*

■ AD (Regs. J1/2/3)

Requirements are specified for fireplace components which are illustrated in Figure 46.

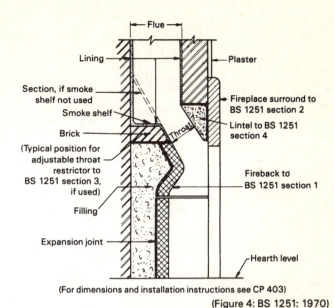

(For dimensions and installation instructions see CP 403)

(Figure 4: BS 1251: 1970)

Figure 46 *Typical assembly of open fire components*

BS 3376: 1982 *Solid mineral fuel open fires with convection, with or without boilers*

Constructional and performance requirements and methods of test are specified for all types of open fires with convection, with or without boiler, capable of burning coke. Both overnight burning and intermittent types of appliance are included. For an appliance of this type the fuel capacity should not be less than 0.013 m³ for an appliance with a boiler or 0.010 m³ for an appliance without a boiler. Details are given for determining the fuel capacity.

Requirements are specified for bottom grates, deepening bars and plates, front firebars and fall plate, closure plate, ashpan and ashpit, ignition burners, air control, boiler (if fitted) and boiler flue, sealing of firebox, connection to chimney, tools, finish, fixing, throat restrictor, marking and installation and operation. Section two details performance requirements and section three covers methods of thermal tests, banking and slow-burning tests.

BS 3378: 1972 *Room heaters burning solid fuel*

The standard deals with the constructional requirements and testing of room heaters designed to burn fuel with the doors closed. They may or may not incorporate a boiler and may have manual or thermostatic control. The rated outputs (space heating and water heating) of the room heaters can be calculated from the formula given in the standard. Any appliance with a refuelling interval of less than four hours will be deemed not to comply with this standard. For home feed appliances and those intended to burn smokeless fuel whose bulk density exceeds 640 kg/m³, the minimum refuelling interval shall be 6 hours. Generally the fuel capacity should be not less than 0.010 m³. Further requirements are specified for front firebars, bottom grate, ashpan and ashpit, combustion controls, door, boiler, flue outlet and flueways, chimney sweeping, stand-in room heaters, convection chambers, general construction, operating tools, instructions and marking.

Section two details performance requirements, and section three the test procedures.

BS 4834: 1972 *Inset open fires without convection*

Constructional and performance requirements and methods of test are specified for inset open fires with or without boilers. The standard applies to all solid fuel burning inset open fires not specifically designed to give space heating by convection.

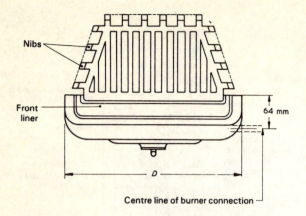

(Figure 1: BS 4834: 1972)

Figure 47 *Typical inset open fire*

The appliance should be designed for use with either fireplace components as specified in BS 1251 assembled in accordance with CP 403, or with special fireplace components which shall be supplied with it. BS 1251 specifies fireplace components for use with fires nominally sized 350, 400 and 450 mm. A fire of any other size will thus require special components.

In order that the firefront may fit with the fireplace surround the dimension D in Figure 47 should be within ± 3 mm of the nominal size.

Other requirements are given for front firebars and fallplate, deepening bar and plates, closure plate, air control, ashpan and ashpit, integral and under bar ignition burners, boiler and boiler flue, chimney throat restrictor, tools, finish, fixing to hearth, instructions and marking and electrical controls. Sections on performance tests and methods of test are also included.

BS 6539: 1984 *Fireguards for use with solid fuel appliances*

The construction is specified for fireguards for use with the types of appliance which incorporates an open fire, including combination grates, or a closed fire including room heaters and stoves installed in a fireplace recess at floor level or on a superimposed hearth within 100 mm of floor level. The fitting of the fireguard is also described including design and dimensions.

BS 3248: 1986 *Sparkguards for use with solid fuel appliances*

This specification covers the design, construction and performance for guards intended to reduce the probability of sparks reaching and igniting nearby combustible material.

BS 5871: 1980 *Code of practice for the installation of gas fires, convectors and fire/back boilers (2nd family gases)*

This code is concerned with the installation of space heating appliances burning gas, mainly intended for heating single rooms in domestic and other premises. In addition, it presents information on the installation of gas fires when combined with back boilers.

The space heaters dealt with are available in four basic types, known as radiant gas fires, radiant convector gas fires, gas convectors and fire/back boilers.

Fire/back boilers are available for two purposes. The back boiler may be intended for providing domestic hot water only, or for central heating with or without domestic hot water.

Attention is drawn to the fact that many of the practices recommended in this code are obligatory under the Gas Safety Regulations 1972 and, therefore, persons using the code should be fully conversant with these regulations.

Any appliance described in this code can be used to heat a room or internal space to a desired temperature level, but the type chosen will depend on the user's personal preference; it should be based on the knowledge of the range of appliances available, the use to which the room will be put and the period of usage.

Gas fires, convectors and fire/back boilers are available with rated heat inputs in the approximate ranges given in Table 24.

Table 24 *Rated heat inputs*

Radiant fire	5 kW to 6 kW
Radiant/convector fire	4 kW to 8 kW
Flued convector	2 kW to 15 kW
Flueless convector (domestic)	up to 3 kW
Flueless convector (greenhouse)	1 kW to 4 kW
Fire/back boilers:	
fire	4 kW to 8 kW
boiler	4 kW to 22 kW

(From text, BS 5871: 1980)

BS 4876: 1984 *Performance requirements for domestic flued oil-burning appliances (including test procedures)*

A comprehensive range of performance requirements are specified for appliances up to and including 44 kW capacity, used for hot water supply and for space-heating purposes. Test procedures and measurement methods are also described. The heating appliances are classified into five classes. Classes 1–4 relate to appliances with types of vapourizing burners, class 5 relates to appliances employing on/off pressure-jet burners.

BS 3999 *Methods of measuring the performance of household electrical appliances*

Part 14: 1982 *Electric room heaters other than storage heaters*
This part covers the performance of direct-acting electric room heaters of the portable, stationary, fixed, built-in, or ceiling-mounted types. The principle characteristics of these heaters likely to be of interest to the user are listed and defined. The standard also describes methods of determining warming up time, temperature rise and regulation.

(57) Air conditioning, ventilation

The Building Regulations 1985, Part E, applies. In this section the standards are concerned with testing and rating, air conditioning appliances, fan testing, specifying flanges for fans, environmental cleanliness, and room air conditioners. The code of practice covers general aspects of design.

BS 5720: 1979 *Code of practice for mechanical ventilation and air conditioning in buildings*

■AD (Reg. F1)

In recent years the industry has undergone rapid development and services within buildings have become much more complex. Today they often account for over 50 per cent of the initial capital cost. The services engineer is now recognized as an influential member of the building team. In this context there had been identified a need for an overall guide to the whole complex process of ventilating and air conditioning a modern building written from the standpoint of the services engineer but with allied professionals in mind.

It is hoped that this code will be used by all those concerned with ensuring that a client obtains what he expects to receive, and who wish to understand the interrelation of the multitude of actions necessary to achieve that end. The decision that the code should be broadly based inevitably means that some users will not be engineers. It has been necessary therefore to include brief descriptions of certain systems and items of equipment which, it is hoped, will make the code intelligible to those without the specialist training of the services engineer.

This code deals with the work involved in design, installation, commissioning, operation and maintenance of mechanical ventilation and air conditioning systems. The recommendations made in this code recognize the need to optimize the use of energy, reduce hazards and minimize effects detrimental to the environment. The increasing involvement of British engineers in projects overseas is noted and some guidance given in that context.

BS 2852 *Testing for rating of room air conditioners*

A method of rating the performance of single package and split system room air conditioners of capacities up to 7 kW employing air- and water-cooled condensers is described. It also details a method of testing the performance characteristics of these room air conditioners.

Part 1: 1982 *Cooling performance*
Room air conditioners used for cooling are dealt with in this part. Units designed for use with additional ducting are not included, but, if inlet or outlet ducting is supplied as an integral part of the assembly, tests for that particular assembly can be carried out in accordance with this standard. Test conditions, instruments, cooling capacity tests, measurements of air flow and performance tests are all specified.
Note: Tests are limited to those using a room calorimeter.

BS 3899: 1965 *Refrigerated room air conditioners*

This standard prescribes the general construction requirements for refrigerated room air conditioners up to 10.6 kW capacity. It defines room air conditioners and refrigerating systems and specifies the type tests and production tests that must be carried out on the units.

Requirements are specified for construction for refrigerant system, casing and fan system. Section three deals with electrical equipment and section four production tests. Further sections deal with type tests and marking and information.

BS 4773 *Methods for testing and rating air terminal devices for air distribution systems*

This testing and rating standard has been designed to produce information by means of which the characteristics of similar air terminal devices made by various manufacturers can be compared. The effects of integral damper closures have been omitted.

Part 1: 1971 *Aerodynamic testing*
This part deals with all types of elements of air diffusion, such as grilles, registers, diffusers, etc. Elements concerned with air distribution are not considered. The aerodynamic characteristics of air terminal devices can be specified by two basic parameters: the total pressure loss caused by the insertion of the device at the termination of a duct and, for supply devices, the envelope of the jet issuing from the device. The standard provides information on methods to measure these parameters.

Part 2: 1976 *Acoustic testing*
This part deals with methods of testing and rating for sound power emission from these devices. It gives instructions for calculations and for the interpolation and extrapolation of test results. Only relatively small air terminal devices are dealt with.

BS 4788: 1972 *Rating and testing of refrigerated dehumidifiers*

Test conditions are specified for determining performance characteristics of dehumidifiers of the refrigerated type. Details are given regarding the standard conditions on which ratings are based and the methods of testing to be applied for the determination of various ratings.

Requirements are specified for rating and testing of three types of dehumidifiers as set out in Table 25.

Table 25 *Capacity rating conditions*

Type designation	A	B	C
Air temperature:			
dry-bulb	5 °C	15 °C	35 °C
wet-bulb	1.4 °C	9.7 °C	26.2 °C

(From Table 1: BS 4788: 1972)

BS 4856 *Methods for testing and rating fan coil units, unit heaters and unit coolers*

For the purposes of this standard the following definition applies to:
1 Unit heaters.
2 Unit coolers.
3 Fan cool units.

Definition: fluid-to-air heat exchange apparatus through which air is passed by their electrically powered fan systems. The units may or may not contain filters.

Part 1: 1972 *Thermal and volumetric performance for heating duties: without additional ducting*
This part deals with methods of carrying out thermal and volumetric tests on forced convection units containing fluid-to-air heat exchangers and incorporating their own fans. The units are for heating applications and tests are to be carried out on units in an essentially clean condition. The primary fluids are water, steam and heat transfer fluid (excluding primary refrigerants); the range of operating conditions for the units are defined.

The general approach to the test methods described has been to consider the simplest practical method of carrying out the measurements without any unnecessary sacrifice of accuracy. The main test method permits thermal rating to be carried out in a large open space, and does not make any attempt to relate the primary fluid heat transfer with the heat transferred to the secondary fluid. This test method is very desirable when testing certain units that recirculate the heated air, as it allows this recirculation to be measured and corrected for in the test results.

It is appreciated that some of the larger units may not be suitable for testing in an open laboratory because it may be impossible to obtain steady state conditions and to this end a second test method has been introduced where the heat is ducted away from the unit. The test is necessarily more complex involving the calibration of the test chamber.

The standard relates to equipment with capacities of up to the equivalent of 75 kW.

Part 2: 1975 *Thermal and volumetric performance for cooling duties: without additional ducting*
Methods of carrying out thermal and volumetric tests of unit coolers without additional ducting are covered. The unit coolers operate with or without condensation on the coils, and are of the type used for cooling and dehumidifying purposes under frost-free conditions of operation. The cooling medium used is water or other heat transfer fluid (excluding volatile refrigerants). The range of approximate air volume flow rates is between 25×10^{-3} and 5 m³/s.

The primary fluids used are water, brine, glycol, heat transfer fluid, and this standard applies to units having operating temperatures of primary fluid within the range 0 to 27 °C.

The standard specifies performance characteristics that are to be obtained from a unit. Although the requirements of the methods for individual tests may be followed to determine the performance of a unit at one specified set of conditions, where the performance at conditions other than those of the actual test are to be stated the full schedule of tests specified in the standard have to be made.

Two different methods of thermal test, a gravimetric method and a psychrometric method, are given in this part. If variations in condensate flow rate are within the requirements specified (see clause 8 of this part) it is considered that the gravimetric method provides the data required. If this proviso is not met then the psychrometric test method is used.

The unit cooler psychrometric tests given in this part are very similar to those given for unit heaters in Part 1, with the exception of the latent cooling tests. Two approaches to the latent loading problem are presented, one a fixed point test which will yield accurate comparative data, and a second test series for general rating purposes. The latter is based on the bypass factor method (see, for example, Carrier, Cherne, Grant and Roberts, *Modern air conditioning, heating and ventilating*).

Part 3: 1975 *Thermal and volumetric performance for heating and cooling duties: with additional ducting*

This part deals with methods of carrying out thermal and volumetric tests on units intended for use with additional ducting containing fluid to air heat exchangers and incorporating their own electrically powered fan system. The units may be either for heating or for cooling applications and the latter may be with or without dehumidification under frost-free conditions.

A range of testing conditions are included which encompass the complete performance envelope of the individual item of equipment. The general approach to the test methods has been to consider the simplest practical methods of carrying out measurements without any unnecessary sacrifice of accuracy.

The rating tests described in the standard are for heating units with the fan located upstream of the coil, and for cooling units with the fan in any position. If the fan is located downstream of the coil then for heating units the modified test series described in Appendix A shall be applied.

The standard defines the range of operating conditions for the units and states that the primary medium shall be any of the following fluids:

1 Water.
2 Steam.
3 Heat transfer fluid (excluding volatile refrigerants).

Part 4: 1978 *Acoustic performance: without additional ducting*

Details are given for methods of testing and rating for sound power emission from fan coil units, unit heaters and unit coolers when used directly in the conditioned space, that is, without ducting. It gives instructions for calculations and for presentation of test results.

Part 5: 1979 *Acoustic performance: with ducting*

This part covers methods of testing and rating for sound power emission resulting from the operation of the air-moving parts of fan coil units, unit heaters and unit coolers when used with ducting. It gives instructions for calculations and for the presentation of results comprising:

1 Sound power radiated from the outlet of a unit.
2 Sound power radiated from the inlet of a unit.
3 Sound power radiated from the casing of a unit.

BS 4857 *Methods for testing and rating terminal reheat units for air distribution systems*

A terminal reheat device is defined as an assembly consisting of a heat exchanger within a casing, having one air inlet. The casing may also contain some or all of the following components:

1 A manual damper.
2 A constant flow rate controller.
3 A sound attenuator.

The casing is so designed that the whole of the air discharged from the device is obtained from the inlet duct.

Part 1: 1972 *Thermal and aerodynamic performance*

The test methods presented in this part of the standard will enable the thermal and aerodynamic performance of a terminal reheat unit to be evaluated at any water and air flow rate and temperature within the range of variables employed for the test. Air flow tests are carried out in accordance with BS 4979 Part 1. Two heat transfer methods are given, one for operation over a limited range and one for a wider range of temperatures. The standard describes testing and rating for high pressure terminal reheat units with or without flow rate controllers. It describes the equipment required and gives instructions for calculation, interpretation and interpolation of results.

Part 2: 1978 *Acoustic testing and rating*

This part specifies methods of acoustic testing and rating of units for:

1 Static terminal attenuation.
2 Sound generation, upstream and downstream of the unit.
3 Radiation of sound from casing.

BS 4954 *Methods for testing and rating induction units for air distribution systems*

Part 1: 1973 *Thermal and aerodynamic performance*

Methods are specified for the test of induction units with water coils for either (or both) heating and sensible cooling duties. It gives instructions for the calculation, interpretation and interpolation of the test results. The test methods enable the thermal and aerodynamic performance of a unit to be evaluated at any water and air flow rate and temperature within the range of the variables employed for the test. The aerodynamic test methods deal with four aspects of the units performance:

1 The pressure loss of the primary air supply.
2 The relationship between the primary air flow rate and the nozzle pressure. Since the inlet velocity profile effects will be small, the data obtained in this test may be used by site engineers to assist them in balancing an air distribution system.
3 The inlet plenum leakage flow rate.
4 The induction ratio.

Two heat transfer methods are given, one for operation over a limited range of temperatures and the other for a wider range of temperatures. Examples of calculation from the test data are included.

Part 2: 1978 *Acoustic testing and rating*

This part deals with methods testing induction units for:

1 Sound power emission.
2 Terminal attenuation.

BS 4979 *Methods for testing and rating air control devices for air distribution systems*

Part 1: 1973 *Aerodynamic testing of constant flow rate assemblies without a heat exchanger*

The function of the assembly considered in this standard is to present a room or duct system with a predetermined constant flow of air at a predetermined temperature. This temperature will be determined by conditions in the space, and, in the case of a single duct box, be regulated at a point in the air conditioning system remote from the box. A dual duct box should not only maintain a constant flow of air but also regulate the temperature of this air by mixing two streams of air. This testing standard takes into account the basic functions of the unit together with air leakage from the unit casing.

Certain aspects of the dynamic performance of the assemblies is dependent upon the system to which the unit is connected, and is therefore difficult to measure in isolation from a duct system. Such considerations have led to the omission of these aspects of the dynamic performance measurements from this standard; it is considered that an assessment of them may be inferred from the assessment of hysteresis obtained from measurements made in the aerodynamic tests.

This part specifies methods for the aerodynamic testing and rating of air control devices without heat exchangers suitable for use with air distribution systems operating at high or low velocity, or high or low pressure.

The tests cover:

1　The leakage past a closed inlet damper.
2　The casing leakage.
3　The characteristics of the constant flow rate controller.
4　The performance of the proportioning damper fitted to a dual duct box.
　　Note: Tests 3 and 4 are designed for boxes fitted with pneumatic actuators only.
5　The degree of the temperature mixing achieved by a dual duct box.

These tests are designed to establish the performance of the air control assemblies. The results will enable the comparison of the suitability of such assemblies when correctly installed in a high or low velocity air distribution system.

Note:　Although single duct units are not strictly constant flow rate assemblies, since it is possible to test them according to this standard, they have been included as a special case.

An example of the derivation of performance data using the tests described in this standard is given in Appendix A.

The test procedures are designed to give information on the characteristics of the control of air flow rate, the efficiency of mixing (dual duct boxes) and data on the compliance of the equipment with specified performance criteria with respect to casing and damper leakage.

Part 2: 1974 *Aerodynamic testing of variable flow rate assemblies without a heat exchanger*

The function of the assemblies considered in this part is to present a room or duct system with a variable volume rate of air flow at a temperature appropriate to the load in the treated space or spaces. The temperature(s) of the air stream(s) entering the assemblies are predetermined at a point in the air conditioning system remote from the boxes. This function is accomplished by:

1　In the case of a single duct variable flow rate box, varying the volume rate of air flow at a constant temperature.
2　In the case of a dual duct variable flow rate box, reducing the volume rate of air flow to a predetermined level and then mixing the two air streams at differing temperatures.

Certain aspects of the dynamic performance of the assemblies are dependent upon the system to which the unit is connected, and are therefore difficult to measure in isolation from a duct system. Such considerations have led to the omission of these aspects of the dynamic performance measurements from this standard; it is considered that an assessment of them may be inferred from the assessment of hysteresis obtained from measurements made in the aerodynamic tests.

This part specifies methods for the aerodynamic testing and rating of variable air flow rate assemblies without heat exchangers suitable for use with air distribution systems operating at high or low velocity or pressure.

The tests included cover only the characteristics of the variable flow rate controller. All other aspects of the testing of variable air flow rate high or low velocity boxes are covered by Part 1 of this standard, including the leakage past a closed inlet damper or variable flow rate controller set for substantially zero flow.

In this part, as in Part 1, the tests are designed for boxes fitted with pneumatic actuators only. These tests are designed to establish the performance of the air control assemblies. The results will enable the comparison of the suitability of such assemblies when correctly installed in a high or low velocity air distribution system.

The test procedures given in Part 1 and this part are designed to give information on the characteristics of the air flow rate control under various conditions imposed by the externally applied signal (simulating the signal from the thermostat). The efficiency of mixing (dual duct boxes) and data on the compliance of the equipment with specified performance criteria with respect to casing and damper leakage, will also be established.

BS 5491: 1977　*Rating and testing unit air conditioners of above 7 kW cooling capacity*

Requirements are specified for test conditions and the corresponding test methods for determining the performance characteristics of unit air conditioners of above 7 kW cooling capacity. It also specifies the standard conditions on which the ratings are based and the test methods to be applied for determining the various ratings. Air conditioners employing air- or water-cooled condensers are within the scope of this standard, which covers the use of air conditioners for cooling but does not cover the performance of such air conditioners when used for heating or humidification. This standard has been prepared in order to specify psychrometric, compressor calibration, volatile refrigerant flow and condenser water methods of test suitable for units of above 7 kW cooling capacity.

BS 848　*Fans for general purposes*

Part 1: 1980 *Methods of testing performance.* This standard deals with the determination of the performance of industrial fans of all types except those designed solely for air circulation, for example ceiling fans and table fans.

Fans are classified for the purposes of this standard according to the installation type or types for which they are intended. There are four standard installation types:

Type A:　free inlet, free outlet.
Type B:　free inlet, ducted outlet.
Type C:　ducted inlet, free outlet.
Type D:　ducted inlet, ducted outlet.

Methods of measurements and calculation for the flow rates, fan pressures and fan efficiencies defined as performance ratings are specified in section one. Compressibility effects are covered up to a maximum pressure ratio of 1:3.

Methods of test for the determination of the corresponding standard performance ratings are described in section two.

Recommendations for the determination of volume flow rate and fan pressure under site conditions are given in section three.

Estimates of uncertainty of measurement are provided and rules for the conversion within specified limits of test results for changes of speed, gas handled and, in the case of model tests, size.

A complete statement of fan performance should include the appropriate fan sound power level. Test methods for determining this quantity are given in Part 2 of this standard.

BS 5285: 1975　*Performance of a.c. electric ventilating fans and regulators for non-industrial use*

This standard specifies the performance of and the corresponding methods of test for ventilating fans for non-industrial use with impellers not exceeding 500 mm in diameter, driven by single phase a.c. motors having a power consumption not exceeding 500 W including any associated regulators for use on single phase a.c. circuits not exceeding 250 V. It covers the performance of ventilating fans for use in walls, windows, kitchens or for attachments to ducts, etc. The standard also covers cooker hoods containing fans.

Requirements are specified for impellers, radio interference suppression, speed regulators, noise level and marking. An appendix lists additional information to be supplied by the manufacturer.

BS 6339: 1983 *Dimensions of circular flanges for general-purpose industrial fans*

This standard details requirements for the above flanges and defines the fans with which they should be used.

BS 5295 *Environmental cleanliness in enclosed spaces*

This standard sets out, in detail, the requirements to which clean rooms, work stations and clean air devices are to conform in order to be certain of achieving the requisite standard of cleanliness. Methods of test and of monitoring to demonstrate these levels are given, together with details of procedures and methods of working which will enable the levels to be maintained.

This standard has quite deliberately been formulated to remain as widely-based and as flexible as possible with the view to embracing the widely varying environmental conditions required in meeting production and usage over the widest possible variety of disciplines demanding environmental control. In putting the standard to work it is up to those responsible for the end-product or process to ensure that the environmental conditions best suited to their work are achieved and maintained, using the standard to specify their selected requirements and, if necessary, using it as a basis in creating for the purpose, their local application standards, codes of practice or similar documents of narrower scope.

Part 1: 1976 *Controlled environment clean rooms, work stations and clean air devices*

At the beginning of this part notes are provided as a warning on explosives, cleaning solvents and radiation in clean rooms. The actual scope of this part of the standard relates to requirements applicable to clean rooms, clean work stations and clean air devices used in the industrial, medical, and pharmaceutical fields to provide controlled environments, suitable for the particular conditions required in manufacture, processing and assembly and in surgery and nursing.

Terminology and definitions are given together with test and other requirements essential to ensure quality, efficiency and, so far as can be achieved, interchangeability.

Some guidance on the selection of classes of clean rooms, work stations and clean air devices is given in Appendix C for the benefit of those who may be inexperienced in clean room technology and who may be looking for a starting point. However, before embarking on the purchase and installation of equipment, it is strongly advised that manufacturers of the equipment should be consulted.

This part lays down requirements for four classes of environmental cleanliness designated according to the degree of control of airborne particulate matter present in the enclosed environment.

Environmental cleanliness should be stated in terms of size and maximum permitted number of airborne particles and is designated Class 1, 2, 3 and 4 environments by the standard with requirements for the four classes specified.

Requirements are specified for air flow, filters, temperature, humidity, lighting and noise. In the section on design and construction the requirements specified apply to clean rooms Classes 1–4. In general mandatory requirements are not stipulated for contained work stations or clean tents, conditions and types. The requirements for clean rooms, work stations or devices are summarized.

Part 2: 1976 *Guide to the construction and installation of clean rooms, work stations and clean air devices*

Guidance is given on the construction, installation and layout of clean rooms, work stations and clean air devices. The foreword includes useful information on selecting classes of environments and air flow and their influence on cost. Requirements are specified in the standard for construction and fitting out, layout, entry ways, lighting, windows, ventilation, work benches, contained work stations, fire and general safety precautions, services, vacuum cleaning equipment, furniture and ante rooms.

Part 3: 1976 *Guide to operational procedures and disciplines applicable to clean rooms, work stations and clean air devices*

This part gives guidance on procedures to be followed in the operation and maintenance of clean rooms to ensure that the specified levels of environmental cleanliness are achieved and maintained while the clean room (work station or clean air device) is in operation.

(59) Parts, accessories, etc. special to piped, ducted services elements

The items in the title are dealt with under separate and particular headings. Where appropriate an introduction has been provided.

Ducts

CP 413: 1973 *Ducts for building services*

This code outlines, with related diagrams, the design and construction of subways, crawlways, trenches, casings and chases for the accommodation of services. In addition to dealing with the precautions to be taken to reduce the fire risk from these ducts it also includes, as an appendix, similar precautions for ventilation duct work. It also makes recommendations regarding the relationship of different services.

Flues

Codes of practice give recommendations for flue design. Standards cover materials for flues, linings and fittings.

BS 6461 *Installation of chimneys and flues for domestic appliances burning solid fuel (including wood and peat)*

Part 1: 1984   *Code of practice for masonry chimneys and flue pipes*

■   AD (Regs. J1/2/3)

This code deals with the construction of new flues whether in chimneys or flue pipes, the operating of which depends on natural draught. The chimneys and flues are specifically suitable for use with all types of domestic solid fuel appliances and may be used with gas- and oil-fired appliances. Recommendations are given for chimneys built of brick, stone, concrete and flue blocks and on materials, components and installation of flue pipes. Guidance is given on remedial action for defective chimneys.

Further recommendations cover chimneys and flue pipes serving appliances with a maximum heat output of 45 kW and the temperature of flue gases leaving the appliance has been assumed not to exceed 500 °C under normal operating conditions.

Part 2: 1984   *Code of practice for factory-made insulated chimneys for internal applications*

Information is provided for the installation of new factory-made insulated chimneys for internal application, of nominal internal diameters 100, 125, 150 and 200 mm. All the chimneys rely on natural draught for their operation, and serve appliances with a maximum heat output of 45 kW, with the flue gases assumed not to exceed a temperature of 500 °C when leaving the appliance.

BS 5854: 1980 *Code of practice for flues and flue structures in buildings*

This code applies to:

1 Linings that are built within a space enclosed by a building.
2 Linings that are built as an integral part of the building.

The flue linings and flue structures are those serving appliances (boilers and air heaters) of 45 kW output and above, burning solid, liquid or gaseous fuels.

The recommendations contained may be used for the design of a flue serving an incinerator, which should be provided with its own individual flue.

This code does not, in general, apply to linings within a free-standing or independent chimney, but many of the conditions and criteria are applicable.

The design of the flue linings and flue structures in buildings is subject to increasing knowledge and experience, and should be undertaken only by those competent to evaluate the many aspects of satisfactory construction and performance.

This code provides the building services engineer and the structural engineer with design criteria, suggested procedures and methods of recommendation for construction, and basic guidance data for the selection of lining materials.

The code also seeks to augment the skills of experienced designers who will need to interpret the information and examples included with appropriate professional expertise, giving due consideration to all the relevant issues involved.

The examples and calculations are given as one form of use of the data provided. They do not preclude other methods of computing satisfactory designs.

BS 5440 *Code of practice for flue and air supply for gas appliances of rated input not exceeding 60 kW (1st and 2nd family gases)*

Part 1: 1978 *Flues*

■ AD (Regs. J1/2/3)

In this part the subject matter covers recent developments and practical experience in the disposal of products of combustion by means of flues. The various flue systems are now classified as individual or shared systems in either room sealed or open flue forms. Particular attention is drawn to changes in terminology arising from the classification: the term 'open flue system' has been introduced to replace 'conventional flue system' and a 'common flue system' is now confined to the situation where open flued appliances are contained in a single room. Flue systems are of two main types, room sealed and open, sub-divisions of these types are shown in Figure 48.

In view of the increasing availability of balanced flue appliances and other forms of room sealed systems, the code recommends that such systems should be employed, wherever practicable as, in general, they have advantages over open flue systems. For open flue systems guidance is given graphically on condensate-free lengths for the various types of individual flues, including concrete block and double walled systems. A method for sizing an individual flue, according to its route and height, is described. Recommendations on the siting of terminals are given. The recommendations relating to materials for flue systems recognize the virtual absence of sulphur in natural gas. Furthermore, attention is drawn to the need to safeguard against debris, which may be released internally from a chimney, and to

make provision of a space for its collection below the point of entry of the products.

This part relates to the choice and installation of any flue which might form part of a gas installation for domestic or commercial purposes. It covers natural and fanned draught flues for appliances with rated heat inputs not exceeding 60 kW and incinerators of up to 0.03 m³ capacity. Flues for industrial appliances and installations requiring specialist attention are excluded.

It also deals with the complete flue equipment from the point of issue of the products of combustion from the appliance to their discharge to the outside air, the general principles being applicable to all types of premises including multi-storied blocks of flats. It also covers flues that were intended originally for appliances burning other fuels but into which gas-burning appliances may be vented.

Part 2: 1976 *Air supply*

■ AD (Regs. J1/2/3)

Recommendations are made for the intake of air into rooms and/or compartments that contain gas appliances and recognizes that adventitious ventilation openings are always present within rooms even after considerable effort has been made to restrict the air change rate. Guidance is given on supply requirements for domestic and commercial gas appliances with input ratings of up to 60 kW. Air vent areas are specified where appropriate, and compartment ventilation requirements are given for appliances installed in purpose-designed compartments.

BS 1181: 1971 *Clay flue linings and flue terminals*

■ AD (Regs. J1/2/3)

Requirements are specified in respect of materials, workmanship, design, construction crushing strength, low permeability and resistance to heat and acid for clay flue linings and flue terminals for use with heating appliances and incinerators and for ventilation. The nominal internal width of side of square linings is given as 185 × 185 mm. The nominal bore of circular linings, bends and terminals covered are 100, 125, 150, 185, 225, 250 and 300 mm. The nominal lengths of flue linings, excluding depth of socket or rebate are 0.3, 0.5, 0.6, 0.9, 1.0, 1.2 and 1.5 m

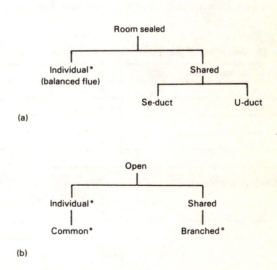

All listed types of flue system may operate under natural draught. Those marked with an asterisk are also used with fanned draught.

(From text, BS 5440: Part 1: 1978)

Figure 48 *Types of flue systems*

BS 1289: 1975 *Precast concrete flue blocks for domestic gas appliances*

■ AD (Regs. J1/2/3)

This specification deals mainly with the manufacture of precast flue blocks. Details of materials, workmanship, surface texture, joints, and a variety of tests are provided. The blocks must conform to the following dimensions which shall be measured in the manner described in the standard:

1 The cross-sectional area of the flueway shall be at least 13,000 mm² and shall remain constant throughout the length of the flueway apart from the entry to, and exit from, the flue block system.
2 The flueway length/width ratio shall not be more than 5:1.
3 The minimum width of the flue shall not be less than 63 mm.
4 The outer wall thickness of any block shall not be less than 25 mm.

An important appendix deals with performance tests for flue components. This has been written to cover the gap existing at present between the specification for precast concrete flue blocks and their use as components of a flue system. The tests are published for the guidance of manufacturers producing new designs of flue blocks.

BS 567: 1973 *Asbestos-cement flue pipes and fittings, light quality*

■ AD (Regs. J1/2/3)

This standard details requirements for light quality asbestos-cement flue pipes and fittings with or without internal acid-resisting coating, intended primarily for use with gas-fired appliances having an input rating not exceeding 45 kW.

They may also be used for ventilation and other purposes. Where it is expected that the material will be subjected to a flue temperature exceeding 260 °C the advice of the manufacturer should be sought.

It is important that there shall be no direct flame impingement on the wall of the flue pipe. Light quality pipes and fittings are not suitable for use with solid fuel and oil-fired appliances.

Composition, manufacture, dimensions and tolerances, standard tests, protection, and sampling arrangements are specified. The flue pipe and fittings covered have nominal diameters of 50, 75, 100, 125 and 150 mm. The nominal lengths of straight pipes in these diameters are 900, 1200 and 1800 mm. Requirements

are specified for bends, tees, taper pieces, sockets and caps.

BS 835: 1973 *Asbestos-cement flue pipes and fittings, heavy quality*

Requirements are specified for composition, manufacture, dimensions and tolerances, and details are given of standard tests, protection and sampling arrangements. The flue pipes and fittings are of diameters from 75 to 600 mm inclusive, with or without internal acid resisting coatings, intended for use with the following types of appliances.

1 Solid smokeless fuel-burning stoves (output rating not exceeding 45 kW).
2 Oil-burning appliances (output rating not exceeding 45 kW).
3 Gas-fired appliances.
4 Incinerators (not exceeding 0.09 m³ in capacity).

It is important that there shall be no direct flame impingement on the walls of the flue pipes. Where it is anticipated that the material will be subjected to a flue temperature exceeding 260 °C the advice of the manufacturer must be sought.

These pipes and fittings may also be used for ventilation and other purposes.

The specification applies to straight pipes of 900 and 1200 mm lengths in all diameters and 1850 mm lengths in diameters 75 to 300 mm inclusive. Requirements are also specified for bends, tees, taper pieces, sockets, caps and cleaning doors.

BS 715: 1970 *Sheet metal flue pipes and accessories for gas-fired appliances*

■ AD (Regs. J1/2/3)

This standard applies to sheet metal flue pipes, fittings and accessories having welded or folded seams, primarily for internal use. The requirements given are based on the use of sheet carbon steel or aluminium, although other metals are not specifically excluded. Section two covers single wall flues and section three covers minimum requirements for lighter twin-wall flue systems than those specified in BS 4543 with air gap insulation.

Appendix A shows typical methods of assembly for pipes, fittings and accessories which are dimensioned in a series of six tables and 14 figures. Included in those is a table of various finishes. The lengths and diameters of the pipes and accessories specified are shown in Table 26.

Table 26 *Sheet metal flue pipes*

Nominal diameter (mm)	Single wall	Twin wall	
50	•	—	
75	•	•	minimum air
100	•	•	gap between
125	•	•	flue lining and
150	•	•	outer casing of 6 mm

Nominal length (mm)	Single wall including spigot	Twin wall including overlap
150	•*	•
300	•	•
450	•*	•
600	•	—
900	•	•
1500	•	•

*Additional length for vitreous enamel.

(From text, BS 715: 1970)

BS 41: 1973 *Cast iron spigot and socket flue or smoke pipes and fittings*

■ AD (Regs. J1/2/3)

This standard covers flue or smoke pipes, and bends, of 100 to 300 mm nominal bore and offsets of 100 to 150 mm nominal bore, and provides an alternative A or B type socket profile to allow interchangeability between pipes manufactured by the sandcast or by the spun process. Fittings are common to both types. The straight pipes are available in overall lengths of 610, 915, 1210 and 1830 mm.

BS 4207: 1982 *Code of practice for monolithic linings for steel chimneys and flues*

Deals with the formulation and installation of monolithic linings for steel chimneys and flues based on materials commonly bonded with hydraulic cements.

Boilers, etc

There are nine standards and three codes of practice relating to boilers. Seven of the standards prescribe requirements for boilers ranging from domestic to industrial and steam generating applications. One covers electrode boilers and another oil-burning equipment for boilers. One code of practice deals with gas boilers, one with oil-firing and the other with stokers. One DD deals with thermal performance.

BS 3377: 1985 *Boilers for use with domestic solid mineral fuel appliances*

Requirements for the materials, construction, pressure testing, information to be supplied by the manufacturer and marking, are specified for normal and high boilers for use with solid-fuel appliances complying with BS 1252, BS 3376, BS 3378 or BS 4834. Appendix A of the standard gives useful guidance on the selection of boilers.

BS 779: 1976 *Cast iron boilers for central heating and indirect hot water supply (44 kW rating and above)*

The information in this standard complies with current practice and applies to cast iron boilers of the following types:

1 Low pressure steam boilers.
2 Hot water central heating boilers for use in open systems.
3 Hot water central boilers for use in pressurized systems. (Steam pressurization is not covered.)

The standard consists of eight sections. Section one gives general requirements for the boilers including the design pressures and flow temperatures for the boilers tested above, with the safety arrangements for pressurized systems. It also includes the fuels which the boilers may use.

Section two covers materials used in the construction of the boiler and components and section three deals with the construction and workmanship involved in manufacture. Section four considers mountings and fittings including safety valves, vent pipes, gauges, thermometers and test valves. Combustion equipment is dealt with in section five and automatic controls, that is water level, automatic firing and overriding controls, are covered in section six. Inspection, testing and marking are detailed in section seven and electrical wiring requirements are specified in section eight.

An appendix gives information on typical international and European categorization of boilers.

BS 855: 1976 *Welded steel boilers for central heating and indirect hot water supply (rated output 44 kW to 3 MW)*

The scope of this standard has generally been extended to cater for new trends in the heating industry, but excludes boilers for direct hot water supply. The standard applies to welded steel boilers (other than boilers with cylindrical shells over 2 m diameter) for which the classification and the design pressures and flow temperatures are given in Table 27.

The standard also covers mountings and appliances and automatic controls where applicable, necessary for safe operation which are not necessarily to be supplied by the boiler manufacturer. Steam boilers are included but hot water boilers pressurized by steam are not.

Section one of this standard deals with such matters as interpretation, conditions of compliance, performance, definitions, dampers and doors, ashpits, openings, inspection and cleaning holes provisions for mountings and boiler assembly.

Section two considers the materials and design stresses. Section three is a major part dealing with design of the shells and components. A number of formulae, figures and tables are given referring to various aspects of the design.

Section four deals with materials and workmanship and mountings, and appliances such as safety valves, pressure valves and thermometers are detailed in section five. Combustion controls, automatic controls for boilers, inspection and testing and electrical wiring are covered in sections six, seven, eight and nine respectively. Appendix A recommends forms of connections and Appendix B gives information which is typical of the European and international categorization of boilers.

BS 2790: 1986 *Specification for design and manufacture of shell boilers of welded construction*

Covers materials, determination of design temperature of components, calculation of scantlings, compensation of openings, design of supports, manufacturing procedures, tolerances, welding, inspection, non-destructive testing for three classes of boiler, and pressure testing. Additional information and details of design and manufacturing considerations in appendices.

BS 4433 *Solid smokeless fuel boilers with rated output up to 45 kW*

The constructional requirements and testing of boilers with rated outputs up to 45 kW are covered by this standard. Part 1

Table 27 *Design pressures and flow temperatures*

Type	Output kW		Maximum operating pressure bar	Maximum working temperature
	Min.	Max.		
Steam	45	1500	2	132 °C
Externally pressurized hot water	45	3000	4.5	132 °C
Vented hot water	45	3000	4.5	100 °C

(Table 1: BS 855: 1976)

deals with boilers fitted with bottom grates, in which the ash is removed from under the firebars and which burn hard coke, gas coke, specially reactive solid smokeless fuels and other smokeless fuels such as anthracite, carbonized briquettes and dry steam coal. Part 2 deals specifically with gravity feed boilers designed to burn small anthracite. Boilers dealt with in these specifications are used for heating water for central heating commonly in conjunction with domestic hot water supply, or for domestic hot water supply only.

Requirements for certain constructional features are given. Tests are described for checking the boiler for:

1 Controllability.
2 Performance at rated output and low load.
3 Ability to withstand accidental over-run.

Part 1: 1973   *Boilers with undergrate ash removal*
A boiler which meets the requirements of this part of the standard will have been type tested with a standard coke and will be deemed to give a satisfactory performance when used with the fuels recommended for its use in the list of 'approved domestic solid fuel appliances'.

Performance standards and test procedures are described in sections two and three respectively. Other requirements are given for fuel capacity, combustion controls, boiler shells, tappings, assembly, installation, operation and maintenance.

Part 2: 1969   *Gravity feed boilers designed to burn small anthracite*
A boiler which meets the requirements of this part of the standard will have been type tested with a standard anthracite and will be deemed to give a satisfactory performance when used with the fuel recommended for its use in the list of 'approved domestic solid fuel appliances'.

Thermostatically controlled cast iron and steel gravity feed central heating boilers designed for burning small anthracite are covered, with integral fuel storage and the fuel feeds by gravity from the storage space to the fuelbed. Ash is normally removed as clinker.

Performance standards and test procedures are described in sections two and three respectively. Other requirements are similar to those listed in Part 1.

CP 3000: 1955   *The installation and maintenance of underfeed stokers*
Guidance is offered in the installation and maintenance of underfeed stokers (ram and screw types) for use with the following types of boilers:

1 Domestic hot water supply.
2 Sectional cast iron or steel.
3 Vertical and horizontal shell.
4 Small water tube.

The code considers the design of boiler rooms, fuel storage and flues and chimneys, and gives recommendations on installation of stokers, automatic safety controls, care and maintenance.

BS 749: 1969   *Underfeed stokers*
Requirements are given for underfeed stokers for all applications except metallurgical or other high temperature furnaces. The stokers are rated up to 550 kg of coal per hour, and may be hopperfed or bunker to boiler types.

The requirements specified include materials, fuel properties, electric motors and transmission gear, conveyor, retort, air supply, coal hopper, lubrication, installation and operation, performance tests and safety requirements.

BS 5410   *Code of practice for oil firing*
The application of oil firing to various plant requires many important decisions to be made at an early stage of planning. It is desirable that there should be recommended requirements so that manufacturers, suppliers, installers, and users of equipment may have a common basis on which to work.

While the code is intended to give guidance on current good practice, the requirements of local authorities, fire authorities and insurance companies should be ascertained.

Part 1: 1977   *Installations up to 44 kW output capacity for space heating and water supply purposes*
Oil burning installations up to 44 kW output capacity are considered for space heating and hot water supply purposes and associated oil tanks of capacity up to 3400 litres. The code also applies, where relevant, to oil-fired cookers where these are connected to flues.

Recommendations are given on types of appliances and burners, oil systems from storage tank to burner, accommodation for boilers and air heaters, and for oil storage tanks for single family dwellings, flues and chimneys, commissioning, maintenance, conversion of existing appliances, and legal requirements.

Part 2: 1978   *Installations of 44 kW and above output capacity for space heating, hot water and steam supply purposes*
Recommendations are given for oil burning systems for boiler and warm air heater plants for space heating, hot water and steam supply purposes, having a total rated output of 44 kW or more. They apply to the oil burning equipment forming part of a multi-fuel installation in which oil is not burnt simultaneously with any other fuel. Relevant sections apply to thermal fluid heaters and to plants of a portable nature (for example as used for emergency or temporary heat supplies).

Recommendations are also given on fuels, selection of burners, oil tanks and equipment, oil handling systems from storage tank to burner, accommodation for installations, chimney and flue systems, electrical equipment, instrumentation, commissioning, maintenance, and safety provisions.

Part 3: 1976   *Installations for furnaces, kilns, ovens and other industrial purposes*
This part covers oil-burning equipment for industrial installations such as furnaces, kilns and ovens. Recommendations are given for the selection, application and installation of burners, tanks, piping systems, accommodation, chimneys, electrical and control equipment.

BS 799   *Oil burning equipment*
Part 2: 1981   *Vaporizing burners*
This part deals with types of vaporizing burners suitable for burning oil conforming to Classes C and D as specified in BS 2869. It specifies requirements for oil vaporizing burners and associated equipment for boilers, heaters, furnaces, ovens and other similar static flued plant such as freestanding space heating appliances for single family dwellings. The types of burner dealt with are as follows:

1 Vaporizing oil burner.
2 Pot burner.
3 Rotary burner.
4 Perforated burner.
5 Fully automatic burner.
6 Semi-automatic burner.

Requirements are specified in this part for fuels, burner systems, oil feed and oil shut off, ignition requirements, air supply, burner construction, control, flame failure, combustion performance and smoke index and electrical supply for the following vaporizing burners:

1 Fully automatic pot-type.
2 Fully automatic rotary.
3 Semi-automatic.

A further section deals with materials and components.

Part 3: 1981 *Automatic and semi-automatic atomizing burners up to 36 litres per hour*
This part specifies requirements for materials from which all component parts of the oil burning equipment shall be constructed, and also deals with such points of component design and plant layout as are fundamental to the proper functioning of such equipment.

The range of equipment includes:

1 Automatic and semi-automatic oil burners of the monobloc type, as defined in Part 6 of this standard.
2 Dual fuel gas/oil burners when using fuel oil.

Section two deals with operation of the oil burner and specifies requirements for oil feed and shut off, preparation of oil for burning, ignition, air supply and control system. Section three covers materials and components. The components considered are oil filters and oil pumps, valves, oil pressure gauges and electrical equipment. This section also specifies painting and identification, operating instructions and marking.

Part 4: 1972 *Atomizing burners over 36 litres per hour and associated equipment for single burner and multi-burner installations*
In this part single burner and multi-burner installations for land and marine purposes are specified, each burner having a maximum burning rate of over 36 litres per hour, and suitable for liquid fuels as specified in BS 2869 and BS 1469. The standard does not apply to gas turbines and internal combustion engines. Definitions are included as part of the classification of the burners.

Oil burner types, for the purposes of this standard, have been classified according to the methods used for atomization of the fuel.

Any of these types can be further classified by the degree to which the sequence of operation is automatic, that is hand control, flame-monitored hand control, partly automatic control, flame-monitored and partly automatic control, fully automatic control.

Details are also given in this part for operating sequences, materials and components, electrical equipment, operating instructions and marking.

Part 5: 1975 *Oil storage tanks*
This part specifies integral tanks which form part of an oil-fired unit, service tanks, and storage tanks of unlimited capacity with a maximum height of 10 m. The requirements are related to tanks constructed of carbon steel. It does not apply to tanks constructed of plastics, galvanized tanks or to tanks other than those constructed of carbon steel. An integral tank is defined as a small tank up to 25 litres capacity which forms an integral part of an oil-fired unit, or appliance. A service tank is an auxiliary tank having a capacity of not more than 1000 litres, which isolates the main storage tank or tanks from the burner installation, and are specified in five types.

The oil storage tanks are specified in two main groups. The first group is dealt with in clause six of the standard and is for tanks not exceeding 10 m in height up to and including 3500 litres capacity specified in four types, with details of cradle support and staying.

Clause seven of the part deals with oil storage, of the second main group, which are defined as oil storage tanks other than those dealt with in clause six, not exceeding 10 m in height. Eleven types are listed.

In general, service tanks and oil storage tanks have the following requirements specified:

1 Pressure conditions.
2 Test conditions.
3 Manholes and inspection openings.

4 Construction and plate thicknesses.
5 Dimensions and position of supports (cradles and stays and struts).
6 Painting, cleaning and marking.
7 Filling pipes and connections.
8 Electric, steam and hot water heaters (second main group of oil storage tanks).
9 Vent pipes.
10 Installation of tanks.

An appendix considers the capacity and overfilling of oil storage tanks. Fifteen tables and twelve figures (four graphs) are used as references by the text.

Part 6: 1979 *Safety times and safety control and monitoring devices for atomizing oil burners of the monobloc type*
This part specifies the safety times and the functions of safety, control and monitoring devices for automatically and semi-automatically operating atomizing oil burners of the monobloc type.

These burners may use liquid fuels the viscosity of which does not exceed 380 mm²/s at 50 °C.

This standard also applies to combined type burners using alternatively liquid or gas fuels when they operate with liquid fuels.

BS 5376 *Code of practice for selection and installation of gas space heating (1st and 2nd family gases)*

Part 2: 1976 *Boilers of rated input not exceeding 60 kW*
The code considers gas-fired central heating boilers utilizing gas for the heating of domestic or commercial premises by the circulation of hot water in open or sealed systems. Recommendations are made on the selection of the boiler and its installation in accordance with currently accepted good practice for domestic and commercial premises, but not on the detailed design or installation of the heating system as a whole; where forced circulation of the heating water is employed, the heating system of which the boiler is part should comply with the recommendations of BS 5449. Where circulation is by gravity, the installation should comply with the recommendations of the CIBS guide.

BS 6644: 1986 *Installation of gas-fired hot-water boilers of rated inputs between 60 kW and 2 MW (2nd and 3rd family gases)*

In the past the conditions to be observed when installing appliances have been published in the form of recommendations. However, it was felt that many of the operations for installations of 2nd and 3rd family gas appliances should be specified to produce a safe installation. This revision of CP 332: Part 3 is therefore presented in the form of a practice specification which deals with the installation requirements for:

(a) hot-water boilers of rated inputs between 60 kW and 2 MW
(b) groups of boilers with individual ratings of 60 kW or less, but with aggregate inputs greater than 60 kW.

The design and installation of any of the associated heating or hot water supply systems are not covered in this standard.

BS 1894: 1952 *Electrode boilers of riveted, seamless, welded and cast iron construction for water heating and steam generating*

The standard applies to boilers for design temperatures not exceeding 286 °C, and is concerned solely with boilers for water heating or for the generation of steam, in which the water is heated by passage of an alternating electric current through the water, the resistance of which to the passage of the current increases under pressure. Safety valves are dealt with at length in this standard. Although electrical safety devices are specified, safety valves are to be regarded as the safety protection against excess pressure. The formulae in this specification give in all cases the minimum scantlings and apply to boilers constructed throughout under competent supervision.

The main recommendations for three boiler types are dealt with under ratings and fillings, mountings, fittings and connections, electrical requirements and construction.

DD 65 *Methods of type testing of heating boilers for thermal performance*

Part 1: 1979 *Direct method*
Detailed requirements are given for the type testing of boilers of all sizes and types for central heating and indirect hot water supply, fired by gas, liquid or solid fuel.

Part 2: 1982 *Indirect method*
Definition, methods of testing, measurements and calculation concerning the indirect method of type testing are all covered by this part of the draft.

Cisterns, tanks, cylinders, calorifiers

Cisterns and tanks are covered by standards specifying different materials, that is, asbestos-cement, cast iron, steel and plastics. Indirect cylinders and calorifiers, combination units, cold water cisterns, and tanks and vessels are also covered.

BS 4213: 1975 *Cold water storage cisterns (polyolefin or olefin copolymer) and cistern covers*

This standard deals with cisterns and covers for the domestic and industrial storage of cold water, and provides methods of test for the evaluation of the properties of cisterns and covers made by any of the available processes. This edition is confined to cisterns produced from polyolefins and olefin copolymers but an outer reinforcing layer of an unspecified composition is now permitted. Covers may be made from polyolefins or olefin copolymers, or from other minerals having an olefin or olefin copolymer layer on the inside face. The standard is applicable to both circular and non-circular cisterns and covers, with a capacity range of 182 to 455 litres (ten sizes).

Because slight changes are necessary in plumbing practice when using thermoplastics cisterns, as opposed to galvanized mild steel and asbestos-cement cisterns, additional information relating to installation has been given in Appendix L. Requirements are provided for cisterns used as expansion cisterns.

The standard also includes details of resistance to deformation, deflection, fatigue, impact, reversion and delamination, tensile strength and elongation at break, and sprue strains.

BS 4994: 1973 *Vessels and tanks in reinforced plastics*

The manufacture of vessels and tanks in reinforced plastics is a wide field, involving a large number of materials, both plastics and reinforcing systems, and widely different methods of manufacture. It is not practicable to cover all aspects in a single specification and this standard covers part of the field, namely, the use of polyester and epoxide resins in wet lay-up systems.

Currently, information on the engineering properties (particularly changes of properties over long periods) of the composites used for the fabrication of tanks and vessels is scattered and meagre. In the absence of details of comprehensive long-term properties, therefore, the material properties used for design are based on short-term tests. Material property data should be presented in the form recommended in BS 4618.

The design method in this standard, being based on the allowable unit loadings is particularly suited to the design of composites of reinforced plastics.

Requirements are specified for the design, materials, construction and workmanship, inspection and testing, and erection of vessels and tanks in reinforced plastics, consisting of a polyester or epoxide resin system reinforced with glass fibres, manu-

factured by the wet lay-up process. Construction both with and without a lining of thermoplastics are included.

The following limitations on pressure and size apply:

1 Vessels subject to internal pressure, product of maximum total effective pressure (bar) and volume (m³) not greater than 10, with an overriding limitation on pressure of 5 bar.
2 Vessels subject to vacuum, product of maximum negative pressure (bar) and volume (m³) not greater than 10, with an overriding limitation on volume of 50 m³.
3 Tanks subjected only to hydrostatic head of liquid contents. No size limitation.

This standard does not apply to:

1 Vessels and tanks operating at temperatures below 0 °C or above 100 °C.
2 Jacketed vessels and tanks.

Vessels subject to external pressure, including buried tanks, shall be given special consideration.

BS 1564: 1975 *Pressed steel sectional rectangular tanks*

This standard was first published in 1949. The present revision was undertaken to provide tank sizes in metric units and to cater in particular for plates which are now being supplied in metric thicknesses. It is pointed out, however, that the sectional dimensions in this revision are interchangeable with the imperial dimensions in the 1949 edition.

Requirements are given for pressed steel sectional rectangular tanks, working under a pressure not greater than the static head corresponding to the depth of the tank, built up of pressed steel plates 1220 mm square used to contain cold water, hot water, potable liquids, certain oils and chemicals. Pressed steel tanks are not recommended for a depth greater than 4880 mm.

For the purposes of this standard cold liquids are defined as those having a temperature not exceeding 38 °C and hot liquids are defined as those having a temperature exceeding 38 °C but less than 100 °C.

In the case of tanks to hold hot liquids, care shall be taken in use to avoid excessive vibration or turbulence. Tanks for temperatures higher than 100 °C should be the subject of mutual arrangement between the purchaser and the manufacturer.

Tanks can also be assembled with all flanges internal with the additions of other components, but because of the difficulty of assembling and maintaining this type of tank they are not preferred. All tanks can be supplied with open or closed top. Detail on tank construction and information on erection and supports is also included.

Table 28 gives the range of basic dimensions and nominal capacities of tanks at the four separate depths.

Table 28 *Tanks: basic dimensions and nominal capacities*

Depth (mm)	Length by breadth range (mm)	Nominal capacity range litres
1220	1220 × 1220 to 8540 × 8540	1818 to 89 102 (21 sizes)
2440	2440 × 1220 to 8540 × 8540	7273 to 178 203 (21 sizes)
3660	3660 × 3660 to 15 860 × 15 860	40 097 to 921 929 (23 sizes)
4880	3660 × 3660 to 15 860 × 15 860	65 462 to 1 229 238 (23 sizes)

(From Tables 1–4: BS 1564: 1975)

Requirements are also specified for flanges, bolting, access, erection, connections and testing.

BS 2594: 1975   *Carbon steel welded horizontal cylindrical storage tanks*

This standard is intended to provide for tanks of adequate safety and reasonable economy, in a range of sizes to suit the requirements of user industries for the static storage of petroleum and other chemical products vented to atmosphere. Tanks intended for the storage of liquids corrosive to mild steel should be suitably protected. When tanks are required for the storage of liquids outside the temperature range $-10\,°C$ to $+150\,°C$, the material and methods of fabrication should receive special consideration.

Dimensions are based on chosen metric capacities. Dished and flanged ends of only four sizes are used which are convenient for the manufacture of compartmented tanks; these are based on metric outside diameters. Imperial dimensions for dished ends are retained for current production purposes, but as and when existing tooling requires renewal it should be replaced to suit the metric sizes specified in this standard.

Due to the current low demand, unflanged ends and flanged ends butt-welded to the shell are not included in this revision. However, if justified by demands from industry, consideration will be given to the reinstatement of either or both of these forms of construction at a future date.

Dimensions for lifting lugs are included along with details of the requirements dealing with welding and testing, and manhole positions.

The above-ground tanks specified in this standard comply with the performance requirements for Type A tanks in BS 799.

The tanks are specified in 18 sizes, the nominal capacities ranging from 5 to 90 m^3. The maximum internal working pressure should not exceed 0.4 bar measured at the top of the tank, and a maximum internal vacuum of 10 mbar. This standard also specifies requirements for saddle supports for above ground tanks, drain and filling points, draw off sockets, manufacture and testing.

BS 1563: 1949   *Cast iron sectional rectangular tanks*

This standard is in imperial units and deals with cast iron sectional rectangular tanks, not working under pressure other than static head, built up of cast iron plates, in the main, either 2, 3 or 4 ft square throughout to contain cold water, hot water, potable liquids, oils and certain chemicals, and of the following types:

1 Type A with external flanges and closed or open top.
2 Type B with internal flanges and closed or open top.

In this standard cold liquids are defined as having a temperature not exceeding 100 °F and hot liquids exceeding 100 °F but not exceeding 300 °F.

BS 2777: 1974   *Asbestos-cement cisterns*

The purpose of the standard is to provide requirements for asbestos-cement cisterns similar to those given in other British Standards for domestic water storage cisterns made from other materials.

It includes a completely revised specification for the allowable compositions of asbestos-cement to accord with the requirements of other British Standards for asbestos-cement products.

As previously, the fittings for attachment of pipes have not been included in the specification, except in so far as space has been allowed for them in the modular coordinating spaces defined in a table in the standard. The requirements of any water undertaking byelaws will apply to the fittings and their position on the cisterns in the same manner as they apply for cisterns made from other materials.

The capacities of cisterns covered by this standard range from 17 to 701 litres. Requirements are also specified for watertightness, water absorption and static strength.

BS 853: 1981   *Calorifiers and storage vessels for central heating and hot water supply*

In preparing this standard, account has been taken of current practice and, in particular, careful attention has been given to the clauses covering scantlings, which lay down the minimum requirements regarded as good practice. While the standard deals fully with the strength and method of construction of calorifiers and storage vessels and also suitable safety devices and methods of pressure testing no provision has been included for testing thermal performance.

The shells of these units are made from copper or carbon steel. Provision is made for the protection from corrosion of carbon steel shells, by galvanizing, sealed zinc spraying or copper lining. This standard covers calorifiers heated by steam, water, heat transfer fluid or electricity, but does not cover calorifiers with steam on the outside of the tube battery.

The calorifiers are classified into Grade A or Grade B, as shown in Table 29. Grade B classification is used for copper units only, the requirements specify less severe operating conditions.

The standard includes comprehensive details, for all materials used, and data and formulae for the design of the various parts of the calorifiers and heater batteries.

BS 1565   *Galvanized mild steel indirect cylinders, annular or saddle-back type*   Part 2: 1973

This part of the standard is the metric (SI) version of BS 1565: 1949. The values in Part 2 represent the equivalent of the values in imperial units in the 1949 edition, rounded to convenient numbers. For the purpose of compliance with this standard, the values in either Part 1: 1949 or this part may be used, provided that one set of values is used consistently.

Two classes and eight sizes of cylinder are specified; Class B is tested to 3.76 bar with a maximum working head of 18 m, and Class C is tested to 1.38 bar with a maximum working head of 9 m. Tables in the standard indicate cylinder dimensions and should be read in conjunction with the accompanying figures. Cylinder sizes range from 109 to 455 litres. All cylinders should be fitted with five screwed connections.

If so ordered by the purchaser, provision can be made for the attachment of a gas circulator.

BS 417   *Galvanized mild steel cisterns and covers, tanks and cylinders*   Part 2: 1973

This part of the standard is the metric (SI) version of BS 417: 1964. The values in Part 2 represent the equivalent of the values in imperial units in the 1964 edition, rounded to convenient numbers. For the purpose of compliance with the standard the

Table 29 *Calorifier classification*

Grade	Maximum working pressure in shell (bar)	Maximum design pressure in the battery (bar)	Maximum operating temperature in shell (°C)	Maximum operating temperature in tube battery (°C)
A	7	17.5	120	300
B	4.5	4.5	90	300

(From text, BS 853: 1981)

values in either Part 1: 1964 or this part may be used provided that one set of values is used consistently.

Requirements are specified in three separate sections for cisterns and cistern covers, tanks, and cylinders. Each section includes such items as dimensions, materials, manufacture, testing pipe connections and galvanizing.

Two grades (A and B) and 20 sizes of cistern are fully dimensioned, in a table, for the range of capacities 18 to 3364 litres, with a length, width and depth dimension of 457, 305 and 305 mm for the smallest cistern to 2438, 1524, and 1219 mm for the largest. Grades A and B refer to the thickness of material used in the manufacture of the various cisterns throughout the full range. Details are also given for covers, and a further table with associated diagrams specifies the type of large cistern requiring stays and the method of staying to be used.

Tables showing the dimensions, capacities, and grading of tanks, which should be manufactured with a hand hole and cover plate, are included. Five tanks form a capacity range of 95 to 155 litres.

Tables showing the dimensions, capacities and grading of cylinders (for vertical installation) with optional hand hole and cover plate are included. Ten cylinders form a capacity range of 73 to 441 litres. A revision is in hand.

BS 699: 1984   *Copper direct cylinders for domestic purposes*

■ AD (Reg. L5)

Copper cylinders of four grades and 16 sizes are specified for storage of hot water. The cylinders are intended for fixing in the vertical position and are all of the type in which the bottom is domed inwards. The four grades specified are given in Table 30.

Table 30   *Grading for copper direct cylinders*

Grade	Test pressure	Maximum working head
1	3.65 bar	25 m
2	2.20 bar	15 m
3	1.45 bar	10 m
4	1.00 bar	6 m

(From Table 1, BS 699: 1984)

The working head is the vertical distance from bottom of cylinder to the water line of the cistern supplying it.

A table shows the basic dimensions of 16 cylinders and should be read in conjunction with accompanying figures. The capacity range is from 74 to 450 litres.

The screwed connections for the pipes must comply with BS 2779 and may be external or internal threads. Cylinder types 0–9E will normally have four pipe connections, types 10–14 normally five pipe connections. If required, provision can be made for a variety of optional features.

The standard recommends the use of the preferred metric sizes of cylinders for new installations.

BS 1566   *Copper indirect cylinders for domestic purposes*

Part 1: 1984   *Double-feed indirect cylinders*

■ AD (Reg. L5)

This part specifies requirements for copper cylinders for the ·storage of hot water where the water is heated indirectly by hot water circulating in a coil-type heat exchanger constructed of tube and mounted inside the cylinder for the transfer of heat to the stored water. Annular type primary heaters are no longer included. Four grades and 16 sizes are specified for cylinders intended for fixing in the vertical position and all are of the type in which the bottom is domed inwards. The grades specified are given in Table 31.

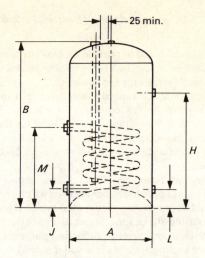

(From Figure 2: BS 1566: Part 1: 1984)

Figure 49   *Indirect cylinder showing the positions of connections for pipes and top-entry immersion heater*

Table 31   *Grading for copper indirect cylinders*

Grade	Test pressure	Maximum working head
1	3.65 bar	25 m
2	2.20 bar	15 m
3	1.45 bar	10 m
4	1.00 bar	6 m

(From Table 1, BS 1566: Part 1: 1984)

The working head is the vertical distance from the bottom of the cylinder to the water line of the cistern supplying it.

Figure 49 illustrates a typical example of a cylinder with five pipe connections. The standard includes details of cylinders with four pipe connections. Tables 1 and 4 in the standard give basic dimensions for the 16 cylinders which have a range of storage capacities from 72 to 440 litres, and if required the cylinders can be supplied with a variety of optional features. The screwed connections for the pipes must comply with BS 2779 and cylinder types 0–9E have four screwed connections, types 10–14 have five screwed connections the threads may be external or internal.

Part 2: 1984   *Single-feed indirect cylinders*

■ AD (Reg. L5)

Three grades and seven sizes of copper cylinders for the storage of hot water are specified. The stored water is heated indirectly by the water circulating in an integral primary heater (annular or coil type) and for which only one feed cistern is required. The feed water to the primary circuit being obtained from within the cylinder through the primary heater. However, whereas double-feed indirect cylinders, in accordance with Part 1, with coil primary heater are preferred for higher primary water operating pressures and higher primary water circulation rates this is not the case with single-feed indirect cylinders which should not be used in sealed systems and which have limited application on direct pump circulation. Coil type primary heaters do not extend the range of application of single-feed indirect cylinders, they allow scope for primary heater design. This standard does not specify in every detail the primary heater design. Manufacturers must ensure their unit design complies with all the relevant requirements.

There are two classes of primary heater:

1 For systems having a primary capacity of not more than 110 litres.

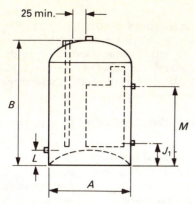

(From Figure 2: BS 1566: Part 2: 1984)

Figure 50 *Single-feed indirect cylinder showing position of connections for pipes and immersion heater*

2 For systems having a primary capacity of not more than 180 litres.

The three grades specified are given in Table 32.

Table 32 *Grading for single-feed indirect cylinders*

Grade	Test pressure	Maximum working head*
2	2.20 bar	15 m
3	1.45 bar	10 m
4	1.00 bar	6 m

* The working head is the vertical distance from the bottom of the cylinder to the water line of the cistern supplying it.

(From BS 1566: Part 2: 1984)

Figure 50 illustrates a typical cylinder.

Tables and other diagrams in the standard show the basic dimensions of the cylinders which come in seven capacities: 86, 104, 108, 130, 152, 180 and 196 litres.

If required by the purchaser, provision can be made for a variety of optional features.

In this part of the standard tests are specified for the isolation of primary and secondary water. Preferred sizes of cylinders for new installations are recommended in both parts.

BS 3198: 1981 *Copper hot water storage combination units for domestic purposes*

■ AD (Reg. L5)

This standard provides details of the essential requirements for hot water storage units of a type which incorporates a cold water feed cistern. These appliances, known as 'combination units', are designed for use with water heating appliances which are connected by pipework, but provision can also be made to use either an electric immersion heater or gas circulator fitted to the unit itself either as an auxiliary or as the sole method of heating. An 'indirect' type of combination unit is intended for service where it is essential that the circulating water is kept separate from the domestic hot water. There is provision for both single-feed and double-feed indirect types. Single-feed indirect units should not be used in sealed systems and they have limited application on direct pump circulation.

The requirements specified are those considered to be necessary to ensure good performance and reliability of the appliance while leaving the manufacturers free to develop actual design and, for this reason, careful consideration has been given to the inclusion of requirements for materials, construction and performance tests rather than to dimensions, which have been omitted as far as possible.

Requirements for direct, double-feed indirect and single-feed

indirect types of combination hot water storage units having hot water storage capacities in a series 65, 115, 130, 140, 150 and 180 litres (preferred sizes) in which, when water is drawn off from the hot water storage vessel there is automatically:

1 Replacement of water withdrawn by that from a cold water feed cistern incorporated in the unit and adjacent to the hot water vessel.
2 Controlled replacement of the water in the cold water feed cistern from the water supply by means of a float operated valve.

The standard defines the following types of combination hot water storage unit:

1 Direct type.
2 Double-feed indirect type.
3 Single-feed indirect type.

It also includes requirements for materials, primary heaters, manufacture, pipe connections, performance requirements. Five appendices cover testing, with three figures showing test apparatus.

Pumps, circulators

BS 3456: Section 2.35: 1975 *Electrical pumps*

Requirements for testing and approval. Substantially agrees with CEE 10, Part 2 Section T.

BS 1394 *Power driven circulators*

This standard is divided into two parts to cover the wide range of applications of glanded pumps and glandless pumps, designed to create a flow of water in piping systems for heating and domestic hot water purposes within a specified pressure and temperature range.

Part 1: 1971 *Glanded and glandless pumps*
Pumps above 200 W and not exceeding 2000 W input at maximum voltage are specified, suitable for operating on single or three phase electrical supply.

All pump units are capable of operating satisfactorily in an environment where the ambient temperature does not exceed 40 °C. They should be capable of operating at the maximum working pressures and maximum temperature ratings corresponding to the type of pump as specified in Table 33. Some useful notes on installation conditions are also included.

Table 33 *Pressure and water temperature ratings*

Type	Maximum water temperature (°C)	Maximum working pressure (gauge) (bar)
Grade 1: glandless and glanded pumps	90	3.0
Grade 2: glandless and glanded pumps	120	4.5
Grade 3: glanded pumps	160	10.0

(Table 1: BS 1394: Part 1: 1971)

Section two of this part of the standard specifies requirements for electrical components, controls and switching devices and wiring necessary for the operation of glandless pumps using a single or three phase electricity supply.

Part 2: 1971   *Domestic glandless pumps*

This part has been developed to provide specific requirements for domestic glandless pumps designed for small bore heating and hot water installations. Consideration has been given to the need for providing a greater degree of safety in the single family dwelling and requirements are specified in section two for the electric equipment and wiring necessary for the operation of these pumps. The power input for the pumps covered in this part of the standard is not to exceed 200 W at maximum rated voltage.

These pumps must be capable of operating at the maximum working pressure and the maximum temperature ratings corresponding to the type of pump as specified in Table 34.

Table 34   *Pressure and water temperature ratings*

Type	Maximum Temperature (°C)	Maximum working pressure (gauge) (bar)
Grade 1: domestic glandless pumps	90	3.0
Grade 2: domestic glandless pumps	110	3.0

(Table 1: BS 1394: Part 2: 1971)

A Grade 1 pump can operate satisfactorily in an environment where the ambient temperature does not exceed 40 °C. A Grade 2 pump can withstand an ambient temperature up to 50 °C.

Pump inlet and outlet branches shall be screwed or flanged, and have dimensions of 25, 40 or 50 mm nominal bore.

Acoustic levels are also specified for this type of pump.

BS 5257: 1975   *Horizontal end-suction centrifugal pumps (16 bar)*

The requirements specify the principal dimensions and nominal duty point of horizontal end-suction centrifugal pumps having a maximum discharge pressure of 16 bar. Additional information and requirements are included concerning suitable pump casing materials, tolerances and surface finishes on shafts and sleeves within the seal cavities, a preferred range of shaft diameters, a 'grid' giving guidance on the selection of suitable pumps for particular duties, and baseplate installations when the pumps are coupled to foot mounted electric motors for installation on a foundation.

Valves, taps, etc.

Of the standards relating to valves, taps, etc. BS 5150 to BS 5160 represent a series of specifications covering a variety of valve types in cast iron. Four standards, BS 6280 to BS 6283 inclusive, are concerned with safety and have been prepared under the direction of the Building Services Standards Committee at the request of the Department of the Environment on the advice of the Standing Technical Committee on water regulations. They are intended to be suitable for citing as deemed to satisfy the relevant regulations or byelaws.

BS 6280, BS 6281 and BS 6282 form a series that specify requirements for devices and arrangements for preventing the backflow or backsiphonage of water in installations.

Six standards deal with draw off taps, including spray and mixing taps. Valves for boilers and radiators are covered by two standards. Copper alloy valves of various types are specified in one of the standards and another three prescribe requirements

for float operated valves. Five standards consider valves and guards for underground control and protection and general purposes. Mixing valves are covered by one standard, as is material for washers, and one standard covers drainage taps. It should be noted that a number of these standards include both SI and imperial units, particularly where tappings and pipe threads are specified, while others are solely in imperial units.

BS 2767: 1972   *Valves and unions for hot water radiators*

Copper alloy valves and unions are specified in this standard. The range of nominal sizes covered is ½, ¾, 1 and 1¼ in, this being the size that corresponds to the pipe size of the thread end of the connection. The valves and unions specified are normally used for a non-shock working pressure up to 4 bar and a temperature of 95 °C. However, metals and metal thicknesses specified in this standard allow valves and unions to be designed for non-shock working pressures of up to 10 bar and a temperature of up to 120 °C. All the valves and unions will normally have one end screwed female and the other end arranged for a tailpiece connection, but other types, such as compression and capillary, and combinations, are not precluded if so ordered. Figure 51 shows typical configurations for valves and unions and illustrates the basic dimensions for the appropriate sizes which the manufacturer's literature should show.

The materials used, and the general design and manufacture are dealt with including the renewable parts, dimensions and marking.

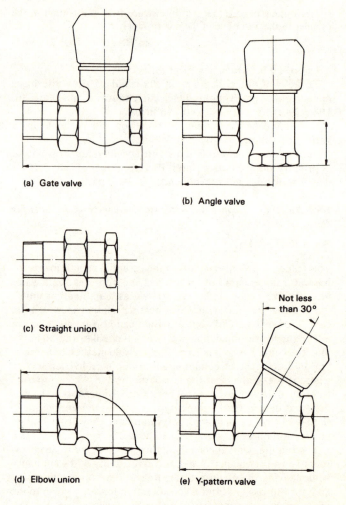

(a) Gate valve

(b) Angle valve

(c) Straight union

Not less than 30°

(d) Elbow union

(e) Y-pattern valve

(Figure 4: BS 2767: 1972)

Figure 51   *Basic dimensions for manufacturers' literature*

BS 6284: 1983 *Thermostatic radiator valves*

Specifies design and performance requirements for thermostatic radiator valves. Suitable test methods for determining the strength, endurance and performance requirements are included. Nominal sizes are 10 and 12, 15, 22 and 28 mm.

BS 6280: 1982 *Method of vacuum (backsiphonage) test for water-using appliances*

This standard describes a method for applying a vacuum test to water-using appliances to determine that they have an acceptable degree of protection against backflow or backsiphonage.

BS 6281: 1981 *Devices without moving parts for the prevention of contamination of water by backflow*

Part 1: *Type A air gaps*
A Type A air gap is defined by the standard as a visible, unobstructed and complete gap measured vertically between the lowest point of discharge of the inlet pipe and spill-over level provided at the associated receiving pipe, cistern, vessel or apparatus into which flow is discharged, and a table of dimensions of such air gaps is included.

This part specifies the characteristics of Type A air gaps for inlet or feed pipes (not draw off taps) of nominal size up to and including DN 159 mm. Air gaps complying with the requirements of this part of the standard are suitable for protection against Class 1 risk, which is that where risk of serious contamination is likely to be harmful to health (continuing or frequent).

Part 2: *Type B air gaps*
This part specifies the characteristics and methods of testing Type B air gaps that are to be built into water appliances at the manufactuers, and supplied by feed pipes of nominal size up to and including DN 159 mm. These types of air gap are between the lowest part of the inlet or feed pipe and the critical level of water is an appliance which does not satisfy Type A air gap requirements, and are suitable for protection against Class 2 risk. A Class 2 risk is defined as risk of contamination by a substance not continuously or frequently present that may be harmful to health.

Part 3: *Pipe interrupters of nominal size up to and including DN 42*
The characteristics and methods of testing pipe interrupter backflow prevention devices are specified. A table gives the range of device diameters which are suitable for use at pressures up to and including 10 bar, and temperatures up to and including 90 °C. Devices meeting the requirements of this part of the standard are suitable for protection against Class 2 risk.

BS 6282: 1982 *Devices with moving parts for the prevention of contamination of water by backflow*

This standard is divided into four parts:

Part 1 *Check valves of nominal size up to and including DN 54*
Part 2 *Terminal anti-vacuum valves of nominal size up to and including DN 54*
Part 3 *In-line anti-vacuum valves of nominal size up to and including DN 42*
Part 4 *Combined check and anti-vacuum valves of nominal size up to and including DN 42.*

All parts specify the characteristics of the particular valves they cover which are suitable for use at pressures up to and including 10 bar and temperatures up to and including 90 °C.

In each case materials, design and performance are dealt with and a table of nominal size range is included. Details of how each valve should be installed and used must be supplied by the manufacturer.

BS 6283: 1982 *Safety devices for use in hot water systems*

This standard is divided into the following parts:

Part 1 *Expansion valves for pressures up to and including 10 bar*
Part 2 *Temperature relief valves for pressures up to and including 10 bar*

■ AD (Reg. G3)

Part 3 *Combined temperature and pressure relief valves for pressures up to and including 10 bar*

■ AD (Reg. G3)

Part 4 *Drop-tight pressure reducing valves of nominal size up to and including DN 54 for supply pressures up to and including 12 bar*

All parts deal with valves of nominal sizes DN 15, 22, 28, 35 and 42 mm and Part 4 includes DN 54.

Specified in each part is design, construction and testing of the valves but application or installation is not covered. However, in each case advice is given on the information to be supplied by the purchaser.

BS 6759 *Safety valves*

Part 1: 1984 *Safety valves for steam and hot water*
Requirements are specified for safety valves for steam and hot water where the set pressure is greater than 1 bar gauge.

It includes requirements for safety valves for boilers, boiler installations and associated pipework systems where the steam pressure exceeds 1 bar gauge or, in the case of hot water boilers, where the rating is 44 kW and above, as well as for boilers pressurized by steam for use in hot water systems which are classified as steam boilers.

Requirements for testing safety valves for determination of their operating and flow characteristics are given.

Recommendations on safety valve mounting, discharge piping and drainage are given in an appendix.

This standard does not cover safety valves for boilers used in open vented hot water systems working at temperatures not exceeding 100 °C, nor safety valves for storage water heaters of the unvented type which normally operate at temperatures not exceeding 82 °C and at pressures not exceeding 10 bar.

BS 759 *Valves, gauges and other safety fittings for application to boilers and to piping installations for and in connection with boilers*

Part 1: 1984 *Valves, mountings and fittings*
Requirements for steam and water fittings excluding safety valves for boiler installations where the steam pressure exceeds 1 bar gauge or, in the case of hot water boilers, the rating is 44 kW and above. It also specifies requirements for fittings for boilers used exclusively for the following:

1 low-pressure steam heating in which the whole of the condensate is returned to the boiler on a closed circuit
2 hot water central heating
3 hot water supply

It deals with valves, boiler blowdown, mountings, water level gauges, high and low water level alarms, pressure gauges, test connections and fusible plugs. Where appropriate, general recommendations relating to the installation of fittings are included for the guidance of users. Additional requirements specific to steam and hot water boilers, arranged for automatic working, are given in section 5.

This part does not cover fittings for boilers used in open vented hot water systems working at temperatures not exceeding 100 °C nor for storage water heaters of the unvented type which normally operate at temperatures not exceeding 82 °C and at pressures not exceeding 10 bar. It will supersede BS 759: 1975 (summarized in the first edition) in December 1987.

BS 1426 and 3461: 1969   *Surface boxes for gas and waterworks purposes*

Cast iron surface boxes for use with gas valves, stand pipes, and regulator chambers, and stop valves and sluice valves on service pipes and water mains are specified. The following duties are covered:

1. Light grade surface boxes for use in situations inaccessible to wheeled vehicles.
2. Medium grade surface boxes for use where heavy commercial vehicles would be exceptional (for example in domestic accesss, verges, footways and cycle tracks).
3. Heavy grade surface boxes for use in carriage ways and capable of bearing wheel loads up to 11.5 tonne.

BS 5834   *Surface boxes, guards and underground chambers for gas and waterworks purposes*

Part 1: 1985   *Guards, including foundation units*
This specification details requirements for pipe type and sectional type guards for use within underground stopvalves.

The guards can be made of grey cast iron, vitrified clay or precast concrete. Foundation units are manufactured from vitrified clay or concrete. The details and dimensions for the various guards and foundation units are illustrated in the standard.

Part 2: 1983   *Small surface boxes*
This part details surface boxes primarily intended for use with gas valves and regulator chambers and for stop valves and sluice valves on service pipes and water mains. The largest size covered has a designated minimum clear opening of 300 mm in diameter. Tables detailing dimensions and design loads are included.

Part 3: 1985   *Large surface boxes*
Requirements are specified for surface boxes with rectangular clear openings, where at least one dimension exceeds 300 mm, manufactured from cast iron, steel, or reinforced concrete. Tables detailing dimensions and design loads are included along with a summary of optional items which may be agreed between manufacturer and purchaser.

BS 2580: 1979   *Underground plug cocks for cold water services*

This standard relates to plug cocks of the type used mostly in Scotland for cold water supply. The plug cocks are suitable for use underground to control the supply of water from the water main to the consumer's premises. The plug cocks are of nominal size ½, ¾ and 1 in (12.7, 19.1 and 25.4 mm), with a key head for use underground. Dimensions which are concerned primarily with the general design have been omitted and only those considered essential for the correct functioning of the plug cock have been specified.

Requirements are stated for the ends of cocks when connecting to copper tube and polythene pipe.

BS 5163: 1974   *Double flanged cast iron wedge gate valves for waterwork purposes*

Valves in accordance with this specification are primarily intended for use with potable water and for operation by a removable key or hand wheel. They include double flanged inside screw, solid wedge, metal or resilient sealed, non-rising stem cast iron wedge gate valves. The flanged ends must comply with BS 4504 and the range of nominal sizes (DN) is from 50 to 600 mm (14 sizes). There are two nominal pressure (PN) designations: PN 10 and PN 16 bar.

BS 5433: 1976   *Underground stopvalves for water services*

Copper alloy screw down stopvalves of nominal sizes ½, ¾, 1½

and 2 in (12.7, 19.1, 38.1 and 50.8 mm) for installation on underground water service pipes are detailed. The nominal size is that corresponding to the pipe size of the thread at the end of the connection. It includes stopvalves with ends screwed internally or externally, the pipe thread being the same nominal size of the valve. Provision is also made for ends for taper pipe threads and threads for light gauge copper tubes and fittings. Details are given of union connections, and valve ends suitable for connecting to copper tube via compression or capillary fittings, and valve ends suitable for connecting to polythene pipe Type 32 and Type 50. The valves may have a crutch or square head for opening and closing.

Illustrations of typical stopvalves showing component parts are given in the standard. Tables also give detailed dimensions of the various component parts for the full range of nominal sizes.

The preferred materials for the component parts are gun metal or bronze or, in addition, cast iron for square heads. However, other metallic materials may be used provided that they are not less suitable than those listed in clause 9.1, not more susceptible to corrosion, completely immune to dezincification and are not of lower mechanical strength. A revision is in hand.

BS 1010   *Draw off taps and stopvalves for water services (screwdown pattern)*

Part 2: 1973   *Draw off taps and above ground stopvalves*
This part of the standard specifies requirements for screwdown pattern draw off taps and stopvalves in nominal sizes of ¼, ⅜, ½, ¾, 1, 1¼, 1½ and 2 in (6.4, 9.5, 12.7, 19.1, 25.4, 31.8, 38.1 and 50.8 mm), pillar taps of the rising types are included in nominal sizes ½, ¾ and 1 in (12.7, 19.1 and 25.4 mm) and non-rising types in nominal sizes ½ and ¾ in (12.7 and 19.1 mm) only.

The following patterns of taps and stopvalves are within the scope of this standard:

1. Bib taps and pillar taps.
2. Above ground stopvalves.
3. Combination tap assemblies.
4. Any type of bib, pillar, or globe* tap or stopvalve including those combining with draining taps, or combination tap, bidet tap, restrictor tap, etc., or any combination of such taps and valves.

The standard includes a list of definitions regarding the taps and valves specified:

1. Screwdown stopvalve.
2. Screwdown tap:
   (a) Bib tap.
   (b) Hose union tap.
   (c) Pillar tap.
   (d) Globe tap.
   Note: The use of the word 'tap' shall be taken to refer to any of the above patterns.
3. Combination tap assembly:
   (a) Single outlet type combination tap assembly.
   (b) Double outlet type combination tap assembly.

Figure 52 illustrates a typical stopvalve, which the standard notes is not intended to indicate exterior design (refer to the summary of BS 5412 and BS 5413 for figures of typical draw off taps).

Generally, when the inlet or outlet of a valve is screwed, the thread whether internal or external should be a BS pipe (parallel) thread complying with BS 2779. However, inlets and outlets when so required can be:

1. Tapped or screwed for taper threads.
2. Tapped or screwed for connecting to light gauge copper.
3. Provided with ends suitable for connecting to copper tube.
4. Tapped or screwed to the purchaser's special requirements.

* The use of a globe tap may contravene the Water Regulations.

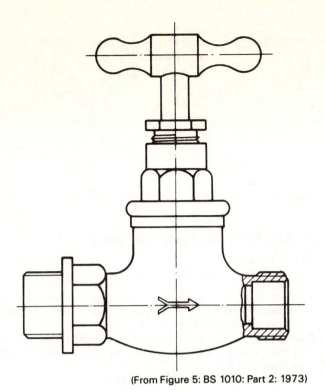

(From Figure 5: BS 1010: Part 2: 1973)

Figure 52 *Stopvalve with BS pipe (parallel) external thread on inlet, compression joint for copper tube on outlet*

BS 5412 *Performance of draw off taps with metal bodies for water services*

BS 5413 *Performance of draw off taps with plastics bodies for water services*

These British Standard performance specifications for draw-off taps have been prepared with the aim of promoting performance, rather than dimensional standards. The previous standard (BS 1010 Parts 1 and 2) has been strictly dimensional with very few performance requirements. These present standards specify the dimensional requirements that are the minimum necessary to ensure satisfactory installation and interchangeability of taps and of certain components. The remaining requirements such as pressure tightness, flow rates, mechanical endurance, etc. are governed by performance criteria.

This publication comprises two separate and distinct standards dealing respectively with draw off taps with metal bodies and draw off taps with plastics bodies. For the sake of convenience and economy, and because requirements for both types of draw off taps are in many respects identical, the two standards have been combined under one cover. Where different requirements apply for certain properties, they are dealt with as specified in clause 4 which is common to all parts of these specifications.

These two standards have been divided into the following five parts:

Part 1 *Dimensional and design characteristics*
Part 2 *Water-tightness and pressure resistance characteristics*
Part 3 *Hydraulic characteristics*
Part 4 *Mechanical and endurance characteristics*
Part 5 *Physio-chemical characteristics: materials, coatings*

These standards conflict only marginally with the draft European Standards that have been circulated for voting. They do, however, include some fittings that are not dealt with in the European drafts, for example single pillar taps and divided flow combination tap assemblies. They also conform in general to the proposals for subsequent parts of the European Standards, so far as these are known. A comment is needed, however, concerning the vital matter of flow rates. The pressures to give minimum flow rates specified in the present standards are those appropriate to United Kingdom installations with their low pressure, cistern-fed systems. It is probable, however, that these requirements will not be appropriate to continental practice where cistern-fed systems are seldom used.

The performances tests in Parts 2, 3 and 4 of these standards are virtually the same for taps with either metal or plastics bodies, except that in clauses 9 and 10 of Part 4 a reduced torque is permitted for tests with plastics bodied taps.

The introduction of performance criteria has also meant that the requirements for material specification can be much less specific and most of the components can be made from a wide range of materials, provided always that they meet the performance tests.

Dimensions are expressed in metric units except that pipe thread designations are in accordance with BS 2779.

Other sizes of taps, as well as above ground stopvalves, are specified in BS 1010 Parts 1 and 2.

The following taps are defined and are common to all parts of these specifications; and all parts consider ½ and ¾ in (12.7 and 19.1 mm) nominal size draw off taps as classified and illustrated in Part 1:

1 Metal tap.
2 Plastics tap.
3 Single tap.
4 Bib tap.
5 Pillar tap.
6 Hose union tap.
7 Combination tap assembly.
8 Single outlet type combination tap assembly.
9 Double outlet type combination tap assembly.

Part 1: 1976 *Dimensional and design characteristics*
The dimensional and design characteristics of ½ and ¾ in nominal size draw off taps are specified. Figures 53, 54 and 55 show classes of taps covered by this part.

Part 2: 1976 *Water-tightness and pressure resistance characteristics*
This part specifies the water-tightness and pressure resistance characteristics, and details are given of four tests:

1 Valve seat and body upstream test.
2 Body downstream test.
3 Hydraulic strength test.
4 'O' ring pneumatic test for taps fitted with 'O' rings for the spindles.

Part 3: 1976 *Hydraulic characteristics*
All taps must be capable of complying with the following requirements which are specified in detail in this part:

1 Hydraulic tests:
  (a) Flow rate test.
  (b) Jet concentration test.
2 Flow characteristics:
  (a) Outlet orifice.
  (b) Flow straightness and aerating devices.

Part 4: 1976 *Mechanical and endurance characteristics*
Test requirements are specified for the resistance of the seat to permanent distortion and any part of the operating mechanism to permanent deflection or loosening when specified torque is applied to the operating member of the backnut and shank to permanent damage when tightened; of the tap to rotation in a circular hole and of the body to bonding.

Two endurance tests are specified, one for the shut-off mechanisms and the other for the swivel outlet if fitted.

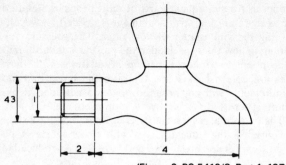

(Figure 2: BS 5412/3: Part 1: 1976)

Figure 53   *Bib tap*

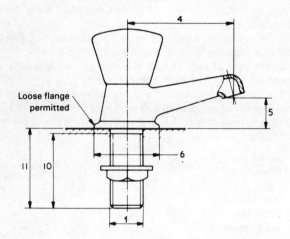

(Figure 1: BS 5412/3: Part 1: 1976)

Figure 54   *Pillar tap*

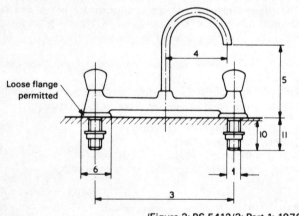

(Figure 3: BS 5412/3: Part 1: 1976)

Figure 55   *Combination tap assembly*

Part 5: 1976   *Physio-chemical characteristics: materials, coatings*
This part includes a section on plastics materials used for structural components in contact with the supply water. The only plastics at present specified in this part is acetal copolymer.

A further section of this part includes non-metallic materials other than those used for structural components in contact with the supply water. In particular, where these materials are thermo-plastic polymers, account has to be taken of the marked dependence on time and temperature of their mechanical and physical properties. It is necessary, when designing components, to use the material manufacturer's long-term data, including those of long-term deformation and long-term strength.

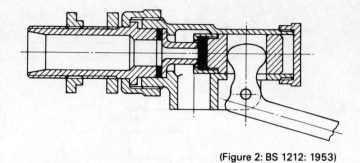

(Figure 2: BS 1212: 1953)

Figure 56   *½ in ballvalve, closed. Sectional elevation*

BS 1212   *Float operated valves (excluding floats)*

Part 1: 1953   *Piston type*
The principal features of the standard valve are:

1 A removable seat, to facilitate the manufacture of this component from special metal or other materials which have high corrosion-resisting qualities.
2 The ability to fit seats with different sized orifices in the same body in order to accommodate varying requirements of water pressure and flow.
3 The easy replacement of worn seats.

The standard provides for a range of seven ballvalve bodies (piston type) and levers of nominal sizes ⅜, ½, ¾, 1, 1¼, 1½ and 2 in (9.5, 12.7, 19.1, 25.4, 31.8, 38.1 and 50.8 mm). The general design of the ballvalve is shown in Figure 56.

The ball valves are made in six different body patterns assembled from standard components whose dimensions are detailed in a series of tables showing the component assemblies for various pressure zones.

Material requirements are specified for brass, gun metal, and bronze for metal parts and nylon for plastic seats.

The inlet connections are screwed externally except when direct connnections are made. The standard provides details for connecting to lead and copper pipes.

A special note is included stating that in the body patterns shown in this standard, there shall be no addition to facilitate the subsequent fittings of a silencing pipe.

Requirements are specified for hydraulic and shutting-off tests and mechanical strength of lever. A method of sizing orifices is given in an appendix.

Part 2: 1970   *Diaphragm type (brass body)*
Features incorporated in this type of float-operated valve are:

1 A separate inlet shank coupled to the valve body.
2 Renewable seats.
3 The use of inlet shanks, body coupling nuts, and seats identical with those specified for 'piston' type valves.
4 The positioning of the water outlet from the body above instead of below the body, so enabling the attachment of discharge arrangements having effective provision against backsiphonage.

The standard covers diaphragm valves in two nominal sizes, ⅜ and ½ in (9.5 and 12.7 mm), having four seat sizes of ⅛, ³/₁₆, ¼ and ⅜ in (3.2, 4.8, 6.4 and 9.5 mm) bore. Figure 57 shows a typical valve.

Material requirements are specified for the various components and cover brass, gun metal, rolled bronze, rubber, plastics, agate and cement.

The standard indicates the seats and floats which should be used with these valves for various water pressures.

Part 3: 1979   *Diaphragm type (plastics body) for cold water services*

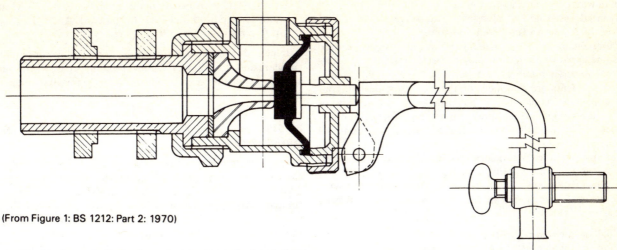

(From Figure 1: BS 1212: Part 2: 1970)

Figure 57 *Diaphragm ballvalve (brass body), closed. Sectional elevation*

This part specifies the dimensional and operational requirements of float-operated valves (diaphragm type) with plastic bodies suitable for use with cold water services. The dimensional requirements are solely those essential to ensure fittings and interchangeability. Features incorporated include:

1 Renewable seats and diaphragm.
2 The water outlet so positioned so as to allow the attachment of discharge arrangements having effective provision against backsiphonage.
3 Performance requirements for components.
4 Requirements for adequacy of flow and positive prevention of backsiphonage.

Materials, workmanship, performance tests and, where appropriate, dimensions and tolerances are specified for float-operated valves (diaphragm type) of ½ in (12.7 mm) nominal size. The valve is capable of accepting flow seat sizes of ⅛, ³⁄₁₆, ¼ and ⅜ in (3.2, 4.8, 6.4 and 9.5 mm) bore. The materials covered are the metal parts of such valves, rubber, plastics and those used for mouldings. Requirements are also specified for distortion and deflection, flow and endurance. A table in the standard indicates seats and floats to be used with those valves at various water pressures.

Common to the two parts is the assurance that valves complying with the requirements of the two parts of this standard will provide the user with the assurance that backsiphonage into the feed pipe should not occur providing the water level is no higher than the horizontal centre line of the valve. A greater level of security against backsiphonage will be achieved where normal shut-off level is arranged to be 35 mm or more below the centre line of the valve.

BS 1415 *Mixing valves* Part 1: 1976 *Non-thermostatic, non-compensating mixing valves*

This part deals only with mixing valves of the manually operated type. It is emphasized particularly that mixing valves of the type described in this part shall be installed in such a manner that both hot and cold supplies are from storage, or from a common source on balanced pressure. Furthermore, unless both the hot and cold waters are supplied at equalized pressures, satisfactory operation may be impracticable and there may be some risk of scalding. When the valve does not incorporate a shut-off facility it is essential to consult the water authority as to its requirements for prevention of cross-flow.

The hot or cold water circuit should be designed so that its supply to other apparatus does not reduce appreciably the pressure and volume available at the inlets of the mixing valve.

In specifying the minimum flow rates of mixing valves, cognizance has been taken of the fact that:

1 The water pressure available at the inlets of the valve will vary from installation to installation.
2 The hydraulic properties of shower heads vary.
3 The rate of discharge from a shower fitting which is considered satisfactory depends upon the individual requirements.

Three categories of minimum flow rates for each size of mixing valve are specified so that purchasers can select the valve most appropriate to their needs and the conditions of installation.

Requirements are specified for performance, materials and method of specifying size of non-thermostatic, non-compensating mixing valves for ablutionary and domestic purposes. The nominal sizes covered are ½ and ¾ in (12.7 amd 19.1 mm), which correspond to the pipe size of the thread of the inlet connections. Three types of mixing valve are defined:

1 Single sequential control.
2 Twin (or dual) control.
3 Single control (or dual) function.

BS 5388: 1976 *Spray taps*

Requirements are specified for the materials, design, construction, dimensions and testing for two forms of spray taps; pillar and bib. Both types with either rising or non-rising spindles should be ½ in (12.7 mm) nominal size. A spray tap is defined as a tap supplied with water at a predetermined temperature, which it delivers at a restricted rate of flow, in the form of a spray. This is achieved by incorporating a flow restrictor of fixed flow or adjustable type to regulate flow and a spray outlet capable of causing the water to assume the specified shape of a diverging spray.

Spray taps provide a quick hygienic method of washing under running water. Their use appreciably reduces the total amount of water used or handwashing. The factors governing the use of spray taps and their associated plumbing systems are numerous. Appendices to this standard set out some basic considerations.

BS 5779: 1979 *Spray mixing taps*

This standard is linked with BS 1010 Parts 1 and 2, BS 1415 Part 1, BS 5388, and BS 5412 and 5413. Spray mixing taps, incorporating a mixing function operated by the user, possess characteristics similar to those of spray taps but are able to accept hot and cold water supplies and mix them for delivery at a temperature to suit the user. The factors governing the use of spray mixing taps and their associated plumbing systems are numerous and guidance is given in an appendix on installation considerations.

Spray taps should normally deliver between 0.03 and 0.06

litres of water per second. Spray mixing taps have therefore been designated 'series 45', which refers to the average rate of flow, that is, 45 ± 15 ml/s (mid-blend position).

It is recognized that non-standard spray taps may be required for some apparatus and there may be some merit in requesting alternative series numbers to be used in these special cases.

Requirements are specified for the materials, design, construction, dimensions, testing and installation of non-thermostatic, non-compensating spray mixing taps for ablutionary purposes. The main dimensional features are illustrated in the standard.

The spray mixing tap is defined as a tap supplied with hot and cold water and incorporating a mixing device operated by the user. The mixed water is delivered at a restricted rate of flow in the form of a spray. There are four other variations considered by the specification:

1 Single sequential control spray mixing tap.
2 Twin (or dual) control spray mixing tap.
3 Single control, twin (or dual) function, spray mixing tap.
4 Combination spray mixing tap.

Details of tests for rate of flow, divergence of spray, sensitivity of control, blended water temperatures, and for devices to prevent cross-tracking intercommunication of supply systems are included in the standard. These tests being fully described in a series of appendices.

BS 2456: 1973 *Floats (plastics) for ballvalves for hot and cold water*

This standard deals with floats for use for all purposes, including use in cold water feed cisterns and expansion systems for hot water apparatus where they may be exposed to temperatures up to a maximum of 90 °C, comprising plastics spherical floats of 102, 114, 127 and 152 mm diameter, and non-spherical floats of equivalent lifting efforts suitable for attachment to the apparatus specified in BS 1212. The floats are classified into types by use of the letters S, NS, and L. The letter S refers to a spherical float, the letters NS refer to a non-spherical float, and the letter L refers to a float having a different length and diameter of screw thread in the boss.

For information regarding the correct size of float to use for a particular size of float valve, or range of pressure, reference should be made to tables in BS 1212.

BS 1968: 1953 *Floats for ballvalves (copper)*

Spherical copper floats of 114, 127, 152, 178, 203, 229, 254, 279 and 304 mm nominal size are specified suitable for attachment to the float-operated valves covered in BS 1212.

BS 3457: 1973 *Materials for water tap and stopvalve seat washers*

Requirements are specified for physical and some chemical properties for materials for seat washers made of rubber, leather or fibre. A seat washer is defined as the disc of material fitted to the washer plate of a water tap or stopvalve in such a manner that on closing the tap or valve it is brought into contact with the seat and closes the orifice against further flow.

Although specifications for rubber, leather and fibre are contained, rubber washers are strongly recommended because they are suitable for use with both hot and cold water. Leather is suitable for cold water only (temperature not exceeding 35 °C), fibre is suitable for hot water only (temperature exceeding 35 °C but not exceeding 100 °C).

BS 2879: 1980 *Draining taps (screwdown pattern)*

Copper alloy bodied taps for draining hot and cold water installations, including heating systems, are specified. The standard covers nominal sizes of ½ and ¾ in (12.7 and 19.1 mm) only for use with water:

1 Up to 70 °C with occasional excursions; up to 90 °C maximum for a period of 1 hour (Type one).
2 Up to a maximum of 120 °C (Type two).

Inlet ends are screwed (or can be fitted with compression or capillary ends for copper). Outlet ends are formed with external serrations or other means of affording grip for attachment of a hose.

BS 5150: 1974 *Cast iron wedge and double disk gate valves for general purposes*

Requirements are specified for flanged and screwed body end cast iron gate valves of the wedge and double disk types, copper alloy faced, resilient seated or all iron. Valves dealt with in this standard may have ends, flanged in accordance with BS 4504 or with internal screw threads in accordance with BS 21. Two types of valve are covered with rising or non-rising stems:

1 Solid or split wedge.
2 Double disk.

For flanged end valves the range of nominal size (DN) is 10 to 1000 mm (twenty-four sizes). For screwed end the range of nominal sizes is ½ to 6 in (12.7 to 152.4 mm) (eleven sizes).

The valves are also designated by nominal pressure (PN) defined as the maximum permissible gauge working pressure in bars at 20 °C as PN 1.6, PN 2.5, PN 4, PN 6, PN 10, PN 16 and PN 25 bar.

Further pressure/temperature ratings are tabulated in this standard but all valves are suitable for continuous use at their PN designation within the temperature range −10 °C to 65 °C.

BS 5151: 1974 *Cast iron gate (parallel slide) valves for general purposes*

This standard covers flanged body end cast iron gate valves of parallel slide type, copper alloy faced, nickel alloy faced and stainless steel faced. The ends are flanged in accordance with BS 4504, and the valve may have rising or non-rising stems.

The range of nominal sizes (DN) is 40 to 1000 mm (nineteen sizes). The valves are also designated by nominal pressure (PN) as PN 10, PN 16 and PN 25 bar.

BS 5152: 1974 *Cast iron globe stop and check valves for general purposes*

This standard specifies requirements for flanged and screwed end cast iron globe and globe stop and check valves, copper alloy faced, nickel alloy faced, stainless steel faced, resilient seated or all iron. It covers the following valves having a rising stem with inside or outside screw:

1 Globe valves:
  (a) Straight.
  (b) Angle.
  (c) Oblique (or 'Y').
2 Globe stop and check valves:
  (a) Straight.
  (b) Angle.

Flanged valves should be flanged in accordance with BS 4504 and threaded ends should be in accordance with BS 21.

BS 5153: 1974 *Cast iron check valves for general purposes*

Swing and lift cast iron check valves, flanged or screwed end, copper alloy faced, nickel alloy faced, stainless steel faced, resilient seated, or all iron, are specified. Flanged ends must comply with BS 4504 and screwed ends with BS 21. The standard deals with the following valve types:

1 Swing (not including tilting disk type):

(a) Straight pattern (for use with the axis of the body end parts horizontal or vertical).

2 Lift:

(a) Straight pattern (for use with the axis of the body end parts horizontal).

(b) Straight pattern (for use with the axis of the body end parts vertical).

(c) Angle pattern (for use where the axes of the body end parts are at 40 °C).

Where swing check valves are used in vertical lines the flow shall be in an upward direction.

For flanged ends the range of nominal sizes (DN) is as follows:

1 *Swing*   10 to 1000 mm (twenty-four sizes)
2 *Lift*   10 to 450 mm (eighteen sizes)

For screwed ends the range of nominal sizes is ½ to 6 in (12.7 to 152.4 mm) (eleven sizes).

The valves are also designated by nominal pressure (PN) as PN 6, PN 10, PN 16, and PN 25 bar.

A table of this standard indicates pressure/temperature range but all valves are suitable for continuous use at their PN designation within the temperature range −10 °C to 65 °C.

BS 5154: 1983   *Copper alloy globe, globe stop and check, check and gate valves*

Two main series are specified (series A and B) differing in their rated maximum temperatures. This standard covers valves:

1 With flanged ends complying with BS 4504.
2 With internal screw threads complying with BS 21.
3 With capillary or compression ends in accordance with BS 864 and BS 2051.

Valves are of the following types having any of the above body ends, integral or renewable body seats and screwed union or bolted bonnets or covers.

1 Globe and globe stop and check valves (of the rising stem type with inside or outside screw):
   (a) Straight.
   (b) Angle.
   (c) Oblique (or 'Y').
2 Check valves:
   (a) Swing (for use with the axis of the body ports horizontal or vertical).
   (b) Lift:
      (i) Piston (straight or angle)
      (ii) Disk (straight, vertical or angle)
3 Gate valves:
   (a) Solid or split wedge.
   (b) Double disk.
   (c) Parallel slide.

For flanged ends the range of nominal sizes (DN) is 10 to 80 mm (nine sizes). For screwed ends the range of nominal sizes is ¼ to 3 in (6.4 to 76.2 mm) (ten sizes).

For capillary or compression ends the range of outside diameters is:

To BS 864 Part 2: 8 to 67 mm (eleven sizes).

To BS 864 Part 3: (compression ends only): ⅜ to 2 in (seven sizes).

To BS 205 Part 1: 10 to 42 mm (thirteen sizes).

The valves are also designated by nominal pressure (PN):

1 Flanged ends: PN 16, PN 20, PN 25, PN 40 and PN 50 bar.
2 Screwed ends: PN 16, PN 20, PN 25, PN 32 and PN 40 bar.
3 Capillary and compression ends: not exceeding those given in the relevant British Standards.

A table in the Standard gives pressure/temperature ratings for valves with flanged or threaded ends.

BS 5155: 1984   *Butterfly valves*

This standard covers requirements for size, rating, design, materials, marking and preparation for transport and storage for double-flanged and wafer-type butterfly valves. A number of test requirements are specified but the standard does not cover installation. Compliance with manufacturers' instructions is necessary. The valves specified are suitable for one or more of the following service applications:

1 Tight shut off.
2 Low leakage rate.
3 Regulating.

and may be one of the following types:

1 Double flanged.
2 Wafer.
   (a) single flange.
   (b) flangeless.
   (c) U-section.

The range of nominal sizes (DN) for PN designated valves is DN 40 to DN 2000 mm (twenty-four sizes) and the nominal pipe size range for class-designated valves is 1½ to 24 in (38.1 to 609.6 mm) (fifteen sizes). The nominal pressure (PN) range for the valves is PN 6 to PN 40 bar (five pressures). The valves specified by nominal pipe sizes have class pressure designated in the range Class 125; Class 150; Class 300 (the class designation of valves are numbers representing the primary service values of the valves in lb/in²). A table in the standard lists a number of materials from which the various components of the valves should be made. All valves must be suitable for continuous use at their rated pressure for the materials within the range −10 °C to +65 °C

BS 5156: 1985   *Diaphragm valves*

This specification details requirements for size, rating, design, materials, marking and preparation for transport and storage for flanged and screwed diaphragm valves with nominal pressure up to PN 16. The nominal size (DN) range for flange valves is DN 10 to DN 300 (fifteen sizes); for valves with screwed internal threads the range is ¼ to 3 in (ten sizes).

Two types of valve pattern are specified:

(a) weir
(b) straight through

and all valves should be suitable for use in a temperature range −5 °C to +5 °C.

BS 5157: 1974   *Steel gate (parallel slide) valves for general purposes*

Flanged body end carbon and carbon molybdenum steel gate valves of the parallel slide type, nickel alloy faced, stainless steel faced and hard metal faced are specified. The ends are flanged to comply with BS 4504. The valves covered have rising stems or non-rising stems and are of either the full bore or venturi pattern. The range of nominal sizes (DN) is 40 to 600 mm (fourteen sizes).

The valves also have the following nominal pressure (PN) designation: PN 16, PN 25, PN 40, PN 64 and PN 100 bar.

Pressure/temperature ratings are specified in a table of this standard. However, all valves are suitable for continuous use at their PN designation within the temperature range of −10 °C to 65 °C.

BS 5158: 1974   *Cast iron and carbon steel plug valves for general purposes*

Requirements are specified for cast iron and carbon steel straight-way plug valves with ends flanged in accordance with BS 4504 or internally screw threaded to comply with BS 21.

Valves may be of the short, regular or venturi pattern, except that in PN 10 and PN 16 bar designations, regular and venturi patterns apply to the long series only.

For flanged ends the range of nominal sizes (DN) is 10 to 600 mm (eighteen sizes). For screwed ends the range of nominal sizes is ¼ to 4 in (eleven sizes).

The valves are also designated by a nominal pressure (PN) and are PN 10, PN 16, PN 25, PN 40, PN 64 and PN 100 bar. Maximum permissible working pressure in bar gauge and operating temperatures shall meet the requirements of BS 4504 and are given in a table of this standard. However, they may be limited by the materials of body linings and lubricants, seat rings, and/or seats. Due to the variety of lining and lubricant materials it is necessary to refer to the manufacturer's recommendations for pressure/temperature ratings. Seats, however, should be capable of withstanding the body test pressure.

BS 5159: 1974   *Cast iron and carbon steel ball valves for general purposes*

The specification covers straight-way ball valves with ends flanged to comply with BS 4504 or with internal screw threads to BS 21. Valves may be 'full bore' or 'reduced bore' or short or long pattern.

For flanged ends the range of nominal sizes (DN) is 10 to 600 mm (twenty sizes). For screwed ends the range of nominal sizes is ¼ to 4 in (eleven sizes).

The valves are designated by nominal pressure (PN) which are PN 10, PN 16, PN 25, PN 40, PN 64 and PN 100 bar. Maximum permissible working pressures in bar gauge and operating temperatures must comply with BS 4504 and are given in a table of this standard. However, these may be limited by the materials of the body seat rings and/or seats. Due to the variety of lining and lubricant materials, reference should be made to the manufacturer's recommendations for pressure/temperature ratings. Seats, however, should be capable of withstanding the body test pressures.

BS 5160: 1977   *Flanged steel globe valves, globe stop and check valves and lift type check valves for general purposes*

This standard deals with outside screw and flanged end valves. It covers valves of the following types:

1 Globe valves:
   (a) Straight.
   (b) Angle.
   (c) Oblique.
2 Globe stop and check valves:
   (a) Straight.
   (b) Angle.
   (c) Oblique.
3 Lift type check valves:
   (a) Straight.
   (b) Angle.
   (c) Oblique.

Flanges must comply with BS 4504. The range of nominal sizes (DN) is 10 to 450 mm (eighteen sizes).

The valves are designated by nominal pressure (PN) and are PN 16, PN 25 and PN 40 bar.

The standard includes a table of pressure temperature ratings, but notes that restrictions may be placed by the manufacturer on valves complying with this standard by reason of valve type, trim material or other factors. All valves, however, shall be suitable for continuous use at their PN designation within the temperature range −10 °C to 120 °C.

Pipes

BS 1710: 1984   *Identification of pipelines*

The colours for the identification of pipes conveying fluids in above ground installations and on board ships are specified on a generic basis. It also includes ducts for ventilation and conduits used for carrying electrical services. The following three methods of identification are included:

1 Basic identification colours only.
2 Basic identification colours and code indications.
3 Basic identification colours used in conjunction with the user's particular colour coding scheme.

Table 35 shows the pipe contents and their basic identification colours. The standard details the method of application and how to indicate direction of flow.

Table 35   *Basic identification colours*

Pipe contents	Basic identification colour	BS colour reference BS 4800*
Water	Green	12 D 45
Steam	Silver-grey	10 A 03
Mineral, vegetable and animal oils; combustible liquids	Brown	06 C 39
Gases in either gaseous or liquefied condition (except air)	Yellow ochre	08 C 35
Acids and alkalis	Violet	22 C 37
Air	Light blue	20 E 51
Other fluids	Black	00 E 53
Electrical services	Orange	06 E 51

* BS 4800 *Paint colours for building purposes*.
Note: The colours given in column 2 are only included for guidance since different colour names may be used by different manufacturers for the same colour reference.

(Table 1: BS 1710: 1984)

When code indications are used they shall be placed at all junctions, at both sides of valves, service appliances, bulkheads, wall penetrations and at any other place where identification is necessary.

The code indications are:

1 The safety colours (see Table 36):
   (a) Red, for fire-fighting.
   (b) Yellow, for warning of danger.
   (c) Auxiliary blue in conjunction with the green basic colour, to denote pipes carrying fresh water, either potable or non-potable.
2 Information regarding the nature of the contents for which the following systems may be used, either individually or in combination:
   (a) Name in full.
   (b) Abbreviation of name.
   (c) Chemical symbol.
   (d) Refrigerant number as specified in BS 4580.
   (e) Appropriate code indication colour bands.

Table 36   *Safety colour references*

Safety colour	BS colour reference BS 4800
Red	04 E 53
Yellow	08 E 51
Auxiliary blue	18 E 53

(Table 2: BS 1710: 1975)

Examples of identification by basic colour and code indications are illustrated. Colour code indication for medical gas services and optional colour code indications for general building services for a range of pipe contents are given, all in appendices.

BS 5383: 1976 *Material marking and colour coding of metal pipes and piping system components in steel, nickel alloys and titanium alloys*

This standard has been prepared following difficulties and dangers resulting from the installation in piping systems in process plant of items of pipe or components which were made from a material other than that intended by the designer.

It requires that for the purpose of identification all piping and piping system components are marked clearly with the details required by the relevant product standard. A simple colour code, either in the form of a strip or by colouring of the printed characters, is also used to identify different groups of materials. These groups have been chosen such that if by error a different material within the same group were used instead of the specified material, it is improbable that catastrophic failure would result. The groups are defined by nominal chemical composition or mechanical properties.

It is intended that the marking and colour code shall be applied by material manufacturers and stockists primarily to materials that are included in British Standards. Its use for other materials conforming to the various material groups, but covered by other than British Standards is not precluded, but in that event purchasers will need to specify their precise requirements for marking and colour coding.

Where confusion might occur the user should ensure that the colour marking applied in accordance with this standard is obliterated after installation.

CP 2010: *Pipelines* (being superseded by)
BS 8010 *Code of practice for pipelines*

Pipeline development almost inevitably affects large numbers of people who own or occupy land along the route. Pipelines there-

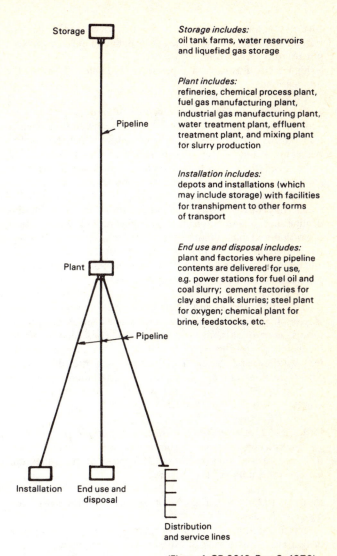

Storage includes:
oil tank farms, water reservoirs and liquefied gas storage

Plant includes:
refineries, chemical process plant, fuel gas manufacturing plant, industrial gas manufacturing plant, water treatment plant, effluent treatment plant, and mixing plant for slurry production

Installation includes:
depots and installations (which may include storage) with facilities for transhipment to other forms of transport

End use and disposal includes:
plant and factories where pipeline contents are delivered for use, e.g. power stations for fuel oil and coal slurry; cement factories for clay and chalk slurries; steel plant for oxygen; chemical plant for brine, feedstocks, etc.

(Figure 1: CP 2010: Part 2: 1970)

Figure 58 *Illustration of the definition of a pipeline*

Table 37 *Present general pipeline applications*

Type of pipeline	Part no. of CP 2010*	Fluid									
		Crude oil and petroleum products	Liquefied petroleum gases	Natural gas	Town gas	Industrial gases	Water	Slurries and sludges	Chemicals	Trade effluents and sewage‖	Brine
Steel with butt-welded joints	2	A	A	A	A	A	A§	A	A§	A§	A§
Steel with other than butt-welded joints	2			A‡	A‡		A§	A	A§	A§	A§
Grey iron and ductile iron	3†			A‡	A‡		A§	A	A	A	A
Asbestos-cement	4†						A	A		A	A
Concrete (prestressed and reinforced)	5†						A	A		A	A
Non-ferrous metals									A	A	A
Plastics				A			A	A	A	A	A

A = the general application.
* Part 1 *Installation of pipelines in land* is applicable to all subsequent parts of the code.
† In course of preparation.
‡ This type of pipeline is used for the conveyance of town and natural gases at lower operating pressures.
§ These applications may require the pipeline to be lined to prevent internal corrosion.
‖ *See also* CP 2005 *Sewerage.*

(Appendix A: CP 2010: Part 2: 1970)

fore involve an encroachment on the rights of the individual, and it is not surprising that pipeline development in most countries is governed by legislation.

Figure 58 illustrates a pipeline, and Table 37 shows the applications.

Part 1: 1966　*Installation of pipelines in land*

This part deals with those aspects of pipeline development which affect the owner and occupier of land through which the pipeline passes and it assumes that every effort will be made to obtain the rights needed by negotiation before application is made for compulsory powers. This part is common to all pipelines irrespective of the materials of which they are constructed or of which they convey. It gives recommendations on the installation of pipelines in land, aquisition and rights of way, construction, operation and maintenance. It includes routing and sections of land and rights of way, pipelaying and reinstatement, inspection and maintenance and a section on abandonment. Under revision as Part 1 of BS 8010.

Part 2: 1970　*Design and construction of steel pipelines in land*

Recommendations are made and guidance is given on the materials, components, design, fabrication, construction, workmanship and testing of steel pipelines. Pipelines jointed by butt-welding and other than butt-welding are dealt with. The code does not apply to pipeline installations which are covered by BS 806, nor piping systems covered by BS 3551. Under revision as Part 2 of BS 8010.

Part 3: 1972　*Design and construction of iron pipelines in land*

Design and constructional recommendations are given for grey iron and ductile iron pipelines. Materials for the pipes and fittings and joints are also covered.

Part 4: 1972　*Design and construction of asbestos-cement pipelines in land*

Recommendations are made for materials for pipes and joints, design and construction of asbestos-cement pipelines.

Part 5: 1974　*Design and construction of prestressed concrete pressure pipelines in land*

The design and construction of pressure pipelines incorporating prestressed concrete pipes are dealt with in this part. Materials for fittings and joints are also considered.

CP 3009: 1970　*Thermally insulated underground piping systems*

This code deals with the work involved in the general designing, planning, prefabrication, transport, installation, maintenance and testing of thermally insulated underground piping systems for conveying or circulating steam, hot or chilled water, heated oils and other fluids. It does not deal in detail with the associated civil engineering and building necessary with this type of installation or with systems which depend upon a very high vacuum for thermal insulation. The main theme of the code is the use of pipe-in-pipe systems of protection and states 'unless a site is unusually or specially protected it is recommended that pipe-in-pipe pressure tight systems with an outer casing of steel, plastics, asbestos-cement, glass, reinforced plastics, or other suitable material be used in order to withstand the pressure and aggression of ground and surface water. Methods using systems other than pipe-in-pipe should be considered only with caution and in a protected site'.

BS 4508　*Thermally insulated underground piping systems*

This standard specifies requirements for thermally insulated underground piping systems for conveying or circulating steam, hot or chilled water, heated oil and other fluids. The standard does not include systems that require a high vacuum in the annulus as a means of insulation. In Parts 1 and 3, details are given for insulation material and how to calculate its thickness. This standard should be used in conjunction with CP 3009.

Part 1: 1986　*Steel cased systems with air gap*

Requirements for design, materials, construction, installation, testing and fault monitoring for steel-cased systems for temperatures exceeding 5 °C.

Part 3: 1977　*General requirements for cased systems without air gap*

This part sets out to define minimum performance requirements for pipe-in-pipe cased systems without air gap, which are being increasingly used especially in district heating schemes for urban and other distribution systems and in cross-country pipelines. Requirements for the construction and installation with the insulated service or product pipe enclosed in a pressure-tight casing. The system is suitable for conveying fluids at a temperature above 3 °C. Clause 9 of this part recognizes the increasing use of fibre reinforced composite (FRC) service and product pipes, and the requirements specified therein will be kept under review pending future experience.

Appendix F contains information on pipe-in-pipe flexible systems, experience in the use of which is limited. Specific testing and inspection requirements are also detailed. Appendices C, D and E cover in depth thermal expansion, strength in the ground and site and soil survey. Eight figures give illustrations of typical assembly and constructional details.

Part 4: 1977　*Specific testing and inspection requirements for cased systems without air gap*

This part deals with requirements for the independent certification of components and assemblies of components in pipe-in-pipe systems with an insulated service or product pipe enclosed in a pressure-tight casing. Specific requirements are stated for the testing, inspection and certification, type tests and inspections, production inspection and tests, test failure, interpretation and system approvals.

BS 6076: 1981　*Tubular polyethylene film for use as protective sleeving for buried iron pipes and fittings*

This standard is based on current practices used in protecting underground iron pipes and fittings from corrosion in aggressive soils. It applies to tubular polyethylene film suitable for the protection of buried duclite iron and grey iron pipes and fittings manufactured in accordance with BS 4772 and BS 4622 respectively. Requirements are specified for the composition and properties of the tubular polyethylene film for use as sleeving and the widths of sleeving to be used according to the nominal diameter of the pipe and the type of flexible joint used.

BS 5886: 1980　*Methods for field pressure testing of asbestos-cement pipelines*

The basic methods of field pressure testing cement pipelines, above and below ground conveying fluids, are specified. The pipes may be with or without internal hydraulic pressure. For pressure pipelines two main types of tests are specified.

The testing of non-pressure pipelines for sewerage and drainage applications will normally be a water test, but should local conditions give rise to difficulty in carrying out this test an air test is specified.

BS 5927: 1980　*Guide for laying of asbestos-cement pipelines*

The standard recommends procedures for the installation of asbestos-cement pipelines for both pressure and non-pressure applications. It covers the types of laying conditions most commonly encountered in practice. Where special or exceptional conditions apply, it is the responsibility of the pipeline designer and the site engineer to give suitable instructions to supplement this standard. Requirements are specified for handling and storage, stringing out, excavation, pipe laying, jointing, house service connections, backfilling and commissioning.

BS 5955 *Code of practice for plastics pipework (thermoplastics materials)*

Part 6: 1980 *Installation of unplasticized PVC pipework for gravity drains and sewers*

This part of BS 5955 sets out information supplementary to that given in CP 301 and CP 2005 on the use of unplasticized PVC (uPVC) pipes and fittings for the conveyance ·by gravity of surface water, foul sewage and subsoil water.

This code relates to unplasticized PVC pipes and fittings manufactured in accordance with BS 4660 in respect of 110 and 160 mm sizes and with BS 5481 in respect of sizes 200 to 630 mm, and used in the construction of gravity drains and gravity sewers.

If it is proposed to use these pipes and fittings with untreated trade waste or with prolonged discharges at high temperature (>60 °C) reference should be made to Part 1 of this code and/or to the manufacturer. It should be noted that it is normally a requirement that the temperature of trade effluent at the point of discharge to public sewers should not exceed 43 °C.

The information given is considered to the good practice in normal conditions in the United Kingdom, but it is appreciated that in certain localities there may be special conditions which will require modifications to these recommendations.

Unplasticized PVC pipes for gravity drains and gravity sewers differ from pipes considered in Part 2 of this code in that they are not normally subject to internal hydraulic pressures except in unusual circumstances, for example when a blockage occurs or in an inverted siphon. However, they are subject to external loads due to the backfill and those transmitted from traffic.

Attention is drawn to the possible hazards involved in the site work of the installation of pipes; due attention should be paid to relevant safety regulations including the Health and Safety at Work etc. Act 1974.

This part of this code is not applicable to pipes laid at depths exceeding 6 m to the top of the pipes.

The code includes charts for determining flow rates of the pipes, details are given on push fit and solvent joints, storage and handling and some notes are provided on installation. A series of diagrams on bedding and jointing details provide useful information.

Part 7: 1983 *Recommendations for methods of thermal fusion jointing*

Gives general guidance on socket fusion, butt fusion and saddle fusion procedures, materials and testing.

BS 4625: 1970 *Prestressed concrete pipes (including fittings)*

This standard deals with the manufacture of prestressed concrete pipes which are designed primarily for the conveyance of water and sewage, and fittings for use with them. Two types of pipe are covered: prestressed concrete cylinder pipes, and prestressed concrete non-cylinder pipes. The standard includes a section on each of these types of pipe and a series of general clauses applicable to all pipes and fittings complying with this standard. A technical specification for fittings is included as Appendix A. The dimensions for the preferred nominal internal diameters are 400 to 1200 mm inclusive in increments of 100 mm, and 1400 to 1800 mm in increments of 200 mm. The standard laid lengths of pipe shall not be less than 4 m for diameters up to and including 500 mm and not less than 4.5 m for pipes over 500 mm diameter. Lengths other than these may be supplied by agreements between purchaser and manufacturer.

BS 486: 1981 *Asbestos-cement pressure pipes and joints*

Requirements are specified for pipes and joints for use under pressure and are applicable both to water cured pipes and to autoclaved pipes in which the binder is partially replaced by ground silica. Certain conditions of manufacture, classification, characteristics, and acceptance tests are defined.

The nominal diameter of the pipes correspond to the internal diameter expressed in millimetres, tolerances excluded. Thirty-seven sizes are included in a range 50 to 2500 mm.

The nominal length of the pipes refers to the length measured between the extremities for pipes with plain ends and to the effective length for socketed pipes. It should preferably be not less than:

3 m for pipes with a nominal diameter equal to or less than 200 mm
4 m for pipes with a nominal diameter exceeding 200 mm.

In special cases shorter pipes may be specified. The nominal length should preferably be a multiple of 0.5 m.

The pipes are classified as follows:

1 Up to nominal diameter of 1000 mm according to the works hydraulic test pressure (TP) which ranges from 5 to 36 bar in twelve steps. The relationship between the bursting pressure (BP) and the works hydraulic test pressure (TP), and the relationship between the bursting pressure (BP) and the hydraulic working pressure (WP) should not be less than the values indicated in Table 38.

Table 38 *Pressure relationships*

Nominal diameters (mm)	BP / TP	BP / WP*
From 50 to 100	2	4
From 125 to 200	1.75	3.5
From 250 to 500	1.5	3
From 600 to 1000	1.5	2.5
From 1100 to 2500	1.5	2.5

* WP includes unavoidable surpressures.   (Table 2: BS 486: 1981)

2 Pipes of nominal diameter exceeding 1000 mm are designed to suit the specific requirements of any particular pipeline. The purchaser's engineer should provide the manufacturer with all the required data for the design of a suitable pipe. Pipes of nominal diameter 600 to 1000 mm may also be designed in this way. The pressure relationship should not be less than those indicated in Table 38.

BS 5949: 1980 *Asbestos-cement pipes and joints for thrust-boring and pipe jacking*

This standard gives specifications relating to pipes and joints for thrust-boring and pipe jacking for applications such as:

1 Ducts to protect other pipes or cables.
2 Sewerage and drainage at atmospheric pressure (accidental overpressures are admitted provided that a sufficient safety factor be maintained in relation to the hydraulic test pressure specification in this standard).

It defines certain conditions of manufacture, classification, characteristics and acceptance tests for these products. The pipes are classified in two classes according to their permissible thrusting load. However, the permissible thrusting load of pipes with nominal diameters above 2000 mm should be agreed between the manufacturer and purchaser. Annex B shows a method of calculating the class of pipe required for thrust-boring in different soils.

The range of nominal diameters, corresponding to the internal diameter, is from 150 to 2500 mm (twenty-eight sizes). The nominal length of pipe is usually 2 m.

Included in the standard are tests for resistance to fissuring, leakage, sweating, crushing and effect of acetic acid.

BS 2035: 1966   *Cast iron flanged pipes and flanged fittings*

In dealing with flanged pipes and fittings this standard covers four classes of pipes and two classes of fittings tests to the pressures specified in Table 39.

Table 39   *Hydrostatic test pressures*

Class		Hydrostatic test pressure at works (bar)	Maximum hydrostatic test pressure after installation (bar)
Pipe	Fittings		
A	—	9	6
B	AB	15	12
C	—	21	18
D	CD	27	24

Note: The specified thickness and pressures for the fittings conform to the last letter of the classification code, that is B and D respectively, though AB fittings are intended for use with Class A or B pipes and CD fittings with Class C or D pipes.

(Table 3: BS 2035: 1966)

Section one specifies requirements for materials, tests, marking, coating, casting, inspection and manufacturer's certificate.

Section two comprises a set of specific requirements set out in tubular form for all relevant dimensions such as diameters, thickness, and length where appropriate. The weight of pipe, flanges and fittings are also specified. The following are dealt with: pipes and flanges, bends, equal crosses, flanged sockets and spigots, tees, radial tees and tapers, angle branches, duck-foot bends and blank flanges. The nominal internal diameter range for all pipes and fittings is from 2 to 48 in (50.8 to 609.6 mm) inclusive.

BS 78   *Cast iron spigot and socket pipes (vertically cast) and spigot and socket fittings*

Part 2: 1965   *Fittings*
The fittings specified shall be cast iron for use with pipes to Part 1 of this standard and BS 1211, but in cases of fittings ordered and supplied with some form of mechanical joint, the body only of the fitting need comply with all the relevant requirements of this standard.

The lengths, shapes, dimensions and (where appropriate) weights for the fittings are specified with related diagrams and tables in section two. The requirements specified refer to a variety of bends, tees, branches, etc.

The standard also includes details of the quality of material and quality control used in casting the fittings, testing, coating and inspection.

BS 1211: 1958   *Centrifugally cast (spun) iron pressure pipes for water, gas and sewage*

The standard covers pipes manufactured in either metal or sand moulds. The requirements common to both methods of moulding are given in section one, those peculiar to metal moulds in section two, and those peculiar to sand moulds in section three. The pipes are produced in three Classes: B, C and D. The class relates the internal nominal diameter to wall thickness, pipe weight and test hydraulic pressure. Tables of dimensions and weights for the particular classes are provided in the standard for a range of nominal diameters from 3 in to 27 in (76.2 to 685.8 mm) inclusive. The pipes are normally provided in four lengths: 12, 13 ft 1½ in, 16 and 18 ft (3.65, 4.34, 4.87 and 5.48 m). The standard also specifies requirements for quality of metal used in casting the pipes, mechanical and hydraulic tests, coating, inspection and gauging.

BS 1387: 1967   *Steel tubes and tubulars suitable for screwing to BS 21 pipe threads*

This standard applies to welded and seamless, screwed and socketed steel tubes and tubulars, and to plain and steel tubes suitable for screwing to BS 21 pipe threads of nominal bores from 6 to 150 mm inclusive. Three thicknesses of tube are provided for as specified in the standard and are designated light, medium and heavy. The tubes may be supplied in random lengths from 4 to 7 m, but exact length can be obtained if so specified.

The standard specifies requirements for joints, materials, galvanizing, hydraulic test and tests on finished tubes. The tubulars specified, that is, pieces, nipples, longscrews, bends, springs and return bends are described in section three with diagrams and related dimension tables. Similar tables provide dimensions and weights of the three classes of pipe.

BS 534: 1981   *Steel pipes and specials for water and sewage*

Requirements are specified for seamless and welded carbon steel pipes and specials and for joints in respect of the pipe end preparation in sizes 60.3 to 2220 mm outside diameter for the conveyance of water and sewage. It includes external and internal protections against corrosive action of the surrounding medium or conveyed fluid. It does not apply to those steel tubes and tubulars with screwed and socketed joints, which are covered by BS 1387, and does not apply to gas pipes.

The pipes and fittings are designated by their outside diameters and Appendix A gives guidance on the minimum thickness considered suitable for general use under normal conditions, with details of masses per unit length and hydraulic test pressures.

Illustrations showing the basic design principle for the more common types of joints appropriate to this standard are given, although the actual details of the joints may differ from one manufacturer to another.

Specials are defined in the standard as 'a fitting made from manipulated or fabricated pipe'. Section four specifies such specials, typical examples of which are shown in five figures.

In section five methods of protecting pipes and specials against corrosion are specified. It covers external protection by bitumen, coal-tar-based and plastics materials, and internal protection by bitumen, concrete and cement mortar.

BS 4772: 1980   *Ductile iron pipes and fittings*

This standard provides for ductile iron pipes produced by the following methods:

1 Centrifugal casting in:
  (a) Metal moulds.
  (b) Sand moulds.
2 Casting in sand moulds.

The standard also applies to ductile iron pipes and fittings having spigots and/or sockets for flexible joints or flanges and also to ductile iron pipes and fittings having other types of joint, the general dimensions of which, except those relating to the joints, are specified in this standard. In view of the increase in the use of cement mortar linings, these are also included in an appendix.

Pipes and fittings are given class designations which comprise a prefix K and a whole number which is the selected coefficient inserted into the formula, given in the standard, used for the calculation of mean wall thickness. Standard pipes with flexible joints or welded on flanges are class K9, standard pipes with screwed on or cast on flanges are class K12.

The ranges of nominal sizes (DN) and lengths for the various pipes are:

1 Pipes with flexible joints K9, DN 80 to 1200 mm (seventeen sizes) in 5.5 m lengths, and DN 900 to 1600 mm (six sizes) in 8 m lengths.

2 Pipes with screwed on flanges K12, DN 80 to 600 mm (eleven sizes) in 4 m lengths.

3 Pipes with welded on flanges K9, DN 300 to 1200 mm in 4 m lengths.

4 Pipes with cast on flanges K12, DN 80 to 1600 mm (nineteen sizes) are normally supplied in short lengths, generally 750 mm long, up to and including DN 250, and 1 m long for the larger sizes.

The class designation for fittings is given as follows:

1 Standard fittings without branches, unless otherwise indicated, shall be class K12.

2 Standard fittings with branches shall be class K14.

Pipeline design considerations may justify or require the use of classes other than those detailed. Provided they meet with the requirements of this specification they will be deemed to comply with this standard.

Hydraulic and hydrostatic pressure tests are detailed in an appendix.

Tables and diagrams specify a comprehensive series in the two grades of fittings.

Details of flexible joints, either of the 'push in' type or of the 'mechanical' type, are not included in this standard since this could restrict their future development.

BS 4622: 1970 *Grey iron pipes and fittings*

Requirements are specified for grey pipes manufactured by centrifugal casting in metal or sand moulds and casting in sand moulds. Grey iron fittings are also covered and this standard is applicable to all grey pipes and fittings having spigots, sockets or flanges as specified, and also to pipes and fittings with other types of joints, the general dimensions of which, except those relating to the joints, conform to this standard. Although increasing use is being made of various forms of mechanical or 'push in' flexible joints, in which the seal is achieved by means of a suitably retained gasket, it is not possible to include such joints in this standard without restricting their future development. The standard therefore specifies lead caulked joints and flanged joints, and includes detailed diagrams and dimensions of such. Flanges for pipes and fittings of 80 to 700 mm nominal internal diameter, designated NP 10 pipes and fittings.

Diameters 80 to 300 mm may be manufactured with flanges, designated NP 16. Caulked lead joints are available through the full range of nominal internal diameters 80 to 700 mm. Screw on flanges can be fitted to pipes of a range of diameters 80 to 600 mm.

There are four classes of pipe specified, wall thickness and mass forming the basis of the classification. Spigot and socket pipes are available in Classes 1, 2 and 3. Standard pipes with screwed on flanges are produced in Class 3 only, but with NP 10 or NP 16 flanges. The standard pipes with cast on flanges can be obtained in Class 3 with NP 10 flanges or Class 4 with NP 16 flanges.

Diagrams and detailed dimensions of all classes of pipe are provided in the specification, and a series of diagrams and tables specify the shape and dimensions of a wide range of grey iron fittings.

The specification also includes details of allowable hydrostatic pressures and hydraulic work test pressures, and external and internal protective coatings.

BS 1740 *Wrought steel pipe fittings (screwed BSP thread)*

Part 1: 1971 *Metric units*

Provisions are made for a range of fittings, with screwed British Standard pipe thread to BS 21 for use with steel tubes to BS 1387 and includes, for the convenience of users, particulars of equal sockets and hexagon backunits as specified in BS 1387.

Fittings of other types and size of outlet not covered by this standard can be made to special order.

Specified in this part are welded and seamless wrought fittings of nominal size 6 to 150 mm inclusive and a variety of types are covered: elbows, tees, crosses, caps, sockets, plugs, bushes and nipples.

Tables of sizes and diagrams illustrate virtually all the fittings mentioned above. Pieces, longscrews, barrel nipples, close taper nipples, running nipples, bends, springs and return bends are covered in BS 1387.

The standard specifies requirements for the steel used in manufacture of the fittings: pressure tests, and hot dip galvanizing. Useful information is also given on the method of specifying outlets.

BS 3600: 1976 *Dimensions and masses per unit length of welded and seamless steel pipes and tubes for pressure purposes*

The tabular information contained in this standard, covering the dimensions and masses per unit length of welded and seamless steel pipe and tubes for pressure purposes, presents within a single cover the dimensions and masses applicable to the present editions of BS 3601–BS 3605 and will also apply to the revised fully metricated versions when they are issued. The dimensional limitations for particular manufacturing processes are given in the appropriate standard in the BS 3601–BS 3605 series. The dimensions of butt-welded tubes and service tubes with screwed and socketed form of joint, or with plain ends suitable for screwing are covered in BS 1387. The dimensions of tubes for boilers and similar plant are detailed in BS 3059. This standard does not apply to pipes for oil and natural gas pipelines.

Tubes detailed in tables of this standard may be specified by nominal sizes or by outside diameters but the outside diameter must always be quoted when ordering except in special for hot finished, cold finished, and hot finished and machined seamless tubes which may be ordered by inside diameter and wall thickness.

BS 3601: 1974 *Steel pipes and tubes for pressure purposes: carbon steel with specified room temperature properties*

This specification covers plain end, welded and seamless carbon steel tubes suitable for general purposes. The tubes are supplied against specified room temperature properties and are subject to the pressure/temperature limitations in the appropriate application standard.

Diameters and thicknesses appropriate to this standard, with the exception of those for butt-welded tubes, should preferably be selected from those given in BS 3600: 1973, or for the use with compression couplings in a table of that standard. Diameters and thicknesses for butt-welded tubes are given in BS 1387: 1967. Tubes complying with the requirements of this standard may also be supplied in accordance with the dimensions given in BS 1600.

The requirements for butt-welded tubes in this standard are generally comparable with those for plain end tubes given in BS 1387. Similarly, service tubes with a screwed and socketed form of joint or with plain ends suitable for screwing and covered in BS 1387, based on pipe threads in accordance with BS 21. Other types of joints are provided for in British Standards such as BS 534, BS 778 and BS 806. Fittings, specials and methods for corrosion protection are covered in BS 534.

The tubes shall be designated by one of the references given in Table 40, which indicates the method of manufacture and the grade of steel. For example, ERW 410 denotes electric resistance welded or induction welded tubes made from steel 410. The number 410 corresponds to the minimum tensile strength of the steel in N/mm².

The tubes may be manufactured by one of the following processes as specified in the standard:

1 Butt-welded.
2 Electric resistance welded and induction welded.
3 Seamless.
4 Submerged arc welded.

The standard further specifies details of materials, mechanical properties, tests, and appearance and soundness.

The range of dimensions in which the tubes are available is dependent upon the method of manufacture, the thicknesses available being also dependent upon the diameter. The dimensional limitations generally applicable to this standard are given in Table 41.

Table 40 *Tube designations*

Method of manufacture		Steel grades applicable		
Butt-welded	BW	320	—	—
Electric resistance welded and induction welded	ERW	320	360	410
Seamless	S	320	360	410*
Submerged arc welded	SAW	—	—	410*

* Steels of higher tensile strength may be supplied by agreement.

(From Clause 3: BS 3601: 1974)

Table 41 *Range of tube designations*

Method of manufacture	Outsize diameter	Maximum thickness
	mm	mm
Butt-welded	6 (nominal size) to 100 (nominal size)	5.4
Electric resistance welded and induction welded*	10.2 to 508	10
Seamless*	10.2 to 457	50
Submerged arc welded	114.3 to 2220	32

* For tubes for use with compression couplings *see* the standard.

(From Clause 5: BS 3601: 1974)

BS 3605: 1973 *Seamless and welded austenitic stainless steel pipes and tubes for pressure purposes*

The general requirements of four types of austenitic steel pipes, suitable for general pressure and corrosion resisting purposes, are detailed in this standard. Separate sections cover the specific requirements for each one of these types of pipe. The types of pipe covered are:

1 Seamless austenitic steel pipes with specific room temperature properties.
2 Seamless austenitic steel pipes with specified elevated temperature properties.
3 Longitudinally and spirally welded austenitic steel pipes with specified room temperature (taken as 20 °C) properties.
4 Longitudinally and spirally welded austenitic steel pipes with specified elevated temperature properties.

Tables of dimensions and masses per unit length of pipes are given in BS 3600, and all the types of steel specified in this standard are suitable for low temperature service. Methods of manufacture and codes for designation purposes are also included, along with the available ranges of external and internal diameters.

BS 6362: 1984 *Stainless steel tubes suitable for screwing in accordance with BS 21 'Pipe threads for tubes and fittings where pressure-tight joints are made on the threads'*

This standard establishes the dimensions and characteristics of seamless and welded austenitic stainless steel tubes with dimensions corresponding to the medium series of ISO 65.

BS 4127 *Light gauge stainless steel tubes*
Part 2: 1972 *Metric units*

Requirements are specified for stainless steel tubes supplied in straight lengths suitable for bending and connection by means of capillary and compression fittings specified in BS 864 in systems where the working pressure does not exceed a gauge pressure of 13 bar.

The full range of nominal sizes is 6 to 42 mm (ten sizes) manufactured by welded or seamless methods. The standard also specifies requirements for the material, and mechanical and hydraulic or pneumatic tests.

BS 2871 *Copper and copper alloys. Tubes*

Part 1: 1971 *Copper tubes for water, gas and sanitation*

■ AD (Reg. H1)

Requirements are specified for copper tubes in the following four different conditions:

1 Annealed copper tubes supplied in coils, suitable for connection by means of compression fittings and capillary fittings for use in micro-bore or mini-bore heating systems, designated Table W.
2 Half-hard copper tubes supplied in straight lengths, suitable for connection by means of compression fittings and capillary fittings, by silver brazing, or by suitable methods of welding, designated Table X.
3 Half-hard copper tubes in straight lengths and annealed copper tubes in coils suitable for burying underground and for connection by means of compression fittings and capillary fittings, by silver brazing, or by bronze or autogenous welding, designated Table Y.
4 Hard drawn copper tubes supplied in straight lengths suitable for connection by means of capillary fittings or non-manipulative type compression fittings (Type A specified in BS 864 Part 2), designated Table Z. (These tubes are not recommended for bending.)

In all cases the tubes are solid drawn.
Tables 42 and 43 show the range of tube sizes and working pressure for the conditions stated above.

Part 2: 1972 *Tubes for general purposes*
Copper and copper alloy tubes are specified for general purposes from 2 mm up to and including 508 mm outside diameters and from 0.4 mm up to and including 8.0 mm thickness. All tubes are solid drawn and may be supplied in one of the following conditions (these requirements apply to round tubes except where reference is made to square or rectangular tubes):

1 M condition. Tubes in the 'as drawn' condition. An 'as drawn' tube is defined as one supplied in the condition of the tube on the completion of the necessary operations to produce the specified diameter and wall thickness.
2 TA condition. Tubes in the temper annealed condition. These tubes will have been heat treated over their full length to an intermediate temper.
3 O condition. Tubes in the annealed condition.
4 ½H condition. Tubes in the half-hard temper produced by cold drawing.

If ordered in coil the tubes shall be annealed. Copper tubes in straight lengths, unless otherwise specified, will be supplied in the M condition.

A table in the standard shows the various designations for the tubes, the material and the condition in which it can be obtained and details of chemical composition and mechanical properties.

The standard includes eight tables of preferred sizes, with

Table 42 *Dimensions and working pressures, Table W tube*

Size of tube (mm)	Preferred thickness (mm)	Other recommended thickness (mm)	Maximum working pressures (bar)	
			for preferred thickness	for other recommended thickness
6	0.6	0.8	90	144
8	0.6	0.8	66·	105
10	0.7	0.8	62	82

(From Table W: BS 2871: Part 1: 1971)

Table 43 *Dimensions and working pressures, Tables X, Y and Z tube*

Size of tube (mm)	Maximum working pressures (bar)			
	Table X	Table Y		Table Z*
		$\frac{1}{2}$ H*	0†	
6	133	188	144	113
8	97	136	105	98
10	77	106	82	78
12	63	87	67	64
15	58	87	67	50
18	56	72	55	50
22	51	69	57	41
28	40	55	42	32
35	42	54	41	30
42	35	45	34	28
54	27	47	36	25
67	20	37	28	20
76.1	24	33	25	19
108	17	29	22	17
133	14			16
159	15			15

* Based on material in $\frac{1}{2}$ H condition (stress = 60 N/mm^2) at 65 °C.
† Based on material in 0 condition (stress = 46 N/mm^2) at 65 °C.

(From Tables X, Y and Z: BS 2871: Part 1: 1971)

maximum working pressures and temperatures as appropriate. They are summarized as follows:

1 Tubes for pipelines for shipbuilding and other engineering purposes. Range of (twenty-seven) tube sizes from 3 to 508 mm inclusive. Tubes supplied in T A, ½ H or O condition.
2 Tubes for purposes other than pipelines. Range of (thirteen) tube sizes from 3 to 50 mm inclusive.
3 Tubes (with plain ends) for steam services (low pressure range). Range of (eighteen) tube sizes from 6 to 219.1 mm inclusive. Working pressure up to and including 7 bar, and maximum working temperature of 205 °C.
4 Tubes with plain ends for steam services (high pressure range). Range of (seventeen) tube sizes from 6 to 291.1 mm inclusive. Working pressure up to and including 17 bar, and maximum working temperature 205 °C.
5 Tubes with screwed ends for steam services (low pressure range). Range of (fourteen) tube sizes from ⅛ to 4 in (3.2 to 101.6 mm) inclusive. Working pressure up to and including 7 bar and maximum working temperature 205 °C.
6 Tubes with screwed ends for steam services (high pressure range). Range of (fourteen) tube sizes from ⅛ to 4 in (3.2 to 101.6 mm) inclusive. Working pressure over 7 bar, up to and including 17 bar and maximum working temperature 205 °C.
7 Tubes for general purposes for pressures up to and including 12 bar. Range of (thirteen) tube sizes from ⅛ to 4 in (3.2 to 101.6 mm).
8 Tubes for general purposes for pressures over 12 bar up to

and including 20 bar. Range of (fourteen) tube sizes from ⅛ to 4 in (3.2 to 101.6 mm).

This part of the standard also specifies requirements for mechanical, pressure and chemical tests, and recommends special requirements for tubes for refrigeration plant.

BS 602, 1805: 1970 *Lead and lead alloy pipes for other than chemical purposes*

In this publication BS 602 and BS 1805 still retain their identity but those clauses which are common to both specifications have been grouped in section one and clauses specific to BS 602 or BS 1805 have been grouped in section two.

Requirements are specified for:

1 Lead pipes in three different compositions (BS 602) in sizes up to and including 125 mm bore intended to be used for the applications listed below:
   (a) Service and distribution pipes to be laid underground.
   (b) Service pipes to be fixed above ground.
   (c) Cold water distributing pipes to be fixed above ground.
   (d) Hot water distributing pipes to be fixed above ground.
   (e) Soil, waste and soil and waste ventilating pipes, and flushing and warning pipes.
   (f) Gas pipes in heavier and lighter weights.
2 Lead, silver, copper, alloy pipes (BS 1805) in sizes up to 40 mm bore intended to be used for the applications (a), (b), (c), and (d) listed above.

Each standard includes tables which state the minimum dimensions of pipe required for a particular application, that is, bore and wall thickness and code number. BS 602 also specifies the three chemical compositions and recommends where they should be used.

CP 312 *Plastics pipework (thermoplastics materials)*

This code of practice has been prepared to present details of comparative physical, chemical and mechanical properties of the various plastic pipes, to guide the selection for different applications and, consequently, to define sound practice in the fabrication and installation of such pipes.

Part 1: 1973 *General principles and choice of materials*
Recommendations are given for the selection of the most suitable materials for thermoplastics pipe systems for particular applications and the general principles applicable to all such systems. Information is given on the materials available and their properties, recommendations on installation above and below ground, pipes for water, soil, waste, rain water and trade effluents (above ground), for gases, gaseous fuel, industrial gases, food and drink other than water and industrial applications. It also includes two tables listing and classifying the resistance of plastics materials to a wide range of chemicals.

Part 2: 1973 *Unplasticized PVC pipework for the conveyance of liquids under pressure*

Guidance is given on the proper application and installation of uPVC. It does not cover reinforced pipe of uPVC used as lining material. Recommendations are given on working and surge pressure, the effects of temperature, limitations, flow properties, jointing, bending, storage, handling and transport, installation, inspection and repairs.

Part 3: 1973   *Polyethylene pipes for the conveyance of liquids under pressure*

This part gives advice on the proper application and installation of polyethylene pipes. It does not recommend the use of this type of pipe for any particular purpose, except to say that polyethylene pipes are slightly permeable to certain gases and are not recommended for use in ground that is, or might be, liable to severe gas contamination.

This part provides similar recommendations for polyethylene pipe as is provided in Part 2 for uPVC pipe.

BS 1972: 1967   *Polythene pipe (Type 32) for cold water services*

Black polythene pipes for use in cold water services and in flush, overflow, warning and waste pipe applications is covered. Requirements are specified for materials, physical and mechanical characteristics, marking, stocking and transport. The range of nominal sizes is ⅜, ½, ¾, 1, 1¼, 1½, 2, 3 and 4 in (9.5, 12.7, 19.1, 25.4, 38.1, 50.8, 76.2 and 101.6 mm) and the pipes are classified by the maximum sustained working pressure as Class B: 6 bar, Class C: 8.9 bar and Class D: 12 bar.

Class C pipes 1 to 3 in (25.4 to 76.2 mm) nominal size and Class D pipes may be threaded in BS 21.

The working pressures given above are based on a water temperature of 20 °C and are the respective maximum for which the pipe is suitable for use, and influences wall thickness. Pipes are normally supplied in coils of 50, 100 and 150 m.

BS 1973: 1970   *Polythene pipe (Type 32) for general purposes including chemical and food industry uses*

Polythene pipe (Type 32) for general purposes and for use in flush, overflow and warning applications is specified. The type designation 32 indicates the recommended maximum working stress for the material in bars at 20 °C when in pipe form. This stress has been used as a basis for calculating the minimum wall thickness.

Details of black pipe and natural pipe materials are specified along with physical and mechanical characteristics, quality control and marking of the pipes.

The range of nominal sizes is ¼, ⅜, ½, ¾, 1, 1¼, 1½, 2, 3 and 4 in (6.4, 9.5, 12.7, 19.1, 25.4, 38.1, 50.8, 76.2 and 101.6 mm) and the pipes are classified by maximum sustained working pressure as Class A: 3 bar, Class B: 6 bar, Class C: 9 bar and Class D: 12 bar.

In the latter two cases certain pipes may be threaded to BS 21. The working pressures given above are based on a water temperature of 20 °C and are the respective maximum for which the pipe is suitable for use, and influences the wall thickness. Pipe can be supplied in random lengths or coils of 50, 100 and 150 m.

BS 2782   *Methods of testing plastics*

(See Table 3, Materials n rubber, plastics, etc).

BS 3284: 1967   *Polythene pipe (Type 50) for cold water services*

Black polythene pipe for use in cold water services, and in flush, overflow, warning and waste pipe applications is specified. Requirements are included for material, physical and mechanical properties, marking, stocking and transport. The range of nominal sizes is ⅜, ½, ¾, 1, 1¼, 1½, 2, 3, 4 and 6 in (9.5, 12.7, 19.1, 25.4, 31.8, 38.1, 50.8, 76.2, 101.6 and 152.4 mm) and the pipes are classified as Class C: 8.9 bar and Class D: 12 bar.

Class C pipes of ¾ to 4 in (19.1 to 101.6 mm) nominal size and Class D pipes may be threaded to BS 21. The working

pressures given above are based on a water temperature of 20 °C and are the respective maximum for which the pipe is suitable for use, and influences wall thickness. Pipes are normally supplied in coils of 50, 100 and 150 m.

BS 6572: 1985   *Blue polyethylene pipes up to nominal size 63 for below-ground use for potable water*

The prime purpose of this standard is to introduce a specification for potable water pipes characterized by a blue colour for use below ground, to distinguish the pipes from other services such as black electrical cables. Requirements are specified for the composition, physical attributes, performance and identification of polyethylene (PE) pipes for use in water services at pressures up to 12 bar at 20 °C in below-ground systems or where protected from sunlight by enclosure in ducts or buildings. The pipes are specified in nominal sizes 20, 25, 32, 50 and 63 mm as straight or coiled pipe. Methods of test and information on quality control testing are given in appendices.

BS 3505: 1968   *Unplasticized PVC pipe for cold water services*

The pipes specified are in nominal sizes up to and including 24 in for use in cold water services. Requirements are provided for materials, dimensions, physical and chemical and mechanical characteristics, marking and stocking and transport. The pipes are classified by maximum sustained working pressure* as Class B: 6 bar, Class C: 9 bar, Class D: 12 bar, Class E: 15 bar and Class 7: see Table 44.

Table 44   *Maximum sustained working pressure for Class 7 pipes*

Nominal size (in)	Pressure (bar)
⅜	44
½	40
¾	32
1	32
1¼	28
1½	25
2	22

(From Table 1A: BS 3505: 1968)

The range of nominal sizes is 3 to 24 in inclusive for Class B (fifteen sizes), 2 to 24 in inclusive for Class C (seventeen sizes), 1¼ to 18 in inclusive for Class D (sixteen sizes) and ¼ to 16 in inclusive for Class E (twenty sizes).

Table 45   *Maximum sustained working pressure for Class 6 and 7 pipes*

Nominal size (in)	Class 6 (bar)	Class 7 (bar)
¼	36	52
⅜	30	44
½	28	40
¾	22	32
1	24	32
1¼	20	28
1½	18	25
2	—	22

(From Table 1: BS 3506: 1969)

BS 3506: 1969   *Unplasticized PVC pipe for industrial uses*

This standard deals with unplasticized PVC pipe up to and

* The working pressure influences pipe wall thickness.

including 24 in nominal size. Classes B, C, D and E are indentical to those specified in BS 3505 while Class O is provided to give dimensions suitable for non-pressure duct applications, and Classes 6 and 7 give dimensions for extra thick pipes for hazardous duty and screw threading. Requirements are included for material, physical and mechanical characteristics, and marking. The pressure* classification for pipes is Class O: non-pressure, Class B: 6 bar, Class C: 9 bar, Class D: 12 bar, Class E: 15 bar, Class 6 and Class 7: see Table 45.

The range of nominal sizes is 1½ to 24 in inclusive for Class O (eighteen sizes), 3 to 24 in inclusive for Class B (fifteen sizes), 2 to 24 in inclusive for Class C (seventeen sizes), 1¼ to 18 in inclusive for Class D (sixteen sizes), ¼ to 16 in inclusive for Class E (twenty sizes), ¼ to 1½ in inclusive for Class 6 (seven sizes) and ¼ to 2 in inclusive for Class 7 (eight sizes).

Pipes are normally supplied in straight lengths of 3, 6 and 9 m.

BS 6437: 1984 *Polyethylene pipes (type 50) in metric diameters for general purposes*

Requirements are specified for the composition, dimensions, performance and marking for two categories of pipes (PE50A and PE50B) in nominal sizes 16 to 500 mm for general purposes including use in the chemical and food industries. The pipes are classified into five classes 2.5, 3.2, 4.0, 6.0 and 10.0, according to pressure rating in bar at a temperature of 20 °C. The type designation (50) indicates the maximum working stress for material in pipe form, in bar at 20 °C, i.e. 50 bar and 20 °C. This stress is used as the basis for calculating minimum wall thicknesses.

BS 4991: 1974 *Propylene copolymer pressure pipe*

Requirements are specified for pressure pipe in the two series:

Series 1: used with potable water, foodstuffs and pharmaceuticals.
Series 2: used with chemicals including water at temperatures up to 100 °C.

The compositions of pipe materials for the two series are detailed. Series 1 may be produced as black or natural pipe and Series 2 is pigmented grey except where it is likely to be exposed continuously to ultraviolet radiation, for example direct sunlight, it must be black.

The dimensions of the pipes are shown in the standard and the range of nominal sizes is ¼ to 24 in (6.4 to 609.6 mm) (twenty-two sizes).

The pipes are classified according to their suitability for maximum sustained working pressure as Class A: 3 bar, Class B: 6 bar, Class C: 9 bar, Class D: 12 bar and Class E: 15 bar.

The pressures given above are based on water at a temperature of 20 °C applied continuously for a period of fifty years. However, if grey pigmented Series 2 pipes are to be used for the transport of non-aggressive fluids (for example water) some variation is allowed and is indicated in this standard. Requirements are also specified for heat reversion, hydrostatic pressure resistance, tensile properties and resistance impact.

BS 5391 *Acrylonitrile-butadiene-styrene (ABS) pressure pipe*

Part 1: 1976 *Pipe for industrial uses*
Requirements are specified for pipe made from ABS polymer for industrial purposes including foodstuffs and pharmaceuticals.

The pipes are designated by the nominal size in eleven sizes from ⅜ to 8 in (9.5 to 203.2 mm) and are classified according to their suitability for threading and for maximum sustained working pressures as follows:

1 Unsuitable for threading: Class B: 6 bar, Class C: 9 bar, Class D: 12 bar and Class E: 15 bar.
2 Suitable for threading in compliance with BS 21: Class T: 12 bar.

The standard specifies requirements for heat reversion, heat ageing, resistance to weathering, impact resistance, and hydrostatic resistance.

BS 5392 *Acrylonitrile-butadiene styrene (ABS) fittings for use with ABS pressure pipe*

Part 1: 1976 *Fittings for use with pipe for industrial uses*
This part specifies requirements for injection moulded pipe fittings made from ABS polymer, for solvent welding to ABS pressure pipe complying with BS 5391. It is usual to manufacture each type of fitting with a single wall thickness appropriate to the maximum pressure class of pipe with which it is intended to be used. The standard includes details of working pressures, dimensions, stress relief, hydrostatic resistance and marking.

BS 5480 *Glass fibre reinforced plastics (GRP) pipes and fittings for use for water supply or sewerage*

Part 1: 1977 *Dimensions, materials and classification*
This part of the standard specifies requirements for materials, dimensions, fittings, joints, classification and marking only. It is for pressure and non-pressure pipe, joints and fittings, made from glass fibre reinforced thermosetting resin, either with or without a thermoplastic liner, intended for conveying above or below ground liquids, including potable and non-potable water, foul sewage and storm water. The pipe may also be used for those industrial wastes for which its suitability has been established. In the case of fittings, materials other than GRP are permitted. This part does not specify quality assurance and type tests, sampling, workmanship, certification, inspection and installation.

All dimensions specified relate to a temperature of 23 °C, and pipes are designated by the nominal internal diameter. Preferred diameters are shown in Table 46.

Table 46

Preferred nominal diameters of pipe (mm)				
25	125	600	1600	3000
32	150	700	1800	3200
40	200	800	2000	3400
50	250	900	2200	3600
65	300	1000	2400	3800
80	400	1200	2600	4000
100	500	1400	2800	

(Table 1: BS 5480: Part 1: 1977)

The straight lengths of pipe normally supplied are 3, 5, 6, 10 and 12 m.

Pipes are classified by the maximum sustained working gauge pressure at which they are suitable for use as 0, 1, 2.5, 4, 6, 10, 12.5, 16, 25, 40 and 60 bar. Pipes suitable for other pressure ratings may be supplied subject to agreement between the manufacturer and purchaser.

A further classification for pipes is their resistance to external load (stiffness). The values of minimal initial specific stiffness are included in the standard.

All fittings made from GRP such as bends, tees, junctions and reducers, must be equal or superior in performance to the pipe of the same classification. For fittings made from other than GRP the standard requires them to have compatible jointing systems and again be equal or superior to the GRP pipe of the same classification.

Joints may be classified in two ways as shown on page 100.

---

* The working pressure influences pipe wall thickness.

1 Rigid joints such as flanged joints, butt and overwrap, socket and spigot with bonding compound, screwed joints.
2 Flexible joints (mechanical) such as rolling or restrained 'O' ring or clamped joints.

Part 2: 1982 *Design and performance requirements*

Requirements related mainly to manufacture are specified for the design and testing of pipes and fittings made from GRP either with or without a thermoplastics liner for the construction of pressure and non-pressure pipelines intended for conveying above or below ground liquids, including potable and non-potable water, foul sewage, storm water, and those industrial wastes for which the suitability of the pipeline has been established by compliance with this standard.

BS 5556: 1978 *General requirements for dimensions and pressure ratings for pipe of thermoplastics materials (metric size)*

BS 5556 is intended to provide a comprehensive series of parameters to be used in the compilation of particular British Standards for thermoplastics pipe. It offers the advantage that appropriate parts of this 'master document' may be selected to meet the particular requirements of individual standards, including those for plastics pipe for non-pressure applications. It is also intended to act in the United Kingdom as a guide to manufacturers and users for pipe not specifically covered by other British Standards.

A table of this standard gives a mathematically derived series of wall thicknesses of pipe that is based on the relationship between stress rating and pressure.

The standard deals with outside diameters, maximum working pressures and stress ratings of circular pipes made of thermoplastics materials, whatever their composition or methods of manufacture, or the purpose for which they are used.

The outside diameters of pipe range from 2.5 to 2000 mm in forty-two sizes. The nominal size of a thermoplastics pipe is its minimum outside diameter.

The limits on diameters for each size of pipe shall be obtained by applying a tolerance appropriate to the application and material in question. The tolerances shall be positive only. Values for tolerances are given in the standards for specific types of pipe.

The pipes are also classified by the maximum sustained working pressure in bars for which the pipe is suitable with appropriate colour marking, as Table 47 shows.

Table 47 *Pressure ratings and colour marking*

Pressure rating		Colour marking
bar	MPa	
1	0.1	} white
2.5	0.25	
3.2	0.32	
4	0.4	} yellow
5	0.5	
6 (6.3)	0.6 (0.63)	} red
8	0.8	
10	1.0	blue
12.5	1.25	green
16	1.6	brown

(Table 2: BS 5556: 1978)

Note: The nominal pressure 6 bar has been chosen as the rounded-off value for 6.3 bar which is the value obtained by the strict application of a series of preferred numbers. However, for calculation purposes, for example of wall thickness, the value 6.3 bar is used.

BS 2598 *Glass plant, pipeline and fittings*

Part 1: 1980 *Properties of borosilicate glass 3.3*

This part of the standard specifies the characteristics of a type of glass designated 'borosilicate glass 3.3' used for the construction of glass plant, pipeline and fittings. Where nominal properties are given they relate, unless otherwise specified, to the range of temperatures 20 to 300 °C.

Part 2: 1980 *Testing, handling and use*

General rules relating to testing, handling and use of glass plant, pipeline, fittings and components are given. This part is not concerned with the design of components. Testing by manufacture and user, receipt and storage, installation, dismantling of plant operation, safety, maintenance, thermal and mechanical conditions and the problem of static electricity are areas covered.

Part 3: 1980 *Pipeline and fittings of nominal bore 15 to 150 mm: compatibility and interchangeability*

The standard specifies the essential requirements for compatibility and interchangeability of glass pipeline and fittings in sizes 15, 25, 40, 50, 80, 100 and 150 mm nominal bore (DN). Sixteen tables and thirty-seven figures set out the requirements for the various parts considered, for example pipe, and fittings such as bends, tees, valves, etc.

Part 4: 1980 *Glass plant components*

The essential requirements are specified for compatibility and interchangeability of components of glass plant, to the extent that these objectives are attainable, bearing in mind the differences in basic design features between the products of different manufacturers. This part not only specifies standardized dimensions but where applicable lists additional information which should be given by the manufacturers either in catalogues or supplied to users on request. The range of nominal bores considered are 80, 100, 150, 200, 225, 300, 400, 450, 600, 800, 1000, 1200 and 1400 mm. All lengths of components shall be multiples of 25 mm if possible.

DD 76 *Precast concrete pipes of composite construction*

Part 1: 1981 *Precast concrete pipes strengthened by continuous alkali-resistant glass-fibre rovings*

This document comprehensively covers centrifugally spun, steam-cured, precast concrete cylindrical pipes, bends and junctions strengthened by continuous alkali-resistant glass-fibre rovings and intended to be used for the conveyance, under atmospheric pressure, of sewage or surface water, and for the construction of culverts. The range of nominal sizes is DN 150 to DN 1800 for the units and they are further defined by minimum crushing strengths, as determined by standard tests, for each nominal size of pipe.

Part 2: 1983 *Precast concrete pipes strengthened by chopped zinc-coated steel fibres*

Precast concrete pipes, bends, and junctions strengthened by chopped zinc-coated steel fibres are the subject of the development draft. The pipes and fittings are intended for the same use as outlined in Part 1 but the range of nominal sizes is DN 375 to DN 1200 by increments of 75. As before, the minimum crushing strengths for each nominal size of pipe are given.

Hose

In this services element a number of standards provide information mainly on types of rubber hose and hose fittings. Three standards, however, consider plastic hoses, and one details methods of test. Because it is felt most of these standards lie outside the terms of reference of this manual a brief summary or title is given of those considered relevant.

BS 5173 *Methods of test for hoses*

Details of tests for rubber and plastic hoses are given in the following parts:

Part 1: 1976 *Measurement of dimensions*
Part 2: 1976 *Hydraulic pressure tests*
Part 3: 1977 *General physical tests*
Part 4: 1977 *Electrical tests*
Part 5: 1977 *Chemical resistance tests*
Part 6: 1977 *Environmental tests*

BS 5118: 1980 *Rubber hoses for compressed air*

BS 6066: 1981 *Thermoplastics hoses for compressed air*

BS 5120: 1975 *Rubber hose for gas welding and allied processes*

BS 5121: 1975 *Rubber sand blast hose*

BS 3212: 1975 *Flexible rubber tubing and hose (including connections where fitted and safety recommendations) for use in LPG vapour phase and LPG/air installations*

Pipe threads

BS 21: 1973 *Pipe threads for tubes and fittings where pressure-tight joints are made on the threads*

This standard specifies pipe threads as follows:

1 *Jointing threads*: these relate to pipe threads for joints made pressure-tight by the mating of the threads; they include taper external threads for assembly with either taper or parallel internal threads.
2 *Longscrew threads*: these relate to parallel external pipe threads used for longscrews (connectors) specified in BS 1387 where a pressure-tight joint is achieved by the compression of a soft material on the surface of the external thread by tightening a backnut against a socket.

The range is from $\frac{1}{16}$ to 6 in (1.6 to 152.4 mm) nominal size inclusive. The $\frac{1}{16}$ in (1.6 mm) size is included since this size of thread is required for fittings: it is not, however, intended to manufacture a $\frac{1}{16}$ in (1.6 mm) size of screwed pipe. An appendix gives details of a parallel external thread required by the Gas Council and Society of British Gas Industries which is for use with parallel internal threads of this standard.

The basic forms of the taper and parallel threads are based on the Whitworth thread form. Diagrams and tables detail shape dimensions, and tolerances. The standard recommends that screw threads should be referred to on drawings and related documents in the following manner: internal taper: $R_c \frac{1}{2}$*, external taper: $R \frac{1}{2}$ and parallel internal: $R_p \frac{1}{2}$.

BS 61: 1969 (1984) *Threads for light gauge copper tubes and fittings*

The specification covers threads intended for use with light gauge copper tubes and associated fittings to BS 2871 Part 2, BS 66 and BS 99 for which BSP threads to BS 21 are not suitable or cannot be utilized due to the thickness being insufficient. The range of nominal sizes of pipe is from $\frac{1}{8}$ to 4 in (thirteen sizes). The threads are designated as shown in the following examples.

* Nominal pipe size.

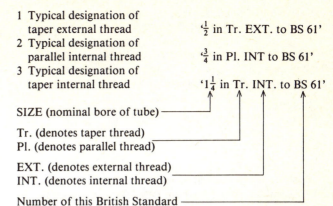

1 Typical designation of taper external thread   '$\frac{1}{2}$ in Tr. EXT. to BS 61'
2 Typical designation of parallel internal thread   '$\frac{3}{4}$ in Pl. INT to BS 61'
3 Typical designation of taper internal thread   '$1\frac{1}{4}$ in Tr. INT. to BS 61'

SIZE (nominal bore of tube)
Tr. (denotes taper thread)
Pl. (denotes parallel thread)
EXT. (denotes external thread)
INT. (denotes internal thread)
Number of this British Standard

(From Clause 5: BS 61: 1969)

BS 2779: 1973 *Pipe threads where pressure-tight joints are not made on the threads*

The parallel screw threads specified are not intended to be used where a pressure-tight seal is to be made. The threads are Whitworth form fastening threads of nominal sizes $\frac{1}{16}$ to 6 in (1.6 to 152.4 mm) inclusive. They are generally used for fastening purposes such as mechanical assembly of the component parts of fittings, cocks and valves, etc. Details of the form of thread and the recommended limits and tolerances are given.

The thread series specified is designated by the letter 'G' and it is recommended that these screw threads be referred to on drawings and related documents as in the following examples for $\frac{1}{2}$ in nominal size: internal threads: G$\frac{1}{2}$, external threads Class A: G$\frac{1}{2}$A and external thread Class B: G$\frac{1}{2}$B (Class B normally used).

If full form internal threads are required the words 'full form' must be added to the designation.

Designation of special truncated Whitworth form threads is by the addition of the letter T, for example G$\frac{1}{2}$A T.

Pipe flanges and bolting

BS 4504 *Flanges and bolting for pipes, valves and fittings, Metric series*

Part 1: 1969 *Ferrous*
This part specifies requirements for circular flanges of the following types and materials with the appropriate bolting:

1 *Integral*: steel, cast iron and malleable cast iron.
2 *Welding neck*: steel.
3 *Plate*: steel.
4 *Screwed boss*: steel and malleable cast iron.
5 *Slip on boss*: steel.
6 *Loose for welded on lapped pipe ends*: steel.
7 *Blank*: steel.

Note 1: Flanges for ductile iron pipes and fittings are specified in BS 4772.
Note 2: Flanges for grey iron pipes and fittings are specified in BS 4622.

Temperature and pressure ratings are given in this standard and are design pressures and temperatures for the materials listed. The pressure ratings for materials are applicable to installations subject to moderate shock as may occur in well designed and efficiently operated boiler feed mains. Where a system may be subject to severe shock it is the responsibility of the purchaser to make suitable allowance when stating the design pressure.

The standard gives comprehensive dimension details in a series of tables and diagrams. The nominal sizes of the flanges are included in a series of ranges from 10 to 4000 mm. The nominal pressure range is from 2.5 mm to 400 bar (gauge) and a temperature range of $-100\,°C$ to $+550\,°C$.

Part 2: 1974 *Copper alloy and composite flanges*
This part specifies requirements for a range of copper alloy flanges of the following types with appropriate bolting:

1 Integral.
2 Slip-on boss for brazing or welding.
3 Slip-on composite for welding.
4 Welding neck composite.

Where slip-on flanges are required for attachment by soft soldering, reference should be made to BS 864.

A series of tables and diagrams detail the dimensions for the various flanges specified. The nominal size range is from 10 to 1800 mm and the nominal pressure range is from 6 to 40 bar and a temperature range of $-200\,°C$ to $+260\,°C$.

BS 4882: 1973 *Bolting for flanges and pressure containing purposes*

General requirements for the bolting for flanges and pressure containing purposes are given with details of dimensions for metric and inch series of bolting. A range of bolting materials are specified including those for nuts and bolts required for service with valves and flanges at elevated and sub-zero temperatures. The materials selected can be used in temperature conditions from $-250\,°C$ to $+750\,°C$. This standard is necessarily largely concerned with stud bolts because of their application to higher temperatures.

Pipe welding

The six specifications outlined in this section are companions and, apart from BS 2910, they consider in detail similar aspects in dealing with their various types of pipe welding. The following list shows the main common subjects covered by BS 1821, BS 2640, BS 2633, BS 4677, and BS 2971, which in turn is followed by a summary of the particular scope of each standard.
Common subjects are:

1 Parent metals.
2 Weld metal (filler rod).
3 Welding equipment.
4 Welding processes or techniques.
5 Assembly for welding.
6 Heat treatment.
7 Inspection.
8 Butt joints.
9 Socket welding.
10 Structural attachments.
11 Flanges.
12 Rectification of faulty welds.
13 Welding procedure approval.
14 Welder approval.

All include a wide range of tables and diagrams to support subjects covered in the text. Appendices detail classes of operating conditions, items for agreement between the contracting parties, and in some cases welding techniques.
Guidance for Class I and Class II operating conditions of pipework are set out in Table 48.

BS 2910: 1973 *Methods for radiographic examination of fusion welded circumferential butt joints in steel pipes*

Requirements are given for the radiographic examination of butt joints in steel pipes primarily in the range 5 mm up to and including 50 mm thick. Recommendations for the radiography of welds in pipes 3 to 10 mm thick when X-rays are not used are also given. Four methods are detailed.

Table 48 *Guidance for Class I and Class II operating conditions*

Service	Class I	Class II
Gases, steam but excluding refrigerants	Over 17 bar or over 220 °C	Up to and including 17 bar and up to and including 220 °C
Liquids excluding refrigerants	Over 17 bar and over 95 °C	Up to and including 17 bar and up to and including 200 °C
	Over 24 bar or over 200 °C	Over 17 bar up to and including 24 bar and up to and including 95 °C
Refrigerants	Over 17 bar or below $-20\,°C$	Up to and including 17 bar and down to and including $-20\,°C$

(From text, BS 1821: 1982 and BS 2640: 1982)

BS 1821: 1982 *Class I oxy-acetylene welding of ferritic steel pipework for carrying fluids*

This standard specifies requirements for both shop and site class I welding of joints in steel pipework of a thickness not exceeding 10 mm intended to carry fluids.

BS 2640: 1982 *Class II oxy-acetylene welding of carbon steel pipework for carrying fluids*

This standard specifies requirements for both shop and site class II welding of joints in steel pipework of a thickness not exceeding 10 mm intended to carry fluids.

BS 2633: 1973 *Class I arc welding of ferritic steel pipework for carrying fluids*

Requirements are specified for shop and site class I arc welding, using manual, automatic or semi-automatic welding processes or combinations of these, of joints in ferritic steel pipework intended to carry fluids. The following processes are dealt with:

1 Manual metal-arc welding.
2 MIG – welding.
3 Active-gas metal-arc welding.
4 TIG – welding.
5 Submerged – arc welding.
6 Flux cored or coated welding.

BS 4677: 1971 *Class I arc welding of austenitic stainless steel pipework for carrying fluids*

The standard covers shop and site class I arc welding, using manual, automatic or semi-automatic fusion welding processes of joints in austenitic stainless steel pipework. The following fusion welding process or combinations of processes as defined by BS 499 are dealt with. They are:

1 Metal-arc welding.
2 MIG – welding (inert gas metal-arc welding).
3 TIG – welding (inert gas tungsten-arc welding).
4 Submerged arc welding.
5 CO_2 flux welding.

BS 2971: 1977 *Class II arc welding of carbon steel pipework for carrying fluids*

Requirements are specified for shop and site Class II arc welding of joints in carbon steel pipework. The standard covers manual, automatic or semi-automatic arc welding or combinations of these processes, but it also allows joints to be made with an oxy-acetylene root run without a backing ring, by agreement between contracting parties.

Pipe couplings

BS 143 and 1256: 1968 *Malleable cast iron and cast copper alloy screwed pipe fittings for steam, air, water, gas and oil*

This revised standard incorporates the specific and common requirements of BS 143 and 1256. It specifies materials, tests and dimensions of plain and reinforced malleable cast iron and cast copper alloy screwed fittings suitable for working pressure up to 13.8 bar in the case of water and up to 10.35 bar in the case of steam air, gas and oil. The standard gives details of types of fittings and size ranges mostly in demand, but is equally applicable to basically similar types of fittings within the size range ⅛ to 6 in provided the standards requirements are complied with.

Two basic designs of fittings are covered by this standard as follows:

1 BS 143 design having BS 21 taper internal and taper external threads.
2 BS 1256 design having BS 21 parallel internal and parallel external threads.

Details of how to specify outlets and fittings with reinforcements are included. A variety of tees, elbows, crosses, bends, sockets, nipples, plugs and caps are dimensioned and illustrated with diagrams.

BS 864 *Capillary and compression tube fittings of copper and copper alloy*

This standard does not attempt the complete dimensional standardization of any of these types of fittings, since the variety in the designs and methods of production already established make any such attempt impracticable, and to do so would also restrict further development. It does, however, specify such dimensions and requirements as are essential to ensure satisfactory installation and performance. It is also complementary to BS 2051, which specifies fittings for use with tubes to BS 2871 Part 2.

Part 2: 1971 *Metric units*

■ AD (Reg. H1)

The following types of tube fittings of copper and copper alloy are defined and specified for use with BS 2871 Part 1, Tables X, Y and Z:

1 Capillary fittings in which the joint is made by the flow of solder by capillary action along the annular space between the outside of the tube and the inside of the socket of the fitting, the size of this annular space being dimensionally accurate within close limits.
2 Compression fittings Type A, in which the joint is made by the compression of a loose ring or sleeve, on the outside wall of the tube.
3 Compression fittings Type B, in which the joint is made by the compression of a manipulated portion of the tube at or near its end against the face of the body of the fitting or against a loose ring or sleeve within the fitting.

This part of the standard applies to the most commonly used types of fittings of nominal sizes ranging from 6 to 54 mm inclusive. Lightweight fittings for waste-pipe systems are not covered by this standard. However, this does not preclude the use of fittings to this standard for waste pipes where considered desirable.

The fittings when assembled with tubing complying with BS 2871 Part 1, Tables X, Y and Z and in accordance with the manufacturer's instructions are suitable for the working service pressures and temperatures as given in Table 49.

Some fittings are suitable for use at higher pressures and temperatures. For such applications the manufacturer of the fitting should be consulted.

In the general section requirements are specified for screwed

Table 49 *Maximum working temperatures and pressures*

Service temperature (°C)	Hydraulic pressure bar	
	Size 6 to 54 mm	Size 67 mm
30	16	10
65	10	6
110	6	4

(Table 1: BS 864: Part 2: 1971)

ends, materials, components made from castings, hot pressings or drawn tube, dimensions, fitting bore, and hydraulic tests for assembled joints. In subsequent sections the design and construction of capillary and compression fittings are covered in detail with the aid of diagrams and tables, some in appendices.

An appendix describes a method of specifying fittings.

Part 3: 1975 *Compression fittings for polyethylene pipes*
This part specifies compression fittings for use with polyethylene pipes complying with the requirements of BS 1972, BS 1973, BS 3284 and BS 3796 for cold water services, and applies to the most commonly used types of fittings for connecting pipes of nominal sizes ranging from ⅜ to 2 in inclusive. Two types of mechanical fittings with bodies and nuts of copper and copper alloy are specified:

1 Compression fittings Type A in which the joint is made by the compression of a loose ring or sleeve on to the outside wall of the pipe, with a suitable internal support.
2 Compression fittings Type B in which the joint is made by the compression of a manipulated portion of the pipe, at or near its end against the face of the body of the fitting or against a loose ring or sleeve within the fitting.

When assembled with specified pipe, and in accordance with the manufacturer's instructions, they should be suitable for the maximum working pressures and temperatures specified in the pipe standards, namely 12 bar at 20 °C.

The requirements specified in the general section of this part are covered by the same headings as in Part 2 except there is no hydraulic type test for assembled fittings. This is now dealt with in a separate section on test requirements.

The design and construction of Type A and B fittings are specified in detail for the nominal sizes ⅜, ½, ¾, 1, 1¼, 1½, and 2 in (9.5, 12.7, 19.1, 25.4, 31.8, 38.1 and 50.8 mm).

An appendix details a method of specifying fittings.

BS 2051 *Tube and pipe fittings for engineering purposes*

The standard does not attempt the complete dimensional standardization of any of the types of fittings covered. (See the preface notes of the complementary standard BS 864). The fittings dealt with in this standard are for use with tubes to BS 2871 Part 2.

Part 1: 1973 *Copper and copper alloy capillary and compression tube fittings for engineering purposes*
This part specifies fittings for use with tubing, for a wide range of engineering purposes. It applies to capillary fittings and compression fittings, Types A and B (see BS 864), in sizes ranging from 4 to 42 mm inclusive. The compression fittings are suitable for use at a pneumatic pressure range of 15 to 115 bar inclusive, a hydraulic pressure range of 30 to 210 bar, up to temperatures of 65 °C. Capillary fittings have a similar range but up to a temperature of 30 °C. Dimensions and design and construction of fittings are included along with porosity and hydraulic tests, and an appendix detailing the methods of designating unequal fittings.

Part 2: 1984 *Olive-type copper alloy compression tube fittings*
Requirements are detailed for tube fittings for use with copper,

copper alloy, aluminium alloy, and steel tubing. It applies to type A compression fittings defined in Part 1 and the fittings are intended for use with tubes also specified in Part 1 of this standard. Dimensions are detailed in eight tables with associated diagrams. Requirements for temperature and pressure are also included.

BS 4346   *Joints and fittings for use with unplasticized PVC pressure pipes*

Part 1: 1969   *Injection moulded unplasticized PVC fittings for solvent welding for use with pressure pipes, including potable water supply*

Requirements are specified for injection moulded uPVC pipe fittings for solvent welding to uPVC pipes conforming to Table 1 of BS 3505 and Table 1 of BS 3506. Socket dimensions from ⅜ to 12 in (9.5 to 304.8 mm) inclusive nominal size are given. Material, stress relief, resistance to sulphuric acid, opacity and hydraulic pressure tests are all dealt with.

Part 2: 1970   *Mechanical joints and fittings, principally of unplasticized PVC*

This part deals with mechanical joints and fittings of the push fit type for use with uPVC pressure pipes complying with BS 3505 and BS 3506. Joints complying with this standard may be either purpose-made sockets formed on pipes themselves, or detachable couplers and other fittings which may either be formed from pipe or injection moulded.

Requirements for stress relief, forming faults, resistance to sulphuric acid, opacity, effect on water, appearance, the elastomeric sealing component and joint dimensions are all specified.

Part 3: 1982   *Solvent cement*

The solvent cement for use with fittings specified in BS 3505, BS 3506, BS 5481 and Part 1 of this standard is covered. It may also be used for jointing products complying with BS 4514, BS 4576 and BS 4660. Details of material, shear strength, long-term pressure and film properties are specified.

BS 4368   *Carbon and stainless steel compression couplings for tubes*

Part 1: 1972   *Heavy series couplings*

Section one gives the general requirements relating to three types of compression couplings for steel tubes for general engineering purposes:

1 Compression couplings, Type A, in which the joint is made and the tube is held by the compression of a ring or ferrule, or part of the coupling on the outside surface of the tube.
2 Compression couplings, Type B, in which the joint is made and the tube is held by the compression of a manipulated portion of the tube at or near its end against the face of the coupling body, or against a loose ring or sleeve within the coupling.
3 Compression couplings, Type C, in which the joint is made by means of a sealing ring (and retaining washer if required) which does not hold the tube. A second ring is included to hold the tube.

Section two specifies detailed dimensions of a range of Type A couplings which, while complying with the requirements of Section one, are also, in general, dimensionally interchangeable with couplings manufactured to DIN 2353 and related German standards.

The couplings are for use with tubes with outside diameters from 6 to 50 mm inclusive. The pressure/temperature ratings for Type B and Type C couplings are subject to agreement between purchaser and manufacturer. Type A couplings in accordance with section two are suitable for use at working pressures given in Table 50, when used between −10 °C and 120 °C.

Table 50   *Tube couplings*

Designation (tube o.d.) mm	Nominal working pressure bar
6 to 20	400
25 to 38	250

(From text, BS 4368: Part 1: 1972)

In section two requirements are specified for a wide range of couplings, elbows, tees, crosses and adaptors.

Part 3: 1974   *Compression couplings for tubes*

Section one gives the general requirements relating to two types of compression couplings for steel tubes for general engineering purposes. The use of tubes of other materials should be subject to agreement between the purchaser and manufacturer.

The two types of compression couplings, Types A and B, are as defined in Part 1.

The couplings are for use with tubes with outside diameters from 6 to 42 mm inclusive. The pressure/temperature ratings are as follows. For temperatures between −10 °C and 120 °C, the minimum working pressures of the couplings, giving a safety factor of 4 under static test conditions at 20 °C, are as follows:

Type A couplings:
Tube sizes up to and including 15 mm   250 bar
Tube sizes from 18 mm up to and including 22 mm   160 bar
Tube sizes from 28 mm up to and including 42 mm   100 bar

Type B couplings:
Tube sizes up to and including 15 mm   250 bar
Tube sizes from 18 mm up to and including 42 mm   160 bar

For applications involving other working temperatures, the working pressure shall be subject to agreement between the purchaser and manufacturer.

In section two of this standard the overall dimensions of Types A and B couplings are specified. Further requirements are specified for a variety of coupling, elbow and tee assemblies and adaptors.

Part 4: 1984   *Type-test requirements*

Requirements for type testing of compression couplings specified in Parts 1 and 3 manufactured in carbon and steel, stainless steel and copper-based alloys.

BS 5114: 1975   *Performance requirements for joints and compression fittings for use with polyethylene pipes*

The performance of joints and compression fittings for use with polyethylene pipes not larger than nominal size 2 in is specified in this standard. The requirements are based on service with normal liquids under pressure. For aggressive liquids it is necessary to establish the resistance to the fluid, of the fitting, in particular the suitability of the sealing ring if fitted. The performance requirements detailed are:

1 Hydrostatic.
2 External pressure.
3 Resistance to pull out of assembled joint.
4 Effect on water.
5 Opacity.

Other requirements for appearance, sampling and marking are included.

BS 6087: 1981   *Flexible joints for cast iron drain pipes and fittings (BS 437) and for cast iron soil, waste and ventilating pipes and fittings (BS 416)*

This standard covers all types of loose couplings and spigot and socket flexible joints which are used as an alternative to caulked joints. Design requirements and types tests are specified. The test requirements relate to:

1 Deflection.
2 Straight draw.
3 Shear resistance.
4 Hydrostatic pressure.

Pipe jointing materials

BS 2815: 1973   *Compressed asbestos fibre jointing*

This specification sets out requirements for the composition, quality, finish, density, and thickness of compressed asbestos fibre jointing for general purposes. It specifies tests for compression, flexibility after accelerated ageing and stress relaxation. Two grades are provided for as follows:

1 Grade A, suitable for use with water, inert gases, inert liquids or steam up to 64 bar and 510 °C.
2 Grade B, suitable for use with water, inert gases, inert liquids or steam up to 16 bar and 230 °C.

Note: The terms 'inert gas' and 'inert liquid' are used to denote gases or liquids which under no circumstances will cause any chemical reaction with any part of the jointing or tend to cause any disintegration.

BS 4375: 1968   *Unsintered PTFE tape for thread sealing applications*

The purpose of this specification is to establish acceptance standards for unsintered polytetrafluoroethylene (PTFE) tape for general engineering applications for use at temperatures up to 250 °C. Requirements are specified for PTFE tape of preferred width of 12 mm and preferred thickness 0.075 mm for use as a pipe thread sealing material and in similar applications. However, material complying with this standard may not be suitable for certain critical applications, for example where contact with high concentrations of gaseous oxygen or liquid oxygen is involved.

BS 6209: 1982   *Solvent cement for non-pressure thermoplastics pipe systems*

Requirements are specified for solvent cement suitable for jointing waste systems complying with BS 5255 except those systems covered in sections four and five of BS 5255. However, this cement is also suitable for jointing products complying with BS 4514, BS 4576 and BS 4660 (see also BS 4346 Part 3).

BS 4865   *Dimensions of gaskets for pipe flanges to BS 4504*

Part 1: 1972   *Dimensions of non-metallic gaskets for pressures up to 64 bar*
This part specifies the dimensions of inside bolt circle and full face gaskets for use with flanges to BS 4504, BS 4622 and BS 4772, in a series of thirteen tables.

For pressures over 64 bar no gasket dimensions have been included since special consideration must be given to the choice of gasket material. This part refers to non-metallic gasket materials. For temperatures over 400 °C, manufacturers should be consulted for compressed asbestos fibre jointing, and over 80 °C for natural rubber and vegetable fibre materials.

Part 2: 1973   *Dimensions of metallic spiral-wound gaskets for pressures from 10 to 250 bar*
Dimensions are specified for gaskets suitable for use with flanges to BS 4504 of nominal size 10 to 900 mm, and design pressures of 10 to 250 bar.

BS 5292: 1980   *Jointing materials and compounds for installations using water, low-pressure steam or 1st, 2nd and 3rd family gases*

This standard deals with the following jointing materials and compounds:

1 Vulcanized fibre jointing.
2 Rubber reinforced jointing.
3 Corrugated metal joint rings.
4 Jointing compounds for use with water and 1st and 2nd family gases.
5 Jointing compound for use with 3rd family gases.
6 Anaerobic jointing compounds for use in appliances using 1st, 2nd and 3rd family gases.

These materials and compounds are for use in connection with screwed, flanged and flat seated joints for any one of the following applications:

1 Cold water up to a test pressure of 20 bar (gauge).
2 Hot water up to a static pressure of 3.5 bar (gauge) and a temperature of 100 °C.
3 1st (excluding coal-based) and 2nd family gases, Types A, B, and C.
4 Saturated steam up to working pressures of 2 bar (gauge).
5 3rd family gas.

Anaerobic compounds are specified for use with 1st, 2nd and 3rd family gases and are for use in appliances only.

In each case conditions of use are specified along with physical and chemical characteristics and where appropriate mechanical properties.

Pipe fixing accessories

BS 3974   *Pipe supports*

Part 1: 1974   *Pipe hangers, slides and roller type supports*
This part of the standard specifies requirements for the design (including dimensions) and manufacture of components for pipe hangers, slides and roller type supports for uninsulated and insulated steel and cast iron pipes of nominal size 15 to 600 mm inclusive, used for transporting fluids within the temperature range −20 °C to +470 °C. Recommendations on design considerations, data, formulae for pipework calculations, methods of fixing and illustrations of typical pipe support assemblies are given in the appendices.

Pipe hanger components are dealt with in section four. A pipe hanger is an assembly comprising:

1 A pipe clip or one piece strap complete with load and clip bolts.
2 A sling rod having a sling eye at the lower end and a spherical washer and nuts at the top end.

Pipe clips are detailed for the full range of sizes and temperatures given above and are fully illustrated and dimensioned. For pipes up to and including 32 mm nominal size and loads up to 70 kgf, a one piece strap may be used up to maximum temperature of 100 °C.

Pipe clips are detailed in this standard for three temperature ranges designated as Range A: −20 °C to 100 °C, Range B: −20 °C to 400 °C and Range C: above 400 °C to 470 °C. Each range is divided into two load carrying series, light and heavy.

Pipe clips have been designed on the basis that they are in direct contact with the pipe but not tightened on to the pipe. To achieve this, distance pieces are mandatory on clips in Ranges B and C but are optional on Range A.

Stress levels in the three ranges are specified and requirements for manufacture and materials are given. Details are also provided for clip and load bolts and distance pieces.

Four types of eye are detailed, all of which are suitable for the temperature range specified above.

The length of sling rods and the extent to which they are threaded at the top shall be such as to suit the individual pipe hanger requirements. The top of each sling rod shall be fitted with two nuts and a spherical washer. Turnbuckles may be used for joining lengths of sling rod together and to provide a convenient method of adjusting the length of the sling rod.

Where the sling rods and sling rod eyes are used with pipe clips in Ranges A, B and C, the safe working load of the complete hanger shall be that given for the pipe clip. Where the sling rods with hot formed eyes are used with pipe clips in Ranges A, B and C, the safe working load of the complete hanger shall be that given for the hot formed eye.

Manufacture and materials for sling rods are specified, with fully dimensioned drawn details.

Section five covers U-bolts, hook bolts and overstraps, which are all illustrated and dimensioned, and section six specifies slider type supports including dimensions. Roller type supports are specified in section seven with details of dimensions and limitations.

Appendices cover design considerations, data and formulae for pipework calculations, recommendations on methods of fixing and (26) illustrations of typical pipe support assemblies.

Part 2: 1978 *Pipe clamps, cages, cantilivers and attachments to beams*

This part gives requirements for the manufacture of further components used in connection with pipe supports. It also gives guidance on design data and formulae for pipe support calculations and methods of fixing in four appendices. This part specifies dimensions of pipe support components and assemblies and is an extension of Part 1. Temperature conditions are specified for certain components in the standard.

Definitions and materials are covered in sections three and four respectively. Section five deals with beam clips and provides full dimensions and loads.

Beam welding attachments are specified in section six. Full dimensions are provided in the standard, with illustrations.

Section seven covers spring cages and sling rod cages and their attachments to universal beams.

Dee shackles are specified in section eight and again dimensions and illustrations are included in the standard.

Section nine tables dimensions for riser pipe clamps of nominal sizes 100 to 600 mm and also gives the maximum permissible load and appropriate temperatures.

Section ten covers support feet indicating how they are constructed. Maximum loads are specified and dimensions for various types of support.

Section eleven gives a number of examples of pipeline anchors and guides and gives guidance on their uses and design. Section twelve deals with the welding of support components and section thirteen with supplementary steelwork.

Part 3: 1980 *Large bore, high temperature, marine and other applications*

Part 3 of this standard specifies design requirements and dimensions for the manufacture of pipe support components that are generally outside the scope of Parts 1 and 2. These are:

1 Carbon steel pipe clips, overstraps and U-bolts for large diameter pipes.
2 Alloy steel pipe clips, U-straps and riser clamps.
3 Copper alloy overstraps and hookstraps.

The overall pipe nominal size ranges is from 10 to 1200 mm for pipeline fluid temperature in the range −196 °C to 570 °C according to type and material.

The pipe support components specified provide for the supporting of pipes manufactured from carbon and alloy steels, cast iron, ductile iron and grey iron spun pipes and copper and copper alloys.

Section one provides design data, material specifications and manufacturing requirements for pipe support components and section two provides dimensional details and safe working loads (where applicable) for pipe support components on a general application basis.

Section three contains additional requirements or restrictions relating to the application to ships' installations of pipe supports detailed in section two. This includes guidance notes, component details, marine range of working temperatures, safe working loads and material specifications not included in Part 1 and elsewhere in this part.

Requirements are specified in sections one and two for pipe support design, temperature ranges for pipe supports, materials, manufacture and heat treatment, protection, pipe clip design data, summary of pipe support components and marking.

Thermal insulation of services

Regulation L4 of The Building Regulations 1985 applies

BS 3958 *Thermal insulation materials*

Part 1: 1982 *Magnesia preformed insulation*
Requirements are specified for preformed insulation slabs, lags and pipe sections, generally suitable for use up to about 315 °C. They cover the composition, sampling and testing, chemical constituents and physical properties, marking and identification. The particular requirements for dimensions can be summarized as follows:

1 *Flat slabs*
  Length: 914 mm
  Width: 150 to 305 mm
  Thickness: 25 to 100 mm
2 *Pipe sections*
  Length: 914 mm
  Diameter: to fit standard pipes of external diameter up to 329 mm
  Thickness: 25 to 75 mm
3 *Bevelled lags*
  Length: 914 mm
  Major width: 75 to 150 mm
  Thickness: 25 to 100 mm
4 *Radius and bevelled lags (curved lags)*
  Length: 914 mm
  Width of outer curved surface: approximately 140 to 170 mm

Part 2: 1982 *Calcium silicate preformed insulation*
This part deals with the composition, moisture content and physical and chemical requirements for two types of calcium silicate preformed insulation.

Type I: slabs radiused and bevelled lags and pipe sections for use at temperatures up to 650 °C or such higher temperatures recommended by the manufacturer.
Type II: slabs and flat bevelled lags for use up to 950 °C or at higher temperatures recommended by the manufacturer.

The dimensions for the standard shapes and sizes are as follows:

1 *Flat slabs*: Types I and II
  Length: 600 to 1000 mm
  Width: 150 to 1000 mm
  Thickness: 25 to 100 mm
2 *Pipe sections*: Type I only
  Length: 914 mm
  Diameter: to fit standard mild steel pipes of external diameters up to 329 mm
  Wall thickness: 25 to 75 mm
3 *Flat bevelled lags*: Types I and II
  Length: 600 to 1000 mm
  Major width: 150 to 166 mm
  Thickness: 25 to 100 mm
4 *Radiused and bevelled lags*: Type I only
  Length: 914 mm
  Width of outer curve: approximately 140 to 170 mm
  Thickness: 25 to 100 mm

Part 3: 1967 *Metal mesh faced mineral wool mats and mattresses*

Mineral wool mats and mattresses for thermal insulation purposes, faced on one or both sides with flexible metal mesh are specified with regard to composition, metal facings and ties, various physical properties, fire classification and alkalinity and corrosive attack.

Standard units are supplied at nominal thicknesses between 25 and 100 mm, in increments of 12.5 mm, with the following approximate dimensions:

Lengths: 1850, 2450 and 2750 mm
Width: 900 mm when faced with woven wire mesh or 600 mm when faced with expanded metal

Part 4: 1982 *Bonded preformed man-made mineral fibre pipe sections*

Requirements are given for the composition, moisture content, physical and chemical characteristics of bonded preformed pipe sections generally for use at elevated temperatures. Ceramic fibres are excluded. The sections are cylindrical or semi-cylindrical. Very large pipe diameters may be catered for by multi-segmental sections. The standard size range is as follows:

Length: 0.5 to 1.2 m
Diameter: to fit standard pipes of external diameter up to 610 mm
Thickness: 19 to 120 mm

The sections may be finished in cotton scrim, cotton canvas, aluminium foil laminate or polyisobutylene sheet.

Part 5: 1969 *Bonded mineral wool slabs (for use at temperatures above 50 °C)*

The products referred to in this part are divided into four groups for use for hot face temperatures up to 230 °C (Group 1A and Group 1B), 540 °C (Group 2) and 800 °C (Group 3) respectively. These slabs do not apply to refrigeration or structural insulation. Requirements are specified for composition, finish, physical properties, fire classification, alkalinity and corrosive attack.

The preferred nominal sizes are:

Length and width (mm)	*Thicknesses* (mm)
1220 × 1220	
1220 × 914	25, 38 or 50
1220 × 610	
914 × 914	
914 × 610	

Part 6: 1972 (1980) *Finishing materials; hard setting composition, self-setting cement and gypsum plaster*

Finishing materials are specified which are prepared for use by mixing with water for application to insulating materials after they have been applied at site to the plant or piping systems. Some of these finishing materials are used for services at temperatures below ambient in which case a vapour barrier is necessary. The materials are normally supplied as dry powders which, when mixed with water in suitable proportions, are applied in plastic form and dried or set in place to form a hard, smooth surface. They are classified into three main types.

1 Hard-setting compositions which sets by the removal of water on heating. Wet covering capacity lies between 50 and 105 m² per 1000 kg at 13 mm thickness.
2 Self-setting cement sets without the application of heat and has a wet covering capacity range of 40 and 95 m² per 1000 kg at 13 mm thickness.
3 Gypsum plaster composition sets without the application of heat and has a wet covering capacity range of 45 and 60 m² per 1000 kg at 13 mm thickness.

The standard specifies requirements for chemical and physical properties, packaging and marking.

BS 5970: 1981 *Code of practice for thermal insulation of pipework and equipment (in the temperature range −100 °C to +870 °C)*

The code explains the basic principles that should be followed in selecting the most suitable insulating systems for specific requirements. It is not practicable to deal with every possible combination of insulating material and finish, so general principles only are indicated. For clarity, the subject has been dealt with in eight main sections covering general considerations, selection of insulating materials and systems, site considerations, methods of applications, finishes, inspection, testing and maintenance, guarantees and design considerations.

Owing to the complexity of the thermal insulation industry and to the wide variation in site conditions, it has been difficult to avoid referring to matters that may be considered to be the subject of contractual arrangement rather than of technical importance; brief mention only has been made of such matters to ensure that they are given appropriate consideration.

The guiding principle in the preparation of this standard has been to give a guide to good current practice while indicating the basic principles by which new materials can be assessed and adapted for use under the widely differing conditions that so often challenge the skill of the insulation contractor.

Several British Standards for the use of thermal insulating materials are available, and these give recommended methods for selecting suitable thicknesses based on a knowledge of the manufacturer's declared value for thermal conductivity at the appropriate temperature of use. They do not attempt to indicate the methods by which appropriate materials may be selected, or by which they may be applied on site. Other standards available, or in course of preparation, deal with methods of test and with the characteristic properties of individual materials.

A series of nine tables and 44 figures, including a number of graphs, are provided in this code supporting and expanding the various aspects considered. Excluded from this standard is the structural insulation of buildings and cold stores, refractory linings in plant, fire-proofing structures, airborne installations, and all external underground mains. However, it may be found to be generally applicable to the insulation of road and rail transport vehicles and of some assistance in marine insulation.

CP 99: 1972 *Frost precautions for water services*

This code is intended to assemble in one publication the essential requirements of good practice and it is published for the guidance of all concerned with the design, construction and maintenance of buildings and other installations in which water services are incorporated.

The general principles involved in protecting water service from frost are outlined and recommendations are given on the location of water pipes and fittings, their protection and insulation.

See also s 51 of the *Public Health Act, 1936*.

BS 5422: 1977 *The use of thermal insulating materials*

This standard is intended to be comprehensive for all temperatures from −40 °C to +650 °C. It contains six sections. Sections one and two are of general application and they include requirements that are common to the remaining sections, which relate to installations for refrigeration, for chilled and cold water supplies, central heating, air conditioning, and domestic hot and cold water supplies, and for process pipework and associated equipment respectively. It does not deal with pipes which are embedded underground or in unventilated ducts, nor does it refer to the insulation of building structures. All the nomenclature is based on the use of SI units except Appendix K, which gives certain units in imperial terms to follow current industrial practice.

For refrigeration and chilled or cold water systems, tables are provided to show the minimum thicknesses that are necessary to avoid condensation of atmosphere moisture on the vapour barrier, or on the external surface of the insulation under specific conditions. Methods of calculation are provided for conditions other than these. Reference is made to cold water systems in both sections four and five and the tables relating to these sections show minimum thicknesses of differing magnitude for protection against freezing. This is because section four covers industrial applications where the conditions of exposure are likely to be severe and the consequences of ice formation within the system relatively serious, whereas section five relates to domestic installations where the water normally is static for shorter periods. Methods of calculation for conditions other than those appropriate to the tables are given in the appendices.

For central heating installations it is preferred that economic thickness shall be applied. However, if it is not convenient to do this then reference should be made to the tables in section five which are based on calculations for intermittent working, that is for an evaluation period of 20,000 working hours (five years at 4000 hours per year). They do not represent uniform heat losses. The thicknesses for domestic hot water services and air conditioning ducts are based on an evaluation period of 40,000 working hours (five years at 8000 hours per year) and again, they do not represent uniform heat losses.

Many users of thermal insulation for process pipework and equipment will wish to calculate thicknesses which are appropriate for their specific requirements, and methods for doing this are given in the appendices. If the purchaser does not wish to indicate any special thickness details, then a table in section six should be used. However, as the thicknesses in this table do not correspond to uniform heat losses, another table shows the magnitude of the heat loss which will result from the application of the indicated thickness, for the size of pipe, the temperature of use, and the thermal conductivity shown.

Other methods of calculation are provided in the appendices so that the correct thicknesses can be ascertained for special requirements, for example for a specified temperature at the point of delivery, etc.

Provision has been made for further revision of the tables of recommended thicknesses, in respect of the conservation of heat, should circumstances render this necessary.

The standard relates to the use of thermal insulating materials within the temperature range $-40\,°C$ to $+650\,°C$. It is restricted to surfaces that do not exhibit appreciable change in temperature as a result of the application of such materials, thus it refers particularly to insulation for process plant, tanks, ducts and pipelines, as well as to the metallic surfaces of boilers and ancillary plant as used for heating fluids or for steam-raising.

Guidance is given for the selection of correct thicknesses and for making the relevant calculation but, for the choice of any particular type of insulating material or for suitable methods of application, reference should be made to CP 3005.

Throughout this standard, unless otherwise stated, reference to the temperature of the surface to be insulated shall be understood to mean the temperature of the fluid inside the pipe, duct or vessel.

Section one contains information which is of general application for the complete standard, that is, scope, definitions and details which are required to permit correct assessment of the work.

Section two includes reference to physical characteristics of general import, thermal conductivity, and to tests for thermal conductivity, thickness, uniformity and for bulk density.

Section three relates to thermal insulation for pipes, ducts, tanks and vessels containing fluid which is maintained at temperatures between 0 and $-40\,°C$. Reference to vapour barriers is also included. It does not relate to particular requirements for refrigeration plant, for insulated compartments, or for non-metallic containment structures.

Section four refers especially to insulation for industrial service, with special application to pipes, tanks and vessels which are used for the conveyance or containment of chilled water (0 to 5 °C) or cold water (normally above 10 °C). Reference to vapour barriers is included. In particular it deals with the use of insulation to prevent freezing of water in pipes, tanks and fittings, and to prevent the condensation of atmospheric moisture on their surfaces.

Section five considers thermal insulation applications for central heating, air conditioning, mechanical ventilation, and hot and cold water supply installations, mainly within buildings, but it can be used for such associated ducts and piping as may be located outside the buildings in the open air.

Reference is made to materials for application to:

1 Direct-fired boilers, calorifiers, hot water cylinders, storage tanks, ducts, pipes and fittings for working temperatures up to but not exceeding 200 °C.
2 Storage vessels, pipes and fittings for cold water supply installations (but excluding application for refrigeration work) and for the purpose of protection against condensation and freezing (see CP 99 and CP 3005).

Section six outlines the use of thermal insulating materials on process pipework and equipment for service temperatures between ambient and 650 °C, but it does not apply to vessels and conveyance systems which are lined internally with protective refractory or insulating material, and it does not refer to pipes which are buried directly in the ground or are contained in unventilated ducts. Tables of recommended thicknesses are given, together with the corresponding heat losses and methods for calculation of thicknesses in special cases are provided.

BS 5241: 1975   *Rigid urethane foam when dispensed or sprayed on a construction site*

This standard specifies requirements for rigid urethane foam which is produced by dispensing or by spraying at the point of final use. Typical examples are the insulation of chemical storage tanks, some specialized buildings and complex pipework. The principal factors are that neither customer nor contractor can have complete control over ambient conditions during the work and that, in general, a substantial contract is involved. It includes a procedure for type approval intended to overcome difficulties which arise during the completion of a contract, in determining the properties of rigid urethane foam when dispensed or sprayed on a construction site. The following main aspects are considered: composition of the foam, appearance, odour, type approval of foam system, quality assurance of dispensed and sprayed foam and a set of requirements the foam must comply with when tested by methods specified in this standard.

The appendices detail burning properties, measurement of foam density and tests for tensile adhesion strength.

BS 5608:   *Preformed rigid urethane and isocyanurate foams for thermal insulation of pipework and equipment*

Requirements are specified for preformed rigid urethane (PUR) and isocyanurate (PIR) foams, and the standard applies to cut, moulded or continuously formed pipe sections and radiused and bevelled lags or slabs. The nominal temperature range for which the insulation material is suitable is $-180\,°C$ to $+140\,°C$.

The following classifications are stated:

PUR 1 and PIR 1 foams: suitable for general use.
PUR 2 and PIR 2 foams: suitable for use where there is a requirement for greater resistance to compressive forces.

The standard includes general requirements for pipe sections, radiused and bevelled lags, moulded components and colour identification. Details are also given of dimensions, composition, condition and appearance, odour, thermal conductivity, compressive strength, closed cell content, burn characteristics and water vapour transmission. Appendices consider the burning properties of the foams and gives recommendations regarding their use and offer some useful notes for designers.

BS 5615: 1985 *Insulating jackets for domestic hot water storage cylinders*

■ AD (Reg. L5)

The standard specifies insulating jackets for use with hot water storage cylinders which comply with the dimensional requirements of BS 699 or BS 1566. Included is a method of test for the thermal performance of a cylinder jacket.

Insulation of combination vessels and factory insulated cylinders are not within the scope of this standard. Requirements for the materials and the design and manufacture of the jackets are specified.

DD 41: 1982 *Methods of test for the determination of composition and physical properties of ceramic fibres for high temperature insulation*

Methods of measurement and determination for a range of ceramic fibre products for use as heat insulating materials are described. Four types of fibre are considered:

1 Type 1000 silica.
2 Type 1250 alumino-silicate.
3 Type 1400 alumino-silicate.
4 Type 1600 polycrystalline alumina.

The number quoted is the maximum operating temperature in °C that the particular fibre is suitable for. The draft includes a table showing the various forms in which the fibre may be produced.

(6–) Services, mainly electrical

(61) Electrical supply

(62) Power

This section covers the whole range of equipment, components and accessories for electrical installations in not only the normal type of domestic and commercial development but also for those in specialized situations. It also includes a number of codes giving guidance on installation practice.

In general the standards are in parallel with and complementary to the provision of the *Regulation for Electrical Installations* published by the Institution of Electrical Engineers with which installations will normally comply.

The analysis of this section may be conveniently considered within the following elemental subdivisions:

1 Equipment and control gear.
2 Cables and cords.
3 Cable enclosures.
4 Accessories.

The standards relating to the various elements comprised in an electrical installation generally prescribe the basic dimensional and other design criteria together with the associated tests to ensure subsequent satisfactory functional performance, safety and durability in normal and, in some cases, stipulated operating conditions. The standards nonetheless permit considerable latitude beyond their provisions, as is indicated by the extensive range of manufactured products complying wholly or predominantly with the same standard.

An important standard relating to the whole of this section is BS 3939. Part 11: 1985 *Architectural and topographical installation plans and diagrams*
This gives graphical symbols, with definitions, for use on electrical, architectural and topographical plans and diagrams.

See also PD 7303: 1981 *Electrical and electronic graphical symbols for schools and colleges*, which includes a wall chart. The Building Regulations 1985 refer to the Electrical Supply Regulations 1937, regulation 22, as an Approved Document.

BS 6396: 1983 *Code of practice for electrical systems in office furniture and office screens*

Guidance is given for both permanent electrical systems to be built in during manufacture and also on the provision of facilities for electrical systems to be added after purchase.

Equipment and control gear

BS 5486: *Factory built assemblies of switchgear and control-gear for voltages up to and including 1000 V a.c. and 1200 V d.c.*

This multi-part standard is concerned with factory-built assemblies of low voltage switchgear and controlgear, the rated voltage of which does not exceed 1000 V a.c. at frequencies 1000 Hz or 1200 V d.c. It also covers assemblies for operation in special service conditions as well as domestic (household) applications.

The provisions relate to the assembly of the switchgear; the individual components and devices comprised in the assembly are the subject of other British Standards.

The various types of factory-built assembly (FBA) defined in Part 1: 1977 are:

Open type FBA: consisting of a supporting structure for the electrical equipment, the live parts of which are accessible.
Dead front FBA: similar to the open type FBA but with a front covering which ensures protection against contact with live parts from the front but not from the other side.

Enclosed FBA: enclosed on all sides with the possible exception of the mounting surface and providing a good degree of protection against contact with live parts.

Cubicle type FBA: an enclosed FBA principally of the floor-standing type which may comprise several sections, sub-sections or components.

Multi-cuble type FBA: a combination of a number of mechanically joined cubicles.

Desk type FBA: an enclosed FBA with a horizontal or inclined control panel or a combination of both.

Box type FBA: an enclosed FBA principally intended to be mounted on a vertical plane – the normal type of small individual units.

Multi-box type FBA: a combination of boxes mechanically joined together with or without a common supporting frame, the electrical connections passing between two adjacent boxes through openings in adjoining faces.

In addition, Part 1 covers in considerable detail the general provisions applicable to all assemblies with respect to:

1 The service conditions in which the assemblies are intended for use.
2 Design and construction covering the mechanical, electrical and safety aspects.
3 Test specifications.

The several other parts of this standard are concerned with the particular requirements for specific assemblies.

Part 2 is concerned with busbar trunking systems (busbars) and is covered in more detail in the section on cable enclosures.

Fuseboards
Part 11: 1979
This part is concerned with the particular requirements for fuseboards for use in systems sharing a rated current not exceeding 200 A for individual outgoing circuits. Consumers' control units which are used for the control and distribution of single phase and neutral installations not exceeding 250 V a.c. and with a maximum load of 100 A are excluded from this part, being the subject of the requirements of Part 13.

Definitions of importance in this part are:

Fuseboard (distribution boards): an enclosure containing busbars with fuses for the purpose of protecting, controlling or connecting more than one outgoing circuit fed from one or more incoming circuits.

Fuseway: within an outgoing unit, it is each pole, in which the protective device is a fuse, that is provided for the connection of a pole on an outgoing circuit.

Pole of a fuseboard: a busbar and associated fuseway connected to a pole of a fuseboard and also the number of outgoing circuits that may be connected.

Number of fuseways per pole: the number of fuseways provided per pole of a fuseboard and also the number of outgoing circuits that may be connected.

The requirements of this part include the provision of one or more nameplates which state the name of the manufacturer, the designation or reference number of the fuseboard, and BS 5486 Part 11. Other information which should be either on the nameplate or obtainable from the manufacturer's list or catalogue is also stipulated.

The limiting dimensions of the enclosures related to a standard design are provided in a table in the standard, the dimensions depending upon the following factors:

1 The number of fuseways.
2 The rating in being the sum of the rated currents of the fuseways per pole multiplied by a diversity factor which takes into account the number of fuseways and the maximum rated current of the outgoing circuit.

3 The arrangement of the poles (that is, the type of electrical system) SP & N, DP, TP, and TP & N.

Recommendations are also made on the preferred numbers and rating of outgoing circuits per pole for each type of fuseboard for the various different arrangements of the poles, depending upon the maximum current ratings of the fuseways per pole. Details are also given for the electrical provisions within the fuseboards and of the test specifications with which the fuseboards must comply.

Miniature circuit-breaker boards
Part 12: 1979
This part is concerned with the particular requirements for miniature circuit breaker boards for use in a.c. systems having a rated current not exceeding 200 A per phase for incoming circuits and 100 A for individual outgoing circuits and where the nominal voltage to each class does not exceed 250 V. As with Part 11, consumers' control units are excluded from this part.

Definitions of importance in this part are: .

Miniature circuit-breaker board (miniature circuit-breaker distribution boards or m.c.b. boards): an enclosure containing busbars and miniature circuit-breakers for the purpose of protecting, controlling or connecting more than one outgoing circuit and which may include an integral isolating switch.

m.c.b. board Type A: an m.c.b. board designed to incorporate both multi-pole and single pole m.c.b.

Miniature air-break circuit-breaker: a compact mechanical device for making and breaking a circuit both in normal conditions (as with a switch) and in abnormal conditions such as those of overcurrent and short-circuit.

The definitions of m.c.b.-way, pole of an m.c.b. board and number of m.c.b. ways per pole are similar to those for fuseboards in Part 11.

Nameplates are required to be attached to the board giving similar information to that stipulated in Part 11 for fuseboards.

The rated current of a miniature circuit-breaker board is that of the incoming circuit. No diversity factor is applied to the board because of the flexibility of selection of rated currents of outgoing circuits and their m.c.b.s. namely 5 (or 6), 10, 15 (or 16), 20, 25, 30 (or 32), 40, 45, 50, 60 (or 63), 80 and 100 A.

The following systems of distribution are preferred:

1 Single pole and neutral.
2 Single pole and switched neutral.
3 Double pole and neutral.
4 Double pole and switched neutral.
5 Triple pole and neutral.
6 Triple pole and switched neutral.

Detailed recommendations are also made with respect to the electrical provisions within the m.c.b. boards and to the test specifications with which the boards must comply.

Consumer units (consumer control units)
Part 13: 1979
This part is concerned with the particular requirements for control units such as are installed in consumers' premises, for the control and distribution of electrical energy principally in domestic consumers' premises, incorporating manual means of double pole isolation on the incoming circuits and on assembly of one or more of the following: fuses, m.c.b.s, or protective devices (residual current or fault voltage-operated).

Units are connected to common busbar(s) with associated multi-terminal neutral bar(s) and multi-terminal protective conductor bar(s).

The means of isolation from the supply may be provided by a switch, an m.c.b. or a protective device (residual current or fault voltage-operated).

Nameplates giving similar information to that required for fuseboards in Part 11 and m.c.b. boards in Part 12 are required.

The rated current of the consumer unit is stated by the manufacturer, taking into consideration the ratings of the components comprised in the assembly. No diversity factor is applied to those units because of the flexibility of selection of outgoing protective devices.

The recommendations include detailed information relating to the mechanical design, electrical components and provisions and test specifications with which the units must comply.

BS 6423: 1983 *Code of practice for maintenance of electrical switchgear and controlgear for voltages up to and including 650 V*

Recommendations representing good practice are set out in this code to provide guidance on those matters which technical knowledge and experience has shown to be important in keeping equipment in an acceptable condition. It is a revision of those clauses in BS 5405: 1976 covering low-voltage apparatus.

The code is intended for use by administrative personnel as well as those actually carrying out the maintenance work. Procedures for the maintenance of the principal components of equipment are included and guidance is given concerning replaceable parts. Safety precautions and procedures for the safe isolation of systems are important parts of this code.

BS 5405: 1976 *Code of practice for the maintenance of electrical switchgear for voltages up to and including 145 kV*

This code of practice covers the whole range of provisions for good maintenance practice for switchgear not exceeding 145 kV, embracing the safety of personnel, frequency of testing and details of the tests to be applied. Although switchgear for voltages exceeding 145 kV may differ significantly from that operating at lower voltages with consequent differences in maintenance and testing procedures, the recommendations of the code with respect to the safety of personnel remain for the most part applicable. Special requirements for the maintenance of flameproof switchgear in respect of safety measures and the maintenance of the flameproof enclosures are excluded from this code. However, other aspects of maintenance covered in the code are appropriate to flameproof switchgear.

BS 5602: 1978 *Code of practice for the abatement of radio interference from overhead power lines*

Information is provided on the factors involved in protecting radio and television broadcasting from interference and may be used when considering means of avoidance or abatement.

BS 951: 1948 *Earthing clamps*

The scope of this standard covers the size ranges, the performance and certain mechanical features of metal clamps intended to be used to provide an appropriate earth continuity conductor and for the purpose of connecting the earthing lead but only for the following duties:

1 To provide a measure of safety for the purpose of returning to the source of supply such leakage current as may flow, or result from a failure of insulation.
2 To provide a path for radio-frequency currents and those from radio interference suppression devices.

The provisions were originally devised to conform with the thirteenth edition of the Regulations for the Electrical Equipment of Buildings and by the Institution of Electrical Engineers. They do not relate to the terminology or practice in the fifteenth edition. Similarly, the dimensions and cables specified in the various tables are in imperial units. Although pipes are no longer used for earthing, the clamps covered by the standard may be used in conjunction with earthing to the metal sheathing of electric cables and with the bonding of pipework.

BS 5345 *Code of practice for the selection, installation and maintenance of electrical apparatus for use in potentially explosive atmospheres (other than mining applications or explosive processing and manufacture)*

This code of practice substantially supersedes CP 1003 and is complementary to BS 5486, which is concerned with the design, construction and testing of apparatus for use in potentially explosive areas.

The recommendations of this code are intended to ensure electrical safety throughout the life of an installation, by one of two methods of installation:

1 By locating the apparatus outside hazardous areas.
2 By ensuring that the apparatus is designed, installed and maintained in accordance with measures recommended for the area in which the apparatus is located.

This code describes the basic safety features of the various types of protection for various operational conditions and recommends the selection, installation and maintenance procedures that should be adopted to ensure the safe use of electrical apparatus in the appropriate hazardous areas.

Part 1: 1976 covers the basic requirements applicable to all situations. Subsequent parts are concerned with the specific types of protection.

Hazardous areas are classified by zones. These zones classifications recognize the differing degrees of probability with which explosive (flammable) concentrations of flammable gas or vapour may arise in installations in terms of both the frequency of occurrence and the probable duration of existence on each occasion. The classifications are as follows:

Zone 0: in which an explosive gas-air mixture is continuously present, or present for long periods.
Zone 1: in which an explosive gas-air mixture is likely to occur in normal operation.
Zone 2: in which an explosive gas-air mixture is not likely to occur in normal operation, and if it occurs it will exist only for a short time.

Areas which are not within these zone classifications are non-hazardous areas for the purposes of this code. Part 2 of this code covers fully the detailed considerations taken into account in determining the appropriate zone classification.

Section two of Part 1 lists the criteria for selection of electrical apparatus, namely:

1 The type of protection required in relation to the zonal classification of the hazardous area in which it will operate.
2 The temperature classification of the apparatus in relation to the ignition temperature of the gases and vapours involved.
3 The apparatus subgroup (where applicable) in relation to the relevant properties of the gases and vapours involved.
4 The apparatus construction and enclosure in relation to the environmental conditions.

Selection of the appropriate type of protection is achieved with regard to the zone of classification.

This part of the code covers in detail general installation requirements including earthing isolation and airing systems, inspection, maintenance and testing, and the properties of flammable liquids, vapours and gases which are listed.

Part 3 and subsequent parts are concerned with the recommendations for the specific installation and maintenance requirements for electrical apparatus with particular types of protection. Each part has sections covering the general principles, selection, installation requirements, inspection, maintenance and testing of the apparatus with the several types of protection.

The parts are as follows:

Part 3: 1979 *Apparatus with type of protection 'd', flameproof enclosure* (of BS 5501 Part 5).

Part 4: 1977 *Apparatus with type of protection 'i', intrinsically safe apparatus and systems* (of BS 5501 Parts 7 and 9).

Part 5: 1983 *Installation and maintenance requirements for electrical apparatus protected by pressurization including continuous dilution and for pressurized rooms*. Provides guidance on the use of electrical apparatus which is protected by pressurization or continuous dilution to prevent any explosive gas atmosphere coming into contact with the electrical apparatus. Supersedes CP 1003 which is being retained to provide a reference guide for existing plants installed according to Parts 1, 2 and 3.

Part 6: 1978 *Apparatus with type of protection 'e', increased safety* (of BS 5501 Part 6).

Part 7: 1979 *Apparatus with type of protection N.*

Part 8: 1980 *Apparatus with type of protection 's', special protection.*

BS 6133: 1982   *Code of practice for safe operation of lead-acid stationary cells and batteries*

The code covers the safety and health aspects associated with the handling, usage and maintenance of lead cells and batteries.

BS 5501   *Electrical apparatus for potentially explosive atmospheres*

This is a comprehensive European standard which covers the requirements for the construction and testing of electrical apparatus for use in potentially explosive atmospheres. Part 1: 1977 gives the general provisions which are supplemented by the subsequent parts which relate to specific types of protection required for different operating conditions.

A number of relevant definitions are worth noting in the context of this standard:

Electrical apparatus: all items applied as a whole or in part for the utilization of electrical energy. These include, among others, items for the generation, transmission, distribution, storage, measurement, regulation, conversion and consumption of electrical energy.

Explosive atmosphere: a mixture of air, under atmospheric conditions of flammable substances in the form of gas, vapour, or mist, in such properties that it can be exploded by excessive temperature, arcs or sparks (that danger is a real one).

Potentially explosive atmosphere: an atmosphere which could become explosive (the danger is merely potential).

Type of protection: the measures applied in the construction of electrical apparatus to prevent ignition of the surrounding explosive atmosphere by such apparatus. The type of protection depends upon the types of gases and vapours which might be experienced in normal operation.

Electrical apparatus for potentially explosive atmospheres may be classified in two groups.

Group 1: electrical apparatus for mines susceptible to fire damp.

Group 2: electrical apparatus for places with a potentially explosive atmosphere other than those in Group 1. The apparatus in this group is subdivided according to the potentially explosive atmosphere. A list of the chemical compounds comprised in each of the subdivisions is provided in an annex to Part 1.

Considerable information is given in Part 1 with respect to the operating conditions, construction, components, design, earthing, testing and marking of the apparatus.

The subsequent parts are concerned with the specific requirement for the construction and testing of particular apparatus with different types of protection as follows:

Part 2: 1977: oil-immersed electrical apparatus, type of protection 'o' in which the protection is provided by the immersion in oil of the apparatus or parts of the apparatus in such a way that an explosive atmosphere above the oil or outside the enclosure cannot be ignited.

Part 3: 1977: pressurized apparatus, type of protection 'p' – in which protection is provided by maintaining, inside the apparatus enclosure, a protective gas at a higher pressure than that of the surrounding atmosphere, the pressure being maintained either with or without a continuous flow of the protective gas.

Part 4: 1977: powder-filled apparatus type of protection 'q' – in which the protection is provided by filling the enclosure of apparatus with material in a finely granulated state so that, in the intended conditions of service, any arc occurring within the enclosure will not ignite the surrounding atmosphere.

Part 5: 1977: apparatus with flameproof enclosure type of protection 'd' – in which the parts which can ignite an explosive atmosphere are placed in an enclosure which can withstand the pressure developed during an internal explosion of an explosive mixture and which prevents the transmission of the explosion to the explosive atmosphere surrounding the enclosure.

Part 6: 1977: increased safety apparatus, type of protection 'e' – in which measures are applied so as to prevent with a minor degree of security the possibility of excessive temperatures and of the occurrence of arcs and sparks in the interior and on the external parts of apparatus which does not provide them in normal service. Luminaires, lampholders, measuring instructions and transformers are covered by these provisions.

Part 7: 1977: intrinsically safe apparatus, type of protection 'i' – in which no spark or any thermal effect produced in the test conditions prescribed in this standard is capable of causing ignition of a given explosive atmosphere.

Part 9: 1982: intrinsically safe electrical systems, type of protection 'l' – a system in this context is an assembly of interconnected items of electrical apparatus described in a descriptive system document, in which the circuits or parts of circuits are intrinsically safe.

BS 229: 1957   *Flameproof enclosure of electrical apparatus*

A flameproof enclosure is defined as one that will withstand, without injury, any explosion of the prescribed flammable gas that may occur within it under practical conditions of operation within the rating of the apparatus (and any recognized overloads, if any, associated therewith and will prevent the transmission of flame such as will ignite the prescribed flammable gas which may be present in the surrounding atmosphere (of BS 5501 Part 5).

The standard classifies the various flammable gases which constitute an explosion hazard in industry into groups according to the appropriate maximum permissible dimensions of joint gaps and other openings in the enclosure of the apparatus.

The requirements of the standard cover those features of design and construction which are considered to be essential or desirable to secure reliability of the enclosure in service.

BS 3955   *Electrical controls for domestic appliances*

Part 3: 1979   *General and specific requirements*

■   AD (Reg. G3)

Requirements and tests are specified for electrical controls either electrically operated or designed to control an electrical function, or both, with a rated voltage not exceeding 500 V and a rated current not exceeding 63 A, for use with a wide range of appliances and apparatus for household and similar general purposes. The standard applies to controls which may be integrated with, or incorporated in or on, appliances and also to independently mounted and freestanding controls. The requirements are, as far as possible, limited to safety requirements although some performance criteria is introduced in order to test the continuance of safety throughout a reasonable period of simulated use of a control.

BS 3456 *Safety of household and similar electrical appliances*

This is an extensive document intended to secure a satisfactory level of safety for a wide range of appliances when they are used in normal conditions. The standard is relevant to this manual in that it specifies requirements for appliances included in (5 –) 'Services, mainly piped, ducted', (6 –) 'Services, mainly electrical' and (7 –) 'Fittings'.

The original particular specifications in the BS 3456 series, designated A2 to B13, have now all been withdrawn with the exception of section A4 *Electrically heated blankets*. Section A1 remains current only in so far as it is referenced in Section A4. The current particular appliance specifications, except for Section A4 and Part C, are in Parts 2 and 3. Part 2 specifications all reference Part 1: 1969 for their general requirements but these are being superseded by the Part 3 specifications which are complete in themselves, and are technically aligned with the corresponding European Committee for Electrotechnical Standardization (CENELEC) harmonization documents (HDs). Part 101: 1978 covers general safety requirements for electrical appliances for household and similar purposes. The relevant requirements of this standard are included in all sections of Part 3, but it is published separately to serve as a guide in those cases where no specification exists for a particular appliance. During the transition period from Part 2 to Part 3 specifications, both remain valid for certification purposes. Part 2 will be withdrawn on the dates determined by CENELEC as those by which national standards which are not aligned with their corresponding HDs must be withdrawn, normally two years after the introduction of the HD.

The following list gives the titles of the various sections of BS 3456 considered relevant to this manual with the appropriate manual element to which they are related. Where Section 2 and Section 3 specifications exist for the same item only Section 3 specifications are quoted.

(52.1) *Refuse disposal*
   Section 3.8: 1979 *Food waste disposal units*
(53.3) *Hot water supply*
   Section 2.7: 1970 *Stationary non-instantaneous water heaters*
   Section 2.21: 1972 *Electric immersion heaters*
   Section 3.9: 1979 *Stationary instantaneous water heaters*
(56.5) *Central heating: warm air distribution*
   Section 2.22: 1972 *Electricaire heaters*
(56.6) *Central heating: Electrical distribution*
   Section 2.26: 1973 *Thermal-storage electric room heaters*
(56.8) *Local heating*
   Section 2.10: 1972 *Room heating and similar appliances*
   Section 2.41: 1977 *Room heating and similar appliances for use in children's nurseries and similar situations*
(57) *Air conditioning, ventilation*
   Section 2.29: 1971 *Ventilating fans*
   Section 2.34: 1976 *Room air conditioners*
   Section 2.39: 1973 *Room humidifiers*
(59) *Pumps*
   Section 2.35: 1975 *Electric pumps*
(64) *Communications, clocks*
   Section 3.10: 1979 *Clocks*
(73) *Culinary fittings*
   Section 2.1: 1972 *Cooking ranges, cooking tables and similar appliances*
   Section 2.23: 1971 *Cooker ventilating hoods*
   Section 2.33: 1976 *Microwave ovens*
   Section 3.4: 1979 *Dishwashers*
(75) *Laundry fittings*
   Section 2.12: 1970 *Spin extractors*
   Section 2.13: 1970 *Tumbler dryers*
   Section 3.2: 1979 *Washing machines*
   Section 3.6: 1979 *Clothes dryers of the rack and cabinet type and towel rails*
   Section 3.7: 1979 *Clothes dryers of the tumbler type*

BS 6266: 1982 *Code of practice for fire protection for electronic data processing installations* (formerly CP 95)

Recommendations are made to installers and users on the protection from fire of the above installations.

BS 6396: 1983 *Code of practice for electrical systems in office furniture and office screens*

Guidance for both permanent electrical systems to be built-in during manufacture, and also on the provision of facilities for electrical systems to be added after purchase.

BS 6204: 1982 *Safety of data processing equipment*

Requirements are specified to ensure the safety of the user when operating or servicing data processing equipment and associated equipment and to ensure the safety of the installed equipment, for operation in offices or special data processing rooms.

Cables and cords

BS 6004: 1984 *PVC-insulated cables (non-armoured) for electric power and lighting*

The cables covered by this standard are those most commonly used in electrical wiring systems in buildings. They are suitable for use with voltages up to 450 V (to earth) and 750 V a.c. (between conductors), and where the combination of ambient temperature and temperature use due to load results in a conductor temperature not exceeding 70 °C and, in the case of a short circuit, the maximum conductor temperature does not exceed 160 °C. These limiting conditions are well in excess of those met in the normal consumer's installations.

A number of cable types have 'harmonized code designations', being designs approved by CENELEC. Others are not 'harmonized' and are designated 'recognized national types', which are regarded as representing a particular requirement in the UK.

The various cables are set out in tables as follows:

Table 1(a), (b) and (c): PVC-insulated, non-sheathed general-purpose cable, single core, 450/750 V.
Table 2: PVC-insulated, non-sheathed cable for internal wiring, single core, 300/500 V.
Table 3: PVC-insulated, PVC-sheathed light cable, circular twin, 3-core, 4-core and 5-core, 300/500 V.
Table 4(a) and (b): PVC-insulated, PVC-sheathed cable, single core, flat twin and 3-core, 300/500 V.
Table 5(a) and (b): PVC-insulated, PVC-sheathed cable with circuit-protective conductor, flat twin and 3-core, 300/500 V.
Table 6: PVC-insulated, PVC-sheathed cable with or without protective conductor, flat twin (alternative conductor versions), 300/500 V.

A guide to the use of PVC-insulated cables for fixed installation is given and guidance to manufacturers for routine testing are given in appendices.

The colours for conductor identification differ according to the type of cable and are indicated in each case with the relevant table.

The standard covers in detail the requirements for the conductors, insulation, external sheath where provided, marking of the cables, construction and physical and electrical tests.

BS 6007: 1983 *Rubber-insulated cables for electric power and lighting*

The rubber-insulated cables covered by this standard are less commonly used than the cables in BS 6004, having rather different properties and applications. They are suitable for use with voltage up to 450 V (to earth) and 750 V a.c. (between conductors), and with different operational temperatures according to the nature of the insulation.

For requirements in the United Kingdom, some of the cables are harmonied code designations and the others are recognized national types (see BS 6004).

BS 6007: 1983 *Rubber insulated cables for electric power and lighting*

Requirements are specified for the construction, electrical properties, mechanical properties and dimensions of non-armoured rubber-insulated cables and flexible cables for operation at voltages up to and including 450 V a.c. to earth and 750 V a.c. between conductors.

The types of cables are set out in tables as follows:

Table 1: Rubber insulated, textile-braided and compounded cable, single core, 450/750 V.
Table 2: Rubber-insulated and sheathed cable, flat twin, 300/500 V.
Table 3: Rubber-insulated and sheathed flexible cable, 3-core and 4-core, 300/500 V.
Table 4: Rubber-insulated and sheathed flexible cable, single core, circular twin, 3-core, 4-core and 5-core, 450/750 V.
Table 5: Rubber-insulated, HOFR-sheathed flexible cable, single core, circular twin, 3-core, 4-core and 5-core, 450/750 V.
Table 6: Rubber-insulated, braided, heat-resistant flexible cable, single core and twisted twin, 300/500 V.

A guide to the use of rubber-insulated cables and guidance to manufacturers on procedures for routine testing is given in appendices.

The conductor used in the cables in all of the tables is tinned, annealed copper, plain or tinned. In the case of those in Table 5, an additional option is for the cores to be protected by a metal other than tin, such as silver.

The conductors may be identified either by colours in or on the insulations or on the braiding. The colours are given with each table.

The standard covers in detail the requirements for the conductors, insulation, external sheath where provided, marking of the cables, construction and physical and electrical tests to be applied.

BS 6207 *Mineral-insulated cables*

Part 1: 1969 in this standard is concerned with copper-sheathed cables with copper conductors and Part 2: 1973 with aluminium-sheathed cables with copper conductors and aluminium-sheathed cables with aluminium conductors.

In each case, the cables are in two classes:

1 600 V (light duty – single, twin, three, four and seven core with or without PVC outer covering (or serving), suitable for use where the voltage between conductors and sheath and between conductors does not exceed 600 V r.m.s., a.c. or d.c.
2 1000 V (heavy duty) – single, twin, three, four and, in the case of cables under Part 1, seven core with or without PVC outer covering (or serving), suitable for use where the voltage between conductors and sheath and between conductors does not exceed 1000 V r.m.s., a.c. or d.c.

In the case of cables under Part 2, the conductor for the light duty cables are of copper and for the heavy duty aluminium.

Each part of this standard covers in detail the conductor insulation, sheath and PVC outer covering, together with the tests to be applied to each element of the cable's construction.

BS 6346: 1969 *PVC-insulated cables for electricity supply*

The cables covered by this standard are for electricity supply mains for general use including underground, where the combination of ambient temperature and temperature rise due to load results in a conductor temperature not exceeding 70 °C.

The cables have two voltage designations, 600–1000 V and 1900–3300 V, in each case the former voltage being that between conductors and armour (when provided) and earth, and the latter between conductors. The range of cables includes those which are unarmoured and sheathed, those which are wire armoured and sheathed, and those which are aluminium strip-armoured and sheathed.

The conductors may be either annealed copper or aluminium copper complying with BS 6360. Their structural form may be:

1 Circular solid.
2 Circular stranded.
3 Circular compacted.
4 Shaped stranded.
5 Shaped solid.

The PVC insulation and its thickness is specified in sections five and six.

The core identification colours are:

Single core: red or black.
Twin core: red, black.
Three core: red, yellow, blue (being connected to the corresponding phases).
Four core: red, yellow, blue and black (black for the neutral and the other colours connected to the corresponding phases).

The armour for the cables may be of two types:

1 Wire – a single layer of galvanized steel wires of specified size.
2 Aluminium strip – a single layer of aluminium strip of specified size.

Both unarmoured and armoured cables have a PVC oversheath.

The standard specifies the test to be applied to the various elements comprising the cable and indicates, in a series of tables, data for a wide range of cables with different numbers of cores, construction and rated voltage.

BS 5467: 1977 *Armoured cables with thermosetting insulation for electricity supply*

These cables are similar to those specified in BS 6346, having similar uses and the same rated voltage.

The differences lie principally in the following:

1 The insulating material which permits the operation of the cables at a maximum sustained conductor temperature of 90 °C.
2 All the cables are armoured.
3 Core identification may be either by number or colours at the manufacturer's option such that:

0 zero = black
1 one = red
2 two = yellow
3 three = blue

Certain differences from BS 6346 also arise in the details of the specification for the oversheath and the tests to be applied to the cable. Data for the full range of cables is given in a comprehensive series of tables.

BS 6480 *Impregnated paper-insulated cables for electricity supply* Part 1: 1969 *Lead or lead alloy-sheathed cables for working voltages up to and including 33 kV*

This standard supersedes BS 480. It details test requirements and dimensions for mass-pregnated, mass-impregnated non-draining, and pre-impregnated paper-insulated cables for operation up to and including 18 kV to metal sheath and 33 kV between conductors. Provision is made for armour and protective covering.

BS 6500: 1984 *Insulated flexible cords and cables*

Requirements and dimensions for insulated flexible cords and cables for operation at voltages up to and including 450 V to earth and 750 V between conductors. The types of flexible cords and cables included:

Table 3: Rubber-insulated, braided cord, twisted twin, 300/300 V.

Table 4: Rubber-insulated, braided cord, circular twin and 3-core, 300/300 V.

Table 5: Rubber-insulated, braided, UDF cord, circular twin and 3-core, 300/300 V.

Table 6: Rubber-insulated, sheathed, ordinary cord, circular twin, 3-core, 4-core and 5-core, 300/500 V.

Table 7: Rubber-insulated, sheathed, screened, sheathed cord, circular twin, 3-core and 4-core, 300/500 V.

Table 8: Rubber-insulated, sheathed cord, single-core, circular twin, 3-core, 4-core and 5-core, 450/750 V.

Table 9: Rubber-insulated, HOFR-sheathed cord, circular twin, 3-core and 4-core, 300/500 V.

Table 10: Rubber-insulated, braided, heat resistant cord, single-core and twisted twin, 300/500 V.

Table 13: PVC-insulated (tinsel conductors) parallel twin cord, 300/300 V.

Table 14: PVC-insulated (wire conductors) parallel twin cord, 300/300 V.

Table 15: PVC-insulated, PVC-sheathed, light cord, parallel twin, circular twin, 3-core, 4-core and 5-core, 300/300 V.

Table 16: PVC-insulated, PVC-sheathed, ordinary cord, parallel twin, circular twin, 3-core, 4-core and 5-core, 300/500 V.

Table 17: PVC-insulated, sheathed, screened, sheathed light cord, circular twin and 3-core, 300/300 V.

Table 18: PVC-insulated, sheathed, screened, sheathed ordinary cord, circular twin, 3-core and 4-core, 300/500 V.

Table 19: PVC-insulated, non-sheathed cord, single-core and twisted twin, 300/500 V.

Table 22: Glass fibre insulated cord, single-core, twisted twin and twisted 3-core, 300/300 V.

Table 23: Glass fibre insulated cord, braided, circular twin and 3-core, 300/300 V.

A guide to the use of insulated flexible cords, and guidance to manufacturers on procedures for routine testing are given in appendices.

The standard covers in detail the requirements for the conductor, insulation screen, sheath, protected sheath, together with the construction and the physical and electrical tests to be applied. Core identification colours are detailed.

BS 6081: 1978 *Terminations for mineral-insulated cables*

This standard, which supersedes BS 4081, specifies requirements for terminations used with mineral-insulated cables complying with BS 6207 Parts 1 and 2 and ensures that complete terminations for use with a given size of cable are interchangeable.

Section three lists a number of definitions, the most important of which are:

Termination: a complete end fitting for a mineral-insulated cable, normally comprising a seal and a gland or a composite sealing/glanding device but excluding the locknut and any necessary junction box or accessory.

Seal: the part of a termination designed to seal the end of the cable against entry of moisture and to insulate the conductor beyond the point where the mineral insulant is terminated – normally comprising a pot, sealant and insulating sleeving.

Gland: the part of a termination designed to secure the cable into a cable entry and may or may not be used to ensure earth continuity depending upon the type. Three types are used:

1 Cable-grip in which the gland is secured directly to the cable.
2 Seal grip in which the gland is secured directly to the seal of the cable.
3 Composite gland and seal.

The sealing pots or enclosure are required to be of a material similar to that of the cable sheath to which it is to be attached to avoid corrosion or electrolytic action. Provision within the standard is made for an earth continuity conductor to be welded, brazed or soldered to the pot or to be secured to the cable sheath.

The sealant or sealing material consists of an insulating, moisture-resisting material which is capable of meeting the insulation and voltage test requirements stipulated in the standard.

The standard also prescribes the insulating sleeving and the disc-type pot closures which may be used.

The seals and their several components have to be capable of continuous operation at maximum operating temperatures of 85 °C, 105 °C, 135 °C and 185 °C.

Details of the design and dimensions of glands together with tables of data for glands for the various types of 600 and 1000 V cable in BS 6207 are specified, together with rigorous tests on the mechanical and electrical qualities of the components in the terminations.

Cable enclosures

Conduits

The several British Standards concerned with electrical conduit are in the process of consolidation. A number of standards covering imperial components have been superseded in part or in whole by later specifications for metric components. Those are now being progressively superseded by standards agreed by CENELEC.

BS 6099 *Conduits for electrical installations*

Part 1: 1981 of this new multi-part harmonized CENELEC standard specifies the general requirements for all types of conduit of circular cross-section for the protection of the conductors and for cables in electrical installations. The particular requirements for specific types of conduit will be the subject of different sections of Part 2. These are in the process of being written.

A number of useful definitions relating to types of conduit are given and conduits are further classified under eight different headings according to:

1 Material: metal, insulating, composite.
2 Method of connection: threadable-plain, non-threadable-plain or corrugated.
3 Mechanical properties in terms of resistance to mechanical stress: very light, medium, heavy, very heavy.
4 Suitability for bending: rigid, pliable, self-recovering, flexible.
5 Temperature given in a table in the standard.
6 Resistance to flame propagation: non-flame propagating, flame propagating.
7 Electrical characteristics: without electrical continuity, with electrical continuity, without electrical insulating characteristics, with electrical insulating characteristics.
8 Resistance to external influences: against ingress of water, against ingress of solid foreign bodies, against corrosive or polluting substance, to solar radiation.

This part covers the requirements relating to marking, construction, mechanical, physical and electrical properties and to testing. Detailed matters concerned with the dimensions and thread of the various types of conduit are contained in the relevant section of Part 2.

Part 2 Section 2.2: 1982 *Rigid plain conduits of insulating material*

This section of Part 2, together with Part 1, supersedes those clauses of Parts 1 and 2 of BS 4607: 1970 relating to rigid plain conduits of insulating material (rigid PVC conduits and conduit fittings – metric units and imperial units respectively). The provisions of those clauses in BS 4607 will remain unchanged during a changeover period of up to two years. The provisions of this section are largely cross-referenced to the general provisions of Part 1 with respect to its detailed characteristics. The data relating to available sizes and their internal diameters are given in Table 51.

Table 51   *PVC conduits*

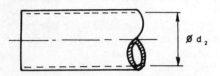

Size	Minimum inside diameter (mm)		
	Light	Medium	Heavy
16	13.7	13.0	12.2
20	17.4	16.9	15.8
25	22.1	21.4	20.6
32	28.6	27.8	26.6
40	35.8	35.4	34.4
50	45.1	44.3	43.2
63	57.0	–	–

Manufacturing length: minimum, 3 m; preferred, 3 or 4 m.

(Standard sheet 1: BS 6099: Section 2.2: 1982)

Other sections to Part 2 will be progressively introduced.

BS 4607: *Non-metallic conduits and fittings for electrical installations*

Part 1: 1984   *Fittings and components of insulating material*
Construction, dimensions and performance of non-metallic conduit fittings and components for electrical installations.

The provisions of two parts of BS 4607 are generally similar to each other in respect of those matters unrelated to dimensions and they cover classification, marking, construction and mechanical, physical and electrical qualities. Part 1, being concerned with metric units, is now more extensively relevant to current installations. Conduits complying with this part are classified as:

Type A: suitable for handling and use at temperature not normally below −5 °C.
Type B: as Type A but at temperatures not normally below −25 °C.

The range of conduit diameters is limited compared with those in the newer BS 6099, being restricted to 16, 20, 25 and 32 mm diameter. Standard sheets are provided for various types of couplers and bends. Fittings not of tubular form, such as circular boxes, are the subject of Part 5.

Part 2: 1970 (1985)   *Rigid PVC conduits and conduit fittings: imperial units.*
This covers the whole range of conduit and conduit fittings with imperial units whether of tubular or non-tubular form. The use of current metric conduit has rendered this part of historical rather than practical interest.

Part 3: 1971 (1985)   *Pliable corrugated, plain and reinforced conduits of self-extinguishing plastics material*

The general provisions of this part are similar to those for conduits in Part 1 particularly with respect to classification, marking, properties and testing.

The range of sizes available, together with relevant dimensional data, is given in the standard.

Part 5: 1982   *Rigid conduits, fittings and components of insulating material*
Components such as circular fittings and covers, and reducers, also rigid conduits other than those specified in Part 1 are set out.

BS 4568: 1970   *Steel conduit and fittings with metric threads of ISO form for electrical installations*

The conduit and fittings described in this standard were intended initially to be an alternative to and eventually to supersede those described in BS 31 with the ultimate object of unification with the standards of other European countries. The scope of this standard is therefore similar to that of BS 31 but certain amendments have been introduced where the requirements of the previous standard needed revision. In some cases the wall thickness of the conduit has been reduced in order to accommodate the ISO thread.

The standard is in two parts, the first being concerned with conduit and those bends and couplers which have been standardized internationally and the second with a wide range of fittings and components not at present standardized internationally but which are extensively used in this country.

Part 1 specifies the requirements for steel conduit and for conduit fittings of steel or malleable cast iron. The conduit and fittings are classified first, according to the method of assembly of conduits with the fittings, namely plain or screwed, and second, according to the type of protection applied:

Class 1: light protection both inside and outside, for example priming paint.
Class 2: medium protection both inside and outside, for example stoved enamel, and drying paint.
Class 3: medium heavy protection, inside as Class 2 and outside as Class 4.
Class 4: heavy protection both inside and outside, for example hot-dip zinc coating, sherardizing.

Conduits may be either solid drawn or seamed by welding and are in two gauges, light and heavy, according to the wall thickness. The light gauge conduit is available only as plain conduit; the heavy gauge may be either plain or screwed.

The requirements of this part cover marking, construction, mechanical properties, resistance to corrosion, electrical continuity and a wide range of tests with which the conduit and fittings must comply.

Details of the conduit for the two gauges are given in Standard Sheets 1 and 2 for light and heavy gauge conduit respectively.

The fittings covered by Part 1 are couplers and bends, both plain and screwed in steel or malleable cast iron. Details are given in a range of standard sheets.

Part 2 is concerned with a wide range of conduit fittings not internationally standardized but designed to be used in conjunction with the conduit and fittings in Part 1. The fittings and components are normally of sheet steel or malleable cast iron but in some cases may be of a wide choice of materials indicated on the appropriate illustrative standard sheet. The provisions with respect to general requirements and conditions, classification, marking and testing are generally the same as those in Part 1. The provisions concerned with the construction of the fittings cover manufacture and the size and location of knockouts.

Twenty-four standard sheets are provided covering a variety of bends, boxes, bushes, couplers, covers, crampets, locknuts, plugs, reducers and saddles.

BS 731 *Flexible steel conduit for cable protection and flexible steel tubing to enclose flexible drives*

Part 1: 1952 *Flexible steel conduit and adaptors for the protection of electric cable*

This part is concerned solely with flexible conduit and adaptors; flexible steel tubing to enclose flexible drives has now been transferred to Part 2.

These types of flexible steel conduit are specified in Section 1 as follows:

Type A: unpacked, of the square locked type of construction, made by helically coiling a formed steel strip. Suitable for use as a mechanical protection to insulated electric cables exposed to normal atmospheric conditions.

Type B: asbestos packed, of similar construction to Type A but provided with a continuous packing of asbestos yarn inserted between the coils. Suitable for use as a mechanical protection to insulated electric cables likely to be exposed to damp conditions or where the temperature precludes the use of rubber.

Type C: rubber packed, of similar construction to Type A but provided with a continuous rubber thread inserted between the coils.

The construction of the three types is illustrated in Figure 59.

The diameters of conduit are in imperial dimensions, namely $3/16$, $1/4$, $5/16$, $3/8$, $1/2$, $5/8$, $3/4$, $7/8$, 1, $1^1/4$, $1^1/2$, $1^3/4$, 2, $2^1/2$, 3 in and full details are given in a table in this standard.

The requirements also cover the materials, workmanship and electrical continuity of the conduits.

Section two covers adaptors in the following categories:

1 Clamp type, having either an internal box thread or internally projecting fins to engage and hold secure the flexible conduit. Fitted with an earthing lug or earthing screw. See Figure 60.

2 Solid type, having either an internal box thread or internally projecting fins. Fitted as with the clamp type with an earthing lug or earthing screw. See Figure 61.

3 Other types, designs other than the clamp or solid types but having dimensions in accordance with those in the dimension table in section one. Fitted with or without earthing provisions.

The requirements also cover the materials threads and their engagement, and workmanship.

Section three outlines tests for flexibility, linear breaking, bend-fracture, crushing and soundness.

BS 4678 *Cable trunking*

This is a multi-part standard covering the different types of trunking in steel, non-ferrous metal and plastics. Because of the large number of different trunking systems currently being manufactured the provisions of this standard do not extend to details of all the fittings used in conjunction with the trunking. The several parts are therefore limited to overall dimensions and to the broad details of construction.

Definitions include:

Cable trunking: a fabricated system of enclosures for the protection of conductors or cables, assembled together by means of connectors or couplers, into which the cables are laid or drawn in. There are minor variations according to the individual part of the standard.

Connector (metal) or coupler (plastic): a device for joining together lengths of cable trunking.

Trunking may have more than one compartment formed by partitions or divides according to need.

Part 1: 1971 is concerned with steel surface trunking normally of square or rectangular cross-section of which one side is removable or hinged, having nominal sizes of 50.0×37.5 mm to

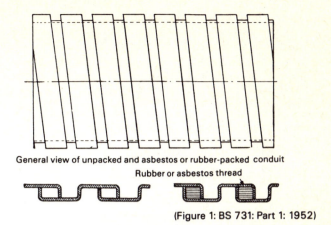

General view of unpacked and asbestos or rubber-packed conduit

Rubber or asbestos thread

(Figure 1: BS 731: Part 1: 1952)

Figure 59 *Packed and unpacked conduit*

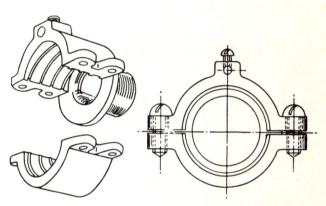

(Figure 2: BS 731: Part 1: 1952)

Figure 60 *Typical example of a clamp type adaptor with external earthing screw (threaded type)*

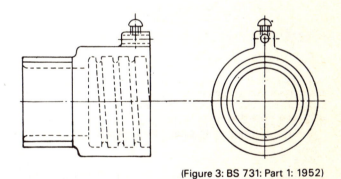

(Figure 3: BS 731: Part 1: 1952)

Figure 61 *Typical example of a solid type adaptor with external earthing screw (threaded type)*

150×150 mm. It excludes bench, flush floor, overhead lighting, skirting or underfloor (duct) trunking.

These classifications of steel trunking are made according to the type of protection against corrosion which is given.

Class 1: light protection inside and out – electroplated zinc.

Class 2: medium protection, as class 1 but with additional protective coating on the outside only – electroplated zinc as Class 1 with stoved enamel or as drying paint externally.

Class 3: heavy protection both inside and out – galvanized.

The requirements cover in addition marking, details of construction including the provision of knockouts, resistance to corrosion and electrical continuity. The sizes of steel surface trunking are given in Table 52.

Table 52   *Sizes, and preferred lengths*

Nominal size	External dimensions
mm	mm
50 × 37.5	50 ± 2.5 × 37.5 ± 2
*50 × 50	50 ± 2.5 × 50 ± 2.5
*75 × 50	75 ± 4 × 50 ± 2.5
*75 × 75	75 ± 4 × 75 ± 4
100 × 50	100 ± 5 × 50 ± 2.5
*100 × 75	100 ± 5 × 75 ± 4
*100 × 100	100 ± 5 × 100 ± 5
150 × 50	150 ± 7.5 × 50 ± 2.5
150 × 75	150 ± 7.5 × 75 ± 4
*150 × 100	150 ± 7.5 × 100 ± 5
*150 × 150	150 ± 7.5 × 150 ± 7.5

Preferred length 3 m; minimum 2 m, maximum 3 m.
Partitions or dividers, nominal thickness 1.0 mm.
*Preferred sizes.

(Table 1: BS 4678: Part 1: 1971)

Table 53   *Sizes and preferred lengths*

External dimensions (excluding flange projections)		Number of compartments
mm		mm
Width	Depth	
75 ± 4	× 25 ± 1.2	One
75 ± 4	× 37.5 ± 2	One
100 ± 5	× 25 ± 1.2	One or two
100 ± 5	× 37.5 ± 2	One or two
150 ± 7.5	× 25 ± 1.2	Two or three
150 ± 7.5	× 37.5 ± 2	Two or three
150 ± 7.5	× 25 ± 1.2	One
150 ± 7.5	× 37.5 ± 2	One
225 ± 11.2	× 25 ± 1.2	Three
225 ± 11.2	× 37.5 ± 2	Three
225 ± 11.2	× 25 ± 1.2	Two
225 ± 11.2	× 37.5 ± 2	Two

Preferred length 3 m; minimum 2 m, maximum 3 m.
Underfloor (duct) trunking to special order having dimensions differing from the above may be deemed to comply with this specification provided it meets all its other requirements.

(From Table 1: BS 4678: Part 2: 1973)

Part 2: 1973 is concerned with steel underfloor (duct) trunking which is laid on a structural floor and subsequently covered by a floor screed. The requirements relate to such trunking with nominal sizes 75 × 25 mm to 225 × 37.5 mm and excludes trunking comprised in Part 1 as well as bench, flush floor, overhead lighting or skirting trunking.

The base of underfloor trunking for this part is defined as that part which is in contact with the floor slab and is not considered to be load-bearing. The classifications for underfloor trunking are according to the degree of protection against corrosion and include only Classes 2 and 3 defined in Part 1.

The provisions with respect to marking, details of construction, resistance to corrosion and electrical continuity are generally similar to those in Part 1.

The sizes of steel underfloor trunking are given in Table 53.

Part 3, which is in the course of preparation, will deal with steel lighting trunking.

Part 4: 1982 is concerned with cable trunking made of insulating material. No specific type of section of trunking is contemp-

lated within this part and consequently the provisions are of a general nature. They are limited primarily to classification, marking, construction and the mechanical, physical and electrical properties of the trunking.

The classifications used are similar to those adopted in BS 6099 Part 1 for conduits, according to:

1 Material.
2 Mechanical properties in terms of resistance to mechanical stress: very light, light, medium, heavy and very heavy.
3 Temperature tolerance defined in a table in the standard related to the lowest temperatures at which the trunking will be stored, transported and used.
4 Electrical characteristics: with or without electrical insulating characteristics and size.
5 Resistance against ingress of solid objects: based upon the nature of the solids to be excluded and the degree of exclusion.
6 Resistance against ingress of water: non-protected, against dripping water, against spraying water, against splashing water and against water jets.
7 Resistance against corrosive or polluting substances: non-protected, low, medium and high protection.

The clauses of this part concerned with mechanical properties are similar to those in BS 6099 Part 1.

The external cross-sectional dimensions for trunking may be selected from 12.5, 16.0, 20.0, 25.0, 32.0, 37.5, 40.0, 50.0, 75.0, 100.0 and 150 mm.

BS 5486   *Factory-built assemblies of switchgear and controlgear for voltages up to and including 1000 V a.c. and 1200 V d.c.*

Part 2: 1978   *Particular requirements for busbar trunking systems (busways)*

The general requirements relating to factory-built assemblies have been mentioned in the previous reference to this standard in equipment and control gear. The particular requirements for busbar trunking systems are the subject of Part 2. The following definitions are worthy of note:

Busbar trunking systems (busways): a conductor system comprising busbars which are spaced and supported by insulating material in a duct, trough or similar enclosure.

Busbar trunking system with predetermined tap-off facilities: a system designed to enable tap-offs units or possibly other connection units to be tapped off at one or more points on the trunking as predetermined by the manufacturer. The connection of tap-off units or other connection units to the busbar system may or may not require this system to be disconnected from the supply.

Busbar trunking system with trolley type tap-off facilities: a system designed to permit the use of roller-type units forming an integral part of the trunking system.

Trunking unit: a unit of a busbar trunking system complete with busbars, their supports and insulation, external enclosure and any fixing and connecting means.

Tap-off unit: an outgoing unit of a busbar trunking system with tap-off facilities.

Expansion unit: a trunking unit intended to permit a certain movement in the axial direction of the busbar trunking system, for example thermal expansion.

Feeder unit: a trunking unit serving as an incoming unit. The connection of the feeder unit to the supply may or may not require the supply to be disconnected.

The requirements stipulate the resistance and reactance values of the systems, the constructional performance and provisions to ensure the correct polarity of the supply at tap-off units. A comprehensive range of tests to verify the electrical, mechanical and constructional adequacy of the systems is also detailed.

BS 4108: 1973 *Pitch-impregnated fibre conduit*

This standard is concerned with pitch-impregnated fibre conduits suitable for cables for electrical and communication services and for use above or below ground or embedded in concrete. The conduits are classified according to wall thickness in two gauges:

1 Gauge L (light) – for use above or below ground but only when surrounded with a concrete casing.
2 Gauge H (heavy) – for use above or below ground without a concrete surround but it must have suitable support such as that provided by a bed of granular material if the concrete surround is to be omitted below ground.

The material used in the manufacture of the conduits must consist of a preformed felted fibrous structure with pitch, bitumen or no other less suitable compound. Couplings, defined as a short hollow cylinder for connecting two conduits, or conduit and fitting, of equal nominal bore, must be made of the same material as the conduit, polypropylene or other plastics material no less suitable, or mineral fibre moulded from an inert aggregate mixed with an inorganic cement and impregnated with pitch, bitumen or other no less suitable material.

The nominal sizes of pitch-impregnated fibre conduits are 50, 75, 90, 100, 125 and 150 mm.

The stock lengths of conduits are normally not less than 1.5 m and not more than 3.5 m. Lengths of conduits, subject to a tolerance of ± 25 mm, include the length of tapered parts where these are provided. Three types of joint are specified each with a table of detail:

1 Snap ring – for heavy gauge, not available for 50 diameter conduits.
2 Taper coupling – for light and heavy gauge.
3 Spigot and socket – for light and heavy gauge.

In addition, the standard covers marking and the wide range of tests with which the conditioned materials must comply.

BS 2484: 1961 *Cable covers (concrete and earthenware)*

The cable covers which are the subject of this standard are intended to give both a warning of the presence of an underground electric cable and to protect the cables against blows from excavating tools. They are most frequently used with service cables.

The standard is in three parts. The first relates to precast reinforced concrete, the second relates to precast unreinforced concrete cable covers and the third relates to earthenware (burnt clay) cable covers.

The requirements of Parts 1 and 2 are substantially the same with the exceptions of a clause relating to the provision of reinforcement in Part 1 and of the dimensions of the covers.

The materials which may be used for both reinforced and unreinforced covers are:

1 Cement – ordinary or rapid-hardening Portland cement, or Portland-blast furnace cement. High alumina cement may be used with the agreement of the purchaser.
2 Aggregates
   (a) Coarse or fine aggregate from natural sources complying with BS 882.
   (b) Air-cooled blast furnace clay coarse aggregate for concrete complying with BS 1047.
   (c) Any other aggregate agreed with the purchaser.
   (d) Pulverized fuel ash with the approval of the purchaser and provided the covers pass the appropriate test.

Other provisions in Parts 1 and 2 are concerned with protection from frost, moulding (or casting), tolerances, interlocks between covers, lettering and testing. The dimensions for reinforced concrete cable covers are given in Table 54 and those for unreinforced concrete in Table 55 (imperial dimensions are

Table 54 *Dimensions of reinforced concrete straight covers*

Nominal length	Width	Thickness Peaked type To apex	At outer edges	Flat type
mm	mm	mm	mm	mm
457	114	51	25	38
457	152	51	25	38
457	178	63	38	51
457	229	63	38	51
457	254	63	38	51
610	457	63	38	51
762	381	63	38	51
914	152	63	38	51
914	178	63	38	51
914	229	63	38	51
914	254	63	38	51
914	279	63	38	51
914	305	63	38	51
914	330	63	38	51

Note: Arch type cable covers of which Figure 65 shows a typical design, are obtainable from some manufacturers. Such covers of necessity depart dimensionally from this standard but should otherwise comply with its relevant requirements.

(From Table 1: BS 2484: 1961)

Table 55 *Dimensions of unreinforced concrete straight covers*

Nominal length	Width	Thickness Peaked type To apex	At outer edge	Flat type
mm	mm	mm	mm	mm
457	114	51	25	38
457	152	51	25	38
	152	63	38	51
up to	178	63	38	51
610	229	63	38	51
mm	254	63	38	51
length	279	63	38	51
	305	63	38	51
	350	—	38	51

(From Table 2: BS 2484: 1961)

(Figure 1: BS 2484: 1961)

Figure 62 *Typical arch type cover*

omitted). The cross-sections of cable covers may be either peaked or flat and typical arrangements of reinforcing rods and transverse reinforcement are given. An alternative cross-section, the arch type cable-cover, which is shown in Figure 62, is obtainable from some manufacturers and necessarily departs dimensionally from the provisions of this standard. Such covers should, however, comply with the other requirements.

Radius covers are required to be either of a similar cross-section to the straight cover, or flat and reversible, to form right or left-hand bends as required by the purchaser.

Part 3 relates to cable covers made of burnt clay so made and fired that they are true in shape, well burnt throughout and free from detrimental cracks.

The dimensions and breaking loads for earthenware covers are also given in this standard. As in Part 1 and 2, the cross-sections may be packed or flat, with similar provisions with respect to arch type covers.

BS 6053: 1981   *Outside diameters of conduits for electrical instal-lations and threads for conduits and fittings*

This standard specifies the items noted in the title and is applicable to all kinds of conduits independent of their material and their nature (rigid, flexible, plain or threaded) taking into consideration all existing conduit entries and the metric threads.

Accessories

BS 5733: 1979   *General requirements for electrical accessories*

As its title indicates, this standard specifies general requirements for electrical wiring accessories for installation purposes and for associated plugs and portable accessories, not specifically covered by current British Standards, which are designed for use in single phase a.c. or d.c. circuits in which the voltage between conductors exceeds extra low voltage (Band 1) and does not exceed 250 V a.c. or d.c. and the rated current does not exceed 45 A.

It does not therefore override any of the provisions, even though it may duplicate them, of other British Standards concerned with particular accessories nor does it apply to electronic devices or accessories for industrial use.

Six definitions are worth noting because of their general connotation:

Accessory: a device associated with the wiring of an installation. This definition is particularly loose compared with that in the IEE Regulations which excludes current-using equipment.
Adaptor: an accessory for insertion into a socket outlet, containing metal contacts, to accommodate one or more plugs.
Plug: an accessory intended for connection to a flexible cord or cable which can be engaged manually with a socket outlet, and which has current carrying pins which may be exposed when not engaged.
Shutter: a movable device comprising one or more components intended to provide automatically an insulating screen to protect live contacts of accessories from access which would otherwise be exposed when a cooperating device is withdrawn when not in normal use.
Fixed accessory: an accessory designed to be part of and permanently connected to a fixed installation.
Portable accessory: an accessory designed for use other than as part of a fixed installation.

Section six requires accessories to have indelible markings covering BS 5733 (where applicable), manufacturer's name or trademark where applicable, rated current, rated voltage, a.c., d.c, or a.c./d.c., identification of terminals, that is line = L, neutral = N, and earth = $\frac{1}{=}$ or $\frac{1}{=}$ E and 'fuse' or 'fused' where fuse links are incorporated. Section ten covers a number of important precautions against electric shock.

Section sixteen requires flexible cables or cords entering an accessory to do so through one hole groove or gland and to be secured by a proper anchorage to prevent strain on the terminal connections and mechanical damage to the cable or cord. The acceptable forms of anchorage are specified.

BS 4662: 1970   *Boxes for the enclosure of electrical accessories*

This standard covers boxes of metal or insulating material intended to be recessed into a wall, ceiling or similar flat surface. Some of the boxes may be suitable for surface mounting. See also BS 1363 for accessories complying with that standard.

Metal boxes must be appropriately protected against rust and corrosion, the type of protection depending upon degree of exposure to deleterious elements.

The provisions cover in detail the design and construction of the boxes including dimensions, thickness of walls, the size, number and position of 'knockouts' for conduit connections, position of lugs, earthing provisions, mechanical strength and marking.

The principal dimensions for the types of box are size UA1, and UA2 for size 16, 20, and 25 conduit, and size UA3, and UA4 for size 20 and 25 conduit.

BS 6220: 1983   *Junction boxes for use in electrical installations with rated voltages not exceeding 250 V*

Requirements for junction boxes of surface- or flush-mounting types for use in fixed wiring installations in a.c. and d.c. circuits where the rated voltage does not exceed 250 V and where the conductors are not subject to mechanical tension in normal use. It covers junction boxes having fixed terminals with capacity for the connection of PVC-insulated and sheathed cables complying with the requirements of BS 6004, and having copper conductors of cross-sectional area up to and including 10 mm^2.

This standard does not apply to junction boxes for use in conditions where special protection against the ingress of dust or moisture is required.

A junction box is classified according to:

(a) the number of terminals as declared by the manufacturer;
(b) the nominal conductor capacity of the terminals, as declared by the manufacturer, which is one of the capacities shown in a table.
(c) the method of mounting (e.g. surface or flush).

Specialized accessories

BS 4343: 1968   *Industrial plugs, socket-outlets and couplers for a.c. and d.c. supplies*

This standard gives information on a wide range of accessories for industrial applications, indoors or outdoors, agriculture or on board ship. The accessories are for single phase and three phase supplies with a voltage between phases not exceeding 750 V and a frequency not exceeding 500 Hz or for d.c. supplies with a rated current up to 125 A.

BS 4573: 1970   *2-pin reversible plugs and shaver socket outlets*

Electric shavers are normally with 2-pin reversible plugs, since the polarity of the connection is of no consequence.

The shaver socket-outlets covered by this standard have a restricted rating of 200 mA for use only on voltages of 200 to 250 V, are shuttered and more particularly, are for use only in rooms other than bathrooms. Normally, the outlets will be designed to accommodate British, American, continental and Australian plugs. Shavers connected to a supply by means of these shaver outlets are not isolated from the mains.

This standard covers the safety precautions which must be provided (similar to those in BS 5733), materials, design, construction, marking and testing of the accessories. Of particular note is the requirement that the shaver outlet must incorporate a manual or self-resetting overload device, not being a fuse, limiting current to 200 mA. A fuse complying with BS 646, not exceeding 1 A rating, may be fitted to protect the overload device against the prospective short circuit current.

BS 4177: 1967   *Cooker control units rated at 30 A and 45 A, 250 V single phase only*

This standard is concerned with units primarily intended to control electric cookers and comprising a switch of 30 or 45 A rating to control the cooker and an auxiliary circuit comprising a switch and socket-outlet for the connection and supply of a portable appliance.

Three forms of cooker control unit are envisaged:

1 Comprising a mains switch of 30 or 45 A rating for the cooker circuit and an auxiliary circuit switch of 13 A rating and a socket-outlet for a fused plug complying with BS 1363.
2 Comprising a similar mains switch to 1 but fitted with luminous indicators and the auxiliary circuit with a 15 A switch and a 15 A socket-outlet complying with BS 546 protected by a fuse within the unit.
3 Comprising components similar to 1 or 2 but with the dimensions of the unit other than those prescribed in this standard.

The limiting maximum external dimensions for units of forms 1 or 2 are 152.4 mm wide, ± 3.2 × 139.7 mm high, ± 3.2 × 55.6 mm deep for flush type units. No depth is specified for surface type units.

The standard covers in addition the material for the units, cable openings, accessibility of components and marking in respect of the British Standard number, manufacturer's name, switch rating, polarity and identification of the cooker switch.

BS 3676: 1963   *Switches for domestic and similar purposes (for fixed or portable mounting)*

The majority of switches used in a normal electrical installation will comply, either wholly or in part, with this standard which covers types having a rating up to and including 45 A for use in a.c. and d.c. circuits up to 250 V. It also relates to switches for the control of lighting fittings and those incorporated in cords or in lampholders.

Section three provides a number of definitions the most important of which include surface switch, semi-recessed switch, flush switch, ceiling switch, plate mounting type switches and grid mounting type switches.

Switches are further classified according to their electrical function, namely:

1 Single pole, one way.
2 Double pole, one way.
3 Single pole, two way and off.
4 Single pole, two way.
5 Intermediate.

Section four indicates the standard current ratings in amperes, namely 1, 2, 3, 5, 10, 13, 15, 20, 30 and 45.

Section five requires switches to be marked (as in BS 5733) in respect of the British Standard number, manufacturer's name, rated voltage and current and, if not suitable for use in d.c. supplies, either 'a.c.' or 'a.c. only'.

The standard stipulates the design factors and electrical tests to be applied to the switches and manufacturers will normally indicate routinely which test requirements are satisfied by each switch.

BS 3052: 1958   *Electric shaver supply units*

Shaver socket outlets complying with BS 4573 are connected direct to the mains and, consequently, the risk of a high prospective short circuit current renders those accessories unsuitable for use in bathrooms. The shaver supply units covered by this standard incorporate a mains isolating transformer with separate input and earth-free output windings and an output socket or sockets rated at more than 30 V r.m.s. a.c. and not more than 250 V a.c.

Load limiting and earth fault protection is given by means of either:

1 Thermal and/or magnetic trip with either manual or self resetting mechanism connected in the transformer primary.
2 Design of the transformer so that overload protection is inherent in the design.

The provision of overload protection by means of a fuse, resistor or reactor is expressly excluded. These accessories are therefore suitable for use in all locations including bathrooms.

The output sockets are required to receive British, American and European 2-pin plugs. They are frequently designed also to accept Australian plugs.

The standard covers in detail the transformer, trip and other safety precautions as well as the materials, design, construction, marking and testing of the units including a humidity test and rigorous tests on the transformer windings.

BS 1363: 1984   *13 A fused plugs and switched and unswitched socket-outlets and boxes*

The introduction of ring mains and certain radial final circuits as specific exemptions from the rules relating to the number of outlets permissible in final circuits exceeding 15 A, necessitated the use of plugs and associated socket-outlets of a pattern in which non-fused plugs were unobtainable. The accessories complying with this standard meet that requirement. They have now largely superseded the accessories under BS 546.

Conditions of use, definitions, construction and tests, including those related to non-rewireable plugs and portable socket outlets. Appendices include construction of a calibrated link and a test plug for the temperature-rise test.

The title of this standard, reinforced by comment in section 1.1, suggesting that the plugs are rated at 13 A, is singularly inapposite and contributes to the popular and dangerous misconception about the fuse rating of these plugs. The cartridge fuse links used should comply with BS 1362, which contemplates 3 and 13 A ratings. The fuse rating should be of the correct value to provide protection to the appliance connected to the supply through the plug.

The plug pins are of rectangular section and their disposition, dimensions and polarity are stipulated. The standard covers in detail the safety precautions which must be provided (similar in large measure to those in BS 5733), the materials, design, construction, marking and testing of the accessories, ensuring interchangeability and electrical and mechanical endurance.

BS 546: 1950   *Two-pole and earthing-pin plugs, socket-outlets and socket-outlet adaptors for circuits up to 250 V*

In the early final circuits not exceeding 15 A rating, protection to the circuit and the appliances connected thereto was provided solely at the distribution board at the beginning of the circuit. The number of outlets on the circuit was limited by the assumed aggregate demand of the outlets within the current rating of the circuit. Protection to appliances connected to such circuits was not provided at the plugs used in connection with socket-outlets, although fused plugs were available optionally.

The socket-outlets and associated plugs used for such circuits are covered by this standard. Although largely superseded by socket-outlets and plugs covered by BS 1363, these accessories are frequently used where it is desired to limit the current ratings available to the consumer, as in hostels.

This standard covers plugs (fused and non-fused), socket-outlets (shuttered and non-shuttered) and fused socket-outlet adaptors (shuttered and non-shuttered). See BS 5733 for definitions.

The plugs are provided with three round pins, with ratings of 2, 5, 15, and 30 A, determining the dimensions of the pins and their disposition.

The standard covers at some length the interchangeability, materials, design and construction safety provisions (which are complementary to those in BS 5573) for both plugs and socket-outlets.

All accessories complying with BS 546 must be marked (as in BS 5733) with the British Standard number, the manufacturer's name or trademark and, additionally, in the case of plugs, the pin polarity markings and if fused; in the case of socket-outlets the current rating and terminal polarity markings; in the case of adaptors, the current rating of the plug portion, the word fused and the maximum total loading.

The fuse links used with accessories complying with this standard are covered by BS 646: 1977 and where they are fitted the accessory should be marked with the words 'use correct fuse-links'. This is an attempt to ensure that an appliance having a rating less than that of the circuit fuse should not be 'protected' by an overrated fuse at the accessory.

BS 67: 1969   *Ceiling roses*

Ceiling roses provide terminations for the permanent wiring of an electrical lighting installation with connection facilities for pendant drops. This standard covers ceiling roses of the surface or semi-recessed types for use in circuits not exceeding 250 V and not exceeding 5 A.

The surface type ceiling rose has a seating surface so that when mounted it projects wholly outside the surface on which it is mounted. The semi-recessed type is designed to have its base partially sunk into a standard small circular conduit box.

The standard covers the materials, construction and cable entry provisions of ceiling roses.

Cord grips for the flexible cord are required in order to prevent damage to the insulation and the accessories must be indelibly marked (as in BS 5733) with this British Standard number, manufacturer's name and terminal identification symbols.

BS 5101   *Lamp caps and holders together with gauges for the control of interchangeability and safety*

Part 1: 1975   *Lamp caps*
Part 2: 1975   *Lamp holders*
Part 3:   *Gauges*
Part 4: 1980   *Lamp caps, lampholders and gauges used in the United Kingdom but not specified in Parts 1, 2 or 3.*

BS 5042   *Specification for lampholders and starter holders*

Part 1: 1981   *Bayonet lampholders*
Requirements and tests are set out for B15 and B22 lampholders in this part. It also contains details of marking and construction with a guide to improve the control of operating temperature.

Part 2: 1978   *Edison screw lampholders*
Ratings, marking, dimensions, construction and tests for electrical and mechanical strength and heat resistance. Applies to E10, E14, E27 and E40 thread sizes.

Part 4: 1973 (1980)   *Built-in lampholders and starterholders for tubular fluorescent lamps*
Specifies dimensional and performance requirements for built-in starterholders used with glow starters and built-in lampholders for use with tubular fluorescent lamps provided with caps G5, G20, G13 and G10q intended for use in circuits connected to an a.c. supply not exceeding 250 V to earth and not exceeding 660 V when the lamp is removed.

(63)   Lighting services

The standards within this section comprehensively cover all aspects of lighting services from the general to the particular, ranging from practice and nomenclature to details of luminaires and the various types of lamp which may be used in them. See also Table 4 Activities, requirements (N) light, dark.

BS 6100   *Glossary of building and civil engineering terms*

Part 3: Section 3.4: 1985   *Lighting*

Defines terms for natural and artificial lighting considered relevant to building and civil engineering.

BS 4727   *Glossary of electrotechnical, power, telecommunications, electronics, lighting and colour terms*   Part 4   *Terms particular to lighting and colour*

BS 4727 combines, in one glossary, terms and definitions used in the several branches of electrical engineering. It is divided into four parts of which the fourth is concerned with terms peculiar to lighting and colour.

Part 4 is subdivided into three groups of terms as follows:

01: 1971 *Radiation and photometry* – with sections on radiation, photometry, quantities and units, optical properties of matter, and radiometric, photometric and colorimetric measurement.
02: 1971 *Vision and colour technology* – with sections on the eye and vision, colour rendering, colorimetry, fundamental concepts and quantities, and tables of spectral tristumulus values for the CIE 1931 and 1964 supplementary standard colorimetric observer.
03: 1972 *Lighting technology terminology* – with sections on illumination, lamps, components of lamps and auxiliary apparatus, and luminaires and their components.

In each case, the terms and definitions are in close agreement with those in the *International Electrotechnical Vocabulary* prepared jointly by the Commission Internationale d'Eclairage (CIE) and the International Electrotechnical Commission (IEC). For BS 8206 *Lighting for buildings* see Table 4 (N).

BS 4533   *Luminaires*

BS 4533 is currently undergoing substantial general revision. The various parts and sections which have been published in the present series are identical with the relevant sections of the IEC publication 598, *Luminaires*. The standard is applicable to luminaires for use with tungsten filament, tubular fluorescent and other discharge lamps on supply voltages not exceeding 1000 V and is, in general, concerned with safety requirements.

Part 101 of the 1981 edition is concerned with the general requirements for the classification and marking of all luminaires and for their mechanical and electrical construction, together with related tests.

A number of important and basic definitions are given:

Luminaire: apparatus which distributes, fillets or transforms the light transmitted from one or more lamps and which includes all parts necessary for supporting, fixing and protecting the lamps but not the lamps themselves, and where necessary circuit auxiliaries together with the means for connecting them to the supply.
Ordinary luminaire: without special protection against dirt or moisture.
General-purpose luminaire: not designed for a special purpose. Examples are pendants, fixed luminaires for surface mounting and spotlights. Examples of special luminaires are those for rough usage, photo and film applications and swimming pools.
Adjustable luminaire: either fixed or portable, the main part of which can be turned or moved by means of joints, raising and lowering devices, telescopic tubes or similar devices.
Basic luminaire: the smallest number of assembled parts that can satisfy the requirements of any of the sections of Part 102.
Combination luminaire: consisting of a basic luminaire in combination with one or more parts which may be replaced by other parts or used in a different combination with other parts and changed either by hand or with the use of tools.
Fixed luminaire: which cannot easily be moved from one place to another, either because the fixing is such that the luminaire

can only be removed with the aid of a tool, or because it is intended for use out of easy reach; ceiling luminaires and pendants are examples.

Portable luminaire: which can easily be moved from one place to another while connected to the supply.

Recessed luminaire: intended by the manufacturer to be fully or partly recessed into a mounting surface. The term applies both to luminaires for operation in enclosed cavities and to luminaires for mounting through a surface such as a suspended ceiling.

Basic insulation: insulation applied to live parts to provide basic insulation against electric shock.

Supplementary insulation: independent insulation applied in addition to basic insulation in order to provide protection against electric shock in the event of a failure of basic insulation.

Double insulation: comprising both basic insulation and supplementary insulation.

Reinforced insulation: a single insulation system applied to live parts, which provides a degree of protection against electric shock equivalent to double insulation.

Section two of this part is concerned with the classification of luminaires, under three headings, according to the type of protection against electric shock, the degree of protection against dust and moisture and the material of supporting surface for which the luminaire is designed.

Class O (applicable only to ordinary luminaires)
A luminaire in which the protection against electric shock relies upon basic insulation.

Class I
A luminaire in which protection against electric shock does not rely on basic insulation only, but which includes an additional safety precaution in such a way that means are provided for the connection of accessible conductive parts to the protective (earthing) conductor in the fixed wiring of the installation in such a way that accessible conductive parts cannot become live in the event of a failure of the basic insulation.

Class II
A luminaire in which protection against electric shock does not rely on basic insulation only but in which additional safety precautions such as double insulation or reinforced insulation are provided, there being no provision for protective earthing or reliance upon installation conditions.

Class II luminaires may be of three types:

1 Having a durable and substantially continuous enclosure of insulating material which envelops all metal parts with the exception of nameplates, screws and rivets which are isolated from live parts with insulation which is at least equivalent to reinforced insulation. Such luminaires are termed insulation-encased Class II.
2 Having a substantially continuous enclosure of metal, in which double insulation is used throughout, except for those parts where reinforced insulation is used because the application of double insulation is manifestly impracticable. Such luminaires are termed metal-encased Class II.
3 Being a combination of 1 and 2.

Class III
A luminaire in which protection against electric shock relies on supply at safety extra-low voltage (SELV) and in which voltages higher than those of SELV are not generated.

The classes according to the degree of protection against ingress of dust and moisture are in accordance with the system explained in the IEC publication 529, *Classification of Degrees of Protection Provided by Enclosure*. The luminaires are classified by means of 'IP numbers'. The symbols which are used in marking are given in Table 56.

The classes according to the material of the supporting surface for which the luminaire is designed are based upon whether the luminaires are primarily intended for direct mounting on normally flammable surface or is suitable only for mounting on non-combustible surfaces. The classes and any associated references or symbols used in marking are as follows:

Suitable for direct mounting only on non-combustible surfaces.	No symbol is used but a warning notice is required, indicating that the luminaire is not suitable for mounting on a normally flammable surface.
Without built-in ballasts or transformers, suitable for direct mounting on normally flammable surface. With built-in ballasts or transformers, suitable for direct mounting on normally flammable surfaces.	Symbol thus F

The remaining sections deal in considerable depth with the various aspects of the design, construction and tests for luminaires as follows:

Section 1.4 *Construction* – general requirements for the various components, electrical connections, insulation, mechanical strength, durability and tests
Section 1.5 *External and internal wiring* – method of connection to supply, internal provisions for cables and cords, bushings and anchorages
Section 1.6 *Terminations*
Section 1.7 *Provision for earthing* – earth connections, terminals, tests
Section 1.8 *Protection against electric shock* – general provisions with regard to safety
Section 1.9 *Resistance to dust and moisture* – tests for ingress of dust and moisture and for humidity

Table 56 *Degrees of protection for luminaires*

First figure	Protection (solids)	IP	Symbol
2	Ordinary	2 X	none
4	1 mm probe	4 X	none
5	Dust-proof	5 X	✦
6	Dust-tight	6 X	✦

Second figure	Protection (water)	IP	Symbol
0	Ordinary	X 0	none
1	Drip-proof	X 1	●
3	Rain-proof	X 3	▣
4	Splash-proof	X 4	⚠
5	Jet-proof	X 5	⚠ ⚠
7	Water-tight (immersible)	X 7	●●
8	Pressure water-tight (submersible)	X 8	●● .m

IP numbers are usually combinations of the two above figures, example IP54 dust-proof and splash-proof.

Section 1.10 *Insulation resistance and electric strength* – tests for insulation resistance and electric strength, measurement of leakage current

Section 1.11 *Creepage distances and clearances* – criteria to ensure that live parts and adjacent metal parts are adequately spaced

Section 1.12 *Endurance test and thermal test* – selection of lamps and ballasts for testing, details of test requirements

Section 1.13 *Resistance to heat, fire and tracking* – details of test requirements for resistance to heat, to flame and ignition and to tracking.

Section 1.14 *Nipples for lampholders*

Section 1.15 *Screwless terminals and electrical connections* – definitions, general requirements, and mechanical and electrical tests

Part 102 is divided into individual sections each of which covers the particular requirements for the various types of luminaire as follows:

Section 102.1 *Fixed general purpose luminaires*
Section 102.2 *Recessed luminaires*
Section 102.3 *Luminaires for road and street lighting*
Section 102.4 *Portable general-purpose luminaires*
Section 102.5 *Floodlights*
Section 102.6 *Luminaires with built-in transformers for filament lamps*
Section 102.18 *Luminaires for swimming pools and similar applications*

The sections follow a standard format each covering scope, general test requirements, definitions, classification, marking, construction, creepage distances and clearances provisions for earthing, terminals, external and internal wiring, protection against electric shock, endurance and thermal tests, resistance to dust and moisture, insulation resistance and electric strength, resistance to heat fire and tracking. Some sections include certain special provisions outside the standard format.

Section 103.1 deals with the performance requirements of luminaires, covering the light distribution from road-lighting lanterns. Other sections may be published later to include the performance requirements of other types of luminaire. The provisions of section one relate to Group A and B lighting installations and lighting installations in the vicinity of aerodromes (as defined in BS 5489 Parts 2, 3 and 8 respectively).

BS 5225 *Photometric data for luminaires*

Part 3: 1982 *Method of photometric measurement of battery-operated emergency lighting luminaires*
Details are covered on the photometry of the above luminaires which is used in the derivation of lighting scheme planning data. The reporting of measurement and application of correction factor differ from Part 1, which considers laboratory conditions, procedures and instrumentation for measurement on single general-purpose luminaires and methods of measuring luminance and illuminance.

BS 5266 *Emergency lighting*

This standard is being developed in a number of parts, each concerned with various aspects of emergency lighting.

Part 1: 1975 is a code of practice relating to the provision of electric emergency lighting in most types of premises, other than private domestic premises, cinemas and existing premises to which the provisions of CP 1007 *Maintained lighting for cinemas* have been applied by the enforcing authority. The content of Part 1 recommends standards for the clear indication and safe level of illumination of escape routes in the event of failure of the normal supply and proposed minimum continuous periods of operation of such emergency lighting based on the size, life and usage of the premises.

Part 2, when published, will supersede CP 1007 *Maintained lighting for cinemas* and will include requirements for other types of premises to which the general provisions of CP 1007 are currently applied, for example dance halls, ballrooms, licenced bingo premises and ten-pin bowling establishments.

Part 3: 1981 *Small power relays (electromagnetic) for emergency lighting applications up to and including 32 A* is the first of possibly a number of parts specifying the requirements for items of equipment used in emergency lighting systems. This part specifies performance characteristics of relays capable of transferring an emergency lighting load from a normal source of supply to an emergency supply when the normal source of supply fails, or connecting an emergency lighting load when de-energized, and disconnecting an emergency lighting load when energized.

BS 559: 1955 *Electric signs and high-voltage luminous-discharge-tube installations*

This standard relates to low and medium voltage signs (excluding exit signs for cinemas, etc.) irrespective of the lamp employed, and high voltage discharge tube installations up to and including 5 kV to earth, whether used for publicity, decorative or general lighting purposes, either for external or for internal use. The voltage bands used are those laid down in the Electricity Supply Regulations 1937 and not those in the fifteenth edition of the Regulations for Electrical Installations issued by the Institution of Electrical Engineers.

The provisions of the standard cover in detail the construction of the installations, the electrical apparatus and the wiring.

BS 889: 1965 *Flameproof electric lighting fittings*

This is another standard which is dated by the use of the term 'lighting fitting'. It is in four parts each concerned with different types of flame luminaires intended for use in situations where explosive mixtures of air and flammable gases or vapours may occur, as follows:

Part 1 *Fittings using well-glasses, bulkhead dished or flat glasses*
Part 2 *Fittings incorporating glass tubes to enclose tubular fluorescent lamps*
Part 3 *Fittings incorporating clear or opal acrylic plastics tubes to enclose tubular fluorescent lamps*
Part 4 *Portable handlamps and particular type of screened flexible cable approved for use therewith*

Each part covers the design, components, testing and marking of the luminaires.

BS 161: 1976 *Tungsten filament lamps for general service (batch testing)*

The recommendations of this standard apply to ordinary incandescent lamps for general lighting purposes having a nominal life of 1000 hours, a rated wattage of 25–1500 W inclusive, a rated voltage of 240 V, bulbs, clear (all wattages) or internally frosted (25–300 W inclusive) and caps, normal bayonet or Edison screw.

The scope of recommendations covers the technical requirements for the lamps and the methods of test to be used in determining the quality and interchangeability of the lamps on a scientific basis.

The standard comprises some five sections.

Much important information is found in appendices including among others, tables showing the dimensions for lamps and the minimum initial burner outputs. See Table 57.

The values in Tables 58 and 59 are those for voltages standardized in the IEC publication 38, *IEC Standard Voltage* (other values for 12 further voltages are given).

Table 57 *Dimensions for lamps*

Dimensions are given in mm

Rated wattage W	Caps for which the dimensions are given	Diameter			Light-centre length 130 × 121.5 mm		Overall length max.	
		Bulb max.	Neck		Nominal	Tolerance	With bayonet cap	With screw cap
			min.	max.				
25	B22/25 × 26	62	32	34	To be		108.5	110
40	or	62	32	34	declared		108.5	110
60	E27/27	62	32	34	by the		108.5	110
	E26/24*				manufacturer			
100		62	32	34		± 3	108.5	110
150		82	32	40		± 4	165	166.5
200	E27/27 E26/24*	82	32		130	± 4		166.5
300	E27/30 E26/24	91			133	± 4		184
300	E40/41 E39/41*	91			138	± 4		189
300	E40/45	111.5	49		178	± 5		240
500	E39/41*	111.5	49		178	± 5		240
1 000		151.5	49		225	± 8		309
1 000		131.5	49		202	± 6		275
1 500		171.5	49		250	± 8		344

*Not interchangeable.

(Appendix C: BS 161: 1976)

Table 58 *Minimum rated lumens: lamps of normal luminous flux*

Voltage V	Wattage W									
	25	40	60	100	150	200	300	500	1000	1500
	Lumens									
110	225	445	770	1 420	2 360	3 250	5 050	8 900	19 300	30 000
115	225	440	760	1 420	2 340	3 250	5 000	8 900	19 300	30 000
127	220	425	750	1 380	2 300	3 200	4 950	8 800	19 100	29 600
220	220	350	630	1 250	2 090	2 920	4 610	8 300	18 600	29 000
230	220	345	620	1 240	2 070	2 900	4 580	8 250	18 500	28 800

(From Table IIIA: Appendix D: BS 161: 1976)

Table 59 *Minimum rated lumens: lamps of high luminous flux*

Voltage V	Wattage W			
	25	40	60	100
	Lumens			
110	265	500	840	1580
115	265	500	840	1580
127	260	490	820	1560
220	230	415	715	1350
230	230	415	710	1340

(From Table IIIB: Appendix D: BS 161: 1976)

BS 5971 *Safety and interchangeability of tungsten filament lamps for domestic and similar lighting purposes*

The two parts of this standard apply to tungsten filament lamps which have:

1 Pear-shaped, mushroom-shaped, candle, round and reflector or other bulb shapes where the lamps are intended to serve the same purpose as any lamps with the foregoing bulbs.
2 A rated wattage of up to and including 200 W.
3 A rated voltage of 50 to 250 V inclusive.
4 B 15d, B 22d, E 14 and E 27 caps.
5 Clear, frosted, internally and externally coated and reflector-ized finishes.

Part 1: 1980 specifies requirements and test for the lamps as regards their marking, safety in normal use and their inter-changeability.

Part 2: 1980 specifies a method of assessment of compliance with the requirements of Part 1.

BS 1853 *Tubular fluorescent lamps for general lighting service*

There are two parts to this standard. Part 1: 1979, which is identical to the IEC publication 81, covers internationally specified lamps. Part 2: 1979 covers lamps used in the United Kingdom and which are not included in Part 1.

A tubular fluorescent lamp is defined as 'a low pressing mercury discharge lamp of tubular form, either straight or U-shaped or curved, in which most of the light is emitted by a layer of fluorescent material excited by the ultra-violet radiation from the discharge'.

Many of the requirements in the two parts are identical, Part 2 being cross-reference to Part 1. The provisions of the standard cover the sampling, marking, mechanical, physical and starting characteristics, requirements and conditions of test for electrical and luminous characteristics and for life, and conditions for compliance. The electrical, luminous and dimensional charac-teristics of the several lamps are contained in a series of sheets in each part.

Three types of lamp are covered in Part 1, namely:

1 Lamps with preheated cathodes operated with the use of a starter.

2 Lamps with preheated cathodes operated without the use of a starter.
3 Lamps with non-preheated cathodes operated without the use of a starter.

A digest of some of the information in the data sheets for lamps in this part is shown in Table 60.

Table 60   *Tubular fluorescent lamp data*

Sheet no.	Lamp rating	Cap	Method of starting	Cathode type
81-1EC-1020-1	4 W	G 5	Starter	Pre-heated
81-1EC-1030-1	6 W	G 5		
81-1EC-1040-1	8 W	G 5		
81-1EC-1050-1	13 W	G 5		
81-1EC-1110-1	20 W	G 13		
81-1EC-1150-1	25 W	G 13		
81-1EC-1210-1	30 W (T8)	G 13		
81-1EC-1220-1	30 W (T12)	G 13		
81-1EC-1310-1	40 W	G 13		
81-1EC-1550-1	65 W	G 13		
81-1EC-1710-1	80 W	G 13		
81-1EC-1780-1	85 W	G 13		
81-1EC-1930-1	125 W	G 13		
81-1EC-2130-1	22 W	G 10q		
81-1EC-2230-1	32 W	G 10q		
81-1EC-2350-1	40 W	G 10q		
81-1EC-2810-1	90 W	G 20		
81-1EC-4110-1	20 W	G 13		High-cathode resistance
81-1EC-4210-1	30 W (T8)	G 13		
81-1EC-4220-1	30 W (T12)	G 13		
81-1EC-4310-1	40 W	G 13		
81-1EC-4710-1	80 W	G 13		
81-1EC-4780-1	85 W	G 13		
81-1EC-4930-1	125 W	G 13		
81-1EC-5110-1	20 W	G 13	Starter less	Low-cathode resistance
81-1EC-5210-1	30 W (T8)	G 13		
81-1EC-5220-1	30 W (T12)	G 13		
81-1EC-5225-1	30 W (T12)	G 13 **		
81-1EC-5310-1	40 W	G 13		
81-1EC-5325-1	40 W	G 13 **		
81-1EC-5350-1	40 W	G 10q		
81-1EC-5520-1	60 W	R 17d		
81-1EC-5550-1	65 W	G 13		
81-1EC-5760-1	85 W	G 13		
81-1EC-5770-1	87 W	R 17d		
81-1EC-5920-1	112 W	R 17d		
81-1EC-8110-1	20 W	Fa6		Non pre-heated
81-1EC-8290-1	39 W	Fa8		
81-1EC-8310-1	40 W	Fa6		
81-1EC-8470-1	57 W	Fa8		
81-1EC-8650-1	75 W	Fa8		

** Low starting voltage lamps (LSV).

(From BS 1853: Part 1: 1979)

Two types of lamp are covered in Part 2:

1 Lamps with preheated cathodes operated with the use of a starter.
2 Lamps with preheated cathodes operated without the use of a starter.

Four rated colours are specified for Part 1 lamps:

Daylight: corresponding to a correlated temperature of approximately 6400 K (equivalent to Standard Colour in Part 1).
Cool white: corresponding to a correlated colour temperature of approximately 4200 K (equivalent to Standard Colour 2 in Part 1).
White: corresponding to a correlated colour temperature of approximately 3450 K.

Warm white: corresponding to a correlated colour temperature of 2950 K (equivalent to Standard Colour 3 in Part 1).

A digest of some of the information in the data sheets for lamps in this part is shown in Table 61.

BS 3767: 1972   *Low pressure sodium vapour lamps*

This is technically equivalent to the IEC publication 192, second edition, and relates to low pressure sodium vapour lamps of the integral type, both U-shaped and linear, operating on a.c. mains at 50 Hz or 60 Hz with a ballast satisfying the requirements of BS 4782.

The requirements in the standard cover the marking, physical characteristics and starting of the lamps together with the conditions of test for their electrical and luminous characteristics which are detailed in appendices. The electrical and dimensional requirements of the lamps are contained in a series of data sheets.

BS 3677: 1982   *High pressure mercury vapour lamps*

This standard specifies the requirements for such lamps with or without a red connecting fluorescent coating, operating on a.c. mains with a ballast complying with BS 4782. It is technically equivalent to the IEC publication 188.

A high pressure mercury vapour lamp is one in which the light emission is produced by an electric discharge in mercury vapour at high pressure with or without the assistance of a fluorescent or translucent coating which may be on the inner surface of the outer bulb.

The requirements of the standard cover the making, physical starting and luminous characteristics of the lamps together with the various tests for compliance.

The electrical and dimensional characteristics are contained in a series of data sheets, a digest of which is shown in Table 62.

In addition, maximum lamp outlines are given which, if observed, will facilitate mechanical acceptance of lamps in luminaires.

(64)   Communications

Three codes of practice consider the selection and installation of communication systems in buildings. Clocks are dealt with in sections of BS 3456 (see section (– 6) 'Services, mainly electrical').

BS 6100   *Glossary of building and civil engineering terms*

Part 3: Section 3.2 Subsection 3.2.1: 1984   *Internal communication*
Gives definitions of certain terms relevant to the construction industry, for telecommunications, security equipment and other communication systems.

BS 6506: 1984   *Code of practice for installation of private branch exchanges for connection to the British Telecommunications public switched telephone network*

This standard deals with the installation of private branch exchanges (PBX) for direct or indirect connection at the users premises to analogue interfaces of the British Telecommunications public switched telephone network (PSTN).

Although this standard is intended primarily for the installer of a PBX it includes recommendations and advice directed towards the supplier, user, maintenance personnel and to designers and architects of buildings intending to house PBXs.

BS 6330: 1983   *Code of practice for the reception of sound and television broadcasting*

Gives guidance for obtaining good reception of sound and tele-

Table 61 *List of specific lamp types included in this standard*

Sheet number	Lamp rating	Cap	Method of starting	Cathode type	
1853 – 01	15 W (T8)	G 13	Starter	Preheated	
1853 – 02	40 W	G 13	Starter	Preheated	
1853 – 03	75 W	G 13	Starter	Preheated	
1853 – 04	100 W	G 13	Starter	Preheated	
1853 – 20	60 W	G 10q	Starter	Preheated	
1853 – 40	50 W	G 13	Starterless	Preheated	High-cathode resistance
1853 – 41	65 W	G 13	Starterless	Preheated	High-cathode resistance
1853 – 42	75 W	G 13	Starterless	Preheated	High-cathode resistance

(From Clause 4.2: BS 1853: Part 2: 1979)

Type 62 *Lamp characteristics*

Sheet no.	Rated wattage	Lamp Voltage	Current	Bulb diameter (D1) (mm)	Neck diameter (D2) (mm)	Overall length (L) mm	Cap
1.1	50	95	0.61	56	35	130	E26 or E27
2.1	80	115	0.80	81	40	166.5	E26 or E27
3.1	125	125	1.15	91	43	185.5	E26 or E27
4.1	175	130	1.50	91	53	211	E39 or E40
5.1	250	130	2.13	91	53	227	E39 or E40
6.1	400	135	3.25	122	58	292	E39 or E40
7.1	700	265	2.80	152	66	368	E39 or E40
8.1	700	140	5.40	152	66	368	E39 or E40
9.1	1000	265	4.00	181	66	410	E39 or E40
10.1	1000	145	7.50	181	66	410	E39 or E40
11.1	1000	135	8.00	181	66	410	E39 or E40
12.1	2000	270	8.00	187	70	445	E39 or E40

(Digest S2: BS 3677: 1982)

vision broadcasting in buildings. Includes recommendations for the provision of aerial systems and cabled distribution systems, accommodation for equipment and cables and protective measures against certain hazards. General guidance is given on the broadcast services available and on satisfactory completion and handing over of systems.

CP 1022: 1973 *The selection and accommodation of telephone, telegraph and data communication services*

Structural and accommodation requirements for telephone, telegraph and data communications equipment, installed in new or existing private premises are considered. No restriction is laid upon the range and size of units or the application of special features. The code applies to installations in temperate climates and buildings of all types of construction. Included is information on the facilities and systems provided and on materials and methods recommended with appropriate structural design considerations.

BS 6259: 1982 *Code of practice for planning and installation of sound systems*

Guidance is given on the design, construction, use and maintenance of sound distribution systems for installation in buildings and outdoor stadia. The code includes sections dealing with equipment, materials, design, system characteristics, sources of sound output, amplification, reproduction from discs, tapes and films, reproduction of broadcast programmes, synthetic and voice signals, methods of control, power supplies, earthing, cables, wires, ducts, structural accommodation, safety, work on use, inspection, testing and maintenance.

(66) Transport

This section deals with the various forms of mechanical vertical and horizontal transportation systems found in buildings, such as lifts, paternosters, escalators and passenger conveyors. The applications range not only from those found in normal circumstances but also those concerned with the needs of the disabled and infirm.

A number of new standards are being introduced as international standards and are expected to supersede or at least complement those which are based upon British practice.

BS 6100 *Glossary of building and civil engineering terms*

Part 3: Section 3.2 Subsection 3.2.2: 1984 *Internal transport* Defines certain terms relevant to construction for lifts, escalators, and other conveyors.

BS 2655 *Lifts, escalators, passenger conveyors and paternosters*

This is a standard covering all aspects of the design, construction, safety, testing and modernization of the various forms of vertical transportation provided in buildings. Some of the standard has already been rendered obsolescent by BS 5655 Part 1 which is a European standard and Part 5 takes account of international standards. A transitional period is contemplated during which the provisions of BS 5655 will progressively supersede this standard. In the meantime much remains in force.

The parts are as follows:

Part 1: 1970 *General requirements for electric, hydraulic and hand-powered lifts*
Part 4: 1969 *General requirements for escalators and passenger conveyors*

Part 5: 1970 *General requirements for paternosters*
Part 6: 1970 *Building construction requirements*
Part 7: 1970 *Testing and inspection*
Part 8: 1971 *Modernization or reconstruction of lifts, escalators and paternosters*
Part 9: 1970 *Definitions*
Part 10: 1972 *General requirements for guarding*

Four definitions in Part 9 are fundamental to this standard, namely:

Lift: an appliance for transporting persons or goods between two or more levels by means of guided car moving in a substantially vertical direction and travelling in the same path in both upward and downward directions.

Escalator: a power drive incline moving storage used for raising or lowering passengers.

Passenger conveyor: a passenger carrying device on which passengers stand or walk and in which the passenger carrying surface remains parallel to its direction or motor and is uninterrupted.

Paternoster: a continuous running appliance for transporting in a substantially vertical direction, in which a number of cars are suspended by two endless chains attached to the cars diagonally so that the car floors are substantially horizontal when changing direction at the extremities of travel.

Part 1 applies to electric hydraulic and hand-powered passenger lifts, goods lifts and service lifts suspended by ropes or chains or supported by direct-acting ram and employing a guided lift car. It does not apply to lifting platforms and road vehicle lifting machines having a vertical travel not exceeding 2.00 m (6 ft 6 in), amusement devices, strap hoists, builders' hoists, conveyors or similar apparatus used for raising, piling or tiering. Section one requires a safety factor of not less than five for all parts of the lift.

Section two and section four were both rendered obsolescent by the publication of BS 5655 Part 1. They have been superseded after a transitional period ending on 31 May 1984.

Sections five and six deal with the specific requirements of different types of lift, namely hydraulic lifts and hand-powered lifts.

In each case the section covers the requirements for the lift cars, lift machines, principal components of the installation, controls, safety provisions and electrical installation.

Part 4 specifies in separate sections the requirements for escalators and passenger conveyors.

Section two covers escalators specifying the design requirements, steps, landing plates, combplates, balustrading, guards at ceiling intersections, handrails, driving machines, safety factors, operating and safety devices, machinery specs, main switches and wiring, controllers, lighting and making.

The requirements applying to passenger conveyors are given in section three under a similar list of headings to those in section two. A number of the provisions are in fact cross-referenced to section two.

Part 5 is concerned with the engineering and safety requirements of paternosters. The maximum speed is limited to 0.4 m/s or 80 ft/min. The specific requirements in section two of this part cover guides and fixings, car frames, car capacity and loading, car enclosures, loading entrances, shaft screening and lighting, suspension, driving machinery and sprockets, load and warning plates, controller, operation and operating devices, suppression of radio and television interference, circuit breaker or main switch and wiring.

Part 6 has six sections which cover the building construction requirements for escalators, lifts, passenger conveyors and paternosters, those for lifts being subdivided into powered lifts and handpowered lifts. The sections are as follows:

Section 1 *General*
Section 2 *Passenger and goods lifts (lowered)* – now rendered

obsolescent by the introduction of BS 5655 Part 1. See the comments of section two relating to electric passenger or goods lifts
Section 3 *Service lifts (powered)*
Section 4 *Hand-powered lifts*
Section 5 *Paternosters*
Section 6 *Escalators and passenger conveyors*

Each section covers in detail constructional requirements of the various types of installation within the building together with provisions concerned with fire protection.

Part 7 specifies at length the requirements for testing and examining new and modified equipment covered by Parts 1, 4 and 5, differentiating between the tests and examinations carried out at the time of commissioning and subsequent periodic examinations. Because of the introduction of BS 5655 Part 1 the tests prescribed by Part 7 of BS 2655 are rendered obsolescent and will, in any case, not apply to any installation scheduled for commissioning after 31 May 1984, except in the case of modernization, where it can be shown that compliance with BS 5655 is not reasonably practicable.

Part 8 covers the engineering and safety requirements which must be incorporated, as far as may be reasonably practicable, in old lifts, escalators and paternosters during modernization or reconstruction so that the parts of installation affected by such changes should comply with Parts 1, 4 and 5.

The modernization or reconstruction of lifts commissioned after 31 May 1984 will require compliance with BS 5655 Part 1. Until that time, however, compliance with the requirements of either standard is permitted. In view of the fact, however, that the reconstruction of existing lifts imposes space limitations which may render compliance difficult or impossible, special provisions are permissible to meet certain site conditions often present in buildings that have been in use for many years. Any deviation from the requirements where compliance is not reasonably practicable must secure a minimum acceptable standard of safety.

Part 9 contains some ten definitions, each definition being identified with the type of installation with which it is associated.

Part 10 (rendered obsolescent by BS 5655) is concerned with the guarding of moving parts and protection against hazards from electrical equipment and relates to installations covered by Parts 4 and 5 of this standard.

BS 5655 *Lifts and service lifts*

This standard, which is still being developed, deals with permanently installed new lifts.

It does not cover the lifts which come under the following headings: paternosters, rack and pinion elevators, screw driver elevators, mine lifts, theatrical lifts, appliance with automatic caging, skips and lifts and hoists used for building and public works, sites, ships' hoists, platforms for exploration or drilling at sea, construction and maintenance appliances.

At the moment some ten parts are designated and the publication of further parts is anticipated.

Part 1: 1979 *Safety rules for the construction and installation of electric lifts*
Part 2: 1983 *Hydraulic lifts*
Part 3 *Safety rules for the construction and installation of electric service lifts* (in preparation)
Part 4 *Safety rules for the construction and installation of hydraulic service lifts* (in preparation)
Part 5: 1981 *Dimensions of standard electric lift arrangements*
Part 6: 1985 *Code of practice for selection and installation*
Part 7: 1983 *Manual control devices, indicators and additional fittings*
Part 8: 1983 *Eyebolts for lift suspension*
Part 9: 1985 *Guide rails*
Part 10 *Testing and inspecting electric and hydraulic lifts* (in preparation)

Part 1 has rendered obsolete and will ultimately supersede a number of parts and sections of parts of BS 2655. The requirements of Part 1 apply to all relevant lift installations scheduled for commissioning since 31 May 1984.

The object of this part of the standard is to define safety rules related to passenger goods and service lifts with a view to safeguarding people and objects against the risk of accidents associated with the operation of lifts and service lifts. Towards this end, it covers in considerable detail the design, mechanical, electrical and durability aspects of lift construction while assuming that all components are correctly designed, well manufactured and well maintained.

The contents are comprised in some seventeen sections:

Section 0 *Introduction*
Section 1 *Scope and field of application*
Section 2 *References*
Section 3 *Definitions*
Section 4 *Symbols and abbreviations*
Section 5 *Lift well*
Section 6 *Machine and pulley rooms*
Section 7 *Landing doors*
Section 8 *Car and counterweight*
Section 9 *Suspension*
Section 10 *Guides, buffers and final limit switches*
Section 11 *Clearance between car and the lift well wall facing the car entrance*
Section 12 *Machines*
Section 13 *Electric installations and appliances*
Section 14 *Protection against electric faults, controls and priorities*
Section 15 *Notices and operating instructions*
Section 16 *Examination tests, register and servicing*

Extensive amplification of the requirements is contained in seven appendices.

Part 2 specifies requirements for permanently installed new hydraulic lifts, serving defined levels having a car designed for the transportation of persons and/or goods. It also includes the associated construction requirements of the building within which the lifts are installed.

Part 5 specifies dimensions to permit the accommodation of passenger lift installations. Lift speeds appropriate to normal United Kingdom practice can be found in CP 407.

In addition this part gives preference to centre opening doors while permitting single sliding doors for a limited period.

The dimensions specified in Part 5 cover the nine dimensions of cars and the lift wall, door entrance dimensions of landing doors and the dimensions of the machine room and landings. These are summarized in Table 63 and Figure 63 which show the structural configuration of the installation.

Part 6 gives recommendations for electric and hydraulic lifts manufactured to comply with the requirements of other parts of this standard. It paraphrases many of the requirements in and should be read in conjunction with other parts of this standard.

Section two of this code gives general guidance on the procedure to be adopted in obtaining a lift installation that is satisfactory from the aspects of operation, safety and maintenance, and also on the exchange of information between the lift contractor and other trades providing various service facilities.

Lifts selected in accordance with these recommendations are generally suitable for use by disabled persons; it may, however, be necessary to specify additional features to suit certain disabilities (see BS 5810 and BS 5619).

The building requirements for the equipment covered by BS 5655: Parts 1 and 2 have been brought together in section three because of their interest to the architect or other person responsible for specifying the details of building construction, this last-mentioned function not being the prime responsibility of the lift contractor. Additional building work requirements (such as fixings, cutting away for switches and making good) are

not covered by BS 5655: Parts 1 and 2; reference should be made to the drawings supplied by the manufacturer of the equipment.

Electric lifts are dealt with in section four and hydraulic lifts in section five.

Section six provides guidance on the use and installation of observation lifts, which are increasingly being installed in modern buildings. Since specific requirements for this type of lift are not included in the current editions of BS 5655: Parts 1 and 2, appendix C has been included to provide guidance in the design and installation of observation lifts.

Part 7 considers essential features for manual control devices and indicators when lifts are constructed and installed taking into account the control system adopted. Three basic types of control system are specified in terms of devices to be provided for users to operate the lift and the indicators to indicate to users the function of the lift, i.e.

Table 1 for lifts under single push button control
Table 2 for lifts under down collective control
Table 3 for lifts under full collective control

Also included are minimum requirements for handrails and the identification of telephones installed in lift cars.

Part 8 specifies the materials, dimensions, test requirements and safe working loads for eyebolts. Eight nominal sizes are listed covering wire rope diameters in the range 6 mm to 22 mm inclusive.

Part 9 details the grades and quality, the dimensional characteristics and tolerances and the surface finish of nine sizes of tee-section guide rails and their fishplates. In addition the designation system for the guide rails is defined. Appendix A provides instructions to lift contractors on how to evaluate the forces and stresses in guide rails and this enables the contractor to select the appropriate rails and correct fixing spaces for each installation.

BS 5656: 1983 *Safety rules for the construction and installation of escalators and passenger conveyors*

Specifies safety requirements for new escalators and passenger conveyors to safeguard passengers and maintenance personnel against injury. Covers the mechanical and electrical construction of the machine, the relevant, structural feature of the building in which it is to be installed, examination and testing. Supersedes BS 2655: Part 4 which is obsolescent.

BS 5900: 1980 *Powered homelifts*

A homelift is defined as 'a permanent lifting equipment, installed to serve defined landing levels in a private dwelling or residential home, that comprises a car, whose dimensions and means of construction clearly permit the access of passengers and/or passenger in a wheelchair, running rigid vertical guides'. The requirements of this standard identify minimum safety rules related to the design, construction, installation, operation and maintenance of electrically powered suspended homelifts which are to be specifically used by disabled persons with a view to safeguarding against the risk of accidents associated with the operation of such equipment, and cover testing, inspection and testing.

Homelifts do not normally travel a vertical distance greater than 12 m. Those having a partially enclosed car are suitable for use only in private dwellings. Those having a totally enclosed car may be used in both private dwellings and residential homes but in the latter case, the lift well would also need to be totally enclosed.

BS 5965: 1980 *Manually driven balanced personal homelifts*

The definition of a homelift in this standard is substantially the same as powered homelifts in BS 5900. However, those complying with this standard are suitable for installation and use only in private dwellings.

Table 63 *Dimensions for general purpose passenger lift installations*

Typical applications For the carriage of passengers in banks, office buildings, hotels, etc.
Entrances Power operated, two panel centre opening, sliding doors.
Standard speeds (see note 1) These speeds are as follows:

(a) two speed $v = 1.00$ m/s
(b) variable speed $v = 1.00$ m/s and 1.60 m/s

Rated load Q	No. of passengers	Rated speed v	Car internal sizes			Well min. dimensions		Clear entrance		Pit depth P_h	Headroom S_h	Machine room min. dimensions (see note 2)			
			Width C_w	Depth C_d	Height C_h	Width W_w	Depth W_d	Width E_w	Height E_h			Area R_a	Width R_w	Depth R_d	Height R_h
kg		m/s	mm	mm	mm	mm	mm	mm	mm	mm	mm	m²	mm	mm	mm
630	8	1.00	1100	1400	2200	1800	2100	800	2000	1700	4000	15	2500	3700	2600
		1.60									4200				
800	10	1.00	1350	1400	2200	1900	2300	800	2000	1700	4000	15	2500	3700	2600
		1.60									4200				
1000	13	1.00	1600	1400	2300	2400	2300	1100	2100	1800	4200	20	3200	4900	2700
		1.60													
1250	16	1.00	1950	1400	2300	2600	2300	1100	2100	1900	4400	22	3200	4900	2700
		1.60													
1600	21	1.00	1950	1750	2300	2600	2600	1100	2100	1900	4400	25	3200	5500	2800
		1.60													

(Table 4: BS 5655: Part 5: 1981)

Note 1: The dimensions specified in this table are also valid for rated speeds lower than those stated.
Note 2: Select dimensions for R_w and R_d

(a) which are equal to or greater than those specified, and
(b) whose product produces an area which is equal to or greater than that specified for R_a.

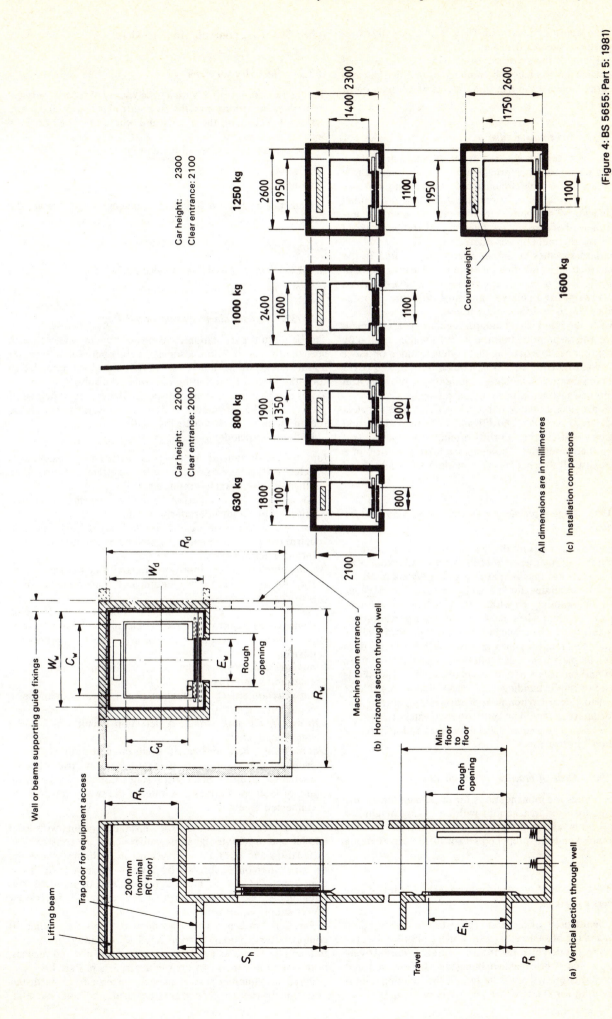

Figure 63   *Layout of general purpose passenger lift installations*

These homelifts are hand-wound. They do not normally travel a vertical distance greater than 6 m.

The provisions of the standard are designed to ensure that homelifts, which are to be used by nominated disabled persons are safeguarded against the risk of accidents which may occur during their use.

BS 5776: 1979 *Powered stairlifts*

The power driven stairlifts covered by this standard are for use on stairways within, or on internal stairways giving access to a private dwelling. In suitable circumstances, such equipment may be used in a residential home or similar establishment provided for persons who by reason of age, infirmity or other circumstances are in need of care and attention not otherwise available to them; or for the mentally disordered.

The standard specifies minimum safety rules related to the design, construction, installation, operation and maintenance of the stairlift which are to be used specifically for disabled persons travelling between fixed points in a normal domestic environment with a view to ensuring safety in use.

Both in BS 5965 and this standard, regulations are framed, however, on the assumption that the stairlifts will be used only by persons either capable of using them safely unaided or under the supervision of a competent able-bodied person, and cover the design considerations, building requirements, full technical specification and testing, inspection and servicing.

An appendix gives guidance to intending purchasers to select and specify an appropriate stairlift and to remind them and owners of new and existing stairlifts of additional factors that will require their attention. The guidance takes the form of a useful checklist. Reference is also made to BS 5900 and BS 5965.

BS 6440: 1983 *Code of practice for powered lifting platforms for use by disabled persons*

The minimum safety rules for the design, construction, installation, operation and maintenance of fixed powered lifting platforms whose platform may be partially or totally enclosed.

Platforms are intended for use solely by disabled persons, whether sitting, standing or within a wheelchair and accompanied by an attendant when necessary, for transportation between fixed levels, which may include intermediate levels, where the maximum height of the platform above the lowest level does not exceed 1.98 m. It is intended that the equipment is for fixed installation and for access to and use in or about private dwellings, private or public buildings and places, and be capable of operation in an indoor environment of normal temperature and humidity or alternatively in an outdoor environment.

This code also details some special features and actions for consideration by purchasers.

BS 5323: 1980 *Code of practice for scissor lifts*

The code contains recommendations for the design and safety requirements for fixed installations with a working height not exceeding 1.98 m above ground or floor level, and mobile vehicle mounted and self-propelled scissor lifts of any working height.

BS 6037: 1981 *Code of practice for permanently installed suspended access equipment*

The recommendations of this code relate to the construction, installation and use of an access system which comprises a working platform suspended on ropes from a securely mounted overhead structure. It may be capable of being raised or lowered, and of being moved laterally across the face of the building, and is customarily used for maintenance and window cleaning.

(68)   Security, control, other services

(68.2)   Security services

This section is concerned with a wide variety of security services and safety provisions, ranging from intruder alarms and alarm systems to safeguard the elderly and others who live at risk, to security glazing.

The standards may be subdivided into:

1 Alarms.
2 Protection.

Detection and alarm systems in connection with fire are the subject of section (68.5), 'Fire protection services'.

Alarms

BS 8220   *Safety of buildings against crime*

Part 2   *Offices and shops* is in draft.

BS 4737   *Intruder alarm systems in buildings*

This is a multi-part standard, at present under review, which specifies the construction, installation and operation of intruder alarm systems using audible and remote signalling, intended to form the basis for the contract between the subscriber and an alarm company but it does not specify the extent or degree of protection to be provided, nor does it necessarily cover all the requirements for a particular installation.

Definitions include:

Intruder alarm system: an electrical installation designed to detect and signal the presence, entry or attempted entry of an intruder into protected premises.
Protected premises: that part of a building to which protection is afforded by an intruder alarm system.
Subscriber: a person or organization utilizing the services of an alarm company for the installation and/or maintenance of an intruder alarm system.
Alarm company: an organization prepared to enter into a contract for the provision, installation and/or maintenance of an intruder alarm system.
Detection circuit: a circuit connecting one or more detection devices to the control equipment of an intruder alarm system, or a circuit connecting a detection device to a processing device.
Closed detection circuit: a detection circuit which is in an alarm condition when it is open.
Open detection circuit: a detection circuit which is in an alarm condition when it is closed.
Single-pole detection circuit: a detection circuit which has a single conductor.
Double-pole detection circuit: a closed detection circuit so arranged that throughout its length there are two adjacent conductors in different electrical states and such that an alarm and/or fault condition is generated if the two conductors are connected together.

Part 1: 1986 is concerned with installed systems with local audible and/or remote signalling, and specifies the construction, installation and operation of systems in buildings where the principal interconnections are by physical conductors. Such systems consist of one or more detectors, one or more control equipments, one or more warning devices and the necessary power supply equipment.

Part 2 is concerned with systems with remote signalling. It comprises two sections: Section 2.1: 1977 covering the installation and Section 2.2: 1977 covering maintenance and records, both similar in content to their counterparts in Part 1.

Part 3 has a number of sections each concerned with particular detection devices designed to greater alarm conditions, namely:

Section 3.1: 1977 *Continuous wiring* – taut wires operating when the wiring is broken.

Section 3.2: 1977 *Foil on glass* – metallic foil fixed to a glass surface, operating when the glass is broken across the lie of the foil.

Section 3.3: 1977 *Protective switches* – a switch device associated with a movable part such as a door or window operating when the movable part is opened.

Section 3.4: 1978 *Radiowave Doppler detectors* – a detector operating in response to Doppler frequency effect produced by the reflection of radio waves from a moving person.

Section 3.5: 1978 *Ultrasonic movement detectors* – a detector operating in response to the reflection of ultrasonic waves from a moving person.

Section 3.6: 1978 *Acoustic detectors* – a detector intended for installation in a strong room, operating in response to air-borne sounds resulting from a physical attack on the structure.

Section 3.7: 1978 *Passive infra-red detectors* – a detector operating in response to a change in ultra-red radiation level when a person enters and moves in the area of volume of coverage.

Section 3.8: 1978 *Volumetric capacitive detectors* – a detector operating in response to the change (or rate of change) in capacitance when a person enters and moves in the area or volume of change.

Section 3.9: 1978 *Pressure mats* – a mat operating when the weight of a person is placed upon it.

Section 3.10: 1978 *Vibration detectors* – a sensor operating in response to vibration resulting from a physical attack on the structure to which it is fitted.

Section 3.11: 1978 *Rigid printer-circuit wiring* – conductors printed on to a base material operating when a conductor is broken or cut.

Section 3.12: 1978 *Beam interruption detectors* – a detector operating when a beam of radiation between a transmitter and a receiver is completely interrupted.

Section 3.13: 1978 *Capacitive proximity detectors* – a detector operating in response to the change (or rate of change) in capacitance resulting from the proximity of a person to the protected object.

Section 3.14: 1978 *Deliberately operated device* – a device generated by the subscriber in the event of an emergency.

Part 4 deals with codes of practice related to intruder alarm systems. Section 4.2: 1986 gives recommendations for preventative and corrective maintenance and keeping records for the range of systems covered in Parts 1 and 2.

BS 6707: 1986 *Specification for intruder alarm systems for consumer installation*

Components and performance of 'do-it-yourself' intruder alarm systems in kit form or as self-contained units. Marking, labelling and instruction requirements with an appendix giving appropriate advice regarding planning installation and use of a system for inclusion in the instruction manual.

BS 4166: 1967 *Automatic intruder alarm terminating equipment in police stations*

Intruder alarm systems may, apart from generating local signals, be connected direct to police stations.

This standard specifies the requirements for the provision, installation and maintenance of directly connected intruder alarm equipment in police stations and stipulates the dimensions, appearance and mounting to ensure that all such units will be identical regardless of manufacturer.

BS 5979: 1981 *Direct line signalling systems and for remote centres for intruder alarm systems*

This standard specifies the requirements for direct line signalling systems between an intruder alarm system complying with

BS 4737 Part 2, and a named remote centre other than a police station. It is intended to apply to those systems with dedicated communication channels comprising wire or cable signalling links but other forms of link are not excluded if they comply with the requirements of this standard. Although the provisions of this standard are not specifically related to direct line signalling systems to police stations, they should none the less be adopted, when appropriate, in specifying the requirements for such systems.

The provisions cover the requirements for signalling from protected premises, central stations, annunciation equipment, satellite stations, and collector points. It is, however, necessary to take account of all applicable local and national legal and other requirements which may bear upon the design and construction of installations covered by this standard.

BS 5613: 1978 *Recommendations for alarm systems for the elderly and others living at risk*

This standard is designed to assist in the selection of alarm systems suitable for elderly persons and others considered to be living at risk. Specific disabilities, such as blindness and deafness, which involve particular problems, are excluded and require special consideration where appropriate.

An alarm system essentially comprises an alarm device and a switch to operate it but, particularly in the context of this standard, it is essential to provide for a response to the alarm.

Alarm systems complying with this standard are not intended as fire alarms or to serve in the place of fire alarm systems.

The standard is divided into four sections.

Section one *introduction* provides four important definitions:

Fixed alarm system: a system consisting of an alarm-activating device (or devices) in the form of a manually operated switch connected by a cable to a separate alarm unit, in which each activating device is fixed or constrained by a flexible cable and the alarm unit is fixed in position.

Alarm signal: the auditory or audio-visual signal resulting from the operation of an alarm-activating device.

Habit-circle device: an alarm-activating device set to operate automatically at the end of a predetermined time period unless the timing mechanism is reset involuntarily by the user during the normal course of daily activity or by the voluntary action of operating a switch.

Radio-triggered alarm system: a system in which the alarm signal unit is activated by a radio transmission from a portable triggering device.

Section two *general considerations* outlines the objectives of the alarm system such that a person in need may receive prompt help in an emergency.

To this end, the essentials of an alarm system are that an alarm signal can be given, an effective response can be obtained and the system be designed to minimize false alarm signals.

The emergency situations which have to be covered are categorized as follows:

1 Where the person is able to operate an alarm-activating device.

2 Where the person is able to operate an alarm-activating device but is immobile.

3 Where the person is able to operate the alarm-activating device and is mobile.

The choice of the type of alarm signals and the siting of the alarm unit are discussed in general principle, bearing in mind the need to take into account the circumstances peculiar to each case, not least the type of supervision provided.

Three types of supervision are specified:

Full: a twenty-four hour coverage by a designated person with specific responsibility for those at risk.

During a limited period of time: coverage for a limited period of

time not being for twenty-four hours, by a designated person with responsibility for those at risk during that period.
Non-designated: where responsibility for a response may be placed upon neighbours or volunteers.

Sections three, four and five detail the particular requirements for the activating device, alarm unit, safety, instructions for operation and maintenance of different alarm systems:

Section three *Manually operated fixed alarm systems*
Section four *Automatically-triggered alarm systems*
Section five *Electromagnetically-triggered alarm systems*

BS 8220   *Guide for security of buildings against crime*

Part 1: 1986   *Dwellings*
Further parts dealing with other types of building will be issued in due course. The term 'dwelling' as used in this document does not include residential buildings categorized as being within the purpose group 'Institutional' by the Building Regulations. These types of building will be covered in a later part. Guidance is given on security measures aimed at deterring burglars from entering dwellings and at helping to prevent criminal damage to dwellings, whether new or existing, and whether single or multiple units.

The recommendations have been so prepared they can be used by residents as well as architects, builders, designers, housing managers, manufacturers and specialists.

General guidance is given in Section 1; Sections 2, 3, 4 and 5, deal with securing windows and rooflights; securing external doors; glass, plastics, glazing sheet and glazing; and intruder alarm systems respectively. A series of thirty-four figures gives comprehensive details of devices and techniques.

BS 5357: 1976   *Code of practice for the installation of security glazing*

This code of practice is designed to give guidance to those responsible for installations involving the use of security glazing which is defined as a glazing material affording protection against a specified level of attack. BS 5051 specifies the levels of attack for bullet-resistant glazing.

Recommendations are made for installing anti-bandit glazing (framed) and bullet-resistant glazing (framed and unframed) for internal use.

The principles applicable to security glazing are such that the glazing should not be dislodged from its position during attack and that the rest of the installation should offer at least equal protection.

BS 5544: 1978   *Anti-bandit glazing (glazing resistant to manual attack)*

This standard specifies the minimum performance requirements and test methods for that type of security glazing, called anti-bandit glazing. Anti-bandit glazing is intended to delay access to a protected space, such as showcase, shop window or premises for a short period of time. In cases where protection for personnel is required, security glazing should be chosen of a grade which will give adequate protection against the attack-threat. Hence anti-bandit glazing under this standard is unlikely to meet the requirements of BS 5051 for bullet resistance, but bullet resistant glazing to that standard will probably provide adequate resistance to manual attack.

The materials which may be used for anti-bandit glazing include:

1 Rigid plastics.
2 Laminates of glass with one or more plastics interlayers.
3 Laminates of glass incorporating high tensile steel wire mesh in a plastics interlayer.
4 Glass and/or plastics bonded with one or more plastics interlayers.

5 Any combination of the above.

BS 5051   *Security glazing*

This standard specifies the requirements and type approval methods for security glazing resistant to specified levels of attack by firing bullets. It is in two parts:

Part 1: 1973 *Bullet-resistant glazing for interior use*
Part 2: 1979 *Bullet-resistant glazing for exterior use*

In each case, the requirements cover through-vision, classification of panels in respect of levels of attack, provision of panel test pieces for type testing, performance requirements and marking. Part 2 also covers security-glazed windscreens for road vehicles.

(68.5)   Fire protection services

This section is concerned with fire detection and manual and automatic fire alarm systems in various types of building. The standards comprising this section are being progressively revised. Those agreed by the European Committee for Standardization and which are accepted as British Standards, will be embodied in BS 5445 *Components of automatic fire detection systems*. Those peculiar to Britain will be included in BS 5839 *Fire detection and alarm systems in buildings*. In the transitional period a number of individual standards will remain in force. See also Table 4 Activities, requirements (K) *Fire, explosion*.

BS 5445:   *Components of automatic fire detection systems*

Only parts of this European standard have been produced; the remainder will be published as soon as they have been approved. The ultimate coverage of the standard is intended to be as follows:

Part 1: 1977 *Introduction*
Part 2: – *Control and indicating equipment*
Part 3: – *Fire alarm devices*
Part 4: – *Power supplies*
Part 5: 1977 *Heat sensitive detectors – point detectors containing a static element*
Part 6: – *Heat sensitive detectors – rate of rise point detectors without a static element*
Part 7: 1984 – *Point-type smoke detectors using scattered light, transmitted light or ionization*
Part 8: 1984 – *High-temperature heat detectors*
Part 9: 1984 *Methods of test of sensitivity to fire*

It is intended that the standard should specify requirements, test methods and criteria against which the effectiveness and reliability of the component parts of an automatic fire detection system can be assessed. Recommendations for the installation, siting and maintenance of such systems are outside the proposed scope of this standard.

Part 1 definitions include:

Fire detector: that part of an automatic fire detection system which constantly or at frequent intervals, monitors suitable physical and/or chemical phenomena for detection of fires in the area under surveillance. The detectors are categorized according to:

1 The phenomenon detected – heat, smoke and gas flame.
2 The way they respond to the phenomenon detached – static, when the magnitude of the phenomenon exceeds a certain value for a sufficient time; differential, when the magnitudes of the measured phenomenon at two or more places exceeds a certain value for a sufficient time; and rate of rise, when the rate of change of the measured phenomenon exceeds a certain value for a sufficient time.
3 The configuration of the detector, that is the value of the

vicinity within which the detector responds to the phenomenon point, multi-point and line.

4 The resettability – resettable in which the detector may be restored from its alarm state to its normal state of readiness without the renewal of any component, self-resetting, remotely resettable or locally resettable; non-resettable (with exchangeable elements); and non-resettable (without exchangeable elements).

Part 5 is concerned with the extensive range of requirements, test methods and performance criteria for heat sensitive (point) detectors, both resettable and non-resettable, containing a static element.

Part 7 deals with the requirements, test methods and performance criteria for point-type, resettable smoke detectors that operate using scattered light, transmitted light, or ionization. For other types of smoke detectors or those working on different principles this standard should only be used for guidance.

Part 8 specifies the requirements, tests and performance criteria for point-type, heat-sensitive detectors that:

(a) have high response temperatures;
(b) contain at least one element having a static response threshold;
(c) have heat-sensitive elements (excluding elements having auxiliary functions, e.g. characteristic correctors) that are not closer than 15 mm to the mounting surface of the detector.

Part 9 describes test fires to which fire detectors are to be subjected with the aim of providing information as to the response behaviour expected from fire detectors under genuine fire conditions. The detectors to be tested are subjected to test fires, which are typical of certain categories of fire and, viewed as a whole, cover the majority of the fires which occur in practice.

BS 3116 *Automatic fire alarm systems in buildings*

Part 4: 1974 *Control and indicating equipment*
This part will no doubt be superseded in due course by BS 5445 Part 2. It specifies requirements for electrical control and indicating equipment for installation at premises protected by an automatic fire alarm system. It also covers indicating equipment at remote manned centres, that is centres which are permanently manned and at which appropriate action will be taken immediately on receipt of any fire alarm or fault warning.

A general definition of an automatic fire alarm system at protected premises indicates that it may consist of a number of trigger devices connected to control and indicating equipment, which is deemed to have primary and secondary functions, namely:

1 To give a fire alarm in response to the operation of the trigger devices.
2 To indicate the existence of faults within the system.

The alarm which is given is required to be provided by up to five means:

1 At least one internal alarm sounder.
2 At least one external alarm sounder.
3 A visible indication in the indicating equipment.
4 A visible indication for each zone in which a trigger device operates (which may be combined in 3).
5 A signal transmitted to a remote manned centre where such a centre is used.

Fault warnings must be given by particular means whenever failure or, in some cases, disconnection occurs.
In the case of equipment for remote manned centres (other than local authority fire brigade stations and control rooms) the requirements demand that the operation of the trigger devices should be indicated by an audible alarm and a visible indication in the equipment, identifying the origin.

Fault warnings must be given by similar means to those for fire alarms whenever failure and, in some cases, disconnection occurs.

The standard gives specific requirements in respect of sounders, visual indicators, protection and power supplies for the equipment together with stipulations with regard to its construction, reliability and an extensive range of tests.

BS 5446 *Components of automatic fire alarm systems for residential premises*

Part 1: 1977 *Point-type smoke detectors*
Part 1 is concerned with the performance requirements and tests for smoke detectors in automatic fire alarm systems installed for the purpose of protecting of life in premises in which regular provision is made for people to sleep. Such premises include hotels, boarding houses, nursing homes, homes for the elderly and handicapped, hospitals and other institutional premises. Additional parts to this standard are contemplated particularly in respect of power supplies and control and indicating equipment which may be used as alternatives to those specified in BS 3116 Part 4.

Smoke detectors are designed primarily to be suitable for the protection of life in residential situations; they may not be suitable for other applications.

Three types of smoke detector are defined:

1 Fixed sensitivity – in which the response threshold cannot be manually varied subsequent to manufacture without breaking a seal or similar validating component. The response threshold represents the smoke concentration at which the detector changes to its alarm condition.
2 Self-contained (single station) – comprising a unit capable of operating in itself as a complete smoke detection system. Such devices are likely to provide satisfactory protection only in situations of small risk.
3 Adjustable sensitivity – in which the response threshold can be varied within specified limits without permanent indication of such variation.

The standard specifies marking, data to be supplied on or with the detector, constructional requirements and some fifteen tests covering different aspects of performance.

BS 5839 *Fire detection and alarm systems in buildings*

Part 1: 1980 *Code of practice for installation and servicing*
This part has superseded CP 1019. Additional parts are envisaged and will eventually supersede BS 3116 Part 4 and BS 5446 Part 1.

This part spans the planning, installation and servicing of fire detection and alarm systems in and around buildings in temperate climates such as that of the United Kingdom.

It covers systems from simple installations with one or two manual call points to complex installations with automatic detectors, manual call points, control and indicating equipment and connection to the public fire service. It also covers systems capable of providing signals to initiate, in the event of fire, the operation of ancillary services such as fixed fire extinguishing systems but does not cover the ancillary services themselves. It does not cover the installation of single or interconnected self-contained detectors having a power supply and alarm sounder within one unit, street fire alarms, the 999 emergency call system, automatic sprinkler installations and extinguishing systems whether or not they can give an alarm, nor manually or mechanically operated sounders.

The topics in the code include among others:

Design considerations: circuit design, zones, audible and visual alarms, the several types of triggering device, control and indicating equipment, power supplies and wiring systems.
Structural accommodation: ducts and channels, siting of equipment and builders' work in connection with the installation.

Workmanship, installation and testing: wiring systems, equipment, inspection, testing and commissioning.
User responsibilities: supervision and maintenance of records.
Servicing: procedures for routine and regular inspection.
Self-contained detectors: see BS 5446 Part 1.

Part 2: 1983 *Manual call points*
This part supersedes BS 5364 Part 1 and deals with the requirements of and methods of test for manual call points and their mounting boxes for use in electrical fire alarm systems. The requirements are intended to ensure similarity in the method of use and reliability of operation.

Fire protection

This section embraces those standards which are concerned with fires and fire-fighting, including the terms and symbols used and fire-fighting equipment and installations. Several of the standards are in the process of revision and their contents may be embodied in a revised form in new composite standards, some of which may incorporate agreed European standards or at least reflect them.

BS 4547: 1972 *Classification of fires*

This European standard classifies the different types of fire in terms of the nature of the fuel supporting the combustion. The classifications are useful in differentiating between the types of fire in the context of fire-fighting by means of an extinguisher and in simplifying spoken or written reference to them. The types of fire are as follows:

Class A: fires involving solid materials, usually of an organic nature in which combustion normally takes place with the formation of glowing embers.
Class B: fires involving liquids and liquefiable solids.
Class C: fires involving gases.
Class D: fires involving metals.

BS 4422 *Glossary of terms associated with fire*

There are five parts to this standard each of which provides a glossary of terms in specialist contexts in the field of fire engineering, fire prevention and fire technology.

The aim is to provide a set of simple basic definitions which will be correct in any context but each of which is capable of extension for specific purposes for use by the specialist.

The several parts and their subject contents are as follows:

Part 1: 1969 *The phenomenon of fire* – covering general terms relating to fire.
Part 2: 1971 *Building materials and structures* – covering terms for building elements with relevance to fire.
Part 3: 1972 *Means of escape.*
Part 4: 1975 *Fire protection equipment* – covering terms relating to the very wide range of fire protection equipment.
Part 5: 1976 *Miscellaneous terms* – covering terms largely concerned with organization equipment and operations of the fire service.

BS 1635: 1970 *Graphical symbols and abbreviations for fire protection drawings*

The intention of this standard is to provide a set of symbols and abbreviations which will be of use to:

1 The field worker or surveyor by whom the symbols can be used in place of longhand notes.
2 The draughtsman by whom the symbols may be used in place of elaborate pictorial portrayal or written description of the items involved.
3 The reader who will wish to read and interpret the information with minimum difficulty.

The contents are divided into five sections:

1 Basic symbols and abbreviations – features indicated by lines, wall openings and means of escape.
2 Fire protection symbols – fixed fire-fighting equipment, (internal, external and automatic), fire warning systems (manual, manually operated, internal telephone, public address system and emergency lighting system) services and main controls.
3 Structural symbols for small-scale drawings – walls, wall-opening, roofs and floor openings.
4 Miscellaneous symbols for small-scale drawings – structures, etc.
5 Fire protection symbols for small-scale drawings – fixed and water supplies.

The use of the symbols and abbreviations is illustrated in typical plan drawings appended to the standard.

BS 5499 *Fire safety signs, notices and graphic symbols*

Part 1: 1984 *Fire safety signs*
The purpose of this standard is to extend the basic framework concerning safety colours and safety signs in BS 5378 with regard to fire. The following definitions are important in interpreting the provisions:

Fire safety sign: a sign that gives a message about fire safety by a combination of geometric form, safety colour and symbol or text (i.e. words, letters, numbers) or both.
Safety colour: a colour to which a specific safety meaning or purpose is assigned.
Safety symbol: a pictorial representation used on a safety sign.

Five types of fire safety sign are identified (see Figure 64):

1 Warning signs.
2 Mandatory signs.
3 Prohibition signs.
4 Fire equipment signs.
5 Safe condition signs.

Requirements for standard shapes, colours, safety symbols, and lettering layout and sizes are also specified.

Examples of each sign, together with standard wording, are listed in tables in this standard.

BS 5306 *Fire extinguishing installations and equipment on premises*

This standard is a revision of CP 402: 101: 1952 and ultimately will comprise a number of parts which taken together are intended to cover all the main types of extinguishing medium and systems in current use, and therefore will form a comprehensive guide to all aspects of the subject.

The parts published to date are:

Part 0: 1986 *Guide for the selection of installed systems and other fire equipment*
Part 1: 1976 *Code of practice for hydrant systems, hose reels, and foam inlets*
Part 2: 1979 *Code of practice for sprinkler systems*

■ AD (Regs. B2/3/4)

Part 3: 1985 *Code of practice for selection, installation and maintenance of portable fire extinguishers*
Part 4: 1985 *Specification for carbon dioxide systems*
Part 5 *Halon systems*
   Section 5.1: 1982 *Halon 1301 total flooding systems*
   Section 5.2: 1984 *Halon 1211 total flooding systems*

Each of the systems identified may form only a part, albeit an important part, of the total fire protection facilities of a building or of particular plant. The need to consider a number of systems which may be complementary or supplementary to each other is stressed.

(a) A warning sign

(b) An obligation sign

(c) A prohibition sign

Fire hose reel

(d) A fire equipment sign

Push bar to open

FIRE EXIT

(e) Escape signs

(Figure 1: BS 5499: Part 1: 1978)

Figure 64 *Types of sign*

Part 0 is a guide to the selection, installation and maintenance of automatic water sprinkler and spray systems, carbon dioxide and Halon systems, foam and extinguishing powder systems. It gives guidance on installed equipment for fire service use, and on the application of portable fire extinguishers. It complements the more detailed information given in the other specialized parts of this standard.

Part 1 covers good practice in matters affecting the planning, installation, testing and upkeep of fire hydrant systems including wet and dry rising mains, hose reels and foam inlets on premises.

The provisions are subdivided into nine sections each dealing with specific aspects of the installation.

Part 2 is a code of practice which deals with the provision of automatic sprinkler systems together with their essential supplies and their maintenance. It does not cover other systems having an affinity with sprinkler systems such as drenches, deluge sprinklers, etc. Sprinkler systems are designed to provide an automatic means of detecting and extinguishing or controlling a fire by water in its early stages by an installation of overhead pipes on to which sprinkler heads are fitted at intervals. A sprinkler head is a heat operated valve designed to open at a predetermined temperature and to discharge water under

pressure from the installation directed in a specific pattern by a deflector in the head. The flow of water from the installation also causes an alarm to sound. As only the sprinkler head(s) in the immediate vicinity of the fire open, water damage during the extinguishing of the fire is reduced to the minimum while the remainder of the building remains protected.

The provisions are subdivided into nine sections each dealing with specific aspects of the installation.

Part 3: 1985 is a code of practice for selection, installation and maintenance of portable fire extinguishers. It deals primarily with portable fire extinguishers conforming to BS 5423 which can be carried by one person and which are used for the protection of buildings and other premises and their contents. Much of the content is applicable extinguishers used for other purposes.

Part 4 gives recommendations for the provision of carbon dioxide fire extinguishing systems in buildings or industrial plant. Such a system is designed to convey carbon dioxide from a central source on the premises as and when required for the extinction of fire or the protection of particular plant or parts of the premises against possible fire risk.

The provisions are subdivided into five sections each dealing with specific aspects of the installation.

Part 5 Section 5.1 gives recommendations for Halon 1301 total flooding fire extinguishing systems in building or plant. Such a system consists of an installation designed to convey Halon 1301 from storage containers by pipes or otherwise for the protection of particular plant or parts of the premises against possible fire risk. While Halon 1301 is a recognized effective medium for the extinction of flammable liquid fires and fires in the presence of electrical risks, there are hazards for which it is not suitable and certain circumstances in which its use requires special precautions, for example in fires involving chemicals containing their own supply of oxygen, reactive metals, metal hydrides or metal amides, chemicals capable of undergoing thermal decomposition and solid materials in which fires quickly become deep seated.

The provisions cover the characteristics, use and hazards to personnel of Halon 1301, planning, contract arrangements, contract drawings, design, operations, and maintenance of the system and it constituent parts.

Part 5: Section 5.2 gives recommendations for the design, installation, maintenance and safety of Halon 1211 total flooding fire extinguishing systems in buildings or plant. Such a system consists of an installation designed to convey Halon 1211 from storage containers for the protection of particular plant or parts of the premises against possible fire risk. Such systems may be piped or otherwise connected. Explosion suppression systems are not covered. Factual data on the characteristics of Halon 1211 and the types of fire for which it is a suitable extinguishant is provided. Two methods of operation, viz, manual and automatic are described. Advice is given on the selection of a system and on the operational method with detailed recommendations on the design, maintenance and efficient operation of installation. Reference is made also to the part which these systems should play in general schemes of fire protection of premises, having regard to safety as well as efficiency. It should be remembered that in the planning of comprehensive schemes there may be hazards for which this medium is not suitable. Advice on these matters can be obtained from the appropriate fire authority or other enforcing authorities.

BS 5173 *Methods of test for rubber and plastics hose and hose assemblies* in 2 parts (5 sections) is relevant.

BS 5041 *Fire hydrant systems equipment*

The five parts of this standard each deal with particular aspects of fire hydrant systems equipment. They provide detailed requirements for most of the special items required for wet and dry risers described in CP 402 or BS 5306, depending upon which of the two is relevant.

The several parts and subject matter are as follows:

Part 1: 1975 *Landing valves for wet risers*
Part 2: 1976 *Landing valves for dry risers*
Part 3: 1975 *Inlet breechings for dry riser inlets*
Part 4: 1975 *Boxes for landing valves for dry risers*
Part 5: 1974 *Boxes for foam inlets and dry riser inlets*

Important definitions are:

Dry riser (dry rising main): a vertical pipe installed in a building for fire-fighting purposes, fitted with inlet connections at fire brigade access level and outlet connections at specified points, which is normally dry but capable of being charged with water by pumping from fire service appliances.
Wet riser (wet rising main): a vertical pipe installed in a building for fire-fighting purposes, permanently charged with water from a pressurized supply, and fitted with valves and outlet connections at specified points.
Breeching: a unit at an inlet of a dry riser fitted with either two or four connections leading to a common pipe. This unit is usually contained within a box as described by BS 5041 Part 5.
Landing valve: an assembly comprising a valve and outlet connection from a wet or dry riser.
Box (for landing valves): a form of construction which can enclose a landing valve when positioned on the face of a wall, with a duct or in such a way as will complete the existing structure to form an enclosure.
Box (for foam inlets and dry riser inlets): a box containing the inlets of foam inlets or water mains, installed in or within the boundaries of the site of a building, preferably recessed in a wall, with inlets normally at street level through which foam or

water can be pumped to provide a supply at discharge points situated at various levels in the building.

In each case the various parts specify in detail matters relating to design and manufacture, materials, dimensions, certificates and testing (where appropriate) and marking.

The three types of valve in Part 1 are classified by pressure ratings

Low pressure (LP): up to 10 bar, 62.5 mm (2½ in) diameter.
High pressure (HP): up to 20 bar, 62.5 mm (2½ in) diameter and other sizes.

Part 2 specifies the requirements for copper alloy gate valves generally complying with the requirements of BS 1952 or BS 5154, and intended for use on dry rising mains only. The valves are of nominal size 62.5 mm (2½ in) and are to be fitted with an instantaneous female outlet.

Part 3 specifies the requirements for two-way and four-way inlet breechings intended for dry risers only. The breechings are required to be fitted with male instantaneous connections and to be of such size that they can readily be accommodated in boxes for dry risers complying with Part 5.

The boxes covered by Part 4 are intended to be suitable for enclosing landing valves complying with Part 5. The requirements relate also to the frames, doors and glazing of the boxes. The ruling dimensions of the boxes are as shown in Figure 65.

Part 5 specifies the requirements for boxes for foam inlets or dry risers, manufactured in a choice of materials to suit a particular application. Typical drawings of boxes are shown in Figures 66 and 67.

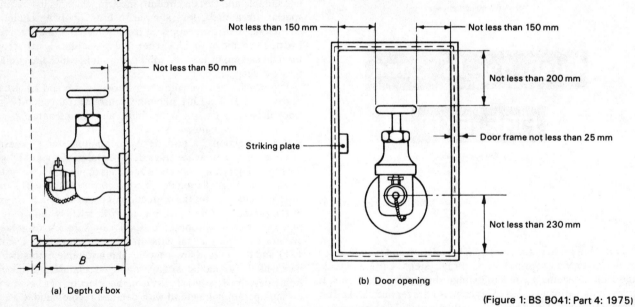

(a) Depth of box

(b) Door opening

(Figure 1: BS 5041: Part 4: 1975)

Figure 65 *Ruling dimensions of box*

Figure 66 *Typical drawing of box for two foam inlets*

(Figure 1: BS 5041: Part 5: 1974)

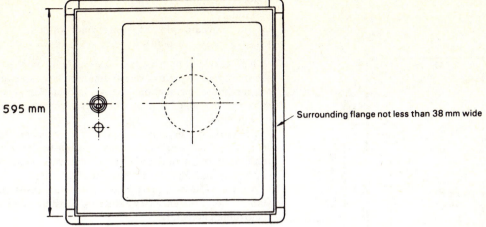

595 mm

Surrounding flange not less than 38 mm wide

(Figure 2: BS 5041: Part 5: 1974)

Figure 67 *Typical drawing of box for dry risers (four inlets)*

BS 5274: 1985 *Fire hose reels (water) for fixed installations*

Fire hose reels, if in proper condition, provide a most effective fire fighting facility in installations as a continuous supply of water is made readily available.

This standard specifies the requirements for fire hose reels for fixed installations permanently connected to a water supply and designed to facilitate the swift withdrawal of the hose in any direction, generally horizontal. The requirements have been framed to ensure that the equipment can be manipulated by one person, while at the same time ensuring reasonable robustness for long life, efficient operation and avoidance of excessive maintenance.

Tests are included to verify the satisfactory performance of individual reel and valve subassemblies after manufacture. The hose reels are described as manual, that is those which are operated by opening a manual inlet valve, and automatic types, that is those which open the inlet valve automatically by action of drawing the hose off the hose drum. Section 1 covers definitions and requirements for the complete fire hose reel assembly. Section 2 deals with the reel and valve subassembly.

BS 3169: 1981 *First aid reel hoses for fire-fighting purposes*

The hoses covered by this standard are for use on fire-fighting vehicles and on hose reels for fixed installations complying with BS 5274.

Two types according to working pressure are available, each in both 19 and 25 mm nominal bore:

Type A: design working pressure 15 bar.
Type B: design working pressure 40 bar.

The construction of the hoses comprises a seamless rubber lining, a textile reinforcement and an elastomeric cover which must be black or red.

Details are given of the construction, dimensions and toler-- ances, physical properties, performance requirements and marking of the hoses.

BS 5423: 1980 *Portable fire extinguishers*

This standard specifies the requirements for rechargeable and non-rechargeable metal bodied portable fire extinguishers containing an extinguishing medium which can be expelled by the action of internal pressure and directed on to a fire. The extinguishers are classified according to the medium used, namely water, foam, powder, carbon dioxide or halon. A portable extinguisher is one which is designed to be carried and operated by hand and which in working order has a mass exceeding 23 kg.

The following types of portable fire extinguisher are defined:

Stored pressure type: in which the expellent gas is stored with the extinguisher medium in the body of the extinguisher as a whole, and the body of the extinguisher is permanently pressurized.
Chemical reaction type: in which two (or more) chemicals are allowed to react to produce an expellent gas when the operating mechanism is actuated.
Gas cartridge type: in which the pressure is produced by means of compressed or liquefied gas released from a gas cartridge attached to, or fitted into, the extinguisher.
Freestanding: designed to stand vertically on a flat horizontal surface.

The provisions of the standard are subdivided into seven sections each dealing with particular aspects of the extinguishers.

BS 750: 1984 *Underground fire hydrants and surface box frames and covers*

Two classifications of underground fire hydrants suitable for a maximum working pressure of 16 bar gauge are given in this standard, namely:

1 Wedge gate type (see Figure 68)
2 Screw-down type (see Figure 69)

Details are given of the requirements for each type of hydrant as well as general requirements applicable to both. The hydrants must comply with requirements detailed in the figures associated with the valve types and information included in tables regarding materials and dimensions. Appendices A and B give guidance for the purchaser; Appendices C and D outline tests which form part of the requirements of this standard. Surface box frames and covers with test procedures are also included, stipulating dimensions, materials, design features, type and production requirements.

BS 3251: 1976 *Indicator plates for fire hydrants and emergency water supplies*

This standard specifies requirements for indicator plates made from a variety of materials, together with all removable characters and spacer pieces supplied with them. A character is defined as a term which includes all letters, digits, arrows and other indicating marks on the front face of the plates and may be flush, raised recased or removable.

Four types of plate are identified:

Class A: hydrant indicator plates for general use except on roads of motorway standard.

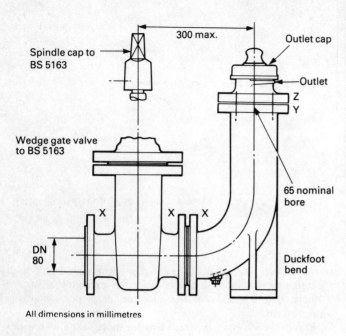

All dimensions in millimetres

(Figure 68: BS 750: 1984)

Figure 68   *Fire hydrant: wedge gate type*

Class B: hydrant indicator plates for use on roads of motorway standard.

Class C: indicator plates for emergency water supplies (EWS).

Class D: indicator plates for motor bypass valves.

Section two of the standard deals in detail with the design of the four types of plate covering dimensions, character sizes and the method of presentation of the information. The required colour of the plates is, in all cases, black characters on a canary background.

The materials of which the plates may be manufactured are steel, cast iron, aluminium alloy and plastics. The provisions relating to the manufacture of the indicator plates cover the characters and their fixing, finish and protective painting.

A series of tests is given to ensure impact resistance, colour stability and resistance to weathering, flexibility and security of removable characters.

(68.6)   Lightning protection

BS 6651: 1985   *Code of practice for protection of structures against lightning*

The risk, greatest at 7+ flashes to the ground per km² per year within a 50 km radius of Colchester, Essex and reducing to under 1 flash per km² in Northern Ireland, the Western peninsulars of Wales and Scotland, general elements of design, basic considerations and system design are covered. Inspection, testing, records, maintenance and upkeep are particularly important.

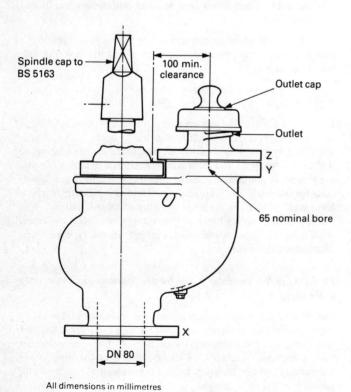

All dimensions in millimetres

(Figure 69: BS 750: 1984)

Figure 69   *Fire hydrant: screw-down type*

(7–) Fittings

BS 5304: 1975 *Code of practice for safeguarding of machinery*

This code of practice identifies and describes methods of safeguarding dangerous parts of machinery and indicates the criteria to be observed in the design, construction and application of such safeguards. It does not cover non-mechanical hazards and sources of danger. The code is fully documented and illustrated. A full reading of the code is recommended for those involved in safeguarding machinery.

BS 5910 *Methods of test for surface finishes for furniture*
Part 1: 1980 *Assessment of surface resistance to cold liquids*

This standard is concerned with the surface finish to furniture during manufacture and the appropriate tests and liquids.

(71) Circulation fittings

(71.1) Notice boards, signs

BS 559: 1955 *Electrical signs and high voltage luminous-discharge-tube installations*

This standard is concerned with the construction, materials of construction, fixing, protection, earthing and wiring to such medium and low voltage manufactured signs and high voltage discharge-tubes up to 5 kV to earth for internal or external use.

BS 1376: 1974 *Colours of light signals*

This standard specifies the colours of light signals for all purposes. Based upon transport signalling requirements it is applicable to signal colours for other purposes.

BS 2560: 1978 *Exit signs (internally illuminated)*

The specification for the manufacture of internally illuminated box type 'Exit' signs is given in this standard.

BS 3275: 1960 *Glass for signs and recommendations on glazing for signs*

This standard specifies the requirements for glass used in box and panel signs.

BS 3510: 1968 *A basic symbol to denote the actual or potential presence of ionizing radiation*

This standard is covered in Table 4 'Activities, requirements', under section (Q7) 'Radiation protection'.

BS 4218: 1978 *Self-luminous exit signs*

Self-energized luminous exit signs requiring no external source of power are covered in this standard.

BS 4781 *Self-adhesive plastics labels for permanent use*

Part 1: 1973 *General purpose labels*

Part 2: 1979 *Requirements for stringent conditions*
Self adhesive labels are covered by these standards.

BS 5378 *Safety signs and colours*

Part 1: 1980 *Colour and design*
This part specifies the colour and design for safety signs. A compendium of colour backgrounds and standard signs for prohibition, warning, mandatory and safety signs are given, together with their meanings. This part is recommended reading.

Part 2: 1980 *Colorimetric and photometric properties of materials*
This part specifies the above properties of materials used for safety signs.

Part 3: 1982 *Additional signs to those given in BS 5378: Part 1*
This part gives further examples of safety signs following principles laid down in Part 1. Advice on selection and use of safety signs is also given. This part is recommended reading.

BS 5499 *Fire safety signs, notices and graphic symbols*
Part 1: 1978 *Fire safety signs*

The colour signs are the same as those given in BS 5378 Part 1: 1980, but this standard is only concerned with fire safety.

BS 6034: 1981 *Public information symbols*

This standard specifies the image content of thirteen symbols, and is recommended reading.

(71.3) Doormats

BS 4037: 1966 *Coir doormats*

This standard is in three parts, the latter two giving dimensions for mats for general purposes (nine, from 610 × 355 mm to 1220 × 760 mm) and for service requirements (five, from 610 × 355 mm to 1830 × 1220 mm).

(73) Culinary fittings

Thirty-seven codes and standards are covered in this section (see also BS 3456 in section (6 –) 'Services, mainly electrical'), namely:

BS 3705: 1972 *Recommendations for provision of space for domestic kitchen equipment*

BS 5957: 1980 *Recommendations for modules for the coordinating dimensions of catering equipment using containers to BS 4874*

BS 6222: *Domestic kitchen equipment*

Part 1: 1982 *Coordinating dimensions*
This part specifies the coordinating dimensions for kitchen equipment in domestic dwellings. It supersedes the dimension clauses in BS 1195: Parts 1 and 2, which are being amended accordingly.

BS 1195 *Kitchen fitments and equipment*

Part 1: 1973 *Imperial units with metric equivalents*

Part 2: 1972 *Metric units*

BS 1206: 1974 *Fireclay sinks. Dimensions and workmanship*

BS 1244 *Metal sinks for domestic purposes*

Part 1: 1955 *Imperial units with metric equivalents*

Part 2: 1982 *Stainless steel sink tops (excluding inset sinks)*
The manufacture, quality, marking, materials, sizes and finish are covered by this standard.

BS 3380: 1982 *Wastes (excluding skeleton sink wastes) and bath overflows*

BS 3402: 1969 *Quality of vitreous china sanitary appliances*

BS 3456   *Safety of household and similar electrical appliances*

Section 2.27: 1973   *Dish-washing machines*
Testing, rating, protection, heating strength and hazard protection in manufactured goods are covered in this section.

Section 2.30: 1971   *Food waste disposal units*
This section specifies the manufacture of disposal units.

Section 3.4: 1979   *Dishwashers*
This section gives the complete specification for manufacture of household units.

Section 3.8: 1979   *Food waste disposal units*
This section gives the complete specification for manufacture of household units.

BS 5809: 1980   *Safety and efficiency of the gas heating equipment of commercial dishwashing machines*

The manufacture, rating, performance, safety and testing of the gas water heating associated with a commercial dishwasher are given in this standard.

BS 4086: 1966   *Recommendations for maximum surface temperatures of heated domestic equipment*

Recommended surface temperatures where they may come in contact with the body accidentally, or with the hand during normal operation of the equipment, are given in this standard.

CP 403: 1974   *Installation of domestic heating and cooking appliances burning solid fuel*

This code covers five categories of burners and lists all the relevant British Standards, British Regulations and bye-laws. As a supplement to general building construction knowledge, this code is recommended reading.

BS 1252: 1981   *Domestic solid fuel free standing cookers with integral boilers*

The manufacture, installation and testing of boilers are covered by this standard.

BS 1846   *Glossary of terms relating to solid fuel burning equipment*

Part 1: 1968   *Domestic appliances*

BS 3250   *Methods for the thermal testing of domestic solid fuel burning appliances*

Part 1: 1973   *Flue loss method*

Part 2: 1961   *Hood method*
This part is the same as Part 1, but it covers the aspirated hood method of measurement.

BS 3300: 1974   *Kerosine (paraffin) unflued space heaters, cooking and boiling appliances for domestic use*

This standard specifies the construction, operation, safety requirements and tests.

BS 4876: 1972   *Performance requirements and test procedures for domestic flued oil burning appliances*

BS 4353: 1968   *Gas catering equipment for educational establishments (LASMEC modular units)*

This standard specifies the performance, testing, safety and finish of four main categories of cooking appliance.

BS 5258   *Safety of domestic gas appliances*

Part 2: 1975   *Cooking appliances*

■ AD (Regs. J1/2/3)

This part covers the safety requirements and methods of testing of cooking appliances.

BS 5314   *Gas heated catering equipment*

This standard specifies the requirements and tests for each of the appliances listed in the following parts:

Part 1: 1976 *Ovens*
Part 2: 1976 *Boiling burners*
Part 3: 1976 *Grillers and toasters*
Part 4: 1976 *Fryers*
Part 5: 1976 *Steaming ovens*
Part 6: 1976 *Bulk liquid heaters*
Part 7: 1976 *Water boilers*
Part 8: 1979 *Griddle plates*
Part 9: 1979 *Boiling pans*
Part 10: 1982 *Heated rinsing sinks*
Part 11: 1979 *Hot cupboards*
Part 12: 1979 *Bains-marie*
Part 13: 1982 *Brat pans*

BS 5386   *Gas burning appliances* (see also Table 1: 53.3)

Part 3: 1980   *Domestic cooking appliances burning gas*

■ AD (Regs. J1/2/3)

This part defines the construction, performance, tests and marking of cooking appliances.

Part 4: 1983   *Built-in domestic cooking appliances*
Specifies construction, performance, test methods and marketing of hotplates, ovens, grills and cookers, individually or in combination, burning 1st, 2nd and 3rd family gases.

BS 6172: 1982   *Code of practice for installation of domestic gas cooking appliances (2nd family gases)*

Recommendations for the selection and installation of cookers or separate ovens, hot plates and grills are given in this standard. It supersedes CP 334 Part 1: 1962.

BS 6173: 1982   *Code of practice for installation of gas catering appliances (2nd family gases)*

Recommendations given in this standard cover all catering establishments except fish and chip shops.

BS 3999   *Methods of measuring the performance of household electrical appliances*

Part 5: 1968   *Electric cookers*

Part 11: 1972   *Dish-washing machines*

Part 15: 1983   *Microwave cooking appliances*
Principal performance characteristics and the standard method of measuring such performance are covered in this standard.

BS 4167   *Electrically-heated catering equipment*

This standard is largely parallel with BS 5314, but the parts still relevant are:

Part 3: 1969 *Grillers, grillers on ranges, toasters*
Part 4: 1970 *Deep fat fryers*
Part 5: 1969 *Steaming ovens*
Part 6: 1969 *Bulk liquid heaters*
Part 7: 1969 *Water boilers*
Part 8: 1969 *Griddles and griddle grills*
Part 9: 1969 *Boiling pans*

Part 10: 1970 *Sterilizing sinks*
Part 11: 1970 *Hot cupboards*
Part 12: 1971 *Bains-marie*

The general requirements and tests to establish a satisfactory standard of safety and performance for each of the appliances listed above are given.

BS 5784: *Safety of electric commercial catering equipment*

Part 1: 1979 *Particular requirements for ranges, ovens and hob elements*

Part 3: 1984 *Griddles and griddle grills*
Safety requirements for electrically operated griddles and griddle grills not intended for household use. Applicable to the electrical part of appliances making use of other forms of energy and to the influence of non-electrical parts on electrical parts.

BS 2501: 1976 *Commercial refrigerated storage cabinets of the closed reach-in type*

This standard deals with the manufacture, internal capacities, performance and testing of storage cabinets.

BS 2502: 1979 *Manufacture of sectional cold rooms (walk-in type)*

This standard deals with the construction, internal capacities and performance of a sectional cold room within a building but does not cover the associated refrigerating plant.

BS 4434 *Requirements for refrigeration safety*

Part 2: 1976 *Particular requirements for small refrigerating systems for use in household appliances*

BS 5643: 1979 *Glossary of refrigeration, heating, ventilating and air conditioning terms*

CP 334 *Selection and installation of town gas cooking and refrigerating appliances.*

Part 3: 1971 *Refrigerators*
This standard is virtually obsolete in the United Kingdom.

BS 5258 *Safety of domestic gas appliances*

Part 6: 1975 *Refrigerators and food freezers*

BS 922 and 1691: 1959 *Electrical refrigerators and food freezers for household use*

This standard specifies the construction, performance, capacities, compressor ratings and testing of electrical refrigerators and food freezers.

BS 3999 *Methods of measuring the performance of household electrical appliances*

Part 10: 1972 *Food freezers*

Part 13: 1976 *Frozen food storage compartments in refrigerators and frozen food storage cabinets*

BS 5071: 1974 *Food and drink vending machines*

This standard does not apply to vending machines which cook food as part of the cycle nor to machines which heat food or liquids by radio frequency electromagnetic energy.

BS 3831: 1964 *Vitreous enamel finishes for domestic and catering appliances*

This standard applies to vitreous enamel finish to sheet steel and cast iron with the exception of baths which are covered by

BS 1189 (cast iron) and BS 139 (sheet steel) for domestic purposes.

(74) Sanitary, hygiene fittings

The scale of provision, performance, siting, design and installation are the subject of Part G of the Building Regulations 1985. A group of standards, of which two, BS 3380 and BS 3402, are considered in section (73), 'Culinary fittings'.

BS 4118: 1981 *Glossary of sanitation terms*

This standard gives full glossary of terms and definitions for all aspects of sanitation including water supply (hot and cold), sanitary appliances, above ground drainage (including roofs), underground drainage (including private treatment plants and connection to sewerage systems). This standard is recommended reading.

BS 6465 *Sanitary installation*

Part 1: 1984 *Code of practice for scale of provision, selection and installation of sanitary appliances*

■ AD (Reg. G4)

This part deals with requirements of sanitary appliances in the following:

(a) dwellings;
(b) accommodation for elderly people;
(c) residential homes for elderly people;
(d) office buildings and shops;
(e) public conveniences;
(f) factories;
(g) schools and higher educational establishments;
(h) cinemas, concert halls, theatres and similar buildings used for public entertainment;
(i) hotels;
(j) restaurants and canteens;
(k) public houses;
(l) swimming pools.

The requirements for sanitary appliances in hospitals and other health buildings are covered by the general recommendations of this standard. However, for the scale of provision, ergonomic data and the special requirements for appliances in hospitals, the various guidance documents produced by the Department of Health and Social Security should be followed. These include:

Building notes – especially 'Common Spaces'
Activity Data Base
Component Data Base

This part does not purport to deal in detail with hot or cold water supplies, for which reference should be made to CP 310, or with sanitary pipework, for which reference should be made to BS 5572.

Attention is directed to Acts, Byelaws, Regulations and any other Statutory requirements relating to sanitary appliances, the water supplies thereto and the drainage therefrom.

BS 1189: 1986 *Baths made from porcelain and enamelled cast iron*

This standard covers the marking, materials, design and construction of baths. The standard also includes a useful appendix of information to be supplied when ordering.

BS 1390: 1972 *Sheet steel baths for domestic purposes*

This standard covers the same requirements as for BS 1189: 1986 and uses the same appendix for ordering purposes.

BS 4305: 1972 *Baths for domestic purposes made from cast acrylic sheet*

This standard specifies the properties of the material and manufacturing requirements and uses the same appendix from BS 1189: 1986 for ordering purposes.

BS 6340 *Shower units*

This standard is being published in a number of parts to provide guidance to consumers on their choice and installation of showers to ensure that the units when installed perform satisfactorily. The parts published to date are:

Part 1: 1983 *Guide on choice of shower units and their components for use in private dwellings.*
Part 2: 1985 *The installation of shower units.*
Part 3: 1985 *Prefabricated shower enclosures and shower cabinets.*
Part 4: 1984 *Shower heads and related equipment.*
Part 5: 1983 *Prefabricated shower trays made from acrylic materials.*
Part 6: 1983 *Prefabricated shower trays made from porcelain-enamelled cast iron.*
Part 7: 1983 *Prefabricated shower trays made from vitreous-enamelled sheet steel.*
Part 8: 1985 *Prefabricated shower trays made from glazed ceramic.*

BS 1188: 1974 *Ceramic wash basins and pedestals*

This standard specifies the manufacturing requirements and permissible deviations from the nominal size for basins with or without back skirtings.

BS 1329: 1974 *Metal hand rinse basins*

This standard covers the manufacturing requirements for both rectangular or round bowl basins.

BS 5506 *Wash basins*

Part 1: 1977 *Pedestal wash basins. Connecting dimensions*

Part 2: 1977 *Wall hung basins. Connecting dimensions*
The aim of both these parts is to specify the connecting characteristics and dimensions of wash basins, whatever material is used in their manufacture.

Part 3: 1977 *Wash basins (one or three tap holes). Materials, quality, design and construction*
This part specifies the materials, quality, design and construction of wall hung and pedestal wash basins with one or three tap holes in the platform. It is restricted to vitreous china at this date.

BS 5505 *Bidets*

Part 1: 1977 *Pedestal bidets, over rim supply only. Connecting dimensions*

Part 2: 1977 *Wall hung bidets, over rim supply only. Connecting dimensions*
The aim of both these parts is to specify the connecting characteristics and dimensions whatever the material of manufacture.

Part 3: 1977 *Vitreous china bidets, over rim supply*
This part gives the specifications for the quality, workmanship and functional dimensions other than connecting dimensions.

BS 1125: 1973 *WC flushing cisterns (including dual flush cisterns and flush pipes)*

This standard specifies the manufacture, construction, testing and marking for both a single 9 litre flush and a dual 4.5 litre or 9 litre flush.

BS 1254: 1981 *WC seats (plastics)*

This standard specifies the requirements for plastics WC seats and covers for use with WC pans.

BS 5503 *Vitreous china washdown WC pans with horizontal outlet*

Part 1: 1977 *Connecting dimensions*
Connecting dimensions for pedestal washdown WC pans with independent and close coupled cisterns are given in this part.

Part 2: 1977 *Materials, quality performance and dimensions other than connecting dimensions*
This part covers pedestal washdown WC pans as described in Part 1.

BS 5504 *Wall hung WC pans*

Part 1: 1977 *Wall hung WC pan with close coupled cistern. Connecting dimensions*

Part 2: 1977 *Wall hung WC pan with independent water supply. Connecting dimensions*

Part 3: 1977 *Wall hung WC pan. Materials, quality and functional dimensions other than connecting dimensions*

BS 5627: 1984 *Plastics connectors for use with horizontal outlet vitreous china WC pans*

This standard specifies the plastics connectors to discharge pipework systems of various materials for both new and existing installations.

BS 2081 *Closets for use with chemicals*

Part 2: 1981 *Permanent installations*
This part specifies those features necessary to ensure that permanently installed chemical closets are made from suitable materials, give adequate service as regards operation, load-bearing capacity and impact resistance, and safeguard public health and welfare.

BS 1876: 1972 *Automatic flushing cisterns for urinals*

This standard specifies the manufacture, materials, marking, design, performance and testing of cisterns. Included is a table, indicating the number of stalls which can be served by various size cisterns. See Table 64.

Table 64 *Nominal size of cisterns*

Nominal size	Nominal size of outlet nipple BSP	Number of stalls or equivalent width of slab served
litres	mm	
4.5	25*	1
9	25*	
13.5	25	3
18	32	4
22.5	32	5
27	38	6

*This size may be reduced to 19 if so required by the purchaser.

(From BS 1876: 1972)

BS 4880 *Urinals*

Part 1: 1973 *Stainless steel slab urinals*

This part gives the materials, dimensions, workmanship and performance requirements for stainless steel slab urinals.

BS 5520: 1977 *Vitreous china bowl urinals (rimless type)*

This standard specifies the materials, quality, design and dimensions of vitreous china bowl urinals (rimless type).

BS 1439: 1961 *Industrial paper towelling and · dispensing cabinets*

(75) Cleaning, maintenance fittings

CP 335 *Selection and installation of miscellaneous town gas appliances* Part 1: 1973 *Domestic laundering and miscellaneous appliances*

Recommendations for the provision, siting and installation of a number of appliances are given. This standard covers items from washing machines to gas pokers.

BS 3456 *Safety of household and similar electrical appliances*

Part 2 *Particular requirements*

Section 2.9: 1970 *Clothes drying cabinets and towel rails*
This section does not include tumbler dryers.

Section 2.11: 1970 *Electric clothes-washing machines*
Washing machines powered by electricity with or without water heating and integral means of water extraction and clothes drying are covered in this section. It does not include machines in which the water is heated by other than electrical means.

Section 2.12: 1970 *Spin extractors*
Household spin extractors with a load capacity not exceeding 10 kg of dry textile material are covered in this section. This limit does not apply to spin extractors incorporated in a washing machine.

Section 2.13: 1970 *Tumbler dryers*
Household electrically heated tumbler dryers including those incorporated in washing machines are covered in this section.
   All of the appliances listed above are defined, and specification for testing, rating, classifying, marking, safety, construction and electrical supply are shown in each section.

Part 3: 1979 *Complete particular specifications*

Section 3.2: 1979 *Washing machines*

Section 3.6: 1979 *Clothes dryers of the rack and cabinet type and towel rails*

Section 3.7: 1979 *Clothes dryers of the tumbler type*

BS 3999 *Methods of measuring the performance of domestic electrical appliances*

Part 4: 1967 *Electric clothes drying cabinets and racks*

(76) Storage screening fittings

BS 6396: 1983 *Code of practice for electrical systems in office furniture and office screens*

Guidance is given for both permanent electrical systems to be built in during manufacture and also on the provision of facilities for electrical systems to be added after purchase.

BS 826: 1978 *Steel single tier bolted shelving (angle upright type)*

This standard specifies materials, finish, method of construction, essential dimensions, safety, bracing, rigidity of bays, testing and erection techniques.

BS 4345: 1968 *Slotted angles*

BS 4680: 1971 *Clothes lockers*

This standard gives three types of clothes locker used for industrial and commercial purposes. It does not apply to lockers designed for special applications.

(76.7) Blinds
BS 3415: 1961 *Mechanical performance of venetian blinds*

This standard is concerned with the testing of prototype mechanical blinds and the simulation of average conditions of use.

(8–) Loose furniture

(84) Sanitary loose equipment

BS 2081 *Closets for use with chemicals* Part 1: 1980 *Portable and transportable types*

This specification ensures that portable and transportable chemical closets give adequate service and safeguard public health and welfare.

(90) External elements, other elements

This section begins with some very useful standards covering the cultivation and maintenance of trees. Then follows a group of standards on fencing in various materials including electric fencing. Precast concrete kerbs, channels, edgings and flagstones for paving and road work are also dealt with. Finally, a group of 14 standards dealing with asphalts, roadstone matrices, tars, bitumens and emulsions is given. Pavers are covered in Table 2 Constructions, forms F Brickwork, blockwork.

BS 3936: *Nursery stock*

This standard is dealt with in Table 2 'Construction, forms', under section W 'Plants, etc.'.

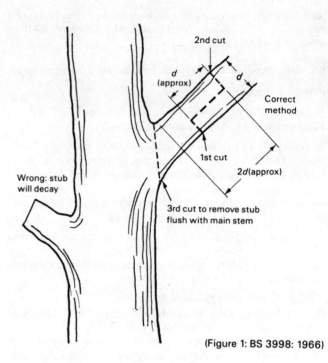

(Figure 1: BS 3998: 1966)

Figure 70 *Pruning of large branches*

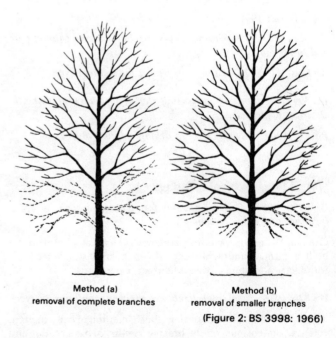

Method (a)
removal of complete branches

Method (b)
removal of smaller branches

(Figure 2: BS 3998: 1966)

Figure 71 *Lifting of crown*

BS 3998: 1966 *Recommendations for tree work*

This standard describes and illustrates a number of operations which might prove to be necessary in tree work such as cuts, pruning, lifting of crown, cleaning and repair work, bracing, feeding and tree removal.

Figures 70 and 71 demonstrate the character of this standard.

An appendix lists general safety precautions.

BS 4043: 1966 *Recommendations for transplanting semi-mature trees*

Modern landscaping often requires the movement of semi-mature trees in order to achieve the end effect of a proposed environment as quickly as possible.

This standard gives a list of trees which are suitable for transplanting and defines a semi-mature tree in terms of its size and weight. Generally such trees are between 6 and 15 m in height weighing between 250 kg and 10 tonne.

BS 5236: 1975 *Recommendations for the cultivation and planting of trees in the extra large nursery stock category*

This standard deals with trees of intermediate size, smaller than semi-mature trees as defined in BS 4043, but larger than nursery stock and suitable for transplanting and growth for amenity purposes.

The recommendations cover propagation, lifting, packaging, labelling and planting.

Appendices cover methods for securing trees and guidelines on maintenance. Good diagrams are provided of which Figure 72 is typical.

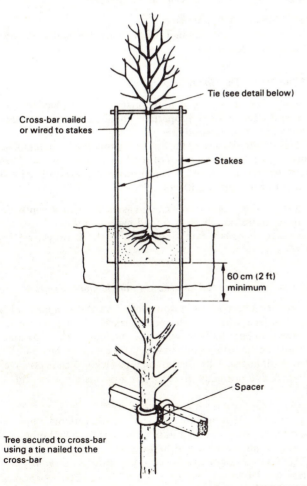

Tie (see detail below)

Cross-bar nailed or wired to stakes

Stakes

60 cm (2 ft) minimum

Spacer

Tree secured to cross-bar using a tie nailed to the cross-bar

(Figure 6: BS 5236: 1975)

Figure 72 *Securing by double staking*

BS 1722 *Fences*

This is an extremely long and comprehensive standard giving recommendations for all types of fencing in all appropriate materials. Recommendations cover such matters as components and materials, fittings, leases, posts, gates, protective treatment and erection procedures. The thirteen parts are:

Part 1: 1972 *Chain link fences.*
 Supplement No 1 (1974): *Gates and gateposts used in conjunction with chain link fences.*
Part 2: 1973 *Woven wire fences.*
Part 3: 1973 *Strained wire fences.*
Part 4: 1972 *Cleft chestnut pale fences.*
Part 5: 1972 *Close-boarded fences including oak pale fences.*
Part 6: 1972 *Wooden palisade fences.*
Part 7: 1972 *Wooden post and rail fences.*
Part 8: 1978 *Mild steel (low-carbon steel) continuous bar fences.*
Part 9: 1979 *Mild steel (low-carbon steel) fences with round or square verticals and flat posts and horizontals.*
Part 10: 1972 *Anti-intruder chain link fences.*
Part 11: 1972 *Woven wood fences.*
Part 12: 1979 *Steel palisade fences.*
Part 13: 1978 *Chain link fences for tennis court surrounds.*

BS 3470: 1975 *Field gates and posts*

This standard covers field gates and posts in timber, timber and concrete and steel together with appropriate fittings. Information includes dimensions, design, construction and protective treatment.

BS 4092 *Domestic front entrance gates*

Information specifying dimensions, material and constructional requirements for single and double metal front gates in tubular frame and mild steel or wrought iron flat frame construction.

The standard states the functional requirements with which a design shall comply but does not specify detail design.

Heights, widths and clearances are specified. Materials, construction, dimensions of components, hanging and latching fittings and protective treatments are also covered.

BS 4102: 1971 *Steel wire for fences*

The steel wires to be used in chain link, woven wire and barbed wire are specified. Galvanized wire and plastic coated wire are also covered. Preferred sizes of wire and mesh and preferred widths for chain link and woven wire fences are given.

BS 5709: 1979 *Stiles, bridle gates and kissing gates*

The details of stiles (post, rails and steps) together with bridle gates and kissing gates are specified. Materials, dimensions, posts, latches, hinges and protective treatments are covered.

BS 340: 1979 *Precast concrete kerbs, channels, edgings and quadrants*

This standard covers a range of sections, lengths and radii available in the above components for use in the construction of carriageways and footways. Materials, finishes, colours, casting and curing are specified together with dimensional tolerances.

	Typical Sizes and Sections
Kerbs	305 × 150 rounded, full batter, half batter
	255 × 125 rounded, full batter, half batter and square
	150 × 125 rounded, half batter and flat
	175 × 125 rounded
Edgings	50 × 255, 205 and 150 half-round, square, chamfered and bullnosed (all sizes in mm)

BS 368: 1971   *Precast concrete flags*

Flag stones in precast concrete are now extensively used in constructing footways and other paved areas. Materials, finish, colour, casting and curing are specified together with dimensions and tolerances. Water absorption limits and strength requirements are also laid down.

Sizes are: 600 ($^{+0}_{-4}$) × 450, 600, 750 and 900 ($^{+0}_{-2}$) × 50 and 65 thickness (all in mm)

Various tests are covered in the appendices.

BS 435: 1975   *Dressed natural stone kerbs, channels, quadrants and setts*

The materials, finishes, dimensions and other requirements for the above items in natural stone are covered.

BS 5931: 1980   *Code of practice for machine laid in situ edge details for paved areas*

Concrete and asphalt can be extruded in moulds to form features such as kerbs or channels.

This standard gives details of concrete and asphalt mixes suitable for this process together with constructional details. The choice as to when to use machine laid concrete is a matter of economics.

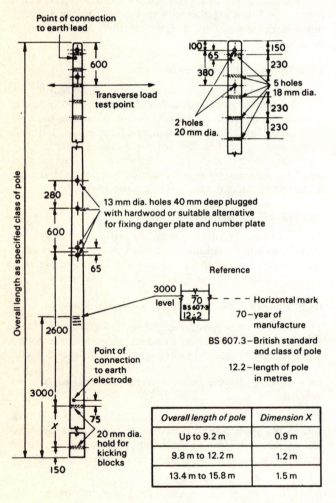

Figure 73 *Elevation of typical pole in direction of line indicating holes and markings*
Note: This drawing gives information on holes and markings only and should not be used as a basis for design. All dimensions are in millimetres unless otherwise stated

BS 607   *Concrete poles for electrical transmission and traction systems*   Part 2: 1970   *Metric units*

The poles, which may be reinforced or prestressed concrete, are to be suitable for electrical transmission and traction line supports including telegraph lines but not concrete street lighting columns (these are dealt with in BS 1308).

The standard begins by specifying the materials of the concrete mix and methods of casting, curing and maturing the poles. The earthing devices are also defined.

The ultimate transverse loads to be carried are defined and special requirements relating to reinforced concrete as opposed to prestressed concrete are specified.

Testing procedures are laid down and the special care of poles exposed to the possibility of impact from vehicles is covered.

Figure 73 shows a typical elevation of such a pole.

BS 1990   *Wood poles for overhead lines (power and telecommunication lines)*   Part 1: 1984   *Softwood poles*

The increased range of species of timber acceptable for use are specified.

The standard covers felling, preparation of poles, waterborne preservative treatment and pressure creosoting. There are tables giving recommended sizes for poles in terms of length to diameter and butt end diameter. The marking of poles giving length, classification and other information vital to the user is carefully laid down.

The appendix gives details of the various tests required to verify the strength and suitability of the poles.

BS 63   *Single-sized roadstone and chippings*

Part 2: 1971   *Metric units*
This standard is covered in Table 3 'Materials' under section p 'Aggregates, loose fills'.

BS 76: 1974   *Tars for road purposes*

Tar is defined as a viscous liquid, black in colour, having adhesive and waterproofing properties, obtained by the destructive distillation of coal, wood, etc.

This standard specifies the essential properties of a number of viscosity grades of two types of road tar as given below. These types differ mainly in their setting properties as controlled by the content of flux oil and its volatility.

1 Surface dressing tars, designated as the S series, are intended to set more rapidly than coated macadam tars.
2 Coated macadam tars, designated as the C series, are less volatile.

BS 434   *Bitumen road emulsions (anionic and cationic)*

Anionic emulsion is one in which the anion of the emulsifier is at the interface with the bitumen particle which is negatively charged, and normally in which the aqueous phase is alkaline.

Cationic emulsion is one in which the cation of the emulsifier is at the interface with the bitumen particle which is positively charged, and normally in which the aqueous phase is acid.

Part 1: 1984   *Bitumen road emulsions*
This specifies requirements for anionic and cationic emulsions used for the preparation and treatment of road and other surfaces carrying wheeled and foot traffic.

Anionic road emulsions are classified in order of stability into:
Class A1: labile.
Class A2: semi-stable.
Class A3: stable.
Class A4: slurry seal (subdivided into slow setting and rapid setting).

Cationic road emulsions are classified into:
Class K1: rapid acting.
Class K2: medium acting.
Class K3: slow acting.
Methods of test are appended.

Part 2: 1984 *Code of practice for use of bitumen road emulsions*
This part provides guidance on the general aspects of use of anionic and cationic bitumen emulsions on road and other surfaces carrying wheeled and foot traffic, other applications such as blowing and stabilization, not appertaining directly to the trafficked surface.

BS 594: *Hot-rolled asphalt for roads and other paved areas*

Rolled asphalt (hot process) is defined as a material used as a dense wearing course, base course or roadbase material. It consists of a mixture of aggregate and asphaltic cement which, when hot, can be spread and compacted.

Part 1: 1985 *Constituent materials and asphaltic mixtures*
This part specifies requirements for hot-rolled asphalt laid as wearing course, base course or roadbase for road and other paved areas, excluding heavy-duty airfield pavements. It includes guidance on the selection of asphalt mixtures and their ingredients.

Part 2: 1975 *Transport, laying and compaction of rolled asphalt*
This part sets out requirements and recommendations for the transportation, laying and compaction of rolled asphalt and includes directions for preparation of substrate and finishing or wearing course.

BS 598 *Sampling and examination of bituminous mixtures for roads and other paved areas*

This 3-part standard is covered in Table 3 'Materials', under section s 'Bituminous materials'.

BS 1446: 1973 *Mastic asphalt (natural rock asphalt fine aggregate) for roads and footways*

Mastic asphalt is defined as a type of asphalt composed of suitably graded mineral matter and asphaltic cement in such proportions as to form a coherent, voidless, impermeable mass, solid or semi-solid under normal temperature conditions but sufficiently fluid when brought to a suitable temperature to be spread by means of a float.

This standard specifies requirements for mastic asphalt with natural rock asphalt fine aggregate for roads and footways. Recommendations for laying, information for enquiries and/or orders are appended.

BS 1447: 1973 *Mastic asphalt (limestone fine aggregate) for roads and footways*

This standard specifies requirements for mastic asphalt with limestone fine aggregate for roads and footways. Recommendations for laying, information for enquiries and/or orders are appended.

BS 1984: 1967 *Gravel aggregates for surface treatment (including surface dressings) on roads*

This standard is covered in Table 3 'Materials', under section p 'Aggregate, loose fills'.

BS 2499: 1973 *Hot applied joint sealants for concrete pavements*

This standard is covered in Table 3 'Materials', under section t 'Fixing and jointing agents'.

BS 3262: 1976 *Hot-applied thermoplastic road marking materials*

This standard specifies white and yellow thermoplastic materials which are melted and applied hot to roads, by screeded or sprayed application, as thin superimposed markings for centre lines, edge lines, pedestrian crossing stripes, etc. It does not apply to road inset materials.

BS 3690 *Bitumens for building and civil engineering*

Part 1: 1982 *Bitumens for road purposes*
Part 1 specifies the requirements for penetration grade bitumens and cut-back bitumens which are suitable for use in road construction and maintenance in the United Kingdom. The bitumens are classified into a number of grades with appropriate designation and properties.

This part does not cover bitumen emulsions or bitumen mixtures containing lake asphalt, coal tar or pitch; such materials are specified in BS 434, BS 594, BS 1446, BS 1447 and BS 4987.

Advice on handling and packaging, and in sampling and testing, is appended.

Part 2: 1982 *Bitumens for industrial purposes*
Part 2 specifies the requirements for penetration grade, cut-back, oxidized grade and hard grade bitumens which are suitable for use in industrial applications in the United Kingdom.

This part does not cover bitumen emulsions or bituminous solutions containing petroleum solvents (other than cut-back bitumens); such materials are specified in BS 534, BS 743, BS 747, BS 988, BS 1863, BS 2499, BS 2832, BS 3416, BS 3634, BS 4147, BS 5493, CP 102, CP 144 and CP 2010.

Advice on handling and packaging, and on sampling and testing is appended.

Part 3: *Bitumen mixes*
This part specifies classification, composition and properties of pitch-, tar- and lake asphalt-bitumen mixes that are suitable for use in road and industrial applications relevant to the United Kingdom climate, conditions and application techniques. Each mixture is classified into a number of grades for each of which the appropriate designation and properties are specified. Appendices give advice on handling, packaging, sampling and testing.

BS 4987: *Coated macadam for roads and other paved areas*

This standard deals with the composition, manufacture, testing, transport and laying of roadbase, basecourse and wearing course coated macadam.

Part 1: *Constituent materials and mixtures* is in preparation

BS 5212: 1975 *Cold poured joint sealants for concrete pavements*

This standard is covered in Table 3 'Materials', under section t 'Fixing and jointing agents'.

BS 5273: 1975 *Dense tar surfacing for roads and other paved areas*

This standard specifies composition, manufacture, testing and transport of dense tar surfacing (DTS), defined in BS 892 as a hot process wearing course material consisting of aggregate, filler and road tar, in such gradings and proportions that when spread and compacted it provides a close textured impervious mixture.

CI/SfB Table 2: Constructions, forms

A Preliminaries and general conditions (no entry)

B Demolition and shoring work (no entry)

C Excavation and loose fill work (no entry)

D Cast *in situ* **work** (no entry)

F Blockwork and brickwork

BS 6100 *Glossary of building and civil engineering terms* is here, as elsewhere, a useful guide, especially Part 5: Masonry, and Section 5.3: 1984 Bricks and Blocks. BS 6270 *Cleaning and surface repair of buildings* (see Table 4 (W2)). BS 4513: 1969 *Lead bricks for radiation shielding* and BS 3379: 1975 *Flexible urethane foam for load-bearing applications*, cover the burning characteristics, handling and application of block, sheet, strip and moulded material mainly used for upholstery; both deserve mention.

BS 3921: 1974 *Clay bricks and blocks* (see next entry)

■ AD (Regs. A1/2 and H1)

The standard is in three sections: general, bricks and blocks for walling and hollow blocks for structural floors and roofs.

Section one *general*
Section one defines the scope as extending to bricks and blocks manufactured from clay (including brickearth and shale).

Modular metric bricks are not included but they are covered by DD 34.

Section two *bricks and blocks for walling*
Bricks and blocks are defined as follows:

Brick: a walling unit not exceeding 337.5 mm in length, 225 mm in width, or 112.5 mm in height.

Block: a walling unit exceeding in length or height the sizes specified for bricks.

Varieties of brick and block are:

Common – suitable for general building work but having no special claim to give an attractive appearance.
Facing – specially made or selected to give an attractive appearance when used without rendering or plaster or other surface treatment of the wall.
Engineering – having a dense and strong semi-vitreous body conforming to defined limits for absorption and strength.

The *qualities* of brick and block are:

Internal quality bricks and blocks suitable for internal use only (may need protection on site during winter).
Ordinary quality less durable than special quality but normally durable in the external face of a building.
Special quality durable even when used in situations of extreme exposure where the structure may become saturated and be frozen, for example retaining walls, sewerage plants or pavings.

It should be noted that engineering bricks or blocks normally attain the standard of durability of 3. Facing and common bricks or blocks may do so, but this should not be assumed unless claimed by the manufacturer.

Types of brick and block are:

Solid – in which holes passing through, or nearly through, a brick or block do not exceed 25 per cent of its volume, or in which frogs (depressions in the bed faces of a brick) do not exceed 20 per cent of its volume.
Perforated – in which holes passing through the brick or block exceed 25 per cent of its volume.
Hollow – in which holes passing through the brick or block exceed 25 per cent of its volume, there being no limitation on the size of the holes.
Cellular – in which cavities (holes closed at one end) exceed 20 per cent of the volume of the brick or block.

Cellular bricks and blocks are normally made by pressing, perforated and hollow bricks and blocks by extrusion. Perforations and hollows may be either perpendicular to the bed face (V-type) or parallel to the bed face (H-type).

Special shapes are defined as shapes other than the normal rectangular prism, and *standard specials* are special shapes that are in general use and may be available from stock. These are detailed in BS 4729.

Formats, with the exception of the widths of blocks, include the thickness of a mortar joint equal to 10 mm. The standard format and the block formats are given in Table 65.

In addition, half blocks, 140 mm long, and three-quarter blocks, 215 mm long, are available for bonding.

Compliance for dimensions of bricks is based on a sample of twenty-four, the limits prescribed in Table 66 and of blocks on a sample of ten, of which no more than two may exceed permissible deviations prescribed in Table 67.

Requirements are also given for compliance for out of squareness (blocks), compliance for bowing or twisting (blocks), and maximum deviations on dimensions.

A classification of strength and absorption in accordance with the requirements of CP 111 *Structural recommendations for load-bearing walls* or Building Regulations is given in Table 68.

Facing and common bricks and blocks of ordinary quality. Requirements are given for finish, notes on durability, and on strength, where, unless a higher strength is agreed, the compres-

Table 65 *Standard format (bricks and blocks)*

Designation	Work size		
	Length	Width	Height
Bricks	mm	mm	mm
225 × 112.5 × 75	215	102.5	65
Blocks			
300 × 62.5 × 225	290	62.5	215
300 × 75 × 225	290	75	215
300 × 100 × 225	290	100	215
300 × 150 × 225	290	150	215

(From Tables 1 and 2: BS 3921: 1974; also
BS 3921: 1985)

sive strength of bricks should not be less than 5.2 N/mm² and of blocks not less than 2.8 N/mm².

Liability to efflorescence and *frost resistance* are covered in a note.

Facing and common bricks and *blocks of special quality.* Requirements are given for finish, strength, soluble salts content, where limits are stated for sulphate, calcium, magnesium, potassium and sodium, liability to efflorescence, where, when tested in accordance with the standard, no sample shall develop efflorescence worse than moderate, and frost resistance. The best evidence of ability to withstand frost damage is provided by brickwork which has been in service for some three years, but two other options are given – the exposure of sample panels for not less than three years, or, exceptionally, a brick or block with either a strength not less than 48.5 N/mm², measured in accordance with the standard, or a water absorption not greater than 7 per cent measured in accordance with the standard, may be deemed to be frost resistant.

Bricks and blocks for internal walls. Requirements are given for finish; strength, with the acceptable lower compressive strength of bricks and blocks for non-load-bearing partitions of not less than 1.4 N/mm²; and liability to efflorescence.

Section three *hollow blocks for structural floors and roofs defined as blocks designed to be used as filler blocks in reinforced concrete floors* (Table 69)

Requirements are also given for compliance for dimensions – as for walling blocks, compliance for out of squareness, compliance for bowing or twisting, finish and strength, where the compressive strength of blocks for structural floors and roofs, when tested in accordance with the standard, should be not less than 14.0 N/mm² (unless higher strengths are agreed to make use of the block strength for design purposes).

BS 3921: 1985 *Clay bricks*

This current standard is reported upon in unorthodox fashion because its 1974 predecessor is referred to in the Authorized Document under the Building Regulations 1985 (Regulations A1/2 and H1). The main changes are first summarized, then new sections are set out.

Changes:

1 *Coverage of clay blocks* omitted (they are no longer made).
2 *Types* redefined (now *solid, cellular, perforated* and *frogged*).
3 *Size* is extended (to give a maximum for one brick)
4 *Format* coverage is reduced (225 × 112.5 × 75 mm only, with 200 × 100 × 75 mm in the separate BS 6649).
5 *Durability* (six new designations).
6 *Frost resistance* (three new categories).
7 *Load-bearing classification* (omitted).
8 *Water absorption* (only one test: the 5 h boil method).
9 *Facing bricks* (a visual acceptability guide introduced).
10 *Ordering* (a checklist included).
11 *Suction* (a test is included).

Table 66 *Limits of size (twenty-four bricks)*

Work size (see Table 68)	Overall measurement of twenty-four bricks	Limits of size	
		Maximum	Minimum
mm	mm	mm	mm
215	5160	5235	5085
102.5	2460	2505	2415
65	1560	1605	1515

(From Table 3: BS 3921: 1974; also BS 3921: 1985)

Table 67 *Permissible deviations in sizes (individual blocks)*

Work size	Permissible deviations in size
mm	mm
Less than 125	± 2.5
125 to 225	± 3.0
Greater than 225	± 5.0

(From Table 4: BS 3921: 1974)

Table 68 *Strength and absorption: bricks*

Designation	Class	Average compressive strength not less than	Average absorption boiling or vacuum per cent weight not greater than
		N/mm² (= MPa)	
Engineering brick	A	69.0	4.5
	B	48.5	7.0
Load-bearing brick	15	103.5	
	10	69.0	
	7	48.5	
	5	34.5	No specific requirement
	4	27.5	
	3	20.5	
	2	14.0	
	1	7.0	
Bricks for damp proof courses	d.p.c.	As required	4.5

(Table 6: BS 3921: 1974)

Table 69 *Standard formats (floor blocks)*

Designation	Work sizes		
	Length	Width	Height
	mm	mm	mm
300 × 300 × 75	295	295	75
300 × 300 × 100	295	295	100
300 × 300 × 125	295	295	125
300 × 300 × 150	295	295	150
300 × 300 × 175	295	295	175
300 × 300 × 200	295	295	200
300 × 200 × 225	295	295	225
300 × 300 × 250	295	295	250

(Table 7: BS 3921 1974)

Summary: An introduction discusses water absorption, durability and tolerances. The *scope* covers these properties, dimensions, compressive strength, soluble salt content, efflorescence, sampling and methods of classification for clay bricks used for walling – and possibly paving – with mortar beds as recommended in BS 5628.

One *size* only is included, a co-ordinating size (including joints and tolerances) of 225 × 112.5 × 75 mm and a work size of 215 × 102.5 × 65 mm.

Sizes of voids determine *types: solid* (no holes, cavities or depressions); *cellular* (no holes, but may have frogs or cavities exceeding 20% of the gross volume); *perforated* (holes not exceeding 25% of the gross volume in aggregate, 10% individually, and aggregate thickness of solid material at least 30% of width) and *frogged* (indent(s) not over 20% of gross volume).

Dimensional deviations are as in Table 71, but no single brick may exceed the co-ordinating size.

Durability. Three categories of *frost-resistance* are distinguished as *frost-resistant* (F), durable in any location, even when saturated and/or subject to repeated freeze-thaw; *moderately frost-resistant* (M), durable except in such situations; and *not frost-resistant* (O), requiring protection during construction and suitable for internal use only. Two categories of *soluble salt content* are distinguished: *low* (L) and *normal* (N) (no limit).

Efflorescence. Four categories are distinguished, based on coverage when tested: *nil, slight* (to 10%), *moderate* (10–50%), and *heavy* (over 50%, or powdering/flaking of surface): the last not acceptable under the standard.

Compressive strengths and *water absorption* (see Table 68).

Sampling procedures are set out for the tests which are used for the properties and which are the subject of detailed appendices. A *random* sample, from a consignment of not more than 15 000 bricks, is preferred to *representative* sampling, though the techniques for stacks or banded packs of the latter are considered.

Marking of the delivery note, invoice or supplier's certificate extends to the name or mark of the manufacturer; this BS; the type (solid, cellular, hollow or perforated) and the name (e.g. Red Multi).

Apart from the appendices dealing with tests for the above properties, others cover:

Appearance: a 'reference panel' exhibiting not less than 100 faces and 'sample panels' (which should not differ significantly viewed from 3 m);

Checklist for ordering: (a) type; (b) durability; (c) requirements for structural use (1) compressive strength, (2) water absorption, (3) category for manufacturing controls; (d) special requirements for tolerance, if any; (e) additional requirements such as colour, texture and acid resistance; (f) quantity – including type and number of specials; and (g) handling requirements.

Quality control procedures for manufacturers in relation to compressive strength and dimensions.

DD 34: 1974 *Clays bricks with modular dimensions* (see next entry)

■ AD (Reg. A1/2)

This draft is in two sections: general and modular bricks for walling.

Section one *general*
This section is the same as BS 3921: 1974.

Section two *modular bricks for walling*
This defines units and varieties, qualities and types substantially as BS 3921: 1974.
Formats are tabulated to include the thickness of a mortar joint. See Table 70.
Compliance for dimensions is as BS 3921: 1974, and the limits of size are similarly prescribed for a sample of 24 bricks. See Table 71.
Certain handmade and stock bricks are identified as giving difficulty, and it may be that tolerances will be altered.
Other requirements are largely as in BS 3921: 1974.

Table 70 *Modular formats: clay bricks*

Designation	Work size		
	Length	Width	Height
mm	mm	mm	mm
300 × 100 × 100	288	90	90
200 × 100 × 100	190	90	90
300 × 100 × 75	288	90	65
200 × 100 × 75	190	90	65

(Table 1: DD 34: 1974; also BS 6649)

Table 71 *Limits of size (twenty-four bricks)*

Work size (see table 73)	Overall measurement of twenty-four bricks	Limits of size	
		Maximum	Minimum
mm	mm	mm	mm
65	1560	1605	1515
90	2160	2205	2115
190	4560	4626	4494
288	6912	7012	6812

(From Table 2: DD 34: 1974; also BS 6649)

BS 6649: 1985 *Clay and calcium silicate modular bricks*

This succeeds DD 34 (above) and DD 59 (below): and see also BS 4729. It specifies requirements for modular bricks of a 200 × 100 × 75 mm format (work sizes 100 mm less). The two DDs remain as approved documents under the Building Regulations 1985, Regulation A1/4. The sampling for clay bricks (24 bricks) is as BS 3921: 1985 and for calcium silicate bricks (10 bricks) as BS 187: 1978, and the relevant limits of manufacturing size are as in Tables 70 and 71.

BS 4729: 1971 *Shapes and dimensions of special bricks*

In a foreword, reference is made on coping units to BS 3789 (see Table 1 'Building elements' under section (31) 'Secondary elements to walls') and to the possible simplification in the range if no frogs are present.

In an appendix the relationship between the sizes of the special bricks likely to be required for brickwork construction and standard bricks is shown.

Table 72 *Sizes: calcium silicate bricks*

Sizes	Length	Width	Height
	mm	mm	mm
Co-ordinating size	225	112.5	75
Work size	215	102.5	65
Maximum limit of manufacturing size	217	105	67
Minimum limit of manufacturing size	212	101	63

(Table 1: BS 187: 1978)

BS 187: 1978 *Calcium silicate (sandlime and flintlime) bricks*
■ AD (Reg. A1/2)

The standard covers calcium silicate bricks of all classes, but not lime-based bricks made with calcined shale, slag or other materials made by a similar process or the colour and texture of bricks, which should be the subject of special agreement.

Definitions (see also Table 3 'Materials') of units follow BS 3921, but include *frogs*: depressions in the bed faces of a brick; *solid brick, cavities and cellular brick; load-bearing brick*: a brick which is suitable for brickwork bearing significant loads and conforming to defined limits for strength; and, in respect of dimensions, *facing brick, common brick* and *special brick shapes*. Definitions are: *co-ordinating size*: the size of a co-ordinating dimension; *work size*: a size of a building component specified for its manufacture, to which its actual size should conform within specified permissible deviations of the work size; *limits of size*: the extreme permissible manufacturing sizes between which the actual size should lie. *Mean strength* is defined as the arithmetic mean of the strengths of a stated number of specimens; *standard deviation* as a measure of the variation of the strength of a sample; and *predicted lower limit* as the value below which the mean strength of a further sample, taken from the same consignment of bricks as the test sample, is likely to fall with a probability of approximately 1 in 40. See Table 72.

Materials are defined as essentially an intimate and uniform mixture of sand consisting predominantly of quartz or uncrushed siliceous gravel or crushed siliceous gravel or rock or a combination of such materials, with a lesser proportion of lime, mechanically pressed together and combined by the action of steam under pressure.

Sandlime (natural sand) and *flintlime* (where a substantial proportion of crushed flint is included) are distinguished, and suitable pigmentation is permitted.

Forms of bricks are solid, or cellular (*note*: excluding the perforated and hollow types in BS 3921). Solid bricks may have frogs in one bed face or be of a simple rectangular prism form without frogs. Perforations or cavities are to be perpendicular to the bed face.

Bricks of non-standard dimensions or design may be agreed, and are deemed to comply with this standard provided that they comply with all other requirements.

If, when measured in accordance with the standard, more than one of the ten bricks fails to comply with any dimension, or any one of the ten bricks has any one dimension exceeding the maximum limit of manufacturing size by more than 2 mm, or less than the minimum limit of manufacturing size by more than 2 mm, then the bricks sampled do not comply with this standard.

Appearance. Load-bearing bricks and facing bricks are to be free from visible cracks and noticeable balls of clay, loam and lime. Facing bricks, the colour, darker when wet than dry, and texture are to be agreed and to be reasonably free from damaged arrises.

Classification and compressive strength. Any consignment of bricks, when sampled and tested in accordance with the standard, is to conform to the appropriate compressive strength requirements for the specified designation and strength class, in respect both of mean strength and of predicted lower limit of strength calculated as described in the standard.

When only the designation of brick is specified, that is load-bearing, facing or common brick, then the mean compressive strength and the predicted lower limit are to be not less than the values for the lowest strength class for that designation shown. See Table 73.

Drying shrinkage. Any consignment of bricks, other than common bricks, when sampled and tested in accordance with the standard is to have a drying shrinkage of not more than 0.040 per cent.

Drying shrinkage of bricks used under permanently damp conditions is generally of little significance.

Table 73 *Compressive strength classes and requirements*

Designation	Class*	Mean† compressive strength of ten bricks not less than	Predicted lower‡ limit of compressive strength not less than
		N/mm²	N/mm²
Load-bearing brick or Facing brick	7	48.5	40.5
	6	41.5	34.5
	5	34.5	28.0
	4	27.5	21.5
	3	20.5	15.5
Facing brick or common brick	2	14.0	10.0

Editor's notes
*Classes as in BS 3921.
†For design purposes.
‡Of statistical significance in sampling.

(From Table 2: BS 187: 1978)

The delivery note, invoice or supplier's certificate is to identify the manufacturer, strength, class, dimensions, and this BS number.

A proportion of the bricks in each delivery *may* also be colour-marked by the manufacturer to show the strength class. Colours are Class 7, green, Class 6, blue, Class 5, yellow, Class 4, red, and Class 3, black.

Recommendations on the use of calcium silicate bricks. The selection of the appropriate class of bricks and class of mortar for a particular use depends on a number of factors. See Tables 74 and 75 for the appropriate classes of mortar and minimum strength class of bricks. For guidance on other aspects reference should be made to BS 5628 *Code of practice for the structural use of masonry* Part 1 *Unreinforced masonry* and CP 121 *Walling* Part 1 *Brick and block masonry*.

Precautions should be taken prior to laying to keep bricks clean and dry.

DD 59: 1978 *Calcium silicate bricks with modular dimensions*
See BS 6649 above.

■ AD (Regs. A1/2)

Sizes of modular bricks for walling, which otherwise comply with BS 187, are given in Table 76.

Not more than one of the ten bricks in a sample should fail to conform to the limits of size given in Table 77. If more than one brick fails, a fresh sample should be measured and, if more than one fails again, the batch should be rejected.

BS 3056 *Sizes of refractory bricks*

Intended eventually to comprise eight parts, four published to date.

Part 1: 1985 *Multi-purpose bricks*
This tabulates sizes for eight shapes: (a) squares, (b) splits, (c) tiles, (d) straight, (e) side-arch bricks, (f) end-arch bricks, and (g) crown bricks; for five classes of refractory: 'F' (fireclay), 'HA' (high alumina), 'B' (basic), 'S' (silica), and 'I' (insulating). Appendices detail standard constructions and the numbers of units for many of these.

Part 2: *Bricks for use in glass-melting furnaces*
Shapes and classes are again set out, a wider range of each than in Part 1, additional shapes being 'blocks' and additional classes: 'Z' (zircon), 'F/S' (fused silica), 'AZS' (fusion cast), and 'VC' (vacuum cast) sillimanite refractories; with appendices on constructions and quantities.

Table 74 *Mortar mixes*

Increasing strength	Increasing ability to accomodate movements, e.g. due to settlement, temperature and moisture changes	Mortar designation	Type of mortar (proportion by volume, see note 1)		
			Cement:lime: sand (see note 2)	Masonry cement: sand (see note 3)	Cement: sand with plasticizer (see note 3)
		(i)	1:0 to $\frac{1}{4}$:3	—	—
		(ii)	1:$\frac{1}{2}$:4 to 4 $\frac{1}{2}$	1:2 $\frac{1}{2}$ to 3 $\frac{1}{2}$	1:3 to 4
		(iii)	1:1:5 to 6	1:4 to 5	1:5 to 6
		(iv)	1:2:8 to 9	1:5 $\frac{1}{2}$ to 6 $\frac{1}{2}$	1:7 to 8
		(v)	1:3:10 to 12	1:6 $\frac{1}{2}$ to 7	1:8

→ Increasing resistance to frost attack during construction

Direction of change in properties is shown by the arrows

← Improvement in bond and consequent resistance to rain penetration

Note 1: The proportions given are for lime putty which is a mixture of dry hydrated lime and water allowed to mature, and dry sand. If hydrated lime is batched when dry, the volume may be increased by up to 50%, if necessary, to obtain adequate workability.

Note 2: In the case of cement: lime: sand mortars, the term 'lime' refers to non-hydraulic or semi-hydraulic lime.

Note 3: The masonry cement mortars, plasticized mortars and hydraulic lime mortars that are included in a given designation are of approximately equivalent strength to the corresponding cement: lime: sand type.

(From Table 7: BS 187: 1978)

Table 75 *Minimum quality of calcium silicate bricks and mortars for durability*

Element of construction		Minimum quality of bricks class (see note 1)	Appropriate mortar designation (see note 2)	
			When there is no risk of frost during construction	When freezing may occur during construction
Inner-leaf of cavity walls and internal walls	unplastered	2	(iv)	(iii)
	plastered	2	(v)	(iii)
Backing to external solid walls		2	(iv)	(iii)
External walls including the outer-leaf of cavity walls and facing to solid construction	above damp proof course (d.p.c.) near to ground level	2	(iv)	(iii)
	below this d.p.c. but more than 150 mm above finished ground level	2	(iii)	(iii)
	within 150 mm of ground or below ground	3	(iii) (see note 4)	(iii) (see note 4)
External freestanding walls (see note 3)		3	(iii)	(iii)
Parapets	unrendered	3	(iii)	(iii)
	rendered	3	(iv)	(iii)
Sills and copings of bricks		4	(ii)	(ii)
Earth-retaining walls (see note 5)		4	(ii) (see note 3)	(ii) (see note 3)

Note 1: The classification of bricks is given in Table 73.

Note 2: The designation of mortars is that given in Table 74.

Note 3: Where sulphates are present in the ground water, the use of sulphate-resisting cement for the mortar may be necessary.

Note 4: An effective and continuous d.p.c. should be provided at the top of the walls, as well as just above ground level.

Note 5: Walls should be backfilled with free-draining materials as recommended in the Civil Engineering Code of Practice no. 2: *Earth-retaining Structures*, published by the Institution of Structural Engineers, 1951. This is to be revised by BSI and published as a British Standard.

(From Table 8: BS 187: 1978)

Table 76 *Sizes of modular bricks for walling*

Co-ordinating sizes (mm)			Work sizes (mm)		
Length	Width	Height	Length	Width	Height
300	100	100	290	90	90
200	100	100	190	90	90
300	100	75	290	90	65
200	100	75	190	90	65

(Table 1: DD 59: 1978; also BS 6649)

Table 77 *Limits of manufacturing size: modular bricks*

Work size (mm)	Limits of manufacturing size (mm)	
	Maximum	Minimum
65	67	63
90	92	88
190	192	187
290	293	287

(Table 2: DD 59: 1978; also BS 6649)

Part 4: 1985 *Bricks for elastic arc furnace roofs*
Sizes, standard constructions and quantities.

Part 5: 1985 *Bricks for blast furnace walls*
A range of tapered bricks for linings comprising five lengths (230, 300, 345, 375, 450 mm), all 150 mm wide but tapering to 130, 145 or 150 mm and normally 76 mm high. An appendix details the design radii for the resulting construction.

BS 6677 *Clay and calcium silicate pavers for flexible pavements*

Part 1: 1986 *Specification for pavers*
Requirements for clay and calcium silicate pavers: Type PA intended for use in flexible pavements for landscaping and pedestrian applications; and Type PB and in flexible pavements used by pneumatic tyred vehicles. Gives dimensions, tolerances, transverse breaking load, skid resistance value. Appendices give commonly available work sizes, methods of sampling and methods of test.

Part 2: 1986 *Code of practice for design of lightly trafficked pavements*
Recommendations for the design of lightly trafficked flexible pavements (pavements carrying not more than 1.5 million standard axles during their design life). Selection of pavers; sub-base, roadbase, bedding course and wearing surface; drainage; finished tolerances.

Part 3: 1986 *Method for construction of pavements*
Describes a method for the construction of flexible pavements designed in accordance with BS 6677: Part 2 incorporating clay or calcium silicate pavers complying with BS 6677: Part 1.

BS 6073 *Precast concrete masonry units*

This standard is in two parts.

Part 1: 1981 *Precast concrete masonry units*
■ AD (Regs. A1/2 and B2/3/4)

This part specifies materials, tolerances and minimum performance levels for these units. It covers solid (including autoclaved aerated concrete), cellular and hollow units not exceeding 650 mm in any work size dimension.

Units in which the height exceeds the length or six times the thickness are outside the scope of this standard, as are precast concrete paving blocks.

A range of definitions include *masonry unit*: a block, a brick or a fixing unit; *block*: a masonry unit which when used in its normal aspect exceeds the length or width or height specified for bricks; *brick*: effectively as in BS 3921; *fixing unit*: a masonry unit of the same dimensions as a brick which permits the easy driving of, and provides a good purchase for, nails or screws.

Three types of blocks are distinguished. They are:

Solid block – a block which contains no formed holes or cavities other than those inherent in the material; and including autoclaved aerated blocks.
Cellular block – a block which has one or more formed holes or cavities which do not wholly pass through the block.
Hollow block – a block which has one or more formed holes or cavities which pass through the block.

Types of brick, which resemble in general terms those in BS 3921, are perforated brick, hollow brick and cellular brick.
Sizes of brick resemble in general terms those in BS 187.
Compressive strength is determined as the average value of the crushing strengths of ten masonry units.

The composition is considered under the headings of binders, aggregates and admixtures.

Binders, either *binders specified in British Standards*: lime, ordinary and portland blast pulverized fuel ash, rapid-hardening portland cement, furnace cement, or sulphate resisting portland cement. Note that the proportion, by mass, of lime to cement should not exceed 10 per cent unless the units are autoclaved, and similarly that the proportion of p.f.a. to cement should not exceed 35:65; or *other binders*: ground granulated blast furnace slag (to a maximum proportion to cement of 65:35), and limes not complying with the requirements of BS 890 which, for autoclaved masonry units, should be finely ground to prevent inclusion of lumps in the finished units.

Aggregates, either *aggregates specified in British Standards*: foamed or expanded blastfurnace slag, natural aggregates, air-cooled blastfurnace slag, furnace clinker, lightweight aggregates, or pulverized fuel ash. Note that grading requirements are generally relaxed and in the case of p.f.a. when used for autoclaved aerated blocks there are wider relaxations; or *other aggregates*: granulated blastfurnace slag made by the rapid cooling of iron slag, containing not more than 50 per cent of calcium oxide; or bottom ash from boilers fired with pulverized coal, complying with the requirements given for furnace clinker (Class A or Class B) in BS 1165; or milled softwood chips.

For autoclaved aerated blocks, the use of aggregates as defined in clause 2 of BS 882, 1202 is permitted.

Admixtures where complying with BS requirements, and with particular limits on calcium chloride are permitted.

Dimensional requirements and *tolerances* are given in respect of end and bedding surfaces, the external shell thickness of blocks (to be not less than 15 mm or 1.75 times the nominal maximum size of the aggregate, whichever is the greater), and dimensional deviations.

The *strength of blocks* is dealt with in two ways. Blocks of thickness 75 mm or greater, sampled and tested for compressive strength are to have an average crushing strength of ten blocks not less than 2.8 N/mm² and a corresponding lowest crushing strength of any individual block not less than 80 per cent of that figure (that is 2.24 N/mm²).

Blocks of thickness less than 75 mm, when tested for transverse strength, are to have an average transverse strength of five blocks not less than 0.65 N/mm².

The *strength of bricks* sets two conditions: the average crushing strength of ten bricks, not les than 7.0 N/mm²; and the corresponding coefficient of variation for the sample, not to exceed 20 per cent.

Strength of fixing units. Two conditions are set: the average

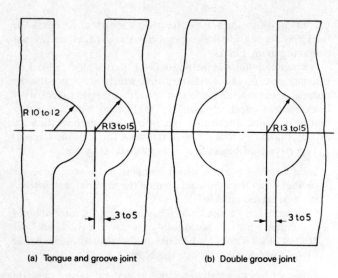

(a) Tongue and groove joint   (b) Double groove joint

All dimensions in millimetres

(Figure 1: BS 6073: Part 2: 1981)

Figure 74   *Typical profiled ends of blocks*

crushing strength of ten units, not less than 2.8 N/mm²; and the corresponding coefficient of variation for the sample, not to exceed 20 per cent.

Drying shrinkage of a sample of masonry unit other than fixing units is not to exceed 0.06 per cent except for autoclaved aerated concrete blocks (0.09 per cent).

Certification is provided for.

Identification of masonry units on the relevant documents and, desirably, on any wrapping covers the manufacturer comprising this BS, dimensions and type of unit.

There are appendices on the measurement of dimensions and on the determination of compressive strength, transverse strength and drying shrinkage.

Part 2: 1981   *Method for specifying precast concrete masonry units*

This part gives a method for specifying precast concrete masonry units complying with the requirements of Part 1 and describes the compliance procedure for the special category of manufacturing control.

Generally, it states that the purchaser is to specify masonry units in terms of basic requirements, and additional and optional requirements. Basic requirements are set out (compliance with Part 1; size, and strength where above the minimum). See Tables 78 and 79. Additional and optional requirements are those in Appendix A (d) to (i). See Figure 74.

Table 79   *Work sizes of bricks*

Thickness (mm)		90	103
Length	Height		
mm	mm		
290	90	x	
215	65		x
190	90	x	
190	65	x	

Note: This range covers three of the four modular sizes in DD 59, and the rationalized metric size in BS 187.

(Table 2: BS 6073: Part 2: 1981)

A guide for compressive strength for design purposes is included, and reference is made to BS 5628 *Code of practice for the structural use of masonry*, in Part 1: 1978 of which are graphs for the same purpose.

Blocks (N/mm²) 2.8, 3.5, 5.0, 7.0, 10.0, 15.0, 20.0, 35.0.
Bricks (N/mm²) 7.0, 10.0, 15.0, 20.0, 30.0, 40.0.

Note: It should be noted that the brick classes differ from those in BS 3921 and BS 187.

The following particulars cover the essential details to be given by the purchaser to the manufacturer for an enquiry and order to be fully understood.

(a) Quantity.
(b) Work size dimensions and thickness in the order of length × height × thickness.
(c) Compressive strength of blocks 75 mm or greater in thickness or of bricks.
(d) Type of masonry unit.
(e) Specific requirements for constituent materials.
(f) Special shapes and/or tolerances.
(g) Requirements for additional properties.
(h) Whether special category of manufacturing control is required.
(i) Whether additional means of identification is required.
(j) Handling requirements, such as palletization, strapping or mechanical off-loading.

There are further appendices on a routine rapid control test and on the determination of block density, concrete density and net area of hollow blocks.

BS 6457: 1984   *Reconstructed stone masonry units*

Materials, tolerances and minimum performance levels for reconstructed stone masonry units intended to resemble and to be used for similar purposes as natural stone, and intended to be used primarily on the external face of masonry constructions. It

Table 78   *Work sizes of blocks*

Thickness (mm)		60	75	90	100	115	125	140	150	175	190	200	215	220	225	250
Length	Height															
mm	mm															
390	190	x	x	x	x	x		x	x		x	x				
440	140	x	x	x	x			x	x		x	x			x	
440	190	x	x	x	x			x	x		x		x	x		
440	215	x	x	x	x	x	x	x	x	x	x	x	x	x	x	x
440	290	x	x	x	x			x	x		x	x	x			
590	140		x	x	x			x	x		x	x	x			
590	190		x	x	x			x	x		x	x	x			
590	215		x	x	x		x	x	x	x		x	x		x	x

(Table 1: BS 6073: Part 2: 1981)

covers homogeneous units manufactured using casting, extrusion or pressing techniques and not exceeding 650 mm in any work size dimension, excluding the thickness of any profile on a textured face.

This standard does not cover masonry units consisting of a facing material and a backing concrete as specified in BS 1217.

The constituents of a masonry unit are:

1 *Cementitious binders*:
Ordinary and rapid-hardening Portland Cement (BS 12)
Portland – blastfurnace cement (BS 146: Part 2)
Sulphate-resisting Portland Cement (BS 4027)
Ground granulated blastfurnace slag (no BS yet)
Pulverized-fuel ash (BS 3892)
Lime (BS 890)

2 *Aggregates*:
Foamed or expanded blastfurnace slag (BS 877: Part 2: 1973)
Natural aggregates (BS 882: 1983)
Lightweight aggregates (BS 3797: Part 2: 1976)
Pulverized-fuel ash (BS 3892: Part 1 or Part 2)

3 *Admixtures may be added*:
Accelerating, retarding and water-reducing agents (BS 5075: Part 1) and air-entraining agents (BS 5075: Part 2)
Pigments (BS 1014)
Calcium chloride (BS 3587)

Masonry units should not exceed 650 mm in any work size dimension, excluding the thickness of any profile on a textured face.

The maximum dimensional deviations are: length +3 mm, −5 mm; height +3 mm, −5 mm, and thickness at bed level (fair-faced rectangular units only) +2 mm, −4 mm.

The delivery note, invoice or supplier's certificate supplied with a consignment of masonry units should record:

(a) name, trademark or other means of identification of the manufacturer;
(b) the number of this British Standard, ie. BS 6457: 1984;
(c) the colour and finish of the units.

G Large block, Panel work

Two relevant standards, but of such disparate applications as to make generalization meaningless.

BS 3717: 1972 *Asbestos-cement decking* and CP 199 *Roof deckings* Part 1 *Asbestos-cement* are covered in Table 1 'Building elements' under section (27) 'Roofs'.

BS 4022: 1970 *Prefabricated gypsum wallboard panels*

This deals with non-load-bearing panels – in practice dry partitioning units consisting of two gypsum wallboards conforming to BS 1230 separated by a core formation. The core is attached to the boards by an adhesive. See Table 80 for sizes.

Requirements are specified for testing, and a resistance to impact of 68 N is required. Certification by the manufacturer, or test records acceptable to a purchaser, may be required.

Table 80 *Preferred sizes and tolerances: gypsum wallboard panels*

Length	Permissible deviation	Width	Permissible deviation	Thickness	Permissible deviation
mm	mm	mm	mm	mm	mm
1800				38.1	
2350	+0	600	+0	50*	+0
2400	−6	900	−6	57.2	−3
2700		1200		63.5	
3000				100	

* Available in length 2350 mm and width 900 mm only.

(Table 1: BS 4022: 1970)

BS 3809: 1971 *Wood wool permanent formwork and infill units for reinforced concrete floors and roofs*

The standard does not specify the form and design dimensions of the units.

The units, whether composite or solid, consist essentially of wood wool and inorganic cementing agents, mechanically mixed together, pressed and adequately matured.

The form and texture are prescribed, as are permissible deviations of work sizes.

The density of moulded material in the air-dry condition is to be not less than 320 kg/m³ in the case of solid units or 400 kg/m³ in the case of hollow units.

The weight of units per square metre in the air-dry condition is not to exceed that stated by the manufacturer by more than 10 per cent.

The unit is to be capable of supporting a static load of 4.5 kg supported from any point on the soffit when using the method of attachment recommended by the manufacturer.

In an appendix it is stated that walkways or scaffold boards bearing on the tops of the units should always be used and no load should be applied directly to the units.

Until the concrete slab has attained sufficient strength to be self-supporting the units should be supported in such a manner that the span and incidental construction loads do not exceed those recommended by the manufacturer.

H Section work

Standards are grouped into seven sections: bars generally; steel bars, angles and sections; steel tubes; aluminium and aluminium alloy sections and tubes; copper, alloys and jointing strip; wood; and polythene and rubber gaskets.

Bars generally

BS 4229   *Recommendations for metric sizes of non-ferrous and ferrous bars*

Part 1: 1967   *Non-ferrous bars*

Part 1 covers metric sizes for round, square and hexagonal bars of aluminium alloys, copper and copper alloys and nickel and nickel alloys. Other sizes may be selected by consulting PD 6481: 1977 *Recommendations for the use of preferred numbers and preferred sizes*.

Recommended metric sizes for aluminium and aluminium alloy round bars are 3 ($\times$ 1) to 10 ($\times$ 2) to 22 ($\times$ 3) to 28, 30, 32 and 35 ($\times$ 5) to 80 ($\times$ 10) to 140 ($\times$ 20) to 200 mm.

Recommended metric sizes for aluminium and aluminium alloy square bars are 3 ($\times$ 1) to 6 ($\times$ 2) to 12, 16, 20, 25 and 30 ($\times$ 10) to 60 ($\times$ 20) to 120, 160 and 200 mm.

Recommended metric sizes for copper and copper alloy round bars are as aluminium etc. up to 100 mm only (excluding 75 mm).

Recommended metric sizes for copper and copper alloy square bars are 3 ($\times$ 1) to 6 ($\times$ 2) to 22, 25, 30, 32, 36, 40, 46, 50, 55 and 60 ($\times$ 10) to 100 mm.

Recommended metric sizes for nickel and nickel alloy round bars are as aluminium, etc.

Recommended metric sizes for nickel and nickel alloy square bars are as copper, etc. to 60 mm, then ($\times$ 5) to 90 ($\times$ 10) to 140 ($\times$ 20) to 200 mm.

Recommended metric sizes for hexagon bars for aluminium and aluminium alloys, copper and copper alloys and nickel and nickel alloys, measured mid-face round face are 3.2, 4, 5, 5.5, 7, 8 and 10 ($\times$ 1) to 14, 17, 19, 22, 24, 27, 30, 32, 36, 41, 46 and 50 ($\times$ 5) to 100 mm.

Recommended metric sizes for copper and copper alloy rectangular bars in the range 10 to 100 mm are 10 $\times$ 1.6 to 8, 12 $\times$ 1.6 to 10, 16 $\times$ 1.6 to 12, 20 $\times$ 2 to 16, 25 $\times$ 3 to 20, 30 $\times$ 3 to 25, 40 $\times$ 3 to 30, 50 $\times$ 3 to 40, 60 $\times$ 4 to 50, 80 $\times$ 4 to 60 and 100 $\times$ 4 to 80 mm.

Recommended metric sizes for aluminium and aluminium alloy rectangular bars in the range 10 to 250 mm are 10 $\times$ 3 and 6, 12 and 1.6 $\times$ 2.5 to 10, 20 $\times$ 2.5 to 6, 25 $\times$ 1.6 to 16, 30 and 40 $\times$ 2.5 to 12, 50 $\times$ 3 to 12, 60, 80 and 100 $\times$ 3 to 25, 120 and 160 $\times$ 6 to 16 and 200 and 250 $\times$ 10 and 16 mm.

Part 2: 1969   *Ferrous bars*

Part 2 covers metric sizes of round, square and hexagonal bars of non-alloy steel and alloy steels, including stainless steels.

The ranges are primarily intended for the guidance of engineers and other users of steel bars and do not necessarily include sizes which may be produced for further processing.

Recommended metric sizes for hot-rolled non-alloy steel round bars are (first choice) 6 ($\times$ 2) to 12, 16, 20, 25, 30, 32, 35, 40, 42, 45, 48 and 50 ($\times$ 5) to 80 ($\times$ 10) to 200 ($\times$ 20) to 300 mm (with a further forty second choice diameters).

Recommended metric sizes for hot-rolled non-alloy steel square bars are (first choice) 7 ($\times$ 1) to 18 ($\times$ 2) to 24, 25, 28, 30, 32, 35, 38, 40, 42 and 45 ($\times$ 5) to 80 ($\times$ 10) to 150 mm (with a further twenty-four second choice diameters).

Recommended metric sizes for hot-rolled non-alloy steel hexagon bars measured mid-face to mid-face are (first choice) 10 ($\times$ 1) to 20, 22, 24, 25, 27, 30, 32, 35, 36, 38, 40, 41, 46, 48, 50, 52, 55, 58, 60, 62, 65, 68, 70, 72, 75, 78 and 80 ($\times$ 5) to 100 mm (with a further fifty-one second choice cross-sizes).

Recommended metric sizes for non-alloy bright steel round bars are (first choice) 14, 15, 16, 18, 19, 20, 22, 24, 25, 26, 28, 30, 32, 35, 36, 38, 40, 42, 45, 48, 50, 55, 56 and 60 ($\times$ 5) to 130 ($\times$ 10) to 160 ($\times$ 20) to 200 mm (with a further twenty-six second choice diameters).

Recommended metric sizes for non-alloy bright steel square bars are (first choice) 13 ($\times$ 1) to 16 ($\times$ 2) to 22, 25, 28, 30, 32 and 35 ($\times$ 5) to 80 ($\times$ 10) to 100 mm (with a further eight second choice sizes).

Recommended metric sizes for non-alloy bright steel hexagon bars, measured mid-face to mid-face are (first choice) 12, 13, 14, 17, 19, 22, 24, 25, 27, 30, 32, 36, 41, 46, and 50 ($\times$ 5) to 100 mm (with a further fourteen second choice sizes).

Recommended metric sizes for non-alloy steel round bars for the reinforcement of concrete are 6 ($\times$ 2) to 16, 20, 25, 32 and 40 mm, with 50 mm for hot rolled bars only.

Recommended metric sizes for non-alloy rods for wire drawing are 5.5 ($\times$ 0.5) to 13 mm.

Recommended metric sizes for hot-rolled and bright alloy and stainless steel bars are (first choice) 5 ($\times$ 1) to 28, 30, 32, 33, 35, 36, 38, 39, 40, 42, 45, 48, 50, 52, 55, 56, 58, 60, 62, 64, 65, 68, 70, 72, 75 and 80 ($\times$ 10) to 200 ($\times$ 20) to 300 mm (with a further sixty-seven second choice diameters).

Recommended metric sizes for hot-rolled and bright alloy and stainless steel square bars are (first choice) 5, 5.5 + 6 ($\times$ 1) to 28, 30, 32, 35, 36, 38, 40, 42, 45, 46, 48, 50, 52, 55, 58, 60, 62, 65, 68, 70, 72, 75 + 80 ($\times$ 10) to 150 mm (with a further fifty-five second choice sizes).

Recommended metric sizes for hot-rolled and bright alloy and stainless steel hexagon bars, measured mid-face to mid-face are (first choice) 3.2*, 5.5*, 7, 8, 10 ($\times$ 1) to 20, 22, 24, 25, 27, 30, 32, 35, 36, 38, 40, 41, 46, 48 + 50 ($\times$ 5) to 75, 78 + 80 ($\times$ 5) to 100 mm (with a further twenty second choice sizes).

Recommended metric sizes for hot-rolled steel flat bars range from 10 $\times$ 3 to 7, to 450 $\times$ 15 to 60 mm.

Recommended metric sizes for bright steel flat bars range from 12 $\times$ 10 to 160 $\times$ 6 to 50 mm.

Steel bars, angles and sections

The general basis of design for steelwork is set out in standards and codes of practice discussed more fully in Table 1 'Building elements' under section (2 –) 'Structure, primary elements, carcass'.

BS 4: 1980   *Structural steel sections*

This standard is not merely the earliest standard still in being but it also incorporates BS 1. Originally in imperial units, it is now in metric units (compare with BS 4848).

This standard sets out dimensions, tolerances and certain properties of hot-rolled structural steel sections. A section is designated by the serial size (nominal size) in millimetres and the mass per unit length in kilograms per metre. Mass and length tolerances for all sections are given. See Table 81.

Lengths are 'specified' lengths ± 25 mm, or, when a minimum length is specified $+50$, -0 mm of that minimum length; or 'exact' lengths, cold sawn to within ± 3.2 mm.

In all cases, the significant properties extend beyond physical dimensions, and are available set out in detail in the handbooks issued by the major fabricators.

BS 2994: 1976   *Cold-rolled steel sections*

This standard sets out dimensions, mass and geometrical properties of the basic ranges of eight simple and three compound types of cold-rolled steel section. See Table 82.

Dimensions and tolerances are prescribed.

* 5.5 mm and below bright bars only.

Table 81 *Hot-rolled steel sections*

Steel sections	Serial sizes	Steel sections	Serial sizes
Universal beams	A range of twenty serial sizes *from* 914 × 419 and 305, *to* 254 × 146 and 102, and 203 × 133 mm, each in two to four masses.	Structural tees cut from universal beams	A range of nineteen serial sizes *from* 305 × 457 *to* 133 × 102 mm, each in two to five masses.
Universal columns	A range of six serial sizes (and a column core, 427 × 424.4) *from* 356 × 406 and 368 *to* 152 × 152 mm, each in three to seven masses.	Structural tees cut from universal columns	A range of six serial sizes *from* 406 × 178 *to* 152 × 76 mm, all but the largest in three or four masses.
Universal bearing piles	A range of four serial sizes 356 × 356, 305 × 305, 254 × 254 and 203 × 203 mm, each in two to eight masses.	Rolled tees	Serial sizes 51 × 51 × 6.92 × 4.76 and 44 × 44 × 4.11 × 3.14 (last figure kg/m) (other mm).
Joists with taper flanges	A range of nineteen rollings *from* 254 × 203 and 114 *to* 76 × 76 mm.	Channels	A range of seventeen serial sizes *from* 432 × 102 *to* 76 × 38 mm.

(From Tables 5–12: BS 4: 1980)

Table 82 *Cold-rolled steel sections*

Cold-rolled steel sections	Designations and sizes	Cold-rolled steel sections	Designations and sizes
Equal angles	Designations for $A \times A \times t$ *from* $20 \times 20 \times 1.2$ *to* 2 *to* $100 \times 100 \times 3$ to 6 are set out. A sizes are 20, 25, 30, 40, 50, 60, 70, 80, 100 (all in mm).	Outwardly lipped channels	Designations for $B \times A \times C \times t$ *from* $40 \times 50 \times 10$ to 20×1.6 to 3 *to* $80 \times 100 \times 15$ to 30×2 to 5 are given (all in mm).
Unequal angles	Designations for $A \times B \times C$ *from* $20 \times 15 \times 1.2$ to 2 *to* $100 \times 50 \times 3$ to 6 are set out. $A \times B$ sizes are 20×15, 30×15, 30×20, 40×20, 40×25, 50×25, 60×30, 80×30, 80×50, 100×30, 100×50 (all in mm).	T sections	Designations for $B \times D \times t$ *from* $25 \times 15 \times 1$ to 1.6 *to* $80 \times 80 \times 1.2$ to 3 are given (all in mm).
Plain channels	Designations for $D \times B \times t$ *from* $20 \times 20 \times 1.2$ to 2 *to* $100 \times 100 \times 2$ to 6 are set out. $D \times B$ sizes are 20×20, 25×25, 30×30, 40×40, 50×50, 60×60, 80×80, 100×100 (all in mm).	Z sections	Designations for $D \times B \times t$ *from* $40 \times 20 \times 1.6$ or 2 *to* 150×40 or 60×3 to 5 are set out. $D \times B$ sizes are 40×20, 50×25, 50×30, 75×25, 75×40, 100×25, 100×40, 130×40, 130×60, 150×40, 150×60 (all in mm).
Plain channels	Designations for $D \times B \times t$ *from* $30 \times 15 \times 1.2$ or 1.6 *to* $250 \times 80 \times 4$ to 6 are set out. $D \times B$ sizes are 30×15, 30×20, 40×15, 40×20, 40×25, 50×25, 50×40, 60×30, 60×40, 60×50, 70×30, 70×40, 80×25, 80×40, 80×50, 80×60, 90×40, 90×50, 100×40, 100×50, 100×60, 120×50, 120×60, 140×60, 150×50, 180×50, 200×50, 200×80, 250×50, 250×80 (all in mm).	Lipped Z sections	Designations for $D \times B \times C \times t$ *from* $120 \times 45 \times 20 \times 1.6$ to 2.5 *to* $250 \times 75 \times 25 \times 3$ or 4 are set out. $D \times B$ sizes are 150×45, 130×50, 140×50, 150×50, 165×50, 180×60, 190×60, 200×60, 215×75, 230×75 and 250×75 (all in mm).
Inwardly lipped channels	Designations for $D \times B \times C \times t$ *from* $25 \times 25 \times 8 \times 1.2$ or 1.6 *to* $100 \times 100 \times 15$ to 25×2 to 5 are set out. $D \times B$ sizes are 25×25, 30×30, 35×35, 40×40, 50×50, 60×60, 80×80, 100×100 (all in mm).	Plain channels back-to-back	Designations from $D \times 2B \times t$ *from* $100 \times 80 \times 1.6$ to 4 *to* $250 \times 160 \times 4$ to 6 are set out. $D \times 2B$ sizes are 100×80, 120×100, 150×100, 180×100, 200×100, 200×160, 250×100 and 250×160 (all in mm).
Inwardly lipped channels	Designations for $D \times B \times C \times t$ *from* $30 \times 15 \times 10 \times 1.2$ or 1.6 *to* 250×50 or 80×20 or 25×3 to 5 are set out. $D \times B$ sizes are 30×15, 40×20, 50×25, 50×40, 60×30, 60×40, 70×25, 70×30, 70×40, 80×40, 80×50, 90×40, 90×50, 100×40, 100×50, 100×60, 120×50, 120×60, 140×60, 150×50, 180×50, 180×80, 200×50, 200×80, 250×50, 250×80 (all in mm).	Inwardly lipped channels back-to-back	Designations of $D \times 2B \times C \times t$ *from* $100 \times 80 \times 10$ to 20×1.6 to 3 *to* $250 \times 160 \times 20$ to 25×3 to 5 are set out. $D \times 2B$ sizes are 100×80, 100×100, 120×100, 150×100, 180×100, 200×100, 200×160, 250×100 and 250×160 (all in mm).
Outwardly lipped channels	Designations for $B \times A \times C \times t$ *from* $30 \times 30 \times 10 \times 1.2$ or 1.6 *to* $100 \times 100 \times 15$ to 30×2 to 6 are set out (all in mm).	Inwardly lipped channels lip-to-lip	Designations of $D \times 2B \times C \times t$ are identical with those above.

(From Tables 1–14: BS 2994: 1976)

BS 4848 *Hot-rolled structural steel sections*
Part 2: 1975 *Hollow sections (there is no Part 1)*

A foreword identifies that the adoption of new ranges of sections based on metric units will be influenced in time by ISO.

In all parts, properties are set out.

Hot-rolled structural hollow steel sections are of three types:

1 Circular, from 21.3 to 457 mm.
2 Rectangular, from 50 × 30 to 450 × 250 mm.
3 Squares, from 20 × 20 to 400 × 400 mm.

A hollow section is designated by its outside dimensions and thickness in millimetres and by the symbols CHS for circular hollow sections and RHS for rectangular (including square) hollow sections. Tolerances are set out. See Table 83.

Part 4: 1972 *Equal and unequal angles (there is no Part 3)*
Part 4 presents the British Standard range of metric sizes of equal and unequal angles, from ISO/R 657 *Dimensions of hot-rolled steel sections* Part 1 *Equal leg angles* and Part 2 *Unequal leg angles*. See Table 84.

Three standards deal with steel bars or rods for reinforced concrete, namely BS 4449, hot-rolled steel bars – conventionally termed 'high tensile reinforcement'; BS 4461, cold-worked steel bars – conventionally termed 'mild steel reinforcement'; and BS 4466, bending dimensions and scheduling. The last also extends to wire and fabric respectively in BS 4482 and BS 4483, discussed in section J 'Wirework, meshwork'.

High tensile bars (BS 4486) for prestressing are considered here, but strand (BS 4759) for prestressing is covered in section J 'Wires, meshes, cords' of this table.

BS 4449: 1978 *Hot-rolled steel bars for the reinforcement of concrete*

This standard covers hot-rolled steel bars for the reinforcement of concrete. It covers plain round steel bars in grade 250 only and deformed high yield steel bars in grade 460/425 only. It also specifies weldability requirements for both grades of steel in terms of the carbon equivalent value.

Steel bars for use as lifting hooks are not included, nor are steel bars produced by re-rolling finished products.

Definitions given include:

Bar: a steel product of plain round or deformed cross-section, as-rolled, including a rod of steel.
Hot rolled deformed bar: a bar which has been so shaped during hot-rolling.
Nominal size.
Nominal density.
Yield stress: the stress measured during the tensile test when the total extension of the gauge length is 0.5 per cent.
Coil.
Length: a piece of nominally straight bar cut to a specified length.
Bundle: two or more coils or a number of lengths together.
Batch: any quantity of bars of one size and grade.
Longitudinal rib.
Transverse rib.
Flash weld.

The nominal sizes of bars given are 'preferred sizes' (see BS 4229).

Requirements are specified for manufacture, chemical composition, quality, weldability.

Bond classification of deformed bars. In this respect two types, are distinguished – by 'performance test' or geometrical form, Type 1, a plain square twisted bar or a plain chamfered square twisted bar; and Type 2, a bar with transverse ribs with a substantially uniform spacing not greater than 0.8φ. Continuous helical ribs may be present.

Table 83 *Hollow sections: hot-rolled steel*

Hollow sections	Designations and sizes
Circular hollow sections	Designations for *D*, *t* and the mass *M* in kg/m are set out. *D* is 21.3, 26.9, 33.7, 42.4, 48.3, 60.3, 76.1, 88.9, 114.3, 139.7, 168.3, 193.7, 219.1, 244.5, 273, 323.9, 355.6, 406.4 and 457 mm, most sizes, with three, four, six or seven thicknesses and therefore masses.
Rectangular hollow sections	Sizes *D* × *B*, *t* and mass *M* in kg/m are set out. *D* × *B* is 50 × 30, 60 × 40, 80 × 40, 90 × 50, 100 × 50 and 60, 120 × 60 and 80, 150 × 100, 160 × 80, 200 × 100, 250 × 150, 300 × 200, 400 × 200 and 450 × 250 mm. All sizes have two to six thicknesses and therefore masses.
Square hollow sections	The equal sizes *D* × *D*, *t* and the mass *M* in kg/m are set out. *D* × *D* is 20 × 20 (× 10) to 100 × 100, 120 × 120, 150 × 150, 180 × 180 and 200 × 200 (× 50) to 400 × 400 mm, all sizes with two to six thicknesses and therefore masses.

(From Tables 1–3: BS 4848: Part 2: 1975)

Table 84 *Equal and unequal angles: hot-rolled steel*

Angle	Designation and size
Equal angles	The designation of size *A* × *A* and *t* gives the mass/unit length in kg/m. Sizes *A* × *A* are 25 × 25, 30 × 30, 40 × 40, 45 × 45 and 50 × 50 (× 10) to 100 × 100, 120 × 120, 150 × 150 and 200 × 200 mm, each size with three or four thicknesses and therefore masses. Some variations in rolling practice are allowed.
Unequal angles	The designation of size *A* × *B* and *t* gives the mass/unit length in kg/m. Sizes *A* × *B* are 40 × 25, 60 × 30, 65 × 50, 75 × 50, 80 × 60, 100 × 65 and 75, 125 × 75, 150 × 75 and 90 and 200 × 100 and 150 mm. All sizes except the 40 × 25 have two or three leg thicknesses and therefore masses. Some variations in rolling practice are allowed.

(From Tables 2 and 3: BS 4848: Part 4: 1972)

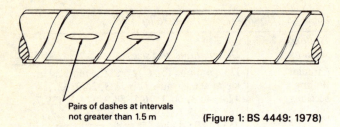

Pairs of dashes at intervals
not greater than 1.5 m   **(Figure 1: BS 4449: 1978)**

Figure 75   *Markings for bars of carbon equivalent greater than 0.51 per cent*
Note: The height and width of the dashes are at least half the size of the cross-section of the ribs

Requirements are specified for checking compliance, routine inspection and testing.

Requirements are specified for certification, testing, with tensile tests, bend tests, the specified characteristic strength (the yield stress below which no more than 5 per cent should fall) and tensile properties.

The specified characteristic strength and elongation of the two grades of steel are as given. The tensile strength of any bar is to be at least 15 per cent greater than the actual yield stress. For steel of grade 250 the yield stress should not exceed 425 N/mm^2.

Requirements are specified for purchaser's tests of chemical composition, weldability, tensile strength, elongation and bending, and verification of specified characteristic strength. See Figure 75 and Tables 85 and 86.

Table 85   *Cross-sectional area and mass: steel bars*

Nominal size	Cross-sectional area	Mass per metre run	
mm	mm^2	kg	
6	28.3	0.222	
8	50.3	0.395	
10	78.5	0.616	
12	113.1	0.888	Preferred
16	201.1	1.579	sizes
20	314.2	2.466	
25	490.9	3.854	
32	804.2	6.313	
40	1256.6	9.864	
50	1963.5	15.413	

(From Table 2: BS 4449: 1978)

Table 86   *Tensile properties: steel bars*

Grade	Nominal size of bar	Specified characteristic strength	Minimum elongation on gauge length L_o
	mm	N/mm^2	%
250	– All sizes	250	22
460/425	– 6 up to and including 16	460	12
	– Over 16	425	14

(From Table 6: BS 4449: 1978)

BS 4461: 1978   *Specification for cold-worked steel bars for the reinforcement of concrete*

This standard covers rolled steel bars, other than plain round bars, cold-worked to such an extent that their yield point has been eliminated, in grade 460/425 only.

Steel bars complying with all the requirements of this standard are readily weldable.

The range of sizes is as in BS 4449.

Definitions are as in BS 4449, together with *cold-worked deformed bar*: a bar which has been cold-worked to comply with the property requirements of this standard and conforms to either the geometrical or performance test classification given, and *yield stress**: the 0.2 per cent proof stress.

The *specified characteristic strength* of bars complying with the requirements of this standard is given. It is based on either not more than 5 per cent of the 0.2 per cent proof stress test results falling lower than the values given or, where applicable, there being no test results below the 0.2 per cent proof stress defined.

Tensile properties are as in BS 4449, with a further requirement in respect of tensile strength:

(a) The tensile strength should be at least 10 per cent greater than the actual yield stress measured in the tensile test.
(b) The tensile strength should be between 5 and 10 per cent greater than the actual yield stress measured in the tensile test.

BS 4466: 1981   *Bending dimensions and scheduling of reinforcement for concrete*

This standard specifies requirements for scheduling, dimensioning and bending of steel reinforcement complying with the requirements of BS 4449, BS 4461, BS 4482 and BS 4483.

Definitions and notations are as in those standards, with the following additions:

Designated fabric: fabric reinforcement where the wire and mesh arrangement can be defined by an identifiable fabric reference, for example as in BS 4483.
Scheduled fabric: fabric reinforcement with a regular wire and mesh arrangement that can be defined by specifying the size and spacing in each direction using the notation shown which assumes that sheets are always viewed with their cross wires uppermost. See Figure 76.

The type and grade of steel bars are identified by the following prefixes:

R: plain or deformed grade 250 bars to BS 4449.
T: type 2 deformed bars of grade 460/425, to BS 4449 or BS 4461.
X: a general abbreviation where the properties required have to be defined.

A typical bar schedule is shown in Figure 77 and a typical fabric schedule is shown in Figure 78.

Dimensioning and referencing is fully discussed.

BS 4486: 1980   *Hot-rolled and hot-rolled and processed high tensile alloy steel bars for the prestressing of concrete*

This standard deals with preferred sizes of smooth or ribbed bars in straight lengths supplied in the hot-rolled or hot-rolled and processed conditions. Two nominal strength levels of steel are specified. Stress-corrosion testing is not specified, and fatigue testing is dealt with in BS 4447.

Definitions given which are significantly different from BS 4449 are:

---

* At variance with the terminology used in some other standards, for example BS 18 *Methods for tensile testing of metals*.

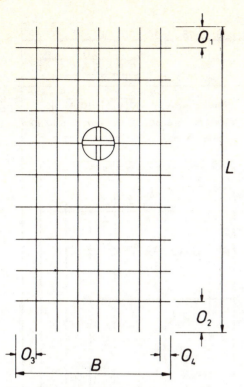

L is the length of the longitudinal wires (which are not necessarily the longer wires in the sheet)

B is the length of the cross-wires

O_1 and O_2 are the overhangs of the longitudinal wires

O_3 and O_4 are the side overhangs of the cross-wires

(Figure 1: BS 4466: 1981)

Figure 76 *Scheduled fabric reinforcement for concrete*

Cast: usually the product of a single furnace charge. Where the furnace contents are tapped into two or more ladles, the product of each ladle may be called a separate cast.

Bar: a steel product produced in straight lengths by hot-rolling of steel and which may be smooth or ribbed. Processed bars are bars subsequently processed by stretching or other forms of cold-working, and which also may have an additional tempering treatment to give the required properties.

Bar tendon: a bar used in prestressed concrete.

Batch: a number of lengths of one nominal size from one cast.

Consignment: any quantity of material prepared at any one time for delivery to one location.

Requirements in respect of manufacture uses, dimensions, properties and statistical requirements are specified. See Table 87.

Requirements for establishment of curves for relaxation at constant strain, sampling and statistical interpretation and routine testing and inspection requirements are specified.

For all other properties, all test results should show compliance with the requirements of this standard.

Steel tubes

BS 6323 *Seamless and welded steel tubes for automobile, mechanical and general engineering purposes*

Part 1: 1982 *General requirements*

The standard covers hot and cold finished seamless and welded steel tubes for use in general engineering industries. Parts 2–8 specify the chemical compositions, mechanical properties, dimensions, dimensional tolerances and technical delivery conditions for each type of tube.

The tubes are designated by:

(a) The number of this British Standard and the part number of the relevant specific requirements, for example BS 6323/2.

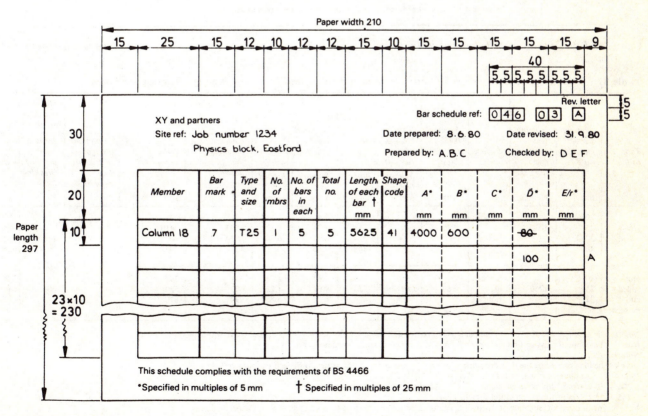

This schedule complies with the requirements of BS 4466

*Specified in multiples of 5 mm   † Specified in multiples of 25 mm

All dimensions in millimetres

(Figure 2: BS 4466: 1981)

Figure 77 *Form of bar schedule for reinforced concrete*

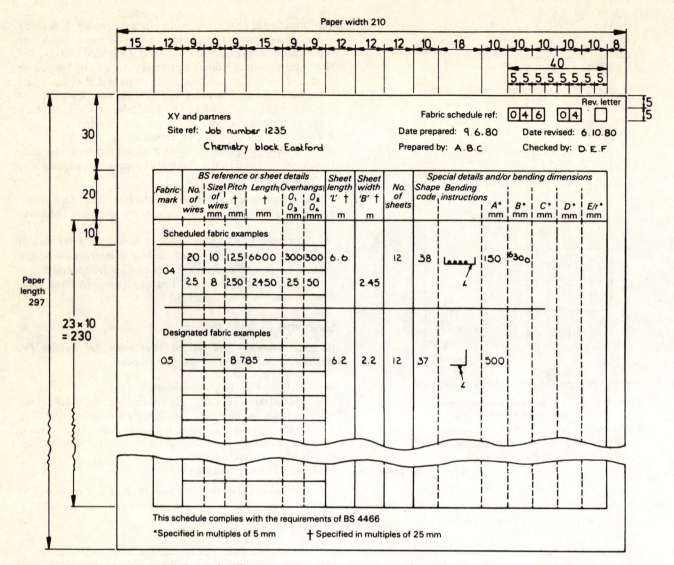

Figure 78 *Form of fabric schedule for reinforced concrete*

(Figure 3: BS 4466: 1981)

Table 87 *Dimensions and properties of hot-rolled and hot-rolled and processed high tensile alloy steel bars*

Type of bar	Nominal size (see note 1) mm	Nominal tensile strength (see note 1) N/mm²	Surface	Nominal 0.1% proof stress (see note 1) N/mm²	Nominal cross-sectional area (see note 2)		Nominal mass (see note 2)		Specified properties			Maximum relaxation at 1000 h	
					Smooth bar mm²	Ribbed bar mm²	Smooth bar kg/m	Ribbed bar kg/m	Characteristic breaking load (see note 4) kN	Characteristic 0.1% proof load kN	Minimum elongation at fracture (see note 6) %	Initial load as % of breaking load %	Value %
Hot-rolled	20	1030	Smooth or ribbed	835	314	349	2.47	2.74	325	260		For all bars	For all bars
	25				491	538	4.04	4.22	505	410	6		
	32				804	874	6.31	6.86	830	670			
	40				1257	1348	9.86	10.58	1300	1050			
Hot-rolled and processed	20	1230	Smooth or ribbed	1080	314	349	2.47	2.74	385	340		60	1.5
	25				491	538	4.04	4.22	600	530	4	70	3.5
	32				804	874	6.31	6.86	990	870		80	6.0

Note 1: The nominal size of bar and nominal tensile strength data are given for designation purposes only.
Note 2: The nominal cross-section and nominal mass data are given for information only.
Note 3: . . . .
Note 4: The load carried by the threaded portion of smooth bars is not to be less than the specified characteristic load.
Note 5: The modulus of elasticity may be taken as
  206 ± 10 kN/mm² for as rolled and as rolled stretched and tempered bars.
  165 ± 12 kN/mm² for as rolled and stretched bars.
Note 6: The minimum elongation at fracture is measured on gauge length of $5.65 \sqrt{S_o}$ where S_o is the original cross-sectional area of the gauge length. If measurement of extension under load is possible, the minimum elongation at maximum load is to be 3.5%. The actual elongation at maximum load need not be measured.
Note 7: The maximum standard deviations expressed as equivalent stress values of load for the various bar size are as follows: nominal tensile strength: 55 N/mm², nominal 0.1% proof stress: 60 N/mm².

(From Table 1: BS 4486: 1980)

Table 88 *Designation of steel tubes: method of manufacture*

Method of manufacture	Reference	Applicable part of BS 6323
Hot finished welded	HFW	2
Hot finished seamless	HFS	3
Cold finished seamless	CFS	4
Electric resistance welded and induction welded	ERW	5
Cold finished electric resistance welded and induction welded	CEW	6
Submerged arc welded	SAW	7
Longitudinally welded stainless	LW	8
Cold finished longitudinally welded stainless	LWCF	8

(Table 1: BS 6323: Part 1: 1982)

Table 89 *Designation of steel tubes: type and grade of steel*

Type	Grade designation reference	Applicable part of BS 6323
Carbon and carbon manganese steels		
0.13 % carbon maximum 280*	1	5 and 6
0.16 % carbon maximum 320*	2	2, 5 and 6
0.20 % carbon maximum 360*	3	2, 3, 4, 5 and 6
0.20 % carbon maximum (case hardening) 360*	3A	4
0.25 % carbon maximum 410*	4	2, 3, 4, 5, 6 and 7
0.23 % carbon maximum 490*	5	2, 3, 4, 5 6 and 7
0.30 to 0.40 % carbon 460*	6	4
0.20 to 0.30 % carbon 1.2 to 1.5 % manganese	7	4
0.40 to 0.55 % carbon 540*	8	3 and 4
Low alloy steels		
244 † manganese molybdenum	9	4
623 † low carbon 1 % chromium 0.25 % molybdenum	10	4
624 † high carbon 1 % chromium 0.25 % molybdenum	11	4
Stainless steels		
409S18 ferritic 11 % chromium titanium steel	12	8
302S17 † austenitic chromium nickel steel	13	8
304S12 † austenitic chromium nickel steel	14	8
304S15 † austenitic chromium nickel steel	15	8
316S12 † austenitic chromium nickel molybdenum (2.5 %) steel	16	8
316S16 †austenitic chromium nickel molybdenum (2.5 %) steel	17	8
321S12 † austenitic chromium nickel stablized steel	18	8

*For carbon and carbon manganese steels this number relates to the minimum tensile strength in N/mm^2 in the hot finished or normalized condition.

† This designation is used in other British Standards.

(Table 2: BS 6323: Part 1: 1982)

(b) The reference from Table 88, indicating the method of manufacture.
(c) The reference from Table 89, indicating the grade of steel.
(d) The reference from Table 90, indicating the delivery condition, where applicable.

Appearance and soundness, dimensions and tolerances, certification by the manufacturer, protection and information to be provided by purchasers are all covered.

Appendices tabulate steel grades, delivery conditions and mechanical properties (the information shown below in the respective parts) and sectional properties of steel tubes.

Parts 2 to 8, summaries of which follow, all cover the scope, general requirements on materials and grades, delivery conditions, chemical composition, mechanical properties, dimensions and dimensional tolerances and sectional properties (in most cases related back to Appendix B of Part 1).

Part 2: 1982 *Specific requirements for hot finished welded steel tubes*
This part deals with four designations (HFW2, HFW3, HFW4, and HFW5) having minimum yield strengths R_e of 195, 215, 235 and 340 N/mm^2 respectively, available with outside diameters of 21.3, 26.9, 33.7, 42.4, 48.3, 60.3, 76.1, 88.9 and 114.3 mm, most in three thicknesses.

Part 3: 1982 *Specific requirements for hot finished seamless steel tube*
This part deals with four designations (HFS3, HFS4, HFS5 and HFS8) having minimum yield strengths of 215, 235, 340 and 340 N/mm^2 respectively, available in twenty outside diameters, from 33.7 to 457 mm, and various thicknesses, most commonly from two to six thicknesses for each size.

Part 4: 1982 *Specific requirements for cold finished seamless steel tubes*
This part deals with ten designations in up to six delivery conditions with minimum yield strengths as given in Table 91, in two series of sizes, series 2 from 5 to 200 mm and series 3 from 14 to 220 mm outside diameter from one to twenty thicknesses each.

Part 5: 1982 *Specific requirements for electric resistance welded and induction welded steel tubes*
This part deals with five designations in up to five delivery conditions with minimum yield strengths are given in Table 92, in three series of sizes: thirty-seven sizes from 13.5 to 457.00 mm; twenty-two sizes from 5 to 140 mm; and six other sizes from 42 to 76 mm (all outside diameters) and each from three to twenty-six thicknesses.

Part 6: 1982 *Specific requirements for cold finished electric resistance welded and induction welded steel tubes*
This part deals with five designations in up to six delivery conditions with minimum yield strengths as given in Table 93, in thirty-one common sizes for outside diameters from 6 to 220 mm outside diameter, each in five to thirteen thicknesses.

Part 7: 1982 *Specific requirements for submerged arc welded steel tubes*
This part deals with two designations (SAW4 and SAW5) with minimum yield strengths of 235 and 240 N/mm^2 respectively, in a range of fifteen sizes from 508 to 2020 mm outside diameter and commonly of three or four thicknesses each.

Part 8: 1982 *Specific requirements for longitudinally welded stainless steel tubes*
This part deals with thirteen designations in one to three delivery conditions with minimum yield strengths as given in Table 94. The sizes are *not* tabulated (but tolerances specified from below 30, to 110 mm outside diameter).

Table 90 *Designation of steel tubes: delivery condition*

Delivery condition	Description	Reference	Applicable Part of BS 6323
Cold finished/hard (cold finished as drawn)	No heat treatment after the last cold finishing process	BK	4, 6
Cold finished/soft (lightly cold-worked)	After the last heat treatment there is a light finishing pass (cold pass)	BKW	4, 6
As welded and sized	No heat treatment after the welding and sizing process	KM	5, 8
Annealed	After the final cold finishing process the tubes are subcritically annealed in a controlled atmosphere	GBK	4, 6
	After welding and sizing, the tubes are subcritically annealed in a controlled atmosphere	GKM	5
	After the final cold finishing or the welding and sizing process, the tubes are subcritically annealed and then descaled mechanically or chemically	GZF	4, 5, 6
Normalized	After the final cold finishing process, the tubes are heated to a temperature above the upper transformation point and cooled. Both stages of heat treatment are carried out in a controlled atmosphere	NBK	4, 6
	After welding and sizing, the tubes are heated to a temperature above the upper transformation point and cooled. Both stages of heat treatment are carried out in a controlled atmosphere	NKM	5
	After the final cold finishing or the welding and sizing process, the tubes are heated to a temperature above the upper transformation point, cooled in air and then descaled mechanically or chemically	NZF	4, 5, 6
Welded and sized (fully softened)	After welding and sizing the tubes are annealed (solution treated) in a controlled atmosphere	GKM(S)	8
	After welding and sizing the tubes are annealed (solution treated) and then descaled mechanically or chemically	GZF(S)	8
Cold finished (fully softened)	After cold finishing, the tubes are annealed (solution treated) in a controlled atmosphere	GBK(S)	8
	After cold finishing the tubes are annealed (solution treated) and then descaled mechanically or chemically	GZF(S)	8

(From Table 3: BS 6323: Part 1: 1982)

Table 91 *Mechanical properties: cold finished seamless steel tubes*

Designation	Delivery condition			
	BK	BKW	GBK + GZF	NBK + NZF
	(minimum yield strengths N/mm^2)			
CFS	360	280	170	215
CFS3A	360	280	170	215
CFS4	415	315	200	235
CFS5	480	385	—	340
CFS6	470	350	300	280
CFS7	560	460	—	—
CFS8	575	470	300	340
CFS9	575	470	—	—
CFS10	575	470	—	—
CFS11	575	—	—	—

(Based on Table 1: BS 6323: Part 4: 1982)

Table 92 *Mechanical properties*

Designation	Delivery condition		
	KM	GKM + GZF	NKM + NZF
	(minimum yield strengths N/mm^2)		
ERW1	200	150	155
ERW2	250	160	195
ERW3	300	170	215
ERW4	350	200	235
ERW5	420	—	240

(Based on Table 1: BS 6323: Part 5: 1982)

Table 93 *Mechanical properties*

Designation	Delivery condition			
	BK	BKW	GBK + GZF	NGK + NZF
	(minimum yield strengths N/mm^2)			
CEW1	320	245	150	155
CEW2	355	260	160	195
CEW3	360	280	170	215
CEW4	415	315	200	235
CEW5	480	385	—	340

(Based on Table 1: BS 6323: Part 6: 1982)

Table 94 *Mechanical properties*

Designation	Delivery condition		
	KM	GKM(S) + GZF(S)	GBK(S) + GZF(S)
	(minimum yield strengths N/mm^2)		
LW12	300	—	—
LW13	450	210	—
LWGF13	—	—	210
LW14	420	185	—
LWCF14	—	—	185
LW15	450	210	—
LWCF15	—	—	210
LW16	420	185	—
LWCF16	—	—	185
LW17	450	210	—
LWCF17	—	—	210
LW18	450	210	—
LWCF18	—	—	210

(Based on Table 1: BS 6323: Part 8: 1982)

Aluminium and aluminium alloy sections and tubes

In respect of aluminium and its alloys, some discussion of the materials and certain applications appear in Table 3 'Materials' under section h 'Metal'.

This section covers four specifications: two, BS 1161 and BS 1474, deal with aluminium alloys for structural purposes and wrought aluminium and aluminium alloys for general engineering purposes respectively, the latter including coverage of extruded round tube, and one, BS 1471, deals specifically with drawn tube. Finally, BS 4300 *Wrought aluminium alloy and aluminium alloys for general engineering purposes* Part 1: 1967 *Aluminium alloy longitudinally welded tube* deals with a mode of fabrication for large diameter tubes, and is not discussed further here.

BS 1161: 1971   *Aluminium alloy sections for structural purposes*

The aluminium alloy is to be selected from the range given in Table 95.

The sizes of the sections and the dimensional tolerances are specified, together with tolerances on straightness and twist, in Table 96. The standard also gives values for area of section, centroid, second moments of area, radii of gyration, moduli of section and torsion constant.

Tolerances on straightness and tolerances on twist are given.

Table 95   *Aluminium alloys suitable for structural use*

Material designation	Condition	0.2 % proof stress min.	Tensile strength min.
(New British alloy designation [international])		N/mm²	N/mm²
NE8 (5083)	O M	125 130	275 280
HE9 (6063)	TE TF	110 160	150 185
HE15 (2014A)	TB TF	230 370	370 435
HE17	TB TF	190 280	300 340
HE30 (6082)	TF	255	295
NE51	O M	85 100	215 215

(From Table 1: BS 1161: 1971)

BS 1474: 1972   *Wrought aluminium and aluminium alloys for general engineering purposes, bars, extruded round tube and sections*

The standard deals with these shapes, made from two grades of aluminium and seven aluminium alloys in various conditions. Definitions include:

Bar: a round, rectangular or polygonal solid section supplied in straight lengths, of not less than 6 mm diameter or minor dimension.

Extruded round tube: a circular hollow extrusion of uniform wall thickness not subject to cold drawing.

Hollow section: an extruded shape other than round, the cross-section of which completely encloses a void or voids, and which is not subjected to cold drawing.

Regular section: a solid drawn or extruded section, not otherwise covered by the definition of a bar, which can be conveniently divided into approximate rectangles with measurable dimen-

sions, for example angles. The ratio of maximum to minimum thickness of such regular sections does not exceed 4:1.

Freedom from defects and condition provisions are largely as in BS 1471.

Sizes (for bars, as in BS 4229) and tolerances are covered.

Regular sections shall include square and rectangular bars, angles, T-sections, I-beams, H-sections, Z-sections, and any other normal types of sections which can conveniently be divided into approximate rectangles with measurable dimensions.

Complicated sections not covered in the standard.

Certification, chemical composition and mechanical properties of aluminium alloy bars, extruded round tube and sections are considered.

The following grades are covered:

Two grades of *aluminium*: 1050A and 1200 (formerly EIB and EIC), each in condition M.

Three grades of *non-heat treated alloys*: 5083 and 5154A (formerly NE8 and NE5), each into conditions O + M, and 5251 (formerly NE4) in condition M.

Four grades of *heat-treatable alloys* 2014A and 6061 (formerly HE15 and HE20) each in two conditions TB + TF, 6063 (formerly HE9) in five conditions O, M, TB, TE and TF and 6082 (formerly HE30) in four conditions O, M, TB and TF.

Conditions are as in BS 1471.

Standard sizes of medium strength general purpose sections are given. Those for equal angles, unequal angles, T and channel sections do *not* correspond with those in BS 1161. See Table 97.

Flat bars and square bars are as given in BS 4229.

BS 1471: 1972   *Wrought aluminium and aluminium alloys for general engineering purposes – drawn tube*

This standard deals with tube made from the grade of aluminium and the same alloys as in BS 1474, though in differing conditions.

Drawn tube is defined as a hollow product of uniform wall thickness, produced by cold drawing from the tube bloom.

The following *conditions* are distinguished:

M: *as manufactured*. Material which acquires some temper from shaping processes in which there is no special control over thermal treatment or strain hardening. (Used in BS 1474).

O: *annealed*. Material which is fully annealed to obtain the lowest-strength condition.

H1–H8: *strain hardened*. Material subjected to the application of cold work after annealing (or hot forming) or to a combination of cold work and partial annealing/stabilizing in order to secure the specified mechanical properties. The designations are in ascending order of tensile strength.

TB: *solution heat-treated and naturally aged*. Material which receives no cold work after solution heat treatment except as may be required to flatten or straighten it. Properties of some alloys in this temper are unstable.

TD: *solution heat-treated, cold-worked and naturally aged*.

TE: *cooled* from an elevated temperature shaping process and *precipitation-treated*.

TF: *solution heat-treated and precipitation-treated*.

TH: *solution heat-treated, cold-worked and then precipitation-treated*.

The schedule is given in full, as it also appears in BS 1474 (with the addition of condition M).

The following materials are distinguished:

Two grades of *aluminium*
    designated 1050A in three conditions: O, H4 and H8
    designated 1200 in three conditions: O, H4 and H8
Three grades of *non-heat-treated alloys*
    designated 5083 in two conditions: O and H2
    designated 5154A in two conditions: H2 and H4
    designated 5251 in two conditions: H2 and H4

Table 96   *Sectional properties*

Sections	Sizes and tolerances	Sections	Sizes and tolerances
Equal angle sections	$a \times b\ (t)$ Two ranges: *Thin range* 50 × 50 (3), 60 × 60 (3.5), 80 × 80 (5), 100 × 100 (6) and 120 × 120 (7) mm. *Thick range* 30 × 30 (2.5), 40 × 40 (3), 50 × 50 (4), 60 × 60 (5), 80 × 80 (6), 100 × 100 (8) and 120 × 120 (10) mm.	Equal bulb angle sections	$d \times b\ (t)$ 50 × 50 (2.5), 60 × 60 (3), 80 × 80 (4), 100 × 100 (5) and 120 × 120 (6) mm.
Unequal angle sections	$a \times b\ (t)$ Two ranges: *Thin range* 50 × 38 (3), 60 × 45 (3.5), 80 × 60 (5), 100 × 75 (6), 120 × 90 (7) and 140 × 105 (8.5) mm. *Thick range* 50 × 38 (4), 60 × 45 (5), 80 × 60 (6), 100 × 75 (8), 120 × 90 (10) and 140 × 105 (11) mm.	Unequal bulb angle sections	$d \times b\ (t)$ 50 × 37.5 (2.5), 60 × 45 (3), 80 × 60 (4), 100 × 75 (5), 120 × 90 (6) and 140 × 105 (7) mm.
Channel sections	$a \times b\ (t_1 \text{ and } t_2)$ 60 × 30 (5 and 6), 80 × 35 (5 and 7), 100 × 40 (6 and 8), 120 × 50 (6 and 9), 140 × 60 (7 and 10), 160 × 70 (7 and 10), 180 × 75 (8 and 11), 200 × 80 (8 and 12) and 240 × 100 (9 and 13) mm.	Lipped channel sections	$a \times b\ (t)$ 80 × 40 (2.5), 100 × 50 (3.13), 120 × 60 (3.75) and 140 × 70 (4.38) mm.
I sections	$a \times b\ (t_1 \text{ and } t_2)$ 60 × 30 (4 and 6), 80 × 40 (5 and 7), 100 × 50 (6 and 8), 120 × 60 (6 and 9), 140 × 70 (7 and 10) and 160 × 80 (7 and 11) mm.	Bulb tee sections	$d \times b\ (t)$ 75 × 90 (3), 100 × 120 (4), 125 × 150 (5) and 150 × 180 (6) mm.
T sections	$a \times b\ (t)$ 50 × 38 (4), 60 × 45 (5), 80 × 60 (6), 100 × 75 (8) and 120 × 90 (10) mm.		

(From Tables 2–10: BS 1161: 1977)

Four grades of *heat-treatable alloys*
    designated 2014A in two conditions: TB and TF
    designated 6061 in three conditions: H4, TB and TF
    designated 6063 in three conditions: O, TB and TF
    designated 6082 in two conditions: TB and TF

Tolerances and requirements in respect of defects are set out. The range of sizes comprises 5, 10, 14, 20 (× 5) to 80 (× 10) to 310 mm outside diameter, and with three to twelve wall thicknesses available for each size.

Copper, alloys and jointing strip

As with steel and aluminium and their alloys, consideration is included in Table 3 'Materials' section h 'Metal' to the metal, its

alloys and certain applications. One specification, BS 2874, is discussed here while BS 1878, covering jointing strip for expansion joint, is considered in Table 3 'Materials' section h 'Metal'.

BS 2874: 1969   *Copper and copper alloys. Rods and sections (other than forging stock)*

This standard deals with rods having a diameter, or sections with width across flats, of not less than 1.6 mm.

The materials include copper, copper alloys, brasses, phosphur bronze, aluminium bronze, leaded nickel brass and leaded nickel silver, and copper-silicon.

Requirements in respect of condition (which is of very considerable importance in respect of working and performance), tolerances on square rod (except for certain of the brasses), dimensions and tolerances are set out, and requirements are

Table 97 *Sectional properties: aluminium and alloys*

Sections	Sizes and dimensions
Equal angles	Leg lengths (thicknesses) 10 (3), 12 (1.6 and 3), 16 (3), 20 (1.6 and 3), 25 (1.6, 3 and 6), 30 (1.6 and 3), 40 (3 and 6), 50 (3, 6 and 10), 60 (3 and 6), 80 (3, 6 and 10) and 100 (6 and 10) (all mm).
Unequal angles	Leg lengths (thicknesses) 12 × 10 (1.6), 16 × 12 (1.6), 20 × 12 (1.6 and 3), 25 × 12, 25 × 16 and 25 × 20 (all 1.6 and 3), 30 × 16, 30 × 20 and 30 × 25 (all 3), 40 × 12, 40 × 20, 40 × 25 and 40 × 30 (all 3), 50 × 20 (3), 50 × 25 (1.6, 3 and 6), 50 × 40 (3 and 6), 60 × 25 (3), 60 × 40 (6), 80 × 25 (3), 80 × 40 (3), 80 × 50 (3 and 6), 100 × 25 (3), 100 × 50 (6) and 100 × 80 (6) (all mm).
T sections	Dimensions $A \times B$ (thicknesses) 12 × 12 (3), 20 × 20 (3), 25 × 25 (3), 40 × 40 (3), 50 × 50 (6), 80 × 80 (6) and 100 × 100 (6) (all mm).
Channels	Dimensions web (A) × flange (B) (thickness) 10 × 10 (1.6), 12 × 12 (1.6 and 3), 20 × 10 (1.6), 20 × 12 (3), 20 × 20 (3), 25 × 12 (3), 25 × 20 (3), 25 × 25 (1.6 and 3), 30 × 20 (3), 30 × 30 (3), 40 × 25 (3), 40 × 40 (3), 50 × 25 (3 and 6), 50 × 40 (6), 50 × 50 (3 and 6), 60 × 30 (6), 80 × 25 (3), 80 × 40 (6), 80 × 50 (3 and 6) and 100 × 25 (6), 100 × 50 (6) (all mm).
Z sections	Dimensions web (A) × flanges (B) (thickness) 25 × 25 (3), 30 × 20 (1.6), 40 × 25 (3) and 50 × 25 (3) (all mm).

(From tables in Appendix C: BS 1474: 1972)

specified for chemical composition and mechanical properties. The relevant tests are set out.

Wood

Wood and wood products are largely covered in Table 3 'Materials' section i 'Wood' where the ranges of standard sizes, structural members in softwood and hardwood given in BS 4471 and BS 5450 will be found. One joinery standard is included here.

BS 584: 1967   *Wood trim (softwood)*

This standard covers architraves, skirtings, picture rails, cover fillets, quadrant, half-round and scotia moulds.

Sizes (measured with a 20 per cent moisture content), tolerance (± 0.5 up to 400 mm, ± 1 mm over 40 mm) finish, quality of timber (to BS 1186), moisture content and particulars are prescribed.

Two designatory letters are used, one for *purpose*, namely 'A' for architraves, 'S' for skirtings and 'P' for picture rails, with a *prefix* 'C' for chamfered, 'R' for rounded or 'B' for bevelled (so that RA stands for rounded architrave). Scotias have the single designatory letter 'S', quadrants 'Q', half-rounds 'HR' and cover fillets 'C'.

Dimensions in mm precede (thickness) and follow (width) the designatory letters, except for scotias, half-rounds and cover fillets, which show width only (for example C33).

The ranges comprise 13 × 45 and 20 × 70 sizes of all three architrave mouldings (example 20 RA 70), eight sizes from 13 × 70 to 20 × 170 for all three skirting mouldings (example 20 CS

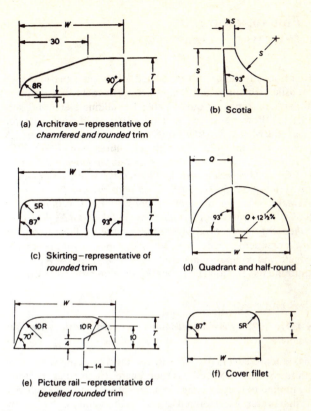

(a) Architrave – representative of *chamfered and rounded* trim

(b) Scotia

(c) Skirting – representative of *rounded* trim

(d) Quadrant and half-round

(e) Picture rail – representative of *bevelled rounded* trim

(f) Cover fillet

Figure 79   *Typical mouldings: wood trim*

140), 13 × 45 and 13 × 70 for all three picture rail mouldings (example 13 BP 70), 13, 20 and 27 for scotias (example 5S7), 11, 13 and 20 for quadrants (example Q13); 33 and 45 for half-rounds (example HR 45); and 33 and 45 for cover fillets – both 11 mm thick, of rounded profile (example C45) (all in mm). See Figure 79.

Timber quality should be to BS 1186 Part 1. Moisture content should be either as required by BS 1186 Part 1, ie 14 to 17 per cent or, exceptionally, 20 per cent. Finish and limits of manufacturing tolerances are specified.

Polythene and rubber gaskets

BS 4255   *Rubber used in preformed rubber gaskets for weather exclusion from buildings*   Part 1: 1986   *Non-cellular gaskets*

Requirements for solid (non-cellular) rubber sealing and/or glazing gaskets for location in buildings where resistance to weathering and to ozone and permanent deformation under load are prime essentials. It classifies five classes (A–D and L) of hardness, the requirements and tests for each. The applications for these are: A–D for U-channels; L for lock-type (zipper) strip, although D is normally used for the locking strip itself. (Part 2 – see Table 3 Materials t fixing and jointing materials).

BS 2919: 1968   *Low and intermediate density polythene rod for general purposes*

This standard deals with characteristics generally, and identifies three grades of polythene for pipe purposes – Grades X, Y and Z, of decreasing density and increasing inert flow index respectively.

I Pipework (no entry)
J Wire work, mesh work

Other relevant standards to be noted for special situations such as tensile structures and temporary work include a range of standards on ropes set out in Table 1 'Building elements', section (62) 'Power services' and BS 4102: 1971 *Steel wire for fences* and BS 2873: 1969 *Copper and copper alloys. Wire*. A group of four standards deal with glass fibres, namely BS 3396 *Woven glass fibre fabrics for plastics reinforcement*, BS 3496: 1973 *Glass fibre strand mat for the reinforcement of polyester resin systems*, BS 3691: 1969 *Glass fibre rovings for the reinforcement of polyester and of epoxide resin systems*, and BS 3749: 1974 *Woven glass fibre roving fabrics of E glass fibre for the reinforcement of polyester resin systems*. For temporary work a number of standards also cover ropes, cords and twines of single and composite materials. See, also, Table 4 'Activities requirements', section (B2) 'Temporary non-protective works'.

Wires and cords

BS 4391: 1972 *Recommendations for metric basic series for metal wire*

This standard covers first, second and third preference sizes for both ferrous and non-ferrous round wires (defined as 'customarily limited to those having diameters of 13.5 mm and below'). The first preference – termed 'choice' in the standard – covers 30 diameters from 0.020 to 16.0 mm, the second choice interpolates a further 29 diameters, and the third choice interpolates a further 58 to 117 in total.

BS 1052: 1980 *Mild steel wire for general engineering purposes*

This standard covers wire, of round and other cross-sectional shapes, between 0.122 and 13.2 mm diameter or equivalent cross-sectional area. Three *conditions of supply* – finally annealed, mild drawn or rolled and hand drawn or rolled – are defined, and five *conditions of finish* – amended by agreement, bright, galvanized, coppered and tinned – are specified.

Information to be supplied by the purchaser is set out in considerable detail.

The standard also covers the quality (chemical analysis and defects), coatings (to be subject to agreement), dimensions and tolerances, tensile strength and ductility.

In respect of tensile strength, the standard states that for drawn or rolled wire of 0.25 mm diameter (and below) the minimum and in other cases the maximum and minimum range of 160 N/mm² are to be specified by the purchaser. The limits for ranges of tensile strength values are given in Table 98.

Packaging and marking requirements include provision for corrosion protection, labelling and for delivery in coil, bundles of coil or bundles of lengths form.

BS 443: 1982 *Testing zinc coatings on steel wire and for quality requirements*

This standard covers galvanized wire of circular section in diameters from 0.23 to 10 mm inclusive and products fabricated from them and lays down standards for nominal mass, uniformity and adhesion of zinc coating, and the methods of testing for these properties.

The standard makes no reference to the quality of the wire itself. It does not apply to articles made from wire which have been galvanized after fabrication.

BS 4482: 1985 *Cold reduced steel wire for the reinforcement of concrete*

Nominal sizes of 5 (19.6), 6 (28.3), 7 (38.5), 8 (50.3), 9 (63.6), 10 (78.9) and 12 (113.1) mm (areas in mm² in brackets) are

Table 98 *Limits for ranges of tensile strength values: wire*

Condition of supply	Limits on tensile strength range	
	Lower N/mm²	Upper N/mm²
Finally annealed	280	500
Mild drawn or rolled	330	550
Hard drawn or rolled	500	950

(Table 3: BS 1052: 1980)

Table 99 *Nominal wire sizes*

Nominal wire size	Nominal area	Nominal mass
mm	mm²	kg/mm
5	19.6	0.154
6	28.3	0.222
7	38.5	0.302
8	50.3	0.395
9	63.6	0.502
10	78.5	0.616
12	113.1	0.888

(From Table 1: BS 4482: 1985)

described (Table 99) and the manufacture, chemical composition, quality and tolerances given. Two types of deformed wire are distinguished: Type 1 square twisted or chamfered square twisted (including 'indented'), and type 2 ribbed. Testing and certification are set out: the tests detailed in appendices. Bundles or coils are the delivery forms.

BS 1554: 1981 *Stainless and heat-resisting steel round wire*

In section one the standard specifies the requirements for stainless and heat-resisting steel round wire, supplied in coils or in straight lengths, suitable for general engineering purposes. It is generally applicable to wire sizes in the range from 0.05 mm up to and including 13 mm diameter.

Information to be supplied by the purchaser is set out in detail.

The condition of finished wire, and the method of supply are covered.

Requirements are specified for selection of test pieces, for testing and for tolerances on diameter.

Packing and identification is prescribed.

Section two sets out specific requirements for three classes of wire. These are ferritic chromium steel, martensitic steels and austenitic chromium nickel steels. The chemical composition and the condition of material are described for each class.

Three strength ranges are identified, within one or two of which given steels will be found in their hardened and tempered states. These are 550 to 700 N/mm², 700 to 850 N/mm², and 850 to 1000 N/mm².

An appendix deals with product analysis and permitted variations.

BS 4757: 1971: *Nineteen-wire steel strand for prestressed concrete*

Definitions include:

Strand: any length of the finished material which comprises nineteen-wire spun helically in two layers around one of their number as a centre wire.

Length of lay: the longitudinal distance, or pitch, of one complete helix. (Elsewhere this is specified as between twelve and sixteen times the nominal diameter.)

Equal lay construction: the wires in the strand are so spun that they all have an equal lay length. It follows that all the wires in all layers are in parallel with each other.

Coil or reel: one continuous length of finished strand wound in close packed concentric rings, termed a reel when supported on a suitable former. (Elsewhere this is specified as being 1.5 m minimum for 'as spun' strand, 900 mm minimum for 'treated' strand.)

Production length: the maximum length of strand which can be manufactured without welds having been made in the wires after patenting.

Parcel: any quantity of finished strand presented for examination and test at any one time.

Information to be supplied by the purchaser is detailed.

Manufacture of strand is given in some detail.

The wire used is to be cold drawn from patented plain carbon steel and the chemical composition and condition is controlled.

The stranding process with two layers of wire around a centre wire, is spun with a right-hand equal lay in each layer and a lay length of between twelve and sixteen times the nominal diameter. The wires should be capable of being held in position at a cut end without excessive binding. The finished strand is to be wound on to suitable reels.

Jointing of strand is prohibited, but welds may be made in the individual wires prior to patenting.

Surface condition is dealt with by forbidding lubricant or the like, but permitting superficial rust.

Routine inspection and testing is required and a record of the test results, kept by the manufacturer, is to be available for inspection.

The manufacturer is to provide dated test certificates prepared from these results.

Requirements are specified for tensile, load-extension and relaxation tests.

Identification details to be included on a label are set out.

'As spun' strand and 'treated' strand are separately discussed. In the case of treated strand, the final heat treatment determines the characteristic relaxation, which allows a smaller diameter strand.

Normal relaxation. The strand is subject to a low temperature heat treatment as a continuous linear process, and then rewound on to reels or into coils having core diameters of not less than 900 mm, to ensure that the strand will pay off substantially straight.

Low relaxation. A further process follows, which will reduce the relaxation to that given in Table 100. A colour code identification of the low relaxation strand in coil is permissible, provided the surface area affected by the marking is an insignificant proportion of the total surface of the strand in the coil.

BS 5896: 1980 *High tensile steel wire and strand for the prestressing of concrete*

This standard has three sections: general, cold-drawn wire and strand.

Section one *general*

Types of prestressing wire and strand are defined:

Cold-drawn wire: is produced in coil form from hot-rolled rod treated to make it suitable for cold drawing. The surface is smooth and may be covered by a residue of drawing lubricant; by subsequent mechanical processes the wire may be indented or crimped and a final stress-relieving treatment is carried out on the wire by a method of relaxation.

Strand: is made from cold-drawn wire. The seven-wire strand consists of a straight core wire around which are spun six helical wires in one layer. Strand is given a final stress-relieving treatment before winding into coil form.

Steel making requirements are specified, as are the *properties* of prestressing steels, which are:

Geometrical properties: defined by a nominal dimension, characteristic of the section, with specified tolerances or other appropriate criteria.

Mechanical properties: specified characteristic value, either:
specified characteristic breaking loads and specified characteristic 0.1 per cent proof loads; or
specified characteristic tensile strength and specified characteristic 0.1 per cent proof stress.

The relevant terms, and elongation and ductibility, are defined, as are the requirements for establishment or curves for isothermal relaxation.

Technological properties set out are:

Wire condition: the finished material is to be free from defects, in manufacture, that would impair the performance as a prestressing tendon. Longitudinal surface defects are acceptable provided that their depth is less than 4 per cent of the nominal diameter of the wire. Rusted steels, apart from those with a thin film of rust, are not to be supplied. The limitations on the presence of welds for each product are specified.

Inspection and certification provisions are detailed, with alternatives of manufacturers' test certificates or purchaser testing.

On request, purchasers may obtain, from the manufacturers, maximum and minimum load-extension diagrams (showing maximum and minimum values of modulus of elasticity), for a consignment.

Section two *specific requirements for cold-drawn wire*

This distinguishes plain, indented, or crimped wire, which is supplied in coils, either:

1 As drawn on the wiredrawing machine in coils of internal

Table 100 *Physical and mechanical properties of strand*

Nominal diameter of strand mm	Tolerance on diameter mm	Nominal area of steel mm^2	Nominal mass per 1000 m run kg	Specified characteristic load kN	Maximum relaxation after 1000 h from an initial load of 70% of the specified load characteristic %	80% %
25.4) 28.6 'as spun' } 31.8)	+ 0.6 − 0.25	423 535 660	3350 4240 5240	659) 823 } 979)	9	14
18 'treated'	+ 0.5 − 0.25	210	1650	370	2.5 (low relaxation) 3.5 7 (normal relaxation) 12	

(Adapted from Tables 2 and 3: BS 4757: 1971)

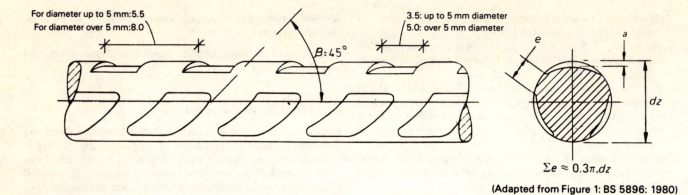

(Adapted from Figure 1: BS 5896: 1980)

Figure 80   *Indentations: cold drawn wire*

Note: One line of indentations is at a contrary angle to the others

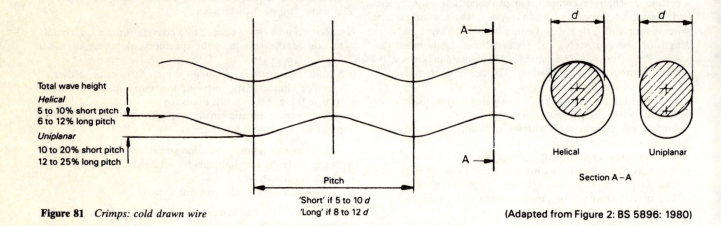

Figure 81   *Crimps: cold drawn wire*

(Adapted from Figure 2: BS 5896: 1980)

diameter approximating to that of the wiredrawing capstan: or

2 Straightened and stress-relieved with two classes of relaxation. The straightened wire may be supplied in cut lengths.

The wire is ordered and designated as BS 5896/2, wire, nominal tensile strength, nominal diameter, D = as drawn, P = straightened, E = smooth, I = indented, C = crimped and class of relaxation (relax 1 or relax 2).

In respect of manufacture, the standard covers material, types of deformation and their constraints, and prohibits welds.

Delivery requirements cover coil diameter (1.5 m for 5 mm wire, 1.25 mm for smaller diameter wires and 2.0 m for larger diameter wires), curvature of straightened wire, and requirements are specified for manufacturers' inspection; and purchaser's acceptance testing for non-certified material, while the properties are set out. See Figures 80 and 81.

Properties of smooth wire, indented wire and crimped wire are prescribed.

Section three   *specific requirements for strand*

High tensile steel wire strand is given a stress relieving heat treatment to produce either of two classes of relaxation. The strand may be seven-wire standard strand, seven-wire super strand, or seven-wire drawn strand.

The strand is ordered and designated as BS 5896/3, seven-wire strand, for example standard, super or drawn strand, nominal tensile strength, nominal diameter and class of relaxation (relax 1 or relax 2) (see BS 4757).

In respect of manufacture, the standard covers material, the stranding process defects, welds, stress-relieving heat treatment and drawn strand.

Delivery requirements cover coil size (800 or 950 diameter) and curvature of strand.

Requirements are specified for manufacturers' inspection, and purchaser's acceptance testing for non-certified material, and properties are set out. See Tables 101, 102 and 103.

BS 4483: 1985   *Steel fabrics for the reinforcement of concrete*

Factory-made fabrics manufactured from plain or deformed wires to BS 4449, BS 4461 or BS 4482. The standard *enquiry* or *order* comprises: (a) 'BS 4483', (b) the BS for the wire quality, (c) the wire sizes and mesh arrangement (see table), (d) the sheet dimension and (e) the number of sheets. The stock sheet size is 4.8 × 2.4 m (see Table 104). Process of manufacture, quality controls, tolerances and tests are included. An appendix gives the notation of fabrics, indicating the forms of schedules and drawings.

BS 405: 1945   *Expanded metal (steel) for general purposes*

This is an imperial standard but metric equivalents are given in the Table.

Mesh sizes are based on the shortway of the diamond centre to centre of intersections.

Requirements are specified on the quality of steel, manufacture, dimensions, weights and tolerances on these, cold bend tests, condition, sheet size, weight and tolerance, and marking (by tags on each bundle). See Table 105.

BS 1369: 1947   *Metal lathing (steel) for plastering*

This standard is in imperial units, but gives metric equivalents (given here). It covers four types of metal lathing (steel), as follows:

Plain expanded.
Ribbed expanded.

Table 101 *Dimensions and properties of cold-drawn wire: tolerances, ductility tests and relaxation also given*

Nominal diameter	Nominal tensile strength	Nominal 0.1% proof stress	Nominal cross-section	Nominal mass	Specified characteristic breaking load	Specified characteristic 0.1% proof load	Load at 1% elongation	Minimum elongation at max. load $I_o = 200$ mm
mm	N/mm²	N/mm²	mm²	g/m	kN	kN	kN	
7	1570	1300	38.5	302	60.4	50.1	51.3	For all
7	1670	1390			64.3	53.4	54.7	wires
6	1670	1390	28.3	222	47.3	39.3	40.2	3.5%
6	1770	1470			50.1	41.6	42.6	
5	1670	1390	19.6	154	32.7	27.2	21.8	
5	1770	1470			34.7	28.8	29.5	
4.5	1620	1350	15.9	125	25.8	21.4	21.9	
4	1670	1390	12.6	98.9	21.0	17.5	17.9	
4	1770	1470			22.3	18.5	19.0	

(Adapted from Table 4: BS 5896: 1980)

Table 102 *Dimensions and properties of cold-draw wire in mill coil: tolerances, ductility tests and relaxation also given*

Nominal diameter	Nominal tensile strength	Nominal cross-section	Nominal mass	Specified characteristic breaking load	Specified characteristic load at 1% elongation
mm	N/mm²	mm²	g/m	kN	kN
5	1570	19.6	154	30.8	24.6
5	1670			32.7	26.2
5	1770			34.7	27.8
4.5	1620	15.9	125	25.8	20.6
4	1670	12.6	98.9	21.0	16.8
4	1720			21.7	17.4
4	1770			22.3	17.8
3	1770	7.07	55.5	12.5	10.0
3	1860			13.1	10.5

(Adapted from Table 5: BS 5896: 1980)

Table 103 *Dimensions and properties of strand: tolerances, constriction and relaxation also given*

Type of strand	Nominal diameter	Nominal tensile strength	Nominal steel area	Nominal mass	Specified characteristic breaking load	Specified characteristic 0.1% proof load	Load at 1% elongation	Minimum elongation at max. load $L_o \geqslant 500$ mm
	mm	N/mm²	mm²	g/m	kN	kN	kN	
7-wire standard	15.2	1670	139	1090	232	197	204	For all
	12.5	1770	93	730	164	139	144	strands
	11.0	1770	71	557	125	106	110	3.5%
	9.3	1770	52	408	92	78	81	
7-wire super	15.7	1770	150	1180	265	225	233	
	12.9	1860	100	785	186	158	163	
	11.3	1860	75	590	139	118	122	
	9.6	1860	55	432	102	87	90	
	8.0	1860	38	298	70	59	61	
7-wire drawn	18.0	1700	223	1750	380	323	334	
	15.2	1820	165	1295	300	255	264	
	12.7	1860	112	890	209	178	184	

(Adapted from Table 6: BS 5896: 1980)

Table 104   *Preferred range of designated fabric types and stock sheet size*

Fabric Tolerance	Longitudinal wires			Cross wires			
	Nominal wire size	Pitch	Area	Nominal wire size	Pitch	Area	Mass
	mm	mm	mm²/m	mm	mm	mm²/m	kg/m²
Square mesh							
A393	10	200	393	10	200	393	6.16
A252	8	200	252	8	200	252	3.95
A193	7	200	193	7	200	193	3.02
A142	6	200	142	6	200	142	2.22
A98	5	200	98	5	200	98	1.54
Structural mesh							
B1131	12	100	1131	8	200	252	10.9
B785	10	100	785	8	200	252	8.14
B503	8	100	503	8	200	252	5.93
B385	7	100	385	7	200	193	4.53
B283	6	100	283	7	200	193	3.73
B196	5	100	196	7	200	193	3.05
Long mesh							
C785	10	100	785	6	400	70.8	6.72
C636	9	100	636	6	400	70.8	5.55
C503	8	100	503	5	400	49	4.34
C385	7	100	385	5	400	49	3.41
C283	6	100	283	5	400	49	2.61
Wrapping mesh							
D98	5	200	98	5	200	98	1.54
D49	2.5	100	49	2.5	100	49	0.77
Stock sheet size	Longitudinal wires			Cross wires			Sheet area
	Length 4.8 m			Width 2.4 m			11.52 m²

(Table 1: BS 4483: 1985)

NOTE. Values are subject to specified tolerances

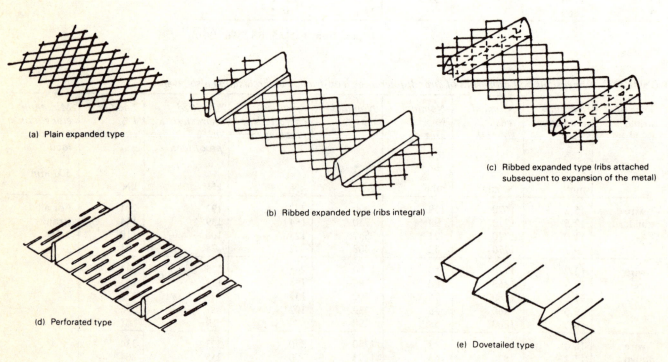

(a) Plain expanded type

(b) Ribbed expanded type (ribs integral)

(c) Ribbed expanded type (ribs attached subsequent to expansion of the metal)

(d) Perforated type

(e) Dovetailed type

(Figures 1–5: BS 1369: 1947)

Figure 82   *Types of metal lathing for plastering*

Table 105 *Summary of dimensions (weights, sectional area SWM and sheet sizes also shown)*

Reference	Nominal size of mesh		Dimensions of strands	
	SWM	LWM	width	thickness bars
	mm	mm	mm	mm
XM1 to XM10	152	400	11 to 3	6 to 3
XM 11 to XM 20	114	305	13 to 3	6 to 3
XM 21 to XM 33	76	200	13 to 3	6 to 3
XM 41 to XM 51	38	114	10 to 2	5 to 18 BG
XM 61 to XM 69	25	76	5 to 2	3 to 20 BG
XM 70 to XM 79	19	62	6 to 2	5 to 24 BG
XM 80 to XM 86	13	38	3 to 2	16 BG to 22 BG
XM 90 to XM 105	10	43	6 to 2	16 BG to 22 BG
XM 110 to XM 125	6	29	6 to 2	16 BG to 22 BG
XM 130 to XM 132	5	21	2	20 BG to 24 BG
XM 140 to XM 150	3	11	2 to 1	20 BG to 27 BG

(From Clause 5: BS 405: 1945)

(a) With ribs forming an integral part of the expanded sheet.
(b) With ribs attached subsequent to expansion of the sheet.
Perforated.
Dovetailed.

Typical illustrations of these types of lathing are shown in Figure 82.

Material, manufacture for each type, freedom from defects, sizes of mesh (at least two spans of mesh per 29 mm in one direction, apertures not less than 5 mm), sizes and weights of sheet and tolerances on these are all specified. The surface coating is of paint, and certification is covered.

BS 1485: 1971 *Galvanized wire netting*

This standard deals with netting, having meshes of hexagonal shape, either woven from galvanized wire or woven from annealed wire for galvanizing after fabrication.

The wire (to BS 1052), galvanizing and size of rolls (normally 50 m long) are specified. Tables deal with wire sizes and designations and tolerances on mesh and width.

Available meshes are 10, 13, 19, 25, 31, 38, 50, 75 and 100 mm, the last two with choice of selvedge, and in wire from 22 and 19 for the smaller meshes to 16, 15 and 14 for the larger gauges. Almost all are available 900 mm wide, most also 600, 750, 1050 and 1200 mm wide, and the range of widths extends from 300 to 1800 mm.

K Quilt work (no entry)
L Flexible sheet (work proofing)

Three standards are summarized below. BS 3408: 1977 *Tarpaulins*, is discussed in Table 4 (B3); BS 743: 1970 *Materials for damp proof courses* and BS 6515: 1984 *Polyethelene damp proof courses for masonry are* in Table 1 Building elements (29) and (20) respectively.

BS 747: 1977 *Roofing felts*

■ AD (Regs. B2/3/4)

Five classes of roofing felt are distinguished, each subdivided into several types.

Class 1 bitumen felts (fibre base)
Types:
1B fine surfaced bitumen felt.
1E mineral surfaced bitumen felt – the chippings having some weathering and decorative value.
1F reinforced bitumen felt – with a hessian fabric incorporated.

The felts comprise a sheet of animal or vegetable fibres forming an absorbent base, saturated with bitumen, and with sand or mineral granules as a surfacing.

In the case of type 1B, the surfacing is intended to prevent the felt from sticking, in its roll form. Three 'masses' (kg/10m²) are prescribed, 14 kg/10m² intended for sheds, etc. and 18 and 25 kg/10m² for the lower layer or layers of built-up roofs laid to CP 144.

In the case of type 1E, the surfacing enables use as an external layer on sloping roofs, facilitated by a granule-free margin for adhesive jointing (or in 'strip slate' or 'strip shingle' form). The standard mass is 38 kg/10m².

Type 1F is designed as a sarking or underlay to tiling or slating on a pitched roof, or as a vapour barrier. It is also available with a reflective aluminium foil, laid on the underside.

The standard mass is 15 kg/10m² (13 kg/10m² in the case of aluminium faced felt).

Class 2 bitumen felts (asbestos base)
Types:
2B fine granule surfaced bitumen asbestos felt.
2E mineral surfaced bitumen asbestos felt.

The characteristics and uses correspond to the equivalent Class 1 felts, but the base contains at least 80 per cent of asbestos fibre. The masses prescribed are 18 kg/10m² for Class 2B and 38 kg/10m² for Class 2E.

Class 3 bitumen felts (glass fibre base)
Types:
3B fine granule surfaced bitumen glass fibre felt.
3E mineral surfaced bitumen glass fibre felt.
3G venting base layer bitumen
3H glass fibre felt.

The characteristics and uses of Type 3B and 3E resemble the equivalent Class 1 and 2 felts. The base in all cases is glass fibre – inert, but incapable of being saturated, so that behaviour is somewhat different. Types 3G and 3H have a perforated base, to give partial bond as the first layer of a built-up roof, Type 3G with coarse granules on one face, surfacing on the other, Type 3H with surfacing on both faces, and, in all cases, lapping margins for jointing.

The masses are 18 kg/10m² for Type 3B, 28 kg/10m² for Type 3E, 32 kg/10m² for Type 3G and 17 kg/10m² for Type 3H.

Class 4 sheathing felts and hair felts

Types:
4A (i) black sheathing felt (bitumen).
   (ii) brown sheathing felt – three grades available.
4B (i) black hair felt.
   (ii) brown hair felt.

These felts are based on a 'batt' of flax, jute or the like (Types 4A), cow hair or the like (Types 4B).

Sheathing felts are used as underlays for mastic asphalt roofing and flooring laid to CP 144 and CP 204 (see Table 1: Building elements (3 –) 'Secondary elements'), or as sarking felts under metal roofing (see CP 143 Parts 11, 12, 13 and 15).

Hair felts are used for heat insulation and sound absorption among other purposes.

The masses are for a standard roll 810 mm wide and 25 m long, and are 17 kg/roll for Type 4A(i), 25, 20 and 17 kg/roll for the grades in Type 4A(ii) – brown sheathing felt (no. 1 inodourous), (no. 2 inodourous) and unqualified, respectively – and 41 kg/roll for Types 4B(i) and 4B(ii).

Packages. Rolls are 1 m wide for felts in Classes 1–3 and 810 mm wide for class 4, and in lengths from 10 to 25 m. The package shows the manufacturer, BS number, felt type, nominal length, width and mass. A colour code margin of up to 50 mm on the underside is used for the heavier masses of Type 1B and Type 1E (white), Types 2B and 2E (green) and Types 3B and 3E (red).

Class 5 bitumen felts (polyester base)
non-oxidized bitumen coating (5B, 5U and 5t).

The particular technical benefits conferred by bitumen polyester roofings are:

(a) an improvement in the capability of the build-up roof covering to accommodate deformations;
(b) an increase in the puncture and general mechanical damage resistances of the covering;
(c) a higher nail holding or nail anchorage capability by virtue of the increased tear resistance of the polyester reinforcement.

These felts are made from a base consisting of polyester fibres which are needled and chemically bonded (method 1) or, alternatively, spun bonded (method 2) to form a strong reinforcing carrier for the bituminous roofing.

Two distinct types of felt are covered in class 5. The main strength and performance requirements of the top layer are provided by the use of a 350 g/m² polyester base, the properties of which are fully detailed. Also covered is a special light weight underlayer of improved strength achieved by the use of a 125 g/m² base.

BS 1521: 1972   *Waterproof building papers*

This standard distinguishes two classes of waterproof building papers. Each class is divided into two grades and each grade into two types as follows:

Class A. For such purposes as the prevention of draughts or the ingress of water into wall or pitched roof structures, but not for damp-proof courses.
Grades: Grade A1, having higher tensile strength and bursting strength test requirements; and Grade A2, having lower tensile strength and bursting strength test requirements.
Class B. For temporary purposes, such as for the protection of concrete during curing or as an underlay to concrete to prevent moisture being absorbed by the base.
Grades: Grade B1, having a higher bursting strength test requirement, and Grade B2, having a lower bursting strength test requirement.

All grades are subdivided into the following types: those which are not reinforced with fibres (A1, A2, B1, B2); and those which have fibrous reinforcements (A1F, A2F, B1F, B2F). In the latter case the standard requires a minimum of eighteen strands per 300 mm, each way.

The paper is supplied in standard rolls of 50 m length and in multiplies of 50 m and in widths of 1000, 1250, 1500, 2000 and 2150 mm but special widths and half-length rolls may be supplied.

The material is to be free from visible defects and should not become sticky provided that the roll is properly stacked on end and not laid flat. Papers are likely to vary in permeability to water vapour.

Marking, by BS number, grade of paper and length of roll (m) is required on the roll, its wrapping, or a label.

BS 4016: 1972   *Building papers (breather type)*

Standard rolls are of 46 m length and in multiples of 50 m and in widths of 1000 and 1500 mm, or specially ordered widths or half-rolls.

Requirements are specified for freedom from defects, permeability, resistance to water penetration, bursting strength and pH. Marking is substantially similar to BS 1521.

M Malleable sheet work (no entry)
N Rigid sheet overlap work

A group of relevant codes of practice, especially CP 143, BS 5247, and BS 5534, is outlined in Table 1 'Building elements' section (47) 'Roof finishes'. BS 5950 *Structural use of steelwork in building* Part 4: 1982 *Code of practice for design of floors with profiled steel sheeting* deals with floors spanning in the direction of ribs.

Internal inconsistencies are evident, with the ghosts of imperial dimensions evident, for example in the nomenclature of BS 3083, and in the referencing of numbers and size of corrugations – where '8/3' in BS 3083 and '8 × 3' in BS 4868 refer to similar profiles with 3 in modules. Although BS 4943: 1973 has been withdrawn, Table 106 remains as a valuable guide.

BS 680 *Roofing slates* Part 2: 1971 *Metric units*

Characteristics required are that roofing slates are of reasonably straight cleavage and ring true when struck. The slates must be rectangular, but the head corners may be shouldered with one-quarter of the width and one-quarter of the length. The grain should run longitudinally and not transversely. They may contain naturally ingrained stripes. The surface shall be such as to permit proper laying of the slates.

Designations. *Uniform length* slates, supplied to one of the sizes listed below, of uniform or varying widths (recommended) as agreed. The minimum width of any slate is to be not less than half its length. Slates may be graded or ungraded. *Random* slates and *peggies* within the range of lengths specified are suitable for laying in diminishing courses. The width may vary, but should not be less than half the length for any particular slate. They should be graded.

Thickness. Slates supplied as graded are selected so that any one lot of 100 slates does not exceed in thickness by more than 25% any other lot of 100 slates of the same nominal length.

The terms (such as "Best" "Second" "No. 1" etc.), applied by the quarries denote the thickness grading of slates of each particular description. These must not be used to compare slates produced from different veins of rock.

A marketing description covers the name, description, thickness (graded or ungraded), length and width (and ranges where appropriate).

Tests prescribed include water absorption, wetting and drying tests, and for slates intended for use under conditions of severe or moderate atmospheric pollution by sulphurous or other acid fumes, a sulphuric acid immersion test.

For randoms and peggies twenty-one length ranges are pre-

Table 106 *Maximum span (i.e. distance between centres of purlins or sheeting rails) for short, medium and large span sheets (for general guidance)*

| Functional use | Sheet type | Maximum permissible span | |
		Roof	Vertical
		mm	mm
Minor, industrial and residential	Short span	1500	2100
General and industrial	Medium span	2100	2700
	Medium span decking	3000	–
Large span industrial	Large span	3000	3300
	Large span decking	4500	–

(From Table 2: BS 4943: 1973)

Table 107 *Standard lengths and widths of uniform length slates*
Maximum and minimum manufacturing sizes are ± 5 mm of the work size

| Work size (mm) | | | | | |
Length	Width		Length	Width	
610	355	405	305	330	255
610	305	405	255	330	205
560	305	405	230	330	180
560	280	405	205	305	255
510	305	355	305	305	205
510	255	355	255	305	150
460	305	355	205	255	255
460	255	355	180	255	205
460	230	330	280	255	150

(From Table 1: BS 680: Part 2: 1971)

scribed, the maximum corresponding to the lengths in Table 107, the minimum one-half to three-quarters as long.

BS 473 and 550: 1971 *Concrete roofing tiles and fittings*

The standard allows for any surface texture or colour desired by the purchaser, while ensuring that the physical and mechanical properties of the tiles are satisfactory.

Concrete roofing tiles and concrete slates have been divided into two groups:

1 Group A – double-lap (non-interlocking).
2 Group B – single-lap (interlocking).

Concrete plain or interlocking tiles are to be marked with the name of the manufacturer, trademark, or other means of identification.

Requirements are specified for cement, aggregate, pigments, colour, freedom from defects, surface coatings, nail hole sizes and alignments, and for transverse strength and permeability.

Fittings of similar quality to and matching the tiles with which they are laid are to comply with the general requirements and be consistent in cement content and thickness to the tiles with which they are used.

In respect of Group A products the dimensions of nibs, whether two or one provided, are specified.

Where tiles are manufactured for use in vertical tiling, the hanging side of the nibs are to be such that the tile will support itself. (Certain patterns in this group are fixed by nailing only and are not provided with nibs.)

Dimensions of Group A double-lap (non-interlocking) concrete tiles and concrete slates are given as, typically, $267 \pm 3 \times 165 \pm 3$ and $457 \pm 5 \times 330 \pm 5$, the minimum thickness 9.5 mm. Longitudinal and cross cambers (where present) and squareness are specified.

In respect of Group B products, the nib or nibs are again specified.

The lower edge of each tile is to be designed to fit closely the profile of the tile immediately below.

Dimensions of Group B single-lap (interlocking) concrete tiles and concrete slates are given as, typically, $381 \pm 5 \times 229 \pm 5$, $413 \pm 5 \times 330 \pm 5$, $420 \pm 5 \times 330 \pm 5$ and $430 \pm 5 \times 380 \pm 5$, the minimum thickness 9.5 except in the interlocking portion (6.3) and the minimum size lap 25 (all mm).

This standard does not inhibit the manufacture of other sizes than those given in either group.

BS 402: 1979 *Clay plain roofing tiles and fittings*

Certain plain tiles are manufactured nibless and/or in irregular sizes, shape, colour and camber, to meet special requirements. This standard is not intended to provide for such tiles in these respects and its issue is not intended to exclude their use.

Longitudinal camber
half-thickness to
half-thickness +3

13·15

25 - 45

5 · 7

10 - 15

Continuous nib,
or two nibs
each 20 min.

7 - 13

Cross-camber
unlimited

Worksize 265×165,
both ±3

(280×175 available)

(Inverted isometric view)

All dimensions in millimetres

Figure 83   *Clay plain roofing tiles to BS 402*

The tiles are either hand made or machine made, as may be specified, and are manufactured from well weathered or well prepared clay or marl. The tiles are to be well burnt throughout and free from fire cracks, true in shape, dense, tough and, when broken, show a clean fracture. The colour or colours as agreed, with either two nibs or one continuous nib. See Figure 83.

Requirements are specified for sampling, transverse strength and water absorption.

Certification and testing are covered.

Fittings include the following:

Eaves tiles and *top course tiles*: 215 mm long, *Tile-and-a-half tiles*: 248 mm wide (two nibs or continous nib). *Hip tiles** 7 to 10 mm diameter nail holes: angular round pattern (semi-bonnet), bonnet (granny bonnet).
Valley tiles*
Ridge tiles: 300 or 450 mm, minimum 15 mm thick.
Vertical angle tiles: right- and left-handed, external and internal square, hexagonal and octagonal.
See Figure 84.

* Standard pitches 40 ° (×2½ °) to 52½ °.

BS 690   *Asbestos-cement slates and sheets*

Part 2: 1981   *Asbestos-cement and cellulose-asbestos-cement flat sheets* (there is no Part 1)

This part distinguishes asbestos-cement sheets of two categories intended for both interior and exterior use and cellulose-asbestos-cement sheets of three categories for interior use only. They may be natural colour or pigmented.

Asbestos-cement sheets: semi-compressed sheets:

Category 1, semi-compressed sheets, minimum bending strengths 13 N/mm² parallel and 16 N/mm² at right angles to the asbestos fibres, minimum density 1.2 g/cm³.
Category 2, fully-compressed sheets, minimum bending strengths of 20 and 28 N/mm² and density 1.6 g/cm³

Cellulose-asbestos-cement sheets:
Category 0, minimum bending strengths of 6 and 9 N/mm² and density 0.8 g/cm³ (not presently manufactured in the United Kingdom).
Category 1, semi-compressed, minimum bending strengths of 12 and 16 N/mm² and density 1.0 g/cm³.
Category 2, fully-compressed, minimum bending strengths of 16 and 20 N/mm² and density 1.3 g/cm³.

Lengths and widths are not prescribed, but an appendix gives ranges available, from 1500 to 3050 mm long and 900 to 1500 mm wide. Tolerances are prescribed.

The thickness range is from 3 to 25 mm (but no sheets over 12 mm are manufactured in the United Kingdom).

Identification, sampling and inspection are covered.

Part 3: 1973   *Corrugated sheets*

This part distinguishes unreinforced symmetrical and asymmetrical corrugated sheets of straight, longitudinal cranked and curved configuration normally used for pitched roofing and wall cladding. They may be left in natural colour or pigmented to BS 402.

Classification is both *geometrical* according to the height of corrugations and *mechanical* according to load-bearing capacity.

Geometrical classification. The height of the corrugations is the height measured from the upperside of the valley to the

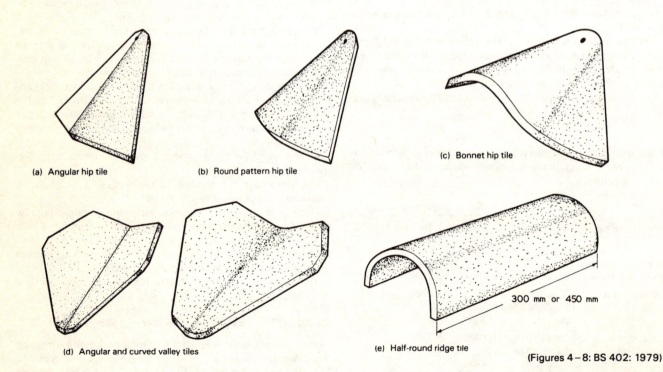

(a) Angular hip tile

(b) Round pattern hip tile

(c) Bonnet hip tile

(d) Angular and curved valley tiles

(e) Half-round ridge tile

300 mm or 450 mm

(Figures 4 – 8: BS 402: 1979)

Figure 84   *Types of tile*

upperside of the crown. Profile Class 1, height 30 to 15 mm, class 2, height 50 to 30 mm and Class 3, height 90 to 50 mm are used for pitched roofing and cladding, Class 4, height 90 to 50 mm is used for pitched roofing only, and Class 5, height 50 to 45 mm is used for cladding only. See Table 109.

Mechanical classification. The minimum load-bearing capacity, when tested in accordance with BS 4624, is given in Table 108.

General appearance and finish requirements are set out, and tolerances specified. Requirements are specified for impermeability and frost resistance.

Marking on the sheets is required, to show the date of manufacture.

Part 4: 1974   *Slates*

This part covers slates, normally used for roofing and wall cladding. The requirements for the composition, general appearance and finish, geometrical characteristics, bending strength, impermeability, frost resistance, and density are as in Part 2.

Dimensions of slates are 600 × 350 or 300 and 500 × 250 mm, all × 4 mm thickness (for fully compressed slates), 600 × 300 × 6.5 mm thickness (for semi-compressed slates). Three holes are normally pre-drilled. Tolerances are specified.

Part 5; 1975   *Lining sheets and panels*

This part covers symmetrical and asymmetrical corrugated lining sheets of straight, longitudinal cranked and curved configuration. These are normally used as over purlin/rail linings to weathering membranes for either roofing or vertical cladding.

Requirements include composition (natural, pigmented or coated) and classification, by geometrical and mechanical capacity.

Geometrical classification is defined as in Part 3. Profile class A, height 30 to 18 mm is used for pitched roofing and cladding, and class B, height 30 to 18 mm is used for cladding only.

Mechanical classification. The minimum load-bearing capacity, when tested in accordance with BS 4624, is given in Table 110.

General appearance and finish requirements are set out.

Characteristics given include geometrical characteristics: the length, 75 mm less than the appropriate top weathering sheet, and thickness, 5.5 mm minimum, with similar tolerances to those in Part 3, and with similar mechanical and physical characteristics.

Part 6: 1976   *Fittings for use with corrugated sheets*

This part details eaves, apex, verge, and movement joint fittings, fittings for corners and openings, and a range of miscellaneous fittings including louvre, side closure piece, flashing pieces and a soaker flange sheet. Not all are available for all profile classes.

BS 3083: 1980   *Specification for hot-dip zinc coated corrugated steel sheets for general purposes*

Dimensions are specified in direct metric equivalents of the imperial units in order to ensure uniformity with existing profiled sheets.

Three separate types of sheet are classified according to the thickness (mass per unit area) of zinc coating. The more heavily coated sheets give a higher degree of corrosion protection of the base steel.

The dimensional requirements relate to the most commonly required sheets (those having 76.2 mm corrugations).

Requirements are specified for the method of manufacture, the quality of hot-dip zinc coated steel sheet (lower yield stress for design purposes 210 N/mm²), freedom from defects, surface treatment (a chemical passivation treatment) and marking.

Coating mass per unit area is tabulated for 350, 450 and 600 g/m² coatings, with test requirements.

Coating adherence is required to be such that there is no

Table 108   *Bending strength: corrugated sheets*

Profile class	Symmetrical N/m	Asymmetrical N/m
1	1450	—
2	4400	3000
3	7440	7400
4	10000	10000
5	—	3800

(From Table 2: BS 690; Part 3: 1973)

Table 109   *Sheet lengths and thicknesses*

Length	Profile class				
	1	2	3	4	5
mm					
3050	x	x	x	x	x
2900	x	x	x		x
2750	x	x		x	
2600	x	x			x
2450	x				
2425		x	x	x	
2275		x			x
2125	x	x	x	x	x
1975	x	x	x	x	x
1825	x	x	x	x	x
1675	x	x	x		x
1525	x	x			x
1375	x				
1225	x				
Thickness mm	5.5	6	6	9	6

Note: A constant parallel thickness is given for all classes; with constant vertical thickness of 7.5 also specified for class 2.

(Table 3: BS 690: Part 3: 1973)

Table 110   *Minimum load-bearing capacity*

Profile class	Symmetrical and asymmetrical N/m
A	2000
B	1000

(From Table 2: BS 690: Part 5: 1975)

flaking of the zinc coating after corrugating the sheets, or curving after corrugating.

If curved sheet is required, the radius of curvature shall be agreed. Ordering thickness in mm is as tabulated in an appendix: 0.425, 0.50 (× 0.10) to 1.00, 1.20, 1.60 + 2.00 mm. Widths on the profiles are shown in Figure 85.

At sides: one, one and a half, and two corrugation overlaps are possible.

Tolerances are specified for length, depth or corrugation and thickness.

BS 4868: 1972   *Profiled aluminium sheet for building*

This specification deals with sheet of aluminium alloy to BS 1470 NS3–H8 (tensile strength 175 N/mm²) or BS 4300–6–NS31–H6 (tensile strength 185 N/mm² minimum), in any of the three profiles shown. See Figure 86.

Dimensions, thickness, tolerances, freedom from defects and finish are specified. For the commonest, corrugated type S, 8, 10 and 12 corrugations (specified in widths in multiples of 3 in, for the metric sizes are imperial translations), give the following

work sizes in mm: *8 × 3* – 610 (1 corrugation lap), 572 (1½ corrugation laps), and 533 (2 corrugation laps) (all ± 5); *10 × 3* – 762 (1 corrugation lap), 724 (1½ corrugation laps), and 686 (2 corrugation laps) all (± 5); *12 × 3* – 914 (1 corrugation lap), 876 (1½ corrugation laps) and 838 (2 corrugation laps) (all ± 6). See Figures 87 and 88.

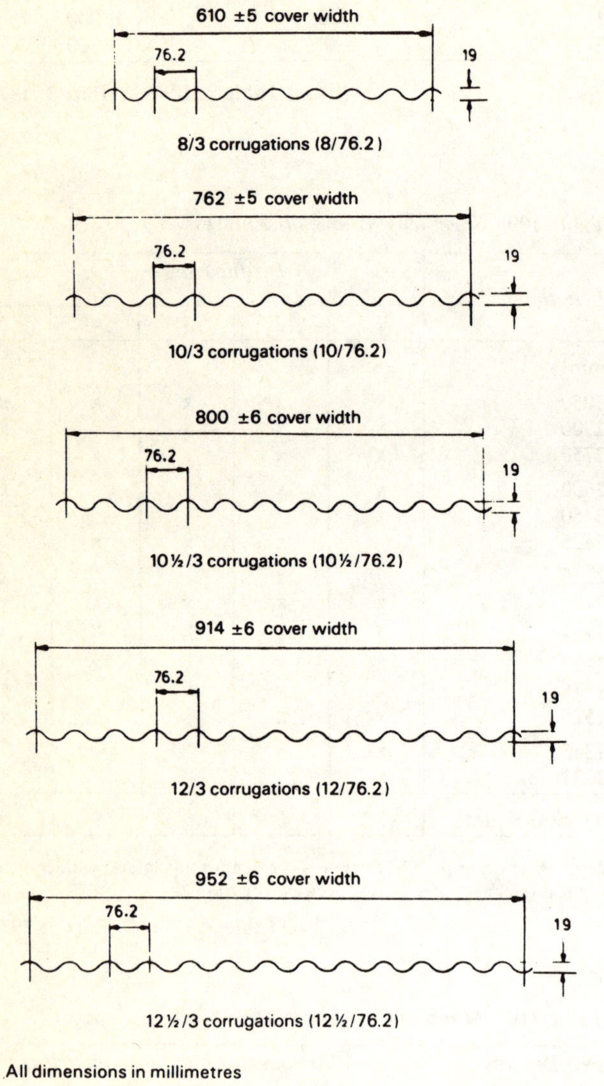

BS 4154   *Corrugated plastics translucent sheets made from thermo-setting polyester resins (glass fibre reinforced)*

Part 1: 1985 *Material and performance requirements*
The materials and acceptable surface films and coatings are specified, together with requirements on freedom from defects. Properties include *bolt shear resistance, load deflection, hardness, light diffusion* and *light transmission*, all the subject of tests set out in appendices. *Tolerances* in sheets to 5 m long are −0 + 10 mm; longer sheets −5 + 15 mm; width + 5 mm. *Squareness* and *thickness* are also regulated. *Marking* (maker's name and/or trademark and BS number) and *certification*, are presented.

Part 2: 1985 *Profiles and dimensions*
Eight profiles are scheduled, each with details of overall width of sheet; pitch and height of corrugation. They are: 1, 'standard 3', 750 wide; 2, to match 6 in, 1086 wide; 3, 'double six M', 1300 wide; 4 'Monad', 1090 wide; 5 'Major tile', 1140 wide; (all five to match fibre cement) 6, '10/3' to match steel sheet, 8/3 wide; 7, 'A7' to match aluminium sheet, 932 wide; and 8, 'WA6' to match steel or aluminium sheet 959 wide (all mm).

BS 4203   *Extruded rigid PVC corrugated sheeting*

Part 1: 1980   *Performance requirements*
The fragile nature of the material, that it softens at temperatures above those met with in normal service and the need to comply with the relevant Building Regulations are among the issues stressed in a foreword.

The specification covers material and performance of unreinforced PVC sheeting produced to the desired proile by extrusion and forming, of the following three types (only Type A is required to comply with the requirements for light transmission):

Type A: transparent (natural)
Type B: transparent (tinted or coloured)
Type C: translucent or opaque.

Requirements are specified for material, colour fastness, and head stability.

Thickness is given as a minimum of 1.30 for profile depths of 55 and under, 1.40 for profile depths above 55, with −4 per cent tolerance (all in mm). Dimensions are measured at 23 ± 2 °C.

Requirements are specified for retention of profile, strength and light transmission, and marking if prescribed.

Figure 85   *Profiles for corrugated sheets*

610 ±5 cover width
76.2   19
8/3 corrugations (8/76.2)

762 ±5 cover width
76.2   19
10/3 corrugations (10/76.2)

800 ±6 cover width
76.2   19
10½/3 corrugations (10½/76.2)

914 ±6 cover width
76.2   19
12/3 corrugations (12/76.2)

952 ±6 cover width
76.2   19
12½/3 corrugations (12½/76.2)

All dimensions in millimetres

(Adapted from Figure 1: BS 3083: 1980)

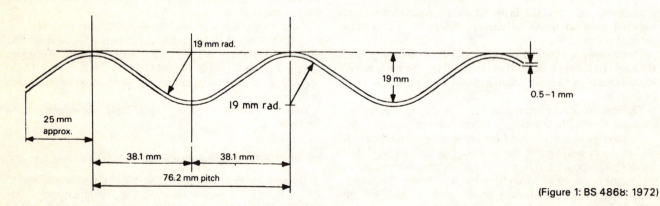

Figure 86   *Profiled aluminium sheet: corrugated Type S (sinusoidal)*

19 mm rad.
19 mm rad.
19 mm
0.5–1 mm
25 mm approx.
38.1 mm   38.1 mm
76.2 mm pitch

(Figure 1: BS 4868: 1972)

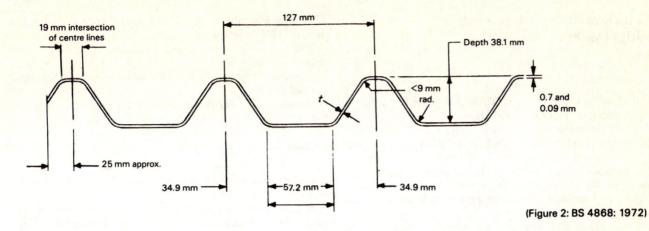

(Figure 2: BS 4868: 1972)

Figure 87 *Profiled aluminium sheet: Type A (asymmetrical trapezoidal)*

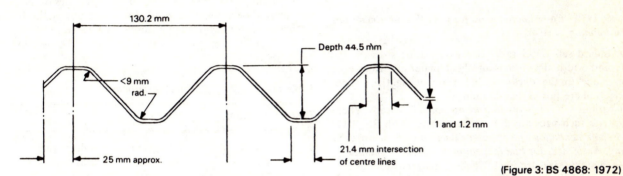

(Figure 3: BS 4868: 1972)

Figure 88 *Profiled aluminium sheet: Type B (symmetrical trapezoidal)*

Part 2: 1980 *Profiles and dimensions*
This gives seven profiles and their related dimensions for unreinforced rigid PVC corrugated sheeting. These are: Profile 1: *Standard 3 in*, to match asbestos-cement, Profile 2: to match 6 in asbestos-cement, Profile 3: *A7* profile corresponding to troughed aluminium sheet, Type A of BS 4868, Profile 4: *Doublesix*, to match asbestos-cement, Profile 5: *Monad*, to match asbestos-cement; Profile 6; *Major tile*, to match asbestos-cement; and Profile 7: *Doublesix metric* to match asbestos-cement.

P Thick coating work (no entry)
R Rigid sheet work

Metal sheets are dealt with in Table 3 'Materials' section h 'Metal', and glass in Table 3 and elsewhere.

BS 4606, reconciles rigid flat sheets with BS 4011 in dimensional terms. Two standards, BS 690 and BS 3536, deal with asbestos fibre-based products (and we scarcely need reminding of the particular care in their working and use now known to be necessary). BS 1230 deals with gypsum plasterboard, and a group of five standards, deals with plywoods, blockboard and laminboard.

Four standards deal with fibre and particle materials. Eight deal with plastics in various forms and for differing applications. Two only of a group on glass and glazing appear here, namely BS 4031 on X-ray protective glass and BS 5713 on double glazing units (for others see, for example Table 3 'Materials').

BS 4606; 1970   *Co-ordinating sizes for rigid flat sheet materials used in building*

This standard sets out a range of co-ordinating sizes for the length and width dimensions of sheet materials. Reference is also made to the thickness dimension of rigid flat sheet materials, where this exceeds 25 mm.

For various materials other sizes are manufactured. Where appropriate such sizes are to be in accordance with BS 4011: 1966 *Recommendations for the co-ordination of dimensions in building. Basic sizes for building components and assemblies.*

Co-ordinating sizes for rigid flat sheet materials set out are; width, any of 600, 900, or 1200 mm and length, any of 1800, 2400, 2700 or 3000 mm.

BS 3536   *Asbestos insulating boards and asbestos wallboards*

Part 2: 1974   *Metric units*
(Part 1 is the imperial version)
This part deals with boards of two types:

1 *Asbestos insulating boards* – essentially for use where thermal insulation and fire protection are the paramount characteristics.
2 *Asbestos wallboards* – these properties are of less importance because of a higher material density and are intended primarily for wall linings and for partitions.

Both types are intended mainly for interior use but may be used externally when suitably protected against moisture. Moulded pieces should have the same basic characteristics as the boards themselves.

For certain specialized purposes a screw-holding test may be appropriate, and a test method is given in the standard.

Composition is given as a close and homogeneous mixture consisting solely of asbestos fibre, suitable mineral agents and inorganic fillers, pigmented or coated if required, and non-combustible as defined in BS 476 Part 4.

Insulating boards to have a density not exceeding 900 kg/m³ and a thermal conductivity not exceeding 0.175 W/(m °C). Asbestos wallboards to have a density from 900 kg/m³ to 1450 kg/m³ and a thermal conductivity not exceeding 0.360 W/(m °C).

General appearance and finish and geometrical characteristics are set out.

Asbestos insulating boards are available in thicknesses of 6, 9, 12, 16, 19, 22, 25, 28 and 30 mm, and asbestos wallboards in thicknesses of 3, 4.5, 6, 9 and 12 mm.

Lengths and widths for asbestos insulating boards under 15 mm are 1200, 1500, 1800 and 2100 each × 600 or 1200 mm, and from 15 to 30 mm, 2400, 2700 and 3000 each × 600 or

1200 mm. For asbestos wallboard lengths both are 2400 and 3000 × 1200 mm width.

Tolerances on dimensions, thickness, squareness and straightness are given.

Mechanical characteristics for minimum bending strengths are laid down.

Manufacturer's certificate, and arrangements for sampling, inspection and acceptance are given.

BS 1230   *Gypsum plasterboard*

Part 1: 1985   *Plasterboard excluding materials submitted to secondary operations* (Part 2 will deal with plasterboard for secondary operations.)

This part specifies requirements for gypsum plasterboard intended to be used as a vertical or horizontal lining in buildings, excluding that which has been subjected to secondary manufacturing operations. It includes gypsum plasterboard manufactured to receive either direct surface decoration or gypsum plaster finishes.

The standard specifies the general characteristics of the gypsum plasterboard together with appropriate test methods and defines types for various applications. See Table 111.

Table 111   *Types of gypsum plasterboard*

Type	Description	Use
1	Gypsum wallboard	Linings to walls, ceilings and partitions to receive decoration
2	Gypsum base wallboard	Linings to walls, ceilings and partitions to receive veneer finishes
3	Gypsum moisture resistant wallboard	Linings where there is a risk of limited exposure of the board to moisture
4	Gypsum moisture repellent wallboard	Linings where there is a risk of limited exposure to moisture on the surface of the board
5	Gypsum wallboard F	Linings, as in type 1, but where improved fire protection performance is required
6	Gypsum baseboard	Linings to walls, ceilings and partitions, to receive a gypsum plaster
7	Gypsum baseboard F	Linings as in type 6 but where improved fire protection performance is required

NOTE 1. Whilst gypsum wallboard is not intended as a plaster base, the back of the board can receive gypsum plaster.

NOTE 2. The designation F indicates the inclusion of mineral fibres and/or other additives.

(Table 1 of BS 1230 Part 1: 1985)

This part covers *construction* – a gypsum core with suitable paper liners; *marking* – this BS number, the *type* and *description, manufacturer* and *source* of gypsum; the *tests* and the *requirements*.

Sizes are: Gypsum wallboard (types 1, 2, 3, 4 and 5) width, 600, 900, or 1200 $^{+0}_{-5}$; length, 1800, 1829, 2286, 2350, 2400, 2438, 2700, 3000, 3300 or 3600 $^{+0}_{-5}$; thickness, 9.5 ±0.5, 12.5, 15, 19 or 25 m ±0.6, all mm.

Gypsum baseboard (types 6 and 7) width 400 and 900, $^{+0}_{-8}$; length 1200, 1219, 1350, 1372, 1800, 1829, 2000 or 2032 $^{+0}_{-6}$; thickness 9.5 or 12.5 ±0.6, all mm.

An appendix sets out dimensional requirements.

Another appendix gives breaking load tests: tabulated in Tables 112 and 113.

Table 112 *Minimum breaking load: gypsum wallboard*

Board thickness	Breaking load	
	Transverse direction	Longitudinal direction
mm	N	N
9.5	170	405
12.5	230	535
15	260	620
19	305	765
25	380	1000

(Table 2 of BS 1230: Part 1: 1985)

Table 113 *Minimum breaking load: gypsum baseboard*

Board thickness	Breaking load	
	Transverse direction	Longitudinal direction
mm	N	N
9.5	125	180
12.5	165	235

(Table 3 of BS 1230: Part 1: 1985)

BS 1088: 1966 *Marine plywood manufactured from selected untreated tropical hardwoods*

This standard deals with plywood with a bond of WPB quality (see BS 1455) between the plies and made from veneers, treated or untreated, having a suitable prescribed level of resistance to fungal attack.

Species of timber permitted are:

(a) Those of which the heartwood is classed as moderately durable, durable or very durable. Core veneers only may be made from timber of lower durability providing they are treated with preservatives in accordance with BS 4079.
(b) Small proportions of sound sapwood are not deemed a defect unless the purchaser specifically requires their exclusion.
(c) Gaboon or Okoume (Aucoumea klaineana), classed as non-durable, may be used provided that the name of the timber is included in the mark specified.

Requirements are specified for manufacture and quality of veneers, core veneer, and edge joints.

Three-ply construction is not to be used in assemblies exceeding 8 mm thick when bonded but before sanding.

Requirements are specified for manufacture, bonding, scarf joints in board, and moisture content.

Finishing: boards are to be sanded or scraped on both sides equally unless specially agreed.

Dimensions of plywood boards *along* the grain of the face veneer are quoted first. Length, width and thickness tolerances and squareness are specified.

Each board is marked on the back or edge with the particulars including manufacturer, country of manufacture, this BS number and the bonding and thickness. Where the plywood is manufactured of Gaboon or Okoume (Aucoumea klaineana) the name Gaboon is shown as, for example, BS 1088 WBP GABOON. If of unbalanced construction, the word UNBALANCED should be shown as for example, BS 1088 WBP UNBALANCED. If some or all of the core plies are treated veneers, additional particulars are to be given.

BS 6566 *Plywood*

Part 1: 1985 *Construction of panels and characteristics of plies including marking*
This part covers the *construction, characteristic marking* and *classification* of plywood. *Marking* has five basic elements (this BS number, manufacturer; appearance grade; bond performance, durability class and any treatment), and further details of subsequent treatment. The classification relates to: (a) constitution; (b) glueing type; (c) surface finish; (d) durability; (e) shape; (f) homogeneity or mixture of wood in plies; (g) grain direction of outer plies; (h) grade of outer plies; and (i) use for which the plywood is suitable.

Seven or more other parts are in preparation.

BS 1455: 1972 **Plywood manufactured from tropical hardwoods**

Definitions are as in BS 565 (see Table 4 'Activities, requirements' section (Agh) 'Glossaries'), with the following modifications: *Rotary cut*, peeled from a rotating log, and *sliced*, flat cut.

Plywood is graded according to the appearance of the face and back, each being assessed separately after the board has been made.

Grade 1 veneer is of one or two pieces (joined approximately in the middle of the board) of firm smoothly cut veneer, reasonably matched for colour, and free from knots, worm and beetle holes, splits, dote, glue stains, filling or inlaying of any kind or other defects. No end joints are permissible.

Grade 2 veneer presents a solid surface free from open defects. When jointed, veneers need not necessarily be matched for colour or be of equal width. A few sound knots and occasional minor discoloration and slight glue stains and isolated pinholes* not along the plane of veneer, occasional splits not wider than 0.8 mm at any point and not longer than one-tenth of the length of the panel or slightly opened joints filled with a suitable filler are all permissible, as are neatly made repairs consisting of inserts of the same species as the veneer, which present solid, level, hard surfaces and are bonded with an adhesive equivalent to that used for bonding the veneers. No end joints are permissible.

Grade 3 veneer may include wood defects, including wormholes, which are excluded from Grades 1 and 2 in number and size which do not impair the serviceability of the plywood. It may also include manufacturing defects, such as rough cutting, overlaps, gaps or splits, provided these do not affect the use of the plywood. No end joints are permissible.

Other grades, appropriate to the end use, may be supplied.

Standard general requirements for plywood are specified. All plywood thicker than 10 mm to be of not less than five plies. The core in three ply to be not more than 60 per cent of the total

*Pinholes may be excluded, by agreement.

thickness. For panels with more than three plies, the faces, and all plies running in the same direction as the faces, to have a total or combined thickness of not less than 40 per cent and not more than 65 per cent of the total thickness of the panel. In the dry state, no face ply to be thicker than 3 mm and no inner ply to exceed 5 mm.

Four types of adhesives are distinguished:

Type WBP: weather and boil-proof. Adhesives of the type which by systematic tests and by their records in service over many years have been proved to make joints highly resistant to weather, micro-organisms, cold and boiling water, steam and dry heat.

Type BR: boil resistant. Joints made with these adhesives have good resistance to weather and to the boiling water test, but fail under the very prolonged exposure to weather that Type WBP adhesives will survive. The joints will withstand cold water for many years and are highly resistant to attack by micro-organisms.

Type MR: moisture-resistant and moderately weather-resistant. Joints made with these adhesives will survive full exposure to weather for only a few years. They will withstand cold water for a long period and hot water for a limited time, but fail under the boiling water test. They are resistant to attack by micro-organisms.

Type INT: interior. Joints made with these adhesives are resistant to cold water but are not required to withstand attack by micro-organisms.

Delamination (not accepted), the removal of metal clips, and requirements in respect of scarf joints in boards are specified, and a moisture content of 8 to 12 per cent is required at the time of leaving the factory.

Permissible deviations on dimensions are tabulated.

Boards are to be sanded or scraped both sides unless otherwise agreed.

Each board is to be marked near an edge on the back with the manufacturer's name or trademark, country of manufacture, the number of this British Standard (that is BS 1455), grade for face and back (for example 2–3) (special reference to ungraded veneers), bonding (that is, WBP, BR, MR or INT), and work size thickness of board.

BS 4512: 1969 *Methods of test for clear plywood*

This standard relates to clear plywood, defined as that manufactured from veneers containing no strength-reducing defects. The methods are not generally suitable for commercial plywood but may be used with reservations set out in some detail. It covers procedures for measuring the mechanical properties of plywood. The tests described may be used to obtain data for design purposes, to determine the effect on strength of various treatments or of various factors in processing, to ascertain properties in relation to grain or fibre direction in the material, to compare the properties of different species and for other similar purposes.

Methods are described for determining the following properties: static bending, compression, tension, panel shear, modulus of rigidity, rolling shear, panel impact, moisture content and density.

Tests of the glue in plywood are not included as they are covered in BS 1203.

BS 4079: 1966 *Plywood made for marine use and treated against attack by fungi, insects and marine borers*

This standard covers plywood made from veneers of defined quality with a bond of WBP quality between the plies and treated with preservatives, to give protection against risks such as decay and marine borers, one or both of which may occur in fresh water, temperate sea water, and tropical sea water, together with high risk of insect attack including termites.

The plywood is to comply with the requirements of BS 1088 except for that standard's limitations as to species, mycological test, moisture content, finishing and marking requirements.

Requirements are specified for treatment against specified hazards.

Marking provisions are as in BS 1088, with the number of this standard substituted, and reference to the appropriate treatment following the bonding, for example BS 4079/WBP/T1/2.

BS 3444: 1972 *Blockboard and laminboard*

Where the term 'blockboard' is used in this specification the provision refers equally to laminboard.

Definitions include:

Blockboard: a composite board consisting of a core made up of strips of wood, each not more than 25 mm wide, laid separately or glued or otherwise jointed together to form a slab, to each side of which is glued one or more outer veneers with the direction of the grain of the core strips running at right-angles to that of the adjacent veneers.

Cross grain: boards where the grain of the face veneers runs at right angles to the longer axis of the board.

Face: that surface of blockboard on which the grade or quality is chiefly judged. Where both surfaces are of the same quality, both are described as faces.

Laminboard: as blockboard, but the core strips each not more than 7 mm thick.

Long grain: a term applied to boards where the grain of the face veneers runs parallel to the longer axis of the board.

Ply: an individual layer in a sheet of blockboard, either the core or a veneer. In the case of the veneers, usually a play is a single veneer.

Veneer grading is determined by the appearance of the face and back, each being assessed separately after the board has been made, and not when in the form of veneer. The following grades are specified:

Grade S veneer: specially selected grade to be the subject of agreement.

Grade 1 veneer: one or more pieces of firm, smoothly cut veneer. When of more than one piece, well jointed and matched for colour.

Grade 2 veneer: presents a solid surface free from open defects. When jointed, veneers need not necessarily be matched for colour, or be of equal width.

No end joints are permitted for either grade. Unless otherwise specified the veneers are Grade 2.

Thickness of veneer, core construction and manufacturing requirements are specified.

Bonding terms and the designatory letters used in marking the blockboard are types BR, MR and INT, largely as in BS 1455.

The use of a durable glue does not in itself impart durability to the wood, and it is recognized that the description of the bonding does not necessarily refer to the blockboard as a material.

Delamination is not permitted, and requirements are specified in respect of conditioning and surface stability, as are permissible deviations on dimensions.

Boards are to be sanded or scraped both sides unless otherwise agreed between manufacturer and purchaser.

Marking is again as in BS 1088, with this standard number substituted.

BS 1142 *Fibre building boards*

Part 1: 1971 *Methods of test*

This standard sets out methods of test for sheet material usually exceeding 1.5 mm in thickness, manufactured from fibres of lignocellulosic material, with the primary bond from the felting of the fibres and their inherent adhesive properties. Other agents may be added.

Four basic types are distinguished by density:

1 Softboard – equal to less than 350 kg/m³.
2 Medium board (including panelboard) – greater than 350, equal to or less than 800 kg/m³.
3 Medium density fibre board – greater than 800 kg/m³.
4 Hardboard – greater than 600 kg/m³.

Part 2: 1971 *Medium board medium density fibreboard (MDF) and hardboard*
Definitions and coding given are:

Code	Type	Density	Edge marking
TE	Tempered hardboard	(over 960 kg/m³)	2 red stripes
TN	Tempered hardboard		1 red stripe
S	Standard hardboard	(over 800 kg/m³)	1 blue stripe
LME	Low density medium board	(350–560 kg/m³)	2 white stripes
LMN	Low density medium board		1 white stripe
HME	High density medium board	(560–800 kg/m³)	2 black stripes
HMN	High density medium board		1 black stripe
MDF	Medium density fibreboard	(over 600 kg/m³)	3 black stripes

The suffixes E and N represent 'extra' and 'normal' density respectively.

Flame retardant (shown by an additional yellow stripe), type FR is hardboard and medium board that has been treated to reduce the rate at which flame will spread across the surface.

Requirements are set out for bending, water absorption, response to humidity change, dimensions and tolerances.

The boards, tested in accordance with the requirements of Clause 2 of BS 476 Part 7: 1971, are classified into one of the following groups:

1 Boards giving the same flame spread classification on both faces:
Class 1A, both faces comply with Class 1 ⎫ in Table 1
Class 2A, both faces comply with Class 2 ⎬ Surface spread of
Class 3A, both faces comply with Class 3 ⎥ flame test of BS
Class 4A, both faces comply with Class 4 ⎭ 476 Part 7: 1971
2 Boards giving a higher flame spread classifications on one face than on the other:
Class 1B, one face complies with Class 1 ⎫ in Table 1
Class 2B, one face complies with Class 2 ⎬ Surface spread of
Class 3B, one face complies with Class 3 ⎥ flame test of BS
Class 4B, one face complies with Class 4 ⎭ 476 Part 7: 1971

With these Type 'B' boards, the face having the superior performance is the unmarked face.

Note that surfaces treated or processed to give such a performance may need special preparation before decoration, and that this may affect performance.

Verification of compliance is by one of the following methods: manufacturer's certificate of compliance, records of quality control tests carried out by the manufacturer, or tests using the methods described in Part 1 of this standard, on samples drawn from the consignment under consideration. A method for selection of samples for consignment testing is given.

Marking by a colour coding on all but small boards is as shown in the table at the start of this part.

Appendices table ranges of possible performance levels of hardboard for bending, absorption after immersion, and dimensional response to humidity change; and deal with the use of medium board and hardboard in flat roofs (generally type TE only).

Part 3: 1972 *Insulation board (softboard)*
Definitions include:

Softboard: fibre building board having a density not exceeding 360 kg/m³.
Insulating board: fibre building board of a homogeneous or laminated nature with a density not exceeding 350 kg/m³ and a mean thermal conductivity not exceeding 0.058 W/(m °C).
Bitumen impregnated insulating board: fibre building board impregnated with bitumen during or after manufacture (to improve resistance to moisture), having a density not exceeding 400 kg/m³ and a mean thermal conductivity not exceeding 0.065 W/(m °C).
Insulating board tile: insulating board formed as a tile with the dimensions of any side not exceeding 1220 mm and normally 9.5 to 25 mm in thickness. The tiles may have square, bevelled, kerfed, rebated, or tongued and grooved edges.
Flame retardant insulating board (type FL.R): insulating board that has been treated to reduce the rate at which flame will spread across its surface.

Requirements for insulating boards or tiles cover permissible deviations in squareness, size and straightness of boards or tiles. Standards for bending strength, deflection and effects of relative humidity for insulating boards and bitumen humidity for insulating boards and bitumen impregnated insulating boards are tabulated.

Requirements for special purpose boards or tiles include:

(a) Flame retardant insulating boards and tiles (type FL.R).
  (i) In respect of the 'surface spread of flame' classification, as in Part 2, where both faces have the same classification, Types 1A, 2A and 3A; and where the faces differ, Types 1B2, 1B3, 1B4, 2B3, 2B4 and 3B4, in each case the prefix and suffix giving the relevant class numbers.
    The face of these Type B boards having the superior performance is the unmarked face.
  (ii) FL.R boards and tiles are tested in accordance with the requirements of BS 476 Part 7, in respect of the fire propagation index of performance.
    Those having an index of performance not exceeding 12 and a subindex not exceeding 6 are designated as Class 0 boards or tiles.
(b) Acoustic boards and tiles – insulating board material which has been processed to increase the sound absorption coefficient over any range of frequencies.
(c) Sarking and sheathing boards – insulating boards normally bitumen impregnated, fixed to a roof or a wall respectively, capable of contributing to their weather resistance and thermal insulation and, in the case of sheathing boards, capable of contributing to the racking resistance of timber framed structures.

Standards of water absorption and vapour permeability are set out.
Verification of compliance is as in Part 2.
Marking by a colour coding, again as in Part 2, on the edges of boards 1220 × 1500 mm or larger, is as follows:

Insulating board – one black stripe.
Bitumen impregnated insulating board – one red stripe.
Sarking and sheathing boards – two red stripes.

Special marking provision is made for type FL.R flame retardant softboards, the marking being on the inferior face.

BS 4046 *Compressed straw building slabs* Part 2: 1971 *Metric units* (Part 1 deals with imperial units)
Compressed straw slabs defined by reference to the type of lining (see below) are for use in building construction for such purposes as roof decking, supported on open framing of timber, steel, or reinforced concrete, as partitions in timber or metal framing, as inner lining to walls of brick, metal or other materials, as infill panels to curtain walling, as permanent shuttering and as ceilings nailed to joists or suspended in metal tees.

Compressed straw slabs for thermal insulation purposes only (such as lagging of water tanks) fall outside the specification.
An appendix gives advice on the use of the slabs.
Form and texture are specified.
Dimensions are 1800, 2400, 2700, 3000 and 3600 × 1200 × 50 mm. Tolerances are set out.
Four types of lining, which may be of paper, fabric, plastics, or a combination of these securely bonded to each surface, are distinguished. These are:

1 Plain.
2 Roofing (showerproof), meeting the requirements of sub-clause 3e (resistance to water penetration) of BS 1521.
3 Class 1, treated to meet the requirements of Class 1 (resistance to spread of flame) specified in BS 476 Part 7.
4 VB (vapour barrier), treated to limit water vapour permeability not exceeding 0.066 g/s MN when tested in accordance with BS 2972 Section 12.

Properties include weight, 17.0 to 22.0 kg/m³, moisture content, 14 to 20 per cent, density, 340.0 to 440.0 kg/m³, bending strength and thermal conductivity, not more than 0.108 W/(m °C).
Marking, with BS 4046, is optional.

BS 5669: 1979 *Wood chipboard and methods of test for particle board*

Four types of wood chipboard, made from particles of wood bonded with synthetic resin and/or organic binder, are distinguished, either by their properties or by their intended use, as follows:

Type I: standard, generally up to 25 mm thick.
Type II: flooring.
Type III: improved moisture resistance, which recovers acceptable strength after short periods in wet or humid conditions.
Type II/III: combining the strength properties of Type II with the improved moisture resistance of Type III. This may be used for flooring.

This standard does *not* cover requirements for extruded particle board, flaxboard, waferboard, flakeboard or particle board other than wood chipboard. These terms are defined.
Dimensional tolerances, strength, swelling, resistance to impact, stiffness and total extractable formaldehyde are also prescribed.
Relevant limits for manufacturers' control charts for Types I, II and III board are given in the standard and consumers' acceptance limits for these three types are given.
Maximum joist centres for flooring are for 18 or 19 mm thickness, 450 mm and, for 22 mm thickness, 610 mm.
Size of boards is not prescribed, though BS 4330 and BS 4606 are recommended as guides.
Freedom from foreign matter which might cause excessive damage to woodworking tools, moisture content (7–13 per cent), thermal conductivity (not greater than 0.14 W/(m K) (0.12 kcal/m h °C)), surface spread of flame (not lower than Class 3 in Part 7 of BS 476) and dimensional stability are regulated.
Verification of compliance is preferably through quality control tests carried out by the manufacturer.
Marking, on the board, a label or a delivery note, identifies this standard, the manufacturer, and the type of board.
Edge marking, similar to that in BS 1142 is for Type 1, black stripe, Type II, red stripe, Type III, green stripe and Type II/III red and green stripes.
Methods of test for particle board are specified in an appendix.
Appendix C, which is advisory in status, contains recommendations for the selection and application of boards for specific purposes. It stresses that they have to be carefully selected and correctly handled and installed, with appropriate protection, for example, from damp. Chipboard is subject to moisture movement, not always completely reversible. Apart from general movement, the effects of moisture may include surface roughening, edge swelling and loss of structural strength. The appendix continues with detailed advice on storage and handling, design, fixing and laying, for flooring, structure and roofing applications.

BS 1105: 1981 *Wood wool cement slabs up to 125 mm thick*

Such slabs are of wood fibres, chemically treated, mixed with Portland cement, compressed, matured and accurately trimmed to size. Edge channel-reinforced, prefelted and prescreeded slabs are also covered. the slabs are of three types:

Type A: slabs intended for non-load-bearing application, for example partitions, ceilings, wall linings, roof insulation and permanent shuttering.
Type B: slabs with a work size thickness of not less than 50 mm possessing a greater strength than Type A slabs and intended for use in roof construction providing that safety precautions are taken. They are also suitable for the purposes indicated for Type A slabs.
Type SB: as Type B, but with greater resistance to impact, and intended for roof constructions not subject to Regulation 36(1) of the Construction (Working Places) Regulations 1966.

Requirements are specified for manufacture, materials, form and texture and tolerances.
Nominal thicknesses are prescribed, in an airdry state, as 25, 38, 50 64, 75, 100 and 125 mm, with corresponding densities.
Thermal conductivity, where the slab thickness is 25 or 38 mm, is not to exceed 0.1 W/(m K), and, where the thickness is 50 mm or greater, is not to exceed 0.093 W/(m K).
Sound absorption properties are set out, in an appendix, for 25, 50 and 75 mm slabs on solid backing and on 50 mm square battens at 600 mm centres.
Marking and manufacturers' certificates are covered. Type B slabs are marked with a white line on one short edge, Type SB slabs with a white and a green line on one short edge.

BS 2572: 1976 *Phenolic laminated sheet and epoxide cotton fabric laminated sheet*

Section one *general*
The standard covers sheet material of thicknesses within the ranges given in Table 114.

Definitions include:

Phenolic laminated sheet: consisting of superimposed layers of paper, felt, fabric or veneer which have been coated or

Table 114 *Ranges of sheet thickness: laminated sheet*

Types	Range* of nominal thicknesses mm		
A1, A3, A4	1.6	to	100
A2	0.8	to	25
F1, F2	0.4	to	100
F2/1, F3	0.8	to	100
F4, F5	0.8	to	25
F6	0.8	to	80
P1, P2, P2/1, P3, P4	0.4	to	50
P3/1	0.4	to	40
W1, BW1	5.0	to	100
UW1	5.0	to	50

* The full range: 0.4, 0.5, 0.6, 0.8, 1.0, 1.6, 2.0, 2.5, 3 (× 1 to) 6 (× 2 to) 16, 20 (× 5 to) 50 (× 10 to) 100 mm.

(From Clause 1: BS 2572: 1976)

impregnated with a thermosetting phenolic resin and bonded together under heat and pressure. Other ingredients, for example, colouring matter, may be incorporated.

Directions A and B: two directions in the plane of a sheet which are mutually at right angles. For fabric and wood-based laminates these directions are related to the surface layer of fabric or wood veneer. One of these directions is parallel either to the warp threads of a fabric, or to the grain of a wood veneer. For paper or felt reinforced sheet, one of these directions is parallel to the edge of the sheet.

Epoxy bonded cotton fabric sheet: consisting of layers of cotton fabric impregnated with a thermosetting epoxide resin, bonded under heat and pressure. Again, other ingredients, for example colouring matter, may be added.

Classification is into two classes, the first having four groups, of which three are subdivided into types, the second class with only two types:

Class 1: sheets in which the mechanical properties in both directions are of the same order (except for group W).
Group A, with asbestos reinforcement: Type A1 of felt, Type A2 of asbestos paper and Types A3* and A4* of woven asbestos cloth.
Group F*, with cotton, or cotton/synthetic fibre mixture, fabric reinforcement comprising Types F1, F2, F2/1, F3, F4 and F5 and epoxide Type F6.
Group P, with cellulose paper reinforcement comprising Types P1, P2, P2/1, P3, P3/1 and P4.
Group W, with wood veneer reinforcement comprising Type W1. (These have significant directional strength differences.)
Class 2: wood veneer reinforced. Type UWI, with maximum directional strength differences and Type BWI, with lesser differences.

Colour is to be natural unless otherwise agreed.

Section two *requirements*
Appearance and workmanship, flatness, preferred nominal thicknesses and permissible deviations, machinability and resistance to hot oil are specified. The last does not apply to sheet of Types P3/1, A1, A2, A3 or A4, although Types A1, A2, A3 and A4 are subject to the alternative test requirement for crushing strength after hearing.

Requirements are specified for the physical properties of both classes.

BS 3757: 1978 *Rigid PVC sheet*

This standard covers PVC sheet of nominal thickness 0.25 mm and above. Rigid PVC sheet is classified into six types as shown in Table 115, and is available in a wide range of colours. Types A and B are manufactured by press lamination or press surfacing and Types C and D by calendering or extrusion.

Rigid PVC sheet is defined as consisting of polyvinyl chloride and/or copolymers of vinyl chloride of which the major constituent is vinyl chloride, suitably compounded with other ingredients.

General requirements for appearance, thickness, tolerances and length and width measurement requirements are given.

The range of thicknesses is 0.25, 0.7, 0.75, 1 ($\times$ 0.5 to) 5, 6, 8, 9, 10, 12, 18 and 24 mm with prescribed tolerances.

In respect of characteristics in fire, horizontal burning characteristics of a test specimen when exposed to a small flame, and retention of embossed surface after heating, are specified.

Performance requirements are specified for resistance to delamination, softening point, impact strength, tensile strength, elastic modules in bend and dimensional change at 120 °C.

For certain specialized applications, additional test requirements may be appropriate. These include electrical properties, mechanical properties at temperatures other than 23 °C, mechanical properties after ageing, notch sensitivity (impact strength), colour fastness to light and resistance to specific chemicals. See Table 116.

BS 3794 *Decorative laminated sheets based on thermosetting resins*

Part 1: 1982 *Specification*
This standard sets out requirements and a classification for decorative laminated sheets according to their performance and main recommended applications, and also provides requirements for materials with special characteristics, for example postformability or defined reaction to fire.

Requirements are given for those types of material that are most commonly used, but additional types may be added as required. The specified limit values apply to the types of material most commonly used, but it may be possible, within each classification, to obtain variants having much higher performance.

The materials are characterized by their decorative surfaces, which are relatively hard and resistant to wear, scratching, impact, boiling water, domestic stains and moderate heat. They are intended for interior applications and are ready for use. The back surface of sheets having only one decorative face is manufactured so that it is suitable for adhesive bonding to a substrate.

Decorative laminated sheet is defined as consisting of layers of fibrous sheet material (for example paper) impregnated with thermosetting resins and bonded together by means of heat and a pressure of not less than 5 MPa ($= 5$ N/mm^2), the outer layer or layers on one or both sides having decorative colours or designs.

A classification is set out (see Part 2), with the suffixes 'S' for standard, 'P' for postformable and 'F' for a defined reaction to fire.

Requirements and methods of test are specified for appearance, dimensional stability, formability, reaction to fire and resistance to surface wear, boiling water, dry heat, impact, cracking, scratching, stains, colour change in artificial light and cigarette burns. The properties include colour and pattern, surface finish, and thickness.

Part 2: 1982 *Methods of determination of properties*
This sets out methods of test for determination of the properties of decorative laminated sheets. Table 116 gives the classes and their applications (see reference to suffixes in Part 1).

Table 115 *Type descriptions: rigid PVC sheet*

Type	Description and general applications
A1 C1	General purpose sheet suitable for most applications and fabricating techniques
A3 C3	Sheet similar to Types A1 and C1 but with specific impact strength. The chemical resistance of these types may be inferior to that of Types A1 and C1
B	Sheet particularly suitable for deep vacuum forming. These types are generally characterized by a lower softening point and the maximum service temperature of articles made from them may consequently be reduced

*The numbers of the threads per unit length, warp and weft, of the fabric reinforcements in Types A3 and A4, and all types in Group F, determine the type.

(Table 1: BS 3757: 1978)

Table 116 *Application characteristics: rigid PVC sheet*

Class	Performance category	Typical applications
HD (heavy duty)	Materials with greater resistance to abrasion than Class HG	Flooring, and supermarket checkout counters
HG (horizontal, general purpose)	Materials of high performance for general use in horizontal applications, and for use in vertical applications requiring particularly high performance	Kitchen working surfaces, restaurant and hotel tables, heavy duty doors and wall coverings, interior walls of public transport vehicles
VG (vertical, general purpose)	Materials of less high performance than Class HG, for general use in vertical applications, and for use in some horizontal applications where only moderate performance is required	Kitchen front panels, wall coverings, shelves
VL (vertical, light duty)	Materials of moderate performance for use in vertical applications where the requirements are less demanding than in Class VG	Exposed side components of cupboards
CL (cabinet liner)	Materials of moderate performance but with lower standards of surface appearance, colour fastness and resistance to heat and moisture than in Class VL, for use in vertical applications not normally exposed to light or view	Interior components of cupboards

(Table 1: BS 3794: Part 2: 1982)

BS 3837: 1977 *Expanded polystyrene boards*

This standard deals with cut, moulded or extruded boards not less than 13 mm* thick for use at temperatures up to 80 °C for cut or moulded boards and temperatures up to 75 °C for extruded boards.

Six *grades* are given. These are:

SD: standard duty.
HD: high duty.
EHD: extra high duty.
UHD: ultra high duty (only Type A).
SHD: special high duty (only Type A).
ISD: impact sound duty.

Types are:
Type N: a cellular structure consisting substantially of closed cells.
Type A: is similar to Type N, but meets the additional requirement that, when tested in accordance with BS 4735, specimens of 150 × 50 × 13 mm, subjected to a small flame, show an extent of burn of less than 125 mm.

The following *board structures* are described:

Cut board: board cut from a block moulded from expanded beads
Moulded board: board moulded from expanded beads, that has surface skins.
Extruded board: board moulded from expanded beads, that has surface skins.
Extruded board: board extruded, that has surface skins.†
Cut extruded board: board obtained by cutting extruded board into boards of lesser thickness.†
Compressed board: cut board of grade SD that has been compressed and then allowed to recover to a thickness less than its original thickness, thus reducing its compressive stress to within a range defined for grade ISD making it suitable for impact sound absorption.

Standard board sizes are: length, 1220 and 2440 mm, width, 610 and 1220 mm and thickness, 13, 25, 38 and 50 mm.
Tolerances are given.
Identification is by a colour code, differentiating grades and types.
Requirements are tabulated in respect of close breaking strength, compressive stress, water vapour transmission, thermal conductivity, dimensional stability and burning characteristics.

BS 4840 *Rigid polyurethane (PUR) foam in slab form*

(Part 1: 1985 relates to applications to vehicles)

Part 2: 1985 *PUR foam for use in refrigerator cabinets, cold rooms and stores*
This part covers composition and form, and tolerances: thickness, ± 15; length or width (up to and including) 100: ± 1, 1000 ± 15, 2000 ± 2.5, 4000 ± 5, over 4000 + 10 (all mm).
Three important appendices:
A *Guidance for designers* (increase in thermal conductivity over time; the need for moisture and vapour barriers; conversion risks at interface of PUR and metal; risks with certain adhesives; and fire performance).
B *Burning properties*
C *Guidance intended to minimize fire hazard* (need for good housekeeping standards; stringent fire precautions, including 'no smoking' rules; briefing employees; consultations with HM Inspectorate of Factories; fire drills; liaison with Fire Authority; fire protection system; installation and protective facings, compliance with fire regulations; fire precautions and notifications if large quantities are used).

BS 4841: *Rigid urethane foam for building applications*

Part 1: 1975 *Laminated board for general purposes*
This standard considers boards consisting of a core of rigid urethane foam bonded to two flexible facings of minimum thickness 12 mm. The boards are to be essentially flat and show no significant areas of lack of adhesion between facings and foam core. Suitable facings are flexible cellulose-based materials such as paper, which may be coated with a plastics material. The core material is to consist of rigid urethane foam with a substantially closed cell structure.
These boards are suitable for use within the cavity of heavy

*In thicknesses of less than 13 mm, the specification should be a matter for agreement.
†Not all combinations of these grades, types and structures are available; in particular, extruded and cut extruded board is not available in SD, HD, EHD and ISD grades. On the other hand, UHD and SDH grades are only available in Type A.

construction cavity walls and as insulation under screeds, but are not recommended for use in ceiling and roofing insulation. In particular, they should not be used in situations where they are liable to be directly exposed to flame in the event of fire. The finished construction must be checked in relation to fire properties under The Building Regulations or similar requirements.

Dimensions are 2400 × 1200 × 12 mm upwards.

Requirements are specified for thermal conductivity of foam core (maximum 0.024 W/(m K)), compressive strength/stress of core, water vapour permeability of core, dimensional stability and burning characteristics.

An appendix dealing with burning properties is essentially similar to BS 4840.

Part 2: 1975 *Laminated board for use as a wall and ceiling insulation*

This part deals with laminated boards similar to those described in Part 1, but suitable for use as ceiling and wall linings where thermal insulation is required.

The finished construction must be checked in relation to fire properties under the Building Regulations, etc.

Applications and provisos include:

1 The boards are not normally suitable for use in cold-store construction.
2 In wall constructions where the boards are applied to a non-combustible substrate, they are to be protected on the exposed surface by 9.5 mm plasterboard or by two coats of gypsum plaster giving a total thickness of at least 12 mm.
3 In wall constructions where the boards are not applied directly to a non-combustible substrate, they are also to be suitably protected against the spread of flame within the cavity.
4 In ceiling construction where the boards are applied to a non-combustible substrate, they are to be protected on the lower surface by a texturing compound which, when tested in accordance with BS 476 Part 7, confers Class I rating in respect of spread of flame.
5 In ceiling construction where the boards are not applied to a non-combustible substrate, a texturing compound is not acceptable unless the lower faces of the boards are first protected by 9.5 mm plasterboard or by two coats of gypsum plaster giving a total thickness of at least 12 mm to prevent fire breaking into the cavity.

The boards may be finished, if required, by conventional plastering, texturing or painting techniques or by any suitable combination of these.

Dimensions (2400 × 1200 × 12 mm upwards) and tolerances are prescribed.

Boards are marked on the non-finish face with the BS number and the instruction 'Finish shall be applied on opposite face'.

Requirements are specified for thermal conductance (maximum 1.87 W/m²K), compressive strength/stress of core, water vapour permeance, burning properties, dimensional stability and stiffness in bending.

An appendix is essentially similar to the appendix in Part 1. A further appendix gives general notes for the end-user.

BS 4965: 1974 *Decorative laminated plastics sheet veneered boards and panels*

This standard deals with composite boards (of standard sizes) and panels (cut or specially made) for interior use.

They are made up of various core materials veneered on one side with a decorative laminated plastics sheet. The reverse side may be

1 Veneered with a decorative laminated plastics sheet.
2 Veneered with a non-decorative sheet.
3 Not veneered.

Definitions include:

High humidity: ambient relative humidity of 80 per cent or higher.
Normal humidity: ambient relative humidity of 40 to 80 per cent.
Low humidity: ambient relative humidity of 40 per cent or lower.

Classification is in four basic types, and the special forms of each with Class 1 resistance to surface spread of flame under BS 476 Part 7, as follows:

1 Type H – for use in heavy duty applications where conditions require resistance to impact damage and also to sustained periods of high humidity and frequent wetting; and Type H/S, as for Type H*.
2 Type LH – for use in light duty applications where the risk of impact damage is minimal but where conditions require resistance to sustained periods of high humidity and frequent wetting; and Type LH/S as for Type LH*.
3 Type HN – for use in heavy duty applications where conditions require resistance to impact damage but not to sustained periods of high humidity and frequent wetting; and Type HN/S, as for Type HN*.
4 Type LN – for use in light duty applications where the risk of impact damage is minimal and where conditions do not require resistance to sustained periods of high humidity and frequent wetting; and Type LN/S, as for Type LN*.

When low humidity conditions are anticipated, specifiers are to require raw materials to be suitably conditioned before bonding.

A table of typical applications is given in an appendix, for guidance only. See Table 117.

Material requirements for each type are as follows:
Type H:
Veneers: both faces with decorative laminated sheet.
Cores: plywood, Type BR of BS 1203; tempered hardboard of homogeneous construction, or asbestos board, perpendicular tensile strength of not less than 400 k Pa.
Adhesive: Type BR of BS 1203 or, where used in virtually continually wet conditions, Type WBP of BS 1203.
Edges: effectively sealed.
Type H/S: as Type H, but veneers 1.5 mm thick and fire spread resistant (in the case of the backing sheet, this is optional).
Type LH: as Type H, but veneers 0.5 mm thick.
Type LH/S: as Type H/S, but veneers 0.5 mm thick.
Type HN:
Veneers: one face or both faces.
Cores: one of seven materials – plywood, blockboard, laminboard, particle board, asbestos-cellulose board or asbestos board.
Adhesive: adequate to a standard set out.
Type HN/S: as Type HN, but veneers on one or both sides as Type H/S.
Type LN: veneers as Type LH, otherwise as Type HN.
Type LN/S: veneers as Type LH/S, otherwise Type HN.

In all cases relevant BS references and preparation requirements are given.

Appearance, the examination of surfaces by the reflected light method described, matching of colour and appearance are all covered.

Dimensional tolerances, and requirements in respect of straightness of edges, squareness and flatness are set out.

Marking requirements are prescribed (manufacturer, BS number, type).

---

*The suffix 'S' relating to surface spread of fire.

Table 117 *Typical applications: decorated laminated plastics sheet*

Type	Typical applications	Typical areas of use	Typical conditions of use
H	Wall linings, doors, partitions, horizontal working surfaces	Toilet, changing and shower cubicles, dairies, breweries, abattoirs etc.	Prolonged periods of high relative humidity of over 80% and/or frequent surface washing with water which may include detergents and disinfectants
LH	Ceiling panels, light duty wall linings and partitions, fitments etc.		
H/S	Ships bulkheads linings and divisions, wall linings, doors	Hospitals, schools, shipbuilding and public transport where there is a requirement for surface spread of flame to Class 1 of BS 476 Part 7	Prolonged periods of high relative humidity of over 80% where some surface condensation and occasional washing can be expected
LH/S	Ceiling panels Vertical surfaces		
HN	Horizontal working surfaces to furniture and fitments Heavy duty panelling, doors	Shops, supermarkets, offices, schools, hospitals, public buildings and transport, kitchen, bathroom and other domestic applications	Normal industrial and domestic application where occasional surface condensation and/or washing can be expected
LN	Ceiling panels, light duty wall linings, partitions, fitments etc.		
HN/S	Shoplifting, lift-car linings, lift shafts, wall linings, doors	Supermarkets, public transport and areas in public buildings where there is a requirement for surface spread of flame to Class 1 of BS 476 Part 7	
LN/S	Ceiling panels, body side linings, vertical surfaces		

(From Appendix E: BS 4965: 1974)

Table 118 *Size limitations for production units*

Glass thickness mm	Cavity width mm	Maximum larger dimension mm	Maximum smaller dimension except for squares mm	Maximum area m²	Maximum square mm
3	5 to 12	2110	1270	2.4	1270
4	5 to 6	2420	1300	2.86	1300
	8 to 20	2440	1300	3.17	1300
5	5 to 6	3000	1750	4.00	1750
	8 to 10	3000	1750	4.80	2100
	12 to 20	3000	1815	5.10	2100
6	5 to 6	4550	1980	5.88	2000
	8 to 10	4550	2280	8.54	2440
	12 to 20	4550	2440	9.00	2440
10	6	4270	2000	8.54	2440
	8 to 10	5000	3000	15.00	3000
	12 to 20	5000	3180	15.90	3250
12	12 to 20	5000	3180	15.90	3250

(Table 1: BS 5713: 1979)

Table 119 *Typical thermal transmittances of units*

Air space (mm)	Conditions of exposure		
	Sheltered W/(m² K)	Normal W/(m² K)	Severe W/(m² K)
5	3.3	3.5	4.0
6	3.2	3.4	3.8
9	3.0	3.2	3.5
12	2.8	3.0	3.3
20	2.8	2.9	3.2

(From Table 2: BS 5713: 1979)

Typical thermal transmittances for hermetically sealed double-glazing units under varying conditions of exposure are given. See Table 119.

The standard does not apply to units incorporating a plastics-covered annealed glass.

Materials are prescribed. .

Size limitations for production units are subject also to considerations set out in CP 152, but Table 116 is a guide.

Dimensional tolerances are given.

Marking with the manufacturer and this BS number is required legibly and permanently in such a way that the marking can be seen after the units are installed.

Performance requirements given include:

1 No evidence of contamination on the interior glass surfaces.
2 No indication of leakage at the seal.
3 No evidence of frost or condensation on the interior glass surfaces.
4 No evidence of fogging or contamination on the interior glass surfaces after being tested by ultraviolet exposure.
5 A minimum of eleven of the twelve units tested in accordance with weather cycling and high humidity cycling tests specified shall show no evidence of condensation or frost on the interior glass surfaces.

In each case the relevant test procedure is described. An appendix deals with performance and includes typical thermal transmittances of double-glazed units for different conditions of exposure.

BS 4031: 1966 *X-ray protective lead glasses*

This standard distinguishes two types of lead glass for protection against X-radiation and a method of measuring the lead equivalent of the glasses in which the transmission of the glass is compared with the transmission of lead sheets of appropriate thickness under identical conditions of X-radiation.

BS 5713: 1979 *Hermetically sealed flat double glazing units*

This standard deals with aspects of factory made units. The detail of units is not specified. Symmetrical and asymmetrical units (equal or unequal glass thickness) are distinguished.

For guidance on the correct choice of glazing for a particular application, for instance where safety or wind loading requirements need to be considered, CP 152 should be consulted.

S Rigid tile work

The relevant codes of practice are BS 5385 for wall tiling and CP 202 for tile and slab flooring. See also BS 4131: 1973 *Terrazzo tiles* (dealt with in Table 1 'Building elements' under section (43) 'Floor finishes').

BS 6431   *Ceramic floor and wall tiles*

The majority of parts are European standards. The drafting is particularly careful and repetitious. *Sizes are given commonly in centimetres.*

Part 1: 1983 *Classification and marking including definitions and characteristics.*
   The scope, intended normally for 'best commercial quality' or 'first quality' extends to mosaics, factory slabs, pavers and accessories.
Characteristics for floors and walls are distinguished and include dimensions and surface quality, physical properties and chemical resistance. 'Split tiles' (split after lining) are distinguished from 'single tiles'.
Marking of tiles or their packing must show: manufacturer and country of origin; quality; BS, EN (European) or national standard, nominal and work size – prefixed with M if modular; and whether surface is glazed (GL) or matt unglazed (UGL).
Specification and *ordering* are also covered – the former the subject of examples cited in later parts.

Part 2: 1984   *Extruded ceramic tiles with a low water absorption (E ≤ 3%). Group A1*
Sizes: (modular) M30 × 30, M30 × 15*, M25 × 25*, M25 × 12.5*, M25 × 6.25, M20 × 20*, M20 × 10*, M20 × 5*, M15 × 15* and M10 × 10* (all cm). Work sizes are $^{-5}_{-10}$ mm $^{-3}_{-11}$ mm for single extruded tiles).

Notes: 1. In all cases the manufacturer specifies the thickness.
   2. The sizes given are for *split tiles*.
(*Sizes for *single extruded tiles*).
   For non-modular tiles, the sizes commonly available differ, from 24 × 11.5 to 24 × 7.3 or 21.9 × 6.6 cm for split tiles; 30 × 15 to 10 × 10 or 20 × 5 cm for single tiles.
   A typical specification is 'Extended split tile EN 121 A1 M 25 cm × 12.5 cm (W 240 mm × 115 mm) GL', or 'Extruded quarry tile EN 121 A1 M 20 cm × 10 cm (W 193 mm × 95 mm) EGL'.

Part 6: 1984 (EN 176)   *Dust-pressed ceramic tiles with a low water absorption (E ≤ 3%) Group B1*
Sizes (modular) M10 × 10, M15 × 15, M20 × 10; M20 × 15, M20 × 20, M30 × 30 (work sizes $^{-2}_{-5}$ mm). Non-modular common sizes range from 40 × 30 to 15 × 7.5 cm (work sizes ± 2% or 5 mm).
   A typical specification is 'Dust-pressed tile EN 176 B1 M 15 cm × 15 cm (W 147 mm × 147 mm) GL'.

Part 9   *Dust-pressed ceramic tiles with a water absorption of E. < 10%. Group B111*
These tiles are not intended for use where there is severe mechanical load, or where conditons of frost may apply. The surface may be smooth, profiled, wavy or finished in some other way: glossy, matt or semi-matt (GL). Sizes (modular) M10 × 10, M30 × 15, M25 × 25, M20 × 20, M20 × 15, M20 × 10, M15 × 15, M15 × 7.5, M10 × 110 cm (work sizes $^{-1.5}_{-5}$ mm).
   Non-modular common sizes range from 40 × 40 to 10.8 × 10.8 and 15 × 7.5 cm (work size ± 2 mm).
   A typical specification is 'Dust-pressed tile EN 159 B111 M15 cm × 15 cm (W 148 mm × 148 mm) GL'.
   The remaining parts so far issued deal with tests:

Part 10: 1984   *Method for determination of dimensions and surface quality*
Part 11: 1983   *Method for determination of water absorption*
Part 12: 1983   *Method for determination of modulus of rupture*
Part 14: 1983   *Method for determination of resistance to deep abrasion*
Part 15: 1983   *Method for determination of linear thermal expansion*
Part 16: 1983   *Method for determination of resistance to thermal stock*
Part 17: 1983   *Method for determination of crazing resistance. Glazed tiles*
Part 18: 1983   *Method for determination of chemical resistance. Unglazed tiles*
Part 19: 1984   *Method for determination of chemical resistance. Glazed tiles*
Part 20: 1984   *Method for determination of resistance to surface abrasion. Glazed tiles*
Part 21: 1984   *Method for determination of moisture expansion using boiling water. Unglazed tiles.*

T Flexible sheet work

A very wide category, within which the inclusions and exclusions must be arbitrary, is covered in this section. Sectional List 16 excludes floor finishes, which are dealt with in Table 1 'Building elements' under section (43) 'Floor finishes', proofing sheets, which are dealt with in Section L, and furnishing fabrics. Yet mention is made of BS 4815: 1972 *Glossary of generic names for man made fibres*, BS 3119: 1959 *Method of test for flameproof materials*, BS 3120: 1959 *Performance requirements of flameproof materials for clothing and other purposes*, BS 3121: 1959 *Performance requirements of fabrics described as of low flammability* BS 2963: 1958 *Tests for the flammability of fabrics*, and BS 6249 *Materials and material assemblies used in clothing for protection against heat and flame* Part 1: 1982 *Flammability testing and performance* and rightly so, for the burning and flame-spread characteristics of drapings and furnishings significantly influence the performance of buildings in fire. These will not be considered here but are covered in Table 4 'Activities, requirements' under section (K) 'Fire'. BS 3379 is mentioned in section F, BS 1763, BS 2739, BS 3012, BS 4023 and BS 4646 all deal with plastics, and are considered here. BS 5803 which covers thermal insulation matting in pitched roof spaces, is set out in Table 4 (M).

BS 1763: 1975 *Thin PVC sheeting (calendered, flexible, unsupported)*

This standard distinguishes such sheeting up to and including 400 μm (micrometres) thick, classified as follows:

Type 1A: general purpose unprinted single or laminated thin sheeting with a plain or embossed surface.
Type 2A: thin sheeting of Type 1A, printed.
Type 1B: unprinted single or laminated thin sheeting with a plain or embossed surface complying with the requirements for distance of travel of flame given in the standard.
Type 2B: thin sheeting of Type 1B, printed.

In type references odd numbers apply to unprinted sheeting and even numbers to printed sheeting.
The standard does not apply to transparent polished sheeting, often referred to as 'glass clear' sheeting.
The term 'film' is sometimes used in a general sense, but it is recommended that this term should not be applied to PVC sheeting above 75 μm nominal thickness.
Definitions include *printed sheeting, embossed sheeting, plain frosted (mat) or polished PVC sheeting, laminated sheeting* and *roll of sheeting* (not less than 10 m length) sheeting. *Film* should be used only for sheet up to 75 μm thick.
Requirements are specified for visual examination and physical properties.
Marking is provided for by a label giving the name and/or trademark of the manufacturer, the number of this British Standard and type reference of the sheeting (and if laminated and/or embossed), nominal thickness and dimensions, and date of manufacture, if intended for printing. Further information is encouraged.

BS 2739: 1975 *Thick PVC sheeting (calendered, flexible, upsupported)*

This standard distinguishes sheeting in the nominal thickness range 250 to 900 μm inclusive, classified as follows:
Type 99: very low stiffness general purpose unprinted single or laminated thick sheeting with plain or embossed surface.
Type 100: sheeting of Type 99, printed.
Type 101: low stiffness general purpose unprinted single or laminated thick sheeting with plain or embossed surface.
Type 102: sheeting of Type 101, printed.

Type 103: medium stiffness general purpose unprinted single or laminated thick sheeting with plain or embossed surface.
Type 104: sheeting of Type 103, printed.
Type 105: high stiffness general purpose unprinted single or laminated thick sheeting with plain or embossed surface.
Type 106: sheeting of Type 105, printed.

As in BS 1763, odd numbers apply to unprinted and even numbers to printed sheeting.
The standard again does not apply to 'glass clear' sheeting.
The difficulty of defining 'stiffness' is discussed. Such properties as tensile strength, elongation at break and low temperature extendability all have a bearing on stiffness. The temperature and thickness will also affect the stiffness of a sample of sheeting as assessed by handling.
The definitions given are consistent with BS 1763.

BS 3012: 1970 *Low and intermediate density polythene sheet for general purposes.*

This standard covers sheet not less than 0.5 mm thick for general purpose including pipe fabrication, chemical, food and building industry uses.
Requirements are specified for the composition, freedom from defects, dimensions of sheets and rolls, and heat reversion.
Polythene sheet is supplied in black for general use, essential where the sheet may be exposed to direct sunlight, or natural for use where the sheet will not be exposed to direct sunlight.
Sheet dimensions and tolerances – still in imperial units from $^{1}/_{16}$ in upwards – generally about ± 10 per cent on thickness and $^{-0}_{+6}$ mm on length and width, are set out.
Tensile strength is required to be not less than 11.2 N/mm² for use with pipe or rod, 9.8 N/mm² otherwise, with a minimum elongation at break of 350 per cent.
Marking of each sheet or package is by strongly adhesive green tape or a suitably painted or stamped mark, showing manufacturer, British Standard number and the grade.

BS 4646: 1970 *High density polythene sheet for general purposes*

This standard covers sheet of nominal thickness not less than 0.5 mm for general purposes including pipe fabrication, chemical, food and building industry uses.
Requirements are specified for composition, freedom from defects, and dimensions.
Colours, sheet dimensions and tolerances are as in BS 3012.
Tensile strength is required to be not less than 19.0 N/mm² and the elongation at break should be not less than 150 per cent.
Requirements are specified in respect of heat reversion.
Marking of each sheet or package is by strongly adhesive coloured tape or a suitably or stamped mark showing the manufacturer and British Standard number.

BS 4023: 1975 *Flexible cellular PVC sheeting*

This standard covers sheets up to 25 mm in thickness for use in applications involving welding (for example padding and quilting). Sheets may be welded together. Two types of sheeting are specified:

Type 1: physically blown material, largely of open cell structure.
Type 2: chemically blown material, largely of closed cell structure, the former air-permeable, the latter usually impermeable.

Flame retardant characteristics cannot be included because no generally accepted method of test for flammability is available, but efforts to devise such a method are being made. Sheeting with such characteristics is normally coloured pink or printed with the appropriate identification.

V Film coating and impregnation work (no entry)
W Planting work

Only top soil, peat as the basic initial dressing, turf and (in outline) the most relevant planting for new building work will be touched upon here.

BS 4428: 1969 *Recommendations for general landscape operations (excluding hard surfaces)*, BS 5236: 1975 *Recommendations for the cultivation and planting of trees in the extra large nursery stock category*, BS 4043: 1966 *Recommendations for transplanting semi-mature trees* and BS 5837: 1980 *Code of practice for trees in relation to construction* form a basic source of information for the landscaper. External works, including pavements, 'hard' landscapes, fences and gates are covered in Table 1 'Building elements' under section (90) 'External works'. The relevant glossary is BS 3975 **Glossary for landscape work;** Part 4: 1966 *Plant description* and Part 5: 1966 *Horticultural, arboricultural and forestry practice.*

BS 3882: 1965 *Recommendations and classification for top soil*

This standard deals with top soil for general landscape work purposes. The standard also classifies top soil in relation to three particular characteristics – texture, reaction (lime content) and stone content – which it may sometimes be desirable to specify fairly closely. It is primarily concerned with top soil, as dug, which is to be imported on to a site.

An appendix gives notes on some relevant methods of test for top soil. Another appendix lists the information to be given for the purpose of an order or an enquiry.

BS 4156: 1967 *Peat*

This standard sets out pH values, moisture, content, ash, particle size and marking required for peat produced for general horticultural and landscape purposes.

BS 3969: 1965 *Recommendations for turf for general landscape purposes*

This standard deals with turf for general landscape purposes, such as lawns. The standard does not specify all the requirements of turf specially grown or specially selected for purposes such as bowling greens or golf greens. A coarser turf, not complying with the requirements of this standard, may be entirely satisfactory for areas where quality is less important, such as for children's playing areas or for the prevention of erosion on banks.

BS 3936 *Nursery stock*

Part 1: 1980 *Trees and shrubs*
This part deals with trees and shrubs, including woody climbing plants and conifers, that are suitable to be transplanted and grown for amenity.

Part 2: 1978 *Roses*
This part deals with rose plants that are grafted or budded on to a rootstock and are suitable for transplantation and growth for amenity purposes.

Miniature roses on their own roots are outside its stock.
The following types of rose plants are distinguished:

1 Bush and shrub roses.
2 Climbing, rambler and pillar roses.
3 Standards, half standards and weeping standards.
4 Dwarf roses.
5 Miniature roses.

Because of the natural variability of the plants and because the list of available varieties is constantly changing, no attempt is made to identify varieties with types.

Part 5: 1985 *Poplars and willows*
Covers four species of white poplars and aspens, eleven species of black poplar, five species of Balsam poplars and fifteen species of willow; including dimensions, condition and marking.

Part 10: 1981 *Ground cover plants*
Shrubs (including conifers) and herbaceous perennials (including grasses) are covered in this part.

The remaining parts in print are Part 3: 1978 *Fruit*; Part 7: 1960 *Bedding plants grown in boxes or trays*; Part 9: 1968 *Bulbs, corms and tubers*; and Part 11: 1984 *Container grown culinary herbs.*

X Work with components

This particular section includes two very large subsections: (Xt6), covering fasteners; and (Xt7), covering hardware. Four other standards justify mention. They are:

BS 4479: 1969 *Recommendations for the design of metal articles that are to be coated*

This standard sets out the design considerations for electroplating, anodic oxidation, chemical conversion, hot dipping and metal spraying. It does not cover the use of the above processes to provide coatings for engineering applications, such as heavy deposition, hard anodizing or building-up by metal spraying.

BS 4342: 1968 *Glossary of terms used in mechanized and hand sheet metal work and metal box making*

BS 4169: 1970 *Glued-laminated timber structural members*

Manufacture is expected to be carried out in a suitably equipped workshop under the supervision of properly qualified personnel, and the standard lists facilities for which provision needs to be made.

The standard deals with structural components manufactured from separate pieces of timber arranged in laminations parallel to the axis of the member, the individual pieces being assembled with the grain approximately parallel, and glued together to form a member which functions as a single structural unit.

Timber may be any of the softwoods and hardwoods set out, selected and graded in accordance with CP 112, any lamination not over 47 mm thick, or regulated moisture content. Temperature, the use of mixed species (permitted), and conversion (both quarter-sawn and flat-sawn permitted, in mixed use) are all discussed.

Three types of adhesive are permitted:

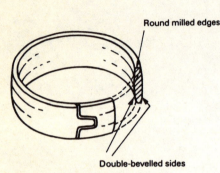

(a) Split-ring with bevelled sides

Connectors nos. 1b and 1c
67 and 102 mm internal diameter
19 and 25.5 mm deep
13 and 19 mm diameter bolt
51 and 96 mm square washer
(3 and 5 mm thick)
Connector no. 1a as 1b, but parallel sides

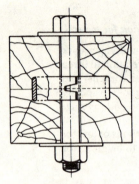

(b) Split-ring connector unit
(may also have bevelled sides)

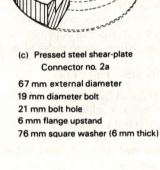

(c) Pressed steel shear-plate
Connector no. 2a

67 mm external diameter
19 mm diameter bolt
21 mm bolt hole
6 mm flange upstand
76 mm square washer (6 mm thick)

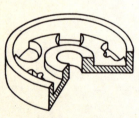

(d) Malleable cast iron shear-plate
connector no. 2b

102 mm external diameter
9 mm diameter bolt
21 mm bolt hole
11 mm upstand
76 mm square washer (6 mm thick)

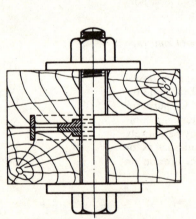

(e) Two shear-plates used back to back as in a
demountable structure

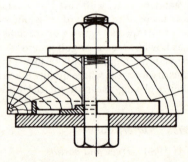

(f) Shear-plate connector unit for timber-to-metal joint

(g) Double-sided round toothed-plate
connector

Connectors nos. 3c, 3d, 3f and 3h
38, 51, 67 and 76 mm diameter
20, 20, 18 and 18 g thick
9, 12, 12 and 12 mm diameter bolts
11, 14, 14 and 14 mm diameter bolt holes
9, 9, 9 and 10 mm high teeth
38, 38, 51 and 51 mm square washers (all 6 mm thick)

Figure 89 *Connectors for timber*

Casein adhesives: Type A of BS 1444, for interior structures, with a moisture content of 18 per cent

Urea formaldehyde adhesives: Type MR of BS 1204 Part 1, used only for interior conditions with a wider moisture content, but temperature below 50 °C

Resorcinol and phenolic adhesives: Type WBP of BS 1204 Part 1, suitable for both interior and exterior structures without restriction on temperature and humidity conditions (except cold setting phenolic adhesives – not suitable for service conditions of high temperature and high humidity).

Requirements are specified for laminations, joints and gluing, and preservative and flame retardant treatment. A revision is in hand.

BS 6446: 1984 *Manufacture of glued structural components of timber and wood-based panel products*

Sets out requirements for the manufacture of structural compo-

nents (e.g. box beams, single-web beams, stressed-skin panels, glued gussets) made from separate pieces of timber. Plywood or tempered hardboard that are glued together and for which the continued integrity of the glued joint is essential for satisfactory performance in service. Requirements are specified for production facilities, materials, types of joint, production, product control, preservative and flame retardant treatments and storage.

Components manufactured in accordance with this Standard are not suitable for use in service conditions where they are exposed directly to the weather, e.g. marine structures. The standard does not apply to glued-laminated timber structural members (see BS 4169) or finger joints in structural softwood (see BS 5291) (in Table 3 Materials, i wood).

Recommendations on the design of components are given in BS 5268 *Structural use of timber* Part 2: 1984 (see Table 1 Building elements (–2) structures, etc.).

Prior to production the manufacturer must obtain details of the service conditions and the anticipated equilibrium values of

(h) Single-sided round toothed-plate

Connectors nos. 3a, 3c, 3e, 3g and 3j
38, 51, 67, 76 and 95 mm diameter
20, 20, 18, 18 and 16 g thick
9, 12, 12, 12 and 19 diameter bolts
11, 14, 14, 14 and 21 mm bolt holes
6, 7, 9, 10 and 11 mm high teeth
38, 38, 51, 51 and 83 mm square washers
(all 6 mm thick)

(i) Double-sided round toothed-plate connector unit

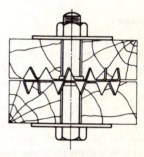

(j) Two single-sided round toothed-plates used back to back as in a demountable structure

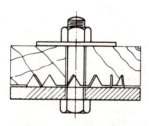

(k) Single-sided round toothed-plate connector unit for timber-to-metal joint

(l) Double-sided square toothed-plate

Connectors nos. 4b, 4d, 4f, 4h and 4k
38, 51, 67, 76 and 89 diameter
18, 18, 16, 16 and 16 g thick
11, 14, 14, 14 and 22 mm bolt holes
6, 6, 9, 9 and 13 mm high teeth
38, 51, 57, 76 and 89 mm square or round washers (3, 3, 3, 5 and 5 mm thick)

(m) Single-sided square toothed-plate

Connectors nos. 4a, 4c, 4e, 4g and 4j
38, 51, 67, 76 and 89 mm diameter
18, 18, 16, 16 and 16 g thick
11, 14, 14, 14 and 22 mm bolt holes
6, 6, 9, 9 and 13 mm high teeth
38, 51, 57, 76 and 89 mm square or round washers (3, 3, 3, 5 and 5 mm thick)

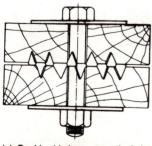

(n) Double-sided square toothed-plate connector unit

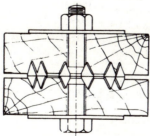

(o) Two single-sided square toothed-plates used back to back as in a demountable structure

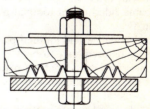

(p) Single-sided square toothed-plate connector unit for timber-to-metal joint

(Figures 1–16: BS 1579: 1960)

moisture content and submit the following details to the client for agreement: the types of material; preservative and flame-retardant treatments; the moisture content of the component in service; the dimensions of individual pieces and the component; the deviations assembled component dimensions; the method of assembly; the location of joints and splices; the camber; and the surface finishes.

The species or type and grade of timber, plywood and tempered hardboard will be selected from those for which mechanical properties are given in BS 5268: Part 2.

Each component is marked with the following:

(a) the name, trade mark or other means of identification of the manufacturer;
(b) the reference related to the records of production.

The mark is positioned so that it is accessible in the final construction except where visual appearance requirements dictate otherwise.

Components are to be marked to show the orientation of the component in service where this is critical.

Xt6   Fasteners

This subsection is further subdivided into a sequence of nuts, screws, bolts, washers and kindred fastenings for wood and metal, rivets and the like, and specialized fixings. Dealt with elsewhere are wall ties (Table 1 'Building elements', section (21) 'Walls') and pipe hangers and like (Table 1, section (59) 'Parts accessories'). A significant number of imperial standards remain, in obsolescent form, reflecting the need of the maintenance side of the building industry to continue to have replacement components matching existing work. They are not separately dealt with here; in general differences from metric standards are merely dimensional.

BS Handbook 44: 1982 *Threaded fasteners* covers much of the material. One standard (BS 1579) deals with timber connectors, two standards with general issues, two standards deal with 'black' bolts and screws and the like – the term 'black' implying comparatively wider tolerances than 'precision' or machine screws etc., which are considered in a group of thirteen standards. Rivets are dealt with in five standards, of which three are included here, and specialized fitments are dealt with in a further five standards.

Throughout this section, figures in brackets refer to *non-preferred* sizes (see BS 3643: ISO Metric screw threads Part 1: 1981 *Principles and basic data*).

BS 1579: 1960   *Connectors for timber*

This standard distinguishes nine types of connector units for timber (see Figure 89(a) – (p)).

(a) One split-ring, with bolt, washers and nut.
(b) Two-shear plates, with bolt, washers and nut, to be used back-to-back.
(c) One shear-plate with bolt, washer and nut, for use in conjunction with a steel strap or plate in timber-to-metal joint.
(d) One double-sided round toothed-plate with bolt washers and nut.
(e) Two single-sided round toothed-plates with bolt, washers and nut, to be used back-to-back.
(f) One single-sided round toothed-plate with bolt washer and nut, for use in conjunction with a steel strap or plate in a timber-to-metal joint.
(g) One double-sided square toothed-plate with bolt, washers and nut.
(h) Two single-sided square toothed-plates with bolt, washers and nut, to be used back-to-back.
(i) One single-sided square toothed-plate with bolt, washer and nut, for use in conjunction with a steel strap or plate in a timber-to-metal joint.

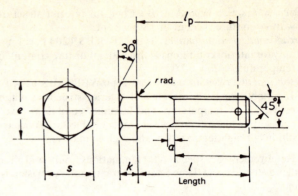

(Figure 3: BS 4190: 1967)

Figure 90   *Hexagon head bolt*

BS 4190: 1967   *ISO metric black hexagon bolts, screws and nuts*

BS 916: 1952, BS 1769: 1951 and BS 2708: 1956 deal with the imperial equivalents (the latter extending to square headed bolts etc.).

This standard deals with items in diameters from 5 to 68 mm inclusive. Larger sizes are touched on, in Appendix C. Material, manufacture and mechanical properties are given, accepted finishes ('black' and 'partly machined') and dimensional requirements are included which are largely identical to those in BS 3962.

Lengths of bolts and screws are as shown in Figure 90, tolerances are specified, and the range is given in Table 120.

Ends of bolts and screws may be chamfered or rounded.

Screw threads in this and subsequent standards as are set out in BS 3643 (see introduction to this section).

Table 120   *List of sizes (non-preferred sizes are given in brackets) ISO metric nuts, etc.*

Nominal size and thread diameter	Pitch of thread	Nominal size and thread diameter	Pitch of thread
d	(Coarse pitch series)	d	(Coarse pitch series)
M5	0.8	M30	3.5
M6	1	(M33)	3.5
M8	1.25	M36	4
M10	1.5	(M39)	4
M12	1.75	M42	4.5
M16	2	(M45)	4.5
M20	2.5	M48	5
(M22)	2.5	(M52)	5
M24	3	M56	5.5
(M27)	3	(M60)	5.5
		M64	6
		(M68)	6

Note: M5 not available with turned shank. (From text BS 4190: 1967)

Chamfering and facing are prescribed, the standard chamfer being 30 °; bearing faces optionally machined, bolt and screws with an optional 'washer face' (see Figure 91).

Bolts with split pin holes will be supplied only when specially ordered.

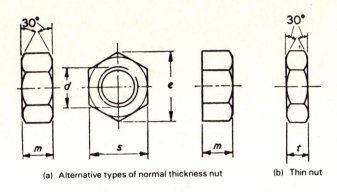

(a) Alternative types of normal thickness nut   (b) Thin nut

(Figures 6 and 7: BS 4190: 1967)

Figure 91 *Types of nut. Sizes correspond with bolts in Figure 100*

Table 121 *Strength grade designations for steel bolts and screws*

Strength grade designation	4.6	4.8	6.9
Tensile strength Rm minimum, kgf/mm² (N/mm²)*	40 (392)*	40 (392)	60 (588)
Yield stress Ro minimum, kgf/mm² (N/mm²)	24 (235)	32 (314)	—
Stress at permanent set limit $R_{0.2}$ minimum, kgf/mm² (N/mm²)	—	—	54 (538)

*SI interpretation.

(Adapted from Table 7: BS 4190: 1967)

The strength grade designation system for steel bolts and screws consists of two figures: the first one-tenth of the minimum tensile strength in kilograms/force per square millimetre, and the second one-tenth of the ratio between the minimum yield stress (or stress at permanent set limit $R_{0.2}$) and the minimum tensile strength, expressed as a percentage. See Table 121.

Requirements are specified for material, manufacture and mechanical properties.

The strength grade designation system for steel nuts is a number which is one-tenth of the specified proof load stress in kilograms/force per square millimetre. See Table 122.

Table 122 *Strength grade designations for steel nuts*

Strength grade designation	4	6
Proof load stress kgf/mm² (N/mm²)*	40 (392)*	60 (588)

*SI interpretation.

(Adapted from Table 8: BS 4190: 1967)

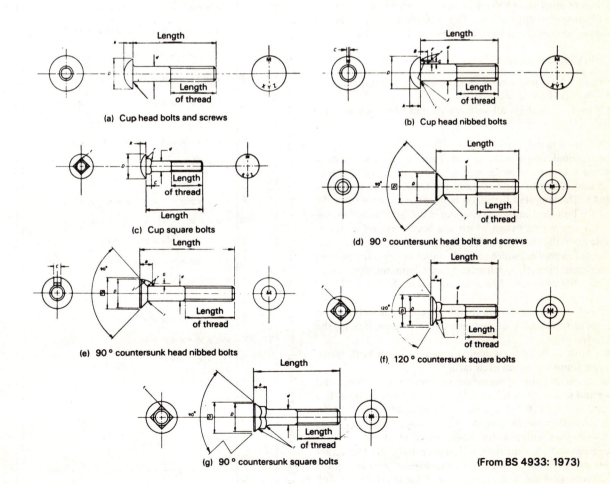

(a) Cup head bolts and screws

(b) Cup head nibbed bolts

(c) Cup square bolts

(d) 90° countersunk head bolts and screws

(e) 90° countersunk head nibbed bolts

(f) 120° countersunk square bolts

(g) 90° countersunk square bolts

(From BS 4933: 1973)

Figure 92 *Types of bolt and screw. ISO metric black cup and countersunk bolts, etc.*

It is recommended that the grades of nut to be used with each grade of bolt or screw should be (bolt first) 4.6 + 4, 4.8 + 4, 6.9 + 6.

Marking and identification is restricted to bolts and screws of 6 mm and larger; not nuts.

Complete designation for the purpose of an enquiry or order is set out, and closely follows that in BS 3692.

BS 4933: 1973 *ISO metric black cup and countersunk head bolts and screws with hexagon nuts*

BS 325: 1947 deals with the imperial equivalent.

This standard covers seven types of bolts (see Figure 92):

a Cup head bolts with nibs.
b Cup head nibbed bolts.
c Cup head square neck bolts.
d 90° countersunk head bolts and screws.
e 90° countersunk head bolts and nibs.
f 120° countersunk head square neck bolts.
g 90° countersunk head square neck bolts.

The standard covers similar issues to BS 4190, and this summary is confined to diagrams and ranges.

The range of sizes in all cases comprises M5, M6, M8, M10, M12, M16, M20 and M24 (for details see the summary of BS 4190).

BS 3692: 1967 *ISO metric precision hexagon bolts, screws and nuts*

BS 1768: 1963 and BS 1083: 1965 deal with the imperial equivalents.

This standard covers diameters from 1.6 to 68 mm inclusive.

Material and manufacture, including the method of production, is covered. Mechanical properties are given only in respect of carbon or alloy steel bolts, screws and nuts, which are not to be used for special applications. The dimensional requirements also apply to non-ferrous and stainless steel bolts, screws and nuts.

Finishes are normally:

Heat-treated bolts and screws: customarily dull black, or *Bright-finished bolts and screws*.

Nuts may be bright on all surfaces or dull black when heat-treated.

Other finishes may be agreed, see BS 3382.

The nominal length of bolts and screws is defined. Ends of bolts and screws may be chamfered or rounded. The form of thread and diameters and associated pitches are as set out in BS 3643. The length of thread on bolts is the distance from the end of the bolt (including any chamfer or radius) to the leading face of a screw ring gauge which has been screwed as far as possible on to the bolt by hand. In the case of screws an alternative definition applies, which gives clearance beneath the head of two and a half times the pitch up to 52 mm diameter, three and a half times the pitch over that size. See Tables 127 and 128 for sizes.

Bolt and screw heads have a chamfer of approximately 40° on their upper faces and a washer face or full bearing face on the underside.

Nuts have a chamfer of approximately 30° on both faces. They are countersunk on each face.

The strength grade designation system for steel bolts and screws and nuts is as in BS 4190, but with a greater range. See Tables 124, and 126 for bolt and nut combinations.

The strength grade designation system for steel nuts is again as in BS 4190, but with a wider range. See Table 125.

Marking and identification is required only for the larger items (above 6 mm diameter) in the higher strength grade designations (8.8 for bolts and screws, 8 for nuts) are set out.

Information to be given for the purpose of an enquiry or order is set out.

Table 123 *Standard nominal lengths and preferred sizes of metric black hexagon bolts and screws*

Nominal size and thread diameter	12	14	16	20	25	30	35	40	45	50	55	60	65	70	75	80	85	90	100	110	120	130	140	150	160	170	180	190	200	220	240	260	280	300	325	350	375	400	425	450	475	500
M5	×	×	×	×	×	×	×	×	×	×																																
M6	×	×	×	×	×	×	×	×	×	×	×	×	×																													
M8	×	×	×	×	×	×	×	×	×	×	×	×	×	×	×	×																										
M10			×	×	×	×	×	×	×	×	×	×	×	×	×	×	×	×	×																							
M12				×	×	×	×	×	×	×	×	×	×	×	×	×	×	×	×	×	×	×	×																			
M16				×	×	×	×	×	×	×	×	×	×	×	×	×	×	×	×	×	×	×	×	×	×	×	×	×	×													
M20					×	×	×	×	×	×	×	×	×	×	×	×	×	×	×	×	×	×	×	×	×	×	×	×	×	×	×	×										
(M22)						×	×	×	×	×	×	×	×	×	×	×	×	×	×	×	×	×	×	×	×	×	×	×	×	×	×	×	×	×								
M24							×	×	×	×	×	×	×	×	×	×	×	×	×	×	×	×	×	×	×	×	×	×	×	×	×	×	×	×	×							
(M27)								×	×	×	×	×	×	×	×	×	×	×	×	×	×	×	×	×	×	×	×	×	×	×	×	×	×	×	×	×						
M30									×	×	×	×	×	×	×	×	×	×	×	×	×	×	×	×	×	×	×	×	×	×	×	×	×	×	×	×	×					
(M33)										×	×	×	×	×	×	×	×	×	×	×	×	×	×	×	×	×	×	×	×	×	×	×	×	×	×	×	×	×				
M36											×	×	×	×	×	×	×	×	×	×	×	×	×	×	×	×	×	×	×	×	×	×	×	×	×	×	×	×	×			
M39												×	×	×	×	×	×	×	×	×	×	×	×	×	×	×	×	×	×	×	×	×	×	×	×	×	×	×	×	×		
M42													×	×	×	×	×	×	×	×	×	×	×	×	×	×	×	×	×	×	×	×	×	×	×	×	×	×	×	×	×	
(M45)														×	×	×	×	×	×	×	×	×	×	×	×	×	×	×	×	×	×	×	×	×	×	×	×	×	×	×	×	×
M48															×	×	×	×	×	×	×	×	×	×	×	×	×	×	×	×	×	×	×	×	×	×	×	×	×	×	×	×
(M52)																×	×	×	×	×	×	×	×	×	×	×	×	×	×	×	×	×	×	×	×	×	×	×	×	×	×	×
M56																	×	×	×	×	×	×	×	×	×	×	×	×	×	×	×	×	×	×	×	×	×	×	×	×	×	×
(M60)																		×	×	×	×	×	×	×	×	×	×	×	×	×	×	×	×	×	×	×	×	×	×	×	×	×
M64																			×	×	×	×	×	×	×	×	×	×	×	×	×	×	×	×	×	×	×	×	×	×	×	×
(M68)																				×	×	×	×	×	×	×	×	×	×	×	×	×	×	×	×	×	×	×	×	×	×	×

Standard nominal lengths (l)

Screws only ← → Screws and bolts ← → Screws and bolts

NOTE 1: Sizes shown in brackets are non-preferred.
NOTE 2: The inclusion of dimensional data in this standard is not intended to imply that all of the products described are stock production sizes. The purchaser is requested to consult with the manufacturer concerning lists of stock production sizes.

(Table 13: BS 4190: 1967)

Table 124 *Strength grade designation of steel bolts and screws*

Strength grade designation	4.6	4.8	5.6	5.8	6.6	6.8	8.8	10.9	12.9	14.9
Tensile strength R_m min. kgf/mm² (N/mm²)*	40 (392)*	40 (392)	50 (490)	50 (490)	60 (588)	60 (588)	80 (784)	100 (980)	120 (1176)	140 (1372)
Yield stress R_0 min. kgf/mm² (N/mm²)	24 (238)	32 (314)	30 (294)	40 (392)	36 (353)	48 (471)	–	–	–	–
Stress at permanent set limit $R_{0.2}$ mm kgf/mm² (N/mm²)	–	–	–	–	–		64 (627)	90 (882)	108 (1058)	126 (1235)

*SI interpretation. (Adapted from Table 2: BS 3692: 1967)

Table 126 *Recommended bolt and nut combinations*

Grade of bolt	4.6	4.8	5.6	5.8	6.6	6.8	8.8	10.9	12.9	14.9
Recommended grade of nut	4	4	5	5	6	6	8	12	12	14

(Table 4: BS 3692: 1967)

Table 125 *Strength grade designations of steel nuts*

Strength grade designation	4	5	6	8	12	14
Proof load Stress kgf/mm² (N/mm²)*	40 (392)*	50 (490)	60 (588)	80 (784)	120 (1176)	140 (1372)

*SI interpretation. (Adapted from Table 3: BS 3692: 1967)

ISO metric precision hexagon bolts and screws include all dimensions shown in Figure 93.

ISO metric precision hexagon nuts and thin nuts, and a range corresponding to bolts, include all dimensions shown in Figure 94.

ISO metric precision hexagon slotted nuts and castle nuts and a range corresponding to all bolts from M4 inclusive upwards, include all dimensions shown in Figure 95.

Tolerances on the standard nominal lengths of bolts and screws are tabulated and diagrams and tables in an appendix show methods of marking.

BS 4168 *Hexagon socket screws and wrench keys – metric series*

BS 2470: 1973 is the imperial equivalent.

This standard deals with eight types of screws with ISO metric

Table 127 *List of sizes (as BS 4190 with the addition of M1.6 to M4)*

Nominal size and thread diameter d	Pitch of thread (coarse pitch series)	Nominal size and thread diameter d	Pitch of thread (coarse pitch series)
M 1.6	0.35	M24	3
M 2	0.4	(M27)	3
M 2.5	0.45	M30	3.5
M 3	0.5	(M33)	3.5
M 4	0.7	M36	4
M 5	0.8	(M39)	4
M 6	1	M42	4.5
M 8	1.25	(M45)	4.5
M10	1.5	M48	5
M12	1.75	(M52)	5
(M14)	2	M56	5.5
M16	2	(M60)	5.5
(M18)	2.5	M64	6
M20	2.5	(M68)	6
(M22)	2.5		

Note: Sizes shown in brackets are non-preferred.

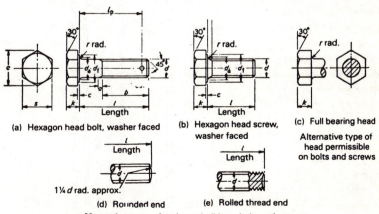

(a) Hexagon head bolt, washer faced

(b) Hexagon head screw, washer faced

(c) Full bearing head
Alternative type of head permissible on bolts and screws

1¼ d rad. approx.

(d) Rounded end

(e) Rolled thread end

Alternative types of end permissible on bolts and screws

(Figures 2–6: BS 3692: 1967)

Figure 93 *ISO metric precision hexagon bolts and screws*

Table 128 *Preferred standard sizes of ISO metric precision hexagon bolts and screws*

All dimensions in millimetres

Nominal size and thread dia. d	Standard nominal lengths (l)
M1.6	
M2	
M2.5	
M3	
M4	
M5	
M6	
M8	
M10	
M12	
(M14)	
M16	
(M18)	
M20	
(M22)	
M24	
(M27)	
M30	
(M33)	
M36	
(M39)	
M42	
(M45)	
M48	
(M52)	
M56	
(M60)	
M64	
(M68)	

Standard nominal lengths (l): 5, 6, (7), 8, (9), 10, (11), 12, 14, 16, (18), 20, (22), 25, (28), 30, (32), 35, (38), 40, 45, 50, 55, 60, 65, 70, 75, 80, 85, 90, (95), 100, (105), 110, (115), 120, (125), 130, 140, 150, 160, 170, 180, 190, 200, 220, 240, 260, 280, 300, 325, 350, 375, 400

Screws only — Bolts and screws

Note 1: Sizes and lengths shown in brackets are non-preferred.
Note 2: X indicates first choice length.
Note 3: O indicates second choice length.
Note 4: The inclusion of dimensional data in this standard is not intended to imply that all of the products described are stock production sizes. The purchaser is requested to consult with the manufacturer concerning lists of stock production sizes.

(Table 21: BS 3692: 1967)

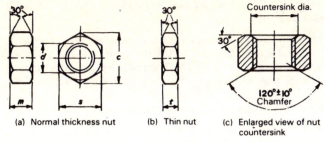

(a) Normal thickness nut   (b) Thin nut   (c) Enlarged view of nut countersink

(Figures 7 – 9: BS 3692: 1967)

Figure 94 *ISO metric precision nuts and thin nuts*

threads and wrench keys for use with them. The eight types are:

Part 1: 1981 *Cap screws*
Part 2: 1981 *Set screws with flat point*
Part 3: 1981 *Set screws with cone point*
Part 4: 1981 *Set screws with dog point*
Part 5: 1981 *Set screws with cup point*
Part 6: 1982 *Button head screws*
Part 7: 1982 *Shoulder screws*
Part 8: 1982 *Countersunk head*
Part 9: 1983 *Wrench keys.*

They are variously available in range from M1.6 or M3 to M12, M20, M24 or M36.

BS 4174: 1972 *Self-tapping screws and metallic drive screws*

This standard deals with ferrous and non-ferrous tapping screws and metallic drive screws.

Three types of screw are distinguished: thread forming screws, thread cutting screws and metallic drive screws.

Thread forming screws are for application in materials which allow sufficient plastic deformation to enable the thread to be formed by displacement without the removal of any material. Types are:

Type AB; with widely spaced threads and gimlet points, intended for use in light sheet metal, metal-clad and resin-impregnated plywood, soft plastics, etc.
Type B: with widely spaced threads and blunt, slightly tapered points, intended for use in light and heavy sheet metal, non-ferrous castings, soft plastics, metal-clad and resin-impregnated plywood, etc.
Type A: with widely spaced threads and gimlet points. The pitch is coarser than for Types AB and B. They are primarily intended for use in light sheet metal, metal-clade and resin-impregnated plywood, soft plastics, etc. Now obsolescent, and it is recommended that Type AB be substituted.

Thread cutting screws are for application in materials which do not allow plastic deformation to an extent sufficient for thread

forming screws, but may be used in materials which do allow plastic deformation and may have the advantage of a lower driving torque than thread forming screws and sometimes the further advantage of a standard machine screw thread form. Types are:

Type BT: primarily intended for use in light and heavy sheet metal, non-ferrous castings, plastics, die castings, metal-clad and resin-impregnated plywood, asbestos and other compositions.
Type Y: primarily intended for use in plastics, die castings, metal-clad and resin-impregnated plywood, asbestos and other compositions.
Type D: suitable for use in such materials as aluminium, zinc, and lead die castings, steel sheets and shapes, cast iron, brass, plastics, etc.
Type T: used as Type D.

Metallic drive screws are designated Type U. Primarily for use in cast iron, metal shapes and plastics, these screws are hammered or forced into the appropriate holes and are intended for making permanent fastenings.

Material and manufacture may be of steel, heat treated, which must comply with the test requirements of this standard, or corrosion-resistant steel, brass, monel and aluminium, but screws made from these materials should not be subject to the test requirements of this standard.

Finishes include plated or other protective and/or decorative finish. Length of screws is defined and tolerance requirements are specified. Requirements are specified for screw threads, diameter of unthreaded shank, radius under head and testing.

Designation for ordering is given.

Screw sizes (mm) and the relevant further dimensions to BS 3643, shown in Table 129, are set out for the following head styles.

80 ° countersunk head screws 'C' 2.
80 ° truncated countersunk head screws 'C'.
80 ° raised countersunk head screws 'R'.
80 ° truncated raised countersunk 'R' head screws.
(All four diameters 2 (× 2) to 16.)
Panhead screws 'P' 2 (× 2) to 16.
Mushroom head screws 'M' 4 (× 2) to 14.
Recessed flange head screws 'M' 4 (× 2) to 14.
Hexagon head screws 'H' 4 (× 2) to 16.
Round head Type U metallic drive screws 00, 0, 2 (× 2) to 6, 7, 8 (× 2) to 14.

BS 4183: 1967 *Machine screws and machine screw nuts*

BS 450: 1958 and BS 1981: 1974 deal with the imperial equivalents.

This standard covers screws and nuts having ISO metric threads.

The generic term 'screws' has been adopted here as applying

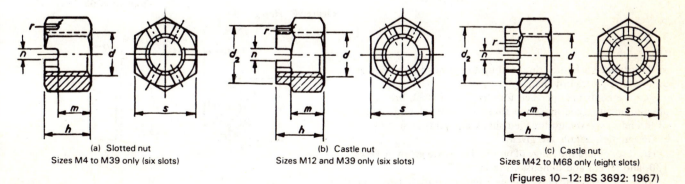

(a) Slotted nut
Sizes M4 to M39 only (six slots)

(b) Castle nut
Sizes M12 and M39 only (six slots)

(c) Castle nut
Sizes M42 to M68 only (eight slots)

(Figures 10 – 12: BS 3692: 1967)

Figure 95 *ISO metric precision hexagon slotted nuts and castle nuts. Sizes correspond with bolts and screws in Figure 93*

Table 129 *Types of screws and type designations for tapping screws and metallic drive screws (the length from an appendix)*

Thread contour	Type of screw	Type designation for tapping screws and metallic drive screws
	Thread forming	AB Length 4.5 to 50 mm
	Thread forming	B (formerly Z) Length 3.2 to 5.0 mm
	Thread cutting	T (formerly 23) Length 4.5 to 45 mm
	Thread cutting	Y Length 6.5 to 25 mm
	Thread cutting	D (formerly 1) Length 4.5 to 45 mm
	Thread cutting	BT (formerly 25) Length 4.5 to 45 mm
	Drive	U Length 3.2 to 25 mm
	Thread forming	A Not recommended, use Type AB Length 4.5 to 50 mm

(From BS 4174: 1972)

BS 4186: 1967 *Recommendations for clearance holes for metric bolts and screws*

This standard tabulates three series of clearance holes for metric bolts and screws, from 1.6 to 150 mm diameter. The series are *close fit*, *medium fit* and *free fit*. Tolerances are set out. Comment is made that medium fit will suit the majority of applications.

BS 4219 *Slotted set screws – metric series*

Part 1: 1985 *Slotted set screws with flat point*
Part 2: 1985 *Slotted set screws with cone points*
Part 3: 1985 *Slotted set screws with long dog points*; and
Part 4: 1985 *Slotted set screws with cup points*.
This standard covers screws having ISO metric coarse pitch series threads with first choice diameters in the range M1.2 (1.2 mm) to M12 (12 mm) inclusive M1.6 to M12 in Part 3.

The materials given are: *steel*, class 14H or 22H to BS 6104: Part 3; *stainless steel* class A1–50 to BS 6105 or *non-ferrous metal*.

A range of twenty lengths (nineteen preferred) from 2 to 50 mm is given. A range of twelve nominal sizes from M1.2 to M12 is given.

BS 4395 *High strength friction grip bolts and associated nuts and washers for structural engineering*

Part 1: 1969 *General grade*
This part deals with one (general) grade of quenched and tempered hexagon head bolts and their associated nuts and washers for use in structural engineering in a range of nominal sizes from M12 (12 mm) to M36 (36 mm) inclusive. Mechanical properties are specified. Full details of tests, inspection procedure and provisions for marking are also included.

The term 'high strength friction grip bolts' relates to bolts of high tensile steel, used in conjunction with high tensile steel nuts and quenched and tempered steel washers, which are tightened to a predetermined shank tension in order that the clamping force thus provided will transfer loads in the connected members by friction between the parts and not by shear in or bearing on the bolts or plies of connected members.

The mechanical properties of bolts are set out in Table 131.

The dimensions for hexagon head bolts are shown in Figure 96 and given in Table 132.

Washer dimensions are the same as those given for nuts. See Figure 97 and Table 133.

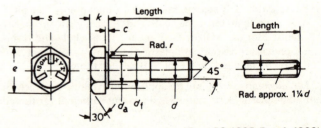

Figure 96 *Hexagon bolts*   (From BS 4395: Part 1: 1969)

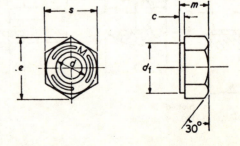

Figure 97 *Hexagon nut*   (From BS 4395: Part 1: 1969)

to the products whether threaded up to the head or having an unthreaded portion of shank.

Requirements are specified for strength of steel, brass, and aluminium alloy, coating, screw threads, nominal length, length of thread in screws, unthreaded shank and ends of screws.

Designation details are given.

Head styles and the range of nominal sizes are given in Table 130, and length and dimensions in mm.

Nuts are given in eleven sizes (nine preferred, two non-preferred) in two styles, hexagonal and square, M1.6 to M10.

Table 130 *Head styles, nominal sizes and indication of lengths: machine screws and nuts*

Head styles	Nominal sizes	Lengths
Slotted countersunk head machine screws	M1, M1.2, (M1.4),	1.5 to 200 (2 to 60 normally available)
Recessed countersunk head machine screws	M1.6, M2, (M2.2),	38 preferred, 12 non-preferred.
Slotted raised countersunk head machine screws	M2.5, M3, (M3.5),	1.5 to 200 (2 to 50 normally available)
Recessed countersunk head machine screws (Slotted and recessed panhead machine screws)*	M4, (M4.5), M5,	38 preferred, 12 non-preferred.
Recessed countersunk head machine screws Slotted cheese head machine screws	M6, M8, M10, M12, (M14), M16, (M18), M20	5 to 100 (5 to 60 normally available) 24 preferred, 8 non-preferred.

*Only the range from M2.5 to M10, inclusive.

(Tables 2 and 10–16: BS 4183: 1967)

Table 131 *Mechanical properties of bolts (hardness requirements also included): general grade friction grip bolts*

1	2	3		4	15	16	Standard nominal lengths†	
Nominal size and thread diameter d	Pitch of thread p	Diameter of unthreaded shank d			Thickness of head k			
	(coarse pitch series)	Maximum		Minimum	Maximum	Mininum	Minimum	Maximum
M 12*	1.75	12.70		11.30	8.45	7.55	40	300
M 16	2.0	16.70		15.30	10.45	9.55	50	300
M 20	2.5	20.84		19.16	13.90	12.10	60	300
M 22	2.5	22.84		21.16	14.90	13.10	65	300
M 24	3.0	24.84		23.16	15.90	14.10	70	300
M 27	3.0	27.84		26.16	17.90	16.10	75	500
M 30	3.5	30.84		29.16	20.05	17.95	85	500
M 36	4.0	37.0		35.0	24.05	21.95	100	500

*Non-preferred.
†From the appendix.

(Table 5: BS 4395: Part 1: 1969)

Table 132 *Dimensions of hexagon head bolts (in mm): high strength friction grip bolts*

1	2	3	5	7	9	10
Nominal size and thread diameter d mm	Pitch of thread (coarse pitch series) p mm	Tensile stress area A_s mm²	Ultimate load minimum kN	Yield load or load at permanent set limit $R_{0.2}$ minimum kN	Proof load minimum kN	Elongation after fracture per cent minimum
M 12*	1.75	84.3	69.6	53.5	49.4	12
M 16	2.0	157	130	99.7	92.1	12
M 20	2.5	245	203	155	144	12
M 22	2.5	303	250	192	177	12
M 24	3.0	353	292	225	207	12
M 27	3.0	459	333	259	234	12
M 30	3.5	561	406	313	286	12
M 36	4.0	817	591	445	418	12

*Non-preferred. Only to be used for the lighter type of construction.

(Table 4: BS 4395: Part 1: 1969)

Table 133 *Dimensions of hexagon nuts (in mm): high tensile steel nuts*

1	2	7		8	9	10		11
	Pitch of thread p	Diameter of washer df			Depth of washer face c	Thickness of nut m		Proof load†
Nominal size and thread diameter d	(coarse pitch series)	Maximum	Minimum		Maximum	Maximum	Minimum	kN
M 12*	1.75	22.00	19.91		0.4	11.55	10.45	84.3
M 16	2.0	27.00	24.91		0.4	15.55	14.45	157
M 20	2.5	32.00	29.75		0.4	18.55	17.45	245
M 22	2.5	36.00	33.75		0.4	19.65	18.35	303
M 24	3.0	41.00	38.75		0.5	22.65	21.35	353
M 27	3.0	46.00	43.75		0.5	24.65	23.35	459
M 30	3.5	50.00	47.75		0.5	26.65	25.35	561
M 36	4.0	60.00	57.75		0.5	31.80	30.20	817

*Non-preferred.
†From another table in this standard.

(Table 8: BS 4395: Part 1: 1969)

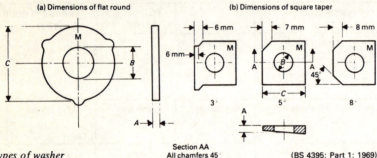

Figure 98 *Types of washer*

Dimensions and tolerances for three types of washer – plain washers, taper washers and clipped washers – are set out. The sizes correspond with bolts and nuts. See Figure 98.

An appendix gives a test programme covering tensile strength, yield stress or stress at permanent set limit of 0.2 per cent, percentage elongation after fracture, stress under proof load, strength under wedge loading and hardness.

Part 2: 1969 *Higher grade bolts and nuts and general grade washers*
This part covers higher grade (strength grade 10.9) bolts and their associated nuts (strength grade 12) and washers for use in structural engineering, in a more limited range of nominal sizes than in Part 1 from M16 (16 mm) to M33 (33 mm).

Terminology is as Part 1.

Bolts are marked '109' and nuts are marked '12' for identification. Relevant properties are given in Tables 134 and 135.

The dimensions of hexagon head bolts are as in Part 1, with the different head marking described, and the more restricted size range given. In respect of size M3, p = 3.5, d = 34 to 32 and k = 22.05 to 19.95 (see Table 132).

In almost all respects the requirements and provisions under Part 2 for washers are similar to those under Part 1. A further test method for hardness is included, and the size range is

Table 134 *Mechanical properties of bolts (hardness requirements also included): higher strength friction grip bolts*

1	2	3	4	5	6	7	8	9	10
Nominal size and thread diameter d	Pitch of thread ISO metric coarse series p	Tensile stress area A_s		Ultimate load minimum		Load at permanent set limit $R_{0.2}$ min minimum		Proof load minimum	Elongation after fracture
mm	mm	mm²		kN		kN		kN	% minimum
M 16	2.0	157		154.1		138.7		122.2	9
M 20	2.5	245	. . . .	240.0	. . . .	216	. . . .	190.4	9
M 22	2.5	303		296.5		266		235.5	9
M 24	3.0	353		346		312		274.6	9
M 27	3.0	459		450		406		356	9
M 30	3.5	561		550		495		435	9
M 33	3.5	694		680		612		540	9

(From Table 4: BS 4395 Part 2: 1969)

Table 135 *Mechanical properties of nuts (coarse pitch series)*

Nominal size and thread diameter d	Proof load kilo-newtons
M 16	184.4
M 20	288.4
M 22	356.9
M 24	415.4
M 27	540.0
M 30	660.0
M 33	817.0

(From Table 7: BS 4395: Part 2: 1969)

smaller (and similar to that for bolts and nuts).

In an appendix there is a more restricted range of standard nominal lengths than in Part 1 and they are as follows:

M 16	60–300
M 20	70–300
M 22	75–300
M 24	80–300
M 27	85–500
M 30	100–300
M 33	100–300 (all in mm)

Part 3: 1973 *Higher grade bolts (waisted shank), nuts and general grade washers*
This part covers higher grade (10.9) bolts (waisted shanks) and their associated nuts (grade 12) and washers, for structural engineering, of the same range of sizes as in Part 2. Table 136 gives the different mechanical properties, and Figure 99 shows the general form. See Table 1 Building Elements (2–) Structure, etc.

BS 4929 *Steel hexagon prevailing-torque type nuts*

The standard is in two parts, dealing respectively with metric and imperial units. Only Part 1 is given here.

Part 1: 1973 *Metric series*
This standard covers general dimensions and tolerances of nuts with ISO metric threads in diameters from 3 to 36 mm inclusive – M3 (× 1) to M6 (× 2) to M12 (× 4) to M24, M30 and M36 preferred, M14, M22 and M33 non-preferred.
'Prevailing-torque type nut' is defined as a nut which is fric-

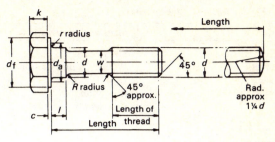

(Figure 2: BS 4395: Part 1: 1969)

Figure 99 *Waisted bolt*

tionally resistant to rotation due to a self-contained prevailing-torque feature and not because of a compressive load developed at assembly against the bearing surface of the nut. It does not imply an indefinite permanence of fixity.

Mechanical properties and performance requirements are given only in respect of steel nuts, with or without non-metallic inserts such as nylon, which are not to be used for special applications such as those requiring weldability, corrosion resistance or the ability to withstand temperatures above 300 °C (120 °C for nuts with non-metallic inserts) or below −50 °C.

Two nut heights are specified, designated 'normal' and 'high' respectively.

The property class designation system is, again, one-tenth of the specified proof load stress.

Property class (kgf/mm²)	Proof load stress (Sp)
8	785
12	1177

Requirements are specified for material, manufacture, mechanical properties, dimensional requirements and performance requirements, marking and identification.

BS 856: 1969 *Wing nuts*

This standard covers wing nuts having ISO metric, ISO inch (unified) and other obsolescent screw threads.

Nominal dimensions for two forms of wing nut blank geometry are specified in the following size ranges:

HS (hot stamped: M3 to M18)
DC (cast: M3 to M18)
CF (cold forged: M3 to M20)

Two types are distinguished: those manufactured from hot brass or other non-ferrous stampings or die castings, malleable

Table 136 *Mechanical properties of bolts (hardness requirements also included): higher grade bolts, waisted shanks*

1	2	3	4	5	6	7
Nominal size d	Pitch of thread	Tensile stress area (waisted shank area)	Ultimate load	Load at permanent set limit $R_{0.2\ min}$	Proof load	Elongation after fracture
			minimum	minimum	minimum	minimum
	mm	mm²	kN	kN	kN	%
M16	2.0	123	120.6	108.5	95.4	9
M20	2.5	194	190.3	171.1	150.5	9
M22	2.5	243	238.4	214.3	188.6	9
M24	3.0	279	273.7	246.1	216.5	9
M27	3.0	369	362.0	325.5	286.3	9
M30	3.5	448	439.5	395.1	347.6	9
M33	3.5	562	551.3	495.7	436.1	9

(Adapted from Table 4: BS 4395: Part 3: 1973)

Table 137 *Dimensional range of rivets*

Material	Sizes and dimensions
Cold forged snap head rivets	Sizes 1–16. With d 16 mm or smaller $D = 1.75\,d$ $K = 0.6d$ L = length
Hot forged snap head rivets	Sizes (14)–(39). With d 14 mm or larger $D = 1.6d$ $K = 0.65d$ L = length
Cold forged universal head rivets	Sizes 1–16. $D = 2d$ $K = 0.4d$ $R = 3d$ $r - 0.6d$ L – length
Hot forged Universal head rivets	Sizes (14)–(39). $D - 2d$ $K = 0.4d$ $R = 3d$ $r = 0.6d$ L = length
Cold forged flat head rivets	Sizes 1–10. $D - 2d$ $K = 0.25d$ L = length
Cold forged 90° countersunk head rivets	Sizes 1–12. $D - 2d$ $K = 0.5d$ (for reference only) L = length
Hot forged 60° countersunk and *raised countersunk* head rivets	Sizes (14)–(39). $D - 1.5d$ $K = 0.43\,d$ (for reference only) $W = 0.2d$ L = length

(From Tables 1–7: BS 4620: 1970

iron castings, or hot steel stampings; and those manufactured by cold forging steel or brass.

BS 4439: 1969 *Screwed studs for general purposes. Metric series*

This standard deals with screwed studs with ISO metric threads in diameters from M3 (3 mm) to M39 (39 mm) inclusive and lengths from 12 to 500 mm.

BS 4320: 1968 *Metal washers for general engineering purposes*

Washers for use with ISO metric bolts, screws and nuts. BS 3410: 1961 is the imperial version.

Section one of this standard relates to bright metal washers and two ranges, from M1.0 to (M39) and M4 to (M39), are distinguished, respectively termed 'nominal diameter' and 'large diameter'.

Section two relates to black steel washers in three ranges, from M5 to (M68), M8 to (M39) and M5 to (M39), respectively termed 'normal', 'large' and 'extra large'.

For both bright and black washers a further range to M150 is also described.

BS 4463: 1969 *Crinkle washers for general engineering purposes. Metric series*

This standard covers metric series crinkle washers suitable for use with metric threaded fasteners in the range M1.6 (1.6 mm) to M20 (20 mm) diameter inclusive.

BS 4464: 1969 *Spring washers for general engineering and automobile purposes. Metric series*

BS 1802: 1951 is the imperial equivalent.

This standard covers washers of helical construction, within the range M1.6 (1.6 mm) to M68 (68 mm) diameter. Dimensions and tolerances are specified for the following types:
Type A: single coil square section.
Type B: single coil rectangular section (with normal ends).
Type BP: single coil rectangular section (with deflected ends).
Type D: double coil rectangular section.

Materials include steel, phosphor bronze, copper silicon and copper beryllium.

BS 4620: 1970 *Rivets for general engineering purposes*

BS 275, BS 641 and BS 1974 are imperial equivalents.

The standard deals with rivets ranging from 1 to 39 mm diameter intended for general engineering purposes.

Materials include mild steel, copper, brass, pure aluminium, aluminium alloys or other suitable metal. See Table 137.

BS 4894: 1973 *Bifurcated rivets for general purpose use*

This standard sets out dimensions of *oval head* and *flat countersunk head* bifurcated rivets, in a metric range for general purpose use. Diameters are 16G, 12G, 11G, 9G, 6G and 3G and lengths are 3.2 to 25.4 mm.

BS 4895: 1981 *Semi-tubular rivets for general purpose use*

This standard covers semi-tubular rivets in steel, brass, copper and aluminium in a range, which extends from 3 to 20 mm and beyond, and three head types are distinguished, oval, bevel countersunk and countersunk.

BS 3572: 1986 *Access fittings for chimneys and other high structures in concrete or brickwork*

Section 1 General
Groups of fittings to provide means of access for inspection and maintenance by steeplejacks and similar trades who normally fit their own ladders – sockets for embedding in concrete and brickwork, cappings for sockets; and screw-in fittings.

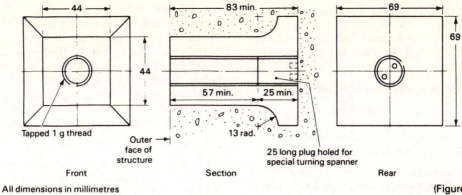

All dimensions in millimetres

(Figure 1: BS 3572: 1962)

Figure 100 *Typical socket for embedding in concrete (brickwork typically 121 mm deep)*

Requirements in respect of materials, workmanship, design, construction and dimensions are specified.

The use of such fittings *inside* chimneys or other structures carrying corrosive gases is not recommended.

Section 2 *Sockets for embedding in concrete*
Materials comprise nickel, gunmetal, 87/7/3/3 gunmetal, aluminium, bronze (copper aluminium), 100% aluminium bronze, nickel-copper, and bronze nickel-copper (100% silicon). The anchorage and fixing is given consideration, and cappings are provided for in Section 4 (see Figure 100).

Section 3 *Sockets for embedding in brickwork*
The scope much as Section 2.

Section 4 *Cappings*

Section 5 *Screw-in hooks*
Screw-in hooks of steel; 19 diameter threads allow for fixing to the sockets. See Figures 101 and 102.

Section 6 *Screw-in eyes, stepirons for embedding in concrete and brickwork*
This part covers stepirons for embedding in concrete and brickwork. Materials comprise aluminium bronze, copper-silicon, phosphor bronze, and nickel copper. See Figure 103.

BS 3678: 1986 *Access hooks for chimneys and other high structures in steel*

This standard covers hooks of similar profile to those in BS 3572, which are intended to be welded permanently to chimneys and other high structures in steel.

An appendix gives general recommendations on the use of access fittings:

(a) Discouraging *internal* access fittings where corrosive gases are present.
(b) Recommending that hooks be used only for temporary ladders and light loads.

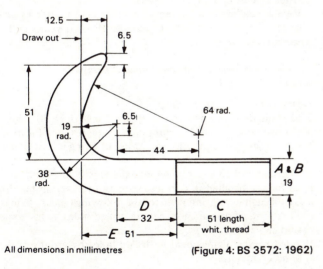

All dimensions in millimetres

(Figure 4: BS 3572: 1962)

Figure 101 *Screw-in hook*

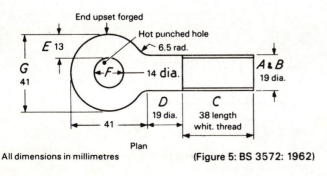

Plan

All dimensions in millimetres

(Figure 5: BS 3572: 1962)

Figure 102 *Screw-in eye*

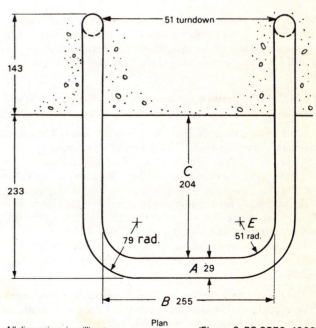

Plan

All dimensions in millimetres

(Figure 6: BS 3572: 1962)

Figure 103 *Stepiron*

(c) Recommending that steeplejacks ladder top pulleys, if used, be limited to 50 kg.
(d) Deprecating the fitting of painters' pulleys and stepirons.
(e) Recommending a vertical alignment at 1.5 m intervals.

BS 5062   *Self-locking safety anchorages for industrial use*

Part 1: 1985   *Self-locking safety anchorages and associated anchorage lines*
This standards deals with self-locking safety anchorages of the following types, whose function is to arrest a fall:

(a) type 1, a device travelling on an anchorage line;
(b) type 2, a device from which an anchorage line pays out.
Definitions include:

Structural anchorages secure points of attachment on a structure to which an anchorage line or a type 2 device may be secured; and
anchorage lines rigid or flexible lines secured to a structure along which a type 1 device travels or a flexible line which unreels from a type 2 device.

Design features cover the design and location of working parts and the protection afforded to them.

Type 1 devices do not rely solely on inertia sensing.

If a device can readily be removed from an anchorage line and inverted, then it either operates in both orientations or must be marked to indicate the correct orientation.

Override of the self-locking feature of the device when in use should not be possible, irrespective of whether a line is slack or taut.

Other clauses deal with metal components, anchorage lines, energy absorbers and performance.

Full maintenance and operating instructions are to be supplied with each device. These include an instruction to carry out a visual inspection and functioning test before each occasion of use and any necessary recommendations for action after the device has been used to arrest a free fall.

Use with a belt, a harness, or both; the type of connector, if any, to be used and information regarding suitable belts and harnesses available on request are required. Marking is prescribed. See BS 1397 *Specification for industrial safety belts, harnesses and safety lanyards* in Table 4: Activities, requirements (81) protection, plant.

Part 2: 1985   *Recommendations for selection, care and use*
This sets out recommendations for the selection of appropriate self-locking safety anchorages, training of users, methods of use, record-keeping, storage and examination and maintenance.

BS 5845: 1980   *Permanent anchors for industrial safety belts and harnesses*

This standard covers eyebolts and ancillary fittings for use as permanent, fixed anchorages for the direct attachment of safety lanyards of industrial safety belts and harnesses and of devices complying with the requirements of BS 5062 and for no other purpose.

Requirements for eyebolts cover materials (steel), form and dimensions, screw threads, workmanship, tolerances, Brinell hardness, testing and inspection. See Figure 104.

An appendix gives recommendations for fixing permanent anchorages for industrial safety belts and harnesses. These include:

1 The use of safety harness and anchorages for the attachment of safety lines should be considered only if no other methods of providing reasonably practicable safe means of access are available.

Where installed in an existing building, the types of wall should be checked.

Safe means of access must be provided for persons carrying out the fixing of sockets and eyebolts.
2 The principles governing the selection of positions for anchorages are set out. Particular consideration is given to fixings in the vicinity of window openings.
3 Selection of type will depend upon the nature of construction of the building. All anchorages should withstand a minimum pull-out force of 5 kN and three samples should be tested to this value in each type of construction.

Recommended types of anchorage are as follows:

(a) Solid brickwork not less than 225 mm thick.	Through-type expanding or chemically bonded.
(b) Cavity brickwork with not less than 100 mm thick outer skin.	Through-type with distance piece.
(c) Cavity walls with lightweight blocks used for the inner lead.	Through-type with distance piece.
(d) 275 mm cavity brickwork.	Through-type with distance piece.
(e) Solid concrete.	Cast-in, expanding, chemically bonded or other sockets.
(f) Structural steel.	Through-type.

For other materials and fixing conditions it is important that specialist advice be sought.

Stability of the wall to provide adequate safety against its collapse if a load from a person falling is applied is essential. In load-bearing structures stability will usually be found, but not in non-load-bearing infill panel walls.

Recommendations are given for fixing; and tests after installation, on each occasion of use and four-yearly (two-yearly in steel structures).

BS 5080   *Methods of test for structural fixings in concrete and masonry*

Part 1: 1974   *Tensile loading*
This standard relates to the method of test only, it is not a performance standard. Interpretation of the results of tests for the purposes of design, selection or use of fixing it is outside its scope.

The standard covers tests under axial tensile forces on structural fixings installed in concrete or masonry used in building and civil engineering, intended for the following types of fixings:
Expanding anchors: anchors held in drilled holes by friction or wedging action.
Bonded fixings: fixings held in drilled holes by grout or other bonding material.
Cast-in fixings: anchor bolts and sockets cast into the material during construction.

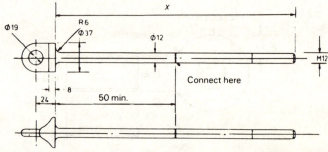

Shank length *X* to be sufficient to locate sockets at correct depth
All dimensions in millimetres   (Figure 1: BS 5845: 1980)

Figure 104 *Eyebolt for chemical, expanded and cast-in sockets*

Channel inserts: slots and channels cast into the material during construction.

The materials in which the fixings above may be installed are concrete, natural stone, cast stone, brick or brick masonry.

The testing agent is to provide a *test certificate* giving the following information for each type and size of fixing:

1 Confirmation that the test has been made in accordance with this standard.
2 The name and location of the testing authority and the date the test was carried out.
3 The specification and description of the base material.
4 The description of the installation of the fixing.
5 The testing procedure if modified.
6 The presentation of results as defined.

BS 1210: 1963   *Wood screws*

This standard prescribes three types of *slotted head* screw available in up to six materials (steel, brass, stainless steel, aluminium, silicon bronze and in one case, nickel copper alloy) and three types of *recessed head* screw, available in steel and brass only. Materials, dimensions and tolerances are among the matters subject to control (see Table 138), and the *designation for ordering* is set out (note that metric conversions are given but British units are regarded as the standard). An appendix lists protective and/or decorative finishes and contains some commentary on them.

Slotted countersunk head wood screws (standard sizes are given below in Table 138).

Standard sizes of slotted countersunk head wood screws.
Length (mm) × screw gauge. (Figure 105)

1 Steel: 4.8 × 1 s.g. *to* 152.4 × 12, 14, 16 and 18 s.g. Most lengths available in up to 12 gauges, but more limited 'preferred' range.

Table 138   *Dimensions of wood screws*

Size of screw and diameter of unthreaded shank		Number of threads per cm	Diameter of head
Screw gauge	D Nominal		V*
	mm		mm
0	1.52	12	3.20
1	1.78	11	3.73
2	2.08	10	4.42
3	2.39	$9\frac{1}{2}$	5.05
4	2.74	$8\frac{1}{2}$	5.84
5	3.10	8	6.63
6	3.45	7	7.39
7	3.81	$6\frac{1}{2}$	8.20
8	4.17	$5\frac{1}{2}$	8.97
9	4.52	$4\frac{1}{2}$	9.75
10	4.88	$4\frac{1}{2}$	10.52
12	5.59	4	12.09
14	6.30	$3\frac{1}{2}$	13.67
16	7.01	3	15.21
18	7.72	3	16.76
20	8.43	$2\frac{1}{2}$	18.31
24	9.86	$2\frac{1}{2}$	21.46
28	11.28	2	24.56
32	12.70	2	27.64

*The dimensions for 'V' are the theoretical diameters of head to sharp corners and are given for design purposes only.

(From Table 1M: BS 1210: 1963)

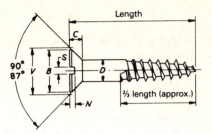

(Figure 1: BS 1210: 1963)

Figure 105   *Slotted countersunk head wood screw*

2 Brass: 6.4 × 0.1, 2, 3, 4 and 6 s.g. *to* 101.6 × 10, 12, 14, 16 and 20 s.g. All lengths available in up to 11 gauges, but more limited 'preferred' range.
3 Stainless steel: 6.4 × 2 *to* 101.6 × 14 and 18 s.g. Most lengths available in up to 8 gauges.
4 Aluminium: 9.5 × 3 and 4 s.g. *to* 76.2 × 12 s.g. Most lengths available in up to 6 gauges.
5 Silicon bronze: 12.7 × 4 and 6 s.g. *to* 127.0 × 18 and 20 s.g. Most lengths available in up to 6 gauges.
6 Nickel-copper alloy: 25.4 × 8 and 10 s.g. *to* 63.5 × 12 s.g. Most lengths available in 2 gauges.

Slotted round head wood screws (standard sizes are given below). The dimensions for screw gauges 0–24, the shank and thread are as for recessed countersunk head wood screws, other dimensions are given in Figure 106.

Standard sizes of slotted round head wood screws.
Length (mm) × screw gauge.

7 Steel: 4.8 × 1 and 2 s.g. *to* 101.6 × 12 s.g. Most lengths available in up to 12 gauges, but more limited 'preferred' range.
8 Brass: 4.8 × 2 s.g. *to* 76.2 × 8, 10, 12 and 14 s.g. Most lengths available in up to 11 gauges, but more limited 'preferred' range.

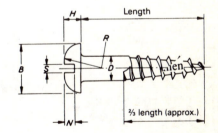

(Figure 2: BS 1210: 1963)

Figure 106   *Slotted round head wood screw*

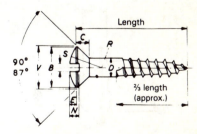

(Figure 3: BS 1210: 1963)

Figure 107   *Slotted raised countersunk head wood screw*

9 Stainless steel: 6.4 × 2 s.g. *to* 76.2 × 10 and 12 s.g. Most lenghts available in up to 6 gauges.
10 Aluminium: 12.7 × 4, 5 and 6 s.g. *to* 38.1 × 8, 10 and 12 s.g. All lengths available in up to 4 gauges.
11 Silicon bronze: 15.9 × 5 s.g. *to* 50.8 × 16 s.g. Most lengths available in 3 or 4 gauges.

Slotted raised countersunk head wood screws (standard sizes are given below). The dimensions for screw gauges 0–24, the shank and thread are as for recessed countersunk head wood screws, other dimensions are given in Figure 107.

Standard sizes of slotted raised countersunk head wood screws. Length (mm) × screw gauge.

12 Steel: 9.5 × 2, 3 and 4 s.g. *to* 50.8 × 8, 10, 12 and 14 s.g. All lengths available in up to 9 gauges, but more limited 'preferred' range.

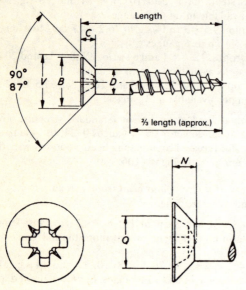

(Figure 4: BS 1210: 1963)

Figure 108 *Recessed countersunk head wood screw*

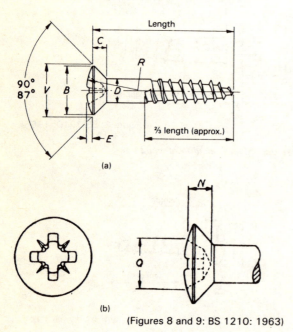

(a)

(b)

(Figures 8 and 9: BS 1210: 1963)

Figure 109 *Recessed raised countersunk head wood screw*

13 Brass: 6.4 × 3 and 4 s.g. *to* 76.2 × 10 s.g. Most lengths available in up to 8 gauges, but more limited 'preferred' range.
14 Stainless steel: 6.4 × 2 s.g. *to* 76.2 × 12 s.g. Most lengths available in up to 7 gauges.
15 Aluminium: 9.5 × 4 s.g. *to* 38.1 × 6, 8, 10 and 12 s.g. Most lengths available in up to 6 gauges.
16 Silicon bronze: 12.7 × 4 s.g. *to* 38.1 × 6 and 8 s.g. Most lengths available in up to 3 gauges.

Recessed countersunk head wood screws (standard sizes are given below). The dimensions for screw gauges 3–16, the shank and thread are as for recessed countersunk head wood screws, other dimensions are given in Figure 108.

Standard sizes of recessed round head wood screws. Length (mm) × screw gauge.

17 Steel: 6.4 × 3, 4 and 6 s.g. *to* 50.8 × 6, 10 and 12 s.g. Most lengths available in up to 7 gauges, but slightly more limited 'preferred' range.
18 Brass: 6.4 × 3 and 4 s.g. *to* 38.1 × 8, 10 and 12 s.g. Most lengths available in up to 5 gauges, but slightly more limited 'preferred' range.

Recessed raised countersunk head wood screws (standard sizes shown below) the dimensions for screw gauges 3–16, the shank and thread dimensions are as for recessed countersunk head wood screws, other dimensions are given in Figure 109.

Standard sizes of recessed raised countersunk head wood screws. Length (mm) × screw gauge.

19 Steel: 9.5 × 3 and 4 s.g. *to* 50.8 × 8, 10 and 12 s.g. All lengths available in up to 5 gauges but markedly more limited 'preferred' range.
20 Brass: 9.5 × 3 and 4 s.g. *to* 63.5 × 10 and 12 s.g. All lengths available in up to 5 gauges, but markedly more limited 'preferred' range.

BS 1202 *Nails*

This standard is in three parts, dealing respectively with steel, copper and aluminium nails.

Part 1: 1974 *Steel nails*
This standard specifies twenty-three types of mild steel *wire nails* and two types of *cut nails*, made from black rolled steel. All nails are required to be straight and true in shape, the surface 'free from excessive oxidation': Wire nails may be bright, galvanized, cement-coated (resin-coated), or an alternative finish such as sherardized, cadmium-plated or lead coated. Cut nails may be as rolled, or galvanized. Dimensions and tolerances for heads, shanks and length are prescribed.

Designation for ordering is given as quantity required by weight, type, finish required, length in millimetres, diameter or dimension 'D' in millimetres and this British Standard number. Figure 110 shows types 1–25.

Schedule of nail types
Table range: length/s (mm) × *shank diameter* (mm) (approximate number of nails per kg)

Wire

1 Round plain head nails: 200 × 8 (13) *to* 15 × 1.40 (4400). Most lengths in 2 to 4 diameters.
2 Round lost head nails: 75 × 3.75 (160) *to* 15 × 1.00 (9400), 50, 60 and 65 nails in 2 diameters.
3 Clout or slate nails: 100 × 4.50 (75) *to* 15 × 2.36 (1540) or 2.00 (2380). Most lengths in 2 to 4 diameters.
4 Extra large head clout or felt nails: 40 × 3.00 (350) *to* 13 × 3.00 (780). All 3 diameter.

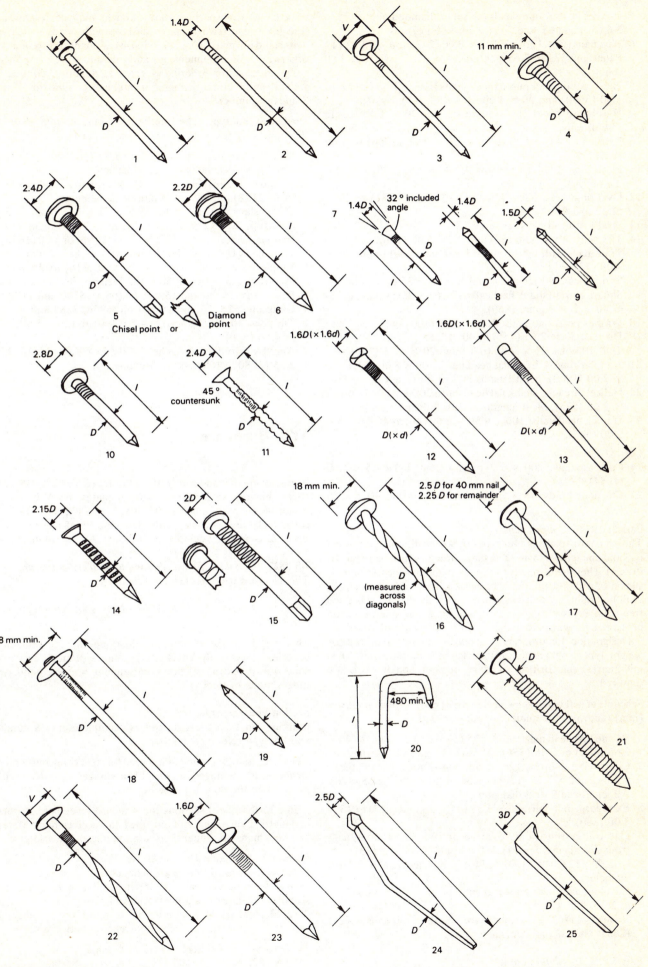

Figure 110 *Steel nails*

(Adapted from figures in BS 1202: Part 1: 1974)

5 Convex head roofing nails (chisel or diamond point): 75 × 5.6 (68) and 65 × 6.00 (66) or 5.60 (79).
6 Pipe nails (chisel point): 100 × 8.00 (24) *to* 50 × 8.00 (44).
7 Panel pins: 75 × 2.65 (290) *to* 15 × 1.25 (6400) or 1.00 (8800).
8 Hard board panel pins (round shank): 25 × 1.60 (2340) or 1.40 (3090) and 20 × 1.60 (3140) or 1.40 (3970).
9 Hardboard panel pins (square shank): 20 × 1.40 square (3470) only.
10 Lath nails: 40 × 2.00 (970) *to* 20 × 1.80 (1750) or 1.60 (2370).
11 Plasterboard nails (jagged shank): 40 × 2.65 (570) and 30 × 2.65 (700).
12 Oval brad head nails: 150 × (7.10 to 5.00) (31) *to* 20 × (2.00 to 1.25) (4500).
13 Oval lost head nails: as serial 12.
14 Tile pegs: 40 × 6.00 (88) and 30 × 6.00 (106).
15 Tram nails with flat or raised head and chisel point: 65 × 8.00 (37) only.
16 Spring head twisted shank nails: 65 × 3.35 (140) only.
17 Square twisted shank flat head nails: 65 × 3.35 square (235) *to* 40 × 2.36 square (860).
18 Washer head slab nails: 100 × 3.35 (100) only.
19 Dowels: 50 × 2.65 (455) *to* 40 × 2.65 (610).
20 Tenter hooks: 25 × 2.36 (690) and 20 × 2.36 (740).
21 Annular ringed shank flat head nails: 200 × 8.00 (13) *to* 20 × 2.00 (1900). Most lengths in 2 or 3 diameters.
22 Helical threaded shank flat head nails: 200 × 8.00 (13) *to* 40 × 2.65 (575). Most lengths in 2 or 3 diameters.
23 Duplex head nails: 100 + 9.50 × 5.60 (46) *to* 45 + 6.50 × 3.00 (345).

Cut
24 Cut clasp nails: 200 × 6.00 narrow stem (11) *to* 25 × 1.60 (1384).
25 Cut floor brads: 75 × 3.35 thickness (100) *to* 40 × 2.36 (396).

Part 2: 1974 *Copper nails*
This standard specifies four types of wire nail, one type of cut nail and one type of roves (a washer, through which nails may be driven). They are normally of copper, but alloys such as copper-silicon or nickel-copper may be agreed. The finish of wire nails shall be bright, cut nails 'as rolled' and nails shall be clean and free from excessive oxidation. Dimensions and tolerances are prescribed for wire nails, but no tolerances for cut nails or roves.

Designation for ordering is given as quantity required, by weight, type, length in millimetres, diameter or dimension 'D' in millimetres, this British Standard number and if roves are required.

Schedule of nail types, showing: length/s (mm) × *shank diameter* (mm) (approximate number of nails per kg)

1 Round lost head nails: 65 × 3.75 (178) or 3.35 (198) *to* 40 × 2.65 (474) or 2.36 (554). All three lengths in 2 diameters.
2 Clout nails (plain or jagged shank): also known as slate, tile or felt nails. 65 × 3.75 (170) or 3.35 (195) *to* 20 × 2.65 (920). All lengths in 2 or 3 diameters.
3 Extra large felt nails: 25 × 3.35 (440) or 3.00 (517) *to* 13 × 3.00 (880).
4 Flat countersunk and rosehead square shank boat nails (round or diamond point): 150 × 6.00 (22) or 5.00 (33) *to* 20 × 2.00 (1237) or 1.80 (1740). Most lengths in 2 to 4 diameters.
5 Cut clout nails: also known as cut slate nails. 50 × 3.00 (275) *to* 25 × 2.00 (1298).
6 Roves: 6.4 D (3520) – suitable for 1.80 diameter nails. 19.1 D (265) – suitable for 5 diameter nails.

Part 3: 1974 *Aluminium nails*
This standard specifies ten types of aluminium round wire nail,

to be made from specified alloys, straight and true in shape and free from 'excessive burrs or flashes', with heads which will 'withstand normal driving'. The finish is as manufactured, unless otherwise agreed. Dimensions and tolerances are prescribed.

Designation for ordering is given as quantity required by weight, millimetres, diameter in millimetres and this British Standard number.

Shedule of nail types, showing: length (mm) × *shank diameter* 'D' (mm) (approximate number of nails per kg)

1 Round plain head nails: 115 × 5.00 (159) *to* 20 × 1.60 (7588). Most lengths in 2 or 3 diameters.
2 Round lost head nails: 75 × 3.75 (448) *to* 40 × 2.64 (1390) or 2.36 (2128), 50 and 40 lengths in 2 diameters.
3 Clout, slate and tile nails: 65 × 3.75 (504) *to* 20 × 3.00 (2300) or 2.65 (2895). Most lengths in 2 to 4 diameters.
4 Extra large head felt nails: 25 × 3.35 (1296) or 3.00 (1636) *to* 15 × 3.35 (1840) or 3.00 (2283). All lengths in 2 diameters.
5 Nipple head roofing nails: 65 × 5.00 (316) *to* 25 × 3.75 (1200) or 3.35 (1410), 50 and 25 lengths in 2 diameters.
6 Panel pins: 25, 20 and 15 × 1.60 (6550, 8790 and 11800).
7 Gimp pins: 25, 20 and 15 × 1.60 (5936, 7588 and 9600).
8 Tile pegs: 40 × 5.00 (450) or 4.50 (490) and 30 × 5.00 (545) or 4.50 (600).
9 Annular ringed shank flat head nails: 75 × 4.00 (345) *to* 25 × 2.65 (2280), 40 lengths in 2 diameters.

Xt7   Hardware

A miscellany of standards, with a glossary (BS 3827). BS 1227 covers hinges, BS 2911 covers letter plates, BS 4112 covers performance requirements, BS 4951, BS 5872 and BS 3621 cover locks and latches (in the last case, thief-resistant) and BS 5725 covers exit devices (panic bolts). All are summarized.

BS 3827 *Glossary of terms relating to builders' hardware*
This has four parts, so far, published.

BS 1227 *Hinges*   Part 1A: 1967   *Hinges for general building purposes*.

This part is in six sections, the first general, the remainder covering respectively knuckle type hinges of steel, cast iron, solid drawn (extruded) brass and aluminium, and band type hinges made of steel.

Section one   *general*
Marking, on each package, covers manufacturer, BS number and BS type reference number.

Note: The 'handling' convention used for steel rising butt hinges, steel falling butt hinges and steel lift-off hinges, is the *hinge* side, from which the door is pushed open.

In all subsequent sections the standard gives both imperial and metric dimensions, but only the latter is given here. Materials, workmanship, dimensions and tolerances are also given.

Section 2   *steel knuckle type hinges*
Seventeen series of hinges are scheduled.

In all the following cases, the open width in mm, number and size of screw holes is among the information given in the standard. Here, the joint length in mm is stated, unless otherwise shown. Note, sadly, the lack of correlation between series.

1 Dimensions of *steel broad butt hinges*: 1A/101, 50.8, 1A/102, 63.5, 1A/103, 76.2, 1A/104, 88.9 and 1A/105, 101.6.

2 Dimensions of *strong steel butt hinges*: 1A/201, 38.1, 1A/202, 50.8, 1A/203, 63.5, 1A/204, 76.2, 1A/205, 88.9, 1A/206, 101.6, 1A/207, 127.0, 1A/208, 152.4.

3 Dimensions of *narrow steel butt hinges*: 1A/301, 25.4, 1A/302, 31.8, 1A/303, 38.1, 1A/304, 50.8, 1A/305, 63.5, 1A/306, 76.2, 1A/307, 88.9, 1A/308, 101.6, 1A/309, 127.0, 1A/310, 152.4.

4 Dimensions of *steel scotch butt hinges*: 1A/401, 101.6, 1A/402, 127.0, 1A/403, 152.4.

5 Dimensions of *extra strong double flap steel butt hinges*: 1A/501, 50.8, 1A/502, 63.5, 1A/503, 76.2, 1A/504, 88.9, 1A/505, 101.6, 1A/506, 127.0, 1A/507, 152.4.

6 Dimensions of *steel rising butt hinges* (specify hand): 1A/601, 76.2, 1A/602, 88.9, 1A/603, 101.6.

7 Dimensions of *steel falling butt hinges* (specify hand): 1A/701, 76.2, 1A/702, 101.6.

8 Dimensions of *steel left-off hinges* (specify hand): 1A/801, 63.5, 1A/802, 76.2, 1A/803, 88.9, 1A/804, 101.6.

9 Dimensions of *steel back flap hinges*: 1A/901, 19.1 1A/902, 25.4, 1A/903, 31.8, 1A/904, 38.1, 1A/905, 44.5, 1A/906, 50.8, 1A/907, 57.2, 1A/908, 63.5, 1A/909, 76.2.

10 Dimensions of *steel square back flap hinges*: 1A/1001, 25.4, 1A/1002, 31.8, 1A/1003, 38.1, 1A/1004, 44.5, 1A/1005, 50.8.

11 Dimensions of *weighty steel tee hinges* (length of tail from centre of pin, mm): 1A/1101, 101.6, 1A/1102, 152.4, 1A/1103, 203.2, 1A/1104, 254.4, 1A/1105, 304.8, 1A/1106, 355.6, 1A/1107, 406.4, 1A/1108, 457.2, 1A/1109, 508.0, 1A/1110, 609.6.

12 Dimensions of *strong steel tee hinges* (length, as serial 11): 1A/1201, 76.2, 1A/1202, 101.6, 1A/1203, 127.0, 1A/1204, 152.4, 1A/1205, 203.2, 1A/1206, 254.0, 1A/1207, 304.8, 1A/1208, 355.6, 1A/1209, 406.4, 1A/1210, 457.2, 1A/1211, 508.0, 1A/1212, 609.6.

13 Dimensions of *medium steel tee hinges* (length, as serial 11): 1A/1301, 254.0, 1A/1302, 304.8, 1A/1303, 355.6, 1A/1304, 406.4, 1A/1305, 457.2.

14 Dimensions of *light steel tee hinges* (length, as serial 11): 1A/1401, 101.6, 1A/1402, 152.4, 1A/1403, 203.2, 1A/1404, 254.0, 1A/1405, 304.8.

15 Dimensions of *weighty steel strap hinges* (length of flap from centre of pin, *and* length of joint, both mm): 1A/1501, 203.2 and 76.2 to 82.6, 1A/1502, 304.8 and 98.4 to 104.8.

16 Dimensions of *medium steel strap hinges* (dimensions as serial 15): 1A/1601, 203.2 and 55.6 to 58.7, 1A/1602, 254.0 and 61.9 to 65.1, 1A/1603, 304.8 and 81.0 to 84.1.

17 Dimensions of *light steel strap hinges* (dimensions as serial 15): 1A/1701, 76.2 and 27.8 to 29.4, 1A/1702, 101.6 and 31.0 to 32.5, 1A/1703, 127.0 and 31.0 to 32.5, 1A/1704, 152.4 and 38.1 to 41.3, 1A/1705, 203.2 and and 44.5 to 47.6 (light bent pattern steel strap hinges also).

Section three *cast iron knuckle type hinges*
Three series of hinges are scheduled:

18 Dimensions of *cast iron butt hinges*: 1A/1801, 63.5, 1A/1802, 76.2, 1A/1803, 101.6.

19 Dimensions of *cast iron using butt hinges* (specify hand): 1A/1901, 76.2, 1A/1902, 101.6.

20 Dimensions of cast iron falling butt hinges (specify hand): 1A/2001, 76.2, 1A/2002, 88.9.

Section four *solid drawn (extruded) brass knuckle type hinges*
Nine series of hinges are scheduled:

21 Dimensions of *brass broad butt hinges*: 1A/2101, 38.1, 1A/2102, 50.8, 1A/2103, 63.5, 1A/2104, 76.2, 1A/2105, 101.6.

22 Dimensions of *strong brass butt hinges*: 1A/2201, 63.5, 1A/2202, 76.2, 1A/2203, 88.9, 1A/2204 and 1A/2205 both 101.6 (open widths vary).

23 Dimensions of *brass washered hinges* (specify type of washer): 1A/2301 and 1A/2302 both 76.2, 1A/2303 and 1A/2304 both 88.9, 1A/2305 and 1A/2306 both 101.6 (open widths vary), 1A/2307, 127.0, 1A/2308, 152.4.

24 Dimensions of *brass projection hinges*: 1A/2401, 76.2, 1A/2402, 88.9, 1A/2403, 101.6 (add suffix 'W' if washered, and 'L' if plain pin).

25 Dimensions of *brass rising butt hinges* (specify hand): 1A/2501, 76.2, 1A/2502, 1A/2503, both 101.6 (open widths vary), 1A/2504, 127.0.

26 Dimensions of *brass falling butt hinges* (specify hand) (as 25, but prefix 1A/26 . . .).

27 Dimensions of *brass backflap hinges*: 1A/2701, 25.4, 1A/2702, 31.8, 1A/2703, 38.4, 1A/2704, 44.5, 1A/2705, 50.8, 1A/2706, 63.5, 1A/2707, 76.2.

28 Dimensions of *brass counter flap hinges*: 1A/2801, 31.6 1A/2802, 38.1.

29 Dimensions of *brass lift-off hinges* (specify hand): 1A/2901 and 1A/2902 both 76.2 (open widths vary), 1A/2903, 88.9 1A/2904, 101.6.

Section five *steel band type hinges*
Four series are scheduled:

30 Dimensions of *light steel hook and band on plate with curled eye* (length and width of band, mm): 1A/3001, 152.4 and 31.75, 1A/3002, 203.2 and 31.75, 1A/3003, 254.0 and 31.75, 1A/3004, 304.8 and 31.75, 1A/3005, 355.6 and 38.10, 1A/3006, 406.4 and 38.10, 1A/3007, 457.2 and 38.10, 1A/3008, 508.0 and 45.45, 1A/3009, 609.6 and 45.45.

31 Dimensions of *heavy steel hook and band on plate* (dimensions as serial 30): 1A/3101, 254 and 38.1, 1A/3102, 304.8 and 38.1, 1A/3103, 355.6 and 44.5, 1A/3104, 406.4 and 44.5, 1A/3105, 457.2 and 50.8, 1A/3106, 508 and 50.8, 1A/3107, 609.6 and 57.2, 1A/3108, 685.8 and 63.5, 1A/3109, 762.0 and 63.5.

32 Dimensions of *light steel reversible hinges* (dimensions as serial 30): 1A/3201, 203.2 and 31.75, 1A/3202, 254.0 and 31.75, 1A/3203, 304.8 and 31.75, 1A/3204, 355 and 4.76, 1A/3205, 406.4 and 4.76, 1A/3207, 457.2 and 4.76.

33 Dimensions of *heavy steel reversible hinges* (dimensions as serial 30): 1A/3301, 254.0 and 38.1, 1A/3302, 304.8 and 38.1, 1A/3303, 355.6 and 44.5, 1A/3304, 406.4 and 44.5, 1A/3305, 457.2 and 50.8, 1A/3306, 508.0 and 50.8, 1A/3307, 609.6 and 57.2, 1A/3308, 685 and 63.5, 1A/3309, 762.0 and 63.5.

Section six *extruded aluminium knuckle type hinges*
One series is scheduled:

34 Dimensions of *extruded aluminium washered butt hinges*: 1A/3401 and 1A/3402, both 76.2, 1A/3403 and 1A/3404, both 88.9, 1A/3405 and 1A/3406, both 101.6 (open widths in these cases vary), 1A/3407, 152.4.

BS 2911: 1974 *Letter plates*

This standard includes performance requirements for letter plates of three different types of construction:

Type 1: letter plates with outward opening flap, closed by gravity action.

Type 2: letter plates with outward opening flap. closed by spring action.

Type 3: letter plates with inward opening flap, gravity or spring action.

Materials, finishes, design features and workmanship are discussed.

Dimensions given are: The aperture of a letter plate: 250 ± 10 × 38 ± 1.5 mm.

Fixing arrangement: suitable for use with doors of any thickness between 35 and 60 mm.

Fixing bolts or studs: ISO metric M6 (coarse pitch) or equivalent.

The fixing centres which are to be 300 ± 1.5 mm, and on the centre line of the aperture within a tolerance of 3.5 mm.

The torque required to open the flap, a suitable test rig for its determination, and marking are specified.

An appendix discusses standard height and fixing recommendations. For domestic premises, a standard height is prescribed, 760 mm (lower edge) and 1450 mm (upper edge) above outside level, with an 'ideal' 1070 mm for the centre line. The distance from a letter plate to a lock should be at least 400 mm for security reasons.

BS 3621: 1980   *Thief resistant locks*

This standard deals with thief resistant locks intended for fixed mounting on hinged or sliding doors. The door and frame should be of adequate length.

Provision is made for locks having claw. or hook bolts, mounted on hinged or sliding doors, and for locks having spring bolts, or dead bolts of either single or multiple throw, mounted on hinged doors.

Design requirements include the use of *concealed* or *locked* fixing screws, where key-operated from both sides, adequate security from each, and handles or knobs to be capable of disconnection or otherwise rendered ineffective by dead locking.

Requirements are specified for sampling and test methods for corrosion resistance and workmanship, operation of security mechanism, security against cutting, strength and the indelible marking of locks.

In addition to the above tests, and to ensure compliance with the design features required, the locks are to be submitted to a panel of locksmith experts.

BS 4112: 1967   *Performance requirements for hardware for domestic furniture*

Requirements are specified for compression stays, tension stays, friction stays, cabinet bolts, castors, cupboard and door catches, roller bolts, magnetic catches, door tracks and runners, drawer runners, grilles and vents for kitchen furniture, knock down fittings, locks, hinges, mirror movements, glides and slides, shelf supports, hanging rails, handles, knobs, mirror clips and corner clips.

BS 4951: 1973   *Builders' hardware: lock and latch furniture (doors)*

This standard covers dimensions, performance tests and workmanship for lever and knob furniture for use with locks and latches for doors. The dimensional requirements only apply to furniture for mortice locks and latches complying with BS 455.

Dimensions and fixing systems are:

Bolt fixing systems: for which dimensions are set out.

Screw fixing systems: which should have screws which shall not foul the lock or latch case.

Other fixing systems: deemed to comply provided they meet the performance requirements.

Keyhold centre dimensions and keyhole dimensions are given.

Delineation of measurement for three forms of lever, three forms of knob and three forms of plate are given.

The spindle is to be 6.7 mm square and of such a length that the engagement of the spindle into the levers or knobs is not less than 12 mm into each side simultaneously, when fitted to doors of 33 mm to 46 mm finished thickness.

Test requirements are specified for strength of return mechanism strength for furniture and methods of fixing and durability of the mechanism.

Marking requirements are set out.

BS 5872: 1980   *Locks and latches for doors in buildings*

This standard sets out tests and levels of performance for locks and latches. Two categories are distinguished: 'A' for housing and 'B' for public and other buildings which are more robust. For locks and latches for doors used in housing the standard also specifies dimensions. Locks and latches for fire doors are not included.

Category A: dimensions of locks and latches are given in diagrams which cover cylinder rim night latch, horizontal mortice lock, upright mortice lock and bathroom lock, striking plates for upright mortice lock and bathroom locks, mortice latch (flat case), mortice latch (tubular case) and bored lock or latch set.

Category B: the dimensions for locks and latches are at the discretion of the manufacturer.

Requirements are specified for sampling and testing.

BS 5725   *Emergency exit devices*   Part 1: 1981   *Panic bolts and panic latches mechanically operated by a horizontal pushbar*

Definitions include:

Anti-thrust device: a device to prevent a panic bolt head being levered out of its floor socket.

Automatic catch: a device to hold a panic bolt in the withdrawn position after it has been actuated and to release the bolt automatically on closure of the door.

Dogging mechanism: a device fitted to a panic bolt or panic latch for holding the bolt heads in the withdrawn position until reset manually.

Door selector (co-ordinator): a device designed to permit a pair of doors with rebated meeting stiles to close in the correct sequence.

Locking attachment: a mechanism for opening or securing an emergency exit device from the outside without in any way overriding the action of the panic bolt or panic latch from the inside.

Materials and finishes are specified.

Design features, including operation by a push-bar, the use of single and double push-bars (the latter where double doors have meeting-style rebates) and panic latches are set out.

Typical applications of panic bolts and panic latches are illustrated.

Unless a locking attachment has been fitted, no panic bolt or panic latch is to be capable of being operated from the outside. The design of panic bolts include easyclean floor sockets, and anti-thrust device. In the case of double panic bolts, either pushbar must release the mechanism. Provision is to be made for the lubrication where necessary of moving parts of the panic bolt or panic latch.

Requirements are specified for dimensions, operating forces, testing, quarterly control and fixings.

An appendix gives recommendations for installation and fixing.

A further appendix gives recommendations for weekly maintenance by the occupier. These are:

1 Inspect and operate, to ensure satisfactory working condition.
2 Ensure that all working parts are lubricated.
3 Ensure that sockets at floor and head are free from obstruction.

Three classes of appearance are distinguished: 'economy', 'industrial', and 'architectural'.

Sizes and tolerances are set out, and inspection, testing, protection of finished members, site gluing and marking are all covered.

BS 6459 *Door closers*

Part 1: 1984 *Specification for mechanical performance of crank and rack and pinion overhead closers*
This standard deals with single-action overhead door closers (with or without backcheck), including their arms and arm linkages, not forming the pivotal or hinged arrangement of the door. They may be either face fixed on the door or transom, or concealed in the door or transom and are used for closing hinged and pivoted doors automatically in a controlled manner.

The requirements specific to door closers for fire doors are not covered (and will be covered in a later part).

Door closers are categorized by size (strength) and class.

Table 139 *Door closer size or strength*

Closer size number	Maximum door leaf width (mm)	Maximum door mass (kg)
2	830	45
3	930	60
4	1030	80
5	1130	110
6	1330	150

Class A: from a minimum opening angle of 45° down to the closed position (operating from 90°)
Class B: from a minimum opening angle of 70° down to the closed position (operating from 90°)
Class C: from a minimum opening angle of 115° down to the closed position (operating from 175°).

Closing moments, tools, instructions, fixings and marking are covered.

Y Formless work (no entry)
Z Joints

Only two standards, the first comprehensive and important, are covered in this section. BS 6100, *Glossary of building and civil engineering terms* Part 4, section 4.4: 1985 *Carpentry and joinery* relates.

BS 6093: 1981 *Code of practice for the design of joints and jointing in building construction*

This code sets out recommendations for the design of joints and the use of jointing products in building construction. Following an analysis of joint functions and of the performance of the parts to be joined, joints are classified on the basis of the movements and inaccuracies they have to accommodate.

An important analysis, derived from ISO 3447 *Joints in buildings – general checklist of joint functions* is tabulated to show design aspects, the main heads being:

1 Environmental factors.
2 Capacity to withstand stress (either during or after assembly).
3 Safety.
4 Accommodation of dimensional deviations.
5 Fixing of components.
6 Appearance.
7 Economics.
8 Durability.
9 Maintenance.
10 Ambient conditions.

The code does not cover rigidly connected joints, joints within components normally made in a factory, the load-bearing functions of structural joints, glazing (see CP 152), joints in service pipes and ducts and their connections to appliances (see the code of practice relevant to the particular service), or methods of test for joints or for jointing products.

BS 6181: 1981 *Method of test for air permeability of joints in building*

This standard sets out the test method to be used in laboratories for assessing the air permeability of non-opening joints in the exterior walls of buildings.

It is applied to joints between components used in the exterior walls of buildings and fixed according to the manufacturer's recommendations, the test, and reporting, is broadly similar to that set out in BS 5368 Methods of testing windows Part 2 (see Table 4 'Activities, requirements', section (H2) modified environments).

CI/SfB Table 3: Materials

e Natural stone

There are two standards available.

BS 6100: *Glossary of building and civil engineering terms*

Part 5: *Masonry*
Part 5: Section 5.2: 1984 *Stone.*
Definitions of geological terms for rocks, minerals and rock structures and of terms for masonry tools, handling equipment and stonework constuction and operations. The terms are arranged by a classifed system in alphabetical order.

BS 6270: *Code of practice for cleaning and surface repair of buildings*

Part 1: 1982. *Natural stone, cast stone and clay and calcium silicate brick masonry*
(See Table 4 (W2)).

f Precast with binder

There are four British standards covered in this section. For reconstructed stone masonry units, see Table 2 Constructions, forms F blockwork and brickwork.

BS 6100: Part 6: Section 6.2: 1986 *Concrete*

This section gives definitions of concretes identified through their properties, formulation, processes used to produce them, and their applications. The terms are arranged systematically in a classified order with an alphabetical index.

BS 1217: 1975 *Cast stone*

Cast stone is defined in this standard as 'any products manufactured from aggregate and cement and intended to resemble in appearance and be used in a similar way to natural stone'. It may be homogeneous or may consist of a facing material and a backing concrete.

The standard specifies requirements for constituent materials, colour and texture, permitted tolerances and slenderness ratio, compressive strength, drying shrinkage and initial surface absorption.

Methods of test for compressive strength, drying shrinkage and initial surface absorption are appended.

BS 4357: 1968 *Precast terrazzo units*

This standard specifies requirements for precast concrete monolithic terrazzo-faced units (other than hydraulically pressed terrazzo tiles covered by BS 4131 (see Table 1 'Buildings elements' section (43) 'Floor finishes')) and units of terrazzo alone including:

1 Floor slabs or pavings.
2 Staircase treads and risers and combined treads, risers and landings.
3 Partitions and components.
4 Wall lining panels, skirtings and window sills.
5 External cladding panels.
6 Shower trays, sink benches, fireplace surrounds and hearths and special applications.

BS 6270 Part 2: 1982 *Concrete and precast concrete masonry*

General guidance for selection of cleaning and surface repair methods for existing and newly erected buildings; the main techniques in common use and recommendations for protection of buildings, operators and public. (See also Table 4 Activities, requirements (W) Operations, maintenance factors.)

g Clay (dried, fired)

g6 Refractories (see also section f 'Precast with binder')

BS 3446: 1962 *Glossary of terms relating to the manufacture and use of refractory materials*

This standard includes the principal terms relating to the manufacture and testing of refractory shapes and to their use in the cement, ceramic, gas, glass, metallurgical and other industries.

h Metal

This section is subdivided into the following sections: general (three documents), iron and steel (17 standards), aluminium and alloys (10 standards), copper, zinc and alloys (six standards) and lead (three standards).

General

CP 3012: 1972 *Cleaning and preparation of metal surfaces*

This code is divided into three sections.

Section one deals with recommended practice for cleaning a variety of metals and alloys when no subsequent coating is required.

Section two deals with cleaning and preparation prior to the application of a comprehensive range of surface coatings.

Section three deals with the various methods of treatment.

PD 6484: 1979 *Commentary on corrosion at bimetallic contacts and its alleviations*

This standard gives:

1 Guidance on the avoidance of situations in which corrosion may arise from the interaction of different metals and alloys at bimetallic contacts.
2 Details of the environmental conditions affecting corrosion at metallic contacts and methods of preventing or minimizing such corrosion.
3 Annotated tables indicating the degree of additional corrosion likely to occur at bimetallic contacts exposed to atmospheric and aqueous environments.

DD5: 1971 *Recommendations for metric plate and sheet thicknesses and width-length combinations for metallic materials*

This draft for development gives recommendations for standard thicknesses of steel and non-ferrous plate and sheet together with standard width/length combinations.

Iron and steel

BS 2094 *Glossary of terms relating to iron and steel*

This standard has the following nine parts:

Part 1: 1954 *General metallurgical, heat treatment and testing terms*
Part 2: 1954 *Steel making*
Part 3: 1954 *Hot-rolled steel produced (excluding sheet, strip and tubes)*
Part 4: 1954 *Steel sheet and strip*
Part 5: 1954 *Bright steel bar and steel wire*
Part 6: 1954 *Forgings and drop forgings*
Part 7: 1956 *Wrought iron*
Part 8: 1956 *Steel tubes and pipes*
Part 9: 1964 *Iron and steel founding*

BS 309: 1972 *Whiteheart malleable iron castings*

This standard covers two grades of castings, namely W410/4 and W340/3, and gives tests and specifications on mechanical properties, hardness, microstructure and freedom from defects. Typical properties are appended.

BS 310: 1972 *Blackheart malleable iron castings*

This standard covers three grades of castings, namely B340/12, B310/10 and B290/6, and gives tests and specifications on mechanical properties, hardness, microstructure and freedom from defects. Typical properties are appended.

BS 1452: 1977 *Grey iron castings*

This standard specifies requirements for seven grades of castings, namely grades 150, 180, 220, 260, 300, 350 and 400 based on tensile strength in N/mm^2. Typical properties are appended.

BS 2451: 1963 *Chilled iron shot and grit*

This standard specifies the size of particles of chilled iron shot and grit, and the method of testing for size. It also specifies material, form, designation and grading, and describes a hardness test.

BS 2789: 1973 *Iron castings with spheroidal or nodular graphite*

This standard specifies requirements for six grades of castings, namely 370/17, 420/12, 500/7, 600/3, 700/2 and 800/2 based on tensile strength in N/mm^2 and elongation.

BS 3333: 1972 *Pearlitic malleable iron castings*

This standard specifies requirements for five grades of castings, namely P690/2, P570/3, P540/5, P510/4 and P440/7 based on tensile strength in N/mm^2 and elongation. Typical properties are appended.

BS 3468: 1974 *Austenitic cast iron*

This standard specifies requirements for nine grades of flake graphite austenitic cast iron and eleven grades of spheroidal or nodular graphite austenitic cast iron intended for use in the manufacture of castings. These grades of material are based on chemical composition and mechanical properties. An appendix gives data on mechanical and physical properties and typical applications.

BS 29: 1976 *Carbon steel forgings above 150 mm ruling section*

This standard specifies requirements for forgings in carbon and carbon manganese steel for shipbuilding and general engineering purposes having tensile strengths between 400 and 760 N/mm^2 and ruling sections greater than 150 mm. It includes steelmaking, composition, forging, heat treatment and testing.

BS 970 *Wrought steels for mechanical and allied engineering purposes*

Part 1: 1983 *General inspection and testing procedures and specific requirements for carbon, carbon manganese, alloy and stainless steels*
Part 1 is structured as follows:

Section one: general inspection and testing procedure
Section two: specific requirements for hot-rolled and normalized steels, for steels supplied as bright bar and for micro-alloyed carbon manganese steels
Section three: specific requirements for through hardening steels including steels capable of surface hardening by nitriding
Section four: specific requirements for case hardening steels
Section five: specific requirements for stainless and heat resisting steels including those supplied as bright bar
Section six: specific requirements for sizes and tolerances

This part is a metricated version and supersedes BS 970 Part 1: 1972, Part 2: 1970, Part 3: 1971 and supplement no. 1 (1973), and Part 4: 1970 excluding the valve steel specifications which will be dealt with separately.

Part 5: 1972 *Carbon and alloy spring steels for the manufacture of hot-formed springs*
This part deals with wrought carbon (including silico-manganese) and alloy steels for manufacture of hot-formed and heat-treated springs.

Part 6: 1973 *SI metric values*
This part specifies SI metric units for use in place of the values specified in imperial units in Part 1 to 5 of BS 970.

BS 1449: *Steel plate, sheet and strip*

This standard deals with steel plate, sheet and strip for automobile and general engineering purposes. Requirements are specified for 3 per cent nickel steel plate and sheet, and eight qualities of carbon spring steel plate, sheet, strip and flat wire, hardening and tempering quality.

Part 1: 1983 *Carbon and carbon manganese plate, sheet and strip*
This part specifies requirements for flat-rolled carbon steel products in both coil and cut length form up to 16 mm thick. Requirements are specified for chemical composition, mechanical properties, dimensions, etc. It includes specific requirements for materials based on formability, minimum strength, temper rolled and other conditions, suitable for heat treatment.

Part 2: 1983 *Stainless and heat-resisting steel plate, sheet and strip*

■ AD (Reg. J1/2/3)

This part specifies requirements for flat-rolled stainless and heat-resisting steel products in both coil and cut form, including plate 3 mm to 100 mm thick, wide strip, sheet from 0.30 mm to less than 3 mm, narrow strip, 0.50 mm to less than 3 mm thick.

BS 2989: 1982 *Continuously hot-dip zinc coated and iron-zinc alloy coated steel: wide strip, sheet/plate and slit wide strip*

This standard specifies requirements for hot-dip zinc coated and iron-zinc alloy coated steel flat-rolled products in forming and structural grades, coated by a continuous process. It applies to products supplied in the forms of wide strip, sheet or plate cut from wide strip and slit wide strip.

Requirements are specified for chemical composition, mechanical properties (tensile properties and end characteristics), coating mass, test methods, dimensional tolerances and geometrical deviations.

BS 3100: 1976 *Steel castings for general engineering purposes*

This standard specifies requirements for carbon, carbon manganese, low alloy, corrosion resisting, heat resisting and high alloy steel castings including chemical composition, mechanical properties (tensile, bend, impact, hardness and intercrystalline corrosion tests), heat treatment, etc. Appendices include comparable steels in BS 1504 and inspection categories. It supersedes twenty-odd former standards.

BS 4232: 1967 *Surface finish of blast-cleaned steel for painting*

This standard specifies first, second and third qualities of surface finish for all steels that are prepared by dry methods of blast-cleaning for the application of paints and non-metallic coatings. It makes recommendations on selection of qualities, methods of control and inspection and blast-cleaning procedures. It includes diagrammatic indications of second and third qualities.

BS 4360: 1979 *Weldable structural steels*

This standard specifies requirements for general and weather resistant structural steels, together with chemical composition and mechanical properties. It also includes dimensional tolerances. It covers requirements for hot-rolled plates, flat bars, wide flats, universal wide flats and bars and for structural steel sections complying with requirements of BS 4848 Parts 2 and 4 and BS 4 Part 1. However, in the case of hollow sections formed from plate and subsequently metal arc welded, it covers only the requirements for the plate material.

BS 5996: 1980 *Methods of testing and quality grading of ferritic steel plate by ultrasonic methods*

This standard describes standard procedures for detecting and estimating the size of discontinuities in steel plate using ultrasonic techniques. It provides a series of grades characterized by the extent of lamination and inclusion cluster content of the plate. It supersedes BS 4336 Part 1A: 1968 and DD 21: 1972.

Aluminium and alloys

BS 3660: 1976 *Glossary of terms used in the wrought aluminium industry*

This standard covers definitions of terms, in alphabetical order, used in connection with the manufacture of wrought aluminium products.

BS 1470: 1972 *Wrought aluminium and aluminium alloys for engineering purposes – plate, sheet and strip*

This standard specifies requirements for plate, sheet and strip made from four grades of aluminium and six aluminium alloys in various conditions. It supersedes BS 395, BS 414 and BS 1477.

BS 1471: 1972 *Wrought aluminium and aluminium alloys for general engineering purposes – drawn tube*

This standard specifies requirements for drawn tube made from two grades of aluminium and seven aluminium alloys. It supersedes BS 385 and BS 386.

BS 1472: 1972 *Wrought aluminium and aluminium alloys for general engineering purposes – forging stock and forgings*

This standard specifies requirements for forging stock and forgings not exceeding 200 mm diameter in one grade of aluminium alloys in various conditions. It supersedes BS 532.

BS 1473: 1972 *Wrought aluminium and aluminium alloys for general engineering purposes – rivet, bolt and screw stock*

This standard specifies requirements for rivet stock of diameter not exceeding 25 mm made from one grade of aluminium and from four aluminium alloys in various conditions, and for bolt and screw stock of diameter not exceeding 12 mm made from four aluminium alloys in various conditions.

BS 1474: 1972 *Wrought aluminium and aluminium alloys for engineering purposes – bars, extruded round tubes and sections*

This standard specifies requirements for solid bars and sections, extruded round tube and hollow sections made from two grades of aluminium and seven aluminium alloys. It supersedes BS 386 and BS 1476.

BS 1475: 1972 *Wrought aluminium and aluminium alloys for general engineering purposes – wire*

This standard specifies requirements for wire made from two grades of aluminium and ten aluminium alloys.

The forms of material covered by BS 1470 to BS 1475 are summarized in Table 140.

Table 140 *Forms of material available*

Material	BS general engineering specification							
	1470 Plate sheet and strip	1471 Drawn tube	1472 Forging stock	1472 Forgings	1473 Rivet stock for forging	1473 Bolt and screw stock for forging	1474 Bars, extruded tube and sections	1475 Wire
1080A	*							*
1050A	*	*	*	*	*		*	*
1200	*	*					*	
4047A								*
4043A								*
3103	*							
5251	*	*	*	*			*	*
5154A	*	*	*	*	*		*	*
5056A					*	*		*
5556A								*
5083	*	*	*	*			*	
6063		*	*	*			*	*
2031			*	*				
2014A	*	*	*	*	*	*	*	*
CLAD 2014A	*							
2618A			*	*				
6061		*				*	*	*
6082	*	*	*	*	*	*	*	

*Material covered by the specification concerned.

(Appendix A: BS 1475: 1972)

BS 4300   *Specification (supplementary series) for wrought aluminium and aluminium alloys for general engineering purposes*

4300/4: 1973   6463 solid extruded bars and sections suitable for bright trim/reflector applications

This standard specifies requirements for solid bars and sections of diameter or minor cross-sectional dimension not exceeding 50 mm in an aluminium alloy suitable for bright trim/reflector applications.

BS 4842: 1972   *Stoving organic finishes in aluminium extrusions and preformed sections for external architectural application*

This standard specifies requirements and methods of test for the organic coatings used for finishing aluminium sections, and also for the finish of the aluminium sections themselves.

BS 6536: 1985   *Continuously hot-dip aluminium/silicon-coated, cold-reduced, carbon-steel and strip*

Requirements for hot-dip aluminium/silicon-coated, cold-reduced, carbon-steel flat products in commercial and drawing grades available in wide strip and sheet in widths from 600 mm to 1540 mm, and strip and cut lengths less than 600 mm wide. It covers products from 0.4 mm to less than 3 mm thick, which are suitable for application where heat and corrosion resistance are required.

Copper, zinc and their alloys

BS 1420: 1965   *Glossary of terms applicable to wrought products in copper, zinc and their alloys*

This glossary includes terms used for wrought products under the groupings:

1 Cast forms.
2 Wrought forms.
3 Processing.
4 Thermal treatment.
5 Finishes.
6 Dimensional, surface and structural characteristics.
7 Packaging.

Temper-designation terms are appended.

BS 2870: 1980   *Rolled copper and copper alloys: sheet, strip and foil*

This standard specifies requirements for rolled copper and copper alloy sheet, strip and foil for general purposes in thicknesses not exceeding 10 mm. It covers five grades of copper and 30 copper alloys. Special requirements are given for specific materials for clocks, watches, instruments, telecommunications, roofing, building, decorative and other purposes.

BS 2875: 1969   *Copper and copper alloys: plate*

This standard specifies requirements for wrought copper and copper alloy plate for general purposes over 10 mm thick. It supersedes BS 1541 and BS 2027.

BS 849: 1939   *Plain sheet zinc roofing*

This standard specifies requirements for material, freedom from defects, stamping, dimensions, gauge, bending test. Also requirements relating to construction and method of laying zinc on different roof forms are given.

BS 1004: 1972   *Zinc alloys for die casting and zinc alloy die castings*

This standard specifies requirements for two zinc die casting alloys (A and B) in ingot form, and the corresponding die castings.

BS 6561: 1985   *Zinc alloy sheet and strip for building*

Requirements for composition, manufacture, dimensions and marking for two types of alloy: a creep-resistant zinc/titanium alloy for roofing, and a soft-temper zinc/lead alloy for flashings. It gives typical available sizes and typical physical and mechanical properties.

Lead

BS 1178: 1982   *Milled lead sheet for building purposes*

■   AD (Reg. H3)

This standard specifies requirements for soft milled lead sheet for roofs, flashings, weatherings, damp-proof courses and similar building work.

BS 6582: 1985   *Continuously hot-dip lead alloy (terne)-coated, cold-reduced, carbon-steel, flat-rolled products*

Requirements for flat products in drawing and forming grades, available in continuous or cut lengths up to 1250 mm wide and over 0.4 mm to less than 3 mm thick. The products are suitable for applications where suitability for soldering and cold forming are required.

BS 5140: 1974 (1981)   *Pewter*

The chemical composition of pewter and solders for the manufacture and joining of pewterware. Compositions apply to alloy in the form of cast ingot, rolled sheet and the fabricated or cast article.

i Wood

There are twelve standards covered in this section.

BS 373: 1957 *Methods of testing small clear specimens of timber*

This standard gives methods of test (moisture contents, specific gravity, static bending test, impact test, compression test, indentation test, shear test, cleavage test, tensile test and shrinkage) using specimens of 20 or 102 mm square cross-section.

BS 881 and 589: 1974 *Nomenclature of commercial timbers including sources of supply*

These standards comprise nomenclature of hardwoods/softwoods and include botanical species, standard names, alternative commercial names, sources of supply and average densities in kg/m³.

BS 1186 *Timber and workmanship in joinery*

Part 1: 1986 *Specification for timber*
This revision incorporates changes necessitated by the need to align the quality of timber requested by the specifier or purchaser with economical selection from suitable commercial grades.

This part specifies requirements for the classification, species, moisture content and quality of softwood and hardwood used in joinery.

Part 2: 1971 *Quality of workmanship*
This part specifies requirements for the quality of workmanship in manufactured joinery suitable for a wide variety of joinery items and of the building needs.

Specifications and requirements for the fit of parts in various details of construction are given for:

1 Fixed joints of framed, edge-to-edge and staircase types.
2 Joints permitting movement for plywood panels, solid panels, bead butt, bead flush panels and joints for matchboard surfaces.
3 Moving parts such as doors and sashes, sliding drawers and flaps.
4 Gluing of joints, surface finish.
5 Laminating and finger jointing.

BS 4047: 1966 *Grading rules for sawn home grown hardwood*

This standard classifies raw material into groups suitable for different purposes. It covers two systems: the cutting system (for timber to be resawn – grades by number and size of rectangular pieces of clean timber obtainable from a board) and the defects system (for timber to be used in the sizes supplied).

BS 4471 *Dimensions for softwood*

■ AD (Regs. A1/2)

Part 1: 1978 *Sizes of sawn and planed timber*
This part specifies dimensions for a range of sawn softwood sizes and provides a table of reductions upon sawn sizes for various categories of products. It covers surfaced constructional timber (Canadian lumber standards or American lumber standards) imported mainly from Canada and in accordance with North American standards. However, it does not cover precision timber.

Part 2: 1971 *Small resawn sections*
This part specifies dimensions of small resawn sections of softwood suitable for roofing battens and counter battens, floor fillets, fixing grounds, noggins, plasterers' laths, etc.

BS 4978: 1973 *Timber grades for structural use*

■ AD (Regs. A1/2)

This standard specifies the two methods of grading timber: visual stress grading and machine stress grading. It does not cover, however, the grading of tropical hardwoods (see BS 5756).

Requirements are given for size, deviations in size, processing reductions, knots, fissures, slope of grain, wane, rate of growth, resin pockets, distortions, worm holes, sapstain and abnormal defects. Illustrations show the principles of knot projection to assess the knot area ratio (KAR) in visual grading and the measurement of other characteristics affecting strength.

BS 5268 *Code of practice for the structural use of timber*

Part 4 *Fire resistance of timber structures*

Section 4.1:1978 *Method of calculating fire resistance of timber members*
This code covers methods of assessing the fire resistance of flexural tension and compression members of solid or glued laminated timber and their joints.

BS 5291: 1984 *Manufacture of finger joints of structural softwood*

Requirements for the manufacture of cut, interlocking, glued finger joints in structural softwood members, for quality control of their manufacture and for assessment of their efficiency ratings.

Requirements are specified for timber, joint spacing, adhesives, moisture content, cutting, gluing and preservative and flame-retardant treatments. It does not cover impressed (die-formed) joints and in the case of laminated timber it applies only to individual laminations.

BS 5450: 1977 *Sizes of hardwoods and methods of measurement*

This standard specifies a range of basic sizes (see Table 141) of sawn hardwood at 15 per cent moisture content with permissible deviations (see Table 142) and the methods of measurement of moisture content and sizes. It includes a table for reductions by

Table 141 *Basic cross-sectional sizes of sawn hardwoods*

Thickness	Width (mm)										
mm	50	63	75	100	125	150	175	200	225	250	300
19			×	×	×	×	×				
25	×	×	×	×	×	×	×	×	×	×	×
32			×	×	×	×	×	×	×	×	×
38			×	×	×	×	×	×	×	×	×
50				×	×	×	×	×	×	×	×
63						×	×	×	×	×	×
75						×	×	×	×	×	×
100						×	×	×	×	×	×

Note: Designers and users should check the availability of specified sizes in any particular species.

(Table 1: BS 5450: 1977)

Table 142 *Permissible deviations from basic sizes of thickness or width*

Basic size	Minus deviation	Plus deviation
mm	mm	mm
Under 25	1	3
25 to 75	2	6
76 to 125	3	9
126 to 300	4	12

(Table 2: BS 5450: 1977)

Table 143 *Reductions from basic sawn size to finished size by processing of two opposed faces*

End use or product	Reduction from basic size to finished size				
	For basic sawn sizes of width or thickness (mm)				
	15 to 25	26 to 50	51 to 100	101 to 150	151 to 300
	mm	mm	mm	mm	mm
Constructional timber surfaced	3	3	3	5	6
Floorings, matchings and interlocked boarding and planed all round	5	6	7	7	7
	5	6	7	7	7
Trim	6	7	8	9	10
Joinery and cabinetwork	7	9	10	12	14

(Table 3: BS 5450: 1977)

manufacturing processes from the basic sawn hardwood sizes, for some end uses and products (see Table 143).

BS 5756: 1980 *Tropical hardwoods graded for structural use*

This standard specifies the permissible limits of characteristics of a single visual stress grade of timber which is designated 'hardwood structural' (HS) grade. Requirements for the HS grade are given for slope of grain, knots, limiting dimensions, longitudinal separation, fissures resin pockets, distortion, insect holes, wane, bark pockets and included phloem, stainfree from decay and other defects.

BS 5820: 1979 *Methods of test for determination of certain physical and mechanical properties of timber in structural sizes*

This standard covers test procedures applying to rectangular and square sections of solid timber dealing with physical (dimensions, moisture content and density), grade determining (visual and machine grading) and mechanical properties (modulus of elasticity in bending, tension and compression, shear modulus, bending, tension and compression strength). See also the related standard, BS 373.

BS 6100 Part 4 *Forest products*

Section 4.1: 1984 *Characteristics and properties of timber and wood-based panel products*

Definitions of terms for anatomical, growth and appearance characteristics; covers knots, conversion and machining, drying and conditioning, imperfections and certain basic aspects of preservation. The terms are arranged systematically in a classified order with an alphabetical index.

Section 4.2: 1984 *Sizes and quantities of solid timber*
Definitions of certain terms related to the sizes and quantities of solid timber. The terms are arranged systematically in a classified order with an alphabetical index.

Section 4.3: 1984 *Wood-based panel products*
Definitions of terms, mainly relevant to the construction industry, applicable to plywood, fibre building board and particle board. The terms are arranged systematically in a classified order with an alphabetical index.

Part 4: Section 4.4: 1985 *Carpentry and joinery*
Definitions of certain terms related to carpentry and joinery. The terms are arranged systematically in a classified order with an alphabetical index.

j Vegetable and animal materials

j5 Cork

BS 6100 Part 4 *Forest products*
Section 4.5: 1984 *Cork*.
Definitions of terms, relevant only to the construction industry, applicable to raw cork, manufactured cork and cork wood, including waste cork and certain products worked from cork. The terms are arranged systematically in a classified order with an alphabetical index.

m   Inorganic fibres (no entry)
n   Rubber, plastics, etc.

There are 16 standards available in this section (see also *Standard List 12* Leather, plastics, rubber).

BS 1755: 1951   *Glossary of terms used in the plastics industry*

This standard covers definitions of terms applicable to chemistry, industrial applications, constituents, properties, moulding processes and other manufacturing processes.

Part 1: 1982   *Polymer and plastics technology*
This part covers definitions of terms applicable to materials and products, processing operations and properties.

Part 2: 1974   *Manufacturing processes*
This part covers definitions of terms applicable to moulding, calendering and embossing, extrusion, film casting, block process, fabric and paper coating and thermoforming.

BS 4901: 1976   *Plastics colours for building purposes*

This standard specifies the colour of opaque plastics products used for building purposes and is summarized in Table 4 'Activities, requirements' under section (G5) 'Colour'.

BS 3227: 1980   *Butyl rubbers compounds (including halobutyl compounds*

This standard specifies requirements for four rubber compounds based on either isobutene (isoprene (butyl) rubber or halogenated isobutene) or isoprene (halobutyl) rubbers, classified by their vulcanized hardness. The compounds are intended for the manufacture of items in the form of extrusions, mouldings, moulded or calendered sheet, or for items cut or punched from sheet.

The vulcanizates do not necessarily have good electrical insulating properties.

BS 3502   *Schedule of common names and abbreviations for plastics and rubbers*

Part 1: 1978   *Principal commercial plastics*
This standard provides a schedule of 33 names and abbreviations of plastics in common use (see Table 144).

Part 3: 1978   *Rubbers and latices*
This part of the standard provides a general classification for basic rubbers, including abbreviations and chemical names (see Table 145).

BS 3532: 1962   *Unsaturated polyester resin systems for low pressure fibre reinforced plastics*

This standard specifies five types of material classified by

Table 144   *Common names and abbreviations*

Common name	Material	Abbreviation
ABS	Acrylonitrile-butadiene-styrene polymer	ABS
Acetal	Polyoxymethylene; polyformaldehyde (a polyacetal)	POM
Acetate	Cellulose acetate	CA
Acrylic	Methylmethacrylate polymer	PMMA
Butyrate	Cellulose acetate butyrate	CAB
Casein	Casein	CS
Celluloid	Cellulose nitrate	CN
Epoxy	Epoxide resin	EP
EVA	Ethylene vinyl acetate copolymer	EVAC
GRP	Glass fibre reinforced plastic based on a thermosetting resin	GRP
Melamine	Melamine-formaldehyde	MF
Nitrate	Cellulose nitrate	CN
Nylon	Polyamide	PA
Phenolic	Phenol-formaldehyde	PF
Polycarbonate	Polycarbonate	PC
Polyester	Polyethylene terephthalate	PETP
	Polybutylene terephthalate	PBTP
Polyester	Unsaturated polyester	UP
Polyethylene Polythene	Polyethylene	PE
LDPE	Low density polyethylene	LDPE
HDPE	High density polyethylene	HDPE
Polypropylene	Polypropylene and copolymers in which propylene is the major constituent	PP
Polystyrene Toughened polystyrene Modified polystyrene	Polystyrene	PS
Polyurethane Urethane	Polyurethane	PUR
PTFE	Polytetrafluoroethylene	PTFE
PVA	Polyvinyl acetate	PVAC
PVA	Polyvinyl alcohol	PVAL
PVC Vinyl	Polyvinyl chloride and copolymers in which vinyl chloride is the major constituent	PVC
SAN	Styrene-acrylonitrile copolymer	SAN
Silicon	Substituted polysiloxane	SI
Reinforced thermoplastic	Thermoplastic material reinforced, commonly with fibre	FRP, FRTP
Triacetate	Cellulose triacetate	CTA
Urea	Ureaformaldehyde	UF

(From BS 3502: Part 1: 1978)

Table 145   *Classification for basic rubbers, based on chemical composition*

Group designations/ chemical composition	Abbreviations/chemical names		Group designations/ chemical composition	Abbreviations/chemical names	
M Rubbers having a saturated chain of the polymethylene type	ACM	Copolymers of ethylacrylate or other acrylates and a small amount of a monomer which facilitates vulcanization	Partly from diolefins	NCR	Nitrile-chloroprene rubbers
				NR	Isoprene rubbers natural
	ANM	Ethylacrylate or other acrylate and acrylonitrile copolymers		PBR	Pyridine-butadiene rubbers
				SBR	Styrene-butadiene rubbers
	CM	Chloropolyethylene		SCR	Styrene-chloroprene rubbers
	CFM	Polychlorotrifluoroethylene		SIR	Styrene-isoprene rubbers
	CSM	Chlorosulphonylpolyethylene		NIR	Nitrile-isoprene rubbers
	EPDM	Terpolymer of ethylene, propylene, and a diene with the residual unsaturated portion of the diene in the side chain		PSBR	Pyridine-styrene-butadiene rubbers
				XSBR	Carboxylic-styrene-butadiene
				XNBR	Carboxylic-nitrile-butadiene
	EPM	Ethylene-propylene copolymer		BIIR	Bromo-isobutene-isoprene
				CIIR	Chloro-isobutene-isoprene
	FPM	Rubbers having fluoro and fluoroalkyl or fluoroalkoxy substituent groups on the polymer chain	Q Rubbers having silicone in the polymer chain	MFQ	Silicone rubbers having both methyl and fluorine substituent groups on the polymer chain
	IM	Polyisobutene		MPQ	Silicone rubbers having both methyl and phenyl substituent groups on the polymer chain
N Rubbers having nitrogen in the polymer chain				MPVQ	Silicone rubbers having methyl, phenyl, and vinyl substituent groups on the polymer chain
O Rubbers having oxygen in the polymer chain	CO	Polychloromethyloxiran (epichlorohydrin elastomer)		MQ	Silicone rubbers having only methyl substituent groups on the polymer chain, such as dimethyl polysiloxane
	ECO	Ethylene oxide (oxiran) and chloromethyloxiran (epichlorohydrin copolymer)		MVQ	Silicone rubbers having both methyl and vinyl substituent groups on the polymer chain
	GPO	Copolymer of propylene oxide and allyl glycidyl ether.	T Rubbers having sulphur in the polymer chain		
R Rubbers having an unsaturated carbon chain, for example, natural rubber and synthetic rubbers derived at least	ABR	Acrylate-butadiene rubbers	U Rubbers having carbon, oxygen, and nitrogen in the polymer chain	AFMU	Terpolymer of tetrafluoroethylene-tri fluoronitrosomethane and nitroso perfluorobutylic acid
	BR	Butadiene rubbers			
	CR	Chloroprene rubbers			
	IIR	Isobutene-isoprene rubbers		AU	Polyester rubbers
	IR	Isoprene rubbers, synthetic		EU	Polyether rubbers
	NBR	Nitrile-butadiene rubbers			

(From BS 3502: Part 3: 1978)

deflection temperature of cast resin under load. Test requirements for laminates, castings and basic resin, and methods of test are provided.

BS 3869: 1965 *Rigid expanded polyvinyl chloride for thermal insulation purposes and building applications*

This standard deals with rigid expanded PVC in the form of blocks, boards and sheets of minimum thickness 12.5 mm for thermal insulation and building applications at temperatures up to 50 °C. Applicable to materials of apparent density 24–48 kg/m³ and over 48 kg/m³. Requirements are specified for cross-breaking strength, compressive strength, water vapour transmission and dimensional stability.

BS 3927: 1965 *Phenolic foam materials for thermal insulation and building purposes*

This standard deals with phenolic foam materials in the form of blocks, boards and sheets of minimum thickness 12.5 mm for building purposes and for thermal insulations up to temperatures of 130 °C. Applicable to materials of apparent density 32 kg/m³ and 56 kg/m³.

BS 4549 *Guide to quality control requirements for reinforced plastics mouldings*

Part 1: 1970   *Polyester resin mouldings reinforced with chopped strand mat or randomly deposited glass fibres*
This part gives recommendations and methods of test for preparation of a scheme to control the quality of mouldings made from a chopped strand mat or randomly deposited glass fibres bonded with filled or unfilled polyester resin.

BS 4618: 1970 *Recommendations for the presentation of plastics design data*

This standard consists of five parts and 22 sections.

Part 1   *Mechanical properties*
This part is subdivided into the following sections:

Section 1.1: 1970   *Creep*
Subsection 1.1.1: 1970   *Creep in uniaxial tension or compression (with particular reference to solid plastics)*
Subsection 1.1.2: 1976   *Creep in flexure at low strains*
Subsection 1.1.3: 1974   *Creep lateral contraction ratio (Poisson's ratio)*

Section 1.2: 1972 *Impact behaviour*
Section 1.3: 1975 *Strength*
Subsection 1.3.1: 1975 *Static fatigue failure caused by a constant force*
Subsection 1.3.3: 1976 *Environmental stress cracking*

Part 2 *Electrical properties*
This part includes the following sections:

Section 2.1: 1970 *Permittivity*
Section 2.2: 1970 *Loss tangent*
Section 2.3: 1975 *Volume resistivity*
Section 2.4: 1975 *Surface resistivity*

Part 3 *Thermal properties*
This part includes the following sections:

Section 3.1: 1970 *Linear thermal expansion*
Section 3.2: 1973 *Heat content*
Section 3.3: 1973 *Thermal conductivity*

Part 4 *Environmental and chemical effects*
This part includes the following sections:

Section 4.1: 1972 *Chemical resistance to liquids*
Section 4.1: 1972 *Resistance to natural weathering*
Section 4.3: 1974 *Resistance to colour change produced by exposure to light*
Section 4.4: 1973 *The effects on plastics of marine exposure*
Section 4.5: 1974 *The effects on plastics of soil burial and biological attack*
Section 4.6: 1974 *The thermal endurance of plastics*

Part 5 *Other properties*
This part includes the following sections:
Section 5.1: 1970 *Density*
Section 5.2: 1970 *Change in linear dimensions with moisture absorption*
Section 5.3: 1972 *Optical properties*
Section 5.4: 1972 *Acoustical properties (mechanical damping capacity)*
Section 5.5: 1974 *Data on diffusion*
Section 5.6: 1975 *Guide to sliding friction*

BS 4735: 1974 *Laboratory methods of test for assessment of the horizontal burning characteristics of specimens no larger than 150 × 50 × 13 mm (nominal) of cellular plastics and cellular rubber materials when subjected to a small flame*

This standard describes a small-scale laboratory procedure for use in controlling manufacturing processes to ensure consistency of production. *This test method is not intended to be used to assess potential fire hazard in use.*

BS 4815: 1972 *Glossary of generic terms for man made fibres*

This glossary gives the generic name with the composition of the polymer and examples, chemical formulae or characteristics.

BS 4935: 1974 *Acrylonitrile-butadiene-styrene (ABS) mouldings and extrusion materials*

This standard provides basic data for control of quality. It gives designations based on five characteristic properties.

1 Acrylonitrile content in the continuous phase.
2 Vicat softening temperature using a force of 49 N.
3 Melt flow index.
4 Izod impact strength.
5 Flexural modulus.

BS 5111: *Laboratory methods of test for determination of smoke generation characteristics of cellular plastics and cellular rubber materials*

Part 1: 1974 *Method of testing a 25 mm cube test specimen of low density material (up to 130 kg/m³) to continuous flaming conditions*
This part describes a small-scale laboratory test for use in product development and monitoring consistency of production. This test is not intended as a measure of potential smoke production in fire situations. For tests on building materials and structures, attention is drawn to DD 36.

BS 5139: 1974 *Classification for polypropylene plastics materials for moulding and extrusion*

This standard provides for the identification of polypropylene plastics by means of a code based on polymer type, melt flow rate, and use and stabilization and additive system. It is not intended to provide engineering data for design purposes nor does it give recommendations on food contact applications. Test methods are specified.

BS 6319 *Testing of resin compositions for use in construction*

Part 1: 1983 *Method for preparation of test specimens*
A general introduction to the testing of resin compositions and describes the procedure to be used for obtaining and preparing samples for test. It is applicable to thermoset cold-curing resin formulations, e.g. epoxide, polyester, acrylic, polyurethane.

Part 2: 1983 *Method for measurement of compressive strength*
The procedure for the determination of compressive strength of specimens of resin-based mortars and concretes in the form of cubes.

Part 3: 1983 *Method for measurement of flexural strength*
The procedure for the measurement of the flexural strength of specimens of resin-based mortars and concretes in the form of rectangular prisms.

Part 4: 1984 *Method for measurement of bond strength* (slant shear method)
A method of determining the strength of the bond between a resin composition and a substrate using a specimen incorporating a scarf joint.

Part 5: 1984 *Methods for determination of density of hardened resin compositions*
Two methods for determining density, one being a simple measurement method and the other using a water-filled pyknometer.

Part 6: 1984 *Method for determination of modulus of elasticity in compression*
A method for the determination of the modulus of elasticity in compression of specimens in the form of rectangular prisms.

Part 7: 1985 *Method for measurement of tensile strength*
A method for measurement of the tensile strength of specimens in the form of dumb-bell shaped briquettes.

Part 8: 1984 *Method for the assessment of resistance to liquids*
A method for assessing the resistance to liquids of resin-based mortars and concrete, using the test for flexural strength described in BS 6319: Part 3.

DD88: 1983 *Method for the assessment of pot life of non-flowing resin compositions for use in civil engineering*

Describes a method for assessing the pot life of a filled-resin composition by determining the time after mixing when the composition fails to wet a filter paper.

BS 2782 *Methods of testing plastics* (see also Table 1: Building elements (59) Parts, accessories etc.)

This standard sets out to define test methods in current use by the plastics industry for determining the quality of its products and includes tests applied to mouldings and extrusion compounds, synthetic resins, reinforced plastics, semi-fabricated products such as sheet, film, rod and tube, and finished articles in the form of mouldings and extrusions. The standard specifies a considerable number of test methods, some in BS 2782: 1970 and others, which are replacing BS 2782: 1970 as they become available, in separate parts. The parts are numbered in groups dealing with thermal properties, electrical properties, mechanical properties, rheological properties and others.

The methods of test are for the following properties:

Part 0: 1982   *Introduction*

Part 1:   *Thermal properties*

■ AD (Regs. B2/3/4)

Method 102C: 1970 Softening point of thermoplastics moulding material,
Methods 120A to 120E: 1976 Determination of the Vicat softening temperature of thermoplastics,
Method 140D: 1980 Flammability of a test piece 550 mm × 35 mm of thin polyvinyl chloride sheeting (laboratory method),
Method 140E: 1982 Flammability of a small, inclined, test piece exposed to an ethanol flame (laboratory method),
Method 508C: 1970 Degree of flammability of thin polyvinyl chloride sheeting,
Method 508D: 1970 Flammability (alcohol cup test).

Part 2: 1982   *Electrical properties*
Part 3: 1982   *Mechanical properties*
Part 4: 1982   *Chemical properties*
Part 5: 1982   *Optical and colour properties*
Part 6: 1982   *Dimensional properties*
Part 7: 1982   *Rheological properties*
Part 8: 1982   *Other properties*
Part 9: 1982   *Sampling and test specimen preparation*
Part 10: 1982   *Glass-reinforced plastics*
Part 11: 1982   *Thermoplastics pipes, fittings and valves*

o Glass

There are five standards set out in this section.

BS 952   *Glass for glazing*

Part 1: 1978   *Classification*
This part classifies soda–lime–silica glasses for building purposes into three groups:

1 *Annealed flat glasses* – including float or polished plate glass, sheet glass, cast or patterned glass and wired glass.
2 *Processed flat glasses* – including toughened or tempered glass, laminated glass, insulating glass units and silvered glass.
3 *Miscellaneous glasses* – including flashed or pot coloured sheet glass, diffuse reflection glass, copper light, bullions, hollow glass blocks, lenses, channel glass and antique glasses.

Terms and definitions, together with details of nominal thickness, weight and tolerance are given. Methods of measurement for thickness and linear dimensions are appended.

Part 2: 1980   *Terminology for work on glass*
This part provides descriptions and illustrations of types of work on glass. The main processes, comprising cutting, obscuring and the various decorating processes are described.

BS 3275: 1960   *Glass for signs and recommendations on glazing for signs*

This standard specifies the requirements (such as quality, marking) for glass for box and panel signs, including toughened and laminated glass. It makes recommendations for the use of glass in these signs, including glazing, fixing, strength of supporting materials and ventilation.

BS 3447: 1962   *Glossary of terms used in the glass industry*

This standard provides classification and definitions of a comprehensive list of terms used in the glass industry, covering types and properties of glass, raw materials, melting, forming and finishing, forms of glass and glassware, imperfections in glass and occupational terms.

BS 4031: 1966   *X-ray protective lead glasses*

This standard specifies essential requirements for lead barium silicate (Type LBS) and lead silicate (Type LS) glasses or protection against X-ray radiation and includes a method of measuring the lead equivalent (see Table 146).

BS 6206: 1981   *Impact performance requirements for flat safety glass and safety plastics for use in buildings*

This standard specifies performance requirements and an impact test method which are intended to reduce the risk of

Table 146   *Typical examples of minimum lead equivalents*

Type of glass and manufacturer's reference	Minimum density	Thickness range of panel	Minimum lead equivalent at stated peak kilovoltage				
			100	150	200	250	300 kV
	g/cm³	mm			mm		
Lead silicate	4.2	6–8	1.3	1.3	1.3	1.3	1.3
	4.2	9–11	2.0	2.0	2.0	2.0	2.0
	4.2	11–13	2.5	2.5	2.5	2.5	2.5
Lead barium silicate	4.6	5–7	1.5	1.5	1.2	1.2	1.2
	4.6	8–10	2.5	2.4	2.0	2.0	2.0

(Table 1: BS 4031: 1966)

cutting and piercing injuries from flat safety glass and safety plastics. It specifies three classes according to behaviour on impact (see Table 147), but does not specify use of these materials or any requirements for their durability.

Table 147 *Classification of safety glass and safety plastics according to behaviour on impact*

Class	Behaviour on impact		
	Drop height 305 mm	Drop height 457 mm	Drop height 1219 mm
A	No breakage, or breaks safely	No breakage, or breaks safely	No breakage, or breaks safely
B	No breakage, or breaks safely	No breakage, or breaks safely	No requirement
C	No breakage, or breaks safely	No requirement	No requirement

(Table 1: BS 6206: 1981)

p Aggregates, loose fills

BS 6100 *Glossary of building and civil engineering terms*

Part 6 *Concrete and plaster*
   Section 6.3: 1984 *Aggregates*
Definitions of terms for natural and manufactured aggregates. The terms are arranged systematically in a classified order with an alphabetical index. It supersedes parts of BS 2787 which is being amended.

BS 63 *Single-sized roadstone and chippings*

Part 1: 1951 *Imperial units*

Part 2: 1971 *Metric units*
This standard covers nominally single-sized aggregates for use in the construction and maintenance of roads, and gives requirements for grading and particle shape (see Table 148) and methods of sampling and test.

BS 812 *Methods for sampling and testing of mineral aggregates, sands and fillers*

Part 1: 1975 *Sampling, size, shape and classification*
Test methods are specified in this part for the determination of the properties of size and shape of mineral aggregates including clay, silt and dust, petrographical classification of aggregates is given and a test method for the determination of shell content of coarse aggregates is included.

Part 2: 1975 *Physical properties*
Test methods are specified in this part for the determination of relative density, water absorption, bulk density, voids, building and moisture content of aggregates.

Part 3: 1975 *Mechanical properties*
Test methods are specified in this part for the determination of the aggregate impact value, aggregate crushing value, 10 per cent fines value, aggregate abrasion value and polished-stone value of aggregates.

Part 4: 1976 *Chemical properties*
Test methods are specified in this part for the determination of the amount of water soluble chloride salts in the aggregate.

Part 101: 1984 *Guide to sampling and testing aggregates*
General guidance on sampling and testing aggregates and procedures for assessing the precision of the methods of test for aggregates.

Part 102: 1984 *Methods of sampling*
Methods for sampling coarse, fine and all-in aggregates. It includes nominal descriptions for materials sampled.

Part 103: 1985 *Methods for determination of particle size distribution*
Two methods for the determination of the particle size distribution of samples of aggregates and fillers by sieving.

Part 105 *Methods for determination of particle shape*
   Section 105.1: 1985 *Flakiness index*
The method for determining the flakiness index of coarse aggregate.

Part 106: 1985 *Method for determination of shell content in coarse aggregate*

Part 119: 1985 *Method for determination of acid-soluble material in fine aggregate.*

Table 148   *Requirements for grading and particle shape*

1	2	3	4	Oversize		Undersize		9	10	11	12	Specified size and oversize
				5	6	7	8					13
Nominal size	Passing BS test sieve	Retained on BS test sieve	Minimum proportion of specified size	All to pass BS test sieve	Maximum retained on BS test sieve quoted in column 2	Passing BS test sieve	Maximum proportion of undersize	Passing BS test sieve	Maximum fines	Passing BS test sieve	Maximum dust	Maximum permissible flakiness index
mm	mm	mm	%	mm	%	mm	%	mm	%	µm	%	
								microns†				
50	50.0	37.5	70	63.0	15	28.0	5	2.36	2	75	1.5	40
40	37.5	28.0	60	50.0	15	20.0	5	2.36	2	75	1.5	40
28	28.0	20.0	60	37.5	15	14.0	7	2.36	2	75	1.5	35
20	20.0	14.0	60	28.0	15	10.0	7	2.36	2	75	1.5	35
14	14.0	10.0	60	20.0	15	6.30	7	2.36	2	75	1.5	35
10	10.0	6.30	65	14.0	15	5.00	10	2.36	2	75	1.5	35
6	6.30	3.35	65	10.0	15	2.36	10	600	2	75	1.5	–
3	3.35	1.70	65	6.30	15	1.18	10	600	2	75	1.5	–

(Table 1: BS 63: Part 2: 1971)

The determination of the amount of acid-soluble material in two fractions of fine aggregate both passing 5 mm test sieve and separated by a 600 mm test sieve.

BS 877   Foamed or explanded blastfurnace slag lightweight aggregate for concrete

Part 2: 1973   *Metric units*

This part specifies requirements for sampling, bulk density (maximum 800 kg/m³ for coarse and 1120 kg/m³ for fine aggregate), grading, sulphate content (maximum 1 per cent as SO_3) and contamination.

BS 882: 1983   *Aggregates from natural sources for concrete*

■ AD (Regs. A1/2 and H1)

Sampling and testing, quality requirements and grading of coarse, fine and all-in aggregate for use in concrete. It gives definitions, information to be provided by the supplier and advice on special considerations and chloride content. (See Tables 149–152.)

Alternatively, a guide to the clay and silt content of sand and crushed gravel fines may be obtained from the field settling test specified in BS 812: Part 1. If the amount of clay and silt as determined by this test is greater than 10% by volume, a decantation test shall be carried out unless a figure higher than 10% by volume represents not more than 3% by mass.

BS 1047: 1983   *Air-cooled blastfurnace slag aggregate for use in construction*

Quality and grading requirements for use in concrete and in other construction materials, stability tests and methods of chemical analysis are appended.

BS 1165: 1985   *Clinker and furnace bottom ash aggregates for concrete*

Requirements for sampling, testing, sulphate content and loss on ignition for two classes (Table 151) of furnace clinker and furnace bottom ash for use as aggregate in concrete.

BS 1199 and 1200: 1976   *Building sands from natural sources*

These standards, published as one document, specify requirements for sampling, testing, quality and grading of sands.

BS 1199: 1976: covers sands for external renderings, internal plastering using mixes of lime and sand (with or without the addition of cement or gypsum plaster), cement and sand (with or without the addition of lime) and for floor screeds of cement and sand.

BS 1200: 1976: covers sands for mortar for plain and reinforced brickwork, blockwalling and masonry.

BS 1198 has been withdrawn.

BS 1438: 1971   *Media for biological percolating filters*

The standard deals with single-sized materials, 63 to 14 mm, including crushed stone, gravel, clinker, coke, slag and other similar materials, for treatment of water, sewage and trade effluents.

Requirements are specified for durability, sizes, descriptions of shape, nature of surface and group classification, flakiness, cleanness, sampling and testing.

BS 1984: 1967   *Gravel aggregates for surface treatment (including surface dressings) on roads*

This standard specifies requirements for grading, particle shape and certain mechanical properties of gravel aggregates for surface treatment (including surface dressings) on roads, and

Table 149 *Coarse aggregate*

Sieve size (mm)	Percentage by mass passing BS sieves for nominal sizes (%)						
	Graded aggregate (mm)			Single-sized aggregate (mm)			
	40 to 5	20 to 5	14 to 5	40	20	14	10
50.0	100	–	–	100	–	–	–
37.5	90–100	100	–	85–100	100	–	–
20.0	35–70	90–100	100	0–25	85–100	100	–
14.0	–	–	90–100	–	–	85–100	100
10.0	10–40	30–60	50–85	0–5	0–25	0–50	85–100
5.0	0–5	0–10	0–10	–	0–5	0–10	0–25
2.36	–	–	–	–	–	–	0–5

(Table 4: BS 882: 1983)

Table 150 *Fine aggregate*

Sieve size	Percentage by mass passing BS sieve (%)			
	Overall limits	Additional limits for grading		
		C	M	F
10.00 mm	100	–	–	–
5.00 mm	89–100	–	–	–
2.36 mm	60–100	60–100	65–100	80–100
1.18 mm	30–100	30–90	45–100	70–100
600 μm	15–100	15–54	25–80	55–100
300 μm	5–70	5–40	5–48	5–70
150 μm	0–15*	–	–	–

*Increased to 20% for crushed rock fines, except when they are used for heavy-duty floors.
Note: Fine aggregate not complying with table 5 may also be used provided that the supplier can satisfy the purchaser that such materials can produce concrete of the required quality.

(Table 5: BS 882:1983)

Table 151 *All-in aggregate*

Sieve size	Percentage by mass passing BS sieve (%)		
	40 mm nominal size	20 mm nominal size	10 mm nominal size
50.0 mm	100	–	–
37.5 mm	95–100	100	–
20.0 mm	45–80	95–100	–
14.0 mm	–	–	100
10.0 mm	–	–	95–100
5.00 mm	25–50	35–55	30–65
2.36 mm	–	–	20–50
1.18 mm	–	–	15–40
600 μm	8–30	10–35	10–30
300 μm	–	–	5–15
150 μm	0–8*	0–8*	0–8*

*Increased to 10% for crushed rock fines.

(Table 6: BS 882: 1983)

recommended limits on the degree of polished-stone value of the aggregate when used for road surfacing.

BS 2451: 1963 *Chilled iron shot and grit*

This standard specifies the sizes of particles of chilled iron shot and grit, and the method of testing for size. It also specifies material, form, designation and grading, and describes a hardness test.

Table 152 *Clay, silt and dust*

Aggregate type	Quantity of clay, silt and dust (max. % by mass)
Uncrushed, partially crushed or crushed gravel	1
Crushed rock	3
Uncrushed or partially crushed sand or crushed gravel fines	3
Crushed rock fines	15 (8 for use in heavy duty floor finishes
Gravel all-in aggregate	2
Crushed rock all-in aggregate	10

Note: The nature of the material passing the 75 μm BS 410 test sieve used in the decantation method differs between crushed rock and gravel or sand.

(Table 7: BS 882: 1983)

Table 153 *Percentage loss of mass on ignition of clinker and furnace bottom ash aggregates*

Class	Use	Percentage loss on ignition
A	Aggregate for use in concrete for general purposes	Not greater than 10
B	Aggregate for use in concrete for interior work not normally exposed to damp conditions	Not greater than 25

(From BS 1165:1985)

BS 3670: 1963 *Methods of sieve analysis of woodflour*

This standard specifies apparatus and procedure for and method of reporting results of sieve analysis of woodflour.

BS 3681 *Methods for the sampling and testing of lightweight aggregates for concrete*

Part 2: 1973 *Metric units*
This standard describes methods of sampling and testing of lightweight aggregates for concrete. The tests cover bulk density, sieve analysis, apparent specific gravity, sulphate content, volatile matter, loss-on-ignition and carbon content.

BS 3797   *Lightweight aggregates for concrete*

Part 2: 1976   *Metric units*
This standard specifies the following aggregates for concrete: exfoliated vermiculite, expanded perlite, pumice, expanded clay, expanded shale and sintered pulverized-fuel ash. Requirements are specified for bulk density, grading, sulphate content and loss-on-ignition.

BS 3892   *Pulverized-fuel ash*

BS 3892 is revised in two parts. Part 1 specifies pulverized-fuel ash with a low sieve residue for use with Portland cement in concrete intended for structural purposes. BS 3892: 1965 has been amended to serve temporarily as Part 2 of this standard and specifies pulverized-fuel ash for use in concrete masonry units, where a higher value of the sieve residue is acceptable.

Part 1: 1982   *Pulverized-fuel ash for use as a cementitious component in structural concrete*
Part 1 specifies requirements for the chemical and physical properties (see Table 154), sampling, testing and certification of pulverized-fuel ash suitable for use with Portland cement in concrete for structural purposes.

Part 2: 1984   *Pulverized-fuel ash for use in grouts and for miscellaneous uses in concrete*
Requirements for chemical and physical properties, sampling, testing and marking and gives recommendations for use.

Table 154   *Specifications for pulverized-fuel ash*

Chemical composition	
loss-on-ignition	7.0 % maximum
magnesia content	4.0 % maximum
sulphuric anhydride (SO$_3$)	2.5 % maximum
Moisture content	0.5 % maximum of mass of ash
Fineness	
retained on 45 μm mesh	
test sieve	12.5 % maximum
Water requirement of a	
mixture of pulverized-fuel	
ash with OPC of that for	
Portland cement alone	95 % maximum

(From BS 3892: Part 1: 1982)

BS 5835   *Recommendations for the testing of aggregates*

Part 1: 1980   *Compatibility test for graded aggregates*
This standard makes recommendations for testing compatibility graded aggregates, particularly those used in road bases and sub-bases. It covers definitions, sampling, preparation of test material, apparatus, test procedure, calculations and reports of results.

BS 410: 1986   *Test sieves*

Sieves for testing the size distribution of granular products in the particle size range 125 mm to 32 μm; aperture sizes for wire cloth and perforated plate (including seven non-ISO sizes for ground holes) in test sieves.
   It lists tolerances and gives relevant definitions and an outline of inspection procedures.

q   Lime and cement binders, mortars, concretes

There are 26 standards, one published document and three drafts for development. For asbestos-cement products see Table 2 'Constructions, forms'. For precast concrete see section f.

BS 6100   *Glossary of building and civil engineering terms*

Part 6   *Concrete and plaster*

Section 6.1: 1984   *Binders*
Definitions of terms for active, latent and blended hydraulic binders, for polymeric binders and for types of lime and gypsum. The terms are arranged systematically in a classified order with an alphabetical index.

Section 6.2: 1986   *Concrete*
Definitions of concretes identified through their properties, formulation, processes used to produce them, and their applications. The terms are arranged systematically in a classified order with an alphabetical index.

BS 890: 1972   *Building limes*

This standard specifies requirements for hydrated lime powder, quicklime and lime putty for use in building, under the following classification:

1 *Hydrated lime (powder)*:
  (a) Hydrated high-calcium lime (white lime).
  (b) Hydrated high-calcium by-product lime.
  (c) Hydrated semi-hydraulic lime (grey lime).
  (d) Hydrated magnesian lime.
2 *Quicklime*:
  (a) High-calcium lime (white lime).
  (b) Semi-hydraulic lime (grey lime).
  (c) Magnesian lime.
3 *Lime putty*:
  (a) High-calcium lime (white lime) putty.
  (b) High-calcium by-product lime putty.
  (c) Semi-hydraulic lime (grey lime) putty.
  (d) Magnesian lime putty

Tests and specifications are summarized in Table 155.

BS 6463   *Quicklime, hydrated lime and natural calcium carbonate*

Part 1: 1984   *Methods of sampling*
Methods for sampling quicklime, hydrated lime, lime putty and natural calcium carbonate.

Part 2: 1984   *Methods of chemical analysis*
Methods for the chemical analysis of quicklime, hydrated lime, lime putty and natural calcium carbonate.

Part 3:   *Physical test methods for quicklime (in preparation)*

Part 4:   *Physical test methods for hydrated lime and lime putty (in preparation)*

BS 12: 1978   *Ordinary and rapid-hardening Portland cement*

■ AD (Reg. A1/2)

This standard specifies requirements for the composition, the manufacture and the chemical and physical properties of OPC and RHPC (see Table 156).

BS 146   *Portland-blastfurnace cement*

Part 2: 1973   *Metric units*
This standard specifies requirements for the composition, the

Table 155 *Tests and specifications for building limes (BS 890)*

	Hydrated lime	Quicklime	Lime putty
Manufacture	(a) By hydration of quicklime with minimal water to produce a dry powder (b) By treatment of calcium carbide with water, as a by-product in the manufacturer of acetylene, followed by drying	By burning a natural rock or other material such that the product can be slaked effectively with water	(a) By treatment of hydrated lime or quick lime with excess water to produce a putty (b) By treatment of calcium carbide with excess water as a by-product in the manufacture of acetylene, followed by other process to produce a putty
Composition	Mainly $Ca(OH)_2$	Mainly CaO	Mainly $Ca(OH)_2$
carbon dioxide, CO_2	Maximum 6 %	Maximum 6 %	Maximum 6 %
Insoluble matter	Maximum 1 %	Maximum 3 %	Maximum 1 %
$CaO + MgO$	Minimum 65 % (Minimum 60 % for semi-hydraulic lime)	Minimum 85 % (Minimum 70 % for semi-hydraulic lime)	Minimum 65 % (Minimum 60 % for semi-hydraulic lime)
MgO	Maximum 4 % (Minimum 4 % for magnesian lime)	Maximum 5 % (Minimum 5 % for magnesian lime)	Maximum 4 % (Minimum 4 % for magnesian lime)
Soluble salts	Maximum 0.5 % (for high-calcium by-product lime)		Maximum 0.5 % (for high-calcium by-product lime)
soluble silica	Maximum 5 % (for semi-hydraulic lime)	Maximum 6 % (for semi-hydraulic lime)	Maximum 5 % (for semi-hydraulic lime)
Fineness residue on 180 μm test sieve total residue on 90 μm test sieve	Maximum 1 % Maximum 6 %	Residue on slaking: residue on 1.00 mm test sieve: Maximum 5 % total residue on 200 μm test sieve: Maximum 7 %	Maximum 1 % Maximum 6 %
Soundness (*not* applicable to high-calcium by-product lime) Le Chatelier test Pat test	Maximum 10 mm expansion Free from pots or pits	Maximum 10 mm expansion Free from pots or pits	Maximum 10 mm expansion Free from pots or pits
Density	Maximum 1.50 g/ml	Maximum 1.45 g/ml	Maximum 1.45 g/ml
Workability (to reach 190 mm spread)	Minimum 12 bumps	Minimum 14 bumps	Minimum 14 bumps
Hydraulic strength (applicable to semi-hydraulic lime)	Standard sand-lime mortar: modulus of rupture at 28 days: 0.7–2.0 N/mm²		

(From BS 890: 1972)

Table 156 *Specifications of Portland cements*

Type / Specifications	OPC (BS 12)	RHPC (BS 12)	LHPC (BS 1370)	SRPC (BS 4027)
Composition	$CaO + SiO_2$, Al_2O_3, Fe_2O_3	$CaO + SiO_2$, Al_2O_3, Fe_2O_3	$CaO + SiO_2$, Al_2O_3, Fe_2O_3	$CaO + SiO_2$, Al_2O_3, Fe_2O_3
Fineness (specific surface)	Minimum 225 m²/kg	Minimum 325 m²/kg	Min 275 m²/kg	Min 250 m²/kg
Chemical analysis				C_3A: Maximum 3.5 %
lime saturation factor	0.66–1.02	0.66–1.02	0.66–1.02	0.66–1.02
insoluble residue	Maximum 1.5 %	Maximum 1.5 %	Maximum 1.5 %	Maximum 1.5 %
MgO	Maximum 4.0 %	Maximum 4.0 %	Maximum 4.0 %	Maximum 4.0 %
SO_3	Maximum 2.5 % (when $C_3A \leqslant 5$ %) / Maximum 3.0 % (when $C_3A > 5$ %)	Maximum 3.0 % (when $C_3A \leqslant 5$ %) / Maximum 3.5 % (when $C_3A > 5$ %)	Maximum 2.5 % (when $C_3A \leqslant 5$ %) / Maximum 3.0 % (when $C_3A > 5$ %)	Maximum 2.5 %
ignition loss	Maximum 3.0 % (temperate) / Maximum 4.0 % (tropical)	Maximum 3.0 % (temperate) / Maximum 4.0 % (tropical)	Maximum 3.0 % (temperate) / Maximum 4.0 % (tropical)	Max 3.0 % (temperate climate) / Maximum 4.0 % (tropical climate)
Compressive strength				
Mortar: 3 days	Minimum 23 N/mm²	Minimum 29N/mm²	Minimum 10 N/mm²	Minimum 20 N/mm²
Mortar: 28 days	Minimum 41 N/mm²	Minimum 46 N/mm²	Minimum 28 N/mm²	Minimum 39 N/mm²
Concrete: 3 days	Minimum 13 N/mm²	Minimum 18 N/mm²	Minimum 5N/mm²	Minimum 10 N/mm²
Concrete: 28 days	Minimum 29 N/mm²	Minimum 33 N/mm²	Minimum 19 N/mm²	Minimum 27 N/mm²
Setting time				
Initial	Minimum 45	Minimum 45	Minimum 1 h	Minimum 45
Final	Maximum 10 h	Maximum 10 h	Maximum 10 h	Maximum 10 h
Soundness	Maximum 10 mm (Maximum 5 mm on retest)	Maximum 10 mm (Maximum 5 mm on retest)	Maximum 10 mm	Maximum 10 mm (Maximum 5 mm on retest)
Heat of hydration			Maximum 250 J/g (7 days) / Maximum 290 J/g (28 days)	

(From standards given above)

Table 157 Specifications of non-Portland cements

Specifications	PBFC (BS 146)	LHPBFC (BS 4246)	SSC (BS 4248)	MASONRY CEMENT (BS 5224)	HAC (BS 915)
Composition	Portland cement clinker + granulated blast furnace slag (maximum 65%)	Portland cement clinker + granulated blast furnace slag (50–90%)	Portland cement clinker or lime + granulated blast furnace slag, (min 75%) + $CaSO_4$	Portland cement + air-entraining agent	$CaO + Al_2O_3$
Fineness (specific surface)	Minimum 225 m²/kg	Minimum 275 m²/kg	Minimum 400 m²/kg		Minimum 225 m²/kg
Chemical analysis insoluble residue	Maximum 1.5 %	Maximum 1.5 %	Maximum 3.0 %		Al_2O_3: Minimum 32 % Al_2O_3/CaO ratio: 0.85–1.3
MgO	Maximum 7.0 %	Maximum 9.0 %	Maximum 9.0 %		
SO_3	Maximum 3.0 %	Maximum 3.0 %	Maximum 4.5 %	Maximum 3.0 %	
S	Maximum 1.5 %	Maximum 2.0 %	Maximum 1.5 %		
ignition loss	Maximum 3.0 % (temperate climate) Maximum 4.0 % (tropical climate)				
Compressive strength Mortar: 1 day					Minimum 42 N/mm²
3 days	Minimum 15 N/mm²	Minimum 8 N/mm²	Minimum 14 N/mm²		Minimum 49 N/mm²
7 days	Minimum 23 N/mm²	Minimum 14 N/mm²	Minimum 23 N/mm²	Minimum 4 N/mm²	
28 days	Minimum 34 N/mm²	Minimum 28 N/mm²	Minimum 34 N/mm²	Minimum 6 N/mm²	
Concrete: 3 days	Minimum 8 N/mm²	Minimum 3 N/mm²	Minimum 7 N/mm²		
7 days	Minimum 14 N/mm²	Minimum 7 N/mm²	Minimum 17 N/mm²		
28 days	Minimum 22 N/mm²	Minimum 14 N/mm²	Minimum 26 N/mm²		
Setting time Initial	Minimum 45	Minimum 1 h	Minimum 45	Minimum 45	Minimum 2 h
Final	Maximum 10 h	Maximum 15 h	Maximum 10 h	Maximum 10 h	Maximum 6 h
Soundness	Maximum 10 mm (Maximum 5 mm on retest)	Maximum 10 mm (Maximum 5 mm on retest)	Maximum 5 mm (Modified method)	Maximum 10 mm	Maximum 1 mm
Heat of Hydration		Maximum 250 J/g (7 days) Maximum 290 J/g (28 days)	Maximum 250 J/g (7 days) Maximum 290 J/g (28 days)		
Air entrainment				Air content 10–25 %	

(From standards given above)

manufacture, sampling and testing of Portland-blastfurnace cement containing not more than 65 per cent by weight of blastfurnace slag (see Table 157).

BS 915   *High-alumina cement*

Part 2: 1972   *Metric units*
This standard specifies requirements for the composition, the manufacture, sampling procedure and tests for fineness, chemical composition, strength, setting time and soundness (see Table 157).

BS 1370: 1979   *Low-heat Portland cement*

This standard specifies requirements for the composition, the manufacture and the chemical and physical properties of LHPC (see Table 156).

BS 4027: 1980   *Sulphate-resisting Portland cement*

This standard specifies requirements for the composition, the manufacture, the chemical and physical properties of SRPC (see Table 156).

BS 4246   *Low-heat Portland-blastfurnace cement*

Part 2: 1974   *Metric units*
This standard specifies requirements for composition, manufacture, sampling and testing of low-heat PBFC containing between 50 and 90 per cent by mass of blastfurnace slag (see Table 157).

BS 4248: 1974   *Supersulphated cement*

This standard specifies requirements for the composition, manufacture, sampling and testing of supersulphated cement (SSC) (see Table 157).

BS 5224: 1976   *Masonry cement*

This standard specifies requirements for the composition, manufacture and testing of masonry cement (see Table 157).

BS 4550   *Methods of testing cement*

This standard is divided into seven parts and eight sections.

Part 0: 1978   *General introduction*
This part gives a list of contents of all parts of BS 4550.

Part 1: 1978   *Sampling*
This part describes methods of obtaining cement samples for testing from bags, drums or other packages, from bulk-delivery vehicles, and from storage silo discharge.

Part 2: 1970   *Chemical tests*
This part gives methods for the chemical testing of cement: insoluble residue, total silica, ammonium hydroxide group, total calcium oxide, alumina, iron oxide, magnesia, sulphuric anhydride, sulphur present as sulphide, total sulphur, loss-on-ignition, minor constituents and free lime, pozzolanicity test for pozzolanic cements, sodium oxide and potassium oxide by flame photometry and chloride.

Part 3:   *Physical tests*
This part includes the following sections:

Section 3.1: 1978 *Introduction*
Section 3.2: 1978 *Density test*
    This is based on the displacement of non-reactive liquid (for example paraffin oil) in a density bottle.
Section 3.3: 1978 *Fineness test*
    This is based on the general Lea and Nurse constant flow rate air permeability method described in clause 6 of BS 4359 Part 2: 1971.
Section 3.4: 1978 *Strength test*
    1 Compressive strength of 100 mm concrete cubes. W/C ratio is 0.60 for all cements, except SSC and HAC, for which W/C 0.55 and 0.45 respectively are used (Table 158).
    2 Comprehensive strength of 70.7 mm mortar cubes (Table 159).

Table 158   *Mixes for concrete cubes*

Mix type	Material	Proportions by mass	Mass	
			6 cubes	9 cubes
			g	g
C1	Cement	1.0	2200 ± 5	3200 ± 5
	Sand	2.5	5500	8000
	Coarse aggregate	3.5	7700 ± 10	11200 ± 10
	Water	0.60	1320 ± 5	1920 ± 5
C2	Cement	1.0	2200 ± 5	3200 ± 5
	Sand	2.5	5500	8000
	Coarse aggregate	3.5	7700 ± 10	11200 ± 10
	Water	0.55	1210 ± 5	1760 ± 5
C3	Cement	1.0	2940 ± 5	4270 ± 5
	Sand	1.875	5500	8000
	Coarse aggregate	2.625	7700 ± 10	11200 ± 10
	Water	0.45	1320 ± 5	1920 ± 5

(Table 2: BS 4550: Part 3: Section 3.4: 1978)

Table 159 *Mixes for mortar cubes*

Mix type	Material	Proportions by mass	All cements other than high alumina cement:mass
			g
V1	Cement	1.0	185 ± 1
	Sand	3.0	555 ± 1
	Water	0.4	74 ± 1
			High alumina cement: mass
			g
V2	Cement	1.0	190 ± 1
	Sand	3.0	570 ± 1
	Water	0.4	76 ± 1

(Table 5: BS 4550: Part 3: Section 3.4: 1978)

Section 3.5: 1978 *Determination of standard consistence*
This is based on the determination of the amount of water required to give a cement paste of standard consistence using the Vicat apparatus. This value of water content is used in the determination of setting times (Section 3.6) and of soundness (Section 3.7). For high alumina cement, this test is not carried out and value of 22 per cent is assumed.

Section 3.6: 1978 *Test for setting times*
The initial and final setting times of cement are determined by using the Vicat apparatus.

Section 3.7: 1978 *Soundness test*
This is based on the Le Chatelier method by measuring the expansion of cement sample, either after immersion in cold and in boiling water or, for supersulphated cement, after immersion in cold water.

Section 3.8: 1978 *Test for heat of hydration*
The heat of hydration of cement is determined calorimetrically based on the difference in the heat of solution between unhydrated and the hydrated cement.

Part 4: 1978 *Standard coarse aggregate for concrete cubes*
This part specifies the source and properties of a standard coarse aggregate to be used with a standard sand for making concrete cubes.

Part 5: 1978 *Standard sand for concrete cubes*
This part specifies the source, preparation and properties of a standard sand to be used with a standard coarse aggregate for making concrete cubes.

Part 6: 1978 *Standard sand for mortar cubes*
This part specifies the source, preparations and properties of a standard sand to be used for making mortar cubes.
Revisions are in hand for Parts 2–6.

BS 3148: 1980 *Methods of test for water for making concrete (including notes on the suitability of the water)*

Two methods of test are described. The tests do not give information regarding the long-term durability of the concrete. An appendix summarizes the present knowledge in the light of which waters may be judged as to their suitability for this purpose.

BS 1926: 1962 *Ready-mixed concrete*

This standard was withdrawn in June 1981 and it is superseded by BS 5328.

BS 1881: 1978 *Methods of testing concrete*

Part 1: 1970 *Methods of sampling fresh concrete*
This part specifies methods of sampling on site and procedures

of mixing and sampling in the laboratory.

Part 5: 1970 *Methods of testing hardened concrete for other than strength*
This part includes determination of modulus of elasticity by an electrodynamic method, changes in length on drying and wetting (initial drying shrinkage, drying shrinkage and wetting expansion) and initial surface absorption of concrete.

Part 6: 1971 *Analysis of hardened concrete*
This part includes methods of sampling, treatment of samples, tests for cement content, aggregate content and grading, original water content, bulk density, type of cement, type of aggregate, chloride content, sulphate content and sulpho-aluminate content.

Part 101: 1983 *Method of sampling fresh concrete on sites*
The method of sampling fresh concrete on site and procedure for determination of sampling errors.

Part 102: 1983 *Method for determination of slump*

Part 103: 1983 *Method for determination of compacting factor*

Part 104: 1983 *Method for determination of Vebe time*
Determining Vebe time of concrete of very low to low workability.

Part 105: 1984 *Method for determination of flow*
Measuring the workability of flowing concrete of high workability using flow table.

Part 106: 1983 *Method for determination of air content of fresh concrete*
Two methods for determination of air content of compacted fresh concrete.

Part 107: 1983 *Method for determination of density of compacted fresh concrete*

Part 108: 1983 *Method for making test cubes from fresh concrete*

Part 109: 1983 *Method for making test beams from fresh concrete*

Part 110: 1983 *Methods for making test cylinders from fresh concrete*
The method for making test cylinders, nominal size of standard test cylinders, preparation of the ends and conditioning of the prepared cylinder.

Part 111: 1983 *Method of normal curing test specimens (20 °C method)*
Normal curing of cubes, beams and cylinders at 20 °C for strength tests at ages of 1 day and over.

Part 112: 1983 *Methods of accelerated curing of test cubes*
Methods of accelerated curing of concrete test cubes at 35 °C, 55 °C and 82 °C.

Part 113: 1983 *Method for making and curing no-fines test cubes*
Making and curing 150 mm test cubes of fresh no-fines concrete made with aggregates of 40 mm nominal maximum size or less.

Part 114: 1983 *Methods for determination of density of hardened concrete*
This part describes the methods for the determination of the density of as-received, saturated or oven-dried specimens.

Part 115: 1986   *Specifications for compression testing machines for concrete*
Requirements for machines used for the testing of concrete specimens in compression. The requirements relate to control and measurement of the load, the geometry and hardness of the machine platens and the means of alignment that ensure correct load application.

Part 116: 1983   *Method for determination of compressive strength of concrete cubes*
This part describes the method for the determination of the compressive strength of concrete cubes. It includes diagrams to show the types of irregular, unsatisfactory failures which can occur.

Part 117: 1983   *Method for determination of tensile splitting strength*
This part describes the method for the determination of the indirect tensile strength of cylindrical, cubic and prismatic concrete test specimens.

Part 118: 1983   *Method for determination of flexural strength*
This part describes a method for the determination of the flexural strength of test specimens of hardened concrete by means of a constant moment in the centre zone using a two-point (or three-point) loading.

Part 119: 1983   *Method for determination of compressive strength using portions of beams broken in flexure (equivalent cube method)*
This part describes the equivalent cube method for the determination of the compressive stength of hardened concrete using portions of beams broken in flexure.

Part 120: 1983   *Method for determination of compressive strength of concrete cores*
This part describes a method for taking cores from concrete and preparing them for testing and for the method for determining their compressive strength. It includes methods of sampling, drilling, preparation of specimens and testing of cores from concrete.

Part 121: 1983   *Method for determination of static modulus of elasticity in compression*
This part describes a method for the determination of the static modulus of elasticity in compression of hardened concrete, on test specimens which may be cast or taken from a structure.

Part 122: 1983   *Method for determination of water absorption*
This part describes a method for the determination of water absorption of concrete specimens cored from a structure or precast component.

Part 201: 1986   *Guide to the use of non-destructive methods of test for hardened concrete*
Brief summaries of a wider range of non-destructive tests for determining the quality of concrete in situ.

Part 202: 1986   *Recommendations for surface hardness testing of rebound hammer*
The functioning of rebound hammers, their applications, the factors influencing readings, method of calibration, test procedure and reporting of results.

BS 4408   *Recommendations for non-destructive methods of test for concrete*

Part 1: 1969   *Electromagnetic cover measuring devices*
The purpose of this part is:

1 To describe briefly electromagnetic cover measuring devices.

2 To give limits of accuracy under particular conditions.
3 To indicate limits of accuracy which may be expected when used under site conditions.
A revision is in hand.

Part 2: 1969   *Strain gauges for concrete investigation*
The recommendations in this part give general guidance common to the use of all gauges. They describe mechanical (including mechanical/optical) gauges, electrical resistance gauges having metal and alloy elements and semi-conductor elements, vibrating wire (acoustic) gauges and inductive displacement transducers. Photo-elastic strain gauges and piezo-electric strain gauges are also mentioned.

Part 3: 1970   *Gamma radiography of concrete*
Caution: It should be noted that radiography of concrete comes within the scope of the Factories Acts and is controlled by the Ionising Radiations (Sealed Sources) Regulations 1961.

The principle of gamma radiography of concrete is similar to that of chest X-rays. The recommendations cover the radiographic inspection of concrete up to 450 mm thick. They deal with the factors affecting the quality of the radiographic image, such as the characteristic and arrangement of the X-ray source (^{60} Co, ^{137} Cs or ^{192} Ir), object and film in space, the film speed, the use of screens, the exposure time and the film development technique.

Part 5: 1974   *Measurement of the velocity of ultrasonic pulses in concrete*
The recommendations in this part deal with the ultrasonic testing of concrete, reinforced and prestressed concrete test specimens, precast components and structures.

The method is based on the measurement of velocity of pulses of longitudinal vibrations passing through the concrete. These measurements may be used to establish:

1 The homogeneity of the concrete.
2 The presence of cracks, voids and other imperfections.
3 Changes in the structure of the concrete which occur with time.
4 The quality of the concrete in relation to standard requirements.
5 The quality of one element of concrete in relation to another.
6 The values of elastic modulus of the concrete.

BS 5328: 1981   *Methods for specifying concrete, including ready-mixed concrete*

■   AD (Regs. A1/2 and C4)

This standard covers methods for specifying prescribed and designed mixes of concrete, both site mixed and ready-mixed, and of checking compliance with specifications.

Prescribed mixes are those for which the purchaser specifies the mix proportions and is responsible for ensuring that these will provide the performances required. Designed mixes are those for which the purchaser is responsible for specifying the required performance and the producer selects the mix proportions to produce this performance.

Strength testing forms an essential part of the judgement of compliance in a designed mix but not in a prescribed mix.

BS 5838   *Dry packaged cementitious mixes*

Part 1: 1980   *Prepacked concrete mixes*

Part 2: 1980   *Prepacked mortar mixes*
Part 1 covers prepacked concrete mixes of two grades: coarse concrete mixes containing aggregate of a nominal maximum size of 20 mm, and fine concrete mixes containing aggregate of a nominal maximum size of 10 mm.

Part 2 covers prepacked cement: lime: sand mortar mixes, and cement: sand mortar mixes for bricklaying, screeding and other building purposes.

BS 6089: 1981 *Guide to assessment of concrete strength in existing structures*

This standard gives guidance on planning and conducting investigations including a description of test methods and interpretation of results. It illustrates the relationship between strength of standard test specimens and that in a structure.

BS 4551: 1980 *Methods of testing mortars, screeds and plasters*

This standard specifies the methods of sampling, analysis, preparation and testing of mortars for bricklaying, screeding, plastering and rendering. It is divided into three sections: general, methods of chemical analysis and aggregate grading, and the interpretation of results, and physical tests such as consistency, water retention, flow, air content, stiffening rate, strength and bulk density.

BS 4721: 1986 *Ready-mixed building mortars*

This standard specifies requirements for ready-mixed lime: sand

for site prepared mortars and plasters (Tables 160 and 161), factory made read-to-use retarded mortars for masonry, plastering and rendering (Tables 162 and 163), factory made ready-to-use retarded mortars for screeds (Tables 164 and 165).

Table 160 *Available lime content of lime: sand mixes*

Category	Limits of available calcium hydroxide (percentage on dry mass)	
Nominal proportions of lime: sand by volume	Minimum	Maximum
	%	%
1:12	1.5	4.0
1:9	2.0	5.5
1:6	3.5	8.0
1:4 $\frac{1}{2}$	4.5	9.5
1:4	6.5	10.5
1:3	9.0	14.0

(Table 1: BS 4721: 1981)

Table 161 *Specified properties of cement gauged mortars*

Category / Nominal proportions of lime to sand by volume	Percentage by mass of cement* to be added to the dry lime:sand mix	Water retentivity / Not less than	Flow / For plastering or rendering / Not more than	Flow / For jointing / Not more than	Air content / Not air entrained / Not more than	Air content / Air entrained / Not less than	Air content / Air entrained / Not more than	Stiffening rate ratio / Not less than	Stiffening rate ratio / Not more than	Compressive strength / 7 days / Not less than	Compressive strength / 28 days / Not less than
	%	%	%	%	%	%	%			N/mm²	N/mm²
1:12	30.0	88	–	135	7	7	12	0.6	1.5	10.7	16.0
1:9	20.0	89	125	135	7	7	12	0.8	1.7	4.3	6.5
1:6	15.0	90	125	135	7	7	15	1.0	2.2	2.4	3.6
1:4 $\frac{1}{2}$	10.0	91	125	130	7	7	15	1.1	2.5	1.0	1.5
1:4	7.5	92	120	125	7	7	15	1.4	3.0	–	–
1:3	0	93	120	125	7	–	–	–	–	–	–

*The cement used shall be ordinary Portland cement complying with the requirements of BS 12 at the time of use.

(Table 2: BS 4721: 1981)

Table 162 *Composition of ready-to-use mortars*

Required mortar / Mortar designation	Nominal proportions by volume / Cement:lime:sand	Nominal proportions by volume / Cement:sand	Nominal proportions by volume / Masonry cement:sand	Mass of original dry materials / Cement	Mass of original dry materials / Lime
				%	%
i	1: $\frac{1}{4}$:3			20.0 t0 25.0	1.0 to 3.0
		1:3		20.5 to 25.0	0
ii	1: $\frac{1}{2}$:4 to 4 $\frac{1}{2}$			14.0 to 19.0	1.5 to 4.5
		1:3 to 4		16.0 to 25.0	0
			1:2 $\frac{1}{2}$ to 3 $\frac{1}{2}$	17.0 to 27.5	0
iii	1:1:5 to 6			11.0 to 15.5	3.0 to 7.0
		1:5 to 6		11.5 to 16.5	0
			1:4 to 5	12.5 to 19.0	0
iv	1:2:8 to 9			7.5 to 10.0	4.0 to 8.5
		1:7 to 8		8.5 to 12.5	0
			1:5 $\frac{1}{2}$ to 6 $\frac{1}{2}$	10.0 to 15.5	0

(Table 3: BS 4721: 1981)

238 *Manual of British Standards in Building Construction and Specification*

Table 163 *Specified properties of ready-to-use mortars*

Mortar designation	Stiffening rate ratio		Compressive strength at 28 days (see note)	Water retentivity	Flow		Air content		
					Not more than		Not air entrained	Air entrained	
	Not less than	Not more than	Not less than	Not less than	For plastering and rendering	For jointing	Not more than	Not less than	Not more than
			N/mm²	%	%	%	%	%	%
i	0.9	1.1	11.0	88	–	135	7	7	12
ii	0.9	1.1	4.5	89	125	135	7	7	12
iii	0.9	1.1	2.5	90	125	135	7	7	15
iv	0.9	1.1	1.0	91	125	130	7	7	15

Note: Extra curing time shall be allowed equal to the specified period of retardation.

(Table 4: BS 4721: 1981)

Table 164 *Ready-to-use screeding mortars*

Designation	Traditional volume proportions cement:sand	Cement by mass of original dry material (see note)
		%
a	1:3	20.5 to 25.0
b	1:4	16.0 to 20.0
c	1:5	13.0 to 15.5

Note: Calculated from chemical analysis in accordance with clause 7.3 of BS 4551: 1980.

(Table 5: BS 4721: 1981)

Table 165 *Specified properties of ready-to-use screeding mortars*

Designation	Traditional volume proportions cement: sand	Stiffening rate ratio		Compressive strengths (see note)	
		Not less than	Not more than	7 days Not less than	28 days Not less than
				N/mm²	N/mm²
a	1:3	0.8	1.2	18.0	27.0
b	1:4	0.8	1.2	12.0	18.0
c	1:5	0.8	1.2	7.5	12.5

Note: Extra curing time shall be allowed equal to the specified period of retardation.

(Table 6: BS 4721: 1981)

Marking BS 4721/4 on or in relation to a product is a claim by the manufacturer that the product has been manufactured in accordance with the requirements of the standard. The accuracy of such a claim is therefore solely the manufacturer's responsibility. Enquiries as to the availability of third party certification to support such claims should be addressed to the Director, British Standards Institution, Maylands Avenue, Hemel Hempstead, Herts HP2 4SQ in the case of certification marks administered by BSI or to the appropriate authority for other certification marks.

PD 6472: 1974 *Guide to specifying the quality of building mortars*

This document is not itself a specification for the supply of mortar; it serves only as a guide to specifying the quality of building mortars. It has four sections. Section one outlines the factors to be considered in deciding the form of the specification and the quality to be specified for a particular job. The specification may be either of the 'prescription' or 'performance' types.

Section two deals with general clauses for all specifications (including storage and preparation, batching of materials, mixing, use of mortar).

Section three gives details for the prescription type of specification and section four for the performance type. Other relevant standards are BS 4551 *Methods of testing mortars, screeds and plasters*, BS 4721 *Ready-mixed lime: sand for mortar*, BS 4887 *Mortar plasticisers* and BS 5224 *Masonry cement*.

BS 4624: 1981 *Methods of test for asbestos-cement building products*

This standard describes methods of test applicable to asbestos-cement building products in the form of symmetrical and asymmetrical section corrugated sheets, flat sheets, pipes, rainwater pipes and slates.

BS 6432: 1984 *Methods for determining properties of glass fibre reinforced cement material*

Determining properties in both uncured and cured states, primarily for quality-control purposes.

BS 6588: 1985 *Portland pulverized-fuel-ash cement*

Requirements for the composition, manufacture, fineness, strength, setting time, soundness, chemical composition, sampling, testing and marking. (See Table 166).

Table 166 *Specifications for Portland pulverized-fuel-ash cement and pozzolanic cement with pulverised-fuel-ash*

Type	Portland pfa cement (BS 6588)	Pozzolanic cement with p.f.a. (BS 6610)
Composition	Portland cement mixed with 15–35 % p.f.a.	OPC mixed with 35–50 % p.f.a.
Fineness (specific surface)	Minimum 225 m²/kg	Minimum 225 m²/kg
Compressive strength mortar		
3 days	Minimum 8 N/mm²	
7 days		Minimum 8 N/mm²
28 days	Minimum 22 N/mm²	Minimum 16 N/mm²
Setting time:		
Initial	Minimum 45 min	Minimum 45 min
Final	Maximum 10 h	Maximum 10 h
Soundness	Maximum 10 mm	Maximum 10 mm
Chemical composition		
MgO	Maximum 4.0 %	Maximum 4.0 %
SO₃	Maximum 3.0 %	Maximum 3.0 %
loss on ignition	Maximum 4.0 % (temperate climates)	Maximum 4.5 % (temperate climates)
	Maximum 5.0 % (tropical climates)	Maximum 5.5 % (tropical climates)

(From standards given above)

BS 6610: 1985 *Pozzolanic cement with pulverized-fuel ash as pozzolana*

Requirements for the composition, manufacture, fineness, strength, setting time, soundness, chemical composition, sampling, testing and marking. See Table 166.

DD83: 1983 *Assessment of the composition of fresh concrete*

Methods for sampling and sample reduction, five methods of analysing fresh concrete: buoyancy method, chemical (GLC) method, constant volume (RAM) method, physical separation (Laing) method and pressure filter (Sandberg) method, and an additional method solely for the determination of water content. It also gives procedures for the assessment of the accuracy and precision of the analysis and procedures for using the test results for compliance purposes.

DD90: 1983 *Volumetric method for determination of compacting factor of fresh concrete*

The compacting factor of concrete of low, medium and high workability. The method applies to plain and air-entrained concrete, made with lightweight, normal weight or heavy aggregates, having a nominal maximum size of 40 mm or less, but not to aerated concrete, no-fines concrete and concrete which cannot be compacted by vibration alone.

DD92: 1984 *Method for temperature-matched curing of concrete specimens*

The method for making and curing concrete cubes at a variable temperature corresponding to that within an *in situ* concrete element.

r   Clay gypsum, magnesia and plastics binders, mortars

r2   Gypsum

There is only one standard on gypsum plasters which are obtained from partial or complete dehydration of gypsum ($CaSO_4.2H_2O$).

BS 1191   *Gypsum building plasters*

Part 1: 1973   *Excluding premixed lightweight plasters*
This part specifies requirements for those plasters which have a definited set due to the hydration of calcium sulphate to form gypsum and which are intended for general building operations and for the manufacture of preformed building products.

Gypsum plasters are classified into:

Class A: plaster of Paris (hemihydrate, $CaSO_4.\frac{1}{2}H_2O$).

Class B: retarded hemihydrate gypsum plaster (containing retarder of set) which is subdivided into:
   Type a: undercoat plaster (plaster for use with sand)
      1 Browning plaster
      2 Metal lathing plaster
   Type b: final coat plaster
      1 Finish plaster
      2 Board finish plaster
Class C: anhydrous gypsum plaster (for finishing only and containing accelerator of set)
Class D: Keene's plaster (for finishing only and containing accelerator of set)

Tests and specifications are summarized in Table 167.

Part 2: 1973   *Premixed lightweight plasters*
This part specifies requirements for premixed lightweight plaster consisting essentially of gypsum plaster and lightweight aggregate used in general building operations.

Premixed lightweight plasters are classified into:

Table 167   *Tests and specifications for gypsum building plasters*

	A Plaster of Paris	B Retarded hemihydrate	C Anhydrous gypsum	D Keene's plaster
Chemical composition (% by weight of plaster)				
Minimum SO_3	35 %	35 %	40 %	47 %
Minimum CaO	$\frac{2}{3}SO_3$	$\frac{2}{3}SO_3$	$\frac{2}{3}SO_3$	$\frac{2}{3}SO_3$
Maximum ($Na_2O + MgO$)	0.2 %	0.2 %	0.2 %	0.2 %
Ignition loss	4–9 %	4–9 %	Maximum 3 %	Maximum 2 %
Maximum free lime		3 %(metal lathing plaster)		
Residue on 1.8 mm BS test sieve	Maximum 5 %	Maximum 1 %	Maximum 1 %	Maximum 1 %
Soundness (Pat test)	The set plaster pats shall show no signs of disintegration, popping or pitting			
Transverse strength (modulus of rupture)				
Minimum	2.5 N/mm²	1.2 N/mm²		
Mechanical resistance (dropping ball test)				
Maximum diameter of indentation		4.5 mm	4.5 mm	4.0 mm
(Linear) Expansion on setting		Maximum 0.2 %		

(From BS 1191: Part 1: 1973)

Table 168   *Tests and specifications for premixed lightweight plasters*

	Type a: Undercoat plaster			Type b: Final coat plaster
	1 Browning plaster	*2 Metal lathing plaster*	*3 Bonding plaster*	
Soluble salt content				
Minimum ($Na_2O + MgO$)	0.25 %	0.25 %	Not limited	0.25 %
Free lime content		Maximum 2.5 %		
Dry bulk density (kg/m³)				
Maximum	640	770	770	
Dry set density (kg/m³)				
Maximum	850	1040	1040	
Compressive strength (N/mm²)				
Minimum	0.93	1.0	1.0	
Mechanical resistance (dropping ball test) Diameter of indentation				4–5.5 mm

(From BS 1191: Part 2: 1973)

Type a: undercoat plasters
  1 Browning plaster
  2 Metal lathing plaster
  3 Bonding plaster
Type b: final coat plater
  1 Finish plaster.

Tests and specifications are summarized in Table 168.

s Bituminous materials

There are 13 standards under this heading. For the use of bituminous materials as road materials see Table 1 'Building elements', section (90) 'External works'.

BS 598 *Sampling and examination of bituminous mixtures for roads and other paved areas*

Part 1: 1974 *Sampling*
This part specifies sampling methods for all types of coated bituminous materials except slurry seal, used in road works and other paved areas. Appendices cover safety, sampling rate and choice of sampling method.

Part 2: 1974 *Testing*
This part specifies methods of testing samples of bituminous mixtures that have been delivered to the testing laboratory, and gives guidance on laboratory safety.
   The tests include water content, binder content and grading of mineral aggregate, hardness number of mastic asphalt and recovery of certain soluble binders for examination.

Part 3: 1985 *Methods for design and physical testing*
Describes design and physical methods of testing all types of coated bituminous mixtures and their constituent materials, except slurry seals, used for roads and other paved areas. The methods include the determination of stability index of pitch bitumen binders, a design method for the composition of wearing-course rolled asphalt, a test for the condition of the binder on coated chippings, the measurement of the temperature of rolled asphalt and the rate of spread of coated chippings, the determination of texture depth and the density of cores. A means for assessing the compaction performance of a roller is also included.

BS 2000 *Methods of test for petroleum and its products*

Part 47: 1983 *Solubility of bituminous binders*
This method is applicable to bituminous binders containing not less than 95 per cent of bitumen in which volatile constituents will not normally be present. If water is present the amount is normally small, and should be removed.
   Solubility of bitumen binders is determined by dissolving a known weight (W_1) of the sample in trichloroethylene or other solvent, followed by filtration through an asbestos filter mat. The insoluble residue is washed, dried and weighted (W_2). Solubility is calculated from the formula:

$$\text{solubility (\% weight)} = \frac{100\,(W_1 - W_2)}{W_1}$$

Caution: *Trichloroethylene* is toxic, hence adequate ventilation should be provided. Although it is non-flammable, in presence of a flame or red hot heating wire its vapour is converted into highly toxic phosphene gas. Consequently smoking and presence of flame etc., should be prohibited. *Asbestos* dust is hazardous when inhaled, even in very small amounts. For this reason, the use of sintered glass crucible is strongly recommended.

Part 213: 1983 *Acidity of bitumen (neutralization value)*
Neutralization value is defined as the quantity of base, expressed in mg of potassium hydroxide required to neutralize the total acidic constituents in 1 g of the sample under the conditions of test.
   It is determined by dissolving the bitumen in a mixture of toluene, alcohol and water, followed by adding a slight excess of alkali and back-titrating the mixture with acid..

Caution: *Toluene* is a toxic, volatile hydrocarbon which is absorbed by inhaling the vapour or through the skin by contact

Table 169 *Grades of mastic asphalt flooring*

Grade Recommended thickness (and see CP 204 Part 2)	I 15–20 mm	II 15–20 mm	III 20–30 mm	IV 30–50 mm
Underlays for other floor coverings	×	×		
Hospital wards	×			
Hospital corridors (foot traffic)		×		
Schools	×			
Shops (floors to take movable racks)	×			
Shops (floors to take fixed racks)		×		
Offices	×			
Factory floors – light		×		
Factory floors – medium			×	
Factory floors – heavy				×
Loading sheds				×
Breweries				×
Railway platforms				×
Domestic floors (either as a finished floor or as an underlay)	×			
Heavily foot-trafficked floors or passageways			×	

(Appendix A: BS 988: 1973)

with the liquid. Consequently avoid skin contact and ensure adequate ventilation.

BS 5094: 1974 *Method of determination of softening point of bitumen and tar in ethylene glycol (ring and ball)*

The ring and ball method is given in this standard. A steel ball of specified weight is placed upon a disk of sample contained within a horizontal, shouldered, metal ring of specified dimensions. The assembly is heated in an ethylene glycol bath at a uniform, prescribed rate and the softening point taken as the temperature at which the sample becomes soft enough to allow the ball, enveloped in the sample material, to fall a distance of 25.4 mm.

This method is applicable to asphalt (bitumen) and tar, including tar pitches, in the range of 30 to 175 °C.

BS 5284: 1976 *Methods of sampling and testing mastic asphalt and pitch mastic used in building*

This standard covers methods of sampling at place of manufacture, from blocks, work site and laid material, sample size and preparation for testing, method of test for hardness number, water and binder content, grading of mineral aggregate and method of binder recovery for further testing.

Safety requirements are appended.

BS 988, 1076, 1097, 1451: 1973 *Mastic asphalt for building (limestone aggregate)*

Requirements are specified in these standards for four types of mastic asphalt for building, composed of ground limestone, coarse aggregate and pigment, if required, incorporated with asphaltic cements.

The types of mastic asphalt are specified in:

BS 988 *Mastic asphalt for roofing (limestone aggregate)*
BS 1076 *Mastic asphalt for flooring (limestone aggregate)*
BS 1097 *Mastic asphalt for tanking and damp-proof courses (limestone aggregate)*
BS 1451 *Coloured mastic asphalt for flooring (limestone aggregate)*

External pavings for situations such as loading bays and balconies are covered by BS 1446, BS 1447, BS 988 and BS 1162.

Grades are given for mastic asphalt floorings according to usage.

Grade I: special hard flooring.
Grade II: light duty flooring.
Grade III: medium duty flooring.
Grade IV: industrial factory flooring.

A guide to the selection of the appropriate grade is given in Table 169.

The composition of mastic asphalt is specified according to Table 170 (for roofing, tanking and damp-proof courses) and Table 171 (for flooring).

BS 6577: 1985 *Mastic asphalt for building (natural rock asphalt aggregate)*

Requirements for roofing, tanking and flooring grades of mastic asphalt for building composed of natural rock asphalt, and coarse aggregate where appropriate, incorporated with asphaltic cements.

Table 170 *Composition by analysis of mastic asphalt*

Property	Percentage by weight of mastic asphalt			
	BS 988		BS 1097	
	minimum	maximum	minimum	maximum
Soluble bitumen	11.0	13.5	12.0	15.0
Passing 75 μm mesh BS sieve	35.0	45.0	38.0	50.0
Passing 212 μm mesh BS sieve and retained on 75 μm mesh BS sieve	8.0	22.0	8.0	26.0
Passing 600 μm mesh BS sieve and retained on 212 μm mesh BS sieve	8.0	22.0	8.0	26.0
Passing 3.35 mm mesh BS sieve and retained on 600 μm mesh BS sieve	12.0	23.0	4.0	17.0
Retained on 3.35 mm mesh BS sieve	0	3.0	0	2.0

(Table 2: BS 988, 1097: 1973)

Table 171 *Composition by analysis of mastic asphalt*

Property	Percentage by weight of mastic asphalt	
	minimum	maximum
Soluble bitumen	12.0	18.0*
Passing 75 μm mesh BS sieve	40.0	56.0
Passing 212 μm mesh BS sieve and retained on 75 μm mesh BS sieve	8.0	25.0
Passing 600 μm mesh BS sieve and retained on 212 μm mesh BS sieve	8.0	32.0

* If the fine aggregate is Irish or Scottish limestone a maximum soluble bitumen content of 19% is permitted.

(Table 7: BS 1076, 1451: 1973)

The composition of mastic asphalt containing natural rock aggregate is specified according to Table 172 (for roofing), Table 173 (for tanking and damp-proof courses) and Table 174 (for flooring).

Table 172 *Composition by analysis of mastic for type R1162 (Roofing)*

Property	Percentage by mass of mastic asphalt			
	Swiss natural rock asphalt		All other natural rock asphalts	
Grading of mineral aggregate using BS 410 test sieves:	min.	max.	min.	max.
Retained on 3.35 mm mesh	0	3	0	3
Passing 3.35 mm mesh retained on 600 μm mesh	14	23	14	23
Passing 600 μm mesh retained on 212 μm mesh	5	15	5	15
Passing 212 μm mesh retained on 75 μm mesh	5	18	5	18
Passing 75μm mesh	40	55	40	55
Soluble bitumen	11	13	14	17

(Table 2: BS 6577: 1985)

Table 173 *Composition by analysis of mastic asphalt for type T1418 (Tanking and damp-proof courses)*

Property	Percentage by mass of mastic asphalt			
	Swiss natural rock asphalt		All other natural rock asphalts	
Grading of mineral aggregate using BS 410 test sieves:	min.	max.	min.	max.
Passing 3.35 mm mesh retained on 600 μm mesh	0	10	0	10
Passing 600 μm mesh retained on 212 μm mesh	5	20	5	20
Passing 212 μm mesh retained on 75 μm mesh	5	20	5	20
Passing 75μm mesh	45	65	45	65
Soluble bitumen	13	16	17	20

(Table 4: BS 6577: 1985)

Table 174 *Composition by analysis of ungritted mastic asphalt for type F1410 (Flooring)*

Property	Percentage by mass of mastic asphalt			
	Swiss natural rock asphalt		All other natural rock asphalts	
Grading of mineral aggregate using BS 410 test sieves:	min.	max.	min.	max.
Passing 600 μm mesh retained on 212 μm mesh	5	20	5	20
Passing 212 μm mesh retained on 75 μm mesh	5	20	5	20
Passing 75μm mesh	45	65	45	65
Soluble bitumen	13	16	16	20

(Table 7: BS 6577: 1985)

BS 1310: 1984 *Coal tar pitches for building purposes*

Coal tar pitch is defined in this standard as the black or dark brown solid or semi-solid fusible and agglomerative residue remaining after partial evaporation or fractional distillation of coal tar and coal tar products.

It describes methods of test based on STPTC (Standardization of Tar Products Tests Committee) and includes appendices on uses of individual grades and health and safety recommendation in handling pitch.

t Fixing and jointing materials

There are thirty-two standards and two drafts for development available under this section, namely soft solders (four standards), glues and adhesives (twelve standards and one draft for development), jointing agents, including sealants (twelve standards and one draft for development) and miscellaneous (five standards).

For pipe jointing materials refer to Table 1 'Building elements', section (59) 'Parts, accessories, etc.'. See also *Sectional List 12* Leather, plastics, rubber.

BS 219: 1977   *Soft solders*

This standard specifies requirements for 25 grades of soft solders for general use and special purpose applications including service at higher temperatures.

Table 175 lists melting characteristics and typical uses of the various grades of solder.

BS 441: 1980   *Purchasing requirements for flux-cored and solid soft-solder wire*

This standard specifies purchasing requirements for round soft-solder wire with or without one or more continuous cores of flux.

Table 175   *Typical uses of solder*

Grade	Tin content %	Starts to melt at °C	Fully molten at °C	Typical uses
Tin	*minimum*			
T1	99.90	Melting point 232	}	Certain food handling equipment, special can soldering, step
T2	99.75	Melting point 232	}	soldering and other special applications
T3	99.00	Melting point 232–		Step soldering
Tin-lead	*maximum*			
A	64	183	185	}
AP	64	183	185	} Soldering of electrical connections to copper
K	60	183	188	} Soldering of brass and zinc
				Hand soldering of electronic assemblies. Hot-dip coating of ferrous and non-ferrous metals. High quality sheet metal work. Capillary joints including light gauge tubes in copper and stainless steel. Manufacture of electronic components. Machine soldering of printed circuits
KP	60	183	188–	Hand and machine soldering of electronic components. Can soldering
F	50	183	212	}
R	45	183	224	} General engineering work on copper, brass and zinc. Can soldering
G	40	183	234	}
H	35	183	244	}
J	30	183	255	} Jointing of electrical cable sheaths
V	20	183	276	} Lamp solder. Dip soldering. For service at very low temperatures
W	15	227	288	} (e.g. less than -60 °C)
Tin-lead-antimony				
B	50	185	204	} Hot-dip coating and soldering of ferrous metals. High quality
M	45	185	215	} engineering. Capillary joints of ferrous metals. Jointing of copper conductors
C	40	185	227–	General engineering. Heat exchangers. General dip soldering. Jointing of copper conductors.
L	32	185	243	Plumbing, wiping of lead and lead alloy cable sheathing. }
D	30	185	248	} Dip soldering
N	18.5	185	275–	} Dip soldering
Tin-antimony				
95A	95*	236	243–	High service temperatures (e.g. greater than 100 °C) and refrigeration equipment. Step soldering
Tin-silver				
96S	96*	Melting point 221–		High service temperatures (e.g. greater than 100 °C)
Tin-lead-silver				
5S	5.25	296	301–	For service both at high (e.g. greater than 100 °C) and very low (e.g. less than -60 °C) temperatures
62S	62.5	Melting point 178–		Soldering of silver coated substrates
Tin-lead-cadmium				
T	50	Melting point 145–		Low melting point solder for assemblies that could be damaged by normal soldering temperatures. Step soldering. For thermal cut outs

* Nominal value.

(Table 2: BS 219: 1977)

Table 176   *Summary of test requirements for flux*

Test	Flux class 1 Inorganic with or without inorganic acids	Flux class 2 Phosphoric acid and derivatives	Flux class 3 Halides of organic compounds	Flux class 4 Organic acids	Flux class 5 5a Activator containing halide	5b Activator not containing halide	Flux class 6 Non-activated rosins	Flux class 7 Other organic compounds
Fluxing performance test	Under consideration	Under consideration	Under consideration	Under consideration	Under consideration	Under consideration	Under consideration	Under consideration
Corrosion				No evidence of corrosion after a period agreed between supplier and purchaser (see Appendix B)	No evidence of corrosion after 3 days (see Appendix B)	No evidence of corrosion after 3 days (see Appendix B)	No evidence of corrosion after 21 days (see Appendix B)	Where applicable, no evidence of corrosion after a period agreed between supplier and purchaser (see Appendix B)
Hardness and homogeneity of flux residue (rosin-based)					Homogeneous hard to the finger nail non-sticky (see Appendix B)	Homogeneous hard to the finger nail non-sticky (see Appendix B)	Homogeneous hard to the finger nail non-sticky (see Appendix B)	
Mould growth resistance					Maximum class 1 BS 2011 Part 2.1J: 1977 (see Appendix B)	Maximum class 1 BS 2011 Part 2.1J: 1977 (see Appendix B)	Maximum class 1 BS 2011 Part 2.1J: 1977 (see Appendix B)	Where applicable maximum class 1 BS 2011 Part 2.1J: 1977 (see Appendix B)
Non-volatile matter					Non-volatile matter to be agreed between supplier and purchaser (see BS 5625)	Non-volatile matter to be agreed between supplier and purchaser (see BS 5625)	Non-volatile matter to be agreed between supplier and purchaser (see BS 5625)	
Halide content (rosin-based)					Maximum halide content to be agreed between supplier and purchaser (see Appendix B)	Maximum halide content to be agreed between supplier and purchaser (see Appendix B)	Maximum halide content to be agreed between supplier and purchaser (see Appendix B)	
Halide content (water-based)	To be agreed between supplier and purchaser (see Appendix B and clause 6.7.3 of BS 5625: 1979)	Maximum 0.05% calculated as chloride (see Appendix B and clause 6.7.4 of BS 5625: 1979)	To be agreed between supplier and purchaser (see Appendix B and clause 6.7.3 of BS 5625: 1979)					
Zinc content	To be agreed between supplier and purchaser (see Appendix B)							
Ammonia content	To be agreed between supplier and purchaser (see Appendix B)							
Acid value				Minimum acid value to be agreed between supplier and purchaser (see BS 5625)	Minimum acid value 160 (see BS 5625)	Minimum acid value to be agreed between supplier and purchaser (see BS 5625)	Minimum acid value 160 (see BS 5625)	Minimum acid value to be agreed between supplier and purchaser (see BS 5625)
Water-extractable acid content (rosin-based)					Acid content to be agreed between supplier and purchaser (see BS 5625)	Acid content to be agreed between supplier and purchaser (see BS 5625)	Acid content to be agreed between supplier and purchaser (see BS 5625)	

(Table 3: BS 441: 1980)

Table 177 *Summary of purchasing requirements*

Test and clause reference	Flux class 1 Inorganic halides with or without inorganic acids	Flux class 2 Phosphoric acid and derivatives	Flux class 3 Halides of organic compounds	Flux class 4 Organic acids	Flux class 5 Activated rosins 5a Activator containing halide	5b Activator not containing halide	Flux class 6 Non-activated rosins	Flux class 7 Other organic compounds
Fluxing efficiency 6.1	Minimum area of spread 0.8 cm^2	Minimum area of spread 3.0 cm^2	Minimum area of spread 1.0 cm^2	Minimum area of spread 1.0 cm^2	Minimum area of spread 1.6 cm^2	Minimum area of spread 1.0 cm^2	Minimum area of spread 0.8 cm^2	Minimum area of spread to be agreed between supplier and purchaser
Corrosion 6.2				No evidence of corrosion after a period agreed between supplier and purchaser	No evidence of corrosion after 3 days	No evidence of corrosion after 3 days	No evidence of corrosion after 21 days	Where applicable, no evidence of corrosion after a period agreed between supplier and purchaser
Insulation resistance 6.3					Minimum 1000 MΩ	Minimum 1000 MΩ	Minimum 1000 MΩ	
Hardness and homogeneity of flux residue (rosin-based) 6.4					Homogeneous hard to the finger nail non-sticky	Homogeneous hard to the finger nail non-sticky	Homogeneous hard to the finger nail non-sticky	
Mould growth resistance 6.5					Maximum class 1 6.3.1 of BS 2011 Part 2.1J: 1977	Maximum class 1 6.3.1 of BS 2011 Part 2.1J: 1977	Maximum class 1 6.3.1 of BS 2011 Part 2.1J: 1977	Where applicable maximum class 1 6.3.1 of BS 2011 Part 2.1J 1977
Non-volatile matter (rosin-based) 6.6					Non-volatile matter to be agreed between supplier and purchaser*	Non-volatile matter to be agreed between supplier and purchaser*	Non-volatile matter to be agreed between supplier and purchaser*	
Halide content (rosin-based) 6.7.2					Maximum halide content to be agreed between supplier and purchaser*	Maximum halide content to be agreed between supplier and purchaser*	Maximum halide content to be agreed between supplier and purchaser*	
Halide content (water-based) 6.7.3	To be agreed between supplier and purchaser		To be agreed between supplier and purchaser					
Halide content (water-based) 6.7.4		Maximum 0.05% calculated as chloride						
Zinc content 6.8	To be agreed between supplier and purchaser							
Ammonia content 6.9	To be agreed between supplier and purchaser							
Acid value 6.10				Minimum acid value to be agreed between supplier and purchaser	Minimum acid value 160	Minimum acid value to be agreed between supplier and purchaser	Minimum acid value 160	Minimum acid value to be agreed between supplier and purchaser
Water-extractable acid content (rosin-based) 6.11					Acid content to be agreed between supplier and purchaser*	Acid content to be agreed between supplier and purchaser*	Acid content to be agreed between supplier and purchaser*	

*Routine batch test for inspection.

(Table 2: BS 5625: 1980)

It covers wire dimensions, flux content, test requirements of solder and flux (see Table 176), inspection and marking.

BS 5245: 1975 *Phosphoric acid based flux for soft soldered joints in stainless steel*

This standard specifies requirements for chemical composition and solderability tests. The flux is considered particularly suitable for making soft soldered capillary joints in stainless steel tube.

BS 5625: 1980 *Purchasing requirements and methods of test for fluxes for soft soldering*

This standard specifies requirements and appropriate test methods for solid, liquid and paste fluxes for use in soldering or 'tinning' with the soft solders listed in BS 219. It classifies soft soldering fluxes according to their active ingredients and describes methods of testing their fluxing efficiency and the properties of their residues.

Purchasing requirements are summarized in Table 177.

BS 647: 1981 *Methods of sampling and testing glues (bone, skin and fish glues)*

This standard specifies the methods of sampling and testing bone, skin and fish glues.

Table 178 lists the tests and summarizes the mass of glue and the volume of water required for each test.

Table 178 *Glue concentrations*

Clause	Test	Mass of glue	Volume of water
		g	ml
6	Moisture content	1	10
7	Jelly strength (see 7.5.2)	15 (7.5)	105 (105)
8	Comparison of jelly strength	5 to 10	50
9	Viscosity	15	105
10	Melting point	37.5	75
11	Setting point	37.5	75
12	Foam: method 1	5	50
	method 2	15	105
13	Keeping quality	5	20
14	pH	1	100
15	Grease	10	15
16	Joint strength in shear	10	15

(Table 1: BS 647: 1981)

BS 745: 1969 *Animal glue for wood (joiner's glue) (dry glue, jelly or liquid glue)*

This standard specifies dry glue (supplied in cakes, pieces, granules, pearls, cubes or powder) and jelly or liquid glue.

Requirements for *dry glue* are specified as follows:

Overlap joint strength in longitudinal shear: minimum 2.65 kN.
Moisture content: maximum 18%.
Chlorides: maximum 2% (calculated as sodium chloride).
pH: minimum 4.0, maximum 8.2.
Odour: not objectionable.
Keeping quality: minimum 6 days without evidence of liquefaction, putrefaction or mould growth.

Requirements for *jelly or liquid glue* are specified as follows:

Overlap joint strength in longitudinal shear: minimum 2.65 kN.
pH: minimum 4.0, maximum 8.2.

BS 1203: 1979 *Synthetic resin adhesives (phenolic and aminoplastic) for plywood*

This standard specifies requirements and test methods for four types of adhesives – three types for external use depending on performance (weather-proof and boil-proof (WBP), boil-resistant (BR), moisture-resistant and moderately weather-resistant (MR)) and one type for internal use (INT).

Requirements are summarized in Table 179.

BS 1204 *Synthetic resin adhesives (phenolic and aminoplastic) for wood*

Part 1: 1979 *Gap-filling adhesives*

Part 2: 1979 *Close-contact adhesives*
This standard specifies requirements for four types of adhesives – three for external use depending on performance and one for internal use.

Requirements are summarized in Tables 180 and 181.

BS 1444: 1970 *Cold-setting casein adhesive powders for wood*

Casein is a protein precipitated from skimmed milk which, when compounded with other reactants, is used as an adhesive for wood. Casein adhesives have a limited degree of water resistance and should be used only for interior applications.

Requirements are specified in this standard for storage properties and adhesive strengths. Sampling and method of test are appended.

BS 3046: 1981 *Adhesive for hanging flexible wallcoverings*

This standard specifies requirements for five types of adhesives

Table 179 *Tabular summary of requirements*

Type of adhesive	Test											
	Boiling water resistance			Hot water resistance			Cold water resistance			Micro-organism resistance		
	Condition	Time	Failing force (minimum)	Condition	Time	Failing force (minimum)	Condition	Time	Failing force (minimum)	Condition	Time	Failing force (minimum)
		h	kN		h	kN		h	kN		weeks	kN
WBP	Boiling water	72	0.90	Not applicable			Water at 15 ± 5 °C	16 to 24	1.10	Humid 25 ± 2 °C	4	1.10
BR	Boiling water	3	0.45	Not applicable			Water at 15 ± 5 °C	16 to 24	1.10	Humid 25 ± 2 °C	4	1.10
MR	Not applicable			Water at 67 ± 2 °C	3	0.90	Water at 15 ± 5 °C	16 to 24	1.10	Humid 25 ± 2 °C	4	1.10
INT	Not applicable			Not applicable			Water at 15 ± 5 °C	16 to 24	1.10	Not applicable		

(Appendix G: BS 1203: 1979)

Table 180   *Tabular summary of requirements*

Type of adhesive	Test														
	Boiling water resistance			*Hot water resistance*			*Cold water resistance*			*Micro-organism resistance*			*Natural ageing*		
	Condition	*Time* h	*Failing force (minimum)* kN	*Condition*	*Time* h	*Failing force (minimum)* kN	*Condition*	*Time* h	*Failing force (minimum)* kN	*Condition*	*Time* weeks	*Failing force (minimum)* kN	*Condition*	*Time* months	*Failing force (minimum)* kN
WBP	Boiling water	6	1.0 / 1.45	Not applicable			Water at 15 ± 5 °C	16 to 24	1.8 / 2.2	Humid 25 ± 2 °C	4	1.3 / 1.8	40 to 60% r.h. 25 ± 2 °C	12	See boiling water and cold water tests
BR	Boiling water	3	0.9 / 1.1	Not applicable			Water at 15 ± 5 °C	16 to 24	1.8 / 2.2	Humid 25 ± 2 °C	4	1.3 / 1.8	40 to 60% r.h. 25 ± 2 °C	12	See boiling water and cold water tests
MR	Not applicable			Water at 67 ± 2 °C	3	1.0 / 1.3	Water at 15 ± 5 °C	16 to 24	1.8 / 2.2	Humid 25 ± 2 °C	4	1.3 / 1.8	40 to 60% r.h. 25 ± 2 °C	12	See hot water and cold water tests
INT	Not applicable			Not applicable			Water at 15 ± 5 °C	16 to 24	1.8 / 2.2	Not applicable			40 to 60% r.h. 25 ± 2 °C	12	See cold water test

(Appendix K: BS 1204: Part 1: 1979)

Note: Where two values are given in the table for minimum failing force, the first limit applies to gap joints and the second to close-contact joint

Table 181   *Tabular summary of requirements*

Type of adhesive	Test														
	Boiling water resistance			*Hot water resistance*			*Cold water resistance*			*Micro-organism resistance*			*Natural ageing*		
	Condition	*Time* h	*Failing force (minimum)* kN	*Condition*	*Time* h	*Failing force (minimum)* kN	*Condition*	*Time* h	*Failing force (minimum)* kN	*Condition*	*Time* weeks	*Failing force (minimum)* kN	*Condition*	*Time* months	*Failing force (minimum)* kN
WBP	Boiling water	6	1.45	Not applicable			Water at 15 ± 5 °C	16 to 24	2.2	Humid 25 ± 2 °C	4	1.8	40 to 60% r.h. 25 ± 2 °C	12	See boiling water and cold water tests
BR	Boiling water	3	1.1	Not applicable			Water at 15 ± 5 °C	16 to 24	2.2	Humid 25 ± 2 °C	4	1.8	40 to 60% r.h. 25 ± 2 °C	12	See boiling water and cold water tests
MR	Not applicable			Water at 67 ± 2 °C	3	1.3	Water at 15 ± 5 °C	16 to 24	2.2	Humid 25 ± 2 °C	4	1.8	40 to 60% r.h. 25 ± 2 °C	12	See hot water and cold water tests
INT	Not applicable			Not applicable			Water at 15 ± 5 °C	16 to 24	2.2	Not applicable			40 to 60% r.h. 25 ± 2 °C	12	See cold water test

(Appendix J: BS 1204: Part 2: 1979)

suitable for hanging flexible wallcoverings and ceiling coverings supplied in roll form.

The types of adhesives are:

Type 1: for use as a low solids adhesive with easy slip showing very low marking and very low tarnishing. Especially suitable for light grammage wallcoverings.
Type 2: normally used as a medium solids adhesive, showing low marking and low tarnishing. Suitable for wallcoverings for all grammages and also for pervious, washable wallcoverings.
Type 3: adhesive with good wet adhesive, particularly suitable for wallcoverings of heavy grammage and also for pervious, washable coverings.
Type 4: adhesive containing fungicide to inhibit mould growth (mould resistant). Suitable for impervious wallcoverings of all grammages.
Type 5: high wet adhesion, high dry strength adhesive, containing fungicide to inhibit mould growth. Suitable for most impervious wallcoverings or special applications, often ready-mixed.

BS 3544: 1962 *Methods of test for polyvinyl acetate adhesives for wood*

This standard describes the following methods of test:

1 Freeze – thaw treatment.
2 Staining properties of the adhesives on wood.
3 Strength of double lap joints under three-point loading in shear, under dry and damp conditions.
4 Resistance of double lap joints to sustained three-point loading, under dry and damp conditions.

Preparation of test pieces for strength tests and a timing device for sustained loading tests are appended.

BS 4071: 1966 *Polyvinyl acetate (PVA) emulsion adhesives for wood*

This standard specifies requirements for resistance to freezing and thawing, freedom from staining, strength, resistance to sustained loading and storage. It refers to the methods of test described in BS 3544.

BS 5270: 1976 *Polyvinyl acetate (PVAC) emulsion bonding agents for internal use with gypsum building plaster*

This standard specifies requirements for PVA emulsion bonding agents for internal use with gypsum building plasters, to improve adhesion to difficult backgrounds or to control high suction as follows:

Solids content: not less than the minimum value stated by manufacturer.
Saponification value: 575–652 (for non-volatile component).
Acid value: maximum 10 (for non-volatile component).
Ash: maximum 2 per cent by mass.
Flexibility: a dry film of the bonding agent 0.05 mm thick shall not show any cracking when bent over a 1.5 mm mandrel at 23 ± 2 °C.
Bond strength: minimum 200 N.

BS 5350: *Methods of test for adhesives*

General Introduction: 1976

Seven groups of tests, sequenced logically.

Group A: Adherends
  Part A1: 1976 *Adherend preparation*

Group B: Adhesives
  Part B1: 1978 *Determination of density*
  Part B2: 1976 *Determination of solids content*
  Part B4: 1976 *Determination of pot life*
  Part B5: 1976 *Determination of gelation time*

  Part B8: 1977 *Determination of viscosity*
  Part B9: 1984 *Determination of resistance to sagging (flow after application)*

Group C: Adhesively bonded joints: mechanical tests
  Part C1: 1986 *Determination of cleavage strength of adhesive bonds*
  Part C3: 1978 (1983) *Determination of bond strength in direct tension*
  Part C4: 1986 *Determination of impact resistance of adhesive bonds*
  Part C5: 1976 *Determination of bond strength in longitudinal shear*
  Part C6: 1981 *Determination of bond strength in direct tension in sandwich panels*
  Part C7: 1976 (1983) *Determination of creep and resistance to sustained application of force*
  Part C9: 1978 (1983) *Floating roller peel test*
  Part C10: 1979 *90 ° peel test for flexible-to-rigid assembly*
  Part C11: 1979 *180 ° peel test for flexible-to-rigid assembly*
  Part C12: 1979 *'T' peel test for flexible-to-rigid assembly*
  Part C13: 1980 *Climbing drum peel test*
  Part C14: 1979 *90 ° peel test for rigid-to-rigid assembly*
  Part C15: 1982 *Determination of bond strength in compressive shear*

Group D: Adhesively bonded joints: environmental tests
  Part D4: 1976 *Determination of staining potential*

Group E: Sampling and analysis of test data
  Part E1: 1976 (1983) *Guide to statistical analysis*
  Part E2: 1979 *Guide to sampling*

Group F: Tests for flooring adhesives
  Part F1: 1983 *Performance tests for flooring adhesives*

Group H: Physical tests on hot-melt adhesives
  Part H1: 1981 *Determination of heat stability of hot-melt adhesives in the application equipment*
  Part H2: 1982 *Determination of low temperature flexibility or cold crack temperature*
  Part H3: 1984 *Determination of heat resistance to hot-melt adhesives*
  Part H4: 1984 *Determination of maximum open-time of hot-melt adhesives – oven method*

BS 5442 *Classification of adhesives for construction*

This standard is in three parts dealing respectively with adhesives for flooring, for internal wall and ceiling coverings, and for use with wood:

Part 1: 1977 *Adhesives for use with flooring materials*
Part 2: 1978 *Adhesives for interior wall and ceiling coverings (excluding decorative flexible materials in roll form)*
Part 3: 1979 *Adhesives for use with wood*

Classifications of adhesives are summarized in Table 182 (for flooring), Table 183 (for internal wall and ceiling coverings) and Tables 184 and 185 (for wood and wood/non wood).

BS 5980: 1980 *Adhesives for use with ceramic tiles and mosaics*

This standard classifies adhesives into five types depending on their chemical composition and physical form and into three classes based on their resistance to water.

The five types and classes follow:

Type 1: hydraulically – hardening mortar.
Type 2: dispersion adhesive.
Type 3: dispersion/cement adhesive.
Type 4: dissolved resin adhesive.
Type 5: reaction resin adhesive.

Class AA: materials with a faster development of water resistance.

Table 182 *Summary of classification of flooring materials/adhesive combinations for general use*

Type of flooring material	Type of adhesive (see key)											
X *indicates a suitable adhesive*	1 Gum spirit	2 Lignin paste	3 Rubber solution	4 SBR emulsion	5 Acrylic emulsion	6 Bitumen solution	7 Bitumen rubber emulsion	8 Epoxy resin	9 Polyvinyl acetate (PVAC emulsion)	10 Polymer modified cement	11 Hot bitumen	12 Unsaturated polyester resin
Cork tiles	X	X	X	X								
Cork tile (PVC faced)	X	X	X									
Cork carpet (complying with BS 810*)	X	X										
Linoleum sheet	X	X										
Linoleum tile (complying with BS 810*)	X ·	X		X								
Linoleum tiles, felt backed (complying with BS 1863†)	X	X		X								
PVC, flexible unbacked sheet and tile (complying with BS 3261 Part 1: 1973‡, type A)			X	X	X				X			
PVC, flexible tiles (complying with BS 3261 Part 1: 1973‡, type B)				X		X	X					
PVC, needle-loom felt backed sheet (complying with BS 5085 Part 1 §)	X			X					X			
PVC, cellular PVC backed sheet and tile				X	X							
PVC, latex-asbestos backed sheet				X	X							
PVC, bitumen felt backed sheet and tile	X			X	X							
PVC, woven hessian backed sheet and tile	X			X	X							
PVC, cork backed sheet	X	X										
‖PVC, (vinyl) asbestos tiles (complying with BS 3260¶)				X		X	X					
‖Thermoplastic tiles (complying with BS 2592**)				X		X	X					
Rubber sheet and tile			X									
Rubber bonded cork sheet and tile			X									
††Felts, needled and similar	X			X					X			
††Textile flooring, cellular PVC backed, sheet and tile				X	X							
††Textile flooring, cellular rubber backed, sheet and tile				X								
‡‡Ceramic tile (complying with BS 1286§§)								X		X		
Wood block							X				X	
Wood mosaic							X					
Covings and stair nosings			X					X				X

* BS 810 *Sheet linoleum (calendered types), cork carpet and linoleum tiles.*
† BS 1863 *Felt backed linoleum.*
‡ BS 3261 *Unbacked flexible PVC flooring* Part 1 *Homogeneous flooring.*
§ BS 5085 *Backed flexible PVC flooring* Part 1 *Needle-loom felt backed flooring.*
‖ This type of flooring should be used on timber substrates only where recommended by the manufacturer of the flooring.
¶ BS 3260 *PVC (vinyl) asbestos floor tiles.*
** BS 2592 *Thermoplastic flooring tiles.*
†† Because of abnormal shrinkage of some types of textile flooring, SBR emulsion should only be used where the material is known to be dimensionally stable.
‡‡ The recommendations for this type of flooring apply only for use on cementitious substrates.
§§ BS 1286 *Clay tiles for flooring.*

(Table 1: BS 5442: Part 1: 1977)

Table 183   *Summary of classification of adhesives for interior wall and ceiling coverings*

Type of adhesive (see key):
1 Acrylic emulsion; 2 Bitumen, hot applied; 3 Bitumen/rubber emulsion; 4 Bitumen/wax; 5 Cementitious; 6 Contact adhesives based on rubber latex or solution; 7 Epoxide resin; 8 Filled rubber solution; 9 Gum spirit; 10 Gypsum plaster; 11 Lignin paste; 12 Polymer-modified cement; 13 Polyvinyl ether solution; 14 Polyvinyl acetate (PVAC) emulsion; 15 Rubber latex; 16 SBR emulsion; 17 Stick pads; 18 Unsaturated polyester resin

Type of covering material	Situation where used W: Walls; C: Ceilings	1	2	3	4	5	6	7	8	9	10	11	12	13	14	15	16	17	18
Ceramics																			
Tiles and mosaics (complying with BS 5385 Part 1*)	W & C	×				×		×	×				×		×	×	×	×	
Plastics																			
Expanded polystyrene: †																			
decorative	W & C	×					×		×	×					×		×		
insulation board (complying with BS 3837‡)	W			×	×				×	×					×				
Decorative laminated plastics sheet (including materials complying with BS 4965§)	W						×		×						×		×		
Polyurethane foam (complying with BS 4841 Part 2‖):																			
rigid, unbacked	W			×					×	×									
rigid, paper-backed	W & C	×							×			×			×		×		
PVC:																			
felt-backed	W & C	×														×	×		
foam-backed	W & C	×															×		
plasticized¶	W & C	×					×		×					×			×		
unplasticized	W & C						×	×	×								×		
Textiles																			
Cellular PVC-backed sheet and tile¶	W & C						×												
Cellular rubber-backed sheet and tile	W & C						×												
Felts, needled and similar	W & C						×												
Timber and related materials																			
Acoustic tiles and insulating board (complying with BS 1142 Part 3**)	W‡‡						×		×	×					×		×		
Cork:																			
decorative	W & C						×			×		×				×			
insulation	W		×	×						×									
Hardboards	W‡						×	×	×								×		
Plywood	W						×	×	×								×		
Timber skirtings and battens	W								×										×
Wood chipboard (complying with BS 2604 Part 2‡‡)	W						×	×	×									×	
Wood-wool slabs (complying with BS 1105§§)	W								×				×						
Miscellaneous																			
Acoustic and decorative tiles of expanded plaster and other mineral compositions	W††												×		×				
Bituminous roofing felts (complying with BS 747‖‖)	W		×																
Foam glass	W		×	×															
Gypsum plasterboard (complying with BS 1230¶¶)	W	×							×		×				×		×		
Leather	W & C						×									×			
Linoleum tiles (complying with BS 810***)	W	×								×		×				×			
Metallic tiles	W & C							×	×										
Rubber	W & C						×		×										

(Table 1: BS 5442: Part 2: 1978)

× Indicates a suitable adhesive.
* BS 5385 *Code of practice for wall tiling* Part 1 *Internal ceramic wall tiling and mosaics in normal conditions.*
† Formulations for use with expanded polystyrene should be free from those solvents which would damage the cell structure of the material. All infaced tiles and sheet shall be continuously bonded overall.
‡ BS 3837 *Expanded polystyrene brands.*
§ BS 4965 *Decorative laminated plastics sheet veneered boards and panels.*
‖ BS 4841 *Rigid urethane foam for building applications* Part 2 *Laminated board for use as a wall and ceiling insulation.*
¶ The manufacturer's recommendations concerning the risk of plasticizer migration should be obtained and followed.
** BS 1142 *Fibre building boards* Part 3 *Insulating board (softboard).*
†† These materials may also be bonded to ceiling surfaces provided that the limit of mass per unit area set by the manufacturer of the adhesive is not exceeded.
‡‡ BS 2604 *Resin-bonded wood chipboard* Part 2 *Metric units.*
§§ BS 1105 *Wood wool slabs up to 102 mm thick.*
‖‖ BS 747 *Roofing felts.*
¶¶ BS 1230 *Gypsum plasterboard.*
*** BS 810 *Sheet linoleum (calendered types), cork carpet and linoleum tiles.*

Table 184 *Summary of classification of adhesives for wood/wood combinations*
Types of adhesive (see key . . .)

Basic classification →	Unmodified natural materials		Synthetic thermoset resins (Heat set and/or acid catalysed)						Miscellaneous multi-component	Elastomers — Solutions in organic solvents (Contact)	Elastomers — Solutions in organic solvents (Gap-filling type)				Thermoplastics — Hot-melt adhesives				Thermoplastics — Latices and emulsions	
Chemical type →	Bone, skin and hide glue	Casein	Phenol-formaldehyde	Resorcinol-formaldehyde	Resorcinol/phenol-formaldehyde	Urea-formaldehyde	Urea-melamine-formaldehyde	Melamine-formaldehyde	Polyvinyl acetate emulsion (cross-linkable)	Polychloroprene	Polychloroprene	Polyacrylonitrile-styrene	Styrene butadiene rubber	Natural rubber	Ethylene vinyl acetate	Polyester	Polyamide	Thermoplastic rubber	Polychloroprene latex	Polyvinyl acetate and polyvinyl acetate copolymer emulsion
Number in key	1	2	3	4	5	6	7	8	9	12	16	17	18	19	20	21	22	23	24	25
Highest suitability of coding	A	A	D	D	D	BC	BC	BC	BC	BC	BC	BC	BC	BC	BC	BC	BC	BC	BC	A
Type of work or structure																				
Plywood / Natural wood veneering — face	A	S	D	S	S	A	BC	BC	S	A					A	S	S	A	A	A
Plywood / Natural wood veneering — edge	A	S				A	BC	BC		A					A	S	S	A	A	A
Laminated beams		A	D	D	D	S	S	S	BC											
Prefabricated trusses		A	D	D	D	S	BC	S	BC											
Roof structures		A	D	D	D		BC													
Window frames	A	A	D	D	D	BC	BC	BC	BC											A
Interior door sets		A				A			BC											
Door manufacture		A	D	D	D	BC	BC	BC	BC											
Furniture manufacture — V-groove joints	A	A				A			BC		S				A	S	S			A
Furniture manufacture — other joints						A	BC		A						A	S	S			A
Assembly on site — joinery	A	A				A	BC		BC		A	A	A	A						A
Assembly on site — furniture	A	A				A	BC		BC		A	A	A	A						A
Assembly on site — structural components†																				

(Table 1: BS 5442: Part 3: 1979)

Table 185 *Summary of classification of adhesives for non-wood sheet material/wood combinations*
Type of adhesive (see key . . .)

Key to number in key (Chemical type / Basic classification):

Synthetic thermoset resins
- Heat set and/or acid catalysed
  - 3 Phenol-formaldehyde
  - 4 Resorcinol-formaldehyde
  - 5 Resorcinol/phenol-formaldehyde
  - 6 Urea-formaldehyde
  - 7 Urea/melamine-formaldehyde
  - 8 Melamine-formaldehyde
- Miscellaneous multicomponent
  - 9 Polyvinyl acetate emulsion (cross-linkable)
  - 10 Epoxide resin
  - 11 Unsaturated polyester

Elastomers
- Solution in organic solvents — Contact type
  - 12 Polychloroprene
  - 13 Butadiene-acrylonitrile
  - 14 Natural rubber
  - 15 Polyurethane
- Solution in organic solvents — Gap-filling type
  - 16 Polychloroprene
  - 17 Polyacrylonitrile-styrene
  - 18 Polybutadiene-styrene
  - 19 Natural rubber
- Hot-melt adhesives
  - 20 Ethylene vinyl acetate
  - 21 Polyester

Latices and emulsions
- 24 Polychloroprene latex
- 25 Polyvinyl acetate and polyvinyl acetate copolymer emulsion
- 26 Acrylate polymer emulsion

Type of work	3	4	5	6	7	8	9	10	11	12	13	14	15	16	17	18	19	20	21	24	25	26
Laminated board manufacture:																						
PVC foil	X	X	X																		X	
melamine decorative laminate			X	X	X	X	X														X	
On-site laminations, face veneering:																						
glass reinforced polyester										X										X		
melamine decorative laminate								X		X	X										X	
PVC										X	X		X								X	X
On-site laminations, edge veneering:																						
melamine decorative laminate					X		X			X	X		X					X	X			
polyester										X	X		X					X	X			
PVC																		X				
ABS																		X				
Stair nosings:																						
rubber										X	X	X		X	X	X	X					
PVC										X	X			X	X	X	X					
aluminium									X					X								
Sheet and galvanized steel sheet								X						X								

X Indicates a suitable adhesive; the choice, however, for any particular class, depends on economic and practical factors

(Table 2: BS 5442: Part 3: 1979)

Class A: materials with a slower development of water resistance.

Class B: materials with no requirement for water resistance.

It also specifies requirements for storage stability, resistance to mould growth, resistance to excessive strain development, tensile adhesion strength, shear adhesion strength, open time and adjustability.

DD 74: 1981   *Performance requirements and test methods for non-structural wood adhesives*

The purpose of this draft is to provide criteria against which adhesives of a given type can be classified and which can be used to check the quality of the adhesive. It covers six durability classes of close-contact and gap-filling adhesives on the basis of the shear strength of test joints, supplementary classification by resistance to sustained load, supplementary requirements for emulsion-based adhesives and animal glues.

BS 217: 1961   *Red lead for paints and jointing compounds*

This standard covers the requirements for red lead for paints and jointing compounds only, and does not cover red lead for other purposes. It specifies three types of red lead:

Type 1: red lead, non-setting, for paints.

Type 2: red lead, ordinary, for paint intended to be mixed on the site and used soon afterwards.

Type 3: red lead for jointing purposes.

Requirements are specified for composition, non-setting properties (Type 1 only), residue on sieve, oil absorption value, colour, matter volatile at 100 °C, matter soluble in water. Sampling and test methods are appended.

BS 544: 1969   *Linseed oil putty for use in wood frames*

This standard specifies requirements for sampling, composition, paintability, workability, consistency, skins and coarse particles, keeping qualities and storage stability and marking. Methods of test are appended.

BS 2499: 1973   *Hot applied sealants for concrete pavements*

This standard covers two main types of hot applied joint sealant: ordinary and fuel-resistant. It specifies properties, methods of test, sampling, recommendations for preparation and use.

Joints are necessary in concrete roads, etc. to prevent excessive stresses being developed in the slabs as a result of expansion and contraction due to temperature and moisture changes.

BS 2571: 1963   *Flexible PVC compounds*

This standard specifies requirements for three classes of PVC compounds, each class being subdivided into a number of different types. It covers the following properties and lays down methods of test: colour fastness to daylight, colour bleeding, appearance, elongation after heating, tensile strength, elongation at break, volume resistivity at 23 °C, effect on polythene, softness, cold bend temperature, cold flex temperature before ageing, cold flex temperature after ageing, deformation under heat, volume resistivity at 60 °C, electric strength at 23 °C, loss on heating, water absorption and water soluble matter.

BS 2919: 1968   *Low and intermediate density polythene rod for general purposes*

This standard specifies requirements for composition, colour, freedom from defects, diameters, lengths, tensile strength and heat reversion. Methods of test are appended.

BS 3712   *Building and construction sealants*

A building sealant is defined as a joint sealant for building and construction, applied by hand, gun, knife, or trowel, or in strip form, or by pouring, and intended to maintain a seal between the sides of a joint which is subject to some degree of movement.

Four parts describe methods of test for the following properties of building and construction sealants.

Part 1: 1985   *Methods of test for homogeneity, relative density, extrudability, penetration and slump*
Part 2: 1973   *Methods of test for seepage, staining, shrinkage, shelf life and paintability*
Part 3: 1974   *Methods of test for application life, skinning properties and tack-free time*
Part 4: 1985   *Methods of test for adhesive in peel, tensile extension and recovery and loss of mass after heat ageing*

BS 4254: 1983   *Two-part polysulphide-based sealants*

A two-part polysulphide-based sealant is a sealant consisting of two components, essentially a component containing polysulphide polymer and a separate component containing the curing agent, which are mixed together before application and cure at ambient temperature to form a rubber-like solid.

Specifies requirements for two grades of two-part polysulphide-based sealant for use in general building and glazing applications, namely pouring grade and gun grade. Test requirements and procedures are given for rheological properties, plastic deformation, application life, adhesion in peel, loss of mass after heat ageing and staining.

BS 4645: 1970   *High density polythene rod for general purposes*

This standard specifies requirements for high density polythene rod for general purposes including pipe fabrication, chemical, food and building industry uses. Requirements specified include composition, freedom from defects, dimensions (diameters), lengths, tensile strength and heat reversion. Methods of test are appended.

BS 5212: 1975   *Cold poured joint sealants for concrete pavements*

This standard covers ordinary (Type N) and fuel-resistant (Type F) cold poured polymer-based sealants for joints in concrete roads, airfields and other exposed pavements. Requirements are specified for application life, shelf life, tack-free time, resistance to flow, recovery after penetration, adhesion and cohesion in tension and compression, resistance to heat ageing and resistance to fuel immersion (for Type F sealants).

BS 5215: 1986   *One-part gun-grade polysulphide-based sealants*

This type of sealant contains a liquid polysulphide polymer and a curing system which is activated by exposure to moisture and which cures to a rubber-like solid. It is used for sealing and glazing applications in building and structures.

Requirements are specified in this standard for rheological properties, recovery, weight loss after heat ageing, staining, adhesion and shelf life. Methods of test are appended.

Refers to BS 5215: 1975 for test methods.

BS 5889: 1980   *Silicone-based building sealants*

A silicone-based sealant consists of a polysiloxane polymer and a chemical curing system which cures to a rubber-like solid with a tack-free surface on exposure to moist air.

This standard classifies silicone-based sealants with two types: Type A (low modulus sealants used for building joints generally) and Type B (high modulus sealants used mainly for glazing and sanitary ware applications). Requirements are specified for skin over time, slump and extrusion rate of uncured sealant, force on extrusion and elastic recovery, weight loss on heat ageing, adhesion and cohesion in tension, staining and adhesion in peel. Methods of test are appended.

DD 69: 1980 *Method for classifying the movement capability of joint sealants*

This draft provides a method for classifying building sealants according to their ability to withstand different degrees of joint movement. The test methods given are not intended to replace test methods at present in BS 4254 and BS 5215.

BS 1878: 1973 *Corrugated copper jointing strip for expansion joints for use in general building construction*

This standard specifies copper strip as a means of providing a weatherproof seal capable of accommodating relative movement between the two sides of the joint or to break rigid continuity in structures for insulation purposes.

Table 186 *Expected service life of sealant types*

Types of sealant	Expected service life
Oleo-resinous Bitumen and rubber/bitumen Butyl	Up to 10 years
Acrylic (solvent) Acrylic (emulsion)	Up to 15 years
1-part polysulphide 1-part polyurethane Silicone 2-part polysulphide 2-part polyurethane	Up to 20 years

Note: Under favourable conditions, the expected service life quoted above may be exceeded.

(Table 2: BS 6213: 1982)

BS 4255 *Rubber used in preformed rubber gaskets for weather exclusion from buildings*

Part 1: 1986 *Non-cellular gaskets* (see Table 2 Constructions, forms (H) section work)

Part 2: 1975 *Cellular gaskets*

Part 1 specifies requirements for non-cellular rubber sealing and/or glazing gaskets for location in buildings where resistance to weathering and permanent deformation under load are prime essentials. Rubber gaskets are classified into five classes (A, B, C, D and E) in terms of hardness. Test requirements are specified for tensile strength, elongation at break, compression set before and after ageing, ozone resistance, stiffening at low temperature and staining. Methods of test are appended.

Part 2 specifies requirements for cellular rubber gaskets and preformed rubber strips for use in buildings. Three types of products are specified: Type 1 (closed cell structure), Type 2 (open cell structure with 'live' skin) and Type 3 (open cell structure). Requirements are specified for composition, finish, dimensions, ozone resistance, water absorption, compression stress-strain, compression set and staining of organic finish.

BS 4243: 1967 *Cork/paper jointing*

This standard specifies requirements for compressible sheet jointing material composed of an intimate mixture of cork granules and cellulosic fibres, from which gaskets can be cut or stamped. The requirements are specified for flexibility, tensile strength, compressibility and compression set, oil absorption, freedom from corrosive impurities, resistance to mould growth and dimensional stability. Methods of test are appended.

BS 4332: 1962 *Composition cork jointing*

This standard specifies requirements for synthetic resin-bonded cork sheet jointing material from which gaskets can be cut or stamped, for general industrial use, excluding automobile use.

Table 187 *Types of sealant failure and possible causes*

Type of failure	Possible causes of failure						
	Incorrectly designed or formed joint or seal profile	Sealant unsuitable for joint type or service conditions	Excessive movement for width of joint or sealant type	Depth of seal	Inadequate surface preparation	Poor application technique	Incorrectly formulated sealant
Adhesion (including spalling)	×	×	×	×	×	×	×
Cohesive (splits, cracks)	×	×	×	× * × †		×	×
Excessive extrusion (during and after periods of joint closure)	×	×	×	× †		×	
Slumping (in vertical joints and horizontal joints in vertical plane)	×	×		× †		×	×
Folding and intrusion	×	×	×	× †			
Chemical attack (in specific environments, e.g. dairies and breweries)		×					
Displacement	×	×		× *	×	×	

*Depth of seal too shallow.

(Table 3: BS 6213: 1982)

Test requirements are specified for thickness, density, flexibility, compressibility and compression set, freedom from corrosive impurities, water-soluble matter, resistance to lubricating oil, petroleum fuel and water, test for resin bond and resistance to mould growth. Methods of test are appended.

BS 6213: 1982 *Guide to selection of constructional sealants*

This standard gives guidance on types of joint sealants and on their selection and correct application to enable proper choice and specification according to joint function and design. It provides information on categories of joints, joint movement and dimensions, and on the geometry, modulus, maintenance (see Table 186) and causes of failure of sealants (see Table 187). It is limited to sealants for use in areas having slow moving vehicular and pedestrian traffic but no areas of more onerous use such as carriageways of roads, airport runways and similar areas.

BS 6214: 1982 *Jointing materials for plasterboard*

Requirements for jointing compounds and tapes for use with tapered edge gypsum wallboard and plank complying with the requirements of BS 1230: Gypsum plasterboard.

u Protective and process/property modifying materials

u1 Anti-corrosive materials, treatments

There are 27 standards, one code and one draft for development under this section, consisting of corrosion protection, including phosphate treatment (two standards, one code of practice and one draft for development), metallic coatings (11 standards), electroplated coatings (six standards), vitreous coatings (five standards) and organic coatings (three standards).

CP 1021: 1973 *Cathodic protection*

Cathodic protection is defined in this code as a means of rendering a metal immune from corrosive attack by causing d.c. current to flow from its electrolytic environment into a metal.

This code deals with the general principles, economic considerations, application to buried structures, ships and immersed structures other than ships, internal protection of plant, safeguarding neighbouring structures, electrical measurements, safety and operation and maintenance.

DD24: 1973 *Recommendation for methods of protection against corrosion on light section steel used in building*

This draft recommends methods of protection against corrosion in temperate climatic conditions for light formed sections used in building and having an arbitrary thickness of up to 5 mm. It includes guiding principles, classification of environments in the United Kingdom, and life requirements and maintenance of various protective schemes. Details of the protective schemes are appended.

BS 3189: 1973 *Phosphate treatment of iron and steel*

This standard specifies five types of phosphate coating (see Table 188) for use with organic coatings and sealants for protection against corrosion or for various engineering applications. It also covers sampling, coating requirements and methods of test.

Table 188 *Typical applications of the various types of phosphate coating*

Type of coating	Typical applications
Type 1A	Protection under sealants. Resistance to wear, fretting and scuffing.
Type 1B	Protection under sealants. Lubricant-carrier in cold forming operations.
Type 2	Use under paints where no subsequent deformation is likely to take place. Lubricant-carrier for less severe forming operations.
Type 3	General use under organic coatings.
Type 4	As Type 3 where either a lower standard of protection is acceptable or maximum formability after organic coating is required.

(Appendix A: BS 3189: 1973)

BS 3745: 1970 *The evaluation of results of accelerated corrosion tests on metallic coatings*

This standard gives a rating system (see Table 189) which provides a means of defining acceptable levels of performance in accelerated corrosion tests where required by other relevant British Standards.

Table 189 *Rating number*

Frequency %	Rating number
0 (no corrosion spots)	10
Over 0–0.25	9
0.25–0.5	8
0.5–1	7
1–2	6
2–4	5
4–8	4
8–16	3
16–32	2
32–64	1
64	0

(From BS 3745: 1970)

BS 5466 *Methods for corrosion testing of metallic coatings*

Part 1: 1977 *Neutral salt spray test (NSS test)*
This part specifies the apparatus, the reagent (50 ± 5 g/l solution of NaCl adjusted to a pH of 6.5–7.2) and the procedure. It does not specify but gives guidance on type of test specimen, exposure period or interpretation of results, which should be covered in coating or product specifications.

Part 2: 1977 *Acetic acid salt spray test (ASS test)*
This part specifies the apparatus, the test solution (glacial acetic acid added to 50 ± 5 g/l NaCl solution to ensure a pH of 3.1–3.3) and the procedure required to ensure reasonable reproducibility especially for decorative coatings of copper + nickel + chromium or nickel + chromium and also anodic coatings on aluminium. It does not specify but gives guidance on type of test specimen, exposure period and interpretation of results.

Part 3: 1977 *Copper-accelerated acetic acid salt spray test (CASS test)*
This part specifies the apparatus, the test solution (NaCl solution containing some $CuCl_2.2H_2O$ and some glacial acetic acid to produce a pH 3.1–3.3) and the procedure. This test is devised for copper + nickel + chromium or nickel + chromium coatings, but is also suitable for anodic oxide coatings on aluminium. It is not reliable for comparison of different types. It does not specify but gives guidance on type of test specimen, exposure period and interpretation of results. Calibration of test conditions is included.

Part 4: 1979 *Thioacetamide test (TAA test)*
This part specifies the apparatus, the reagents and the procedure for assessing the efficiency of tarnish-preventing treatments of silver and gold and for detecting discontinuities in previous metal coatings by exposure to an atmosphere containing volatile sulphides. It gives guidance on the number and type of test specimens, the exposure period and criteria of failure.

Caution: Thioacetamide is a carcinogen; all contact with human skin should be avoided.

Part 5: 1979 *Corrodkote test (CORR test)*
This part specifies the apparatus, reagent and procedure for an accelerated corrosion test mainly applicable to Cu-Ni-Cr or Ni-Cr electroplated parts. It gives guidance on the number and type of specimens, the exposure period and criteria of failure.

The reagent or the corrodkote slurry consists of corrosive salts of $Cu(NO_3)_2.3H_2O$, $FeCl_3.6H_2O$ and NH_4Cl.

Part 6: 1982 *Rating of results of corrosion tests on electroplated coatings cathodic to the substrate*
This part specifies a method of evaluating the condition of electroplated test specimens that have been exposed to corrosive environments for test purposes.

This method is applicable to panels exposed outdoors and to accelerated tests, on decorative and protective coatings that are cathodic to the substrate, for example Ni + Cr or Cu + Ni + Cr on steel or zinc die castings. It is not intended for use with anodic sacrificial coatings such as zinc and cadmium on steel.

It also includes symbols describing defects and dot charts and colour photographs.

Part 7: 1982 *Guidance on stationary outdoor exposure corrosion tests*
This part gives guidance on methods of stationary testing, in natural outdoor atmospheric conditions, of protective metallic, conversion and other non-organic coatings. Results may have to be supplemented with mobile test not included in this standard.

Part 8: 1986 *Sulphur dioxide test with general condensation of moisture*
This Part specifies a method for assessing the resistance of materials or products to condensed moisture containing sulphur dioxide. The method has been found to be suitable for testing metallic and non-organic coatings.

BS 54593: 1977 *Code of practice for protective coating of iron and steel structures against corrosion*

This code specifies recommended methods of protection against corrosion of iron and steel structures. It describes the various methods in detail and gives guidance on how to specify a chosen protective system, how to ensure its correct application and how to maintain it. It does not include specific recommendations for ships, vehicles, offshore platforms, specialized chemical equipment, cladding materials, plastics coatings, cement-mortar linings or weathering steels.

BS 729: 1971 *Hot-dip galvanized coatings on iron and steel articles*

Hot-dip galvanized coating is a coating of zinc or zinc-iron alloy layers, obtained by dipping prepared iron or steel articles in molten zinc.

This standard specifies requirements for hot-dip galvanized coatings on steel articles galvanized after fabrication and on grey and malleable iron castings. It covers composition of zinc in galvanizing bath, appearance and uniformity of coating and coating weight, distortion, cracking and embrittlement of basis metals and repair of damaged areas.

BS 1615: 1972 *Anodic oxidation coatings on aluminium*

This standard deals with anodic coatings on aluminiun, consisting mainly of aluminium oxide, produced by an electrolytic oxidation process during which the aluminium acts as the anode.

It classifies seven grades of anodic coatings in terms of coating thickness. Test methods are specified for coating, thickness, efficiency of sealing, corrosion resistance, abrasion resistance, fastness to light, resistance to heat and weathering of coloured coatings.

BS 2569 *Sprayed metal coatings*

Part 1: 1964 *Protection of iron and steel by aluminium and zinc against atmospheric corrosion*
This part specifies requirements for the composition of coating metal, methods of surface preparation and application of coating, thickness and adhesion, re-treatment of defective areas. Methods of test are appended.

Part 2: 1965 *Protection of iron and steel against corrosion and oxidation at elevated temperatures*
This part specifies five classes of coating for use in service temperature ranges up to 550, 900 and 1000 °C. It specifies requirements for composition of coating materials, methods of

surface preparation and application of coating, thickness and adhesion, subsequent treatment. Methods of test are appended.

BS 3987: 1974   *Anodic oxide coatings on wrought aluminium for external architectural applications*

This standard specifies coating thickness, method of measurement, sealing requirements and method of assessment. It gives guidance on the temporary protection and anodized aluminium and its maintenance when installed in a building.

BS 4761: 1971   *Sprayed unfused metal coatings for engineering purposes*

This standard specifies requirements for sprayed, unfused coatings of metals and metallic compounds applied by combustion gas flame, plasma arc, detonation and similar processes. Requirements are also specified for preparation of components, spraying technique, seating, finishing and inspection.

BS 4921: 1973   *Sherardized coatings on iron and steel articles*

Sherardizing is a diffusion process in which articles are heated in close contact with zinc dust. The process is normally carried out in a slowly rotating closed box at a temperature of 385–425 °C and a coating of zinc-iron alloy layers is produced.

This standard specifies coatings consisting substantially of zinc on steel articles, and on grey and malleable iron castings, applied by the sherardizing process. It deals with the purity of zinc powder, thickness, appearance and adhesion of coating. It gives advice on the condition of the basis metal and the need for post treatments.

BS 4950: 1973   *Sprayed and fused metal coatings for engineering purposes*

This standard relates to the requirements for sprayed coatings, subsequently fused at temperatures approximately within the range 1000–1200 °C, of self-fluxing metals and metallic compounds for engineering purposes applied by combustion gas flame and arc processes.

It covers preparation of components, conditions for spraying and subsequent fusion, finishing and inspection.

It differs from BS 4761 *Sprayed unfused metal coatings for engineering purposes* in that, as the coating is fused to the base, it is not subject to the same restrictions regarding point loading and adhesion.

BS 5411   *Methods of test for metallic and related coatings*

Part 1: 1980   *Definitions and conventions concerning the measurement of thickness*
This part defines terms concerning the measurement of the thickness of metallic and other non-organic coatings on any substrate. It specifies some general rules in the measurement of minimum thicknesses of coatings. It includes the definitions of significant surface, measuring area, reference area, local thickness, minimum local thickness, maximum local thickness and average thickness.

Part 2: 1978   *Review of methods for the measurement of thickness*
This part reviews methods (destructive and non-destructive) for measuring the thickness of metallic and other non-organic coatings on both metallic and non-metallic substrates. It is limited to tests already specified, or to be specified, in other parts of BS 5411.

Part 3: 1976   *Eddy current methods for measurement of coating thickness of non-conductive coatings on non-magnetic basis metals*
This is a non-destructive method applicable to measurements of most anodic oxide coatings but not applicable to all conversion coatings, some of which are too thin to be measured by this method.

Eddy current instruments work on the principle that a high frequency electromagnetic field generated in the probe system of the instrument will produce eddy currents in a conductor over which the probe is placed, and that the amplitude and phase of these currents is a function of the separation between the conductor and the probe.

Part 4: 1986   *Coulometric method for the measurement of coating thickness*
This part specifies a method for measuring the thickness of metallic coatings by the coulometric (anodic dissolution) method using commercial or individually constructed instruments. It specifies coatings to which the method is applicable and lists typical electrolytes appropriate for these.

Part 5: 1976   *Measurement of the local thickness of metal and oxide coatings by the microscopical examination of cross-sections*
This method is destructive and is suitable for the measurement of local thickness of metal coatings, oxide layers and porcelain or vitreous enamels. It is normally used only as a referee method or when the size or shape of the coated article prohibits the use of other methods. Maximum absolute accuracy is $\pm$ 0.8 μm.

Part 6: 1981   *Vickers and Knoop microhardness tests*
This method is applicable to electrodeposited, antocatalytic and sprayed metallic coatings and also to anodic coatings on aluminium when microhardness testing is not suitable because of the large test forces required. The test consists of forcing an indenter into the metal coating and measuring with a microscope the diagonal(s) of the indentation left in the surface after removal of the indenter. A number known on the Vickers and Knoop hardness number is derived from the measurements using given equations.

Part 7: 1981   *Profilometric method for measurements of coating thickness*
This part specifies a method for the measurement of metal coating thickness by first forming a step between the surface of the coating and the surface of its substrate and the measuring the step height using a profile recording instrument. This method is applicable to thickness from 0.01 μm to 1000 μm on flat surfaces and, if precautions are taken, on cylindrical surfaces.

Part 8: 1976   *Measurements of coating thickness of metallic coatings: X-ray spectrometric methods*
This part specifies X-ray emission and absorption methods which are non-destructive methods applicable to the determination of the mass of coating per unit area as well as the coating thickness.

Part 9: 1977   *Measurement of coating thickness of electrodeposited nickel coatings on magnetic and non-magnetic substrates: magnetic method*
This is a non-destructive method based on the magnetic attraction between a magnet and the coating substrate, or the reluctance of a magnetic flux path passing through the coating and the substrate. Magnetic attraction method is applicable to up to 50 μm on non-magnetic substrates. Reluctance method is applicable to thicknesses of up to 1 mm or more.

Part 10: 1981   *Review of methods available for testing adhesion of electrodeposited and chemically deposited metallic coatings on metallic substrates*
This part describes qualitative tests for checking adhesion and indicates the suitability of each test for the most usual type of metallic coatings (see Table 190).

Part 11: 1977   *Measurement of coating thickness of non-*

Table 190 *Adhesion tests appropriate for various coating metals*

Adhesion test \ Coating metal	Cadmium	Chromium	Copper	Nickel	Nickel + chromium	Silver	Tin	Tin-nickel alloy	Zinc	Gold
Burnishing	*		*	*	*	*	*	*	*	*
Ball burnishing	*	*	*	*	*	*	*	*	*	*
Peeling (soldering method)			*	*		*		*		
Peeling (adhesive method)	*		*	*		*	*	*	*	*
File			*	*				*		
Chisel		*		*	*	*		*		
Scribe	*		*	*	*	*	*		*	*
Bending and twisting		*	*	*	*			*		
Grinding and sawing		*		*	*			*		
Tension	*		*	*	*	*		*	*	
Thermal shock		*	*	*	*		*	*		
Extrusion (Erichsen)		*	*	*	*			*		
Extrusion (flanged cap)		*	*	*	*	*		*		
Shot-peening				*		*				
Cathodic treatment		*		*	*					

(Table 2: BS 5411: Part 10: 1981)

magnetic metallic and vitreous or porcelain enamel coatings on magnetic basis metals: magnetic method
This part specifies methods of using magnetic instruments using the attraction between a magnet and the basis metal or the reluctance of a magnetic flux passing through the coating and basis metal.

Part 12: 1981 *Beta backscatter method for measurement of thickness*
This part specifies a method for the non-destructive measurement of coating thickness using beta backscatter gauges. It applies to both metallic and non-metallic coatings on both metallic and non-metallic substrates.

Caution: Radioactive sources used present a potential health hazard. Therefore all rules and regulations of local or national authorities must be observed.

Part 13: 1982 *Chromate conversion coatings on zinc and cadmium*
This part specifies methods for the determination on zinc and cadmium of the presence of colourless chromatic conversion coatings, the presence and quantity of hexavalent chromium in colourless and coloured coatings, the total chromium content per unit area and the satisfactory adhesion of coloured coatings.
These methods are applicable only to chromate conversion coatings which are free from any supplementary coating, such as oil, water or solvent-based polymers, or wax.

Part 14: 1982 *Gravimetric method for determination of coating mass per unit area of conversion coatings on metallic materials*
The coating mass is determined either by weighing the sample before and after dissolving the coating without attacking the substrate, or by weighing the coating after dissolving the substrate without attacking the coating. The mass of the coating divided by the density and the area of the coating gives the average coating thickness. The methods are applicable to phosphate coatings on iron and steel, zinc and cadmium, aluminium and its alloys, and chromate coatings on zinc and cadmium, aluminium and its alloys.

BS 6041: 1981 *Methods of sampling of electrodeposited metallic coatings and related finishes: procedures for inspection by attributes*

This standard establishes sampling plans and procedures for inspection by attributes, that is inspection whereby either the unit of product is simply classified as defective or non-defective, or the number of defects in the unit of product is counted, with respect to one or more given requirements.
It is applicable but not limited to the inspection of end items, components, materials in process and finished products in storage.

BS 1224: 1970 *Electroplated coatings of nickel and chromium*

This standard applies to electroplated coatings of nickel, with or without chromium on steel (or iron), zinc alloy, copper or copper alloys, and aluminium or aluminium alloys, except for the following: coatings applied to machine screw threads, coatings applied to sheet, strip, wire in the unfabricated form, or coil springs, and coatings applied for engineering purposes.
Requirements are specified for appearance, type, thickness of nickel and chromium, adhesion and corrosion resistance.

BS 1706: 1960 *Electroplated coatings of cadmium and zinc on iron and steel*

This standard applies to protective electroplated coatings of cadmium and zinc on iron and steel, except for the following: coatings applied to components having threads of basic major diameter from 0.050 to 0.50 in, coatings applied to sheet, strip, or wire in the unfabricated form.
Requirements are specified for appearance, thickness, adhesion and corrosion resistance for passivated coatings.

BS 6687: 1986 *Electrolytically zinc-coated steel flat-rolled products·*

Requirements for such products up to 2.5 mm thick with coating thicknesses up to 10 μm.

BS 3382   *Electroplated coatings on threaded components*

This standard deals with the plating of small threaded components such as bolts, screws and nuts in various materials with the commoner protective finishes:

Part 1 *Cadmium on steel components*
Part 2 *Zinc on steel components*
Part 3 *Nickel or nickel/chromium on steel components*
Part 4 *Nickel or nickel/chromium on brass components*
Part 5 *Tin on copper and copper alloys (including brass) components*
Part 6 *Silver on copper and copper alloys (including brass) components*
Part 7 *Thicker platings on threaded components*

Parts 1 and 2: 1961 deal with plating thicknesses, sampling, inspection procedures, thicknesses determination, resistance to corrosion, adhesion, porosity, reduction of hydrogen embrittlement, finish and appearance, plating thickness and passivation.

Parts 3 and 4: 1965 deal with resistance to corrosion, adhesion, reduction of hydrogen embrittlement, finish and appearance, plating thickness, sampling, inspection procedures, and thickness determination.

Parts 5 and 6: 1967 deal with plating thicknesses, sampling, inspection procedures and thickness determinations. They are not applicable to components for aircraft, self-tapping screws or wood screws.

Part 7: 1966 deals with plating thicknesses, sampling, inspection procedures, thickness determination. It is not applicable to components for aircraft, self-tapping screws or wood screws.

BS 4601: 1970   *Electroplated coatings of nickel plus chromium on plastics materials*

This standard specifies requirements for electroplated coatings of nickel (with a copper undercoat in many cases) plus chromium on plastics materials for other than engineering purposes.

Requirements are specified for appearance, type and thickness of nickel, type and thickness of chromium, thermal cycling and corrosion resistance tests for various service conditions.

BS 6338: 1983   *Chromate conversion coatings on electroplated zinc and cadmium coatings*

Coatings of zinc and cadmium are chromate treated in order to retard the formation of corrosion products on the surfaces of coatings exposed in corrosive atmospheres. Chromate treatment is particularly effective in retarding the formation of white corrosion products which form on zinc and cadmium coatings under certain conditions.

This standard specifies requirements relating to chromate conversion coatings on zinc and cadmium intended to give protection against corrosion. Finishes for giving particular colours only or specifically to improve paint adhesion are not covered by this standard.

BS 1344   *Methods of testing vitreous enamel finishes*

Vitreous enamel is a glazed surface finish produced by the application of a powdered inorganic glass, dry or suspended in water, to metal parts, and its subsequent fusion.

This standard is subdivided into 19 parts.

Part 1: 1965   *Resistance to thermal shock of coatings on articles other than cooking utensils*

■   AD (Regs. J1/2/3)

This method involves exposing the test specimen to radiant heat (185–195 °C) for about 10 minutes and within 5 seconds quenching the enamelled surface with water at 15–20 °C. After

repeating the procedure six times, the test specimen is assessed by visual examination for signs of flaking-off or crazing.

Part 2: 1975   *Resistance to citric acid at room temperature*
This method involves exposing part of the surface to attack by a 100 g/l citric acid solution for 15 minutes ± 30 seconds. Results are based on appearance and cleanability of the enamelled surface. It is not suitable for matt enamels, enamels that come in contact with hot and strong acids or enamelled articles that are used in the chemical industry.

Part 3: 1967   *Resistance to products of combustion containing sulphur compounds*

■   AD (Reg. J1/2/3)

This method involves saturating the two layers of filter paper disks placed on the cleaned surface of the enamel by adding sulphuric acid solution (20 g H_2SO_4 per litre solution) dropwise and then allowing to stand for 20 ± 1 minutes under cover before washing with running tap water, followed by drying the surface with a clean cloth. A method for classifying results is included.

Part 4: 1968   *Resistance to abrasion*
A method of test for determining the abrasion resistance of vitreous enamel finishes is given, using the abrading charge of steel balls and sand.

Part 5: 1984   *Resistance to detergents*
A detergent is a cleaning material containing a surface active agent used as an aqueous solution, thus including soap alone but excluding abrasive cleaners.

This part gives a method of test for detergent resistance near boiling point. A grading system for assessment in terms of time before loss of gloss is included.

Part 6: 1971   *Resistance to alkali*
This part gives a method of test for determining the alkali resistance of vitreous enamel finishes (on baths, sinks and similar domestic equipment) using 5 per cent sodium carbonate or 10 per cent sodium hydroxide solution for a more stringent test.

Part 7: 1984   *Determination of resistance to heat*

■   AD (Regs. J1/2/3)

A method for determining the resistance of vitreous- and porcelain-enamelled manufactured articles that in service will be subjected to high temperature, for example some cooker components, exhaust pipe silencers, gas heating chimneys.

Part 8: 1975   *Resistance to boiling citric acid*
This part specifies a method of test for the resistance of flat surfaces of vitreous and porcelain enamels to boiling citric acid, by determining the loss in mass per unit area.

Part 9: 1975   *Resistance to boiling water and water vapour*

Part 10: 1975   *Resistance to boiling hydrochloric acid*
This method also allows the determination of the resistance of enamels to the liquid and vapour phases of the corrosive medium, by measuring loss in mass.

Part 11: 1975   *High voltage test for articles for use under highly corrosive conditions*
This is a method for detecting discontinuities in vitreous enamel coatings which extend down to the basis metal, using a d.c. voltage above 2 kV.

Part 12: 1975   *Production of specimens for testing coatings on sheet steel*

Table 191 *Required characteristics*

Pigment	British Standard requirements (see note 1)	Composition: Description or limit	Method of test	Colour and staining power — Methods of test: Appendix D			Matter volatile at 105 °C for powders (see note 2 for dispersions). Method of test: BS 3483 Part B6	Matter soluble in water (see note 3) Method of test: BS 3483 Part C2
				For powders	For dispersions	Requirements		
Chromic oxide green	318	Cr_2O_3 95% minimum	Appendix A or agreed suitable alternative test method	Method 1 or 2	Method 3		0.5% maximum	0.5% maximum
Red iron oxide	3981 Class 1 / Class 3	Fe_2O_3 94% minimum / Fe_2O_3 50% minimum	Appendix B or agreed suitable alternative test method	Method 1 or 2	Method 3		3.0% maximum	3.0% maximum
Carbon black		Amorphous free carbon		Method 2	Method 3	Similar to agreed sample	To be within 2% absolute of the amount stated by the vendor	1.0%
Black iron oxide	3981 Class 8	Fe_2O_3 80% minimum	Appendix B or agreed suitable alternative test method	Method 1 or 2	Method 3		1.5% maximum	2.5% maximum
Yellow iron oxide and iron hydroxide	3981 Class 4 / Class 5 / Class 6	Fe_2O_3 83% minimum / Fe_2O_3 70% minimum / Fe_2O_3 45% minimum	Appendix B or agreed suitable alternative test method	Method 1 or 2	Method 3		4.0% maximum	2.5% maximum
Brown iron oxide and iron-manganese oxide	3981 Class 10 / Class 11 / Class 12	Fe_2O_3 70% minimum / Fe_2O_3 45% minimum / Fe_2O_3 40% minimum	Appendix B or agreed suitable alternative test method	Method 1 or 2	Method 3		4.0% maximum	2.5% maximum
Titanium dioxide white	Anatase type / Rutile type	TiO_2 98% minimum / TiO_2 97% minimum	Appendix C or agreed suitable alternative test method	Method 1 or 2	Method 3		0.5% maximum	0.6% maximum
Phthalocyanine blue	3599/12	Shall consist of copper phthalocyanine CI pigment blue 15 as in Part 1 (Usage section) Volume 2 of the Colour Index and the colour shall be entirely due to this material		Method 2	Method 3	Similar to agreed sample	1.0% maximum	2.0% maximum
Phthalocyanine green	3599/12	Shall consist essentially of polyhalogenated copper phthalocyanine CI pigment green 7, 41, or 43 as in Part 1 (Usage section) Volume 2 of the Colour Index and the colour shall be entirely due to this material		Method 2	Method 3		1.0% maximum	2.0% maximum

Note 1: It should be noted that materials complying with the requirements of the British Standards listed may be of a quality superior to the overall requirements of this standard.
Note 2: For dispersions, the matter volatile at 105 °C shall not vary from the manufacturer's declared value by more than 2% absolute.
Note 3: **The value shall be calculated on the mass of the residue dried at 105 °C.**

(Table 1: BS 1014: 1975)

Part 13: 1975 *Production of specimens for testing coatings on cast iron*

Part 14: 1975 *Apparatus for testing with acid and neutral liquids and their vapours*

Part 15: 1975 *Apparatus for testing with alkaline liquids*

Part 16: 1975 *Resistance to thermal shock of coatings on cooking utensils*
This method determines the behaviour of utensils under sudden changes of temperatures.

Part 17: 1975 *Resistance to hot sodium hydroxide solution*

Part 18: 1981 *Determination of fluidity behaviour: fusion flow test*
This is a comparative method of determining the fluidity behaviour of vitreous and porcelain enamels in the viscous condition during firing.

Part 19: 1984 *Apparatus for determination of resistance to hot detergent solutions used for washing textiles*
Requirements for the apparatus which is used in the method specified in Part 5, above.

BS 3830: 1973 *Vitreous enamelled steel building components*

Requirements are specified for manufacture, including basis metal, design and fabrication and quality, colour and texture of vitreous enamel coating.

BS 3831: 1964 *Vitreous enamel finishes for domestic and catering appliances*

Requirements are specified for the ground coat and cover coat of enamel, the enamel thickness, and imperfections that may or may not be acceptable. Definitions of imperfections are appended. Applicable only to sheet steel or cast iron with the exception of baths.

BS 4900: 1976 *Vitreous enamel colours for building purposes*

This standard is summarized in Table 4 'Activities, requirements' under section (G5) 'Colour'.

BS 4842: 1984 *Liquid organic coatings for application to aluminium alloy extrusions, sheet and preformed sections for external architectural purposes, and for the finish on aluminium-alloy extrusions, sheet and preformed sections coated with liquid organic coatings*

Requirements for liquid coatings before and after their application to aluminium alloys that are to be used externally. Also the pre-treatment of the aluminium alloy. (See also BS 6496 which deals similarly with powder organic coatings for, and finishes on, aluminium-alloy components.)

BS 6496: 1984 *Powder organic coatings for application and stoving to aluminium-alloy extrusions, sheet and preformed sections for external architectural purposes, and for the finish on aluminium alloy extrusions, sheet and preformed sections coated with powder organic coatings*

Requirements for powder coatings before and after their application to aluminium alloys that are to be used externally. It also specifies the pretreatment of the aluminium alloy. (See also BS 4842 and BS 6497.)

BS 6497: 1984 *Powder organic coatings for applications and stoving to hot-dip galvanized hot-rolled steel sections and preformed steel sheet for windows and associated external purposes, and for the finish on galvanized steel sections and preformed sheet coated with powder organic coatings*

Requirements for powder coatings before and after their application to galvanized steel that is to be used externally. It also specifies the pretreatment of the galvanized steel (see also BS 6496). These coatings are not for application to paints (e.g. zinc-rich priming paints) used to repair galvanizing.

u2 Modifying agents, admixtures, etc.

An admixture is often a chemical substance, other than aggregates, cement or water, which is added in small quantities to modify and improve the behaviour of cement, mortar or concrete. The four standards available include the use of pigments, calcium chloride, mortar admixtures and concrete admixtures.

BS 6100: Part 6: Section 6.4: 1986 *Admixtures*

Definitions of admixtures for use in conjunction with hydraulic binders defined in Section 6.1. The terms are arranged systematically in a classified order with an alphabetical index.

BS 1014: 1975 *Pigments for Portland cement and Portland cement products*

This standard specifies requirements for pigments for colouring Portland cement and its products.
Table 191 summarizes the required characteristics.

BS 3587: 1963 *Calcium chloride (technical)*

This standard specifies requirements for two grades of calcium chloride. The first is hydrated calcium chloride suitable for use in solution, for example in the preparation of refrigeration 'brine', in weed killers and in concrete mixes. The second is anhydrous calcium chloride suitable for drying purposes.
Requirements are specified for water insoluble matter, sulphate content, acidity and alkalinity (in the hydrated grade) and calcium chloride content and particle size (in the anhydrous grade). Methods of test are appended.

BS 4887 *Mortar admixtures*

Part 1: 1986 *Air-entraining (plasticizing) admixtures*
Performance and uniformity tests and requirements, information to be provided, and marking. It includes appendices for sampling and testing.
This standard specifies requirements for sampling, testing and performance of materials to be used as mortar plasticizers.
Table 192 summarizes requirements for properties of test mortar.

Table 192 *Requirements for properties of test mortar*

Property	Limiting requirements

Air content (see C.5.1)
    First determination
    (standard mixing)
    Second determination
    (extra four minutes mixing)
	Not less than 15%, nor more than 22%
	The value shall not exceed that for the first determination

Consistence retentivity (see C.5.2)	Not less than 35%
Stiffening time (see C.5.3)	The stiffening time of mix Type 2 shall not exceed that of mix Type 3 by more than three hours, nor be less than that of mix Type 3 by more than one hour.
Strength ratio at seven days	Not less than 15%

(Table 1: BS 4887: 1986)

Table 193 (a) *Performance requirements and tests for test mix concrete A*

Property	Type of admixture				
	Accelerating	Retarding	Normal water-reducing	Accelerating water-reducing	Retarding water-reducing
Compacting factor (see C.3) relative to control mix concrete	Not more than 0.02 below	Not more than 0.02 below	At least 0.03 above	At least 0.03 above	At least 0.03 above
Stiffening times (see C.4) for 0.5 N/mm² for 3.5 N/mm²	More than 1 h At least 1 h less than control mix	At least 1 h longer than control mix –	– –	– –	– –
Minimum compressive strength as % of control mix concrete (see C.5) at 24 h at 7 days at 28 days	125 – 95	– 90 95	– 90 90	125 – 90	– 90 90

Table 193 (b) *Performance requirements and tests for test mix concrete B*

Property	Type of admixture				
	Accelerating	Retarding	Normal water-reducing	Accelerating water-reducing	Retarding water-reducing
Compacting factor (see C.3) relative to control mix concrete	–	–	Not more than 0.02 below	Not more than 0.02 below	Not more than 0.02 below
Stiffening time (see C.4) for 0.5 N/mm² for 3.5 N/mm²	– –	– –	Within 1 h of control mix Within 1 h of control mix	More than 1 h At least 1 h less than control mix	At least 1 h longer than control mix –
Minimum compressive strength as % of control mix concrete (see C.5) at 24 h at 7 days at 28 days	– – –	– – –	– 110 110	125 – 110	– 110 110

Note: The strength requirements take into account the usual variations in cube testing and the limited increase in air content allowed with the test mix concretes.

(Table 1: BS 5075: Part 1: 1982)

BS 5075 *Concrete admixtures*

Part 1: 1982 *Accelerating admixtures, retarding admixtures and water reducing admixtures*
This part specifies requirements and methods of test for five categories of admixture, which may be used to modify one or more properties of hydraulic cement concrete: workability, rate of stiffening and hardening, and strength.

Performance requirements are summarized in Table 193(a) and (b), and admixture uniformity test requirements in Table 194.

Part 2: 1982 *Air-entraining admixtures*
This part specifies the requirements and methods of test for determining the suitability of materials used to entrain a controlled amount of air in concrete, for the purpose of improving its resistance to freezing and thawing and/or modifying its workability.

Performance requirements are summarized in Table 195, and admixture uniformity test requirements in Table 196.

Part 3: 1985 *Superplasticizing admixtures*
A superplasticizing admixture is an admixture that, when added

Table 194 *Admixture uniformity test requirements (BS 5075)*

Characteristic	Test reference	Requirement
Dry material content	D.1	(a) For liquid admixtures: to be within 3% (*m/m*) of the value stated by the manufacturer (b) For solid admixtures: to be within 5% (*m/m*) of the value stated by the manufacturer
Ash content*	D.2	To be within 1.0% (*m/m*) of the value stated by the manufacturer
Relative density	D.3	For liquid admixtures: to be within 0.02 of the value stated by the manufacturer
Chloride ion content	Appendix E	To be within 5% of the value stated by the manufacturer or within 0.2% (*m/m*), whichever is the greater

*As admixtures containing chloride give very variable results for ash content this test and requirement may be waived for admixtures which contain more than 1.0% (*m/m*) of chloride ion.

(Table 2: BS 5095: Part 1: 1982)

to a hydraulic binder concrete, imparts very high workability or allows a large decrease in water content for a given workability. This part specifies the performance requirements and methods of tests for superplasticizing admixtures, which may be used to modify one or more properties of hydraulic binder concrete: the workability, the rate of stiffening and hardening, and the strength.

u3 Materials resisting special forms of attack such as rot, fungus, insects, condensation, etc.

There are 25 standards available, consisting of tar oil types (two standards), water-borne types (four standards), organic-solvent types (two standards) and general (including methods and treatment) (17 standards).

BS 4261: 1985 *Glossary of terms relating to timber preservation*

Definitions of terms relating to the attack of timber by wood-destroying agencies, and to processes for the preservation of timber against such attack. The terms which are grouped into four sections (general, attack by fungi, attack by insects and marine borers, preservative treatments) are listed alphabetically in the index and referred to by numbers.

Table 195 *Performance requirements and tests*

Characteristic	Test reference	Requirements
Repeatibility of air content	B.2	Air contents of three identical and consecutive test mix concrete batches all to be in the range 4.0 to 6.0%, when determined by one operator using one set of apparatus
Stiffening time	B.3	Average times for completion of mixing to reach resistances to penetration of 0.5 N/mm^2 and 3.5 N/mm^2 for the two batches of the test mix concrete to be within 1 h of the corresponding times for the two batches of the control mix concrete
Saturated density	B.5	(a) The 3 day average saturated densities of the six cubes and of the four prisms from the two batches of the test mix concrete to be within 20 kg/m^3 of each other (b) The 28 day average saturated density of the six cubes from the two batches of the test mix concrete to be at least 50 kg/m^3 lower than that of the six cubes from the two batches of the control mix concrete
Compressive strength	B.6	Average compressive strength of the six cubes from the two batches of the test mix concrete to be at least 70% of that of the six cubes from the two batches of the control mix concrete when tested at age 28 days
Resistance to freezing and thawing	Appendix C	The relative length change of at least three of the four prisms of the test mix concrete not to exceed + 0.050 % after 50 cycles of freezing and thawing

(Table 1: BS 5075: Part 2: 1982)

Table 196 *Admixture uniformity test requirements*

Characteristic	Test reference	Requirement
Dry material content	D.1 of BS 5075 Part 1: 1981	(a) For liquid admixtures: to be within 3% (*m/m*) of the value stated by the manufacturer (b) For solid admixtures: to be within 5% (*m/m*) of the value stated by the manufacturer
Ash content	D.2 of BS 5075 Part 1: 1981	To be within 1.0% (*m/m*) of the value stated by the manufacturer
Relative density	D.3 of BS 5075 Part 1: 1981	For liquid admixtures: to be within 0.02 of the value stated by the manufacturer
Chloride ion content	Appendix E of BS 5075 Part 1: 1981	To be within 5% of the value stated by the manufacturer or within 0.2% (*m/m*), whichever is the greater

(Table 2: BS 5075: Part 2: 1982)

BS 5268 *Code of practice for the structural use of timber*
Part 5: 1977 *Preservative treatments for constructional timber*

This part gives recommendations on the requirements for preservative treatment of timber used for structural purposes to protect them from degradation by wood-destroying organisms.

It gives advice on design, treatment and properties of treated timber.

BS 5589: 1978 *Code of practice for preservation of timber*

This code gives recommendations for pre-treatment of timber for protection against biodegradation only, for certain specific uses in the United Kingdom. It recommends processes and treatment levels suited to the severity of the environment of use, and takes into account the natural durability and treatability of the timber employed.

BS 144: 1973 *Coal tar creosote for the preservation of timber*

This standard specifies two types of creosote: Type 1 is for general purposes and Type 2 for telegraph poles and other timbers where 'bleeding' in service is to be avoided.

Requirements are specified for description, density, liquidity, water content, distillation range, extractable phenol content and matter insoluble in toluene.

BS 838: 1961 *Methods of test for toxicity of wood preservatives to fungi*

This standard describes methods of test for initial toxicity, residual toxicity after exposure to leaching and evaporation and toxicity to soft-rot microfungi. These methods are applicable to tar-oil, water-borne and organic-solvent types of wood preservatives.

Descriptions of test fungi and examples of test results are appended.

BS 913: 1973 *Wood preservation by means of pressure creosoting*

This standard specifies processes normally used in the United Kingdom for the preservation of timber by pressure creosoting, involving total immersion of timber in creosote in a closed pressure cylinder. The creosoting methods described are full-cell process (Bethell process) and empty-cell process (Rueping process or Lowry process).

BS 1282: 1975 *Guide to the choice, use and application of wood preservatives*

■ AD (Reg. C4)

This standard describes conditions under which organisms (such as wood-rotting fungi, wood-boring insects, marine borers and termites) are likely to damage timber and gives guidance on selection of preservative treatment. It classifies and describes wood preservatives into three main types: tar oil (TO) type, organic solvent (OS) type and water-borne (WB) type.

Methods of treatment described include pressure impregnation (using full-cell, vacuum/pressure or Bethell process, or empty-cell or Rueping process), low pressure impregnation (using Lowry process), vacuum impregnation, double-vacuum process, liquefied gas process, hot and cold open tank process, immersion, deluging, spraying and brushing, diffusion process and other processes. Existing preservative specifications are listed and factors controlling effectiveness of treatment are given.

BS 3051: 1972 *Coal tar creosotes for wood preservation (other than creosotes to BS 144)*

This standard specifies two types (Type A and Type B) of creosotes consisting of distillates of coal tar obtained by carbonization processes. The two types are of low viscosity and

intended for application by steeping, dipping or brushing.

Requiraeus are specified for description, density, liquidity, limits for water content, distillation, extractable phenols, saturated hydrocarbons, flash point and insoluble matter.

General recommendations for safety and application are given.

BS 3452: 1962 *Copper/chrome water-borne wood preservatives and their application*

This standard specifies requirements for wood preservatives consisting essentially of mixtures of copper sulphate and sodium or potassium dichromate, for application in aqueous solution by pressure or vacuum and pressure processes.

Requirements are specified for proportions of ingredients, characteristics of solution, method of application to timber and minimum net dry salt retentions for protection of timber against various hazards.

BS 3453: 1962 *Fluoride/arsenate/chromate/dinitrophenol water-borne wood preservatives and their application*

This standard specifies requirements for wood preservatives consisting essentially of fluoride/arsenate/chromate/dinitrophenol mixtures for application in aqueous solution by pressure or vacuum and pressure processes.

Requirements are specified for proportions of ingredients, characteristics of solution, methods of application, minimum net dry salt retentions for protection of timber against various hazards.

BS 5056: 1974 *Copper naphthenate wood preservatives*

This standard specifies the composition of two types of copper naphthenate wood preservative solutions and their use for the treatment of timber: Type 1 for general purposes and Type 2 for use on absorbent timbers in small dimensions, preferably for applications by double-vacuum treatment.

General recommendations are given on their use for treatment of timber, including safety aspects.

BS 5217: 1975 *Wood preservatives. Determination of the preventive action against Lyctus brunneus (Stephens) (laboratory method)*

This standard specifies a method of test made on surface treated wood. It is an English language version of European Standard EN 20 and supersedes BS 3653.

This method is applicable to water-insoluble chemicals, or organic water-insoluble formations, or water-soluble materials such as salts.

BS 5218: 1975 *Wood preservatives. Determination of the toxic values against Anobium punctatum (de Geer) by larval transfer (laboratory method)*

This standard specifies a method for the determination of the toxic values of wood preservative against larvae of Anobium punctatum (de Geer), introduced into wood which has been treated previously by full impregnation. It is an English version of EN 21, and with BS 5435 supersedes BS 3651.

This method is applicable to water-insoluble chemicals, or organic water-insoluble formulations, or water-soluble materials such as salts.

BS 5219: 1975 *Wood preservatives. Determination of eradicant action against Hylotrupes bajulus (Linnaeus) larvae (laboratory method)*

This method specifies a method for the determination of the eradicant action of wood preservative against larvae Hylotrupes bajulus (Linnaeus).

This method is applicable to organic water-insoluble formulations or water-soluble materials such as salts.

BS 5434: 1977   Wood preservatives. Determination of the preventive action against recently hatched larvae of Hylotrupes bajulus (Linnaeus) (laboratory method)

This standard specifies a method which involves exposure of specimens of surface treated wood to larvae of Hylotrupes bajulus and compares the resulting attack with that in control specimens not treated with preservative.

The method is applicable to water-insoluble chemicals, or organic water-insoluble formulations, or water-soluble materials such as salts.

BS 5435: 1977   Wood preservatives. Determination of the toxic values against Hylotrupes bajulus (Linnaeus) larvae (laboratory method)

This standard specifies a method involving introduction of larvae of Hylotrupes bajulus into specimens of susceptible wood species treated with a series of concentrates of preservative and determination of their survival rates at fixed intervals of time. Comparisons are made of the results with these from untreated control specimens and derivation of the toxic values for the product under test.

The method is applicable to water-insoluble chemicals, or organic water-insoluble formulations, or water-soluble materials such as salts.

BS 5436: 1977   Wood preservatives. Determination of eradicant action against larvae of Anobium punctatum (de Geer) (laboratory method)

This standard specifies a method involving insertion of larvae into test specimens of a susceptible species of wood. After the larvae are established, treatment with preservative by brushing or spreading and estimation of the subsequent mortality of the insects compared with that in untreated control specimens.

The method is applicable to organic water-soluble formulations, or water-soluble materials such as salts.

BS 5437: 1977   Wood preservatives. Determination of the toxic values against Anobium punctatum (de Geer) by egg-laying and larval survival (laboratory method)

This standard specifies a method which involves exposure of preservative-treated test specimens of wood to female Anobium punctatum and observation of egg-laying, hatching of eggs and survival of larvae.

BS 6239: 1982   Determination of the toxic values of wood preservatives against Reticulitermes santonensis de Feytaud (laboratory method)

BS 6240: 1982   Determination of the preventive action of wood preservatives against Reticulitermes santonensis de Feytaud (laboratory method)

BS 5666   Methods of analysis of wood preservatives and treated timber

Part 1: 1978   *General considerations and sampling and preparation of materials for analysis*
This part gives guidance on the general procedures to be followed in the sampling and preparation for analysis of preservatives and preservative-treated timber. It indicates health and safety hazards and describes a method for the determination of water in treated water.

Part 2: 1980   *Qualitative analysis*
This part describes two types of qualitative tests: those carried out directly on timber sections to detect the presence of copper, chromium, boron, fluoride, tin, zinc and pentachlorophenol by spray or brush application of an appropriate chromogenic

material to the timber surface and those requiring prior preparation of an extract from the timber sample.

Part 3: 1979   *Quantitative analysis of preservatives and treated timber containing copper/chromium/arsenic formulations*
This part describes the spectrophotometric and colorimetric methods for the determination of copper, chromium and arsenic in preservatives and in treated timber containing those water-borne preservative compositions.

Part 4: 1979   *Quantitative analysis of preservatives and treated timber containing copper naphthenate*
This part describes the spectrophotometric and colorimetric methods for the determination of copper naphthenate using zinc dibenzyl-dithiocarbamate.

Part 5: 1986   *Determination of zinc naphthenate in preservative solutions and treated timber*
This part gives two methods: atomic absorption spectrophotometry and colorimetry using dithizone.

Part 6: 1983   *Quantitative analysis of preservative solution and treated timber containing pentachlorophenol, pentachlorophenol laurate, γ-hexachlorocyclohexane and dieldrin*
This part describes gas–liquid chromatographic methods for pentachlorophenol (PCP), pentachlorophenol laurate (PCPL), γ-hexachlorocyclohexane (γ-HCH) and dieldrin, and describes colorimetric methods for PCL and PCPL.

Part 7: 1980   *Quantitative analysis of preservatives containing bis (tri-n-butyltin) oxide: determination of total tin*
This part describes the spectrophotometric and colorimetric methods for the determination of total tin content present in solutions and in treated wood, using catechol violet.

BS 5707   Solutions of wood preservatives in organic solvents

Part 1: 1979   *Solutions for general purpose applications, including timber that is to be painted*
This part specifies requirements for fungicides, insecticides, solvent, appearance, flash point, water content, crystallization, freedom from bloom and tack, penetration factor and designations.

Part 2: 1979   *Pentachlorophenol wood preservative solution for use on timber that is not required to be painted*
This part specifies requirements for composition, solvent, appearance, flash point, water content, crystallization and viscosity.

Part 3: 1980   *Methods of treatment*
This part specifies requirements for selection and preparation of timber for treatment, and describes three methods of treatment: double vacuum process, immersion process, and brushing and spraying.

BS 5761   Wood preservatives. Accelerated ageing of treated wood prior to biological testing

Part 1: 1979   *Evaporative ageing procedure*
This part describes an evaporative ageing procedure, applicable to test specimens of wood previously treated with a preservative, by exposing test specimens to current of air prior to biological testing.

Part 2: 1980   *Leaching procedure*
This part specifies a leaching procedure applicable to test specimens of wood previously treated with a preservative, to evaluate any loss in effectiveness when the specimens are subsequently subjected to biological tests, as compared with test specimens which have not undergone any leaching procedure.

BS 3842: 1965 *Treatment of plywood with preservatives*

This standard specifies treatment by pressure impregnation, diffusion, dipping or surface coating, either after manufacture or at veneer stage, for protection against fungal, marine borer and insect attack. It gives advice on choice of preservative, method of treatment and amenability of wood to impregnation.

BS 4072: 1974 *Wood preservation by means of water-borne copper/chrome/arsenic compositions*

This standard specifies requirements for treatment with water-borne preservatives of copper sulphate, sodium or potassium dichromate and arsenic pentoxide. It covers preservative composition, application and resulting retentions.

u5 Polishes, seals, surface hardeners

There are only two standards for sodium and potassium silicates and two public authority standards for liquid flooring polishes.

BS 3984: 1982 *Sodium silicates*

This standard specifies requirements for alkali content, silica content, matter insoluble in water and iron content of sodium metasilicate pentahydrate of technical quality for industrial use and, in addition, special requirements relating to chloride content and sulphate content of material for service use. It also specifies method of classification for sodium silicate solutions based on silica:alkali ratio and relative density, with optical additional requirement for viscosity.

BS 6092 *Methods for sampling and test for sodium and potassium silicate for industrial use*

Part 0: 1981 *General introduction*
Methods of test are listed in Table 197.

Part 1: 1981 *Determination of solution density at 20 °C*

This part describes methods using density hydrometer and using pyknometer.

Part 2: 1981 *Determination of total solids content*
This part gives a method by drying a test portion followed by heating to 600–650 °C and weighing the residue.

Part 3: 1981 *Determination of silica content (gravimetric method)*

Part 4: 1981 *Determination of carbonate content*
This part gives the gas-volumetric method.

Part 5: 1981 *Determination of total alkali content*
This part gives the titrimetric method: titration with a standard volumetric solution of HCl using methyl orange as indicator.

Part 6: 1981 *Preparation of solution of not readily soluble products and determination of matter insoluble in water*

Part 7: 1981 *Determination of silica content (titrimetric method)*

Part 8: 1981 *Determination of sulphate content*
The gravimetric method by precipitation as barium sulphate is given in this part.

Part 9: 1981 *Determination of iron content*
Photometric method using 1, 10 – phenanthroline is given.

Part 10: 1981 *Determination of matter insoluble in water*
The gravimetric method is again in this part.

Part 11: 1981 *Determination of chloride content of sodium metasilicate*
The titrimetric method using $AgNO_3$ solution and back titration of excess $AgNO_3$ with ammonium thiocyanate solution using ammonium iron (III) sulphate solution as indicator is given in this part.

Table 197 *Methods of test for sodium and potassium silicates: relationship between BS and international series*

BS 6092 Part no.	Corresponding international standard no.	Subject	Type of determination	Relationship of international standard to BS test method
0	–	General introduction (including sampling)	–	Includes the sampling requirements of ISO 1686
–	1686	Samples and methods of test general	–	Not to be implemented
1	1687	Solution density at 20 °C	–	Identical
2	1688	Total solids content	Gravimetric	Identical
–	1689	Calculation of silica/alkali ratio	–	Disapproved by UK
3	1690	Silica content	Gravimetric	Identical
4	1691	Carbonate content	Gas-volumetric	Identical
5	1692	Total alkali content	Titrimetric	Identical
6	2122	Preparation of solutions of not readily soluble products and determination of matter insoluble in water	–	Identical
–	2123	Dynamic viscosity	–	Not implemented. Reference to be made to BS 188
7	2124	Silica content	Titrimetric	Identical
8	3200	Sulphate content	Gravimetric	Identical
9	3201	Iron content	Photometric (1, 10-phenanthroline)	Identical
10	–	Matter insoluble in water	Gravimetric	No equivalent
11	–	Chloride content	Titrimetric	international
12	–	Sulphate limit test	Turbidimetric	standard

(Table 1: BS 6092: Part 0: 1981)

Part 12: 1981   *Limit test for sulphate content of sodium metasilicate·*

The turbidimetric method using BaCl₂ solution and comparing visually with a standard sulphate solution is covered in this part.

PAS 9: 1980   *Metallized polymer floor polish*

This public authority standard specifies requirements or liquid polish suitable for use on all types of non-porous flooring that has good resistance to washing with neutral detergent solutions but may be readily removed from the floor by using a specified stripper.

Test methods for drying time and for slip resistance are appended.

PAS 10: 1980   *Non-metallized polymer floor finish*

This standard specifies requirements for liquid polish, suitable for use on all types of non-porous flooring, that dries to a bright finish, but may be buffed for maintenance purposes.

Test methods are appended.

u6   Water repellents

There are two standards available for silicone-based water repellents, containing silicon-oxygen-silicon links.

BS 3826: 1969   *Silicone-based water repellents for masonry*

This standard specifies performance requirements for silicone-based water repellents which can be applied to masonry free from cracks exceeding 0.15 mm in width, to confer water repellency without appreciable change of colour or appearance other than that imparted by fugitive dye.

Three classes of silicone repellent are specified:

Class A: silicone formulations for clay brickwork, hydraulic cement-based materials and natural and cast stone masonry of a predominantly siliceous nature.

Class B: silicone formulations for natural and cast stone masonry of a predominantly calcareous nature and calcium silicate brickwork.

Class C: aqueous siliconate solution for natural and cast stone masonry of a predominantly calcareous nature.

Requirements are specified for applicant properties and test requirements for early water repellency, absorption of water, evaporation of water, durability and stability. Advice on selection and use is appended.

BS 6477: 1984   *Water repellents for masonry surfaces*

Performance requirements, including a two-year durability test, for four groups of water repellent, defined according to suitability for use on different types of masonry above ground level. Recommendations for application are appended.

v Paints

There are 55 standards, including one public authority standard, made up of general and miscellaneous (five standards), priming paints (seven standards), black paints (tar or bitumen-based) (five standards), methods of test (four standards), solvent (including binders) (10 standards) and pigments (24 standards).

BS 2015: 1965   *Glossary of paint terms*

This standard provides definitions of terms used in the paint industry, including terms describing types of finishes, application and film defects. It includes photographic illustrations of checking, cracking, crazing, alligatoring, crowfooting, a run, colour floating and tears and sagging.

BS 1336: 1971   *Knotting*

This standard specifies requirements for knotting used in the preparation of joinery for painting as an impervious covering for knots and other resinous areas liable to stain superimposed paints.

Requirements are specified for solid content, appearance of solution, drying time of material, appearance of dried film, bleeding, stain prevention and resistance to white spirit.

Methods of test are appended.

BS 3357: 1961   *Glue size for decorators' use*

This standard applies to animal glue in granular or powder form, suitable for use in sizing walls, ceilings and similar surfaces. Type A contains aluminium sulphate, Type B does not. Requirements are specified for residue on sieve, jelly strength and viscosity, chlorides, aluminium sulphate (Type A only), odour, keeping properties, storage properties, instructions for use, marking and sampling.

Test methods not covered by BS 645 are appended.

PAS 32: 1980   *A paint system comprising an undercoat and gloss finish*

This public authority standard relates to good quality paints suitable for brush application, for interior and exterior use as available to the paint trade and drawn from conventional materials such as alkyd, urethane, oleoresinous media or mixtures thereof. Normally the colours will be selected from those listed in BS 4800.

BS 2521 and 2523: 1966   *Lead-based priming paints*

Requirements are specified for composition, sample, consistency, drying time, finish, water content and keeping properties. Methods for the determination of consistency and of drying time are appended.

BS 2521 applies to a brushing lead-based priming paint for exterior and interior woodwork, for use under ready mixed oil-based paints or hard gloss paint systems.

BS 2523 applies to lead-based priming paints for iron and steel (Types A, B and C) for use under ready mixed oil-based paints or hard gloss paint systems.

Type A is intended to be applied within a few weeks of manufacture whereas Types B and C are more suitable for storage.

BS 3698: 1964   *Calcium plumbate priming paints*

This standard applies to calcium plumbate-based priming paints for use on iron, steel, galvanized iron and other structural materials.

It specifies requirements for two types of materials differing mainly in their calcium plumbate contents: composition, sampling, consistency, finish, colour, drying time, flexibilty and adhesion, keeping properties and marking of containers.

Methods of test are appended.

BS 4652: 1971 *Metallic zinc-rich priming paint (organic media)*

This standard gives three types of material (Types 1, 2 and 3) and specifies requirements for sampling, composition, method of application, condition in container, finish, drying time, curing properties (Type 3 only), bend test, resistance to impact, resistance to continuous salt spray, natural weathering, storage properties, packaging and marking of containers.

These priming paints are suitable for use on iron and steel as well as galvanized or zinc-sprayed surfaces.

BS 4756: 1971 *Ready mixed aluminium priming paints for woodwork*

This standard gives two types of materials (Types 1 and 2) and specifies requirements for composition, drying time, flexibility and adhesion, application properties and finish, flash point, water content, keeping properties and marking of containers.

BS 4764: 1986 *Powder cement paints*

Requirements for the composition, colour, film-forming properties and keeping qualities of Portland cement-based paint powder intended for interior and exterior use on porous building structures. Recommendations on use are appended.

BS 5082: 1974 *Water-thinned priming paints for wood*

This standard applies to water-thinned priming paints intended for application by mechanical means and/or by brush to exterior and interior softwood joinery.

Requirements are specified for composition, volatile content, viscosity, hard-drying, appearance of dried film, blocking, low-temperature film formation, blister resistance, opacity, resistance to natural weathering, maximum lead content, colour, compatibility with glazing putty, and keeping properties.

BS 5358: 1976 *Low-lead solvent-thinned priming paint for woodwork*

This standard applies to two types (Types A and B) of priming paint for exterior and interior use on softwood, conforming to the limit for lead as specified in BS 4310.

Requirements are specified for sample, condition in container and consistency, film properties and finish, application properties, drying time, volatile matter content, lead content, danger classification (flash point), artificial weathering, outdoor weathering and recoatability after outdoor weathering.

Methods for outdoor exposure and recoatability after outdoor exposure are appended.

BS 1070: 1973 *Black paint (tar-based)*

Black tar-based paints are applied as a protective rather than a decorative finish on the usual constructional metals as well as other materials.

This standard is restricted to paints for cold application, based on coal tars and carburetted-water-gas tars or blends of these but not containing pigments or extenders. It does not include emulsions, stoving paints or paints designed solely for application by dipping.

Requirements for normal drying (Type A) and quick drying (Type B) paints are given for consistency, application properties and drying time, corrosion resistance, bend test, water content, loss on ignition, flash point and keeping properties.

Test methods are appended.

BS 3416: 1975 *Black bitumen coating solutions for cold application*

This standard specifies requirements for two types of bitumen solutions for cold application, namely Type I, cold applied, for general purposes; Type II, cold applied, for drinking water tanks. Type I is further subdivided into two classes, A and B, differing only in flash point classifications.

These materials are used as protective rather than decorative coating on iron and steel as well as other substrates.

Requirements are specified for sample, consistency, drying time, finish, protection against corrosion, bend test, volatile matter, flash point danger classification, keeping properties and effect on water (Type II only).

Methods of test and recommendations on use are appended.

BS 3634: 1963 *Black bitumen oil varnish*

This material may be expected to retain its gloss to a greater degree than materials specified in BS 3416. It produces a coating for the effective protection of iron and steel, together with a degree of decoration.

Requirements are specified for description, sample, application properties and drying time, finish, protection against corrosion, flexibility, volatile matter, flash point, resistance to fuel oil, resistance to bleeding, and storage properties.

Methods of test are appended.

BS 4147: 1980 *Bitumen-based hot-applied coating materials for protecting iron and steel, including suitable primers where required*

This standard specifies requirements for hot-applied bitumen-based materials, both unfilled and reinforced with inert powdered or fibrous fillers, which will provide protection for iron and steel against corrosion. Requirements for primers are included because the performance of hot-applied coating materials depends on the use of suitable primers.

Different types and grades of material are used for different substrates, conditions of application and service. This standard indicates factors which need to be taken into account in selecting the type and grade for a particular use.

BS 4164: 1980 *Coal-tar-based hot-applied coating materials for protecting iron and steel including suitable primers where required*

This standard specifies requirements for hot-applied coal-tar-based materials both unfilled and reinforced with inert non-fibrous fillers, which will provide protection for iron and steel against corrosion.

Requirements for primers are included because the performance of hot-applied coating materials depends on the use of suitable primers.

Different types and grades of material are used for different substrates, conditions of application and service. This standard indicates factors which need to be taken into account in selecting the type and grade for a particular use.

BS 3900 *Methods of test for paints*

This standard describes procedures, apparatus and related information on widely used test methods for paints, varnishes and similar products. It contains 60 parts, including general introduction and four parts which have now been withdrawn. It describes 46 general test methods for paints so far published.

BS 3900: 1969 *General introduction*
Group A Tests on liquid paints (excluding chemical tests)
Part A1: 1970 *Sampling*
Part A2: 1983 *Examination and preparation of samples for testing*
Part A3: 1986 *Standard panels for paint testing*
Part A5: 1968 *Large scale brushing test*

Part A6: 1986 *Determination of flow time by use of flow cups*
Part A7: 1968 *Determination of the viscosity of paint at a high rate of shear*
Part A8: 1986 *Test for flash/no flash point (closed cup equilibrium method)*
Part A9: 1986 *Determination of flash point (closed cup equilibrium method)*
Part A10: 1976 *Determination of volume of dry coating (non-volatile matter) obtained from a given volume of liquid coating*
Part A11: 1974 *Small scale test for combustibility*
Part A12: 1975 *Determination of density*
Part A13: 1986 *Test for flash/no flash point (rapid equilibrium method)*
Part A14: 1978 *Determination of flash point (rapid equilibrium method)*
Part A15: 1976 (1985) *Determination of quantity of material in a container*

Group B Tests involving chemical examination of liquid paints and dried paint films
Part B1: 1965 (1985) *Determination of water by Dean and Stark method*
Part B2: 1970 (1984) *Determination of volatile matter and non-volatile matter*
Part B3: 1983 *Determination of 'soluble lead'*
Part B4: 1986 *Determination of lead in low-lead paints and similar materials*
Part B5: 1986 *Preparation of acid extracts from liquid paints or coating powders*
Part B6: 1986 *Determination of 'soluble' lead content*
Part B7: 1986 *Determination of 'soluble' antimony content*
Part B8: 1986 *Determination of 'soluble' barium content*
Part B9: 1986 *Determination of 'soluble' cadmium content*
Part B10: 1986 *Determination of hexavalent chromium content of solid matter*
Part B11: 1986 *Determination of total chromium content of liquid matter*
Part B12: 1986 *Determination of 'soluble' mercury content*

Group C Tests associated with paint film formation
Part C1: 1965 *Wet edge time*
Part C2: 1971 (1983) *Surface-drying test (Ballotini method)*
Part C3: 1971 (1983) *Hard-drying time*
Part C5: 1975 *Determination of film thickness*
Part C6: 1983 *Determination of fineness-of-grind*
Part C7: 1982 (1985) *Pressure test for stackability*
Part C8: 1978 (1985) *Print free test*
Part C9: 1982 *Methods for evaluation of the compatibility of product with a surface to be pointed*

Group D Optical tests on paint films
Part D1: 1978 *Visual comparison of the colour of paints*
Part D3: 1975 *Assessment of sheen (withdrawn)*
Part D4: 1974 (1984) *Comparison of contrast ratio (hiding power) of paints of the same type and colour*
Part D5: 1980 *Measurement of specular gloss of non-metallic paint films at 20, 60 and 85 °*
Part D6: 1982 (1985) *Determination of contrast ratio (opacity of light-coloured paints using polyester film*

Group E Mechanical tests on paint films
Part E1: 1970 *Bend test (cylindrical mandrel)*
Part E2: 1970 *Scratch test*
Part E3: 1973 (1979) *Impact (falling weight) resistance*
Part E4: 1976 (1983) *Cupping test*
Part E5: 1973 (1979) *Pendulum damping test*
Part E6: 1974 (1983) *Cross-cut test*
Part E7: 1974 *Resistance to impact (falling ball test)*
Part E8: 1974 (1979) *Resistance to impact (pendulum test)*
Part E9: 1976 (1983) *Buchholz indentation test*

Part E10: 1979 (1983) *Pull-off test for adhesion*
Part E11: 1985 *Bend test (conical mandrel)*
Part E12: 1986 *Indentation test (spherical or pyramidal)*

Group F Durability tests on paint films
Part F1: 1966 *Alkali resistance of plaster primer-sealer*
Part F2: 1973 (1983) *Determination of resistance to humidity under condensation conditions*
Part F3: 1971 (1979) *Resistance to artificial weathering (enclosed carbon arc)*
Part F3: Addendum No. 1: 1978 Notes for guidance on the operation of artificial weathering apparatus to BS 3900 Part F3: 1971
Part F4: 1968 (1985) *Resistance to continuous salt spray*
Part F5: 1972 *Determination of light fastness of paints for interior use exposed to artificial light sources*
Part F6: 1976 (1984) *Notes for guidance on the conduct of natural weathering tests*
Part F8: 1976 *Determination of resistance to humid atmospheres containing sulphur dioxide*
Part F9: 1982 (1985) *Determination of resistance to humidity (continuous condensation)*
Part F10: 1985 *Determination of resistance to cathodic disbonding of coatings for use in marine environments*
Part F11: 1985 *Determination of resistance to cathodic disbonding of coatings for use on land-based buried structures*
Part F12: 1985 *Determination of resistance to neutral salt*
Part F13: 1986 *Filiform corrosion test on steel*

Group G Environmental tests on paint film (including tests for resistance to corrosion and chemicals)
Parts G1, G2, G3 and G4 have been withdrawn
Part G5: 1976 *Determination of resistance to liquids (supersedes G1, G2 and G3)*
Part G7: 1976 *Determination of the effect of heat*

Group H Evaluation of paint and varnish defects
Part H1: 1983 *Designation of intensity, quantity and size of common types of defect: general principles and rating schemes*
Part H2: 1983 *Designation of degree of blistering*
Part H3: 1983 *Designation of degree of rusting*
Part H4: 1983 *Designation of degree of cracking*
Part H5: 1983 *Designation of degree of flaking*

BS 3962 *Methods of test for finishes for wooden furniture*

This standard describes procedures, apparatus and related information on test methods for finishes. It contains six parts:

Part 1: 1980 *Assessment of low angle glare by measurement of specular gloss at 85 °*
Part 2: 1980 *Assessment of surface resistance to wet heat*
Part 3: 1980 *Assessment of surface resistance to dry heat*
Part 4: 1980 *Assessment of surface resistance to cold liquids*
Part 5: 1980 *Assessment of surface resistance to cold oils and fats*
Part 6: 1980 *Assessment of resistance to mechanical damage*

BS 4726: 1986 *Methods for sampling raw materials for paints and varnishes*

This standard draws attention to the safety precautions to be observed and describes procedures for sampling liquid, solid and powder products used in paint manufacture. It describes and illustrates a number of sampling instruments.

BS 242, 243, 259, 632: 1969 *Linseed oil*

These standards, published as one, specify requirements for the following:

BS 243, 632 *Raw linseed oil*
BS 242 *Refined linseed oil*
BS 259 *Boiled linseed oil*

Raw linseed oil is obtained from mature seeds of linseed by expression or solvent extraction and is free from admixture with other oils or fats.

Refined linseed oil is obtained by refined raw linseed oil.

Boiled linseed oil is obtained by incorporating driers in raw or refined linseed oil and heating with or without blowing with air or oxygen.

Requirements are specified for relative density, drying time, refractive index, iodine value, saponification value, ash content, unsaponifiable matter, acid value, foots, phosphoric acid test value. Methods of test appended.

BS 245: 1976   *Mineral solvents (white spirit and related hydro-carbon solvents) for paints and other purposes*

This standard specifies requirements for two types of mineral solvents:

Type A: containing an aromatics content below 25 per cent (v/v).
Type B: containing an aromatics content of 25 to 50 per cent (v/v).

These materials meet the requirements of the Highly Flammable Liquids and Liquefied Petroleum Gases Regulations 1972 as not constituting 'highly flammable liquids'.

Requirements are specified for clarity, undissolved water at 20 °C, odour, colour, volume of condensate recovered, aromatics content, residue on evaporation, neutrality, freedom from objectionable sulphur compounds, aniline point, flash point and viscosity reduction power. Methods of test are appended.

BS 391: 1962   *Tung oil*

This standard defines the properties and methods of testing tung oil for two types known as Type F and Type M, derived respectively from *Aleurites fordii* Hemsley and from *Aleurites montana* Wilson.

Requirements are specified for sample preparation, tests for volatile matter, specific gravity, refractive index, iodine value, saponification value, acidity, unsaponifiable matter, insoluble bromide and a heat test.

BS 4725: 1971   *Linseed stand oils*

Linseed stand oils are polymerized oils obtained from linseed oil by the application of heat only. This standard gives requirements and methods of test for determination of saponification value, unsaponifiable matter, polybromide-forming material, acid value, presence of rosin and of blown oils.

BS 5170: 1975   *Degummed soya bean oil*

Degummed soya bean oil is derived from soya beans by expression or by solvent extraction, or both, followed by degumming.

This standard specifies physical and chemical requirements, method for sampling and sample preparation.

BS 217: 1961   *Red lead for paints and jointing compounds*

This standard specifies three types of red lead:

Type 1: red lead, non-setting, for paints.
Type 2: red lead, ordinary, for paint mixed on site and used soon afterwards.
Type 3: red lead for jointing purposes.

Requirements are specified for composition, non-setting properties (Type 1 only), residue on sieve, oil absorption value, colour, matter volatile at 100 °C and matter soluble in water. Sampling and test methods are appended.

BS 282 and 389: 1963   *Lead chromes and zinc chromes for paints*

These comprise:

BS 282 *Lead chromes*

BS 389/1 *Zinc chrome, Type 1* (including chromates of alkali metals)
BS 389/2 *Zinc chrome, Type 2* (basic zinc potassium chromate)
BS 389/3 *Zinc chrome, Type 3* (basic zinc chromate or zinc tetroxychromate)

Requirements are specified for description, composition, residue on sieve, matter volatile at 100 °C, oil absorption value, colour, staining power and colour on reduction. For zinc chromes, requirements and test method for freedom from impurities are included: limits for sulphates, chlorides, nitrates (Types 2 and 3), limit for water-soluble chromates (Type 2); limit for total water-soluble matter (Type 3).

BS 283: 1965   *Prussian blues for paints*

This standard applies to Prussian blues derived from reaction of solutions of iron salts with ferrocyanide or ferricyanide solutions.

Requirements are specified for sampling, composition, residue on sieve, oil absorption value, colour, staining power, colour on reduction, matter volatile at 100 °C, matter insoluble in water and acidity of aqueous extract.

BS 284–6: 1952   *Black (carbon) pigments for paints*

These comprise:

BS 284   *Carbon black for paints*
BS 285   *Bone black for paints*
BS 286   *Lamp (or vegetable) black for paints*

Requirements are specified for description, residue on sieve, oil absorption value, colour, tone, staining power, loss in weight at 100–105 °C, ash, either extract and matter soluble in water. Sampling and test methods are appended.

BS 303: 1978   *Lead chrome green pigments for paints*

This standard specifies requirements for definition, requirement characteristics, sampling, methods for determination of volatile matter, total lead and acid soluble lead.

BS 314: 1968   *Ultramarine pigments*

This standard specifies three types of pigments:

Type 1: pigments for paint manufacture and similar purposes.
Type 2: pigment for manufacture of plastics materials and rubber.
Type 3: pigments for use as a blueing agent.

Two grades for each type are specified.

Requirements are specified for description, sampling, residue on sieve, oil absorption, colour, staining power (strength) and colour on reduction, dispersibility, matter volatile at 105 °C, heat stability, matter soluble in water, acidity or alkalinity, free sulphur content, manganese content and copper content. Test methods are appended.

BS 318: 1968   *Chromic oxide pigments*

This standard specifies two types:

Type 1: for use in paints, etc.
Type 2: for use in plastics materials.

Two grades are specified for each type.

Requirements are specified for description, composition, sampling, residue on sieve, oil absorption, colour, staining power (strength) and colour on reduction, dispersibility, matter insoluble at 105 °C, colour after heating at 800 °C, heat stability, matter soluble in water, pH value of aqueous extract, resistance to light, chemical resistance, manganese content and copper content. Test methods are appended.

BS 332: 1956 *Liquid driers for oil paints*

This standard applies to liquid driers containing metallic compounds such as linoleates, rosinates or naphthenates. Requirements are specified for strength, suspended matter, colour, appearance of paint film, mixing properties, miscibility with oil, drying properties, flash point, metallic content, keeping properties and sampling. Test methods are appended.

BS 388: 1972 *Aluminium pigments*

This standard specifies four types of aluminium pigments:

Type 1: aluminium powder, leafing.
Type 2: aluminium paste, leafing.
Type 3: aluminium powder, non-leafing.
Type 4: aluminium paste, non-leafing.

Types 1 and 2 are further classified according to water-covering capacity.

Requirements are specified for sampling, description, required characteristics and their tolerances and packing. Test methods are appended.

BS 1795: 1976 *Extenders for paints*

An extender is an inorganic material in powder form with a refractive index usually less than 1.7, used as a constituent of paints to confer special effects and to modify properties such as sedimentation, working and film-forming properties.

This standard specifies the principal requirements and the corresponding methods of test for certain paint extenders.

Types and grades include.

Barytes (Grades a and b).
Whiting (Grades a, b, c and d).
Crystalline calcium carbonate (Grades a, b, c and d).
Dolomite (Grades a, b, c and d).
China clay (Grades a, b and c).
Talc in fibrous form (Grades a and b).
Lamellar form (Grades a, b and c).
Talc containing carbonate, mica (Grades a and b).
Silica, quartzite, Type 1 (Grades a, b, c and d).
Silica, quartzite, Type 2 (Grades a, b, c and d).
Kieselguhr, Type 1 (Grades a, b, c and d).
Kieselguhr, Type 2 (Grades a, b, c and d).
Synthetic calcium silicate, synthetic sodium aluminium silicate, and synthetic silica

Methods of test include comparison of colour, residue on sieve, particle size distribution, matter volatile at 105 °C, loss on ignition, matter soluble in water, pH of aqueous suspension, barium sulphate content, calcium carbonate content, calcium and magnesium contents and silica content. An annex gives normal ranges of absorption values.

BS 1815: 1978 *Titanium dioxide pigments for paints*

This standard specifies two types of titanium dioxide:

Type A: anatase type (Grades A1 and A2).
Type B: rutile type (Grades R1, R2 and R3).

Requirements are specified for description, classification, required characteristics, sampling and determination of titanium dioxide content.

BS 3483 *Methods for testing pigments for paints*

This comprises 24 parts, including a general introduction.

3483: 1974 *General introduction*
The methods are divided into three groups:

Group A   Optical properties
Part A1: 1974 *Comparison of colour*

Part A2: Withdrawn
Part A3: 1974 *Comparison of resistance to light of coloured pigments of similar types to a specified light source*
Part A4: 1974 *Comparison of relative tinting strength (or equivalent colouring value) and colour on reduction in linseed stand oil using the automatic muller*
Part A5: 1974 *Comparison for lightening power of white pigments*

Group B   Physical properties
Part B1: 1974 *Determination of residue on sieve (oil method using pallette knife)*
Part B2: 1974 *Determination of residue on sieve (oil method using automatic muller)*
Part B3: 1982 *Determination of residue on sieve (water method using a manual procedure)*
Part B4: 1974 *Determination of residue on sieve (water method, using a mechanical flushing procedure)*
Part B5: 1974 *Comparison of ease of dispersion (oscillatory shaking method)*
Part B6: 1982 *Determination of matter volatile at 105 °C*
Part B7: 1982 *Determination of oil absorption value*
Part B8: 1982 *Determination of density (pyknometer method)*
Part B9: 1974 *Determination of density relative to water at 4 °C (using a centrifuge)*
Part B10: 1982 *Determination of tamped volume and apparent density after tamping*

Group C   Chemical properties
Part C1: 1980 *Determination of matter soluble in water (hot extraction method)*
Part C2: 1980 *Determination of matter soluble in water (cold extraction method)*
Part C3: 1982 *Determination of acidity or alkalinity of the aqueous extract*
Part C4: 1982 *Determination of pH value of an aqueous suspension*
Part C5: 1974 *Determination of resistivity of aqueous extract*
Part C6: 1974 *Determination of water – soluble sulphates, chlorides and nitrates*
Part C7: 1980 *Comparison of resistance to bleeding*
Part C8: 1980 *Comparison of heat stability*

BS 3699: 1964 *Calcium plumbate for paints*

This standard specifies requirements for calcium plumbate for use in paints: composition, non-setting properties, residue on sieve, oil absorption value, colour and loss in weight at 600 °C, and gives sampling procedure. Appendices give methods of test for the determination of calcium plumbate content, lead and calcium oxide, non-setting properties and loss in weight at 600 °C.

BS 3981: 1976 *Iron oxide pigments for paints*

This standard specifies requirements for iron oxide for use in paints: classification requirements for five colour groups (red, yellow, brown, black and grey), all but the grey being divided into categories according to iron content. Two are further subdivided according to types depending on water-soluble content. Test methods are appended.

BS 3982: 1980 *Zinc dust pigments*

This standard specifies requirements for zinc dust pigment manufactured by a distillation process: composition, residue on sieve, particle size and sampling. It describes methods of test for the determination of total zinc, metallic zinc, lead and cadmium, iron, arsenic and matter soluble in acid.

BS 4313: 1968 *Strontium chromate for paints*

This standard specifies requirements and test methods for strontium chromate for use in paints: sampling, residue on sieve, matter volatile at 105 °C, oil absorption value, water-soluble nitrates and chlorides and water-soluble chromates.

BS 5193: 1975 *Zinc phosphate pigment for paints*

This standard specifies requirements and test methods for zinc phosphate for use in anti-corrosive priming paints and compositions.

BS 4310: 1968 (1979) *Permissible limit of lead in low-lead paints and similar materials*

Sets an upper limit for lead and gives methods for its determination and detection.

w   Ancillary materials

There are five standards relevant to this section, of which three are summarized in other sections.

BS 3148: 1980 *Methods of test for water for making concrete (including notes on the suitability of the water)*

See section q.

BS 3591: 1963 *Industrial methylated spirits*

This standard specifies requirements for residue on evaporation, miscibility with water, alkalinity or acidity, aldehyde and ketone content in relation to industrial methylated spirits of strength between the limits 60 and 74 degrees OP. Methods of test are given and in addition there is a table showing the relation between degrees over proof, specific gravity in air and approximate total alcohol content.

BS 3761: 1970 *Non-flammable solvent-based paint remover*

This standard specifies requirements for non-flammable solvent-based paint remover for application by brush: description, solvent extractable matter, consistency, volatility, water rinsability, effect on wood, flammability, acidity or alkalinity, corrosive effects, toxicity, storage properties, marking of containers and packaging requirements. Methods of test are appended.

BS 3984: 1982 *Sodium silicates*

See section u5.

BS 5270: 1976 *Polyvinyl acetate (PVAC) emulsion bonding agents for internal use with gypsum building plasters*

See section t.

y   Composite materials (no entry)

z   Substances (no entry)

CI/SfB Table 4: Activities, requirements

(A) Administration and management activities, aids

Six of the standards are glossaries, one deals with stationery, two with quality, one with project management and the remaining five cover standardization in the broadest terms.

BS Handbook 3, in four volumes, is a *Summary of British Standards for Building*, including codes of practice, drafts for development, and other publications for building. It is in loose-leaf form, revised twice yearly. The summaries describe specification, ordering, and checking of materials, but not manufacture or testing. The British Standards dealing with administration, management and aids are not specifically dealt with in the handbook, and must be sought under the particular British Standard from the current BSI *Catalogue*.

The other handbook is Handbook No. 22: 1983 *Quality assurance* which contains the full text of the following publications:

BS 4778 *Glossary of terms used in quality assurance*
BS 4891 *A guide to quality assurance*
BS 5233 *Glossary of terms used in metrology*
BS 5750 *Quality systems* (in 6 parts)
BS 5760 *Reliability of systems, equipments and components* (in 2 parts)
BS 5781 *Measurement and calibration systems* (in 2 parts)
BS 6143 *Guide to the determination and use of quality related costs*

The standards covering standardization are:

BS 0 *A standard for standards*
Part 1: 1981 *General principles of standardization*
Part 2: 1981 *BSI and its committee procedures*
Part 3: 1981 *Drafting and presentation of British Standards*

BS 6100   *Glossary of Building and Civil Engineering terms:*

Part 0: 1984 *Introduction*
BS 6100 is large, and growing. Specific parts are referred to elsewhere.

BS 1000: 1963 (1980)   *Guide to the universal decimal classification*
and
BS 1000(M)   *Universal decimal classification (UDC) International Medium Edition*

This is an introduction to the English version of the universal decimal classification (UDC), deriving from the Dewey decimal classification, and is part of the first full English division authorized by the FID, the Hague, Netherlands.

Note: The CI/SfB classification used in this manual is discussed in the preface to this volume.

BS 4462: 1969   *Guide for the preparation of technical sales literature for measuring instruments and process control equipment*

BS 4884   *Technical manuals*

Part 1: 1973 (1983)   *Content*

Part 2: 1974 (1983)   *Presentation*

BS 4940: 1973   *Recommendations for the presentation of technical information about products and services in the construction industry*

This standard deals with the publication of technical literature in the construction industry, its storage and retrieval. There is a demarcation between technical literature and advertising literature.

The standard dealing with stationery

BS 3327: 1970 (1986)   *Stationery for quantity surveying*

This covers sizes, vertical rulings, measurement of column, punching and the binding margin of dimension paper.

BS 4891: 1972   *A guide to quality assurance*

BS 5750   *Quality systems*

■   AD (Reg. 7)

Part 1: 1979   *Design, manufacture and installation*
This part specifies the system to be applied when the technical requirements of material and/or service are specified principally in terms of the performance required where design has not been established. Reliability and other characteristics can then be ensured only by control of all the phases of the work for which the supplier is responsible.

Part 2: 1979   *Manufacture and installation*
This part specifies the system to be applied when the technical requirements of material and/or services are specified in terms of established design and where conformance and specified requirements can be ensured only by inspection and test during manufacture and, as appropriate, installation.

Part 3: 1979   *Final inspection and test*
This part specifies the quality system to be applied when conformance to specified requirements of material and/or services can be adequately established by inspection and tests conducted on the finished material or service.

Part 4: 1981   *Guide to use of BS 5750 Part 1 'Specification for design, manufacture and installation'*
This part provides guidance on the implementation of Part 1 of

the standard, aimed at affording a better understanding of the specification itself as well as assistance in its use, either in implementing or in evaluating such assistance.

Part 5: 1981   *Guide to the use of BS 5750 Part 2 'Specification for manufacture and installation'*

Part 6: 1981   *Guide to the use of BS 5750 Part 3 'Specification for final inspection and test'*

These parts provide guidance on the implementation of Part 2 of the standard, aimed at affording a better understanding of the specification as well as assistance in its use, either in implementing or in evaluating such assistance.

BS 6046   *Use of network techniques in project management*

Part 1: 1984   *Guide to the use of management planning review and reporting procedures*
This emphasizes the importance of pre-contract preparation and organization and cost factors, with review and reporting procedures for the project control phase.

Part 2: 1981   *Guide to the use of graphical and estimating techniques*
Guidance on the two graphical methods of representing the activities in a project: 'activity-on-arrow' and 'activity-on-node'. A checklist highlights the main factors to consider before choosing the network mode. Recommendations on the level of detail to include, conventions and symbols to use, and the estimation of values required for analysing networks are made.

Table 198   *Types of line*

General applications	Description	Line
A1 Visible outlines and edges	Continuous thick	A ——————
B1 Imaginary lines of intersection B2 Dimension, projectors and leader lines B3 Hatching B4 Outlines of revolved sections in plane B5 Initial outlines prior to forming B6 Controlling lines	Continuous thin (straight or curved)	B ——————
C1 Limits of partial or interrupted views and sections, if the limit is not an axis	Continuous thin (freehand, unsuitable for drawing by machine)	C ∿∿∿∿
D1 As for C1	Continuous thin (straight) with zigzags	D ——⋀—— (See note)
E1 Hidden outlines and edges	Broken thin	E - - - - - - - - -
F1 Hidden outlines and edges	Broken thick	F – – – – – – – – (See note)
G1 Centre lines and lines of symmetry G2 Reference lines	Chain thin	G ‑·‑·‑·‑·‑
H1 Cutting planes	Chain thin, thick at ends and changes of direction	H
J1 Indication of lines or surfaces to which a special requirement applies	Chain thick	J ‑·‑·‑·‑·‑
K1 Outlines of adjacent parts K2 Alternative and extreme position of movable parts K3 Centroidal lines	Chain thin double-dashed	K ‑··‑··‑··‑

Note: Although two alternatives are available it is recommended that on any one drawing, only one type of line should be used.

(Table 5: BS 1192: Part 1: 1984)

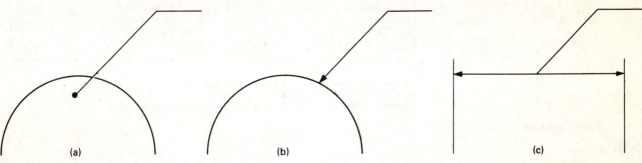

Figure 111   *Termination of leader lines*

(Figure 3: BS 1192: Pt 1: 1984)

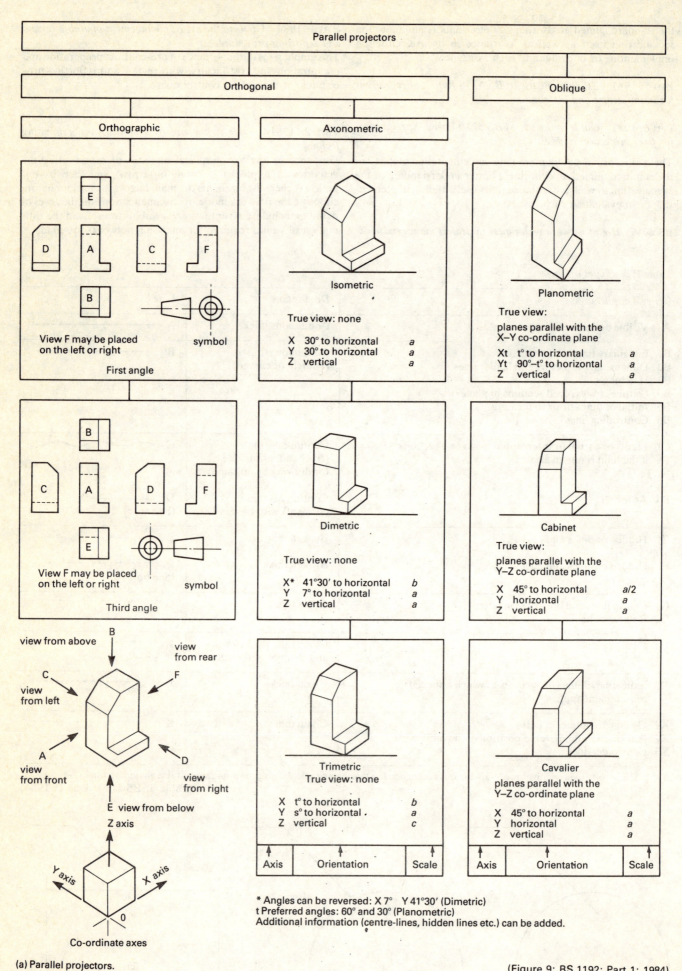

(a) Parallel projectors.

(Figure 9: BS 1192: Part 1: 1984)

Figure 112(a) *Comparison of projection methods*

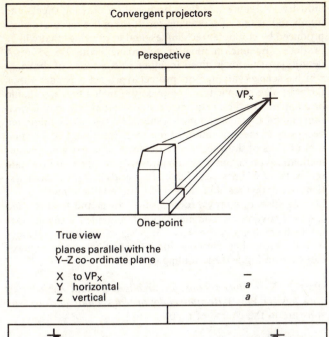

True view
planes parallel with the
Y–Z co-ordinate plane

X	to VP$_x$	—
Y	horizontal	a
Z	vertical	a

One-point

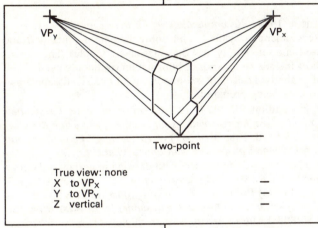

Two-point

True view: none

X	to VP$_x$	—
Y	to VP$_y$	—
Z	vertical	—

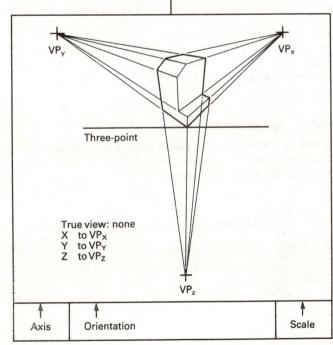

Three-point

True view: none

X	to VP$_x$
Y	to VP$_y$
Z	to VP$_z$

Axis   Orientation   Scale

(b) Convergent projectors.

Figure 112(b) *Comparison of projection methods (concluded)*

Part 3: 1981   *Guide to the use of computers*
Guidance on the application of a computer in project network analysis. Advantages and disadvantages of computer application compared with manual analysis are given together with advice on choice of suitable software package, selection of computing facilities and use of coding systems.

Part 4: 1981   *Guide to resource analysis and cost control*
The use of these two techniques as a natural extension of the use of time analysis as a means of improving the management of projects.

(Agh)   Glossaries

Apart from those referred to under (A) above — in particular BS 6100 — there are numerous standards which provide glossaries of terms. Those glossaries which will be useful to the student are referred to, and in the most relevant cases summarized, under the appropriate subject matter, for example BS 952 *Glass for glazing* Part 1: 1978 *Classification* and Part 2: 1980 *Terminology for work on glass*, summarized in Table 3 Materials (o) 'Glass'.
   Other relevant general standards are listed below.

BS 3138: 1979   *Glossary of terms used in work study and organization and methods (O & M)*

Covers general terms, organization study, method study, work measurement and work performance control. See also BS 3375 *Work study and organization and methods* (in four parts).

BS 3811: 1984   *Glossary of maintenance management terms in terotechnology*

BS 4335: 1972   *Glossary of terms used in project network techniques*

BS 4778: 1979   *Glossary of terms used in quality assurance (including reliability and maintainability terms)*

BS 4949: 1973   *Glossary of terms relating to building performance*

PD 6470: 1981   *The management of design for economic production*

PD 6501   *The preparation of British Standards for building and civil engineering*

Part 1: 1982   *Guide to the types of British Standard, their aims, relationship, content and application*

Part 2: 1984   *Guide to presentation*

Part 3: 1985   *Guide to BSI Committees on the preparation of British Standards for use with the Building Act 1984*

(Aq)   Testing, evaluating

BS 1796: 1796 (1985) *Methods for test sieving* and DD 57: 1978 *Methods of equipment reliability testing* are relevant.

(A1)   Organizing offices, projects

(A1t)   Copying, photocopying, etc.

Relevant references: BS 4187 *Microfiche* Part 1: 1981 *Formats of 60 and 98 frames* and Part 3: 1978 (1985) *Formats of 208,*

270, 325 and 420 frames (except COM), BS 4210 *35 mm microcopying of technical drawings* Part 1: 1977 (1983) *Operating procedures* Part 2: 1977 (1983) *Photographic requirements for silver film* and Part 3: 1977 (1983) *Unitized microfilm carriers*, and BS 5444: 1977 (1983) *Recommendations for preparation of copy for microcopying.*

(A3s)   Site investigation, surveying, including equipment

BS 4035: 1966 *Linear measurement instruments for use on building and civil engineering constructional works. Steel measuring tapes, steel bands and retractable steel pocket rules*
BS 4372: 1968 *Engineers' steel measuring rules*
BS 4484 *Measuring instruments for constructional works*
Part 1: 1969 *Metric graduation and figuring of instruments for linear measurement*

BS 5930: 1981   *Code of practice for site investigations*

This code (formerly CP 2001) deals with the investigation of sites for the purposes of assessing their suitability for the construction of civil engineering and building works and acquiring knowledge of the characteristics of a site that affect the design and construction of such work and the security of neighbouring land and property. This is an extensive code which covers general considerations, objectives, types and extent of site investigation as well as ground water, tests and reports. Description, classification and naming of soils are also covered.

(A3t)   Drawing, drawings including equipment

Those standards and published documents dealing mainly with engineering drawing practice are:

BS 308 *Engineering drawing practice*
Part 1: 1984 *Recommendations for general principles*
Part 2: 1985 *Dimensioning and tolerancing of size*
Part 3: 1972 *Geometrical tolerancing*
BS 499 *Welding terms and symbols*
Part 2: 1980 *Symbols for welding*
BS 1553 *Graphical symbols for general engineering*
Part 1: 1977 *Piping systems and plant*
BS 4466: 1981 *Bending dimensions and scheduling of reinforcement for concrete*
BS 5070: 1974 *Drawing practice for engineering diagrams*
BS 5100: 1974 *Guide to the principles of geometrical tolerancing*
BS 1635: 1970 *Graphical symbols and abbreviations for fire protection drawings*
BS 3939 *Graphical symbols for electric power, telecommunications and electronics diagrams* (in some thirteen parts)

There are also three published documents, namely PD 7304: 1982 *Introduction to geometrical tolerancing*, PD 7307: 1982 *Graphical symbols for use in schools and colleges* and PD 7308: 1980 *Engineering drawing practice for schools and colleges.*

The standard which refers to microfilming is BS 5536: 1978 *Preparation of technical drawings and diagrams for microfilming.*

One of the most valuable standards is the one dealing with construction drawing, namely BS 1192: *Construction Drawing Practice* which is in four parts, two of which have been published and two in the process of production. The standard gives recommendations regarding the production of graphical information needed to provide communication, with accuracy, clarity, economy, and consistency of presentation, between all concerned with the construction industry.

Part 1: 1984   *Recommendation for general principles*
Covers the preparation of all drawings for the construction

industry, including schedules prepared on drawing sheets and numbered as one of a drawing set. It is applicable to drawings produced by computer techniques, and to drawings that will be produced by microfilming in accordance with BS 5536. A definition of terms is given together with a range of drawings which is seen as varying from project to project dependent upon the brief, size, simplicity or complexity of each. Drawings should be complete for their respective purposes; they convey information graphically, and annotation should be kept to the minimum necessary to meet its intended purpose. Selection and designation of sizes of drawing sheets are given together with recommendations on layout, title and information panels, appropriate scales, types of lines (see Table 198), grids and projection systems (see Figures 111 and 112). In addition methods of identification of storeys, rooms, other areas and features and level are covered. Recommendations are made for the manner in which emphasis can be placed upon significant areas, together with dimensioning, methods for indicating tolerance requirements, lettering and the folding of sheets.

(Part 2: *Recommendations for architectural and engineering drawings* and Part 3: *Recommendations for symbols and conventions* are in the course of preparation.)

Part 4: 1984   *Recommendations for landscape drawings*
Recommended symbols and abbreviations are included and used in a series of typical drawings and schedules. The appendices include summaries of information commonly needed and of methods of calculation commonly used when landscape drawings are being prepared.

In addition PD 6479: 1976 *Recommendations for symbols and other graphic conventions for building production drawings* and BS 6430: 1983 *Methods for representing SI and other units in information processing with limited character sets.*

The standards which deal with drawing materials and equipment are BS 1896: 1972 *Sizes of reprographic papers*, BS 2457: 1975 (1983) *Protractors for drawing office use*, BS 2459: 1974 (1983) *Set squares (fixed and adjustable) for drawing office use*, BS 2808: 1969 *Artists' water-colour brushes for local authorities*, BS 3429: 1975 *Sizes of drawing sheets*, BS 4867 *Drawing boards and associated equipment* Part 2: 1972 *Tee squares*, BS 5065: 1974 *Students' drawing boards and other associated equipment*, BS 6381: 1983 *Drawing boards* which supersedes BS 4867 Part 1: 1972 and BS 1347: 1986 *Architects', Engineers' and Surveyors' metric scale rules.*

(A3u)   Specifications

BS 6019: 1980 *Recommendations for performance standards in building: contents and presentation* and PD 6112: 1967 *Guide to the preparation of specifications.*

(A4)   Cost planning, cost control, tenders, contracts (no entry)

(B)   Construction plant, tools

(B1)   Protection, plant

(B1c)   Protective clothing, etc

Footware

The following standards are concerned with the manufacture and specifications for the various types of protective boots and footwear available to industry: BS 1870 *Safety footwear* Part 1: 1979 *Safety footwear other than all-rubber and all-plastics moulded types*, Part 2: 1976 (1986) *Lined rubber safety boots* and Part 3: 1981 *Polyvinyl chloride moulded footwear*; BS 5145: 1984 *Lined industrial vulcanized rubber boots*; BS 5462: 1977 *Lined rubber boots with protection (penetration resistant) midsoles* and BS 6159: 1981 *Polyvinyl chloride lined or unlined industrial boots*.

Clothing

The following standards should be noted:

BS 6408: 1983 *Clothing made from coated fabrics for protection against wet weather*, which deals with the materials, making-up, performance, sizing and marking; BS 1547: 1959 *Flameproof industrial clothing (materials and design)*; BS 5426: 1976 *Workwear*; BS 4171: 1981 *Donkey jackets*; BS 2653: 1955 *Protective clothing for welders* and BS 6629: 1985 *Optical performance of high-visibility garments and accessories for use on the highways*.

These standards generally cover manufacture, testing, care and wearer precautions, and marking.

Gloves

BS 1651: 1986   *Industrial gloves*

Most useful tables of hazards and recommended glove types for protection are contained in the standard, with a plain language description of the glove types.

Three *patterns* are distinguished: 'Clute', 'Gunn' and 'Montpelier' and three groups of material: leather/fabric; plastics; and rubber (see Tables 199 and 200).

Headwear

BS 4033: 1966   *Industrial scalp protectors (light duty)*

This standard is concerned with the shape, manufacture, performance and testing of light-duty helmets.

BS 5240: 1975   *General-purpose industrial safety helmets*

This standard is concerned with manufacture and testing of industrial safety helmets.

Respirators

The following standards are all concerned with the manufacture, performance and testing of various respirators: BS 4771: 1971 *Positive pressure, powered dust hoods and blouses*; BS 2091: 1969 *Respirators for protection against harmful dust, gases and scheduled agricultural chemicals*, these standards recommend respirators against dirt and gases; BS 4275: 1974 *Recommendations for the selection, use and maintenance of respiratory protec-*

Table 199   *Glove types*

Type number	Description
1	Flesh split leather inseam gloves, gauntlets, mitts and one finger mitts
2	Grain leather inseam gloves, gauntlets, mitts and one finger mitts
3	Fabric gloves with leather palms
4	Inseam gloves and gauntlets made wholly from fabric
5	Leather outseam armoured gloves and gauntlets
6	Lightweight PVC supported gloves with a rough finish
7	Lightweight PVC supported gloves with a smooth finish
8	Standard-weight PVC supported gloves with a smooth finish
9	PVC gloves with a granular finish
10	Flock-lined unsupported PVC gauntlets
11	Unflocked, matt finish, unsupported PVC gauntlets
12	Unlined rubber gloves or gauntlets
13	Flock lined rubber gloves or gauntlets
14	Fabric lined rubber gloves or gauntlets
15	Rubber gloves or gauntlets, fabric or flock-lined or unlined with additional rubber reinforcement over the whole or part of the hand

(Table 1: BS 1651: 1986)

tive equipment; respirators with independent air supply; BS 4555: 1970 *High-efficiency dust respirators*; BS 4558: 1970 *Positive-pressure, powered dust respirators*; BS 4667 *Breathing apparatus* Part 1: 1974 *Closed-circuit breathing apparatus*; (oxygen-enriched recirculated apparatus), Part 2: 1974 *Open-circuit breathing apparatus*, open-circuit breathing apparatus (compressed air cylinder), Part 3: 1974 *Fresh-air hose and compressed-air line breathing apparatus*, fresh-air hose apparatus and compressed-air line apparatus (similar to type used by divers), Part 4: 1982 *Escape breathing apparatus*; escape apparatus of a Part 1 or Part 2 type; BS 4001 *Recommendations for the care and maintenance of underwater breathing apparatus* Part 1: 1981 *Compressed-air open-circuit type*.

BS 1542: 1982   *Equipment for eye, face and neck protection against radiation arising during welding and similar operations*

Both gas and electric arc welding operations are covered, as is the need for such protection for those who are observing the operations only.

Special equipment

The following standards should be read in conjunction with entries under (B2) *temporary non-protective works*:

BS 3367: 1980 *Fire brigade and industrial ropes and rescue lines*; BS 1397: 1979 *Industrial safety belts, harnesses and safety*

Table 200   *Classification of hazards and suitable gloves*

Hazard	Typical operations	Suitable gloves	Glove type no.
Heat, but no serious abrasion	Furnace work, drop stamping, casting, forging, handling hot objects	Heat-resistant leather wrist gloves	1, 2
		Heat-resistant leather inseam mitts	1, 2
		Heat-resistant leather gauntlets	1, 2
		Heat-resistant leather gauntlets with canvas cuffs	1, 2
		Felt mitts, palms faced with canvas or heat-resistant leather	3, 4
		Loop-pile gloves or gauntlets	4
Heat and abrasion	Riveting, hot chipping	Heat and abrasion-resistant leather gauntlets and mitts	1, 2
		Fabric mitts with palms faced with canvas or heat and abrasion-resistant leather	3, 4
Heat when a fair degree of sensitivity is required and splashes or splatter of molten metal may occur	Welding, casting, galvanizing	Heat-resistant leather inseam mitts	1, 2
		Heat-resistant leather gauntlets	1, 2
		Heat-resistant leather inseam gauntlets with leather cuffs	1, 2
Sharp-edged materials and objects	Swarf, guillotining metal, blanking, handling metal sheets, handling undressed castings	Leather inseam mitts and gauntlets	1, 2
		Fabric gloves with palms faced with canvas or leather	3, 4
		Supported PVC gloves with granular finish	9
		Reinforced rubber gloves heavy-weight	15
Sharp materials or objects in an alkaline degreasing bath		Supported PVC gloves with granular finish	9
		Reinforced rubber gloves heavy-weight	15
Glass or timber with splintered edges	Glass handling, timber handling, building demolition	Leather gloves and mitts	1, 2, 3
		Loop pile gloves	4
		Supported PVC gloves with granular finish	9
		Reinfoced rubber gloves heavy-weight	15
Very heavy abrasion	Shot blasting	Reinforced natural rubber heavy-weight	15
Heavy abrasion	Handling dressed castings or forgings, bricks, concrete cement, steel stock, heavy duty packaging	Abrasion-resistant leather inseam mitts	1, 2
		Abrasion-resistant grain hide palm split leather-back inseam gloves	2
		Supported loop pile gloves	4
		Abrasion-resistant leather stapled double palm gloves	5
		PVC gloves, granular surface heavy-weight	9
		Reinforced natural rubber gloves	15
Light abrasion	Handling of packaged goods, general labouring	Leather wrist gloves and mitts	1
		Fabric gloves	4
		Fabric gloves with leather palms	3
		Loop pile gloves	4
		PVC gloves	6, 7, 8, 9, 10, 11
		Rubber gloves	12, 13, 14, 15
Solvents*	Degreasing, printing, chemical-manufacturing, paint spraying	Supported PVC gloves rough, smooth, lightweight (excluding open back and knitted wrist styles)	6, 7
		PVC lined gloves smooth and granular finish (excluding open back and knitted wrist styles)	7, 8, 9, 10
		Natural and synthetic rubber gloves and gauntlets	12, 13, 14
Chemicals*	Acids, alkalis, dyes and general chemical hazards not involving contact with solvents or oils	Standard weight PVC gloves	8
		PVC gloves with a granular finish (excluding open-back and knitted wrist styles)	9
		Rubber gloves	12, 13, 14, 15

Table 200 *Classification of hazards and suitable gloves* (cont.)

Hazard	Typical operations	Suitable gloves	Glove type no.
Fats, oils*	Chemical hazards involving contact with oils	Standard-weight supported PVC gloves and gauntlets	8
		Granular finish PVC gloves and gauntlets (excluding open back and knitted wrist styles)	9
		Natural and synthetic rubber gloves and gauntlets	12, 13, 14
Electrical shock		Do not use gloves in this standard but refer to BS 697	
General hazards in food handling	Food industry, canning industry, kitchens, hotels, restaurants	PVC gloves rough or smooth finish	6, 7, 8
		Unsupported PVC gloves	10, 11
		Lightweight or medium-weight natural rubber unlined or lined gloves	12, 13
		NOTE. Constituents of PVC plastisols or rubber latex should conform to relevant food handling regulations.	

* It is important that the purchaser or user should seek advice from the manufacturer before making a final selection of a glove to meet his particular needs. Attention is drawn to the method of test of BS 4724 to assess the resistance to permeation as may be appropriate according to the nature of the liquid composition and the type of glove under consideration.

(Table 13: BS 1651: 1986)

lanyards; and BS 5108: 1980 *Method of measurement of sound attenuation of hearing protectors*. The last covers sound deadening and the conditions under which measurement is taken.

(B2)   Temporary non-protective works

General

BS 3408: 1977   *Tarpaulins*

Materials, behavioural characteristics and manufacture are covered.

BS 3913: 1982   *Industrial safety nets*

This standard covers the manufacture and performance of safety nets. Nets are required to be marked with the maximum distance below working level at which they should be fixed. Students are also directed to read CP 93 for full guidance on the erection, use and limitations of safety nets and the governing regulations.

Scaffolding

BS 1139   *Metal scaffolding*

Part 1: 1982   *Tubes for use in scaffolding*
The materials and the manufacture of both steel and extruded aluminium tube in scaffolding.

Part 2: 1982   *Couplers and fittings for use in tubular scaffolding*
The dimensions and load-carrying capacity of connecting devices for use in erecting scaffolds. (Due for amendment.)

Part 3: 1983   *Prefabricated access and working towers*
The dimensions, load-carrying capacity, fixing and bracing of access towers together with their integral ladders and platforms. (Due for amendment.)

Part 4: 1982   *Prefabricated steel splitheads and trestles*
The requirements of the design and fabrication of steel splitheads and trestles for use as supports for temporary platforms.

BS 2482: 1981   *Timber scaffold boards*

The timbers which may be used, the various thicknesses and the unsupported maximum spans of scaffold boards. See Tables 201, 202 and 203.

DD 72: 1981   *Design requirements for access scaffolds*

Such scaffolds should provide safe and practical access and work place for all users.

BS 5973: 1981   *Code of practice for access and working scaffolds and special structures in steel*

This is a code of practice for the design, construction and use of steel scaffolds. It does not include suspended scaffolds.

The student is strongly recommended to study the standard which has a full definition of terms also many clear useful sketches of good scaffolding practice covering putlog scaffolds, independent tied scaffolds, cantilevered scaffolds, the means of stabilizing and tieing in scaffold systems to the building.

BS 5974: 1982   *Code of practice for temporarily installed suspended scaffolds and access equipment*

This code makes recommendations for the construction and use of such scaffolds and equipment, comprising a working platform, work cage, cradle or safety chain, which are dismantled after the completion of the work for which they were erected.

The student is strongly recommended to read the full standard which contains definitions of terminology and many diagrams of good scaffolding practice.

Ropes and connections

In all the following group, manufacturing, testing and marking are covered.

BS 183: 1972   *General-purpose galvanized steel wire strand*

The standard defines a strand as 'three or more wires twisted together with a uniform lay'.

The direction of lay is right or left hand and is determined by holding the strand vertically and observing the wires. A right-

Table 201   *Timbers for scaffold boards*

Standard name	Botanical species	Other common names
Imported		
Redwood	*Pinus sylvestris*	European redwood
Whitewood	*Picea abies*	European whitewood
	Abies alba	
Canadian species		
combinations		
Douglas fir – larch	*Pseudotsuga menziesii*	Douglas fir
	Larix occidentalis	Western larch
Hem – fir	*Tsuga heterophylla*	Western hemlock
	Abies amabilis	Amabilis fir
	Abies grandis	Grand fir
Spruce – pine – fir*	*Picea mariana*	Black spruce
	Picea engelmannii	Engelmann spruce
	Picea rubeus	Red spruce
	Picea glauca	White spruce
	Pinus banksiana	Jack pine
	Pinus contorta	Lodgepole pine
	Pinus ponderosa	Ponderosa pine
	Abies lasiocarpa	Alpine fir
	Abies balsamea	Balsam fir.
British		
European larch	*Larix decidua*	Larch
Japanese larch	*Larix kaempferi*	Larch
Douglas fir†	*Pseudotsuga menziesii*	
Scots pine	*Pinus sylvestris*	Scots fir

*Spruce – pine – fir also embraces species comprising Eastern Canadian spruce.
†Suitable for machine graded boards only.
Note 1: This table may be amended to include other timbers when information becomes available.
Note 2: The most commonly available timber is imported whitewood.
Note 3: This table list those timbers known to be suitable for use for the production of scaffold boards. No attempt has been made to list timbers in such a manner as to indicate their relative strengths.

(Table 1: BS 2482: 1981)

Table 202   *Cross-sectional sizes: scaffold boards*

Basic		Minimum actual	
Thickness	Width	Thickness	Width
mm	mm	mm	mm
38	225	36	220
50	225	47	220
63	225	60	220

(Table 2: BS 2482: 1981)

Table 203   *Maximum span for scaffold boards*

Basic thickness	Span
mm	m
38	1.5
50	2.6
63	3.25

(Table 3: BS 2482: 1981)

hand lay conforms to the central part of the letter Z and left hand to the central part of the letter S. Seven tensile strength grades, for strands from 1.7 to 23.8 mm diameter are covered.

BS 2052: 1977   *Ropes made from manila, sisal, hemp, cotton and coir*

BS 4048   *Combined wire and fibre ropes*

Part 1: 1966   *Combined ropes*
Part 2: 1966   *Spring lay ropes*

BS 4928   *Man-made fibre ropes*

Part 1: 1973   *Polypropylene ropes (3-strand hawser laid and 8-strand plaited)*
Part 2: 1974   *Polyamide (nylon), polyester and polyethylene filament ropes*

These parts deal with ranges of 3-strand hawser laid ropes and 8-strand plaited ropes.

BS 6125: 1981   *Natural fibre cords, lines and twines*

BS 1214: 1977   *Hessian sandbags and rot-proofed hessian sandbags*

This standard gives the specification for manufacture, rot proofing and testing of three fabric types.

BS 462: 1983   *Wire rope grips*

These include those termed 'bulldog grips', forming an anchorage eye. The range of ropes extends from 3 mm to 56 mm diameter.

BS 5281: 1975   *Ferrule-secured eye terminations for wire ropes*

BS 4340: 1968   *Glossary of formwork terms*

Recommended as a 'technical dictionary' for reference. A clear and concise series of definitions, the standard also clearly indicates preferred terms, alternative terms and deprecated terms in respect of each definition.

BS 5972: 1982 *Code of practice for falsework*

A standard of good practice and, therefore, a recommendation. The code covers structural design, general workmanship and work on site, procedures and technical aspects.

BS 4074: 1982 *Metal props and struts*

While this standard mainly describes and specifies the design and manufacture of adjustable props, the tables of recommended maximum loads are a useful guide (see Tables 204 and 205).

Table 204 *Lengths of props*

Size code	Length fully closed	Length fully extended	Mass (approximate)
	m	m	kg
0	1.07	1.82	15.0
1	1.75	3.12	22.7
2	1.98	3.35	23.6
3	2.59	3.95	26.3
4	3.20	4.87	35.6

(Table 1: BS 4074: 1982)

Table 205 *Lengths of struts*

Size code	Length fully closed	Length fully extended	Mass (approximate)
	m	m	kg
0	0.30	0.48	5.0
1	0.45	0.68	6.4
2	0.68	1.06	9.1
3	1.06	1.67	11.8

(Table 2: BS 4074: 1982)

BS 5507 *Methods of test for falsework equipment*

Part 1: 1977 *Floor centres*
This standard gives the specification and description of test series to determine safe load tables. Essentially it is a laboratory exercise for engineers in order to produce such tables for the extensive use of a system of floor centre falsework.

Part 3: 1982 *Props*
This sets out a test method for props to BS 4074.

Access

BS 1129: 1982 *Timber ladders, steps, trestles and lightweight stagings*

This standard defines the quality of timber and the manufacture.

Classified according to their use as in section 4 and permanently marked as in section 8 both quoted in full:

4 Classification of duty rating
The articles covered by this standard shall be classified according to the general conditions and probable frequency of use as follows.
Class 1 For heavy duty where relatively high frequency and onerous conditions of use, carriage and storage occur. Suitable for industrial purposes.
Class 2 For medium duty where relatively low frequency and

reasonably good conditions of use, storage and carriage occur. Suitable for light trades purposes.
Class 3 For light duty where frequency of use is low and good storage and carriage conditions obtain. Suitable for domestic and household purposes.

8 Markings
8.1 Ladders, steps, trestles and stagings shall be permanently marked with the following particulars:
(a) the name, trade mark or other means of identification of the manufacturer or supplier;
(b) the number of this British Standard, i.e. BS 1129;
(c) the class and duty rating, e.g. Class 1 – Industrial.
8.2 A separate label, except for lightweight stagings, shall include the following wording on a background coloured blue for class 1, yellow for class 2 or red for class 3.
Inspect for damage before use.
Lean at approximately 75° from horizontal (1 m out of each 4 m height).
Ensure firm level base.
Check safety at top.
Avoid electrical hazards.
Avoid over-reaching.
Keep a secure grip.
Never stand on top of swing back steps unless the steps are fitted with a hand or knee rail.
Tie at top and bottom wherever possible.

The manufacturing, testing, marking and precautions are set out.

Temporary services

BS 4363: 1968 *Distribution units for electricity supplies for construction and building sites*

An extensive standard dealing with the necessary switch-gear, transformers and outlet units for incoming power and its distribution around the site, for transportation. The arrangements for demountable parts of the housing to facilitate maintenance, and the means whereby weather tight conditions are achieved, are specified. The markings indicating the dangers are specified. Table 206 gives a general indication of the power supply necessary for various on site uses.

BS 4256 *Oil-burning air heaters* Part 1: 1972 (1980) *Non-domestic transportable, fan-assisted heaters*

The construction operation, performance and safety requirements for flued and unflued heaters designed for use with kerosene, gas oil and domestic fuel oil are specified. (The other parts cover fixed, flued heaters).

BS 2037: 1964 *Aluminium ladders, steps and trestles for the building and civil engineering industries*

Materials and manufacture, but not a classification of these articles for suitability of use, nor a requirement for permanent marking.

The hazard of using metal ladders near power lines or in electrical work with a live system are stressed.

BS 2830: 1973 *Suspended safety chairs and cradles for use in the construction industry*

This standard gives the specification for manufacture, sizing and testing of chairs and cradles.

BS 3143 *Road danger lamps*

The parts listed below are all specifications for the manufacture, materials of manufacture, testing for strength, stability, light output and performance of categories of lamp.

Part 1: 1973 *Kerosene* (sic — now spelt kerosine) *burning lamps* (not suitable for use where explosive atmosphere gases or flammable materials are part of the hazard)

Table 206　*Typical systems voltages at 50 Hz employed on construction and building sites in the United Kingdom and recommended application*

Volts	Phase	Derived from	Special provision	Application
415	3	Supply undertaking		Fixed and transportable equipment above 5 h.p., e.g. crane, hoist, compressor, concrete mixer, and large scale personnel amenities
240	1	Supply undertaking		Site offices, personnel amenities and fixed flood lighting
110	3	415 V transformer	Secondary winding phase to earth 64 V	Transportable equipment up to 5 h.p., e.g. vibrators, pumps, site lighting other than fixed flood-lighting, and hand tools
110	1	240 V transformer	Secondary winding outers to earth 55 V	All portable and trans portable tools up to 2.5 h.p. and site lighting
50	1	Transformer	Secondary winding outers to earth 25 V	Dangerous situations, e.g. tunnelling work or inside bolts
25	1	Transformer	Secondary winding outers to earth 12.5 V	

(Appendix A: BS 4363: 1968)

Part 2: 1973 *Low-intensity battery-operated lamps*
Part 4: 1973 *High-intensity battery-operated beacons* (not suitable where explosive atmospheres are part of the hazard).

(B3)　Transport plant

BS 3810　*Glossary of terms used in materials handling*

Part 2: 1965　*Terms used in connection with conveyors and elevators (excluding pneumatic and hydraulic handling)*
This glossary is of little use to those not concerned with the installation of such systems. The systems described are for bulk handling of granular materials in circumstances such as sand pits, coal depots, etc.

Part 4: 1968　*Terms used in connection with cranes*
Glossary. Much wider than the types of cranes used in the construction industry.

Part 5: 1971　*Terms used in connection with lifting tackle*
A glossary of lifting tackle used to attach a load to a lifting device. Covers hooks, shackles, swivels, components, terminals, slings, chains and ropes.

Part 6: 1973　*Terms used in connection with pulley blocks*
A glossary. The types of hooks and eyes overlap those in Part 5, covers the various forms of rope tackle and chain pulley block.

Cranes

The following group covers the manufacture, characteristics and use of cranes of various types (see also D3).

BS 327: 1964　*Power-driven derrick cranes* (obsolescent)

The information to be supplied by the customer, the structural, safety and motive power specification for manufacture.

BS 357: 1958　*Power-driven travelling jib cranes (rail-mounted, low-carriage type)* (obsolescent)

BS 1757: 1981　*Power-driven mobile cranes*

Covers the siting of the crane on the mobile unit.

BS 2452: 1954　*High pedestal or portal jib cranes*

Little application to the needs of the construction industry.

BS 2573　*Rules for the design of cranes*

Part 1: 1983　*Classification, stress calculations and design criteria for structures*
Part 2: 1980　*Mechanisms*

BS 2799: 1974　*Power-driven tower cranes for building and engineering construction* (obsolescent)

BS 2853: 1957　*The design and testing of steel overhead runway beams*

The minimum requirements for the design, manufacture and testing of such beams.

BS 5744: 1979　*Code of practice for safe use of cranes (overhead/underhung travelling and goliath cranes, high pedestal and portal jib dockside cranes, manually-operated and light cranes, container handling cranes and rail-mounted low carriage cranes)*

The aims of this code of practice are:

1　To describe the principal characteristics of the cranes covered.
2　To draw attention to some of the more common hazards and potential dangers which may be encountered in their use.
3　To recommend general precautions to be taken and procedures to be followed to promote safety in the use of these cranes.

Reference to the British Standard is recommended for those whose occupation is specifically concerned with site equipment or site safety.

Hoists

The following group of standards covers hoists and lifting apparatus.

BS 3125: 1959 *Power-driven mast hoists for materials*

BS 3701: 1964 *Hand-operated plate-sided winches*

All but insignificant loads should be lifted in low gear.

BS 4465: 1969 *Electric hoists for passengers and materials*

None of these three standards deals with fixing the equipment. In the last case the manufacturer is required to test the hoist at the purchaser's premises, before it is put into operation, for both electrical and mechanical and structural safety and suitability.

BS 6405: 1984 *Non-calibrated short link steel chain (grade 3c) for general engineering purposes: Class 1 & 2*

Class 1 is for arduous duties, Class 2 for general duties.

BS 4898: 1973 *Chain lever hoists*

A relevant extract follows:

> **Appendix D**
> **Care and safe use of chain lever hoists**
> Chain lever hoists are precision made and should be treated with appropriate care. Do not drop chain lever hoists from a height.
> Never subject a chain lever hoist to a greater load than the safe working load marked on the hoist. The hoist has been tested to more than this load, but it has been done under carefully controlled conditions. The use of a chain lever hoist at any load greater than the safe working load may result in damage. Attention is particularly drawn to the possibility of overloading a chain lever hoist when pulling loads over uneven ground. Never increase the length of the lever.
> Keep the chains well lubricated along their whole length and especially at the contact points between the links. Where oils and greases are not desirable use a dry lubricant. Failure to maintain correct lubrication reduces the life of a chain. If the chain jumps, does not work smoothly, or marks in use it is probably out of pitch and should be replaced. Before use, examine the chain to ensure that there is no twist. In the case of hoisting on two parts of chain, twist can arise from the chain hook being accidentally turned over. Never load the point of the hook.
> Never use a load chain as a sling, i.e. by back-hooking. Do not tie knots in the load chain or join it by bolts. Do not allow dirt and hard grease to gather in the pockets of the load wheel. Never run the chain out too far. When the maximum range of travel is exceeded an excessive and dangerous load is imposed on the load chain terminal stop.
> Make sure that the brake setting or adjustment is maintained in accordance with the manufacturer's instructions.
> All chain lever hoists should be entered in the appropriate register and submitted to at least the statutory requirements regarding inspection and examination.

BS 5323: 1980 *Code of practice for scissor lifts*

Design and safety requirements for fixed scissor lifts with a maximum working height of 1.98 m above ground or floor level and mobile, vehicle mounted and self-propelled scissor lifts of any working height.

BS 6037: 1981 *Code of practice for permanently installed suspended access equipment*

Guidance on construction, installation and use of equipment to service offices, factories and high-rise residential property is given in this code. It covers both manually and power operated equipment.

BS 6289 *Work platforms* Part 1: 1982 *Code of practice for mobile scissor operated work platforms*

This part is a guide for the design, construction and safe use of such platforms (MSPs) which are movable, self-propelled or vehicle mounted for plant installations, inspection, construction, maintenance and repairs. The work platform can be manual or power operated.

BS 302: 1968 *Wire ropes for cranes, excavators and general engineering purposes*

Included are tables for breaking strain of various ropes and an appendix of terminology and definitions.

BS 330: 1968 *Stranded wire ropes for haulage purposes*

Manufacture. Tables of breaking loads, appendices on handling and maintenance and terminology and definitions are given for 8 to 38 mm diameters.

BS 461: 1970 *Bordeaux connections*

Such connections are a means of splicing two lengths of wire rope or a wire rope to a length of chain, for safe work.

BS 1290: 1983 *Wire rope slings and sling legs for general lifting purposes*

The manufacture and testing, and the safe working loads.

BS 1692: 1971 *Gin blocks*

The manufacture, performance, testing and suspension for loads to 250 kg.

Gin blocks are a simple form of suspended pulley block usually used in connection with fibre ropes, simply suspended and for hoisting and lowering light loads by hand or small portable hand winches. See Figure 113.

Each of the following group deals with manufacture, testing, inspection and certification of the relevant equipments.

BS 2902: 1957 *Higher tensile steel chain slings and rings, links alternative to rings, egg links and intermediate links*

BS 2903: 1980 *Higher tensile steel hooks for chains, slings, blocks and general engineering purposes*

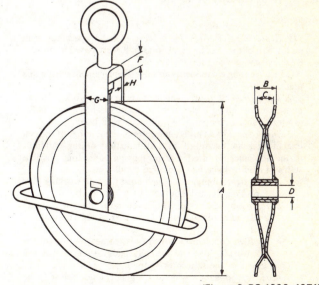

(Figure 3: BS 1692: 1971)

Figure 113 *Gin block section*

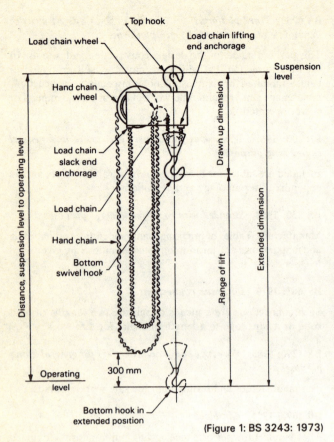

(Figure 1: BS 3243: 1973)

Figure 114   *Chain pulley block components and dimensional definitions*

BS 3032: 1958   *Higher tensile steel shackles*

BS 3551: 1962   *Alloy steel shackles*

Design tables, and requirements for special or unusual shackles not covered by them, are included.

BS 3243: 1973   *Hand-operated chain pulley blocks*

This form of pulley block is found frequently in workshops and sometimes on site. Figure 114 is a typical sketch extracted from this standard together with a general guide to the classification and working capacity of hand operated pulley blocks.

Appendix B

1. *Expected service life.* In the case of hand operated chain pulley blocks that has been taken as five years based upon 250 working days per annum.
NOTE: Wearing components may need replacement during this life.

2. *The frequency of use.* This is based on the product of the number of operating cycles and the length of each cycle, and is given in Table 1 as operating time per day in hours.

3. *State of loading.* This is a measure of the number of times a load of particular magnitude in relation to the working load limit of the appliance, is lifted. For present purposes four possible states of loading have been adopted as follows:

   a. *Very light*: appliances which hoist the safe working load exceptionally, and normally very light loads.
   b. *Light*: appliances which hoist very rarely the safe working load and normally loads of about ⅓ of the safe working load.
   c. *Medium*: appliances which hoist rather frequently the safe working load and normally loads varying between ⅓ and ⅔ of the safe working load.
   d. *Heavy*: appliances which are regularly loaded close to the safe working load.

4. *Conditions of use.* The state of loading may be increased by one grade if justified by severe conditions of use.

Table 1   Class of use

State of loading	Maximum operating time per day (hours)				
	0.125	0.25	0.5	1	2
Very light			IB	IA	II
Light		IB	IA	II	III
Medium	IB	IA	II	III	IV
Heavy	IA	II	III	IV	

In order that the requirements of Table 1 may be met, the safe working loads shall be related to the working load limit as follows:

Classification	Percentage of working load limit
IB and IA	100
II	80
III	63
IV	50

(Table 1 of Appendix B BS 3243)

BS 4018: 1966   *Pulley blocks for use with wire rope for a maximum lift of 25 tonf (250 kN) combination*

BS 4278: 1984   *Eyebolts for lifting purposes*

BS 4283: 1968   *Swivels for lifting purposes*

BS 4344: 1968   *Pulley blocks for use with natural and synthetic fibre roles*

BS 4942   *Short link chain for lifting purposes*

Part 1: 1981   *General conditions of acceptance*

Parts 2 to 6: 1981 deal with various grades of chain.

BS 6304: 1982   *Chain slings of welded construction: grades M(4), S(6) and T(8)*

The requirements, methods of rating and testing of single, two, three and four branch or leg welded chain slings are given.

Earth-moving machinery

Among a large number of standards dealing with earth-moving equipment or plant, the following are seen as of general interest.

BS 6296: 1982   *Glossary of terms for self-propelled crawler and wheel tractors and their equipment used for earth-moving*

BS 5718: 1979   *Glossary of terms for basic types of earth-moving machinery*

Glossaries of terms defining basic types of earth-moving machinery are given. Terms and definitions include the following:

Tractor: a self-propelled crawler or wheeled machine used to exert a push or pull force through a mounted attachment or drawbar.
Loader: a self-propelled crawler or wheeled machine with an integral front-mounted bucket supporting structure and linkage which loads or excavates through motion of the machine, and lifts, transports and discharges material.
Dumper: a self-propelled wheeled machine, having an open body, which transports and dumps or spreads material. Loading is performed by means external to the dumper.
Tractor-scraper: a self-propelled wheeled machine, having a cutting edge positioned between front and rear axles, which cuts, loads, transports, discharges, and spreads material through a forward motion of the machine.
Excavator: a self-propelled machine with an upper structure capable of a minimum of 360° rotation, which excavates,

elevates, swings, and dumps material by action of a bucket fitted to the boom and arm or telescoping boom, without moving the chassis or under carriage during any one cycle of the machine.

Grader: a self-propelled machine having an adjustable blade, positioned between front and rear axles, which cuts, moves and spreads materials usually to grade requirements.

BS 6295   *Dimensions and symbols for earth-moving machinery*

Part 1: 1982   *Glossary of terms for base machine*
Part 2: 1982   *Glossary of terms for equipment*

BS 6685: 1986   *Glossary of terms for loaders used for earth-moving*

Establishes terminology and the content of commercial literature specifications for self-propelled crawler and wheel loaders and their equipment.

BS 2596: 1955   *Components of crawler tractors and earth-moving equipment*

BS 2800: 1957   *Tests for industrial crawler and wheeled tractors (excluding units designed for materials handling in factories)*

These tests include engine performance, drawbar tests, tilting (static), equipment, weight and dimensions.

BS 3318: 1978   *Earth-moving machinery – method for locating the centre of gravity*

This standard covers any condition of loading or position of attachments.

BS 3726: 1978   *Counterbalanced lift trucks. Stability – basic tests*

Basic tests to determine stability of counterbalanced forklift trucks with tiltable or non-tiltable masts.

BS 4337: 1968   *Principal dimensions of hand-operated stillage trucks*

Gives the size of truck and lift. A stillage truck is one where the base is run under a platform holding a load and then mechanically or hydraulically the base jacks up the load which can then be manually transported. Little used in construction work.

BS 4338: 1968   *Rated capacities of forklift trucks*

The rating and marking is given, of trucks to 10 000 kg.

BS 4339: 1968   *Rating of industrial tractors*

The rating of industrial tractors is expressed as the maximum drawbar pull.

BS 4430   *Safety of powered industrial trucks*

Part 2: 1969   *Operation and maintenance*
The operation and maintenance of powered industrial trucks excluding tractors are given. This part is concerned with preventing damage and deterioration of equipment, lessening the risk of accidents and ensuring the safety of personnel.

BS 4436: 1978   *Reach and straddle fork lift trucks – stability tests*

The stability tests for 'reach' and 'straddle' of fork lift trucks to 5000 kg capacity.

BS 5485: 1977   *Maintenance and adjustment tools for earth-moving machinery*

Illustrations of the tools and a table showing the tools necessary and their application to various maintenance items.

BS 5495: 1980   *Laboratory evaluations of roll-over and falling-object protective structures: the deflection-limiting volume for earth-moving machinery*

Laboratory evaluation to reduce the possibility of the operator being crushed in the event of the machine rolling over.

BS 5526: 1985   *Falling object protective structures on earth-moving machinery: laboratory tests and performance requirements*

Tests for protective (FOPS) structures designed to resist impact penetration and impact loading.

BS 5527: 1981   *Roll-over protective structures on earth-moving machinery: laboratory tests and performance requirements*

Tests for (ROPS) protective structures against roll-over of earth-moving machinery particularly crawler loaders, tractors, graders and scrapers.

BS 5528: 1981   *Operator's controls on excavators used for earth-moving*

Requirements, movement directions and actuating forces for the operator's controls in relation to the operator and position on the machine.

BS 5631: 1978   *Earth-moving machinery – seat index point*

The correct padded seat index point.

BS 5635: 1982   *Recommendations for earth-moving machinery – service instrumentation*

Tables of essential and desirable instrumentation to ensure satisfactory operation together with necessary portable tools to check performance at the work site are given.

BS 5768: 1979   *Operating instrumentation for earth-moving machinery*

Mandatory and optional instruments.

Instrumentation at the instrument panel should provide information according to Table 207, where A = mandatory (where applicable) and B = optional.

BS 5796: 1979   *Drain fill and level plugs for earth-moving machinery*

BS 5945: 1980   *Guards and shields for earth-moving machinery*

This standard covers the specification of guards and shields to protect personnel from accidental hazards during operation or servicing arising from mechanical, thermal, chemical or electrical causes.

BS 5982: 1980   *Method for determination of ground speed of earth-moving machinery*

Apparatus and test conditions.

BS 6060: 1981   *Nipple-type lubrication fittings for earth-moving machinery*

BS 6074: 1981   *Method for determination of the volumetric rating of tractor-scrapes for earth-moving machinery*

The method of determining and rating the volume contained in the bowl of tractor scrapers.

BS 6112: 1983   *Recommendations for minimum access dimensions of earth-moving machinery*

Recommendations for working space for the operator for the head, hand, body, arm reach and two handed reach are given.

Table 207   *Operating instrumentation: earth-moving machinery*

Information obtainable	Crawler loaders and dozers	Wheel loaders and dozers	Graders	Tractor scrapers	Self-propelled compactors	Excavators	Off-highway trucks
Engine speed (rotational frequency)	B	B	B	A	B	–	B
Machine speed	–	B	A	A	B	–	A
Amperage and/or voltage	A	A	A	A	A	A	A
Engine coolant temperature	A	A	A	A	A	A	A
Engine oil pressure	A	A	A	A	A	A	A
Brake air pressure	–	A	A	A	A	A	A
Torque converter oil pressure	B	B	B	B	B	B	B
Torque converter oil temperature	A	A	A	A	A	A	A
Transmisson oil pressure	B	B	B	B	B	B	B
Transmission oil temperature	B	B	B	B	B	B	B
Engine fuel pressure	B	B	B	B	B	B	B
Hydraulic oil pressure	B	B	B	B	B	B	B
Hydraulic oil temperature	B	B	B	B	B	B	B

Note 1: Information concerning fuel level and service time are not included in the above table, but are required and should be visible for maintenance purposes on all equipment having an engine. However, location is not required to be on the instrument panel.

Note 2: In the event where information normally required, as given in the table, is not appropriate for a given machine, that information is not required; for example, engine coolant temperate for air-cooled engines, or air pressure for machines having no air-system.

(Table 1: BS 5768: 1979)

BS 6113: 1981   *Method for volumetric rating of dumper bodies used for earth-moving*

BS 6114: 1981   *Method for volumetric rating of elevating scrapers used for earth-moving*

These two standards provide useful information on capacities for different soils.

BS 6124: 1981   *Zones of comfort and reach for controls in earth-moving machinery*

A guide for design to suit operators of all heights and stature.

BS 6197: 1985   *Methods for preservation and storage of earth-moving machinery*

BS 6264: 1982   *Guide to procedure for operator training for earth-moving machinery*

No guidance on assessment of competence or proficiency is given nor does it give guidance on who is responsible for training.

(B4)   Manufacture, screening, storage plant

BS 410: 1976   *Test sieves*

Material and construction of test sieves for use with granular material.

BS 481   *Industrial wire mesh*

Part 1: 1971   *Woven annealed wire cloth with square apertures, plain or twilled weave*
The manufacture and labelling of woven wire cloth of three classes with square apertures in metric sizes, 16 to 0.025 mm.

Part 2: 1972   *High tensile steel wire mesh with square apertures from 125 to 2 mm*

BS 1796: 1976   *Method for test sieving*

The method of test sieving granular materials is fully described. It includes the maximum charge for any one test sieving of any one material, sieving wet and dry materials and the effectiveness of hand and machine sieving. Where laboratory test sieving is to be carried out the standard should be studied.

BS 1305: 1974   *Batch type concrete mixers*

The manufacture, performance and rating of batch type concrete mixers (drum or pan types) but excludes truck type concrete mixers.

BS 3963: 1974   *Method for testing the mixing performance of concrete mixers*

The material content, sampling procedure and assessment of the mixing performance on the basis of the uniformity of water content, fine aggregate content and/or cement content are given. It does not, however, define what constitutes a satisfactory performance.

BS 4251: 1974   *Truck type concrete mixers*

The manufacture, performances and rating, including terms and accessories.

(B5)   Treatment plant

BS 328   *Drills and reamers*

Part 1: 1986   *Specification for twist drills*
Gives dimensions and tolerances for parallel shank, jobber, stub, long and extra long series of twist drills. Also for Morse taper shank and Morse taper shank extra long drills. Tables summarize both imperial and metric sizes for each type of drill.

Part 2: 1972   *Combined drills and countersinks (centre drills)*

BS 328A: 1963   *Twist drill sizes, superseding drill gauge and letter sizes*

A data sheet giving imperial and metric sizes for twist drills.

BS 1983   *Chucks for machine tools and portable power tools*

Part 1: 1969   *Tool-holding chucks*
It includes requirements for machine tools and portable power tools, and on rotational accuracy.

Part 2: 1972   *Work-holding chucks*

BS 5621: 1979   *Dimensions of rotary masonry impact drills with hardmetal tips*

Rotary and rotary impact masonry hardmetal tipped drills, excluding hammer drills.

BS 411: 1969   *Circular saws for woodworking and their attachment*

Information on the type of saw suitable for timber species is included.

BS 3997: 1966 *Classification of woodworking machines and auxiliary equipment*

BS 5741: 1979 *Pressure regulators used in welding, cutting and related processes*

The design, manufacture, testing and marking of pressure regulators used with compressed gases in welding, cutting and related processes.

BS 4019 *Core drilling equipment*

Part 1: 1974 *Basic equipment*
Drilling equipment for drilling holes 30–200 mm and yielding cores of 17–165 mm.

Part 2: 1973 *Concrete drilling equipment*
Holes 18–159 mm diameter, 300 mm long.

BS 5547: 1978 *Portable bore-hole logging equipment (down to 300 m): general characteristics*

Equipment intended for measurement of rock radioactivity.

BS 5791 *Glossary of terms for compressors, pneumatic tools and machines*

Part 1: 1979 *General*
Part 2: 1979 *Compressors*
Part 3: 1984 *Pneumatic tools and machines*

BS 2064 *Diamond abrasive products* Part 2: 1976 *Diamond abrasive circular saws and frame saws*

Circular segmental and continuous rim saws and frame saws with steel cores.

(B6) Placing, pavement, compaction plant

BS 1676: 1970 *Heaters for tar and bitumen (mobile and transportable)*

Heaters for use in roadwork and general construction work. It covers roadworthiness, capacity, construction, safety, performance, certification, instrument fitting and marking.

BS 1707: 1970 *Hot binder distributors for road surface dressing*

Mobile and transportable hot binder distributors (tar/bitumen sprayers).

BS 2096: 1954 *Method of testing oil-fired rotary dryers for use in asphalt and coated macadam plant*

A standard method for testing oil-fired rotary aggregate dryers for both continuous and batch types and for reporting the results for the type and grading of aggregates used in macadam.

BS 3136 *Cold emulsion spraying machines for roads* Part 2: 1972 *Metric units*

The essential mechanical requirements for either mobile or transportable machines spraying emulsion in the surface treatment of roads.

(B7) Hand tools

BS 192: 1982 *Open-ended wrenches*

Dimensional, testing and other requirements for open-ended wrenches within the following limits: Metric: 3.2 to 60 mm; Unified inch size: $^3/_{16}$ to $2^3/_8$ in; British Standard: $^1/_4$ to $2^1/_4$ in; Whitworth: $^3/_{16}$ to 2 in.

BS 1842: 1952 *Double-ended open-jawed spanners for BA hexagon sizes*

The manufacture, testing and marking of double-ended open jaw spanners for BA (British Association) hexagon sizes.

BS 2470: 1973 *Hexagon socket screws and wrench keys. Inch series*

The manufacture, testing, marking and permissible dimension tolerances.

BS 2558: 1954 *Tubular box spanners*

The manufacture, the grading, testing, marking in A/F, W, BA, and permissible tolerances. Metric sizes are included in supplement No. 1: 1968.

BS 2575: 1955 *Square nut spanners (Post Office type)*

The manufacture, testing, size marking and tolerances for open ended spanners intended for square nuts used on outdoors equipment. Commonly called Post Office type. The size is followed by the letter W referring to the nominal bolt diameter together with the nominal fractional size and the letters BS.

BS 2583: 1955 *Podger spanners*

The manufacture, testing, size marking and tolerances for podger spanners (rat tail spanners). These have an open ended spanner at one end and a rat tail taper at the other. The rat tail is often used to force the bolt holes of two steel members into line and for similar heavy work to aid the insertion of a bolt.

BS 3555: 1962 *Ring spanners*

The manufacture, testing, size marking, tolerances, dimensions of material and finish of bi-hexagonal ring spanners of both cranked and flat types, both single and double-ended.

BS 3594 *Pipe wrenches*

Part 1: 1963 *Stillson type wrenches*
Covers manufacture, quality, finish, testing and marking.
    The nominal size of the wrench is the overall length with the jaws fully open. The size of pipe which can be safely handled is shown in column 2 of Table 208. The jaws are fully open when the movable jaw is flush with the back face of the frame as shown in Figure 115.

Table 208 *Dimensions and test loads: Stillson type wrenches*

1	2
Nominal size L	Maximum (safe) capacity D*
in	in
8	1.072
10	1.346
12	1.687
14	1.919
18	2.394
24	3.014
36	4.019
48	5.534

*Equal to maximum outside diameter of black tube to BS 1387 *Steel tubes and tubulars*.

(From Table 1: BS 3594: Part 1: 1963)

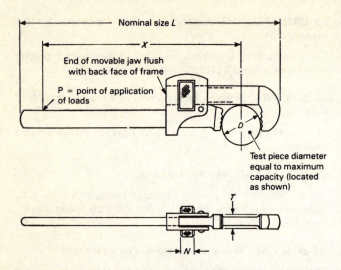

(Figure 2: BS 3594: Part 1: 1963)

Figure 115 *Dimensions of Stillson type wrenches and test data*

Part 2: 1965 *Footprint type wrenches*
The manufacture, dimensions, quality, finish, testing and marking. The nominal size is the overall length of the hook and the maximum safe capacity is shown in Figure 116 and Table 209.

BS 4006   *Socket spanners*

Supplement No. 1: 1968   *Metric sizes*
The nomenclature of the parts, the form, dimensions, material, manufacture, marking, finish and testing of manually operated steel sockets with square drives, the related components and driving handles.

BS 2559   *Screwdrivers*

Part 1: 1971   *Screwdrivers for slotted head screws*
The manufacture, testing, size and marking. The blade shape is internationally agreed and the nominal size is the length of the blade.

Note: Screwdrivers in this part of the standard which have plastic handles are not intended to be used as fully insulated tools. *They are not intended to give any degree of protection against electric shock* (see Part 3).

Part 2: 1973   *Screwdrivers and screwdriver bits for recessed head screws*
The manufacture, testing, sizing and marking.
    The form of the screwdriver head is a point of cruciform section. Screwdriver bits have one end suitable for gripping in the jaws or socket of hand or power operated drivers.

Part 3: 1973   *Insulated screwdrivers*
The manufacture of screwdrivers as described in Parts 1 and 2 *but specially insulated* for use on live electrical apparatus up to

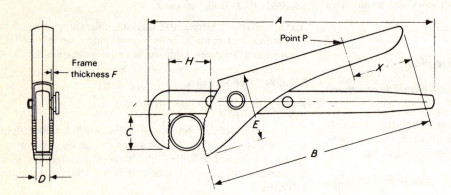

Enlarged view of pivot pin

(Figure 2: BS 3594: Part 2: 1965)

Figure 116 *Dimensions of Footprint type wrenches and test data*

Table 209   *Dimensions, capacities and test loads of Footprint type wrenches*
Dimensions in inches

1	2	3	9	10	13	14	15	16
Nominal size (overall length)	Length of frame	Depth of jaw	Thread diameter UNC or Whitworth	No. of adjusting holes in hook (minimum)	Pitch of holes	Maximum safe capacity	Proof torque	Load position (see Figure 125)
A	B	C					lbf/in	X
6	$4\frac{7}{8}$	1	$\frac{1}{4}$	4	$\frac{3}{8}$	1.346	1000	$1\frac{1}{2}$
7	6	1	$\frac{1}{4}$	4	$\frac{3}{8}$	1.687	1200	$1\frac{1}{2}$
9	$7\frac{1}{4}$	$1\frac{1}{2}$	$\frac{5}{16}$	4	$\frac{5}{8}$	1.919	2400	$1\frac{1}{2}$
12	$10\frac{5}{8}$	$1\frac{7}{8}$	$\frac{3}{8}$	5	$\frac{5}{8}$	2.394	5000	$1\frac{1}{2}$
14	$12\frac{3}{4}$	$1\frac{7}{8}$	$\frac{3}{8}$	5	$\frac{5}{8}$	3.014	7000	$1\frac{1}{2}$

Note: Dimensions are nominal. The values in column 14 are equal to the maximum outside diameter of tubes to BS 1387 *Steel tubes and tubulars suitable for screwing to BS 21 pipe threads*.

(From Table 1 BS 3594: Part 2: 1965)

and including 650 V. The blade insulation, the insulation material and dimensions, testing and marking are included.

Part 4: 1973 *Ratchet screwdrivers*

All of Parts 1 and 2 apply and this part is primarily concerned with the manufacture, testing assembly, finish and marking of a screwdriver with a ratchet of wheels and pawls. This part also applies to ratchets which accept interchangeable bits but does not apply to spiral ratchet screwdrivers (see Part 5).

Part 5: 1974 *Spiral ratchet screwdrivers*

The manufacture, testing, sizing, marking and nomenclature of a spiral ratchet mechanism. The standard specifies three sizes: No. 1 light duty, No. 2 medium duty, and No. 3 heavy duty in relation to slotted headed screws as described in Part 1. The points of screwdriver bit for use on recessed head screws are as described in Part 2.

BS 876: 1981 *Hand hammers*

The manufacture, form, forging, finish, marking, mass, testing and dimension of 11 different forms of hand hammers. A reading of the full standard is recommended. The safe use of hammers is also described.

BS 1919: 1983 *Hacksaw blades*

The manufacture, nomenclature, dimensions and sizing, pitch of teeth, tolerances, testing and marking of low alloy steel and high speed steel, all hard and flexible types for hand use, and high speed steel for power use; and bimetallic types.

BS 3159 *Woodworking saws for hand use*

Part 1: 1959 *Hand saws*

Part 2: 1962 *Tenon and dovetail saws*
The manufacture, classification, details of teeth, marking, and testing taper-ground and flat-ground hand saws for cutting timber. Class 1 and 2 saws are for the use of craftsmen and Class 3 and 4 for general use.

BS 6271: 1982 *Miniature hacksaw blades*

Methods of testing and manufacture.

BS 1943: 1975 *Woodworking chisels and gouges*

Form, nomenclature, manufacture, dimensions, characteristics, testing and marking.

BS 3066: 1981 *Engineers' cold chisels and allied tools*

The nomenclature, manufacture, dimensions, type, form, finish, testing and marking of eight different allied cold chisels. An appendix gives a general illustration of each chisel, the work for which it is suitable and the safe use of such chisels.

BS 3623: 1981 *Woodworkers' metal-bodied planes*

The nomenclature, manufacture, component parts, dimensions, tolerances, testing and marking of eight principal classes of metal-bodied woodworkers planes covering 16 different major forms.
  Figure 117 is a typical illustration from the standard.

BS 1937: 1953 *Engineers' ratchets braces and drilling pillars*

The nomenclature, definitions, manufacture, finish, assembly, dimensions and testing. Ratchet braces of this type are normally used for drills, reamers or similar small tools having Morse taper or square taper shanks.

BS 1978: 1965 *Bit braces*

The nomenclature, manufacture, components, accuracy, finish, testing and marking of bit braces primarily designed for rotating auger bits and bit stock drills. The standard covers both plain and ratchet braces. Figure 118 is a typical illustration from the standard.

BS 2054: 1953 *Augers and auger bits*

The sizes, dimensions, nomenclature, manufacture, form, accuracy, finish, testing and marking of four auger and auger bits as shown in Figure 119, for use in braces to BS 1978.

BS 2556: 1973 *Hand and breast drills*

The dimensions, materials, assembly, finish, strength and performance of hand drills up to 8 mm capacity and breast drills up to 12.5 mm capacity.

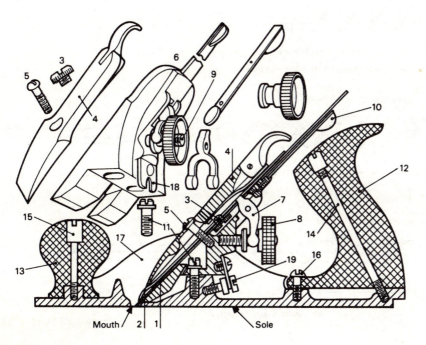

Key

1 Cutter
2 Cap iron
3 Cap screw
4 Level cap assembly
5 Lever cap screw
6 Frog assembly
7 Y adjusting lever
8 Adjusting nut
9 Adjusting screw
10 Lateral adjusting lever
11 Screw and washer for frog
12 Handle
13 Knob
14 Bolt and nut for handle
15 Bolt and nut for knob
16 Screw for handle toe
17 Plane body
18 Clip and screw for frog
19 Adjusting screw for frog

Note: This is a typical design

(Figure 2: BS 3623: 1981)

Figure 117 *Nomenclature of adjustable bench planes*
Note: This is a typical design

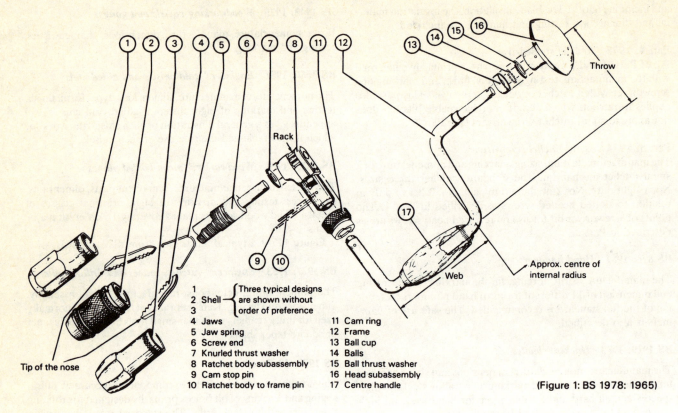

1 ⎫
2 ⎬ Shell Three typical designs
3 ⎭   are shown without
             order of preference
4 Jaws
5 Jaw spring
6 Screw end
7 Knurled thrust washer
8 Ratchet body subassembly
9 Cam stop pin
10 Ratchet body to frame pin

11 Cam ring
12 Frame
13 Ball cup
14 Balls
15 Ball thrust washer
16 Head subassembly
17 Centre handle

(Figure 1: BS 1978: 1965)

Figure 118   *Nomenclature of Type 1 bit brace*

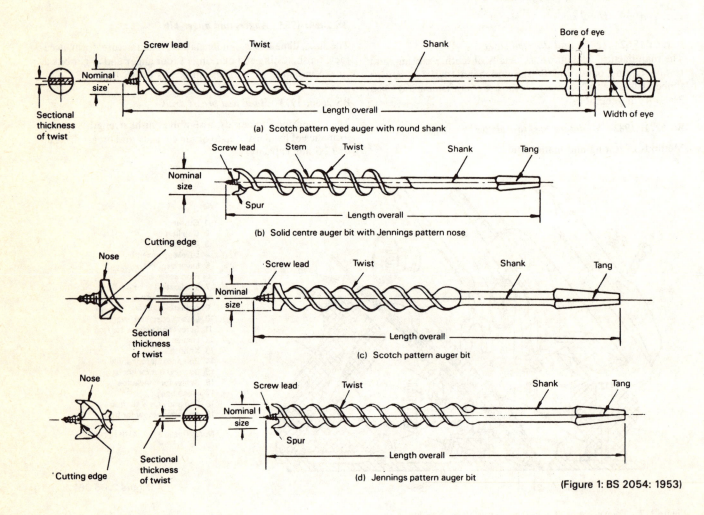

(a) Scotch pattern eyed auger with round shank

(b) Solid centre auger bit with Jennings pattern nose

(c) Scotch pattern auger bit

(d) Jennings pattern auger bit

(Figure 1: BS 2054: 1953)

Figure 119   *Nomenclature of augers and auger bits*

BS 1421: 1947 *Picks, beater picks and mattocks*

The form and dimensions, tolerances, weight, material of manufacture, testing, finishing, marking and inspection, for each implement and for helves.

BS 3388: 1973 *Forks, shovels and spades*

Preferred range of general tools and the dimensions, materials, construction, finish and testing.

BS 4078: 1966 *Cartridge-operated fixing tools*

The design, construction, safety and performance requirements. Included is an appendix of recommendations for the use and maintenance of cartridge operated fixing tools.

BS 2769 1964 *Portable electric motor-operated tools*

The general requirements, special requirements, the classification and normal operating conditions of portable electric motor operated tools for indoor or outdoor use. The standard is limited to tools operating on 250 V a.c. or d.c. for hand held or 440 V d.c. or multi-phase a.c. for other tools. Included are specifications for assembly, dimensions, voltage, classification, testing, insulating and marking.

  BSI certification is recommended for all tools.

BS 673: 1984 *Shanks for pneumatic tools and fitting dimensions of chuck bushings*

The sizes of shanks for use with pneumatic tools and their associated chuck fittings for five main types of shank.

BS 871: 1981 *Abrasive papers and cloths*

The form and dimensions, grading, quality, testing, workmanship and marking of abrasive papers and cloths for both general and technical purpose products and for both metalworking and woodworking.

BS 498 *Files and rasps*

Part 1: 1960 *Rasps and engineers' files*
The manufacture, dimensions, tolerances, testing and marking of twenty-six different rasps and engineer's files. Illustrated.

BS 2939: 1974 *Wire brushes*

The materials, manufacture, sizes and marking of hand and rotary brushes for pneumatic or electric tools and stationary grinders. The range of brushes covered ranges from hand brooms to jewellers' and silversmiths' brushes.

BS 1958: 1953 *Tools for soldered socket-spigot joints for lead and lead alloy pipes*

The necessary kit of tools, their manufacture, size, shape, material and marking.

BS 3087: 1959 *Pliers, pincers and nippers*

General requirements, nominal dimensions, tolerances and weights. The quality and life of the tools is ensured by specified tests. Tables give specific requirements for each type.

BS 3088: 1959 *Adjustable hand reamers with inserted blades*

Ranges of expansion, numbers of blades and general dimensions, features and marking.

BS 3322: 1981 *Carpenter's squares and bevels*

The manufacture, materials, nominal sizes, dimensions, quality, finish, testing and marking.

BS 3823: *Grading of wood handles for hand tools*

Part 1: 1965 *Ash and hickory handles*
The criteria for use in grading handles intended for fitting to general purpose hand tools, giving the requirements for freedom from defects and permissible blemishes which are tolerable in respect of the various grades of handles.

BS 5431: 1976 *Bending springs for use with copper tubes for water, gas and sanitation*

The manufacture, material, dimensions, properties, finish, protection, designation and identification of steel bending springs to support the walls, during bending operations, of copper tubes up to and including 22 mm diameter.

(B8) **Ancillary plant** (no entry)

(B9) **Construction plant, tools** (no entry)

(D) Construction operations

(D1)   Protecting

BS 5228 *Code of practice for noise control on construction and demolition sites*

Part 1: 1984 *Code of practice for basic information and procedures for noise control*
This recommends methods of noise control, and gives guidance on the range of methods for predicting and measuring noise, minimizing the impact of site noise on the neighbourhood, relevant legislation (see also Part 2), and liaison procedures.

Part 2: 1984 *Guide to noise control legislation for construction and demolition, including road construction and maintenance*
This sets out the legislation.

(Part 3 deals with opencast coal workings.)

Part 4: 1986 *Code of practice for noise control applicable to piling operations.*
This code supplements the information given in Part 1 with information especially relevant to piling works. It sets out recommendations for noise control measures which can be adopted to ensure good practice and enable piling by any of the recognized techniques to be carried out economically with as little disturbance to the community as is practicable.

BS 5607: 1978 *Code of practice for the safe use of explosives in the construction industry*

The safe handling, transport and use of blasting explosives and accessories in construction and demolition operations. The use of explosives in special applications such as tunnelling, demolition, excavation and underwater working are all fully covered.
  This is a highly specialized standard and full reading is recommended where the reader is likely to be involved in such operations.

BS 6164: 1982 *Code of practice for safety in tunnelling in the construction industry*

This is a complex standard dealing with all aspects of safety in tunnelling. A full reading of the standard is recommended where reference to such information is required. See also Table 0 'Physical environment', section (18) 'Civil engineering facilities'.

(D2)   Clearing, preparing

BS 6187: 1982 *Code of practice for demolition*

Preliminary procedures, methods of and suitability for various types and elements of structure for demolition and the protective measures. A full reading of the standard is necessary where this type of work is involved.

(D3)   Transporting, lifting (see also 'cranes' in (B3))

CP 3010: 1972 *Safe use of cranes (mobile cranes, tower cranes and derrick cranes)*

All aspects of safe use, installation and dismantling cranes. Requirements for drivers, slingers and signallers, and government regulations and statutory requirements on testing and examination are summarized.

(D4)   Forming: cutting, shaping, fitting

This section is arranged with the relevant glossary (BS 499) followed by *materials and workmanship*; and *testing and certification*.

BS 499 *Welding terms and symbols*

Part 1: 1983 *Glossary for welding, brazing and thermal cutting*
Terms, together with illustrations. The terms are arranged in seven classified sections giving terms common to more than one process; terms relating to welding with pressure; fusion welding; brazing; testing; weld imperfections and thermal cutting. For those with a particular interest in this area a reading of the full standard is recommended.

Part 2: 1980 *Symbols for welding*
The symbols cover the most common types of welds without the requirement for excessive notes on the drawing or the need to show additional views. It is not intended to cover complex welds which are most simply shown by a specific detail drawing. Part 2C: 1980 is a chart of these symbols.

Materials and workmanship

As the titles to most standards indicate the content and the inter-relationship, the majority of this section is a list of these.

BS 638 *Arc-welding power sources, equipment and accessories*

Part 1: 1979 *Oil-cooled power sources for manual, semi-automatic and automatic metal-arc welding and for TIG welding*
Part 2: 1979 *Air-cooled power sources for manual metal arc welding with covered electrodes and for TIG welding*
Part 3: 1979 *Air-cooled power sources for semi-automatic and automatic metal-arc welding*
Part 4: 1979 *Welding cables carrying the welding current in arc welding circuits*
Part 6: 1984 *Safety requirements*

BS 3019 *TIG welding*

Part 1: 1984 *TIG welding of aluminium, magnesium and their alloys*
This identifies the parent metals, consumables, preparation for welding and welding details for TIG (tungsten and inert gas) welding. Appendices set out the selection of filler metal, use of tungsten electrodes, welding equipment and recommended joint details.

Part 2: 1960 *Austenitic stainless and heat-resisting steels*
As Part 1 for austenitic stainless and heat resisting steel plates, sheet and strip bars and forgings, covered electrodes depositing weld metal having a tensile strength of not more than 650 N/mm² (42 tonf/in²).

BS 2493: 1985 *Low-alloy steel electrodes for manual metal-arc welding*

BS 2926: 1984 *Chromium–nickel austenitic and chromium steel electrodes for manual metal-arc welding*

BS 4165: 1984 *Electrode wires and fluxes for the submerged arc welding of carbon steel and medium-tensile steel*

Electrode wires, solid or cored, and fluxes for steels having a tensile strength of not more than 700 N/mm² (45 tonf/in²).

BS 5135: 1984 *The process of arc-welding of carbon and carbon–manganese steels*

Parent metals, consumables, details, preparation and assembly, inspection and testing.

BS 5741: 1979 *Pressure regulators used in welding, cutting and related processes*

For pressure regulators, other than pipeline regulators, for use with compressed gases up to 200 bar (20 MPa) and for the dissolved acetylene used.

BS 1453: 1977 *Filler materials for gas welding*

The requirements and chemicals composition for the most common metals and alloys.

BS 1845: 1984 *Filler metals for brazing*

A range of eight groups of filler metals and alloys.

BS 2901 *Filler rods and wires for gas-shielded arc welding*

Part 1: 1983 *Ferritic steels*
Part 2: 1983 *Austenitic stainless steels*
Part 3: 1983 *Copper and copper alloys*
Part 4: 1983 *Aluminium and aluminium alloys and magnesium alloys*
Part 5: 1983 *Nickel and nickel alloys*

Each part specifies the requirements and chemical composition of packaging and marking.

BS 3571 *General recommendations for manual inert-gas metal-arc welding*

Part 1: 1985 *MIG welding of aluminium and aluminium alloys*
Intended primarily for the manual welding of aluminium base materials 1.6 − 25.4 mm ($^1/_{16}$ − 1 in) thick.

BS 1753 *Brazing*

Part 1: 1986
Joints by brazing 21 different parent metals by seven different heating media. For each a table is provided showing the recommended filler for each parent metal.

BS 1724: 1959 *Bronze welding by gas*

Bronze welding five different parent metals or combinations of any of the five by the use of the combination of three different gases.

Testing and certification

As with the preceding section, titles are seen largely to be self-explanatory.

BS 4870 *Approval testing of welding procedures*

Part 1: 1981 *Fusion welding of steels*
The approval testing of a welding procedure representative of that to be used in production, for the fusion of ferritic steel or austenitic stainless steel but not including cast-to-cast fabrication.

Part 2: 1982 *TIG or MIG welding of aluminium and its alloys*
The approval testing of welding procedures representative of that to be used in production.

Part 3: 1985 *Arc welding of tube to tube-plate joints in metallic materials*
Examination, testing and recording results. A successful operative is approved under clauses 5 and 6 of BS 4871 (which follows).

BS 4871 *Approval testing of welders working to approved welding procedures*

Part 1: 1982 *Fusion welding of steel*

Part 2: 1982 *TIG or MIG welding of aluminium and its alloys*
Both parts specify the requirements for the approval testing of welders to be engaged in fusion welding where the welding procedure does not itelf have to be approved. Part 1 for manual or semi-automatic fusion welding for ferritic steels or austenitic stainless steels and Part 2 for fabrications of sheet, plate and pipe, with 12 test welds.

Part 3: 1985 *Arc welding of tube to tube-plate joints in metallic materials*

The range of processes covers manual, semi-automatic, automatic and mechanised processes. A successful operative is approved under clauses 5 and 6.

BS 3451: 1973 *Methods of testing fusion welds in aluminium and aluminium alloys*

All forms of material including pipes and castings. It covers visual, destructive and non-destructive manual tests together with radiographic testing.

BS 3923 *Methods for ultrasonic examination of welds*

Part 1: 1978 *Manual examination of fusion welds in ferritic steels*
Part 2: 1972 *Automatic examination of fusion welded butt joints in ferritic steels*
Part 3: 1972 *Manual examination of nozzle welds*

The last of these deals with welds and branches to boiler drums and pressure vessels.

BS 4872 *Approval testing of welders when welding procedure approval is not required*

Part 1: 1982 *Fusion welding of steel*
Part 2: 1976 *TIG or MIG welding of aluminium and its alloys*

Part 1 deals with manual or semi-automatic fusion welding for ferritic steels or austenitic stainless steels; Part 2 with TIG or MIG welding of aluminium or aluminium-alloy fabrications.

BS 6072: 1981 *Method for magnetic particle flaw detection*

BS 6443: 1984 *Method for penetrant flaw detection*

These two deal with non-destructive testing techniques.

BS 5289: 1976 *Code of practice for visual inspection of fusion welded joints*

The use of simple measuring devices. Illustrations of good welds and common visual faults are shown.

BS 709: 1983 *Methods of destructive testing fusion welded joints and weld metal in steel*

BS 1140: 1980 *Resistance of welding of uncoated and coated low-carbon steel*

BS 2600 *Radiographic examination of fusion welded butt joints in steel*

Part 1: 1983 *Method for steel 2 mm up to and including 50 mm thick*
Part 2: 1973 *Over 50 mm up to and including 200 mm thick*

BS 2630: 1982 *Resistance projection welding of uncoated low-carbon steel sheet and strip using embossed projections*

This standard covers the testing of resistance projection welding using embossed projections on test specimen.

BS 2996: 1958   *Projection welding of low-carbon wrought steel studs, bosses, bolts, nuts and annular rings*

Tests carried out on production pieces or special test pieces similar to production pieces.

BS 4577: 1970   *Materials for resistance welding electrodes and ancillary equipment*

BS 5135: 1984   *The process of arc welding of carbon and carbon manganese steels*

General requirements for the manual, semi-automatic and automatic (mechanized) metal arc welding of steel, in all forms including circular and rectangular hollow sections.

BS 4206: 1967   *Methods of testing fusion welds in copper and copper alloys*

All forms of material up to 40 mm thick including pipes and castings by both non-destructive and destructive methods.

BS 1723   *Brazing*

Part 1: 1986   *Specification for brazing*
Gives general requirements for brazing and requirements specific to the method of brazing including flame, induction, resistance, furnace, immersion, infra-red electron beam and laser brazing.

Part 2: 1986   *Guide to brazing*
Covers principles, categories of brazed joints, joint design, materials, methods of brazing, economics of brazing and quality assurance. Four categories are distinguished, decreasing in importance.

(D5)   Treatment: drilling, boring

(D6)   Placing: laying, applying

(D7)   Making good, repairing

(D8)   Clearing up

(D9)   Other construction operations (no entries)

(E)   Composition, etc. (no entry)

(F)   Shape, size, etc.

(F1)   Shape (no entry)

(F4)   Size, dimensional co-ordination

PD 6432   *Dimensional co-ordination in building. Arrangement of building components and assemblies within functional groups*

Part 1: 1969   *Functional groups 1, 2, 3 and 4.*
Part 2: 1969   *Functional group 5.*
Components and their application are divided into six functional groups:

1 Structure.
2 External envelope.
3 Internal subdivision.
4 Services and drainage.
5 Fixtures, furniture and equipment.
6 External works.

Components are classified into groups lettered A, B, C and D in order of importance in dimensional co-ordination. The same classification is used in PD 6444 *Recommendations for the co-ordination of dimensions in building* Part 1: 1969 *Basic spaces for structure, external envelope and internal subdivision. (Functional Groups 1, 2 and 3)* and Part 2: 1971 *Co-ordinating sizes of fixtures, furniture and equipment (Functional Group 5).*

Much additional information is to be found in such publications as Design Bulletin 6, *Space in the home* (D of E/HMSO).

The following standards relate to this classification method.

BS 6100:   Part 1: s1.5: ss1.5.1: 1984   Co-ordination of dimensions, tolerances and accuracy

This glossary distinguishes building reference systems and defines dimensions and dimensional and modular co-ordination.

BS 4011: 1966   *Recommendations for the co-ordination of dimensions in building. Co-ordinating sizes for building components and assemblies*

■ AD (Reg. A1/2)

First, second, third and fourth preference sizes are set out as 300, 100 and 50 and 25 mm (the last two up to 300 mm only) in this standard.

BS 4330: 1968   *Recommendations for the co-ordination of dimensions in building. Controlling dimensions*

Definitions in this standard include *controlling dimension*, *controlling line*, *zone*, *controlling zone* and *neutral zone*. Figures 120 and 121 show the use of these.

A framework of 'controlling dimensions' based on BS 4011 is given.

Vertical controlling dimensions are as follows. Note that all dimensions not multiples of 300 mm are second-preference dimensions and are here shown in brackets.

1 *Floor to ceiling heights* ('A' on Figure 120) 1500 and 1800 for agricultural buildings only, 2100 for farm buildings garages and multi-storey car parks (2300), 2400, (2500), (2600), 2700, (2800), (2900) and 3000 (× 300 to) 6600 (× 600 up) (all in mm).
2 *Zones* for floors and roofs ('B' on Figure 120) of (100), (200), (250, for housing only), 300, (400), (500), 600 (× 300 to) 2100 (all in mm).
3 *Floor to floor* and *floor to roof* heights ('C' on Figure 120) of (2600, for housing only), 2700 (× 300 to) 8400 (× 600 up) (all in mm).

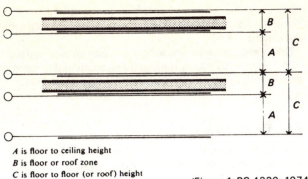

A is floor to ceiling height
B is floor or roof zone
C is floor to floor (or roof) height

(Figure 1: BS 4330: 1974)

Figure 120 *Vertical controlling dimensions*

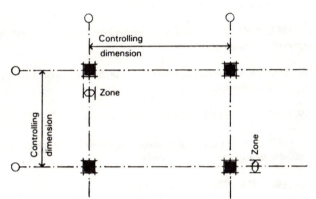

Method A Controlling lines on the axial lines of load-bearing walls and columns

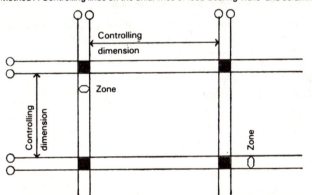

Method B Controlling lines on the boundaries of zones

(Figure 3: BS 4330: 1974)

Figure 121 *Horizontal controlling dimensions*

4 *Changes* in level are recommended as 300 (× 300 to) 2400 (× 600 up) (with 1300, 1400, 1700, 2000 and 2300 for housing only) (all in mm).

Horizontal controlling dimensions are between axes or between zone boundaries (for example column faces). For zones 300 mm and its multiples, as first preference sizes, and 100 mm and its multiples as second preferences, are sizes following BS 4011, and the spacings are 800 (for housing only) and 900 (× 300 up) (all in mm). See Figure 121 and Appendix B of the standard.

BS 4606: 1970 *Recommendations for the co-ordination of dimensions in building. Co-ordinating sizes for rigid flat sheet materials used in building*

This standard is related to BS 4330 and BS 4011, and recom-

mends *widths* of 600, 900 and 1200 mm and *lengths* of 1800, 2400, 2700 and 3000 mm.

BS 4643: 1970 *Glossary of terms relating to joints and jointing in building*

BS 5578 *Building construction – stairs*

Part 2: 1978 *Modular co-ordination: specification for co-ordinating dimensions for stairs and stair openings*
See Table 1 Building elements (24) stairs, etc.

BS 6222: *Domestic kitchen equipment*

Part 1: 1982 *Co-ordinating dimensions*

PD 6446: 1970 *Recommendations for the co-ordination of dimensions in building. Combinations of sizes*

DD 22: 1972 *Recommendations for the co-ordination of dimensions in building. Tolerances and fits for building. The calculation of work sizes and joint clearances for building components* (see also section (F6) tolerance, accuracy)

DD 51 *Guidance on dimensional co-ordination in building* (in eight sections published in 1977)

(F5) Weight

BS 648: 1964 *Schedule of weights of building materials*

The object of this schedule is to standardize the data employed in structural and other calculations. Average weights are given and these are sufficiently accurate for general purposes in calculating dead loads in building work and will be taken as acceptable by all authorities responsible for verifying design calculations. In some instances it has been necessary to include tolerances on each side of the standard weight and there are some cases where, owing to many different densities being produced, it has not been possible to choose a simple notional figure and here a range of values has been given. Some weights are given per m³ whereas others are given per m super for standard thicknesses and other materials such as those of pipes are given per m run of length for standard cross-sections.

The following extract from this standard indicates the method of presentation of this valuable information. No structural designer or builder's agent should be without this standard.

Bronze, phosphor, wrought (BS 369 and 407)	558 lb/ft³	(8938 kg/m³)
Carpet	$0.6 \, {}^{+\,0.1}_{-\,0.2}$ lb/ft²	$(2.9 \, {}^{+\,0.5}_{-\,1.0}$ kg/m²)
Cast stone	140 lb/ft³	(2243 kg/m³)
Cement	90 lb/ft³	(1442 kg/m³)
Concrete		
Aerated	$40 \, {}^{+\,60}_{-\,10}$ lb/ft³	$(641 \, {}^{+\,961}_{-\,160}$ kg/m³)
Brick aggregate	125 ± 10 lb/ft³	(2002 ± 160 kg/m³)
Natural aggregates	144 lb/ft³	(2307 kg/m³)
Lightweight aggregates		
Normal	70 ± 30 lb/ft³	(1121 ± 481 kg/m³)
Structural	$110 \, {}^{+\,15}_{-\,10}$ lb/ft³	$(1762 \, {}^{+\,240}_{-\,160}$ kg/m³)
Heavy weight aggregates e.g. barytes, ilmenite, magnetite, etc.	200 ± 10 lb/ft³	(3204 ± 160 kg/m³)
Steel shot	330 ± 15 lb/ft³	(5286 ± 240 kg/m³)
No-fines	110 ± 5 lb/ft³	(1762 ± 80 kg/m³)
Organic aggregate	80 ± 35 lb/ft³	(1281 ± 561 kg/m³)
Diatomaceous earth	$80 \, {}^{+\,7}_{-\,4}$ lb/ft³	$(1281 \, {}^{+\,112}_{-\,64}$ kg/m³)

Copper

Cast	545 lb/ft^3	(8730 kg/m^3)
Wrought		
Sheet and strip		
0·048 in (18 SWG)	2·2 lb/ft^2	(10·8 kg/m^2)
0·036 in (20 SWG)	1·7 lbft^2	(8·3 kg/m^2)
0·028 in (22 SWG)	1·3 lb/ft^2	(6·3 kg/m^2)
0·022 in (24 SWG)	1·0 lb/ft^2	(4·9 kg/m^2)
Other wrought forms	558 lb/ft^3	(8938 kg/m^3)

Cork

Granular, 0·188 in		
(4·8 mm) size,		
loosely packed	7·5 lb/ft^3	(120 kg/m^3)
Board		
Normal per 1 in		
(25·4 mm) thick	0·9 lb/ft^2	(4·4 kg/m^2)
Semi-compressed		
per 1 in (25·4 mm)		
thick	1·0 lb/ft^2	(4·9 kg/m^2)

(F6) Tolerance, accuracy

BS 5964: 1980 *Methods for setting out and measurement of buildings: permissible measuring deviations*

This standard forms one of a series concerning measurement methods for building, and can be regarded as a frame for further reference standards for all setting-out work. The other documents of this series are currently under preparation.

It deals with the different stages of the setting out work, that is the measuring of the primary framework (traverses, grids, etc.) on the site, the setting out of reference lines (baselines), the transfer (plumbing up) of reference lines to other floors, the setting out of position points and the levelling procedure for these different stages.

It gives values for permissible deviations when measuring and setting out and recommends certain procedures and instruments to be used.

Guidance is given on how inaccuracies can be controlled during the setting out process when using instruments and methods which are currently in common use in building construction.

Definitions include:

Reference points ('primary', 'secondary' and 'position points') which may be related to a *grid* on plan.
Reference levels ('primary', 'secondary' and 'position level') related to levels.
Check measurement, anblock method for relating adjacent local systems.
Discrepancy, deviation, permissible deviation and *tolerance*.

The standard continues by identifying the methodologies and degrees of precision appropriate to various categories of work, typically earthwork without any particular accuracy requirement, earthwork subject to accuracy requirements, *in situ* cast concrete structures, kerbs, etc and precast concrete structures, steel structures, etc.

BS 5606: 1978 *Code of practice for accuracy in building*

This code presents the results of a survey of building accuracy leading to the determination of 'characteristic accuracy' for each of a number of forms of construction, set out in appendices. It shows how such data may be used in specifying permissible deviations. It outlines features of the building process which affect accuracy needing consideration at the design stage and recommends methods for achieving acceptable results during setting out and construction. The code is intended to be applied to building rather than to civil engineering works.

It deals with specifying permissible deviations, design considerations, setting out on site, control of inaccuracy, and (in appendices) the data terms used in the accuracy survey,

reference grids, some typical setting out methods, measuring instruments and their use, and checking and correcting optical instruments.

Tables give characteristic accuracy values determined from a survey and permissible deviations for elements and components of brickwork, *in situ* concrete, precast concrete, steel and timber.

(F7) Dimensional systems

This section deals with conversion of imperial units of measurement and their conversion to the metric systems as follows:

BS 350 *Conversion factors and tables*

Part 1: 1974 (1983) *Basis of tables. Conversion factors*

Supplement No 1: 1967 (1982) (PD 6203) to BS 350 Part 2 *Additional tables for SI conversions*

BS 1957: 1953 *Presentation of numerical values (fineness of expression; rounding of numbers)*

BS 2856: 1973 *Precise conversion of inch and metric sizes on engineering drawings*

BS 3763: 1976 *The International System of units (SI)*

BS 5555: 1981 *SI Units and recommendations for the use of their multiples and of certain other units*

PD 5686: 1978 *The use of SI Units*

BS 5775 *Quantities, units, and symbols*

Part 0: 1982 *General principles* (of the 13 parts, those most general principles relevant to building construction are)
Part 1: 1979 *Space and time*
Part 3: 1979 *Mechanics*
Part 4: 1979 *Heat*
Part 7: 1979 *Acoustics*

(G)   Appearance, etc.

(G1)   Appearance (no entry)

(G4)   Texture, pattern (no entry)

(G5)   Colour

There are nine standards which deal with colour of which the key standard is BS 5252. Of the other eight standards six deal with colours of specific materials or elements of buildings, one with colours for identification, coding and special purposes while the ninth gives a glossary of vision and colour terminology.

BS 5252: 1976   *Framework for colour co-ordination for building purposes*

This standard establishes a framework within which 237 colours have been selected as the source for all building colour standards and the means of co-ordinating them. It is not itself a range of colours for any particular product and is not to be used to specify British Standard colours. A colour is only standardized when it is included in another British Standard, such as those that have been derived for paints (BS 4800), vitreous enamel (BS 4900), plastics (BS 4901) and sheet and tile flooring (BS 4902). Such standards contain only a proportion of the total colours in this British Standard, selected to meet design requirements within relevant technical and economic constraints.

Small scale surface patterns or pronounced texture may prevent a direct match with a colour in this standard. In this event the relevant colours would be reproduced in the derived standards with their identification code together with a clear statement that they are target colours only. In the case of small scale surface patterns, the approximations to the target colours shown are to be in terms of the composite or dominant colours, not in terms of the individual colours making up the pattern.

Colour patterns in the card which accompanies the standard are shown in semi-gloss finish for visual indication of colour in daylight. For matching purposes a fan (BS 5252F) contains larger patches of all colours in this standard.

Because the character of light in which colours are compared affects them comparisons should be made in good diffuse daylight or under an illuminant which meets BS 950 Part 1.

The standard locates and relates 237 colours in terms of selected steps in the visual attributes of hue, greyness and weight.

Hue is the attribute of redness, yellowness, blueness, etc. The framework has 12 horizontal hue rows plus a further row for neutral colours (that is without hue) numbered and named as:

02 red-purple
04 red
06 yellow-red
08 yellow-red
10 yellow
12 green-yellow
14 green
16 blue-green
18 blue
20 purple-blue
22 violet
24 purple
00 neutral

Greyness is the estimated grey content of colours. The framework divides the colours into five groups, lettered A to E, representing steps of diminishing greyness as follows:

Group A: grey.
Group B: nearly grey.
Group C: grey/clear.

Group D: nearly clear.
Group E: clear.

Weight is a subjective term for lightness modified as necessary to produce colours of the same character in different hues.

The framework provides for up to eight vertical columns of colour of equal weight in each greyness group ranging from lightest on the left to darkest or heaviest on the right. The columns are numbered from the left-hand columns of A group (01) to the right hand column of E group (58). The numbering, however, is not regular across eight columns in each group because some column numbers were established as standard in the 1972 edition of BS 4800 and have been retained for convenience of reference.

Thus each colour may be identified by this three part coding system, for example:

Colour code	Hue	Approximate Munsell reference
00A01	Neutral	N8.5
10A03	Yellow	5Y 8/0.5
08B15	Yellow-red	10Y R 9.25/1
12B17	Green-yellow	2.5GY 8/2
04C33	Red	7.5 R 8/4
10C31	Yellow	5Y 9/2
04D45	Red	7.5R 3/10
18E49	Blue	5B 9/2
00E55	Black	N 1.5
00E55	White	N 9.5

The standards dealing with colours of specific materials or elements of buildings are as follows.

BS 4800: 1981   *Paint colours for building purposes*

This standard specifies 100 colours (including black and white) for paints, and their available surface finishes. The colours have been selected from the 237 colours established in BS 5252. Because of technical or commercial limitations the inclusion of a colour in this standard does not necessarily mean that it will be available in all types of paint or in all categories of surface finish or from all manufacturers. A 'basic' selection of 32 colours (including black and white) is expected to be generally available from all manufacturers in all four surface finishes listed below while two supplementary selections should be available in accordance with individual manufacturers' commercial practices – category G (45 colours in full gloss and eggshell and category M (34 colours in matt and silk). Finishes as defined in BS 2015 are given as full gloss, eggshell (semi-gloss), silk (or satin) (semi-gloss) or matt.

BS 4900: 1976   *Vitreous enamel colours for building purposes*

This standard provides 199 colours (including black and white) selected from BS 5252 for vitreous enamels applied to metals for use as vitreous or exterior claddings for building purposes. Appendix A gives approximate Munsell references.

BS 4901: 1976   *Plastics colours for building purposes*

This standard provides 124 colours (including black and white) selected from BS 5252 for colours for opaque plastic products such as laminates and moulded and extruded components. For technical and commercial reasons the availability of each colour for every product is not implied. An appendix gives approximate Munsell references.

BS 4902: 1976   *Sheet and tile flooring colours for building purposes*

This standard provides 143 colours (including black) selected from BS 5252 for the following types of flooring.

Sheet linoleum (calendered types) cork carpet and linoleum tiles to BS 810.

Solid rubber flooring to BS 1711

Felt backed linoleum to BS 1863

Thermoplastic flooring tiles to BS 2592

PVC (vinyl) asbestos floor tiles to BS 3260

Unbacked flexible PVC flooring – homogeneous flooring to BS 3261 Part 1

Backed flexible PVC flooring – needle-loom felt backed flooring to BS 5085 Part 1

Terrazzo tiles to BS 4131

Precast terrazzo units to BS 4357

In situ terrazzo flooring – no British Standard but details in CP 204

Clay tiles for flooring to BS 1286

Ceramic mosaic flooring – no British Standard but details in CP 202

The standard does not deal with carpet or other textile flooring and floor covering. An appendix gives approximate Munsell references.

BS 4903: 1979   *External colours for farm buildings*

This standard provides 40 colours (including black and white) (19 of which are included in BS 4904) for roof and wall sheeting in asbestos cement, steel, aluminium and opaque plastics for external surfaces of farm buildings. For technical and commercial reasons the availability of every colour in every material is not implied. Colours for vitreous enamelled metal extend only to those contained in BS 4900. Equally, colours in this standard for plastics extend only to those in BS 4901 while colours for paint are extracted from BS 4800.

Application of colour range is given, broken down as main wall area and roofs, other wall areas, door and window frames and factory applied colours.

An appendix gives approximate Munsell references.

BS 4904: 1978 (1985)   *External cladding colours for building purposes*

This standard provides thirty-eight colours (including black and white) selected from BS 4252 for external cladding of aluminium, asbestos-cement, opaque glass (used with a back-up wall or similar arrangement), opaque plastics and steel. The standard includes colours for vitreous enamel for building purposes selected from BS 4900 and opaque plastics from BS 4901. An appendix gives approximate Munsell references.

BS 381C: 1980   *Colours for identification, coding and special purposes*

This standard is intended as the principal standard for surface colours for identification, coding and special purposes such as camouflage. The colours include those required by industry, public boards, government departments and other major organizations, as well as colours needed for various visual signalling and coding systems. However, the standard does not include all colours currently specified for identification purposes in other British Standards (see, for example, BS 1710: 1975 *Identification of pipelines*).

A total of 107 colours are given, forty-one are regarded as obsolete and these will be deleted from the next revision.

The standard recommends that when colours are used for identification purposes they should preferably be in association with other distinctive markings such as symbols, banding or wording. Such additional markings may be essential to people with defective colour vision, who, also, can often be helped by a suitable choice of colours.

Appendices list major organizations that use colours from BS 381C and other British Standards that specify colours to BS 381C.

BS 4727   *Glossary of electrotechnical, power, telecommunications, electronics, lighting and colour terms*

Part 4:   *Terms particular to lighting and colour*   Group 02: 1971 (1980)   *Vision and colour terminology*

This standard provides a glossary of terms covering the eye and vision, colour rendering, fundamental quantities and alphabetical index of colorimetry together with tristimulus values for the standard colorimetric observer.

(G6)   Opacity (no entry)

(G7)   Other visuals (no entry)

(G8)   Feel, smell, aural, taste, other (no entry)

(H)   Context, environment

(H1)   Climate, ecological

Although there are no standards under this heading there is one Draft for Development.

DD 93: 1984   Methods for assessing exposure to wind-driven rain.

■   AD (Reg. C4)

This offers two methods for assessing exposure to wind-driven rain, namely the local spell index and the local index method.

(H2)   Modified environments

Two standards deal with the methodology and recording of tests, designed to establish the effectiveness of elements of construction, in this most important of respects.

BS 4315   *Methods of test for resistance to air and water penetration*

This standard is in two independent parts, although both use rigs developed within BRE. In that it prescribes methods of test only, it should not be used or quoted as a specification, for a phrase in respect of a component that it 'conforms to BS 4315 . . .' is meaningless. The same point can be made of all standards solely concerned with test procedures.

Part 1: 1968   *Windows and structural gasket glazing systems*
This part gives methods of test suitable for measuring the air infiltration of windows and for determining the resistance to water penetration of windows under static pressure, and of gasket glazing systems under dynamic conditions, excluding glazing materials such as putty, mastics and sealants.

Requirements are specified for measuring air infiltration of windows (Test A), measuring resistance to water penetration of windows (Test B) and measuring resistance to water penetration of gasket glazing systems (Test C).

The trest rigs, and manner of recording results, are set out.

Part 2: 1970 (1983)   *Permeable walling constructions (water penetration)*
This part gives methods of test for measuring the resistance to water penetration of permeable walling constructions without open joints, under static air pressure. The methods are applicable to constructions which can be built in or fixed into a rigid steel frame, by means of which the wall panel can be transported and secured to the pressure-box test equipment. The first method is also applicable to walling constructions, not built into a steel frame, provided an air-tight seal can be made between the pressure-box and the front face of the panel.

Three methods of assessing the extent of water penetration are specified:

Method A: recording, by time lapse photography, the increase in area of dampness.
Method B: recording the change in weight of the specimen.
Method C: collecting and recording the amount of leakage through the specimen.

BS 5368   *Methods of testing windows*

This standard is in four parts, sequential and linked. Each part has been adopted as a European standard.

Part 1: 1976   *Air permeability test*
This part prescribes an air permeability test of windows to be fitted in exterior walls and supplied in the form of finished units in actual operating conditions. It does not apply to the joints between the windows and surrounding components and material.

Standard pressures given are 50, 100, 150, 200, 300, 400, 500 and 600 Pa (1 Pa = 1 N/m² = 0.102 mm H$_2$O) and can then be increased in steps of 250 Pa exceptionally.

Each window tested is recorded by three indices, as cubic metres of aid per hour passing through:

1   Per metre of length of opening joint.
2   Per square metre of opening light.
3   Per square metre of total surface area of the window.

Part 2: 1980   *Watertightness test under static pressure*
This part sets out methods to be used for the watertightness test under static pressure of windows fitted as in Part 1.

The record will show the pressure at which the leakage is produced and the moment when it appears. The points where the leakage appears are shown on a face view of the window, with an indication of the spraying method used.

Part 3: 1978   *Wind resistance tests*
Wind effects on windows are transmitted, among others, by positive and negative pressures that are conventionally simulated by the following tests.

The tests in this part make it possible to check that, subjected to these effects, the complete window:

1   Has a permissible deformation.
2   Maintains its characteristics.
3   Does not endanger users.

The definitions test used is for 10 seconds exposure at pressures of up to 500 Pa (compare with Part 1), and exceptionally at 250 Pa increments.

The results are expressed graphically as a function of pressure, for each point of measurement. Deformations are expressed in millimetres and pressures in pascals.

Permanent residual deformations are indicated, and damage and functional defects are shown on the sketch of the window.

Part 4: 1978   *Form of test report*
The report is to include:

1   Diagram of the test apparatus or its reference.
2   Details of mounting the test window in its surround.
3   Laboratory ambient air temperature at the time of test and air temperature of the test chamber.
4   A concise description of the window including prescribed information, checked before the tests, and in an annex a sketch of the window elevation (indicating the positions of the hard-ware – hinges, pivots, rollers, unlocking points, etc), and a diagram of the horizontal and vertical sections indicating precisely the location of the weather stripping and the means of water drainage.
5   The results obtained during each test in accordance with the paragraph 'Recording of results' for each test. The report will state that the results are valid only for the conditions under which the test was conducted.

(H4)   Amenities (no entry)

(H6)   Internal environments

The Building Regulations 1985, Part F, apply. Many references are relevant, from those dealing with space standards and planning, to fire-resistance and acoustic performance. Typically BS 5295 *Environmental cleanliness in enclosed spaces* (an AD under Regulation F1) appears in Table 1 Building elements (57) Air conditioning, ventilation.

BS 5925: 1980   *Code of practice for design of buildings: ventilation principles and designing for natural ventilation*

■ AD (Reg. F1)

Originally drafted as CP 3 Chapter 1 (c), this code is complemented by BS 5720 in respect of mechanical ventilation and air conditioning in buildings.

It covers ventilation of buildings for human occupation, gives recommended quantitative air flow rates, and these form the basis for air supply recommendations for different types of buildings and room. The basis for the choice between natural and mechanical ventilation is given.

Two periods of analysis are distinguished:

'TLV-TWA' (threshold limit value-time weighted average): the time weighted average concentration for a normal working day, or 40 hour working week, to which nearly all workers may be exposed continuously without adverse effect.

'TLV-STEL' (threshold limit value-short term exposure limit): the maximum concentration to which workers can be exposed for up to 15 minutes continuously without adverse effects, not more than four such exposures permitted, with at least 60 minutes between.

(H7) Occupancy (no entry)

(J) Mechanics

(J1) – (J3) (no entries)

(J4) Loads, forces

BS 6399 *Design loading for buildings*

Part 1: 1984 *Code of practice for dead and imposed loads*

■ AD (Regs. A1/2)

This document gives the dead and imposed loads which should be taken into account when designing buildings and certain other structures. It applies to new buildings, alterations to existing buildings and existing structures where a change in use is envisaged. It should be noted that it does not cover loads on road or rail bridges (BS 5400), wind loads (CP 3 Chapter V part 2) or structures such as silos, bunkers or water tanks. Nor does it cover machinery vibrations, loads due to lifts or loads encountered during construction.

Where a building involving several floors is under consideration, a reduction is allowed in the imposed loads on the assumption that not all of these will be operating at any one time.

Dead loads (that is loads which constitute the permanent structure) should be calculated using the specific weights given in BS 648 (see (F5) weight).

The imposed (or live) loads which constitute such loads as those resulting from furniture and people are tabulated (see Table 210) for the various uses to which a building may be put. For example the imposed load for a library floor will obviously be much greater than that for a domestic dwelling.

CP 3: *Chapter V Loading*

Part 2 1972 *Wind loads*

■ AD (Regs. A1/2)

Clearly wind loads can be a significant factor affecting the stability of buildings and other structures. This part of the code gives methods for calculating the wind loads when designing buildings and building components.

The area of the country in which the building is to be placed, its degree of exposure and proximity to other buildings will all play a part in affecting the actual wind force on the building.

The necessary information is contained within this document for the design engineer to make an assessment of the wind force. Basic wind speeds are recorded on a map of the United Kingdom and a number of factors and coefficients can then be applied to arrive at a value for the wind pressure. In some cases wind suction may be more critical than wind pressure and the code covers this contingency also.

This part of the code does not apply to buildings or structures of unusual shape or location where special investigations may be necessary to determine wind loads. In any case wind tunnel experimental data may be used in place of the process recommended in this code. This document is highly technical and should only be used by engineers.

Table 211 shows the modification factors resulting from ground roughness considered together with the height of the building for three classes of building A, B and C.

(J5) (no entry)

(J6) Vibration

Background information is provided by **BS 4675** *Mechanical vibration in rotating machinery*. Part 1: 1976 *Basic for specifying evaluation standards for rotating machines with operating speeds*

Table 210 *Extract: Residential occupancy class*

Floor area usage	Intensity of distributed load (kN/m²)	Concentrated load (kN)
Type 1. Self-contained dwelling units		
All	1.5	1.4
Type 2. Apartment houses, boarding houses, lodging houses, guest houses, hostels, residential clubs and communal areas in blocks of flats		
Boiler rooms, motor rooms, fan rooms and the like, including the weight of machinery	7.5	4.5
Communal kitchens, laundries	3.0	4.5
Dining rooms, lounges, billiard rooms	2.0	2.7
Toilet rooms	2.0	—
Bedrooms, dormitories	1.5	1.8
Corridors, hallways, stairs, landings, footbridges, etc.	3.0	4.5
Balconies	Same as rooms to which they give access but with a minimum of 3.0.	1.5 per metre run concentrated at the outer edge
Cat walks	—	1.0 at 1 m centres
Type 3. Hotels and motels		
Boiler rooms, motor rooms, fan rooms and the like, including the weight of machinery	7.5	4.5
Assembly areas without fixed seating, dance halls	5.0	3.6
Bars	5.0	—
Assembly areas with fixed seating*	4.0	—
Corridors, hallways, stairs, landings, footbridges, etc.	4.0	4.5
Kitchens, laundries	3.0	4.5
Dining rooms, lounges, billiard rooms	2.0	2.7
Bedrooms	2.0	1.8
Toilet rooms	2.0	—
Balconies	Same as rooms to which they give access but with a minimum of 4.0.	1.5 per metre run concentrated at the outer edge
Cat walks	—	1.0 at 1 m centres

* Fixed seating is where its removal and the use of the space for other purposes is improbable

(Table 5 BS 6399: Part 1: 1984)

Table 211 *Ground roughness, building size and height above ground, factor S_2*

H	1 Open country with no obstructions			2 Open country with scattered windbreaks			3 Country with many windbreaks, small towns, outskirts of large cities			4 Surface with large and frequent obstructions, e.g. city centres		
	A	B	C	A	B	C	A	B	C	A	B	C
m												
3 or less	0.83	0.78	0.73	0.72	0.67	0.63	0.64	0.60	0.55	0.56	0.52	0.47
5	0.88	0.83	0.78	0.79	0.74	0.70	0.70	0.65	0.60	0.60	0.55	0.50
10	1.00	0.95	0.90	0.93	0.88	0.83	0.78	0.74	0.69	0.67	0.62	0.58
15	1.03	0.99	0.94	1.00	0.95	0.91	0.88	0.83	0.78	0.74	0.69	0.64
20	1.06	1.01	0.96	1.03	0.98	0.94	0.95	0.90	0.85	0.79	0.75	0.70
30	1.09	1.05	1.00	1.07	1.03	0.98	1.01	0.97	0.92	0.90	0.85	0.79
40	1.12	1.08	1.03	1.10	1.06	1.01	1.05	1.01	0.96	0.97	0.93	0.89
50	1.14	1.10	1.06	1.12	1.08	1.04	1.08	1.04	1.00	1.02	0.98	0.94
60	1.15	1.12	1.08	1.14	1.10	1.06	1.10	1.06	1.02	1.05	1.02	0.98
80	1.18	1.15	1.11	1.17	1.13	1.09	1.13	1.10	1.06	1.10	1.07	1.03
100	1.20	1.17	1.13	1.19	1.16	1.12	1.16	1.12	1.09	1.13	1.10	1.07
120	1.22	1.19	1.15	1.21	1.18	1.14	1.18	1.15	1.11	1.15	1.13	1.10
140	1.24	1.20	1.17	1.22	1.19	1.16	1.20	1.17	1.13	1.17	1.15	1.12
160	1.25	1.22	1.19	1.24	1.21	1.18	1.21	1.18	1.15	1.19	1.17	1.14
180	1.26	1.23	1.20	1.25	1.22	1.19	1.23	1.20	1.17	1.20	1.19	1.16
200	1.27	1.24	1.21	1.26	1.24	1.21	1.24	1.21	1.18	1.22	1.21	1.18

Class A. All units of cladding, glazing and roofing and their immediate fixings and individual members of unclad structures.
Class B. All buildings and structures where neither the greatest horizontal dimension nor the greatest vertical dimension exceeds 50 m (165 ft).
Class C. All buildings and structures whose greatest horizontal dimension or greatest vertical dimension exceeds 50 m (165 ft).

(Table 3: CP 3: Chapter V: Part 2: 1972)

from 10 to 200 revolutions per second. Part 2: 1978 *Requirements for instruments for measuring vibration severity.*

BS 6472: 1984   *Guide to evaluation of human exposure to vibration in buildings*

This affords general guidance on human exposure to such vibrations in the frequency range 1 Hz to 80 Hz. Curves of equal annoyance, and the measurement methods used to derive them, are covered.

An appendix deals with conditions leading to adverse comments, and methods of measuring continuous, intermittent and impulsive vibration.

Structural damage, and injury to users of buildings, are *not* covered.

(J7) and (J8)   (no entry)

(K)   Fire, explosion

Regulation B1, Means of Escape, of the Building Regulations 1985 applies

This topic interlocks with fire protection services, covered in Table 1 'Building elements' section (68.5) 'Fire protection services' and emergency lighting, in Table 1 section (63) 'Lighting services'. Four codes of practice – CP 3 Chapter IV, and BS 5908, BS 5588 and BS 6266 are discussed here, together with the important BS 6336 and BS 476, the special section on fire resistance of timber members in Part 4 of BS 5268 and a group of narrower standards.

The glossary of terms in BS 4422 is also dealt with in Table 1 (68.5).

Readers will be aware of the statutory setting, and in particular the Fire Precautions Act 1971, the Housing Act 1980 and the relevant Parts of the Building Regulations 1985. The tests in BS 5803: Part 4 are also relevant—see (M) Heat, cold below.

CP 3   *Code of basic data for the design of buildings:* Chapter IV Precautions against fire

Part 1: 1971   *Flats and maisonettes (in blocks over two storeys)*

■ AD (Reg. B1)

This chapter recommends precautions to be taken when siting, planning or constructing houses and flats having floor areas not exceeding 140 and 93 m² (1500 and 100 ft²) respectively, and any garages which may be nearby. A table is included setting out minimum distances of external walls from site boundaries, and the maximum number of houses or flats that should be contained in a block, having a regard to the degree of fire-resistance and type of construction of the external walls. Recommendations are included on the design, form of construction and grades of fire-resistance, of separating walls erected between individual houses or as fire-stops. Floors, chimneys and roofs are also considered. Guidance is given on the use of fire-stop in hollow constructions and on the provision of means of escape.

Design, construction and equipment of blocks of dwellings to protect occupants in event of fire, by producing safe means of escape and controlling spread of flame and smoke. Recommendations on fire brigade facilities and advice to owners and occupiers.

One and two-storey dwellings entered at ground level from outside any block (that is, not through any main staircase or shared circulation space) are not included.

Part 2: 1968   *Shops and departmental stores* and Part 3: 1968   *Office buildings* have been superseded by BS 5588, Parts 2 and 3.

BS 5908: 1980   *Code of practice for fire precautions in chemical plant*

This code makes recommendations concerning fire hazards in operating chemical plant, and precautions to be taken in design and location of plant items, including change of use and of process. Gives guidance on selection and layout of sites and fire protection.

BS 5588: 1978   *Code of practice for fire precautions in the design and construction of buildings*

Part 1: Section 1.1, 1984   *Single family dwelling houses*

■ AD (Reg. B1)

This important standard is produced as a number of codes of practice with the aim of providing guidance for the designers and the building construction team in their task of incorporating into new buildings or alterations of existing buildings, measures that should in the event of a fire safeguard the lives of people living, working or visiting the building. These measures may also help to protect the building and its contents against the effects of fire.

This code relates to single family houses of any height (any number of storeys) but does not include houses in multiple occupation.

Part 2: 1985   Shops
This code broadly covers premises that would be classed as shops in the Offices, Shops and Railway Premises Act, 1963. It includes shops in the everyday sense of the word, to which the public or a section of the public normally has access; in addition it covers:

(a) larger premises such as department stores, variety stores, supermarkets and hypermarkets;
(b) premises where goods may not necessarily be sold over the counter but in which a trade or business is carried out, such as hairdressers' salons, television rental shops or auction rooms;
(c) cafés, restaurants, public houses and other places of refreshment;
(d) premises where goods are received for treatment or repairs, such as dry cleaners, launderettes and shoe repair shops.

Premises where the activity is more akin to that of an office, such as banks and estate agents, are considered as offices and are dealt with in Part 3. Office accommodation that is ancillary to a shop is dealt with in this code.

This code does not provide guidance on fire precautions in the design and construction of covered and enclosed access areas for pedestrians that are common to a number of shops.

Guidance on fire precautions in such access areas is available from the Home Office and Scottish Home and Health Department.

Part 3: 1983   Office buildings
This document refers to new office buildings and to alterations and extensions to existing offices.

In both parts 2 and 3, appendices provide guidance for managers of shops or office buildings to aid them in making the best use of these design features of the building and acts as a guide to designers in passing to their clients information about the fire precautions designed into a building. In a building that has to have a fire certificate, the advice given may have to be varied in accordance with the conditions of the fire certificate.

Part 4: 1978   Smoke control in protected escape routes using pressurization
This part covers the use of pressurization in buildings for the purpose of smoke control in protected escape routes.

The code is intended to apply to new buildings, though there is no reason why the principles should not be used when existing buildings are to be altered or adapted. It is intended initially for application to protected escape routes in flats and maisonettes, and in offices and shops. It offers a method of protecting escape routes as an alternative to the methods set out in CP 3 Chapter IV.

The principles may be used for other occupancies and purpose groups where the fundamental aim is to keep the protected escape route clear of products of combustion.

This code is not intended to apply to shopping malls and town centre redevelopments. Information on these will be found in the HMSO publication *Fire Prevention Guide 1: Fire Precautions in Town Centre Redevelopments*.

PD 6512   *Use of elements of structural fire protection with particular reference to the recommendations given in BS 5588*

Part 1: 1985   *Guide to fire doors*

Guidance is given on fire doors including shutters and on the performance criteria for fire doors and where fire doors should be used.

BS 6266: 1982   *Code of practice for fire protection for electronic data processing installations (formerly CP 95)*

This code makes recommendations to users and installers of electronic data processing equipment on its protection from fire.

BS 6336: 1982   *Guide to development and presentation of fire tests and their use in hazard assessment*

In the introduction to this standard, the formidable consequences of building fires (over 300,000 per year in the United Kingdom alone) are summarized with 1000 lives lost, thousands more injured and hundreds of millions of pounds worth of damage.

The stated intention is to help a wide range of writers, organizations (including BSI itself) and statutory bodies, designers, fabricators and builders to work in a consistent and coherent way.

The standard sets out the theory of fire behaviour and fire hazard, the assessment of fire hazard and the need for fire tests. It provides guidance on the development of fire tests and on the use of related terminology.

BS 476:   *Fire tests on building materials and structures*

Parts 1 and 2 have been withdrawn. The 1959 edition of Part 3 is included, as it is referred to in the Approved Document under Regulations B2, B3 and B4 of the Building Regulations 1985.

Part 3: 1959   *External fire exposure roof test*
■   AD (Regs. B2/3/4)
___

The 1959 version is the Authorized Document in the Building Regulations, 1985. A summary follows, with the 1975 current version after.

The 1959 part sets out to enable measurement of:

(a) the capacity of a representative section of a roof to resist penetration by fire when the external surface is exposed to radiation and flame (a time-rating being used);
(b) the distance of the spread of flame on the outer surface of the roof covering under certain conditions. The combination of specimens, a preliminary ignition test, fire penetration test and spread of flame test are described.

A prefix 'EXT F' or 'EXT S' indicates *flat* or *sloping* test performance; the first designating letter relates to penetration by flame (A – not penetrated in one hour; B – half to one hour; C – under half hour; D – within a preliminary test); the second letter relates to spread of flame (A – none; B – not more than (533.4 mm) 21 in; C – over 533.4 mm; D – continue to burn for 5 min after flame withdrawal *or* spread more than (467.5 mm) 15 in during the preliminary test) with a suffix 'X' indicating dripping, mechanical failure or holing during one or more of the four tests.

Part 3: 1975   *External fire exposure roof test*
This part sets out tests which are designed to measure:

1 The ability of a representative section of a roof, rooflight domelight and similar components to resist penetration by fire when the external surface is exposed to heat radiation and flame.
2 The extent of surface ignition of the upper surface with and without supporting radiation.

Four test specimens are observed for a preliminary ignition test, and a fire penetration and surface ignition test. The form of a test report is prescribed.

Part 4: 1970 (1984)   *Non-combustibility test for materials*

■ AD (Regs. B2/3/4 and J1/2/3)

This part describes a test for determining whether building materials are non-combustible within the meaning of the definition.

Materials used in the construction and finishing of buildings or structures are classified 'non-combustible' or 'combustible' according to their behaviour in the 'non-combustibility test'. This test is intended for building materials, whether coated or not, but it is not intended to apply to the coating alone.

Requirements are specified for size, number, preparation and conditioning of specimens, apparatus and the test procedure.

The material is deemed non-combustible if, during the test, none of the three specimens either:

1 Causes the temperature reading from either of the two thermo-couples to rise by 50 °C or more above the initial furnace temperature; or
2 Is observed to flame continuously for 10 seconds or more inside the furnace.

The form of a test report is prescribed.

Part 5: 1979   *Method of test for ignitability*
This part sets out a test for the determination of the ignitability characteristics of the exposed surfaces of essentially flat, rigid or semi-rigid building materials or composites, when tested in the vertical position. Requirements are specified for the size and number of specimens, the test procedure, and a test report.

Part 6: 1968   *Fire propagation test for materials*

■ AD (Regs. B2/3/4)

Part 6: 1981   *Method of test for fire propagation for products*

■ AD (Regs. B2/3/4)

This part specifies a method of test, the result being expressed as a fire propagation index, that provides a comparative measure of the contribution to the growth of fire made by an essentially flat material, composite or assembly. It is primarily intended for the assessment of the performance of internal wall and ceiling linings. Both editions are Authorized Documents under the Building Regulations 1985.

The form of a test report is prescribed.

Table 212   *Flame spread classification*

	Flame spread at $1\frac{1}{2}$ minutes		Final flame spread	
Classification	Limit	Tolerance for one specimen in sample	Limit	Tolerance for one specimen in sample
	mm	mm	mm	mm
Class 1	165	25	165	25
Class 2	215	25	455	45
Class 3	265	25	710	75
Class 4	Exceeding Class 3 limits			

(Table 1: BS 476: Part 7: 1971)

Part 7: 1971   *Surface spread of flame test for materials*

■ AD (Regs. B2/3/4)

This part gives two tests, one a large scale test for determining the tendency of materials to support the spread of flame across their surfaces and classifying this in relation to exposed surfaces

of walls and ceilings. The other is a small scale surface spread of flame test suitable for preliminary testing for development and quality control purposes. There is no direct correlation between these two tests. Table 212 shows the classification.

Part 8: 1972   *Test methods and criteria for the fire resistance of elements of building construction*

■ AD (Regs. B2/3/4)

This very important part sets out methods of test and the criteria for the determination of the fire resistance of elements of building construction. The tests are appropriate to the following:

Walls and partitions (load-bearing and non-load-bearing)
Floors
Flat roofs
Columns
Beams
Suspended ceilings protecting steel beams
Door and shutter assemblies
Glazing
Ceiling membranes

The test procedure is that the test element is heated in a furnace whose temperature is controlled to follow, as closely as possible, a time/temperature curve from 556 °C at 5 minutes to 1193 °C at 360 minutes.

Criteria of failure are stability, integrity and insulation.

Stability non-load-bearing constructions. Failure is deemed to occur when collapse of the specimen takes place.

Stability load-bearing constructions. A load-bearing specimen must support the test load during the prescribed heating period and also 24 hours after the end of the heating period. However, should collapse occur during heating or during the reload test the notional maximum period for stability for such a specimen shall be construed as 80 per cent of the time to collapse or the duration of heating if failure occurs in the reload test. In addition, failure for floors, flat roofs and beams is deemed to occur when a specimen deflects in excess of the limits specified.

Integrity. Failure is deemed to occur when cracks or other openings exist through which flame or hot gases can pass which would cause flaming of a cotton wool pad described in the standard.

Insulation. Failure is deemed to occur when the mean temperature of the unexposed surface of the specimen increases by more than 140 °C above the initial temperature, or the temperature of the unexposed surface increases at any point by more than 180 °C above the initial temperature.

Part 10: 1983   *Guide to the principles and application of fire testing*

Part 11: 1982   *Method for assessing the heat emission from building materials*

■ AD (Regs. B2/3/4)

This part sets out a testing and reporting procedure, suitable for simple materials or mixtures of materials, manufactured or natural, provided that they are reasonably homogeneous and it is possible to obtain representative specimens. Non-homogeneous materials may be capable of being tested.

Five representative specimen cylinders, 50 ± 2 mm long and $45 \pm \frac{0}{2}$ mm in diameter, are tested in a furnace at 750 °C.

Part 31   *Methods for measuring smoke penetration through doorsets and shutter assemblies*

Section 31.1 1983   *Method of measurement under ambient temperature condition*
This section describes a method for measuring smoke penetration, as represented by the measurement of air leakage rate,

through doorsets and vertically orientated shutter assemblies under ambient temperature conditions.

This method is used to evaluate the performance of a fire door used for smoke control purposes but gives no information on the fire resistance of a fire door for which the methods described in either BS 476: Part 8 or Part 22 are applicable.

PD 6496: 1981 *A comparison between the technical requirements of BS 476: Part 8: 1972 and other relevant international standards and documents on fire resistance tests.*

The comparison of the test methods is presented in tabular form according to the subject and clause number as given in BS 476 Part 8. Where appropriate to the clause, an analysis is given which highlights the main differences between the compared texts. The clause-by-clause comparisons are grouped into the following main headings: basic test method, walls and partitions, floors and flat roofs, columns, beams, suspended ceilings and glazing.

BS 5268: *Code of practice for the structural use of timber*

Part 4 Section 4.1: 1978 *Fire resistance of timber structures*
This part gives methods of assessing the fire resistance of flexural tension and compression members of solid or glued laminated timber and their joints.

These standards give laboratory tests and are important for designers, but they are not necessarily a guide to performance in use.

BS 2782: 1970 *Methods of testing plastics* (see Table 3 Materials n Rubber, plastics. etc.)

BS 4735: 1974 *Laboratory methods of test for assessment of the horizontal burning characteristics of specimens no longer than 150 mm × 50 mm × 13 mm (nominal) of cellular plastics and cellular rubber materials when subjected to a small flame*

BS 5111 *Laboratory methods of test for determination of smoke generation characteristics of cellular plastics and cellular rubber materials*

Part 1: 1974 *Method of testing a 25 mm cube test specimen of low density material (up to 130 kg/m³) to continuous flaming conditions*

BS 5852 *Fire tests for furniture*

Part 1: 1979 *Methods of test for the ignitability by smokers' material of upholstered composites for seating*
This standard assesses ignitability of material combinations when subjected to either a smouldering cigarette or a lighted match as might be applied accidentally. An appendix gives guidance notes for designers and specifiers.

Part 2: 1982 *Methods of test for the ignitability of upholstered composites for seating by flaming sources*
This standard assesses ignitability of materials combinations when subjected to flaming ignition sources in the form of butane flames or wooden cribs. Appendices give guidance notes for specifiers and operators.

BS 5438: 1976 *Methods of test for flammability of vertically oriented textile fabrics and fabric assemblies subjected to a small igniting flame*

This standard gives three methods for observing and measuring aspects of flammability relevant to apparel fabrics and those fabrics that will be held loosely in an essentially vertical position, for example curtains and drapes. Appendices give notes for users and proposed criteria of acceptance.

BS 6203: 1982 *Guide to fire characteristics and fire performance of expanded polystyrene (EPS) used in building applications*

This standard draws attention to the unsuitability of some standard fire test methods for certain uses of EPS, and the desirability of relevant tests on specific constructions. Recommendations are made on the handling and storage of EPS, and relevant legislation and insurance requirements.

(L)   Matter

(L1)   (no entry)

(L2)   Gases, vapours: condensation

BS 5250: 1975   *Code of basic data for the design of buildings: the control of condensation in dwellings*

■   AD (Reg. F2)

This is a code giving recommendations relating to the control of condensation and mould growth in blocks of flats, maisonettes and houses, including those designed for old people. The recommendations are generally applicable to domestic rooms in other buildings such as hotels and hostels. Communal rooms or kitchens used for other than family purposes are not included. The contents of the code cover factors affecting condensation and mould growth, design for the control of condensation, design assumptions, design and constructional details, work on site, remedial work in existing buildings and the effects of conversion, modernization and change of use of buildings.

(L3) – (L5)   (no entries)

(L6)   Biological

BS 1982: 1968   *Methods of test for fungal resistance of manufactured building materials made of or containing materials of organic origin*

Three tests are set out, and the user is advised on the need for experience in their execution and caution in interpretation of their results. Test 1 is likely to be appropriate for building boards based on woody fibres, Test 2 for organic-based materials, including fibres, felts and papers, used in damp conditions, and Test 3 for materials such as wallpaper used in humid conditions.

(L7)   (no entry)

(L8)   (no entry)

(M)   Heat, cold

(M1)   (no entry)

(M2)   Insulation

The Building Regulations, in Part C, deal with performance, and in Part D, are addressed to the risks of toxicity in cavity fill, and in Part L (Regs. L1 and L2) apply to domestic and non-domestic buildings repectively. See also Table 1 Building elements (56) Space heating.

BS 3533: 1981   *Glossary of thermal insulation terms*   Terminology in use in the industry is assimilated with current technology.

BS 8207: 1985   *Code of practice for energy efficiency in buildings*

This document is produced as a 'head' code which sets out the main principles to be observed when considering energy conservation. Other codes deal more fully with specific building types, such as housing, or with aspects of design that have a strong bearing on energy consumption. The aim of this standard is to promote energy efficiency in buildings and to provide a basis on which the designers of buildings and their clients can work to achieve this aim. Recommendations for the main procedures to be followed to obtain the efficient use of energy in the design and management of buildings are given. They apply to the design of new buildings and the rehabilitation of existing buildings, to the operation and maintenance of buildings, and to all types of buildings including housing.

BS 874: 1973 (1980)   *Methods for determining thermal insulating properties, with definitions of thermal insulating terms*

Methods for determining thermal conductivity, conductance and transmittance of materials are described in this standard along with emissivity and heat capacity per unit mass. The properties of materials may change during their working life and provision is not made for the general requirements of thermal insulating materials. The standard includes definitions of thermal insulating terms. Of these, terms ending in 'ivity' have been used to designate properties normally independent of size or shape, examples being 'conductivity' and 'resistivity'. Each quantity defined may be expressed in a variety of units; consequently no units have been explicitly stated in these definitions. A summary of the chief systems in common use is given in Appendix F. In other appendices four additional methods of measuring thermal conductivity are described.

BS 2972: 1975 (1984)   *Methods of test for inorganic thermal insulating materials*

Twenty-one methods of test are specified in this standard for inorganic thermal insulating materials including preformed plastics, composition, flexible and loose fill materials. For the testing of organic insulating materials reference should be made to BS 4370. The standard makes no attempt to assess the relative values of commercial insulating materials as this type of information can best be supplied by the individual manufacturers who can utilize the most recent technical progress for their own products. However, it is important that claims for technical quality of materials should be related to well established methods of test based on sound fundamental principles, and the purpose of this standard is to provide details of basic tests for the assessment of a range of properties which are likely to be of value to a potential user. It is suggested that the correct way to use this standard is to select those tests which will convey information on the desirable properties for a specific application. All the tests in this standard may not need to be applied in every case.

BS 5617: 1985 *Urea–formaldehyde (UF) foam systems suitable for thermal insulation of cavity walls with masonry or concrete inner and outer leaves*

■ AD (Regs. C4 and D1)

Specified in this standard are the property requirements, the properties of the components and the production parameters of the foam systems suitable for injection into external masonry or concrete cavity walls to provide improved thermal insulation. Twelve appendices, five tables and two figures detail the tests and methods of determining the various properties and requirements.

BS 5618: 1985 *Code of practice for thermal insulation of cavity walls (with masonry or concrete inner and outer leaves) by filling with urea–formaldehyde (UF) foam systems*

■ AD (Regs. C4 and D1)

The successful insulation of external cavity walls still relies on two standards, that is, BS 5617, and this code of practice which is used by the installation contractor to satisfactorily install suitable foam systems.

This code therefore describes recommendations for the installation of urea–formaldehyde (UF) foam systems which are dispensed on site, to fill the cavities of suitably situated and constructed external walls of maximum height 12 m, which have masonry or concrete inner and outer leaves, thereby providing additional thermal insulation to such walls. It defines what are suitably situated and constructed external walls and indicates essential procedures and precautions for the filling process. Walls built of random rubble are not covered by this code.

Appendices deal with criteria for suitability, natural stones, exposure index, driving-rain index, methods for assessing exposure, formaldehyde, flue checks, properties of foam and determination of cavity width. Thirty-one maps, covering the United Kingdom, give values of the driving-rain index.

BS 6232 *Thermal insulation of cavity walls by filling with blown man made mineral fibre*

Part 1: 1982 *Performance of installation systems*

■ AD (Reg. C4)

A series of tests are specified in this part of the standard covering the performance of systems used to install blown man made fibre as thermal insulation in cavity walls with masonry and/or concrete leaves in new and existing buildings. Guidance is given on the essential properties of the materials and equipment, which together comprise the system.

Part 2: 1982 *Code of practice for installation of blown man made mineral fibre in cavity walls with masonry and/or concrete leaves*

■ AD (Reg. C4)

Recommendations are given in this part for the installation of the blown fibre in new and existing cavity walls up to 12 m high (normal three-storey construction) where the leaves are constructed of brick, block, natural stone, cast stone or concrete. It gives criteria for the suitability of walls and indicates essential precautions and procedures for the filling process. Useful information is also included on pre-installation checks and measures, storage and marking.

BS 8208: *Guide to assessment of suitability of external cavity walls for filling with thermal insulants*

Part 1: 1985 *Existing traditional cavity construction*

■ AD (Regs. C4 and D1)

This part gives guidance on factors to be considered when assessing the suitability of existing external cavity walls with masonry and/or concrete leaves for filling with thermal insulants. It applies to cavity walls where:

(a) the height of the cavity wall does not exceed 12 m
(b) vertical members of structural frames do not bridge the cavity
(c) there is no existing cavity insulation

It is published in the form of a guide since it provides a check list of factors to be considered rather than a series of recommendations on what actions to take in the event of defects being discovered.

The purpose of the assessment described in this standard is to identify any defects in the wall which may need to be rectified and to enable consideration to be given to features which may affect the choice of insulation systems or impair the moisture resistance of the wall after filling.

Other parts of this standard in course of preparation will cover other types of construction. Design and construction of buildings intended to incorporate cavity insulation will be covered in an amendment to BS 5628 Part 3.

BS 6676: *Thermal insulation of cavity walls using man-made mineral fibre batts (slabs)*

Part 1: 1986 *Specification for man-made mineral fibre batts (slabs)*
Requirements for batts intended for filling cavities in cavity walls and masonry and/or concrete leaves. Covers composition, tolerances, density, resistance to water retention, wicking, water penetration and settlement; also covers pH value and water-soluble salt content, non-combustability, and thermal conductivity.

Part 2: 1986 *Code of practice for installation of batts (slabs) filling the cavity*
Recommendations for filling cavities using batts in cavity walls with masonry and/or concrete leaves up to 12 m in height (normal three storey construction). Gives criteria for design and construction of walls to be insulated. Indicates essential precautions and procedures for the installation of batts. An appendix gives additional recommendations for installation of batts in buildings exceeding 12 m in height.

BS 5803 *Thermal insulation for use in roof space in dwellings*

Part 1: 1985 *Specification for man-made mineral fibre thermal insulation mats* sets out the requirements for this form of insulation when made from glass, rock or slag. Appendix G gives typical thermal properties of currently available materials.

Part 2: 1985 *Specification for man-made mineral fibre application by blowing* sets out similar requirements for this form of insulation when made from glass, rock or slag.

Part 3: 1985 *Specification for cellulose fibre thermal insulation for application by blowing* sets out installation by blowing.
None of these deal with methods of installation of insulating materials or with the general principles of insulation of pitched roofs which are covered in Part 5.

Part 4: 1985 *Methods for determining flammability and resistance to smouldering* gives methods of test for thermal insulating materials, which may consist of loose-fill granules, beads or fibres, designed to be laid horizontally between joists in lofts or dwellings, whilst Part 5: 1985 *Specification for installations of man-made mineral fibre and cellulose fibre insulation* deals with the requirements for the application of thermal insulation in pitched roof spaces in new and existing dwellings. It covers both the insulation of an uninsulated roof and the application of additional insulation to increase the existing standard of insulation. Insulation at rafter level is not included but advice on this type of installation is given in an appendix.

It gives essential procedures and precautions to be undertaken, and makes recommendations to ensure an adequate installation.

The standard covers fibrous materials that may be substantially inorganic or organic and may be in the form of mats or loose-fill suitable for application by blowing and covers the following situations:

(a) an individual dwelling where the work is carried out by an insulation installer;
(b) a number of dwellings where the work is carried out by an insulation installer;
(c) an individual dwelling where the work is carried out without a contract.

(M3) – (M8)   (no entries)

(N)   Light, dark

See also Table 1 Building elements (63) Lighting services.

In addition to BS 8206, below, BS 4727 *Glossary of electrotechnical, power, telecommunications, electronics, lighting and colour terms* Part 4 *Terms particular to lighting and colour* Group 01: 1971 *Radiation and photometry* and Group 03: 1972 *Lighting technology terminology*, is summarized under section (63) 'Lighting services'.

Two extremely useful drafts for development have been issued, namely DD 73: 1982 *Basic data for the design of buildings: daylight* and DD 67: 1980 *Basic data for the design of buildings: sunlight.*

BS 8206   *Lighting for buildings*

Part 1: 1985   *Code of practice for artificial lighting*
This part gives recommendations for the design, installation and maintenance of artificial lighting systems in buildings. Section 1 describes in general terms the aims of and processes concerned with artificial lighting design, including energy considerations. Section 2 deals with the characteristics of various lamps and their control gear. In Section 3, luminaires and other means of controlling the distribution of light are described together with some aspects of installation. Section 4 considers the particular lighting requirements in various types of building and recommends methods of meeting them, and Section 5 refers to economics and maintenance.

DD 67 and DD 73 which detail the effects of sunlight and daylight respectively on building design are both in the process of being converted into a part or parts of this standard.

DD 73   *Basic data for the design of buildings: daylight*

This is in the process of revision to be part of BS 8206.
DD 73 provides a framework for extending and redrafting CP 3 Chapter 1 Part 1 and incorporates changes in approach to the subject of designing for daylight, arising from the need for a more careful consideration of the combined roles of sunlight, daylight and artificial light in the interests of energy conservation.

In this last respect the use of natural light is so relevant that it is hoped that this draft for development and the parallel DD 67 will together serve to revitalize the combined contribution of skylight and sunlight to the design and quality of buildings.

The integration of artificial lighting sources with daylight has focused attention on the size of view windows, the balance of brightness in the interior and the modelling of form. The study of glare from windows has led to methods by which glare can be predicted. Recommendations are made for standards of quality and quantity of daylight both in spaces that rely on daylight alone during most working hours, and in spaces in which daylight and artificial light are combined. Recommendations are also made for minimum emergency standards in buildings such as hospitals that, although planned for supplementary artificial lighting, are required nevertheless to function in an emergency using available daylight.

This draft is concerned with both the theory and practice of the design of daylighting in buildings and thus has a wider scope than that of CP 3 Chapter 1 Part 1, which it will eventually replace. For guidance and to facilitate reference, recommendations for all aspects of daylighting in specific types of building are given in clauses 8 and 9 (design guidelines and schedule of recommendations) which can be used independently by designers as a direct source of immediately applicable data. The draft also acts as a reference to the many aspects that explain and supplement these specific recommendations.

The body of the text has five headings,

1 Assessment and provisions – clauses 4, 5 and 6 which cover the assessment and provision of daylight, and the design of supplementary artificial lighting.
2 Quality of daylight – clause 7.
3 Design guidance – clause 8 gives general guidance and references for specific building types while clause 9 provides a schedule of recommendations which is extremely valuable.
4 Urban planning – clause 10.
5 Appendices – seven appendices including basic data, method of calculation and a bibliography.

The contents of the draft are cross-referenced under subjects listed under three main headings.

Principles which covers the properties of natural light and distinguishes between sunlight and daylight as well as covering availability and magnitude of light, sky brightness distribution and spectral characteristics of light, access to daylight including side and top lighting, distribution and quality of daylight in spaces including interior daylight and its distribution, daylight and modelling and visual comfort in daylight interiors, supplemented daylight, windows and view, daylighting and energy requirements, and daylighting requirements for lighting and fenestration of spaces together with the requirements for particular activities/spaces.

Standards which covers standards for the provision of daylight to façades, statutory requirements and standards for the quantity and distribution of daylight in buildings including recommended values for interiors with full daylighting or supplemented daylighting and also recommendations for the daylighting of escape routes, standards of illuminance from supplementary lighting and for conservation purposes, standards of limiting glare index for daylighting and artificial lighting, and standards for the area of view of windows.

Calculation and measurement which covers sunlight penetration, thermal and acoustic factors, photometric measurement of daylight factor, surface reflectance values, glass transmittance and other losses, side lighting including average daylight factor over horizontal reference plane, distribution of light from windows, daylight factor at a point, glare; top lighting including glass area for top lighting providing 5 per cent average daylight factor over horizontal reference plane, distribution of top lighting from an acceptably uniform daylight factor and daylight factor at a point, glare.

DD 67 *Basic data for the design of buildings: sunlight*

This is in the process of revision to be part of BS 8206.

DD 67 is concerned with sunlight in and around buildings, the means for its assessment, the criteria by which its adequacy may be judged and environmental consequences arising from its presence.

The term 'sunlight' is generally employed to signify the visible part of the spectrum of direct solar radiation but, as a matter of convenience and semantic simplicity, it is also used in this draft to encompass the total spectrum of solar radiation.

Solar heat gain accompanying the admission of direct sunlight is considered, but the utilization of thermal energy in direct and diffuse radiation does not lie within the scope of the draft and only passing reference is made to it.

The information given and the principles set out are generally applicable to occupied space in all types of building in greater or lesser degree but, in considering levels at which the designer should aim, attention has been directed mainly to residential buildings, offices and schools with some comments on hospital wards.

The effects of sunlight on people and materials are covered together with availability of sunlight and average shadow lengths for the latitudes of London and Edinburgh.

Siting of buildings and the admission of sunlight related to latitudes, time of year, topography, orientation and spacing is given as well as notes on sunlight around buildings. The heating effects and the control of the admission of sunlight with particular attention to windows are covered.

Finally recommendations are made for the admission of sunlight into dwellings, offices and education buildings. For dwellings the recommendation is for a minimum standard of 3 hours of *possible* sunlight on 1 March to be received on the plane of the inside face of the window wall at the centre of the window under consideration with sunlight below the altitude of 5 ° being discounted. Account to be taken of local obstruction such as balconies and similar overhangs.

(P)   Sound, quiet

Part E of The Building Regulations 1985 applies.

Of the standards and codes of practice dealing with sound one covers sound level meters, namely BS 5969: 1981 *Sound level meters*, one standard provides a glossary of terms, namely BS 661: 1969 *Glossary of acoustical terms* and one deals with quantities, units and symbols, namely BS 5775 *Quantities, units and symbols* Part 7: 1979 *Acoustics*. The other nine standards cover various methods of measurement, expression, calculation and rating. These standards include one Authorized Document under the Building Regulations 1985, namely:

BS 2750   *Methods of measurement of sound insulation in buildings and of building elements*

■   AD (Regs. E 1/2/3) apply to Parts 1 and 4

Part 1: 1980 *Recommendations for laboratories*, Part 2: 1980 *Statement of precision requirements*, Part 3: 1980 *Laboratory measurements of airborne sound insulation of building elements*, Part 4: 1980 *Field measurements of airborne sound insulation between rooms*, Part 5: 1980 *Field measurements of airborne sound insulation of façade elements and façades*, Part 6: 1980 *Laboratory measurements of impact sound insulation of floors*, Part 7: 1980 *Field measurements of impact sound insulation of floors* and Part 8: 1980 *Laboratory measurements of the reduction of transmitted impact noise by floor coverings on a standard floor*.

Other standards are: BS 3045: 1981 *Method of expression of physical and subjective magnitudes of sound or noise in air*; BS 3638: 1963 *Method for the measurement of sound absorption coefficients (ISO) in a reverberation room*; BS 4142: 1967 *Method of rating industrial noise affecting mixed residential and industrial areas*; BS 4196: *Sound power levels of noise sources* (6 parts); BS 4198: 1967 *Method for calculating loudness*; BS 6686 *Methods for determination of airborne acoustical noise emitted by household and similar electrical appliances* Part 1: 1986 *General requirements for testing*; BS 5363: 1976 *Method for the measurement of reverberation time in auditoria*; and BS 5821 discussed below.

The code of practice under this heading is very useful indeed.

CP 3 Chapter III: 1972   *Sound insulation and noise reduction*

This code should be considered in conjunction with the other chapters, as certain recommendations in them may be incompatible, or may be reconciled only with difficulty, with recommendations in this chapter. The designer should therefore consider the functional requirements of a building as a whole, and determine which recommendations should have precedence. Attention is particularly drawn to the possibility of increasing the fire hazard in a building by the introduction of acoustic treatments which may assist flame spread.

It cannot be too strongly emphasized that the best defence against noise, both outdoor and indoor, lies in intelligent planning precautions taken before building development begins. If

Table 213   *Octave analyses of some common noises*

Noise	Distance	Octave bands (Hz)								Remarks
		37–75	75–150	150–300	300–600	600–1 200	1 200–2 400	2 400–4 800	4 800–9 600	
	m	Sound-pressure level (dB)								
Large (4 engines) jet air-liner	38	112	121	123	124	123	120	117	109	Maximum values when passing overhead at take-off power. No mufflers
Single-engined jet fighter	38	102	114	116	116	117	115	111	102	Maximum values when passing overhead at take-off power
Large (4 engines) piston-engined air-liner	38	111	117	114	108	107	108	106	97	Maximum values when passing overhead at take-off power
Electric trains over steel bridge	6	94	93	99	99	95	84	81	73	
Kerb side, main road in London at rush hour	5 (average)	78	81	81	79	72	67	63	55	
Electric trains	30	77	77	76	74	73	67	59	54	
Pneumatic drills	38	75	72	72	66	69	71	67	65	In open air
Riveting on large (6 by 4 m) steel plate	2	88	96	105	106	111	109	113	110	
Nylon factory	Reverberant sound	87	86	92	93	97	97	96	87	Up-twisting process
Weaving shed	Reverberant sound	78	71	77	81	86	86	84	78	
Canteen (hard ceiling)	Reverberant sound	52	54	59	67	67	61	55	49	Average levels. Peak values up to 20 dB higher
Typing office with acoustic ceiling	Reverberant sound	68	64	60	56	55	55	53	50	Ten typewriters, one tele-type machine
Male speech	1	52	55	59	66	65	60	52	40	Average values

(Table 1: CP 3: Chapter III: 1972)

such precautions are not taken, the solution to sound insulation or noise reduction problems by structural or technical measures may, in some circumstances, be attainable only at very great cost, if at all. For this reason the section on 'Planning against noise' is placed first.

In each section the problem has been considered under the general headings of outdoor noise and indoor noise. Where possible, recommendations have been made in respect of both. It is not practicable for the code to be entirely consistent, owing partly to the different nature of the problem in varying classes of building, and partly to the comparative lack of data available for a scientific study of certain building types (for example hospitals), as compared with others (for example houses). Much more research needs to be undertaken before a proper scientific assessment of the problem can be made in regard to certain building types, such as hospitals and office buildings.

Finally, a general understanding of the behaviour of sound is necessary in designing for the control of noise. Methods of construction for sound insulation, even the commonest and simplest, may, when conditions depart from normal, be misapplied if this understanding is lacking. For this reason brief explanations and general definitions are given in Appendix A of the properties and behaviour of sound, and how it is propagated and controlled.

The code stresses the importance of planning against noise which should be an integral part of town and country planning proposals ranging from regional proposals to detailed zoning and three-dimensional layouts and road design within built-up areas. Noise nuisance should be fully recognized in zoning regulations.

Noise is either generated by traffic (airborne, road, rail and underground) or it arises from zones and buildings within built-up areas (industry, commerce, offices, public and residential buildings). Planning surveys should examine all the possible causes of noise and consider the various factors making for actual nuisance.

Noise by night, causing disturbance of sleep, is more of a nuisance than noise by day. For this reason factories that work by night are liable to cause serious complaints if housing estates adjoin them.

There are two aspects of defence by planning. The first is to plan so as to keep the noise at a distance. Under this aspect comes the separation of housing from traffic noise by interposing buffer zones, and the protection of schools and hospitals by green belts, public gardens, golf courses, etc. The second is the principle of shading or screening. This consists of deliberately interposing a less vulnerable building to screen a more vulnerable one. It is well illustrated by planning a factory so that the offices and canteen blocks are interposed between the workshops and adjoining houses or schools. Typical noise levels from various sources are shown in Table 213.

Recommendations are given on planning to reduce impact of traffic noise from road, rail and air and the noise from particular buildings or spaces such as school playgrounds and swimming baths.

Specific recommendations are made on site and internal planning and standards of structural insulation for dwellings, educational buildings, hospital buildings, office buildings, industrial buildings, hotels, hostels, law courts and council chambers, libraries, museums and art galleries, churches, indoor swimming baths; laboratories; doctors' surgeries; concert halls and theatres.

Appendices cover properties and behaviour of sound, sound measurement, insulation versus absorption and principles of airborne and impact sound insulation; constructional measures for noise control including effect of window size on the insulation of walls; insulation grades for dwellings; insulation values of walls and floors; noise from aircraft; and legal aspects of noise nuisance.

BS 5821 *Rating sound insulation in buildings and of building elements*

Part 1: 1984 *Method of rating the airborne sound insulation in buildings and of interior building elements*

■ AD (Regs. E1/2/3)

Defines single-number quantities for the airborne sound insulation in buildings and of interior building elements such as walls, floors and doors, and gives rules for determining these quantities from the results of measurements carried out in one-third octave bands according to BS 2750: Parts 3 and 4.

The single-number quantities according to this part are intended for rating the airborne sound insulation and for simplifying the formulation of acoustical requirements in building codes. The required numerical values of the single-number quantities can be specified according to varying needs.

Part 2: 1984 *Method of rating the impact sound insulation*

■ AD (Regs. E1/2/3)

Gives similar information to Part 1, but for impact sound. Annexes also give methods for obtaining single-number quantities for floor coverings from the results of measurements carried out in one-third octave bands according to BS 2750: Part 8 and for bare concrete floors according to their performance in combination with soft floor coverings.

Part 3: 1984 *Method for rating the airborne sound insulation of façade elements and façades*
Gives similar information to Part 1 for façades, façade elements, windows, doors and roofs.

BS 5228: *Code of practice for noise control on construction and demolition sites* (see D1 Protecting, of this table)

(Q) Electricity, magnetism, radiation

(Q1) – (Q6) (no entries)

(Q7) Radiation

Of the standards under this classification, one deals with symbols and signs and one covers glossaries.

BS 3510: 1968 *A basic symbol to denote the actual or potential presence of ionizing radiation*

This standard specifies a symbol recommended for use only to signify the actual or potential presence of ionizing radiation and to identify objects, devices, materials or combinations of materials which emit such radiation.

BS 4727 *Glossary of electrotechnical, power, telecommunications, electronics, lighting and colour terms*

Part 4 *Terms particular to lighting and colour* Group 01: 1971 (1980) *Radiation and photometry*
This standard gives a useful glossary.

Of the remaining six standards one deals with shielding, one with safety, one with radio-active sources and three with materials.

BS 4094 *Recommendations for data on shielding from ionizing radiation*

Part 1: 1966 *Shielding from gamma radiation*

Part 2: 1971 *Shielding from X-radiation*
Both parts provide data adequate for the calculation of shielding barriers against radiation and the data presented has been chosen with the radiation shielding problems of industry in mind. Most of the material has been drawn from existing sources although a certain amount has been measured or calculated separately. All possible contingencies are not covered but data are provided to allow for calculations to be made for a wide range of materials and geometry likely to be encountered. Where possible forms have been simplified to allow calculations to be made by designers who do not have specialist knowledge of radiation shielding.

BS 4803 *Radiation safety of laser products and systems*

Part 1: 1983 *General*

Part 2: 1983 *Manufacturing requirements for laser products*

Part 3: 1983 *Guidance for users*
This standard gives general advice on the selection of materials which may become contaminated by radio-active substances and which require subsequent decontamination. An appendix provides information relating to radiation resistance of materials.

BS 5288: 1976 *Sealed radioactive sources*

This standard specifies the general requirements, production tests, marking, certificates and method of classification of sealed radioactive sources.

BS 4031: 1966 *X-ray protective lead glasses*

This standard specifies requirements for two types (lead barium silicate and lead silicate) of lead glass for protection against X-radiation and includes a method of measuring the lead equivalent of the glasses.

BS 4247 *Surface materials for use in radioactive areas*

Part 1: 1981 *Methods of measuring and evaluating the decontamination factor*

Part 2: 1982 *Guide to the selection of materials*

BS 4513: 1969 (1981) *Lead bricks for radiation shielding*

This standard specifies requirements for the design of the basic bricks of two systems (chevron and rounded mating) of lead shielding brick.

(Q8) (no entry)

(R)   Energy, other physical factors

(R1) – (R7)   (no entries)

(R8)   Durability

CP 3 Chapter IX: 1950 *Durability*

This code gives notes on the design life, satisfactory life, and maintenance requirements of buildings. The causes of deterioration of buildings and installations are analysed and appropriate protective and preservative treatments are recommended. Tables give approximate rates of corrosion of steel and of zinc coatings on steel, recommended protective measures for metals, and a classification of sulphate soil conditions as affecting concrete, with recommended precautionary measures. Classification of water supplies in relation to their effects on metals, and of atmospheric pollution conditions, are included.

An invaluable analysis, which attempted to classify buildings so that the predicted life for the structure and cyclical renewal for components and installations were coordinated. The need for so rational an approach is still evident, but the difficulties are formidable.

Reference should also be made to BS 6100: *Glossary of building and civil engineering terms* Part 1 *General and miscellaneous*, section 1.7.1 1986 *Performance*, BS 8207 *Code of practice for energy efficiency in buildings*, discussed in (M2) Insulation above, and BS 6270: *Cleaning and surface repair of buildings* in (W) Operation, maintenance factors below.

(T)   Application (no entry)

(U)   Users, resources

(U1) – (U2)   (no entries)

(U3)   People

Four standards for special categories of the deserving in the community (two for the elderly, two for the disabled) are covered in this section.

BS 4467: 1969 *Anthropometric and ergonomic recommendations for dimensions in designing for the elderly*

The recommendations in this standard give advice on the dimensions to be incorporated in housing for the elderly. Particular attention is paid to the fact that the elderly differ in average size from the general population, to the fact that their body movements are more restricted (for example climbing or excessive bending should be avoided wherever possible) and that they are more liable to fatigue than younger people. Hence some of these recommendations differ from those laid down in relation to design for the general population. It does *not* deal with the disabled.

This is complemented by BS 5613: 1978 *Recommendations for alarm systems for the elderly and others living at risk*.

BS 5619: 1978 *Code of practice for design of housing for the convenience of disabled people*

Recommendations are given in this standard for ramps, lifts, car parking, garden paths, doors, circulation spaces, floors, windows, kitchens, bedrooms, WCs, bathrooms, stairs and services.

BS 5810: 1979 *Code of practice for access for the disabled to buildings*

The application of this code is to the very widest range of buildings, excluding domestic housing, and to the spaces between them. A special symbol is used to identify and advertise the following:

1 Accessible entrances to buildings.
2 Manageable routes through buildings.
3 Accessible lifts.
4 Accessible lavatory accommodation.
5 Reserved car-parking places.
6 The availability of special services in buildings.

(U4) – (U6)   (no entries)

(U8)   (no entry)

(V)   Working factors   (no entry)

(W)   Operation, maintenance factors

BS 6270 *Cleaning and surface repair of buildings* (See also Table 3, Materials e natural stone)

Part 1: 1982   *Natural stone, cast stone and clay and calcium silicate brick masonry*
This useful code deals with cleaning and surface repair, but not structural repairs. The scope extends to terracotta and faience work. The range of techniques covered includes repointing.

Part 2: 1985   *Concrete and precast concrete masonry*
As with Part 1, cleaning and surface repair techniques are covered, but not structural repairs. Lime stucco, oil mastic, graffito and sand and cement renderings are not covered.

In both parts and in respect of buildings or features of artistic or historical importance, the need for specialist guidance is emphasized. Recommendations for the protection of buildings, operatives and public are included.

(X)   Change, movement, stability factors   (no entry)

(Y)   Economic, commercial factors   (no entry)

(Z)   Peripheral subjects, form of presentation, time, space   (no entry)

Index